Collins

ULTIMATE QUIZ NIGHT

Published by Collins
An imprint of HarperCollins Publishers
Westerhill Road
Bishopbriggs
Glasgow G64 2QT
www.harpercollins.co.uk

HarperCollins Publishers
1st Floor
Watermarque Building
Ringsend Road
Dublin 4
Ireland

First Edition 2022

10 9 8 7 6 5 4 3 2 1

© HarperCollins Publishers 2022
All quizzes copyright Puzzler Media – www.puzzler.com
Images used under licence from Shutterstock.com
ISBN 978-0-00-854160-6

Collins® is a registered trademark of HarperCollins Publishers Limited

Printed and Bound in the UK using 100% Renewable Electricity at CPI Group (UK) Ltd

A catalogue record for this book is available from the British Library.

If you would like to comment on any aspect of this book, please contact us at the above address or online.
E-mail: puzzles@harpercollins.co.uk

MIX
Paper | Supporting responsible forestry
FSC
www.fsc.org
FSC™ C007454

This book is produced from independently certified FSC™ paper to ensure responsible forest management.

For more information visit:
www.harpercollins.co.uk/green

Introduction

What makes a good quiz? A witty and amusing host and a choice of interesting categories are good places to start.

You could combine the hosting talents of Alexander Armstrong and Clive Myrie but you need a great set of questions too.

That's where *Collins Ultimate Quiz Night* comes in. We've taken the hassle out of creating the perfect quiz by providing around 10,000 questions, including 30 picture quizzes, on all manner of subjects in an easy-to-use format.

There's something on offer for everyone, too, from easy questions for those taking their first tentative steps from quizzing base camp right up to super-tricky testers for those experienced trivia travellers heading for the highest peaks of general knowledge.

Let's get going.

The quizzes

The book is divided into two parts, each with 250 quizzes.
Half of the quizzes are based on themes ranging from animals to
art, food to football, science to soap operas and a whole host of
subjects in between. The rest of the quizzes are pot luck and
contain a little bit of everything.

The quizzes in each part of the book are grouped together
depending on how tricky we think they are. The easy ones
come first, followed by medium and finally hard.

Easy

With a wide range of themes on offer in our easy section, you're
bound to find some questions and quizzes easy and others a bit
harder. It's not all straightforward in this section though: watch
out for a few themes that aren't quite as obvious as the title
suggests. Quiz 251 marks the start of the second easy section.

Medium

You'll get a good general knowledge workout when you tackle
our medium quizzes. Classic themes that appeared in the easy
section are repeated here, but you'll most likely need some extra
thinking time to complete the quizzes at this level. The second
medium section starts at Quiz 401.

Hard

You'll really need to work those little grey cells when you
venture into our hard quiz section, so set aside plenty of time.
An enthusiast's knowledge would be a definite advantage on
some of the themed quizzes. When you've toiled your way
through the first section, the second hard section begins at
Quiz 476.

The answers

Each quiz header tells you where the answers are printed.
They're mostly just a couple of pages away, for example the
answers to Quiz 1 appear at the bottom of Quiz 3. The exceptions
are the last two quizzes in each part of the book, which appear at
the bottom of the first two quizzes in that part.

Running a quiz

When you're running a quiz night, there's a great sense of satisfaction to be had in doing a job well, and a little bit of effort beforehand will go a long way to making sure that your quiz goes without a hitch.

❖ Plan: consider how many questions you want to ask in the time available, making sure you leave enough thinking time between questions. Once you've done that, pick a good range of subjects so that there's something for everyone.

❖ Rehearse: Go through all the questions you're going to be asking beforehand, checking any potentially tricky pronunciations and making sure your timings work. Note down all the questions (notes look better in a quiz environment than reading from a book) and answers. Every effort has been made to ensure that all the answers in *Collins Ultimate Quiz Night* are correct. Despite our best endeavours, mistakes may still appear. If you see an answer you're not sure is right, or if you think there's more than one possible answer, then do check.

❖ Paper and writing implements: make sure you prepare enough sheets of paper for everyone to write on, including scrap paper, and have plenty of pens to hand for those who need them.

❖ Prizes: everyone likes a prize. No matter how small, it's best to have one on offer.

Good luck! We hope you enjoy *Collins Ultimate Quiz Night*.

Contents

Easy Quizzes

Easy Quizzes

ANSWERS ON PAGE 3

1. From which protein are human hair, nails and skin made?
2. Which actor starred as the eponymous *Inspector Morse* between 1987 and 2000, as well as DI Jack Regan in *The Sweeney*?
3. Which theoretical physicist wrote the best-selling *A Brief History Of Time*, bringing foundational questions about the universe to the masses?
4. Which TV magician married his assistant Debbie McGee in April 1988?
5. Liam and Noel, brothers and founding members of the Britpop band Oasis, have what surname?
6. Initially sold in the USA and Canada as *Le Car*, which brand of Renault automobile was the highest-selling car in France every year between 1972 and 1986?
7. Which was the final Apollo space mission to launch?
8. In the 2006 film *The Prestige*, David Bowie portrayed which inventor, whose name has latterly become known as an electric car marque?
9. From 1963 until his death in 1981, who were Bob Marley's backing band?
10. Cerys Matthews was the lead singer of which Welsh band that took their name from a psychomotor syndrome?
11. What is the opposite of nocturnal?
12. Schreibvogel, Maldonado and Passage have been the legal surnames of which true crime documentary star and convicted criminal?
13. By area, what is the largest country in the world?
14. What puzzle first appeared in the 2nd November 1924 edition of the *Daily Telegraph*?
15. Which former BBC reporter and "man in the white suit" successfully ran as an MP in the constituency of Tatton in 1997?
16. While it is no longer the capital city, which is the largest city in Nigeria, and the second-largest in Africa?
17. If a dish is described as being *à la Crécy*, which vegetable does it either contain or come served with?
18. Ferrero Rocher and Nutella® are both primarily a mix of chocolate and which nut?
19. In geometry, and also known as a hendecagon, how many sides does an undecagon have?
20. Norville Rogers is the full name of which cartoon slacker, better known by a one-word nickname?

Answers to QUIZ 249 – Pot Luck

1	Brigham Young	11	Gary Player
2	Swaffham	12	19
3	Holocene	13	Dmitri Shostakovich
4	Paige	14	Manaus
5	Miami Dolphins	15	Broad bean
6	Tsesarevich	16	Joan Miró
7	Liver	17	*Emperor*
8	World Games	18	Fyodor Dostoevsky
9	Giles	19	*Yentl*
10	Walking sticks	20	Eris

Easy

1   Which boxing weight is for fighters weighing between 140lbs and 147lbs?
2   How many players are there in a water polo team?
3   In 2000, which country was admitted to the Five Nations rugby union tournament, expanding it to become the Six Nations?
4   A professional stroke play golfing tournament consists of how many rounds?
5   Which Swedish tennis star won 11 Grand Slam singles events in the 1970s and 1980s, but retired aged only 26 due to the resulting burnout?
6   Which snooker legend released an autobiography entitled *Interesting*?
7   What is the oldest golf club in the world?
8   In which track and field sport did Dick Fosbury pioneer a new technique at the 1968 Mexico Olympics that has since become universal?
9   Spanish football clubs named Madrid, Sociedad and Betis all have what prefix, given to them as a symbol of their patronage by King Alfonso XIII?
10 Deported from Australia in January 2022 amid the COVID-19 pandemic, which Serbian tennis player was given the nickname "Novax"?

Medium

11 Which two artistic gymnastic events do women compete in that men do not?
12 Which German comedian originally moved to Britain to work in the marketing department of Wycombe Wanderers FC?
13 Which Irish jockey was the first female to win both the Grand National and the Cheltenham Gold Cup?
14 Football legend Eusebio played for which country?
15 Which English football legend signed with Paris Saint-Germain in January 2013 and gave his salary to charity?
16 How many players are there on each side in an Aussie Rules football game?
17 In cricket, what does LBW stand for?
18 What number shirt did Bobby Moore wear when playing for West Ham United?
19 The NHL is a North American professional league in which sport?
20 How many balls are used in a game of Association Croquet?

Hard

Answers to QUIZ 250 – Music

1	Tom Waits	11	Bananarama
2	*The Million Dollar Quartet*	12	*The Rite of Spring*
3	Harry Styles	13	Technotronic
4	Elvis Costello	14	Cello
5	Mutt Lange	15	Billy Fury
6	*Fire*	16	Captain & Tennille
7	Akon	17	Miles Davis
8	*Blinded by the Light*	18	Nick Kamen
9	Hoobastank	19	Studio 54
10	Bo Diddley	20	John Oates

1   Which TV chef is the daughter of a former British Chancellor of the Exchequer?

2   In 1781, which was the first planet to be discovered by telescope (i.e. not by being visible to the naked eye)?

3   Johnny Knoxville, Steve-O, Party Boy and Wee Man are performers in which stunt crew, known for their eponymous TV series and films?

4   The Anatolian Peninsula comprises most of which modern day country?

5   Who played Inspector Gadget in the 1999 film adaptation of the same name directed by David Kellogg?

6   Georges Braque was instrumental in the development of which early 20th century art movement alongside Pablo Picasso?

7   Beatrice and Benedick were the lead protagonists in which Shakespeare play?

8   Formerly known as the Coyote State, which American state is now known as Mount Rushmore State?

9   At which temperature do the Fahrenheit and Celsius scales meet?

10 Which American dance act had hits in the 1990s with *Gonna Make You Sweat (Everybody Dance Now)* and *Things That Make You Go Hmmm*?

11 Lara Croft was the archaeologist protagonist in which series of adventure games, later turned into a film franchise?

12 Frequently heard at sporting events, *Hit the Road Jack* was a 1962 hit for which blues singer and pianist?

13 The Seas of Tranquillity and Showers can be found where?

14 What is the longest river in Scotland?

15 Which qualitative ordinal scale is used to measure the hardness of minerals, from diamond (10) to talc (1)?

16 Which fictional detective played by Alan Davies lived in a windmill?

17 Bangkok is the capital city of which country?

18 Prior to adopting the Euro, what was the currency unit of Spain?

19 Which luggage company is named after a biblical strongman?

20 Which is the only written number in English that has all its letters in alphabetical order?

Easy

Medium

Hard

Answers to QUIZ 1 – Pot Luck

1	Keratin	11	Diurnal
2	John Thaw	12	Joe Exotic
3	Stephen Hawking	13	Russia
4	Paul Daniels	14	**Cryptic** crossword
5	Gallagher	15	Martin Bell
6	Renault 5	16	Lagos
7	Apollo 17	17	Carrots
8	Nikola Tesla	18	Hazelnut
9	The Wailers	19	Eleven
10	Catatonia	20	Shaggy (from *Scooby-Doo*)

1   Which singer, whose real name is Declan McManus, had a 1979 hit with the new-wave track *Oliver's Army*?

2   Which pop duo consisted of Jimmy Somerville and Richard Coles and were most famous for their cover version of *Don't Leave Me This Way*?

3   Whose debut hit *Return Of The Mack* spent two weeks atop the UK charts in April 1996?

4   Between 1960 and 1964, The Beatles performed live over 1,200 times in which city?

5   Which son of the Bishop of Peterborough hosted *Radio 1's Rap Show* between 1994 and 2013?

6   What links a Boney M song from 1976 and a David Gray song from 2000?

7   A New York farmer named Max Yasgur allowed his dairy farm to be used for which iconic 1969 music festival?

8   Which legendary pop star did Lisa Marie Presley marry in May 1994?

9   Which band's singles include *All the Small Things, What's My Age Again?* and *I Miss You*?

10 Katy Perry sang about "Gurls" from which American state in 2010?

11 Roy Wood left ELO in 1972 to form which rock band, famous for their single *I Wish It Could Be Christmas Every Day*?

12 *When You Wish Upon a Star* is an Oscar-winning song from which 1940 Disney movie?

13 Marvin Lee Aday was the name at birth of which rock singer who died in January 2022?

14 Which legendary musician is in all five of the Rock and Roll, Gospel, Honky Tonk, Rockabilly and Country Music Halls of Fame?

15 Who sang the theme from *Ghostbusters*?

16 *Blackstar* and *Life on Mars* are albums by which late singer?

17 Bill Clinton famously plays which instrument?

18 How is Robyn Fenty better known?

19 Which singer has had UK number ones as a lead artist with *R.I.P.* and as a featured artist with *Hot Right Now*?

20 Wings performed the theme song for which James Bond movie?

Easy / **Medium** / **Hard**

Answers to QUIZ 2 – Sport

1	Welterweight	11	Uneven bars and balance beam
2	Seven	12	Henning Wehn
3	Italy	13	Rachael Blackmore
4	Four	14	Portugal
5	Bjorn Borg	15	David Beckham
6	Steve Davis	16	18
7	St Andrew's Old Course, Scotland	17	Leg before wicket
8	High jump (the "Fosbury Flop")	18	Six
9	Real (meaning Royal)	19	Ice hockey
10	Novak Djokovic	20	Four

1 Named for the author of the first scientific paper on the topic, Daltonism is better known as which affliction?

2 Which company makes Feast ice creams?

3 Which royal palace was built by Cardinal Thomas Wolsey, but is most associated with Henry VIII, to whom Wolsey either gave it or had it seized by?

4 Which historic merchant bank was bankrupted in 1995 by the illicit dealings of rogue trader Nick Leeson?

5 Of the four gospels in the New Testament, which one comes last?

6 How many counties are there in Northern Ireland?

7 Which instruments were "duelling" in a scene from the film *Deliverance*?

8 What are Universal Product Codes more commonly known as?

9 Mandy, Zak and Charity are members of which soap opera family?

10 Which cartoon characters were originally named by their Belgian creator Peyo as *Les Schtroumpfs*?

11 Who was the first boxer to be awarded a knighthood?

12 Which is the only London Underground station whose name contains a Z?

13 Godalming, Dorking, Woking and Leatherhead are all towns in which English county?

14 In the book *The Whispering Land*, the author and naturalist Gerald Durrell recants stories of collecting animals for his zoo founded on which Channel Island?

15 "You'll be a man, my son." is the final line to which Rudyard Kipling poem?

16 Lee Child has written a series of thriller novels about which former American military policeman roaming the country taking odd jobs?

17 In which Shakespeare play does the recurring character of Falstaff die, even though he never appears in it?

18 Which tennis legend was, during his career, known as the "Superbrat"?

19 In which country would you find the Southern Alps?

20 Tynwald is the English name for the legislature of which small self-governing British Crown Dependency island?

Answers to QUIZ 3 – Pot Luck

1	Nigella Lawson	11	*Tomb Raider*
2	Uranus	12	Ray Charles
3	*Jackass*	13	The Moon
4	Turkey	14	River Tay
5	Matthew Broderick	15	Mohs scale
6	Cubism	16	*Jonathan Creek*
7	*Much Ado About Nothing*	17	Thailand
8	South Dakota	18	Peseta
9	-40	19	Samsonite®
10	C&C Music Factory	20	Forty

ANSWERS ON PAGE **8**

1   Which is the only country to pass through both the equator and the Tropic of Capricorn?
2   By area, what is the smallest US state?
3   What is the longest river in Ireland?
4   Known for its tourism, the coastal town of Amalfi is in which country?
5   Northfleet, Chatham and Gravesend are all in which English county?
6   For 34 years between 1977 and 2011, which African country's flag was simply the colour green?
7   What is the state capital of Tennessee?
8   Which African country lies across the Straits of Gibraltar from Spain?
9   What is the only city in Cornwall?
10 What is the capital of Germany?
11 On what peninsula do Spain and Portugal lie?
12 The 188 highest mountains in the world are all found in which continent?
13 Which American city is known as The Windy City?
14 Tunisia gained independence from which European country in 1956?
15 In which English town is Teesside University?
16 The Kruger National Park is located in which African country?
17 La Gomera and El Hierro are two of the lesser-known islands in which group, which also contains Tenerife and Lanzarote?
18 What is the capital city of Finland?
19 What did Ceylon change its name to in 1972?
20 Which is both the world's oldest and deepest lake?

Easy

Medium

Hard

Answers to QUIZ 4 – Music

1	Elvis Costello	11	Wizzard
2	The Communards	12	*Pinocchio*
3	Mark Morrison	13	Meat Loaf
4	Hamburg, Germany	14	Elvis Presley
5	Tim Westwood	15	Ray Parker Jr
6	They both contained Babylon in the title (*Rivers of Babylon, Babylon*)	16	David Bowie
		17	Saxophone
7	*Woodstock*	18	Rihanna
8	Michael Jackson	19	Rita Ora
9	blink-182	20	*Live and Let Die*
10	California		

ANSWERS ON PAGE 9

1   What does a fletcher make?
2   Otitis is inflammation in which body part?
3   The male of which crab species has one front claw far larger than the other?
4   The three-volume historical novel *Ivanhoe* was written by which Scottish author?
5   Pinocchio is swallowed by which animal?
6   Tobey Maguire, Tom Holland and Andrew Garfield have all played which superhero on the big screen?
7   Which Northern Hemisphere tree is also known as the mountain ash?
8   Which star sign would a person be if they were born on April Fool's Day?
9   Jamaican-born fitness instructor Derrick Evans achieved fame in the 1990s under what name?
10 Arkwright, Norman Stanley Fletcher and Lord Rustless were among the roles played on television by which actor, comedian and writer?
11 In which 2004 film does Leonardo DiCaprio star as the eccentric billionaire and cinema mogul, Howard Hughes?
12 Although almost the entire atmosphere of both Venus and Mars consists of it, which gas makes up only 0.04% of Earth's atmosphere?
13 Which acid is used in lead-acid car batteries?
14 Pam St Clement played which *EastEnders* character between 1986 and 2012?
15 In 1971, which theatre opened on Norfolk Street, Sheffield?
16 Who is the only President of the USA to win more than two Presidential Elections?
17 The explorer Ranulph and his third-cousin-once-removed Ralph, an actor, share what surname?
18 What is the only written number in English that has all its letters in *reverse* alphabetical order?
19 Despite two of the letters not even being in the full name, which county's name abbreviates to "Hants"?
20 In carpentry, what does MDF stand for?

Easy

Medium

Hard

Answers to QUIZ 5 – Pot Luck

1	Colour blindness	11	Sir Henry Cooper
2	Walls	12	Belsize Park
3	Hampton Court Palace	13	Surrey
4	Barings Bank	14	Jersey
5	John	15	*If*
6	Six (Antrim, Armagh, Down, Fermanagh, Derry and Tyrone)	16	Jack Reacher
		17	*Henry V*
7	Banjos	18	John McEnroe
8	Barcodes	19	New Zealand
9	The Dingles (*Emmerdale*)	20	Isle of Man
10	The Smurfs		

1 Whose reported last words "fan, fan, rub, rub, drink, drink" are not quite as poetic as what he had said slightly beforehand; "Kiss me, Hardy"?

2 "The car seems OK" were the last words of which Formula 1 driver, moments before his car failed and struck a wall at the 1994 San Marino Grand Prix?

3 Which actress's last words were "I want to be with Carrie", in reference to her daughter, who had died the day before?

4 Which baseball star's last words were "I'll finally get to see Marilyn", referring to his ex-wife?

5 On his deathbed, which playwright was quoted as saying "My wallpaper and I are fighting a duel to the death; one of us has got to go"?

6 Which distiller, dying of blood poisoning reportedly caused by angrily kicking a safe, is said to have requested "One last drink, please"?

7 Eric Garner and George Floyd, two African-American men killed by police, both reportedly said what three-word phrase as their last words?

8 "Leave the shower curtain on the inside of the tub" were reportedly the sage last words spoken by which hotelier?

9 Which singer's last words on 16th August 1977 were reportedly "I'm going to the bathroom to read"?

10 On 14th October 1977, which legendary singer remarked "That was a great game of golf, fellas", then died of a heart attack on his way to the clubhouse?

11 Which Australian Prime Minister reportedly said "I know this beach like the back of my hand" immediately prior to disappearing while swimming at it?

12 "Shoot, coward, you are only going to kill a man." So said which Argentinian Marxist revolutionary to his assassin?

13 Which *Of Human Bondage* author wrote in his final letter, "Dying is a very dull, dreary affair, and my advice to you is to have nothing whatever to do with it"?

14 Which human rights activist urged "Brothers! Brothers, please! This is a house of peace!" to an unruly crowd, before being shot by multiple assailants?

15 Which unrepentant Australian-American actor reportedly went out saying "I've had a hell of a lot of fun and I've enjoyed every minute of it"?

16 "Goodbye, kid. Hurry back" were the last words of which actor to his wife, Lauren Bacall?

17 Which Fascist leader reportedly begged his executioner "Sparami nel petto!" ("Shoot me in the chest!") as his final words?

18 Kurt Cobain's suicide note contained the phrase "it's better to burn out than fade away", taken from lyrics to which Neil Young song?

19 "Get my swan costume ready" were the final words of which ballerina, famous for creating the Dying Swan solo dance?

20 "Let's do it" were the final words of which murderer, the first person executed in the USA for a decade and who campaigned for his own execution?

Answers to QUIZ 6 – Geography

1	Brazil	11	Iberian
2	Rhode Island	12	Asia
3	River Shannon	13	Chicago
4	Italy	14	France
5	Kent	15	Middlesbrough
6	Libya	16	South Africa
7	Nashville	17	Canary Islands
8	Morocco	18	Helsinki
9	Truro	19	Sri Lanka
10	Berlin	20	Lake Baikal

Easy

Medium

Hard

QUIZ 9 – Pot Luck

ANSWERS ON PAGE 11

1 Who played the role of the title character in 1978's *Superman* and 1980's *Superman II*?

2 Rowley Birkin QC, Swiss Toni and Louis Balfour were all characters in which BBC comedy sketch show?

3 "Is this a dagger which I see before me?" is a quote from which Shakespeare play?

4 What is the minimum age one must be to become President of the United States?

5 Terry Gilliam was an animator and occasional actor in which comedy troupe?

6 The cravat takes its name from that of which country, which is known as Hrvatska in its own language?

7 Which biblical prophet received the Ten Commandments at Mount Sinai?

8 Supposedly, the first documented use of "google" as a verb was in 2002 on which supernatural drama series starring Sarah Michelle Gellar?

9 Ronald Wayne co-founded which tech giant, but sold his shares after only twelve days, shares that would now be worth billions?

10 Which entire island nation was awarded the George Cross for resisting a siege against it between 1940 and 1942?

11 What is the name of the United States' five-cent coin?

12 Which Welsh comedian used to wear a pith helmet early in his career, but later became more synonymous with a fez?

13 Which William Shakespeare play is set in the city of Elsinore?

14 Brian Blessed played which character in the TV series *Z-Cars*?

15 What is the stage name of Douglas Trendle, the frontman of two-tone band Bad Manners?

16 Which type of tea is named after a city in India once regarded as a prime tourist destination for the British Raj elite?

17 Hiragana, katakana and kanji are the three alphabets that make up which language?

18 At 232 miles, which is the longest motorway in the UK?

19 Duplicate and Rubber are varieties of which card game?

20 Which type of emergency vehicle often has its name written backwards on the front so it reads properly in rear-view mirrors?

Easy

Medium

Hard

Answers to QUIZ 7 – Pot Luck

1	Arrows	11	*The Aviator*
2	Ear	12	Carbon dioxide
3	Fiddler crab	13	Sulphuric acid
4	Walter Scott	14	Pat Butcher
5	Whale	15	The Crucible
6	Spider-Man	16	Franklin D. Roosevelt
7	Rowan	17	Fiennes
8	Aries	18	One
9	Mr Motivator	19	Hampshire
10	Ronnie Barker	20	Medium density fibreboard

ANSWERS ON PAGE **12**

Easy

1. Who won a Golden Globe for starring as Beth Harmon in the 2020 Netflix miniseries *The Queen's Gambit*?
2. The first two seasons of the Netflix series *Narcos* tell the story of which Colombian drug lord?
3. Piper Chapman, a woman convicted of transporting a suitcase full of drug money, is the lead character in which series?
4. What was the name of the interactive episode of *Black Mirror* released in 2018?
5. In seasons three and four of *The Crown*, who plays Prince Philip?
6. Who plays Emily in the Netflix show *Emily In Paris*?
7. What was Netflix initially called?
8. Per Nielsen, what was the most streamed show on Netflix in 2020?
9. Which Netflix police procedural series is almost entirely set in an interrogation room?
10. Launching in 2015, the comedy series *Grace and Frankie* features which two actresses as the lead characters?
11. In 2013, which became the first Netflix original series to win a primetime Emmy award?
12. Set on the fictional, medieval-inspired landmass known as "the Continent" what series is Netflix's answer to HBO's *Game of Thrones*?
13. Princess Carolyn and Mr Peanutbutter are characters in which animated Netflix series?
14. Linda Cardellini and Christina Applegate starred in which series about two grieving women who bond during therapy?
15. Which legend of late night launched his new venture *My Next Guest Needs No Introduction* on Netflix in 2018?
16. With categories such as "Best Guilty Pleasure" and "Best Hangover Cure" what annual awards show did Netflix used to run?
17. In which Netflix series has Earth frozen over and the last surviving humans live on a giant train circling the globe?
18. What was the spin-off series to *Breaking Bad*?
19. Nick and Vanessa Lachey host which Netflix social experiment series in which single people get engaged before meeting in person?
20. Which French Netflix series of 2021 told the story of a professional thief out for revenge?

Medium

Hard

Answers to QUIZ 8 – Last Words

1	Lord Horatio Nelson	11	Harold Holt
2	Ayrton Senna	12	Che Guevara
3	Debbie Reynolds	13	Somerset Maugham
4	Joe DiMaggio	14	Malcolm X
5	Oscar Wilde	15	Errol Flynn
6	Jack Daniel	16	Humphrey Bogart
7	"I can't breathe."	17	Benito Mussolini
8	Conrad Hilton	18	*Hey Hey, My My (Into the Black)*
9	Elvis Presley	19	Anna Pavlova
10	Bing Crosby	20	Gary Gilmore

ANSWERS ON PAGE 13

1   Alpha is the first letter of the Greek alphabet; what is the last?

2   In terms of both numbers of stations and overall length, which is the shortest London Underground line?

3   In computing, what do the initials IBM stand for?

4   Stonefish, Toadfish and Tadpole Rebecchi are all characters in which Australian soap opera?

5   Dying in 2009, Millvina Dean was the last-known survivor of which maritime disaster?

6   Madonna made a record 85 costume changes in which 1996 musical film?

7   Which animal is the only primate known to hibernate?

8   Which ruler of China launched the Cultural Revolution in May 1966?

9   What is the main ingredient of a frittata?

10 Between 1999 and 2002, the advertising campaign that became known as *Wassup?* advertised which beer?

11 Matthew McConaughey starred as rodeo rider Ron Woodroof in which 2013 film?

12 The first series of the reality show *Popstar to Operastar* was co-hosted by which TV gardener?

13 What colour can be found on the highest number of current national flags, appearing on 148 of them?

14 Moon, Dweezil, Ahmet and Diva are the children of which musician?

15 What is the most common surname in Spain?

16 A gambit is a tactical sacrifice of material for position in which board game?

17 Ernest Hemingway's *Death in the Afternoon* is an exploration into which Spanish traditional physical contest?

18 Which planet in the solar system takes the shortest time to orbit the Sun?

19 Which author, real name Eric Arthur Blair, used the name Edward Burton when deliberately getting arrested for public drunkenness in 1931?

20 An aquifer is an underground store of what?

Easy

Medium

Hard

Answers to QUIZ 9 – Pot Luck

1	Christopher Reeve	11	Nickel
2	*The Fast Show*	12	Tommy Cooper
3	*Macbeth* (spoken by Lady Macbeth)	13	*Hamlet*
4	35	14	Fancy Smith
5	Monty Python	15	Buster Bloodvessel
6	Croatia	16	Darjeeling
7	Moses	17	Japanese
8	*Buffy the Vampire Slayer*	18	M6
9	Apple	19	Bridge
10	Malta	20	Ambulance

Easy

1. The month of January is named after who, the Roman god of beginnings and transitions?
2. Since 1977, which Grand Slam tennis tournament has been held in January every year?
3. On 3rd January 1924, Howard Carter found the sarcophagus of which Egyptian pharaoh?
4. 4th January 1809 saw the birth of which Frenchman, who later invented a reading system for the blind using punch marks in paper?
5. January 1966 saw the election of which woman, the first female Prime Minister of India?
6. Which Emmy-nominated American actress starred as Betty Draper in *Mad Men*?
7. 30th January 1649 saw the execution of who, the first and only monarch executed in Britain's history?
8. On 17th January 1912, Captain Robert Scott arrived at the South Pole, only to find that a Norwegian expedition led by who had gotten there first?
9. Although not inaugurated until January, presidents of the United States have since 1845 been chosen in elections that take place in which month?
10. On 7th January 2015, the offices of which satirical French newspaper were targeted in a terrorist attack?

Medium

11. In Christian religion, folklore considers it unlucky to leave Christmas decorations hanging after which day, the day before Epiphany?
12. Which figure skater was attacked during a practice on 6th January 1994 by the ex-husband of her rival, Tonya Harding?
13. Which building opened on 4th January 2010 in Dubai and became the tallest structure in the world by a significant margin?
14. 27th January 1926 saw the first public display of television by which Scotsman, widely, if not entirely accurately, credited with its invention?
15. On 6th January 2021, a mob of Donald Trump supporters attacked which important American meeting place, the home of the US Senate?
16. Which space shuttle exploded on 28th January 1986, 73 seconds after take-off?
17. Queen Victoria died on 22nd January 1901 in which former Royal residence on the Isle of Wight?
18. Who crashed and died on 4th January 1967 amid a speed record attempt on Coniston Water in the Lake District?
19. 15th January 1967 saw the first edition of which annual American sporting event?
20. What item did bakery chain Greggs introduce in January 2019 to enormous success?

Hard

Answers to QUIZ 10 – Netflix

1	Anya Taylor-Joy	11	*House of Cards*
2	Pablo Escobar	12	*The Witcher*
3	*Orange Is the New Black*	13	*BoJack Horseman*
4	*Bandersnatch*	14	*Dead To Me*
5	Tobias Menzies	15	David Letterman
6	Lily Collins	16	The Flixies
7	Kibble	17	*Snowpiercer*
8	*The Office* (the US version; it was removed from Netflix in 2021)	18	*Better Call Saul*
		19	*Love is Blind*
9	*Criminal: UK*	20	*Lupin*
10	Jane Fonda and Lily Tomlin		

QUIZ 13 – Pot Luck

1. In a leap year, which month gains an extra day?
2. What colour are the seats in the House of Commons?
3. Due to how slowly it rotates, on which planet is a day longer than a year?
4. Which part of the body is also known as the trachea?
5. How many legs do all insects have?
6. What is a young giraffe called?
7. Balmoral Castle is located in which country of the United Kingdom?
8. Caractacus Pott and Lord Skrumshus are characters in which children's novel by Ian Fleming?
9. Aided by Diego Maradona's "Hand of God" goal in their quarter-final, which team won the 1986 FIFA World Cup?
10. Found on the island of Sicily, which is the largest active volcano in Europe?
11. Romaine, butterhead and iceberg are types of which vegetable?
12. Osteology is the study of which part of the human body?
13. What is a zoophobe afraid of?
14. Andrew Holness and Michael Manley have both been Prime Ministers of which Caribbean island state?
15. Which vowel is represented by a single dot in Morse Code?
16. Logan International Airport serves which American city?
17. Which of Queen Elizabeth II's children was born on 10th March 1964?
18. The Old Royal Naval College and St Paul's Cathedral were both designed by which architect?
19. The *Bundesliga* is the top-tier football division in which country?
20. The malleus, incus and stapes bones can be found in which part of the human body?

Easy

Medium

Hard

Answers to QUIZ 11 – Pot Luck

1. Omega
2. Waterloo & City line (two stations, 1.5 miles)
3. International Business Machines
4. *Neighbours*
5. Sinking of the *Titanic*
6. *Evita*
7. Lemur
8. Mao Zedong
9. Egg; it is an omelette
10. Budweiser®
11. *Dallas Buyers Club*
12. Alan Titchmarsh
13. Red
14. Frank Zappa
15. Garcia
16. Chess
17. Bullfighting
18. Mercury (88 days)
19. George Orwell
20. Water

What are the names of these artworks, and the artists who created them?

Easy

1

2

3

4

Medium

5

6

7

8

Hard

Answers to QUIZ 12 – January

1	Janus	11	Twelfth Night (usually 6th January, but it can vary)
2	Australian Open	12	Nancy Kerrigan
3	Tutankhamun	13	Burj Khalifa
4	Louis Braille	14	John Logie Baird
5	Indira Gandhi	15	Capitol Building
6	January Jones	16	Space Shuttle *Challenger*
7	Charles I	17	Osborne House
8	Roald Amundsen	18	Donald Campbell
9	November	19	Super Bowl
10	*Charlie Hebdo*	20	Vegan sausage roll

ANSWERS ON PAGE 17

1 Which supermarket uses the brand and slogan "Taste the Difference"?

2 Bezique is a card game for how many players?

3 What golfing term refers to both the area at the start of a hole, and the little plinth on which the ball is initially stood?

4 A bibliophile is a collector and/or lover of what?

5 What is the young of a swan called?

6 Cuboid and calcaneus bones are found in which part of the body?

7 Which stretch of water separates New Zealand and Australia?

8 Clark Kent and Lois Lane work for which fictional newspaper?

9 Billie Joe Armstrong is the lead singer of which pop-punk band, famous for albums *Dookie* and *American Idiot*?

10 The biggest known volcano in the solar system, Olympus Mons, can be found on which planet?

11 In which year did Queen Elizabeth II's Silver Jubilee take place?

12 Reflecting his primary choices of colour at the time, which Spanish artist had Blue and Rose Periods in the early 20th century?

13 Which fictional scarecrow has a set of interchangeable turnip, mangelwurzel and swede heads?

14 The adrenal glands are situated atop which organs in the human body?

15 Ozzy Osbourne was raised in which city?

16 Which bone is also known as the patella?

17 Which actor and comedian had the catchphrase "...and it's goodnight from him"?

18 Who was the last monarch of England from the House of Tudor?

19 Which German statesman was known as The Iron Chancellor?

20 In the nursery rhyme, who met a pieman going to the fair?

Easy

Medium

Hard

Answers to QUIZ 13 – Pot Luck

1	February	11	Lettuce
2	Green	12	Bones/skeleton
3	Venus	13	Animals
4	The windpipe	14	Jamaica
5	Six	15	E
6	Calf	16	Boston
7	Scotland	17	Prince Edward
8	*Chitty-Chitty-Bang-Bang: The Magical Car*	18	Sir Christopher Wren
9	Argentina	19	Germany
10	Mount Etna	20	Ear

1. What is the name of Barack Obama's wife?
2. In 1919, who became the first female Member of the British Parliament?
3. On 20th November 2014, who became the first female First Minister of Scotland?
4. Who became the first female Vice President of the United States when elected alongside Joe Biden in 2021?
5. Who was the first woman to win any of the Nobel Prizes?
6. In 1932, which American aviator became the first woman to fly solo across the Atlantic Ocean?
7. On 3rd January 1987, who made history by becoming the first woman ever to be inducted into the Rock & Roll Hall of Fame?
8. At the first ever Grammy Awards in 1958, which jazz and pop singer became the first person to ever win two awards?
9. Gertrude Ederle became the first woman to swim what body of water on 6th August 1926?
10. On 16th June 1963, Valentina Tereshkova became the first woman to go where?

11. Who became the first woman to win the Academy Award for Best Director with her 2008 work *The Hurt Locker*?
12. For her work in the 2001 film *Monster's Ball*, who became the first black woman to ever win the Best Actress Oscar?
13. Who, in 1979, became the first ever female Prime Minister of a sovereign European country?
14. In 1893, what became the first self-governing country in the world in which all women had the right to vote in parliamentary elections?
15. In February 2018, Sarah Clark became the first female in the history of British parliament to hold what ceremonial role?
16. In May 2009, who became the first female Poet Laureate?
17. Who, in 2016, became the first woman to represent a major party in a US presidential election?
18. Who, in 1971, became the first Australian woman to lead the world singles tennis rankings?
19. Who, in 1921, became the first woman to win a Pulitzer Prize for her book about New York high society during the 1870s, *The Age of Innocence*?
20. In 2005, although she finished fourth, who became the first woman to ever lead the Indianapolis 500?

Answers to QUIZ 14 – Art

1. *Mona Lisa* – Leonardo da Vinci
2. *The Starry Night* – Vincent van Gogh
3. *Arrangement in Grey and Black No. 1* ("Whistler's Mother") – James Whistler
4. *Girl With A Pearl Earring* – Johannes Vermeer
5. *The Scream* – Edvard Munch
6. *The Persistence of Memory* – Salvador Dali
7. *American Gothic* – Grant Wood
8. *Weeping Woman* – Pablo Picasso

1   Neville Chamberlain was Prime Minister during the reign of which monarch?
2   With what part of their body does a snake "hear"?
3   Which Northern Irish snooker player was known by the nickname "Hurricane"?
4   Which is the largest island in the Caribbean Sea?
5   In *The Taming of the Shrew*, who was the shrew?
6   On a standard dart board, what number lies between 16 and 19?
7   Mary Blige and Homer Simpson both have what middle initial?
8   The original Guggenheim Museum is in which city?
9   *Schwarz* is German for which colour?
10 Which former US President was given the nickname "Dubya"?
11 What is the highest mountain in Africa?
12 Thomas Cromwell, Earl of Essex and high profile lawyer and statesman, was executed during the reign of which monarch?
13 Author Charles Lutwidge Dodgson is better known by which pen name?
14 Which aptly named moon of Saturn is its largest?
15 What is the highest mountain in the Alps?
16 Who sang the theme song to the James Bond film *Skyfall*?
17 In which US state were Bruno Mars, Barack Obama and Nicole Kidman born?
18 What is the capital of Jamaica?
19 Which European city hosted the 2004 Olympic and Paralympic Games?
20 As sung about in *The Sound of Music*, what is the national flower of Switzerland?

Easy

Medium

Hard

Easy

1   Who wrote the iconic 1974 gothic horror novel *Carrie*?

2   Jordan Peele won an Oscar for Best Original Screenplay for which 2017 horror film?

3   What is the name of the "games master"/designer in the *Saw* franchise?

4   Which classic horror movie features a serial killer in a repainted William Shatner mask?

5   Parts of *Psycho*, *Silence of the Lambs* and *The Texas Chainsaw Massacre* were inspired by which real-life killer and bodysnatcher?

6   The demon Pazuzu possesses schoolgirl Regan in which 1973 horror film?

7   In the 1980 original version of *Friday the 13th*, who was the murderer?

8   Walnuts and dead chickens were used to create the gory noises heard in which 1981 cult classic supernatural horror?

9   For which 1996 horror film was a "witch consultant" hired?

10   What was the sequel to Rob Zombie's 2003 comedy horror film *House of 1000 Corpses*?

11   In 1973, *The Exorcist* was the first horror to be nominated for a Best Picture Oscar. In 1975, *Jaws* was second. Which 1991 film was third – and won?

12   Who played Claudia, the little girl that Tom Cruise and Brad Pitt attempt to turn into a vampire, in 1994's *Interview with the Vampire*?

13   In what sort of setting is the classic zombie movie *Dawn of the Dead* set?

14   The real-life story of an Oregonian man's supposedly possessed doll inspired which 1988 supernatural horror film that was remade in 2019?

15   In which 2012 horror film does a disenfranchised medical student enter the extreme body modification community?

16   The villain in *A Nightmare on Elm Street* has what name, which director Wes Craven reused from his former childhood bully?

17   In the *Hellraiser* franchise, who are the demonic antagonists that the series is based around?

18   The culture around which 2014 psychological horror film by Jennifer Kent saw its titular monster becoming an unlikely gay icon?

19   "We all go a little mad sometimes. Haven't you?" So said Anthony Perkins in character as Norman Bates in which 1960 classic?

20   Father Brennan, photographer Keith Jennings and archaeologist Carl Bugenhagen were all characters in which 1976 horror film?

Medium

Hard

Answers to QUIZ 16 – First Ladies

1	Michelle Obama	11	Kathryn Bigelow
2	Nancy Astor	12	Halle Berry
3	Nicola Sturgeon	13	Margaret Thatcher
4	Kamala Harris	14	New Zealand
5	Marie Curie	15	Black Rod
6	Amelia Earhart	16	Carol Ann Duffy
7	Aretha Franklin	17	Hillary Clinton
8	Ella Fitzgerald	18	Evonne Goolagong
9	English Channel	19	Edith Wharton
10	Space	20	Danica Patrick

1 What is the flattened circular organ in the uterus of pregnant mammals that nourishes the foetus through the umbilical cord?

2 Princess Charlotte of Mecklenburg-Strelitz was for 57 years the wife of which British monarch?

3 How many terminals does Gatwick Airport have?

4 Michael Jackson was burned during the filming of an advert in 1984 for which brand of soft drink?

5 Retief Goosen and Ernie Els are golfers from which country?

6 What kind of fruit are James Griece, Cortland and Gala all varieties of?

7 In textspeak, what does IMO stand for?

8 Which Irish rock band were previously known as Feedback and The Hype before settling on their final name in 1978?

9 In rugby league, how many points are awarded for a drop goal?

10 Who won the Golden Boot at the 2002 FIFA World Cup?

11 Which was the first human space flight to land on the moon, doing so in July 1969?

12 The Ten Commandments were revealed to Moses on which mountain?

13 How much is the brown ball worth in a game of snooker?

14 Who is the Greek equivalent of the Roman god of war, Mars?

15 Velma Kelly, Billy Flynn and Roxie Hart are characters in what stage musical?

16 Huey, Dewey and Louie are the nephews of what cartoon character?

17 In 1986, what Swedish rock band had a worldwide hit with *The Final Countdown*?

18 In what 1980s computer game does an amphibian try and cross a busy road?

19 The maxilla and mandible bones form what part of the body?

20 Who served as Mayor of London from 2000 until 2008?

Easy

Medium

Hard

Answers to QUIZ 17 – Pot Luck

1	George VI	11	Mount Kilimanjaro
2	Jawbone	12	Henry VIII
3	Alex Higgins	13	Lewis Carroll
4	Cuba	14	Titan
5	Katherine	15	Mont Blanc
6	Seven	16	Adele
7	J	17	Hawai'i
8	New York City	18	Kingston
9	Black	19	Athens
10	George W. Bush	20	Edelweiss

1   Jon Pertwee, David Tennant and Jodie Whitaker have all played which time-travelling doctor on TV?

2   *Doctor Sleep* was the sequel to which classic horror novel and film?

3   Which Australian drama TV series revolved around the everyday lifesaving efforts of the namesake emergency service?

4   Also known as Eggman, Doctor Ovi Kintobor is the nemesis of which video game character?

5   Boris Pasternak was awarded the Nobel Prize for Literature for which controversial 1957 novel that was banned in his native USSR?

6   Which carbonated soft drink was created in the 1880s by pharmacist Charles Alderton?

7   Which 1998 Eddie Murphy film takes its name and lead character from Hugo Lofting's literary character of the 1920s, but none of the plot?

8   Peter Sellers was the first actor to be nominated for a Best Actor Oscar for portraying three different characters in the same film; which film?

9   Known as the "Father of Medicine", which ancient Greek physician gives his name to the oath taken by doctors?

10 Which paediatrician wrote *The Common Sense Book of Baby and Child Care*?

11 Which dentist and friend of Wyatt Earp is best known for his role in the Gunfight at the O.K. Corral?

12 Short for "ter die sumendum", doctors use the abbreviation TDS to indicate that a prescription should be taken how often?

13 Which *Star Trek* character went by the nickname "Bones"?

14 Which glam rock band formed in London in 1981 is best known for their 1986 cover of Norman Greenbaum's *Spirit in the Sky*?

15 Under the pen name Max Brand, Frederick Schiller Faust created which fictional American medical doctor?

16 George Clooney played Dr Doug Ross in the first five series of which American medical drama?

17 The *Doctor* series of 18 comic novels were written by which British physicist?

18 Which rock band had early 1990s hits with *Two Princes* and *Little Miss Can't Be Wrong*?

19 Which physician, broadcaster, comedian and commentator writes as *Private Eye*'s medical correspondent under the pseudonym "MD"?

20 Which legendary basketball player was known as "Doctor J"?

Answers to QUIZ 18 – Horror Films

1	Stephen King	11	*The Silence of the Lambs*
2	*Get Out*	12	Kirsten Dunst
3	John Kramer or "Jigsaw"	13	Abandoned shopping mall
4	*Halloween*	14	*Child's Play*
5	Ed Gein	15	*American Mary*
6	*The Exorcist*	16	Freddy Krueger
7	Mrs Pamela Voorhees (not Jason!)	17	Cenobites
8	*The Evil Dead*	18	*The Babadook*
9	*The Craft*	19	*Psycho*
10	*The Devil's Rejects*	20	*The Omen*

ANSWERS ON PAGE **23**

1 What is the Spanish word for "tomorrow"?

2 Which Alfred Hitchcock film climaxes atop Mount Rushmore?

3 The 184-metre-high Space Needle is a feature of what US city?

4 The name of which dinosaur literally means "three-horned face"?

5 Angela Lansbury played the detective Jessica Fletcher in what long-running murder mystery series?

6 In linguistics, what is the opposite of a synonym?

7 Which Spanish team did David Beckham leave Manchester United to join?

8 How many years is four score and seven?

9 "The One With Chandler in a Box" was the title of an episode of which American TV sitcom?

10 *The Marriage of Figaro* is an 1786 opera from which Salzburg-born composer?

11 Which Liverpool-based soap opera ran on Channel 4 from its launch in 1982 until November 2003?

12 The term "manga" generally refers to comics, graphic novels or cartoons originating in which country?

13 English mathematician John Couch Adams accurately predicted the existence of which planet, the eighth from the sun, in 1846?

14 New York City's Brooklyn Bridge links Long Island with which other island in the city?

15 *My Booky Wook* is the 2007 memoir from which British comedian, TV presenter and actor?

16 In which city was *Byker Grove* set?

17 In what sport is there a fielding position named "silly point"?

18 The final of the first edition of which competition saw Wanderers beat the Royal Engineers 1-0 in 1872?

19 In which Shakespeare play would you find the characters of Portia, Antonio and Shylock?

20 Which land mammal has the longest tail?

Easy

Medium

Hard

Answers to QUIZ 19 – Pot Luck

1	Placenta	11	Apollo 11
2	George III	12	Mount Sinai
3	Two	13	Four
4	Pepsi®	14	Ares
5	South Africa	15	*Chicago*
6	Apple	16	Donald Duck
7	In my opinion	17	Europe
8	U2	18	*Frogger*
9	One	19	*Jaw*
10	Ronaldo (the Brazilian one, not Cristiano Ronaldo)	20	Ken Livingstone

1. Valentine's Day falls on which day of February?
2. The 6th February anniversary of which singer's birthday is a national holiday in Jamaica?
3. A way of remembering important people and events in the history of the African diaspora, February is also known as which heritage month in the USA?
4. Which band made their American TV debut on *The Ed Sullivan Show* on 9th February 1964?
5. With a namesake film starring Bill Murray, which popular North American tradition is celebrated on 2nd February?
6. Which Australian cricketer was sent home the day before the start of the Cricket World Cup in February 2003 for failing a drug test?
7. Because it has less than 30 days, February is the only month that cannot have which astronomical phenomenon?
8. Britain moved to decimal currency on 15th February of which year?
9. Which man resigned as Liverpool's manager on 22nd February 1991?
10. On 9th February 1996, the IRA ended a 17-month ceasefire by exploding a truck bomb in which area of London?

11. Deep Blue recorded the first ever computer win against human opposition in which board game when it beat Garry Kasparov in February 1996?
12. The 30-year-old ban on the African National Congress was lifted on 2nd February 1990 by which South African President?
13. Who, on 24th February 1867, became the first US President to ever be impeached?
14. On 8th February 1587, who was beheaded on the orders of her cousin, Elizabeth I?
15. Olof Palme was assassinated on 28th February 1986 – which country was he Prime Minister of at the time?
16. Which man, invariably regarded as Britain's most famous landscape designer, died on 6th February 1783?
17. The Irish tradition by which women are allowed to propose to men on 29th February is known as what?
18. On 1st February 2003, which space shuttle disintegrated upon re-entry?
19. Held between the 4th and 11th February 1945, the Crimea Conference to discuss the post-war reorganisation of Germany and Europe was held in which city?
20. The USA signed the Treaty of Guadalupe Hidalgo on 2nd February 1848 that saw them "buy" eight states for $15 million from which country?

Answers to QUIZ 20 – Doctors

1	Dr Who	11	Doc Holliday
2	*The Shining*	12	Three times a day
3	*The Flying Doctors*	13	Dr Leonard McCoy
4	Sonic the Hedgehog	14	Doctor and the Medics
5	*Doctor Zhivago*	15	Dr Kildare
6	Dr Pepper®	16	*ER*
7	*Doctor Dolittle*	17	Richard Gordon
8	*Dr. Strangelove or: How I Learned to Stop Worrying and Love the Bomb*	18	The Spin Doctors
		19	Dr Phil Hammond
9	Hippocrates (the Hippocratic oath)	20	Julius Erving
10	Dr Benjamin Spock		

ANSWERS ON PAGE 25

1. Which British monarch caused a constitutional crisis by abdicating the throne to marry divorced American Wallis Simpson in 1936?

2. Which 'C' is an official count or survey, often of a population?

3. What is the stage name of actor, comedian and potter Michael Pennington?

4. The young of which pesky common household flying insect is known as a leatherjacket?

5. Which year in the 11th century is known in British history as the Year of the Three Kings, because that is precisely what it had?

6. *The Mysterious Island* features the second appearance of Captain Nemo, who originally appeared in which other Jules Verne novel?

7. A bee has how many eyes?

8. Napoleon Solo and Illya Kuryakin were the two lead characters in which 1960s television spy fiction series?

9. A queen bee and a sausage respectively won the first two series of the British version of which televised singing competition?

10. Waco, Austin and Houston are cities in which American state?

11. The saxophone belongs to which family of musical instruments?

12. A statue of 19th century merchant Edward Colston was toppled into which city's harbour on 7th June 2020?

13. *The Fighting Temeraire* was a painting by which British artist, known for his maritime works?

14. In 1819, which poet wrote odes to each of a Grecian urn, melancholy, insolence, autumn, Psyche and a nightingale?

15. Films in which franchise include "__ Camping", "__Doctor" and "__Up The Khyber"?

16. Which unusual bird cannot fly, has hair-like feathers, strong legs and no tail, and is a national icon of New Zealand?

17. For winning the US Open tennis championship as a qualifier, who won the BBC's Sports Personality of the Year award in 2021?

18. In 2021, which actor became the oldest person to travel into space at the age of 90?

19. Ski-Doo is a brand name of what form of transport?

20. In the Bible, who was said to have parted the Red Sea?

Easy

Medium

Hard

Answers to QUIZ 21 – Pot Luck

1	*Mañana*	11	*Brookside*
2	*North by Northwest*	12	Japan
3	Seattle	13	Neptune
4	Triceratops	14	Manhattan
5	*Murder She Wrote*	15	Russell Brand
6	Antonym	16	Newcastle
7	Real Madrid	17	Cricket
8	87	18	FA Cup
9	*Friends*	19	*The Merchant of Venice*
10	Wolfgang Amadeus Mozart	20	Giraffe

Easy

1 According to the company themselves, what is the most popular flavour of Walkers® crisps?

2 What is the American term for what are called crisps in Britain?

3 Which "really cheesy" brand of crisps was advertised for many years as being the only one you could "get a whoosh" with?

4 Advertised with a moustachioed man called Julius, which stackable crisps come in a tube?

5 Gary Lineker has advertised which brand of crisps since 1994?

6 When crisp flavouring was pioneered in 1954, which were the first two flavours created?

7 Which crisps aimed at children come in Pickled Onion, Roast Beef, Chilli Dog and Flamin' Hot flavours, and may or may not be shaped like feet?

8 Which parent company owns Nik Naks®, Skips®, Pop Chips® and Hula Hoops®, and also sells peanuts under this name?

9 Which deep-fried crisp described as "curly potato puffs" on their packaging take their name from musical notation?

10 In the inaugural World Cup of Crisps on Twitter™ in 2012, which fried bacon snack was voted the nation's favourite?

11 Which "quintessentially English" crisps were created in 2002 by farmer William Chase?

12 For the first twenty years of their existence, which alien-shaped snacks sold for only 10p a bag?

13 All bags of crisps have expiry dates that fall on which day of the week?

14 Sheridan Smith, Will Mellor, Natalie Casey and Ralf Little starred in which sitcom about the lives of a group of twentysomethings in Cheshire?

15 Which chocolate bar was known for the first two years of its existence as Rowntree's Chocolate Crisp?

16 Crisp was fifteen lengths ahead at the final fence in the 1973 Grand National, but tired badly and was pipped on the line by who?

17 "When the snow lay round about, deep and crisp and even" is a line from which Christmas carol?

18 Which writer wrote in his memoir *The Naked Civil Servant* that he did no housework, since "after the first four years, the dirt doesn't get any worse"?

19 What was the very fitting name of the hunter, guide and cook who is widely – if not entirely accurately – credited as being the inventor of crisps?

20 Which Major League Baseball 15-year veteran got his unusual nickname from his sister, who thought he looked like the mascot on a cereal packet?

Medium

Hard

Answers to QUIZ 22 – February

1	14th	11	Chess
2	Bob Marley	12	F.W. de Klerk
3	Black History Month	13	Andrew Johnson
4	The Beatles	14	Mary, Queen of Scots
5	Groundhog Day	15	Sweden
6	Shane Warne	16	Lancelot "Capability" Brown
7	Blue moon	17	Bachelor's Day
8	1971	18	Space Shuttle *Columbia*
9	Kenny Dalglish	19	Yalta
10	Docklands	20	Mexico

1 How many players are there in a beach volleyball team?

2 Which English illustrator and author created the Christmas classic children's picture book, *The Snowman*?

3 The Ishihara Test is used to diagnose which visual impairment?

4 Eating what put Snow White to sleep?

5 Which actor had three consecutive films reach number one in 1994, including *The Mask* and *Dumb and Dumber*?

6 A mimosa cocktail is a mixture of citrus juice (usually orange juice) and which alcoholic drink?

7 Which cat with an enormous grin did Alice in Wonderland encounter?

8 How many bottles are there in a magnum?

9 Iron pyrite is also known by which other name?

10 From which country does cognac come?

11 Along with Linas Pauling, which Polish/French scientist is the only person to win Nobel Prizes in two different fields?

12 Which artist reportedly once said that in the future, everybody will be famous for 15 minutes?

13 In 1875, Captain Matthew Webb became the first person to ever swim across which body of water?

14 Jim Davis created which cartoon cat, along with his owner Jon Arbuckle?

15 What name is given to a male chicken?

16 Which Australian model was given the nickname "The Body" by *Time* magazine in 1989?

17 Gnasher is the dog of which cartoon miscreant?

18 In rugby, what name is given to the act of unlawfully driving the ball with the hand or arm towards the opponents' goal line, usually by mistake?

19 Which wax museum opened in London in 1835?

20 Miniature, Toy and Teacup are all breeds of which dog?

Answers to QUIZ 23 – Pot Luck

1	Edward VIII	11	Woodwind as, even though it is made of brass, it is played with a reed
2	Census		
3	Johnny Vegas	12	Bristol
4	Crane fly/Daddy Long Legs	13	J.M.W. Turner
5	1936	14	John Keats
6	*20,000 Leagues Under the Sea*	15	*Carry On*
7	Five	16	Kiwi
8	*The Man From U.N.C.L.E.*	17	Emma Raducanu
9	*The Masked Singer*	18	William Shatner
10	Texas	19	Snowmobile
		20	Moses

1. What distinct colour of paper is the *Financial Times* printed on?
2. *The Guardian* was founded in which city, which used to appear in its name, in 1821?
3. Which London street became known for publishing to the point that by the 20th century, most national newspapers operated from there?
4. After 180 years of paid circulation, which London-centric daily newspaper became a "freesheet" in October 2009 and doubled its circulation?
5. Which short-lived British newspaper ran only between 1986 and 1995?
6. Since 1978, the *Garfield* comic strip has appeared in which British daily newspaper?
7. First published in 1791, which is the world's oldest Sunday newspaper?
8. On 7th July 2011, which British newspaper was shuttered amid a phone-hacking scandal?
9. According to a 13th March 1986 headline in *The Sun*, what did Freddie Starr eat?
10. Which German publication is the best-selling tabloid not only in Germany, but in all of Europe?
11. Which British newspaper has had the motto "Was, is, and will be" appear in every issue since its founding in 1858?
12. For the first three years of its existence between 1785 and 1788, which newspaper was known as *The Daily Universal Register*?
13. Which French national daily newspaper takes its name from a play written in 1778 by Pierre Beaumarchais?
14. What is the name of the official news publication of The Salvation Army?
15. Carl Bernstein and Bob Woodward reported on the Watergate scandal while working for which newspaper?
16. Which daily British publication that launched in 1986 focuses on horse racing, greyhound racing and sports betting?
17. In March 2018, for the first time in 40 years, *The Sun* was knocked off the top of the UK circulation charts by which freesheet?
18. Which annual sporting event was first held in 1903 to improve sales for *L'Auto* newspaper?
19. Which Sunday newspaper was the first in Britain to carry a supplement magazine?
20. Which now-defunct broadsheet – which shares its name with a contemporary tabloid – was the first to have advertisement revenue?

Answers to QUIZ 24 – Crisps

1	Cheese and onion	11	Tyrrell's®
2	Potato chips	12	Space Raiders®
3	Wotsits®	13	Saturday
4	Pringles®	14	*Two Pints of Lager and a Packet of Crisps*
5	Walkers®	15	Kit Kat®
6	Salt and vinegar & cheese and onion	16	Red Rum
7	Monster Munch®	17	*Good King Wenceslas*
8	KP	18	Quentin Crisp
9	Quavers	19	George Crum
10	Frazzles	20	Coco Crisp

Easy

Medium

Hard

1 Making up the BS part of the acronym, the WPBSA is the governing body of which table games?

2 Ted Hughes, Cecil Day-Lewis and Sir John Betjeman all held which honorary literary title?

3 Television chef Phil Vickery married which television presenter in 2000, whom he met on the set of *Ready Steady Cook*?

4 Emperor Napoleon III offered a prize to anyone who could make an alternative to butter, a prize claimed by chemist Hippolyte Mège-Mouriès with his creation of which spread?

5 The Ceremony of the Keys takes place every evening at which historic London landmark?

6 A shepherd's pie is usually made with which meat?

7 Which actor was the first to ever play Doctor Who?

8 Tybalt is a character that appears in which Shakespeare play?

9 Which surname of Irish origin is used to describe a second chance given to a player to perform a certain move or action, for example in golf?

10 Which nuts are traditionally used to make pesto?

11 What 'C' is the name of the spiked metal plates fixed to boots for climbing on ice or rock?

12 The Mercalli scale measures the intensity of what geographical phenomenon?

13 Which animals are the subjects of the Richard Adams novel *Watership Down*?

14 As of 2021, how many American Presidents have been assassinated while in office?

15 Comedians Katy, Jo and Russell all share which surname?

16 Spelunking is the exploration of what, particularly if done as a hobby?

17 In *Dad's Army*, what was Lance Corporal Jones's occupation?

18 Who wrote the 1894 collection of short stories, *The Jungle Book*?

19 *My Bed* was a 1998 artistic installation by which controversial artist?

20 In the Bible, who dies first?

Easy

Medium

Hard

Answers to QUIZ 25 – Pot Luck

1	Two	11	Marie Curie
2	Raymond Briggs	12	Andy Warhol
3	Colour blindness	13	English Channel
4	A poisoned apple	14	Garfield
5	Jim Carrey	15	Rooster
6	Champagne	16	Elle Macpherson
7	The Cheshire Cat	17	Dennis the Menace
8	Two	18	Knock-on
9	Fool's Gold	19	Madame Tussauds
10	France	20	Poodle

Easy

1   Although never crowned and with her legitimacy to the claim disputed, who was "Queen" for nine days in 1553?

2   The *Fifty Shades* book series, beginning with *Fifty Shades of Grey*, was written by which author?

3   Giving his name to a tea, who was UK Prime Minister between 1830 and 1834?

4   The idiom "little grey cells", referring to the brain, was often used by which fictional detective, created by Agatha Christie?

5   Which medical drama series takes its name from an 1858 human anatomy textbook?

6   Greyfriars was a fictional school that formed the setting for the stories of which character created by Frank Richard?

7   The greylag is a species of which animal?

8   With a whisper, Bob Harris presented which BBC television music programme between 1972 and 1979?

9   *Agnes Grey* is an 1847 novel written by which British author?

10 Grey Goose® is a French brand of which alcoholic drink?

11 Which 11-time Paralympic gold medallist was made a Life Peer in 2010?

12 Zane Grey was a leading author in which genre of fiction?

13 Grey Goblin is one of the lesser-known foes of which Marvel comic superhero?

14 A former country club now run as a hotel, Grey Gables is a regular location in which radio drama series?

Medium

15 The fictional character Viscount Greystoke is better known as who?

16 Which actress played Francis "Baby" Houseman in Dirty Dancing?

17 What is the name of the largest intercity bus carrier company in the United States?

18 *Touch of Grey* is the most commercially successful single by which eclectic American rock band, fronted until his death by Jerry Garcia?

19 Which original member of the X-Men, also known as Marvel Girl, has both telepathic and telekinetic powers?

20 In Greek mythology, the Grey sisters (or Graeae) were three sisters who shared only one of which two body parts among them?

Hard

Answers to QUIZ 26 – Newspapers

1	Pink	11	*The Daily Telegraph*
2	Manchester	12	*The Times*
3	Fleet Street	13	*Le Figaro*
4	*Evening Standard*	14	*The War Cry*
5	*Today*	15	*The Washington Post*
6	*Daily Mail*	16	*The Racing Post*
7	*The Observer*	17	*Metro*
8	*News Of The World*	18	Tour de France
9	"My Hamster" (he didn't)	19	*The Sunday Times*
10	*Bild*	20	*The Sun*, a New York-based broadsheet, in 1833

1   On 11th March 2011, a 9.1 magnitude earthquake and subsequent tsunami hit the east of which country?

2   What is the day after Shrove Tuesday called?

3   Who wrote the foundation of evolutionary biology textbook *On the Origin of Species* in 1859?

4   Transylvania is a region in which present day country?

5   Bernie Hamilton starred as police chief Captain Harold Dobey in which crime drama television series of the 1970s?

6   The sausage dog is an alternative name for which breed?

7   Which actress left Hollywood to marry Prince Rainier III of Monaco in 1956?

8   Giving its name to Argentina, argentum is an obsolete Latin name for which chemical element?

9   Which Australian band had albums called *High Voltage*, *TNT* and *Back in Black*?

10 David Prowse portrayed which character in a road safety awareness campaign during the 1970s and 1980s?

11 Ironically, rhotacism is the difficulty in pronouncing which letter of the English alphabet?

12 The national flag of which country features a blue disc with 27 stars and the motto "Ordem e Progresso"?

13 Which is the only capital city in the world that spans two continents?

14 What name is given to the method of hair removal in which strands of cotton are used to pluck unwanted hair?

15 The northernmost tip of which country is geographically closest to the North Pole?

16 Which river's entire 87-mile-long course flows through Aberdeenshire?

17 England's tallest cathedral can be found in which Wiltshire city?

18 What are the sand hazards on a golf course usually called?

19 Which 2006 BBC nature documentary series won four Emmy awards and was narrated for the syndicated Discovery Channel version by Sigourney Weaver?

20 In English, what is the term for a native of the city or principality of Moscow?

Easy

Medium

Hard

Answers to QUIZ 27 – Pot Luck

1   Billiards and snooker (World Professional Billiards and Snooker Association)
2   Poet Laureate
3   Fern Britton
4   Margarine
5   Tower of London
6   Lamb
7   William Hartnell
8   *Romeo and Juliet*
9   Mulligan
10 Pine nuts

11 Crampons
12 Earthquakes
13 Rabbits
14 Four (Abraham Lincoln, James Garfield, William McKinley, John F. Kennedy)
15 Brand
16 Caves
17 Butcher
18 Rudyard Kipling
19 Tracey Emin
20 Abel

In these pictures, both the parent and the child are famous in their own right. Can you name both?

Easy

Medium

Hard

Answers to QUIZ 28 – Grey

1	Lady Jane Grey	11	Baroness Tanni Grey-Thompson
2	E.L. James	12	Westerns
3	Earl Grey	13	Spider-Man
4	Hercule Poirot	14	*The Archers*
5	*Grey's Anatomy*	15	Tarzan
6	Billy Bunter	16	Jennifer Grey
7	Goose	17	Greyhound Lines
8	*The Old Grey Whistle Test*	18	The Grateful Dead
9	Anne Brontë	19	Jean Grey
10	Vodka	20	One tooth and one eye

1   In its own language, which European country is known as *Hellas*?
2   Calligraphy is the art of what?
3   Which river rises in the Himalayas in India and drains into the Bay of Bengal?
4   Which hate group was founded on Christmas Eve 1865 in Pulaski, Tennessee?
5   Small pieces of toasted bread served with soup or salad are known as what?
6   What nonsense word was created by Edward Lear and used as an adjective to describe various items including a hat, cat, goose, wall and a spoon?
7   Which former US Marine and stand-up comedian was the first host of the US version of *Whose Line Is It Anyway*?
8   Created by Judge Henry Fielding, the Bow Street Runners were London's first example of what?
9   Which 2016 film of the DC Extended Universe series saw the first appearance of Margot Robbie as Dr Harleen Quinzel/Harley Quinn?
10 Known as *El Libertador*, which Venezuelan military hero led Venezuela, Bolivia, Colombia, Ecuador, Peru and Panama to independence from the Spanish Empire?
11 Prehension, mastication and deglutition are usually the first three stages of what?
12 What do elephants and giraffes do for only two hours a day?
13 Who played Louise alongside Geena Davis's Thelma?
14 Which 2015 Taylor Swift song shares its name with a Canadian crime drama?
15 The pommel, the seat and the cantle are the three main areas of a what?
16 Zinc and copper combine to make which common alloy?
17 Who was the Greek god of the sea?
18 The creole language of Afrikaans is derived from which European language?
19 Found on the outside of teeth, what is the hardest substance in the human body?
20 Who didn't defeat Truman, despite the premature proclamations of the *Chicago Daily Tribune*?

Easy

Medium

Hard

What are people suffering from the following phobias afraid of?

1. Acrophobia
2. Necrophobia
3. Triskaidekaphobia
4. Ailurophobia
5. Coulrophobia
6. Philophobia
7. Pogonophobia
8. Ochlophobia
9. Anglophobia
10. Hippopotomonstrosesquipedaliophobia
11. Nephophobia
12. Gymnophobia
13. Nomophobia
14. Cynophobia
15. Ornithophobia
16. Cherophobia
17. Hedonophobia
18. Chionophobia
19. Odynophobia
20. Ergophobia

Easy

Medium

Hard

Answers to QUIZ 30 – Celebrity Children

1. Jaden & Will Smith
2. Brooklyn & David Beckham
3. Kris Jenner & Kim Kardashian
4. Kate Hudson & Goldie Hawn
5. Paul & Stella McCartney
6. Cindy Crawford & Kaia Gerber
7. Zoë Kravitz & Lisa Bonet
8. Kiefer & Donald Sutherland
9. Ice Cube & O'Shea Jackson Jr.

1   What is the capital of the American state of California?

2   What drink is also known as "Adam's Ale"?

3   Which is the only mammal capable of true sustained flight?

4   Also referred to as the Hound of Hades, what is the name of the multi-headed dog that guards the gates of the Underworld in Greek mythology?

5   Which Danish toy company is the largest manufacturer of rubber tyres in the world?

6   What is the American term for aubergine?

7   The adjective "haptic" refers to which of the senses?

8   Which legendary comedian and actor won the Best Supporting Actor Oscar for his role as the therapist in *Good Will Hunting*?

9   The Toyota Camry, Corolla and Corona cars all have names that derive from Latin or Japanese words that mean what?

10 In the James Bond movie franchise, what is the single-letter codename of the scientist who produces Bond's gadgets?

11 Which dam on the Colorado river was the largest in the world upon its opening in 1922?

12 Which song from *Pinocchio* was the first from a Disney film to win the Oscar for Best Original Song?

13 In *Rocky*, which type of meat does Rocky Balboa use as a punching bag in his training regime?

14 When the Moulin Rouge opened in Paris, which Post-Impressionist artist was commissioned to paint a series of posters prominently featuring it?

15 What is the slogan of sportswear and equipment manufacturer Nike?

16 Which is the largest brass instrument found in an orchestra?

17 Brazil shares a border with every South American country, except for which two?

18 By area, which is the largest US state?

19 In the film *Gladiator*, who plays the title character?

20 Which statuette weighs 8.5 pounds, is 13.5 inches tall and is made of gold-plated Britannium?

Easy

Medium

Hard

Answers to QUIZ 31 – Pot Luck

1	Greece	11	Eating
2	Handwriting	12	Sleep
3	Ganges	13	Susan Sarandon
4	Ku Klux Klan	14	*Bad Blood*
5	Croutons	15	Saddle
6	Runcible	16	Brass
7	Drew Carey	17	Poseidon
8	Police force	18	Dutch
9	*Suicide Squad*	19	Enamel
10	Simón Bolívar	20	Thomas Dewey

1   The aerospace manufacturer SpaceX was founded by which South African-born entrepreneur?

2   What number is the Roman numeral X equivalent to?

3   The X-Wing is a type of starfighter craft seen in which sci-fi film series?

4   In the NATO Phonetic alphabet, what represents the letter X?

5   Which actor played the title role in Spike Lee's 1992 film, *Malcolm X*?

6   The Xbox range of gaming consoles is manufactured by which technology company?

7   X.com was the precursor to which online payment company?

8   Alongside Chuck D and Flava Flav, Terminator X was the long-time DJ in which pioneering hip-hop group?

9   *XX* was the name of the twentieth anniversary album of which band, best known for hits such as *Rosanna, Hold The Line* and *Africa*?

10 The beer Castlemaine XXXX and its brewer Castlemaine Perkins are based in which country?

11 Steve Brookstein, Shayne Ward and Leona Lewis were the first three winners of which reality television competition?

12 *X Marks the Spot* is a hidden track on the album *A Head Full of Dreams* by which British rock band?

13 Complete the list of the five original X-Men – Cyclops, Marvel Girl, Beast, Angel, _____?

14 Which rapper and singer, real name Montero Hill, broke through with the song *Old Town Road*, later remixed with Billy Ray Cyrus?

15 The Cigarette-smoking Man was a regular antagonist in which science fiction drama series?

16 The X-Pensive Winos were a side project of which legendary British guitarist and songwriter?

17 Although the fourth-least used letter in dictionary entries, X is the third-least used letter in *written* English; which two are used less often?

18 To cure the disease *scrofula* and to show how legitimate he was as a monarch, Charles X of France did what performative act on sufferers?

19 Which extreme sports event organised, produced and broadcast by ESPN with medals for prizes has been held annually since 1995?

20 Rapper and actor Xzibit hosted which car customisation show on MTV between 2004 and 2007?

Easy

Medium

Hard

Answers to QUIZ 32 – Phobias

1	Heights	11	Clouds
2	Death, and anything associated with it	12	Nudity
3	The number 13	13	Not having a mobile phone
4	Cats	14	Dogs
5	Clowns	15	Birds
6	Love	16	Happiness
7	Beards	17	Experiencing pleasurable things
8	Crowds	18	Snow
9	England and the English	19	Pain
10	Long words	20	Work

1. Which alternative medical therapy involves massaging different areas of the foot in the belief they correspond to organs and systems of the body?

2. In the NATO phonetic alphabet, which boy's name represents O?

3. In tennis, what is the term used for a served ball that touches the net, but still lands in the opponent's court, thus neither a live ball nor a fault?

4. Which European country had a population of 3 million in 1741, 8 million in 1841 but barely 4 million in 1941?

5. What does 'RC' stand for in an RC car?

6. A Vitamin D deficiency is the main cause of which childhood soft bone disease?

7. Which then-retired boxer and his pet tiger played a major role in the plot of *The Hangover*?

8. What is the alcoholic ingredient of an Irish Coffee?

9. Shaun Williamson played which *EastEnders* character between 1994 and 2004?

10. Commentating on which aviation disaster prompted Herbert Morrison to spontaneously react "Oh, the humanity!"?

11. Which chemical element has the symbol "Na"?

12. Which Greek Goddess of retribution and indignation shares her name with a ride at Alton Towers?

13. Which Egyptian pharaoh was known as the "boy king"?

14. Eddie Vedder has been the frontman of which rock band since their formation in 1990?

15. On a digital clock, how many LED segments are in a single digit's space?

16. Which Roman Emperor was said to have fiddled while Rome burned?

17. The dong is the currency of which Asian country?

18. What is the name of Sherlock Holmes's landlady and housekeeper?

19. *Hello Kitty* lacks which facial feature?

20. Ho Chi Minh City surrounds which river, which has the same name as the city's former name?

Answers to QUIZ 33 – Pot Luck

1	Sacramento	11	Hoover Dam
2	Water	12	*When You Wish Upon A Star*
3	Bat – possums and flying squirrels glide rather than fly	13	Beef (it is a cow's carcass)
4	Cerberus	14	Henri de Toulouse-Lautrec
5	Lego	15	"Just Do It"
6	Eggplant	16	Tuba
7	Touch	17	Ecuador and Chile
8	Robin Williams	18	Alaska (and by quite some way, too; almost two and a half times bigger than Texas, which is second)
9	Crown	19	Russell Crowe
10	Q	20	Oscar/Academy Award

QUIZ 36 – The Internet

Easy

1. Jerry Yang and David Filo created which search engine in January 1994?
2. Google regularly alters the logo on their home page to commemorate holidays, history and events; what are these novel logos called?
3. Which British computer scientist invented the World Wide Web, the protocol which makes hyperlinked internet navigation possible?
4. In online computing, what does the acronym ISP stand for?
5. Which programming language takes its name from the fact that its creator was reading *Monty Python's Flying Circus* scripts as a hobby?
6. Sales of .tv domain names generates approximately 10% of all government revenue for which small Pacific island nation?
7. An urban legend holds that which US politician claims to have "invented" the internet?
8. Before Facebook, which UK-based social media site sought to reconnect groups of old school mates?
9. Content creator Jonti Pickering, whose early works include *Badger Badger Badger*, goes under what nickname?
10. Amazon acquired which live streaming platform, focusing on live gaming, for $970 million in 2014?

Medium

11. Teenager Gary Brolsma filmed himself dancing to a song entitled *Dragostea Din Te* in 2004; the clip went viral under what tautonym?
12. An early internet meme saw a man called Tay Zonday go viral with which original song of his?
13. 28th April is known on UK Twitter™ as which politician's day, who on that date in 2011 posted just his name as a tweet, mistaking it for the search bar?
14. In 1999, Shawn Fanning and Sean Carter created which pioneering P2P software as a means to swap music files with their friends?
15. Which online word game exploded in January 2022, even though its creator, Josh Wardle, initially made it only for him and his partner to play?
16. Before taking its current name, which company was originally called BackRub?
17. Interest in which American painter and TV host's work has been renewed posthumously via numerous internet memes?
18. Entrepreneur Gabriel Weinberg launched which web browser in 2008 that emphasises user privacy above all else?
19. Which company makes the Firefox web browser?
20. In February 2021, lawyer Rod Ponton appeared before a judge in a Zoom courtroom with what animal filter on, that he could not turn off?

Hard

Answers to QUIZ 34 – X

1	Elon Musk	11	*The X Factor*
2	10	12	Coldplay
3	*Star Wars*	13	Iceman
4	X-ray	14	Lil Nas X
5	Denzel Washington	15	*The X Files*
6	Microsoft®	16	Keith Richards
7	PayPal	17	Q and Z
8	Public Enemy	18	The "Royal Touch"
9	Toto	19	The X Games
10	Australia	20	*Pimp My Ride*

QUIZ 37 – Pot Luck

ANSWERS ON PAGE 39

1   How many are there in a baker's dozen?
2   A Stetson is what type of clothing?
3   Haemoglobin is a protein found in which bodily system?
4   Martin Sheen played US President Josiah "Jed" Bartlet in which TV series?
5   Which budget hotel brand shares its name with a wading bird?
6   In 1984, which tennis player was sued by his own fan club for interfering with its operation?
7   Which term is used to describe words or phrases that are spelled the same backwards as well as forwards?
8   In which forest is the legend of Robin Hood centred?
9   What was the name of the Hunchback of Notre Dame?
10 The Overlook Hotel is the setting of which 1977 Stephen King novel?
11 Ian Hislop took over as editor of which magazine in 1986?
12 Stephen Fry and Noel Edmonds both regularly drive an unlicensed version of which traditionally British vehicle?
13 Who was the only 18th century Queen of Britain?
14 Miso soup comes from which country?
15 The "Lindy Hop" dance is named after which aviation pioneer who completed the first solo transatlantic flight in 1927?
16 Brad Pitt damaged his Achilles tendon playing which character in the 2004 film *Troy*?
17 Which English county is the only one whose name begins with three consonants in a row?
18 What kind of animal is a Labrador?
19 What four-letter name is given to the strongest or central tower of a castle, acting as a final place of refuge?
20 Which Japanese car company manufactures the MX-5/Miata?

Easy

Medium

Hard

Answers to QUIZ 35 – Pot Luck

1   Reflexology
2   Oscar
3   Let
4   Ireland
5   Radio-controlled
6   Rickets
7   Mike Tyson
8   Whiskey
9   Barry Evans
10 The *Hindenburg* disaster
11 Sodium
12 Nemesis
13 Tutankhamun
14 Pearl Jam
15 Seven
16 Nero
17 Vietnam
18 Mrs Martha Hudson
19 Mouth
20 Saigon

Easy

1   Between 1689 and 1814, Britain was in near-constant military conflict with which other imperial power?

2   In 1583, Sir Humphrey Davey claimed which aptly-named Canadian island for Britain, becoming the first part of what would become the Empire?

3   After gaining independence as a nation in 1980, Southern Rhodesia renamed itself to what?

4   The annexation, division and colonisation of most of Africa by seven Western European powers including Britain became known as what?

5   Which 17th century company was formed to trade in the Indian Ocean region, but eventually had near-complete military and administrative control?

6   The trading of what was abolished within the British Empire in 1807?

7   Which Indian lawyer led his country to freedom from British colonial rule in 1947 through his philosophy of non-violence?

8   In 1607, Captain John Smith founded the first permanent English colony in North America, and named it for the King. What was it called?

9   In 1997, Britain relinquished and handed over to China sovereignty of where?

10 The *first* Balfour Declaration, promising Britain would aid the creation of a Jewish state, was signed in which year?

Medium

11 Britain's last territorial claim to date was made in 1955 for which small uninhabited granite islet situated in the North Atlantic Ocean?

12 After 55 years of monarchy, which Caribbean nation in 2021 removed the Queen as head of state and became a republic within the Commonwealth?

13 Because of its key economic and strategic roles in the expansion of the empire, where was known as the "Jewel in the Imperial crown"?

14 The two Opium Wars over trading rights and diplomatic status were fought between Britain and France versus which Asian country?

15 What name was given to the post-war mass immigration to Britain by persons from the former Empire nations to fill labour shortages?

16 Known as Gold Coast prior to leaving, which was the first African country to gain independence from the British Empire in 1957?

17 The Morant Bay rebellion, protesting against injustice and poverty, led to reprisals and the dismissal of the governor of which Empire island nation?

18 Between 1952 and 1960, which revolt against colonial rule helped to hasten Kenyan independence in 1963?

19 Which PM made the 1960 "Wind of Change" speech to the South African Parliament, indicating that Britain would not oppose independence?

20 The *second* Balfour Declaration, conferring equal status on the self-governing dominion states within the Empire, was signed in which year?

Hard

Answers to QUIZ 36 – The Internet

1	Yahoo!	11	*Numa Numa*
2	Doodles	12	*Chocolate Rain*
3	Sir Tim Berners-Lee	13	Ed Balls
4	Internet Service Provider	14	Napster
5	Python	15	Wordle
6	Tuvalu	16	Google
7	Al Gore	17	Bob Ross
8	Friends Reunited	18	DuckDuckGo
9	Weebl or Mr Weebl	19	Mozilla
10	Twitch.tv	20	A cat

1   What term is used in geometry for an angle of less than 90 degrees?
2   What was the real name of David Bowie?
3   Tom Cruise, John Travolta and Kirstie Alley are all outspoken followers of which religion?
4   Which band sued Apple in 2006 for an alleged violation of a contractual agreement not to sell music online?
5   Which is the world's only venomous mammal?
6   Which comedian and interviewer was disparagingly known as "the bubonic plagiarist" for repeated alleged joke-appropriation?
7   Whose works include the 1970 album *The Man Who Sold The World* and the 1976 film *The Man Who Fell to Earth*?
8   Melvin Bragg, A.A. Gill, Giles Coren and Morrissey have all been "winners" of which ignominious literary award?
9   Cerulean, azure and navy are shades of which colour?
10 Which car company's E-Type model was adapted by design firm Vizualtech into a concept car called the Growler?
11 On which racecourse is the Derby run?
12 What is the name of the galaxy we are all in?
13 For a month to contain a Friday the 13th, what day of the week must the 1st fall on?
14 In computing, how many bits are in a byte?
15 Before 1939, what was the official name of Thailand?
16 The name of which Venetian explorer of Asia is used in a call-and-response swimming pool tag game?
17 Which was Ian Fleming's first James Bond novel?
18 English romantic painter George Stubbs was best known for his paintings of which animal?
19 Shakespeare's Hamlet was the prince of which country?
20 Which fruit is dried to make a raisin?

Easy

Medium

Hard

Answers to QUIZ 37 – Pot Luck

1	13	11	*Private Eye*
2	Hat	12	Black cab
3	Circulatory/vascular system	13	Queen Anne
4	*The West Wing*	14	Japan
5	Ibis	15	Charles Lindbergh
6	Jimmy Connors	16	Achilles
7	Palindrome	17	Shropshire
8	Sherwood Forest	18	Dog
9	Quasimodo	19	Keep
10	*The Shining*	20	Mazda

1. Which cartoonist, writer, producer and animator created *The Simpsons*?
2. What is Springfield's neighbouring rival town called?
3. Which late actor voiced the parts of Troy McClure and Lionel Hutz amongst others?
4. Only ever written into the script as "annoyed grunt", what is Homer's catchphrase noise, usually heard after he has done something stupid?
5. Mayor Joe Quimby goes by which nickname?
6. With red hair and a beard, which aggressive and stereotypically Scottish character serves as the school's janitor?
7. What was the name of Ned Flanders's specialist store at the Springfield Mall?
8. What was Maggie Simpson's first word?
9. What was the name of the barbershop quartet that Homer was a part of?
10. A hard worker who resents his nemesis's fortune, which grumpy and irritable power plant employee is the self-declared enemy of Homer?
11. What are the annual Halloween magazine episodes of *The Simpsons* known as?
12. Which is the most popular brand of beer in Springfield, and definitely Homer's favourite?
13. Which 2017 documentary film by Hari Kondabolu caused Hank Azaria to re-examine whether or not he should continue to voice certain characters?
14. Which laconic Jewish comedian played Rabbi Krustofski, Krusty's less-than-proud father?
15. In a bit of a rush, what did Homer use as an emergency engagement ring?
16. In the initial plan for his character arc, Krusty the Clown was supposed to be an alter-ego of which regular character, hence why they look so similar?
17. Who are the only characters on *The Simpsons* with five fingers on each hand?
18. Which bar patron had the worst name Moe had ever heard?
19. What does Ralph Wiggum's cat's breath smell like?
20. Which Mafia member refuses to tell anyone anything, including whether he has a mother and if he had a nice flight?

Easy

Medium

Hard

Answers to QUIZ 38 – British Empire

1. France
2. Newfoundland
3. Zimbabwe
4. The Scramble for Africa
5. The East India Company
6. Slaves
7. Mohandas Karamchand "Mahatma" Gandhi
8. Jamestown
9. Hong Kong
10. 1917
11. Rockall
12. Barbados
13. India
14. China
15. The Windrush Generation
16. Ghana
17. Jamaica
18. Mau Mau Uprising
19. Harold Macmillan
20. 1926

ANSWERS ON PAGE 43

1 The 20th-century confrontations between Britain and Iceland about fishing rights in the North Atlantic Ocean were known as what?

2 Which sport was essentially created at a meeting at the George Hotel, Huddersfield on 29th August 1895?

3 Ichthyosis affects which organ of the human body?

4 A *portière* is a heavy curtain hung across what?

5 What is the name for the pointed ends of a fishing hook that prevent it from being easily extracted?

6 In Britain, which colour of cats' eyes mark the left hand edge of the road?

7 In Indian cuisine, what are dosas and uttapams?

8 Falling back to Earth in 1979, which was the first American space station?

9 The first FA Cup Final played at the old Wembley Stadium was in which year?

10 The phrase "a nation of shopkeepers" to describe England and the English is commonly attributed to which historical figure?

11 Of the 88 keys on a grand piano, how many are black?

12 Which Scottish city is known as the Granite City?

13 The Tall Blacks is the nickname for which country's national basketball team?

14 What term is given to the redundant act of saying the same thing twice in different words, i.e. "adequate enough"?

15 Bill Wright invented which television quiz show based on his experience of being interrogated by the Gestapo?

16 Which American bank note is legally prohibited from being redesigned, due to the effect it would have on the vending machine industry?

17 The silhouette in the iTunes music library is of which singer?

18 Cher, Michelle Pfeiffer and Susan Sarandon were the titular trio in which 1987 American dark fantasy-comedy film?

19 Which tennis star had won eight Grand Slams by the age of 20 but, after being stabbed on the court in 1993, only won one more?

20 Which South American country was named after an Italian city?

Easy

Medium

Hard

Answers to QUIZ 39 – Pot Luck

1	Acute	11	Epsom
2	David Jones	12	Milky Way
3	Scientology	13	Sunday
4	The Beatles	14	Eight
5	Duck-billed platypus	15	Siam
6	Sir David Frost	16	Marco Polo
7	David Bowie	17	*Casino Royale*
8	The *Literary Review's* Bad Sex in Fiction award	18	Horses
9	Blue	19	Denmark
10	Jaguar	20	Grape

Easy

1   Also the seventh-largest island in the world, which is the largest island of Japan?

2   Which former capital city of Japan has a name that is an anagram of the current capital city?

3   Which single-portion meal of Japanese origin is a lunchbox split into compartments to help with portion control and mindful eating?

4   Which crime syndicate originating in Japan is reportedly the world's largest criminal organisation?

5   Which city in Hokkaido, famous for its beer, hosted the 1972 Winter Olympics?

6   Which mountain – the tallest in Japan – is noted for how photogenically symmetrical its cone shape is?

7   Which alcoholic rice wine is the national beverage of Japan?

8   In 2006 and 2009, Japan were the champions of the first two "World Classics" in which sport?

9   What term is used for obsessive fans of Japanese comics and pop culture, particularly anime and manga, to the detriment of other areas of life?

10 Along with Dutch company Phillips, which Japanese technology giant co-developed the CD?

11 Traditionally eaten for New Year, mochi is a cake primarily made of what ingredient?

12 Which member of The Beatles endorsed an apple drink in Japan, on account of the fact that his name means "apple" in Japanese?

13 There has not been a single recorded passenger fatality or injury to date in the history of which high-speed Japanese train?

14 It is customary to avoid saying the word for the number four in Japan, as it is pronounced incredibly similarly to the word for what?

Medium

15 Over 80% of the country's population are said to engage in the practices of which indigenous Japanese religion?

16 Ōkunoshima is a small island in the Hiroshima Prefecture that is overrun with which animal?

17 Bill Murray is having a midlife crisis, travels to Japan and meets Scarlett Johansson in which 2003 film?

18 Which toy was banned in Japan in 1960 due to the required hip movements being deemed inappropriate?

19 Which Japanese mountaineer was the first woman to summit Mount Everest, and the first to climb all "Seven Summits"?

20 Which corner of Tokyo is noted for its vibrant fashion and colourful street art?

Hard

Answers to QUIZ 40 – The Simpsons

1	Matt Groening	11	Treehouse of Horror
2	Shelbyville	12	Duff
3	Phil Hartman	13	*The Problem with Apu*
4	"D'oh!"	14	Jackie Mason
5	Diamond	15	Onion ring
6	Willie	16	Homer Simpson
7	The Leftorium	17	God and Jesus
8	"Daddy"	18	Joey Jo-Jo Junior Shabadoo
9	The Be Sharps	19	Cat food
10	Frank Grimes	20	Johnny Tightlips

1   Who composed 4'33", a "song" consisting of nothing but silence, the idea being that the listener hears only atmospheric noises?

2   Between 2018 and 2021, LadBaby became the first act to ever have four consecutive Christmas number one singles, all of them themed around which food?

3   Bangladesh achieved independence from which other country in 1971?

4   The four treaties and three additional protocols that establish international legal standards for humanitarian treatment in war are named after which Swiss city?

5   Romulus and Remus were – in mythology at least – the founders of which city?

6   Prosciutto is an uncooked, unsmoked and dry-cured ham from which country?

7   Professor Robert Langdon features in novels by which writer?

8   Holden Caulfield is the main character in which novel by J.D. Salinger?

9   Michael Bond was the creator of which fictional marmalade-loving bear?

10 Also often known as Pancake Day, what is the name for the day immediately prior to the beginning of Lent?

11 According to the proverb, what can beggars not be?

12 Which car manufacturer's logo consists of a three-pointed star within a circle?

13 On an analogue clock, which number is opposite number two?

14 Which exercise is a squat thrust with an additional stand between repetitions and is named for its amusingly-named inventor?

15 *Sunflowers*, *Irises* and *Poppy Flowers* were works by which Dutch artist?

16 Which constellation in the northern sky is distinctively shaped like a W?

17 The name of which mode of transport is used to describe overprotective parents?

18 What name is given to the error made when a speaker accidentally transposes the initial sounds or letters of two or more words?

19 Between 1847 and 2005, what obstacle stood on the playing area of Kent County Cricket Club's ground, St Lawrence Park, that players just played around?

20 Cerumen is the technical term for which secretion?

Easy

Medium

Hard

Answers to QUIZ 41 – Pot Luck

1	Cod Wars	11	36
2	Rugby league	12	Aberdeen
3	Skin	13	New Zealand
4	A doorway	14	Tautology
5	Barbs	15	*Mastermind*
6	Red	16	$1
7	Pancakes	17	Bono
8	*Skylab*	18	*The Witches of Eastwick*
9	1923	19	Monica Seles
10	Napoleon Bonaparte	20	Venezuela (after Venice)

Can you identify these European football clubs from their crests alone?

Easy

1

2

3

Medium

4

5

6

7

8

9

Hard

Answers to QUIZ 42 – Japan

1	Honshu	11	Rice (*mochigome*)
2	Kyoto	12	Ringo Starr
3	Bento	13	Bullet train or *Shinkansen*
4	Yakuza	14	Death
5	Sapporo	15	Shinto
6	Mount Fuji	16	Rabbits
7	Sake	17	*Lost In Translation*
8	Baseball	18	Hula Hoop
9	Otaku	19	Junko Tabei
10	Sony	20	Harajuku

1   Jonas Salk earned a Presidential Medal of Freedom for his discovery of a vaccine for which viral disease?

2   Sales of which close-proximity physical game skyrocketed after Eva Gabor played it with Johnny Carson on *The Tonight Show* in 1966?

3   Of the Seven Wonders of the Ancient World, which is both the oldest and the only one to still exist?

4   In which Olympic sport do competitors cross the finishing line backwards?

5   With which gesture did Judas Iscariot identify Jesus to the police force of the Sanhedrin?

6   Supposedly, which sport was invented after ninepin bowling was banned in Connecticut due to its association with gambling?

7   Originating from the name of a Washington DC hotel, which common four-letter word has become a suffix used in the names of scandals?

8   Who was Bugs Bunny's girlfriend?

9   Which snooker player is nicknamed "The Whirlwind"?

10 In which war did the Charge of the Light Brigade occur?

11 How many bones does a shark have?

12 The Old Faithful geyser lies in which American national park?

13 Father Karras from *The Exorcist* and the prophesied Antichrist child in *The Omen* share what name?

14 What is the vegetable called in Britain that is known as *arugula* in the United States?

15 British 20p and 50p coins both have how many sides?

16 Michelle Pfeiffer, Halle Berry and Zoe Kravitz have all played the role of which comic character in film?

17 Which American ice cream brand was given a name that "looked" Danish by its founders, but which does not mean anything in that language?

18 Crocks, whoppers and porkies are synonyms for what?

19 Linen is obtained from the fibres of which plant?

20 Horse's heights are calculated in what measurement, named for part of the human body?

Easy

Medium

Hard

Answers to QUIZ 43 – Pot Luck

1	John Cage	11	Choosers
2	Sausage rolls	12	Mercedes-Benz
3	Pakistan	13	Eight
4	Geneva (The Geneva Conventions)	14	Burpee
5	Rome	15	Vincent van Gogh
6	Italy	16	Cassiopeia
7	Dan Brown	17	Helicopter (parents)
8	*Catcher in the Rye*	18	Spoonerism
9	Paddington Bear	19	A tree
10	Shrove Tuesday	20	Earwax

ANSWERS ON PAGE 48

Name the film that these classic quotes can be heard in.

1   "I am serious. And don't call me Shirley."
2   "You're gonna need a bigger boat."
3   "I'm also just a girl, standing in front of a boy, asking him to love her."
4   "We'll always have Paris."
5   "Gentlemen, you can't fight in here! This is the war room!"
6   "Go ahead, make my day."
7   "I wish I knew how to quit you."
8   "Wax on, wax off."
9   "Good morning, Charlie!"
10 "Nobody puts Baby in a corner."
11 "Just when I thought I was out, they pull me back in."
12 "THIS IS SPARTA!"
13 "You know how to whistle, don't you, Steve? You just put your lips together and blow."
14 "Do you know what Nemesis means?"
15 "I am McLovin!"
16 "Father to a murdered son, husband to a murdered wife. And I will have my vengeance, in this life or the next."
17 "I mean, funny like I'm a clown? I amuse you?"
18 "I'm just one stomach flu away from my goal weight."
19 "You are not special. You're not a beautiful and unique snowflake. You're the same decaying organic matter as everything else."
20 "Why so serious?"

Easy

Medium

Hard

Answers to QUIZ 44 – Football Club Crests

1   Manchester United
2   Newcastle United
3   West Ham United
4   Barcelona
5   Wolverhampton Wanderers
6   Ajax
7   Celtic
8   Real Madrid
9   Leicester City

1. In 1991, who became both the first Briton in space as well as the first privately-funded woman in space?
2. At the 2012 Olympic Games, which event took place on Horse Guards Parade?
3. Giving their name to a sportswear brand, who was the Greek goddess of victory?
4. *Bohemian Rhapsody* and *A Whiter Shade of Pale* both mention which dance in their lyrics?
5. In money slang, how many pounds are there in a pony?
6. Jim Laker in 1956, Anil Kumble in 1999 and Ajaz Patel in 2021 all achieved which Test cricket feat?
7. Which star sign would someone be if they were born on New Year's Day?
8. Which singer's name is an anagram of "Presbyterians"?
9. Which animal features in the logo for Lamborghini?
10. Who was the British king during the American War of Independence?
11. The name of which UK supermarket appears in Chas and Dave's *Rabbit*?
12. The Battle of Agincourt was a part of which war?
13. Hypnophobia is a fear of what?
14. The *Mona Lisa* is on display in which Parisian art gallery?
15. Jeremy Irons voiced which character in the animated movie *The Lion King*?
16. What was the first city in history estimated to have a population of greater than one million?
17. Nitrous oxide is more commonly known by what name?
18. Which three colours make up the German flag?
19. The rupee is the monetary unit in which country?
20. Most episodes of which television programme ended with Zebedee announcing that it was "time for bed"?

Easy

Medium

Hard

Answers to QUIZ 45 – Pot Luck

1	Polio	11	Zero – they are all cartilage
2	Twister®	12	Yellowstone
3	The Great Pyramid of Giza	13	Damien
4	Rowing	14	Rocket
5	Kiss	15	Seven
6	Tenpin bowling	16	Catwoman
7	Gate (after the Watergate Hotel and its related scandal)	17	Häagen-Dazs
8	Lola Bunny	18	Lies
9	Jimmy White	19	Flax
10	Crimean War	20	Hands

Easy

1   Traditionally, what treat is hidden inside a Christmas pudding?

2   How many of Santa's reindeers have names that start with D?

3   Santa's elves are usually depicted with what on the end of their shoes?

4   At what time is the monarch's address to the nation traditionally broadcast in the UK?

5   According to the lyrics of the song, Frosty the Snowman's nose was made out of what?

6   The tradition of Santa Claus wearing a red and white costume is often, but not correctly, attributed to which company?

7   Located in the Indian Ocean, Christmas Island is a territory of which country?

8   How many total gifts were given in the song *The Twelve Days of Christmas*?

9   Ellie Goulding, Gabrielle Aplin, Lily Allen and Tom Odell have all had top ten hits with songs that debuted in Christmas adverts for which company?

10 As described in the poem *A Visit from St Nicholas* by Clement Clarke Moore, how did Santa get back up the chimney?

11 Which Hans Christian Andersen fairy-tale formed the loose basis for the Disney film *Frozen*?

12 What did four Scottish students steal from Westminster Abbey on Christmas Day 1950, breaking it in the process?

13 Lapland, often associated with Father Christmas, is a real sparsely-populated region of which country?

Medium

14 On the Christmas menu in Hungary, what usually replaces turkey?

15 In the Christmas film *Home Alone 2*, who does Kevin run into in a hotel lobby?

16 The film *The Polar Express* was originally a 1985 children's book, written by whom?

17 In centuries past, young women would eat what at Christmas time to ensure they would one day find human husbands?

18 Which country traditionally plays in a so-called "Boxing Day Test" every year?

19 *Stollen* – a fruit bread of nuts, spices, and dried or candied fruit, coated with sugar – is traditionally eaten at Christmas in which country?

20 In Alpine folklore, which horned anthropomorphic figure scares children at Christmas who have misbehaved?

Hard

Answers to QUIZ 46 – Film Quotes

1	*Airplane!*	11	*The Godfather: Part III*
2	*Jaws*	12	*300*
3	*Notting Hill*	13	*To Have And Have Not*
4	*Casablanca*	14	*Snatch*
5	*Dr. Strangelove or: How I Learned to Stop Worrying and Love the Bomb*	15	*Superbad*
		16	*Gladiator*
6	*Sudden Impact*	17	*Goodfellas*
7	*Brokeback Mountain*	18	*The Devil Wears Prada*
8	*The Karate Kid*	19	*Fight Club*
9	*Charlie's Angels*	20	*The Dark Knight*
10	*Dirty Dancing*		

1 Who wrote the controversial erotic novel *Lady Chatterley's Lover*?

2 Which future English monarch evaded Oliver Cromwell's troops by climbing an oak tree?

3 What Beatles song was their first UK no.1 on which neither Paul McCartney nor John Lennon sang lead vocals?

4 In 1982, which 16th century carrack warship was raised from the bottom of the sea near Portsmouth?

5 Stevie Wonder's *Happy Birthday* was written for which activist?

6 Theophobia is the fear of what?

7 Tonto was the sidekick of which fictional former Texas Ranger?

8 What Australian city hosts the largest comedy festival in the southern hemisphere?

9 Which is the only South American country to have English as its official language?

10 Which of golf's four major tournaments is the only one to take place at the same course every year?

11 In the Ultimate Fighting Championship, the fighting arena takes its name from which geometric shape?

12 Which Swedish car company invented the three-point safety seat belt, and gave the patent away for anyone to use?

13 Mick Jagger and David Bowie recorded a cover of which Motown song to raise money for the *Live Aid* famine relief cause?

14 In 1698, Emperor Peter I of Russia instituted a tax on wearing which optional male "look"?

15 Which American sports legend licensed his name for a brand of basketball shoes, as well as athletic, casual and style clothing produced by Nike?

16 Despite it having had 17 new heads and 14 new handles, Trigger from *Only Fools and Horses* claimed to have used the same what for 20 years?

17 "Your mother was a hamster and your father smelt of elderberries" was an insult levied in which comedy film?

18 Wayne and Waynetta Slob were characters in which TV sketch show?

19 *Operation Dynamo* was the 1940 rescue operation of Allied forces from which French beach?

20 In *The Lion King*, what kind of animal is Pumbaa?

Easy

Medium

Hard

Answers to QUIZ 47 – Pot Luck

1	Helen Sharman	11	Sainsbury's
2	Beach volleyball	12	The Hundred Years' War
3	Nike	13	Sleep
4	The fandango	14	The Louvre
5	£25	15	Scar
6	They took all ten wickets in an innings	16	Rome
7	Capricorn	17	Laughing gas
8	Britney Spears	18	Black, red and gold
9	Bull	19	India
10	George III	20	*The Magic Roundabout*

1 J. M. Barrie created which free-spirited and mischievous young boy in 1902?

2 Which F. Scott Fitzgerald character aged backwards?

3 Which 2001 cult classic film starring Jake and Maggie Gyllenhaal tells the story of a troubled teenager who narrowly escapes a bizarre accident?

4 Which actress, model and singer's name at birth was Norma Jeane Mortenson?

5 Which Roman politician and fifth governor of the province of Judaea is best known for being the official who presided over the trial of Jesus?

6 Before starring in *Enchanted* and *Catch Me If You Can*, which actress briefly worked as a Hooters waitress?

7 Which actress caused a stir by appearing naked in the opening scene of 1957's *And God Created Woman*, directed by her then-husband Roger Vadim?

8 Which Indian actress, producer and model was on the receiving end of the 2007 *Celebrity Big Brother* racism scandal?

9 Scientist and inventor Dr Reed Richards is the alter ego of which Marvel superhero?

10 In film set terminology, what name is given to the right-hand person to either the gaffer (lead electrician) or key grip (lead camera set-up)?

11 Which circa 7th century poem about a monster named Grendel is written in 3,182 alliterative lines?

12 French middle-aged literature professor Humbert Humbert is the main protagonist and narrator in which Vladimir Nabokov novel?

13 What is the professional name of the Australian comedian, presenter and actor born Geoff Nugent?

14 Which Shakespeare play contains the longest scene, the longest single word and the longest speech of any of his works?

15 Which large bay straddling France and Spain was the scene of a 1592 naval battle?

16 Which junction where six routes meet is the notional "centre of London" and the point from which distances from London are measured?

17 Which female/male vocal duo had a UK number one hit in December 1982 with *Save Your Love*?

18 What is the capital city of Ethiopia?

19 In 1918, who co-founded the *United Artists* distribution company, giving him complete control over his films such as *Gold Rush* and *Modern Times*?

20 In economics, which 'PPP' allows investors to determine the exchange rate between currencies to trade on a par with the power of the currencies?

Answers to QUIZ 48 – Christmas

1	A silver coin	11	*The Snow Queen*
2	Three (Dasher, Dancer, Donner)	12	The Stone of Scone
3	Bells	13	Finland
4	3pm	14	Fish, often as a soup
5	A button	15	Donald Trump
6	Coca-Cola®	16	Chris Van Allsburg
7	Australia	17	Gingerbread men
8	364	18	Australia
9	John Lewis	19	Germany
10	Put his finger on his nose and nodded [not convinced it works]	20	Krampus

1   In which Scottish city is Waverley train station?

2   "Forgiveness is divine, but never pay full price for late pizza" is a quote from which film?

3   Before the demise of the UK Teletext service, on which page was the subtitle service found?

4   After appearing in a jeans advert, which song by The Clash topped the charts with a 1991 re-release?

5   Australia went to "war" with which bird in 1932?

6   In parts of Hong Kong and China, which quick-growing plant is still to this day used as scaffolding?

7   What word is used for a sentence containing every letter of the alphabet?

8   Russell Brand described which man as being a "pound shop Enoch Powell"?

9   Arthur Dent is the protagonist of which comic science fiction book series?

10   The South Downs Way runs roughly 100 miles between Eastbourne and which Hampshire town?

11   Which tyre company issues an annual guide book with a rating system for establishments, particularly restaurants?

12   The seventh fence on the Aintree Grand National circuit is named for which horse, who won the Grand National in 1967 at odds of 100/1?

13   The name of which Charles Dickens novel is also the stage name of a famous American magician?

14   What is the name for the field study of the properties of moving air and bodies moving through it?

15   Stoichiometry, zymurgy and toxicology are branches of which science?

16   Which Secretary-General of the United States was killed in a plane crash in 1961?

17   After Cardiff, which city is the second most populous in Wales?

18   Which English town is internationally known for its cutlery production?

19   The process of hardening rubber by treating it with sulphur at a high temperature is called what?

20   .JPG, .PNG and .BMP are all extensions for what type of computer file?

Answers to QUIZ 49 – Pot Luck

1	D.H. Lawrence	11	Octagon
2	Charles II	12	Volvo
3	*Yellow Submarine*	13	*Dancing In The Street*
4	*Mary Rose*	14	Beards
5	Martin Luther King	15	Michael Jordan
6	God	16	Broom
7	The Lone Ranger	17	*Monty Python and the Holy Grail*
8	Melbourne	18	*Harry Enfield & Chums*
9	Guyana	19	Dunkerque (Dunkirk)
10	US Masters	20	Warthog

Easy

1   The month of March is named after which god, the Roman god of war?

2   Which patron saint's day is celebrated on 17th March annually?

3   "Beware the Ides of March", a phrase referring to impending betrayal, has its origins in the 15th March 44 BC assassination of which Roman emperor?

4   Which iconic structure opened on 31st March 1889?

5   As told in a film of the same name, the 24th and 25th March 1944 breakout of the *Stalag Luft III* prisoner of war camp was known as what?

6   The March sisters were the focal characters of which coming-of-age novel written by Louisa May Alcott?

7   The invention of the telephone was patented on 7th March 1876 by who?

8   Who wrote the instrumental *Wedding March in C Major*, commonly used at weddings in Western countries?

9   On 1st March 1932, the infant child of which aviation pioneer was kidnapped from his family home?

10 Which massive cache of more than 8,000 sculptured soldiers and 650 horses was discovered on 29th March 1974 by farmers in rural China?

11 Released on 29th March 2019, whose debut album *When We All Fall Asleep, Where Do We Go?* won the 2020 Grammy for Record of the Year?

12 Which Archbishop of Canterbury was executed on the orders of Mary I on 21st March 1556?

13 On 6th March 1987, which ferry capsized moments after leaving the Belgian port of Zeebrugge due to the bow door being left open?

14 On 5th March 1981, which late British inventor released the ZX81 personal computer?

15 "The Million Man March" was a large rally against minority voter suppression held on and around the National Mall in which American city?

16 March, Cambridgeshire was previously the county town of which former administrative county?

17 Which French feature-length nature documentary won the 2006 Oscar for Best Documentary Feature?

18 Which 19th century author wrote *Middlemarch, A Study of Provincial Life*?

19 *Land Of Hope & Glory* originates from the Pomp & Circumstance Marches, written by whom?

20 The annual *March Madness* knock-out tournament is the culmination of the college season in which major American sport?

Medium

Hard

---

1 Food served *au gratin* has what sprinkled on top and grilled?

2 Upon launch in 2004, how much storage space was each user provided on Gmail accounts?

3 Home to approximately 141 million people, which is the world's most populous island?

4 Since 2002, Walkers® crisps sold in black bags have what flavour?

5 Neil Hamilton, Paul Nuttall and Richard Braine have all been leaders of which British political party?

6 Which sport uses the terms "gutter", "turkey", "split" and "alley"?

7 The long, high sea waves caused by a large disturbance (often an earthquake) are called what?

8 Dermatologists specialise in the diagnosis and treatment of disorders of which area of the body?

9 Which organ of the body produces insulin?

10 In the early 20th century, which theoretical physicist published the theories of general relativity and special relativity?

11 Which founding father signed the American Declaration of Independence in writing so big that his name became a by-word for signature?

12 What was the name of King Arthur's sword?

13 Socrates's most famous student was which other fabled Greek scholar?

14 Which three-leaf member of the clover family is a national emblem of Ireland?

15 Sound intensity is measured in which unit?

16 The project which developed the atomic bomb during World War II took its name from which New York City borough?

17 What is the SI unit of electrical power, equal to one joule per second?

18 The star Polaris is more commonly known as what?

19 In which country are the Angel Falls located?

20 Cartographers are people who draw or produce what?

Answers to QUIZ 51 – Pot Luck

1	Edinburgh	11	Michelin
2	*Teenage Mutant Ninja Turtles*	12	Foinavon
3	888	13	*David Copperfield*
4	*Should I Stay Or Should I Go*	14	Aerodynamics
5	Emu	15	Chemistry
6	Bamboo	16	Dag Hammarskjöld
7	Pangram	17	Swansea
8	Nigel Farage	18	Sheffield
9	*The Hitchhiker's Guide To The Galaxy*	19	Vulcanisation
10	Winchester	20	Image files

Easy

1   *Smile* was the platinum-certified 2006 debut single for which recording artist?

2   Eminem won an Academy Award for *Lose Yourself*, the theme song to which of his own movies?

3   *Hey Ya!* was a 2003 worldwide no.1 single for which hip-hop duo?

4   Which 2003 White Stripes single, characterised by distorted vocals, a simple drumbeat and a bass-like riff, became a sports anthem?

5   Which Arctic Monkeys single, their first release from their debut album, went straight to no.1 in 2006?

6   In 2005, the Pussycats Dolls teamed up with which rapper to release the single *Button*?

7   The biggest-selling single of the 2000s was by which singer, who rose to fame on a TV talent show?

8   34 years after he first charted with it, Tony Christie re-released *(Is This The Way To) Amarillo* in 2005 with which comedian in the video?

9   In 2008, Alexandra Burke's cover of which Lou Reed song set the European record for the most singles sold within 24 hours?

10   Miley Cyrus and Joe McElderry released two versions of which song within ten months of each other?

11   The Kings of Leon followed up their 2008 no.1 single *Sex On Fire* with which no.2 hit?

12   Which call-and-response duet by Nelly (OH!) and Kelly Rowland (OH!) charted for 24 weeks (OH!) in the UK, starting in October 2002?

13   Which Jamaican-American singer and songwriter topped the charts internationally with his 2007 debut single *Beautiful Girls*?

Medium

14   Which British boyband made a 21st century comeback with the album *Beautiful World*?

15   What part of Shakira's body does not lie?

16   Formed as Girl's Tyme in 1990, which highly successful trio broke up in 2006?

17   Which singer rose to fame in the noughties with her hits *Hit 'Em Up Style (Oops!)* and *Breathe*, alongside Sean Paul?

18   DJ Pied Piper & The Masters Of Ceremonies asked us which question in 2001?

19   *Don't Call Me Baby* was a 2000 international release for which Australian electronic music duo, named after a road in New York City?

20   Which Californian pop-punk band had a 2006 UK no.1 with their debut single, *No Tomorrow*?

Hard

Answers to QUIZ 52 – March

1   In bingo call terminology, "Danny La Rue" refers to which number?

2   In *The Magic Roundabout*, what does Zebedee have instead of legs?

3   In professional wrestling, to what number must a referee count to end the match when a wrestler is pinned?

4   Nimzo-Indian, Accelerated Dragon, Ruy Lopez and Sicilian Defence are all examples of what?

5   Native to South America, which is the world's largest living rodent species?

6   What name is given to the trough used by builders for carrying bricks?

7   In internet terminology, what does www stand for?

8   *Tacos, burritos* and *quesadillas* originate from which country's cuisine?

9   Which company's product range includes the iPhone, iPad and iWatch?

10 Which heir's assassination led to the start of World War I?

11 Billy Gibbons, Dusty Hill and Frank Beard were the three founding members of which band?

12 The aerial attack by Japan that led to America joining World War II was on which Hawaiian port?

13 Eleven, born Jane Ives and legally named Jane Hopper, is a character in which Netflix science fiction horror drama series?

14 The Musee D'Orsay is a famous museum in which city?

15 *Neighbours* is set in which fictional cul-de-sac?

16 *The Phantom of the Opera* and *Jesus Christ Superstar* are among the musicals by which composer?

17 In 1995, what became the first film created by Pixar, and the first fully computer-animated feature film?

18 The Rijksmuseum of art and history is located in which European city?

19 Which film production house was acquired by Disney from its namesake founder for $4 billion in 2012?

20 Which is the world's longest-running theatre production, having run in London's West End since 25th November 1952?

Easy

Medium

Hard

Answers to QUIZ 53 – Pot Luck

1	Cheese (and/or breadcrumbs)	11	John Hancock
2	1 gigabyte, by far more than the competition at the time	12	Excalibur
		13	Plato
3	Java, Indonesia	14	Shamrock
4	Marmite®	15	Decibels
5	UKIP	16	Manhattan
6	Tenpin bowling	17	Watt
7	Tsunamis	18	The North Star or Pole Star
8	Skin	19	Venezuela
9	Pancreas	20	Maps
10	Albert Einstein		

QUIZ 56 – Brothers

ANSWERS ON PAGE 58

1. Which German authors published folklore and folk tales, popularising stories such as *Cinderella* and *Hansel and Gretel*?
2. Steven Spielberg and Tom Hanks created which 2001 American war drama miniseries?
3. Which sibling filmmakers' canon includes *Raising Arizona, Fargo, The Big Lebowski, Burn After Reading* and *Inside Llewyn Davis*?
4. The Gibb brothers Barry, Maurice and Robin wrote and recorded music for themselves and others under which name?
5. John Belushi and Dan Aykroyd starred as Jake and Elwood in which 1980 musical comedy film?
6. The instrumental song *Jessica*, well known for being the theme tune to *Top Gear*, was written and first performed by who?
7. Sophie Turner, Danielle Deleasa and Priyanka Chopra married the three sibling members of which pop act?
8. The bankruptcy filing of which 161-year-old investment bank was the largest in US history and precipitated the global financial crisis?
9. With hits such as *Bye Bye Love* and *Cathy's Clown*, which singing siblings were pioneers of country rock?
10. Which series of fighting games by Nintendo® brings together characters from various other game franchises?
11. Complete the list of the Marx Brothers: Groucho, Harpo, Chico, Gummo, _____?
12. Jeff "Skunk" Baxter left Steely Dan to join which rock/soul group in 1975?
13. Which sibling singing group wrote the oft-covered hit *Shout* and three years later followed with a cover of *Twist & Shout*?
14. Australian acting brothers Chris, Luke and Liam share what surname?
15. Who is the famous actor brother of Charlie Sheen who, unlike his brother (and father), has acted under his legal Spanish name?
16. Which big beat duo had a 1997 no.1 hit with *Block Rockin' Beats*?
17. Taylor, Isaac and Zac founded which sibling American pop rock band, best known for the 1997 hit song *MMMBop*?
18. Barry and Paul Elliott were better known as which performing duo?
19. In *Legend*, Tom Hardy portrayed both roles in the story of which identical twin brother criminals?
20. Alec, Daniel, William and Stephen are the four members of which sibling acting family?

Answers to QUIZ 54 – 2000s Music

1. Lily Allen
2. 8 Mile
3. Outkast
4. *Seven Nation Army*
5. *I Bet You Look Good On The Dance Floor*
6. Snoop Dogg
7. Will Young (*Evergreen/Anything Is Possible*)
8. Peter Kay
9. *Hallelujah*
10. *The Climb*
11. *Use Somebody*
12. *Dilemma*
13. Sean Kingston
14. Take That
15. Her hips
16. Destiny's Child
17. Blu Cantrell
18. *Do You Really Like It?*
19. Madison Avenue
20. Orson

1   Who in 1962 became the third American in space and the first to orbit the Earth?

2   Mozzarella cheese is made from the milk of which animal?

3   What was The Beatles' first no.1 single in the UK?

4   Which Frenchman conquered England in 1066?

5   "All children, except one, grow up" is the opening line to which celebrated novel?

6   Which American president gave the famous speech known as the Gettysburg Address?

7   Who won gold medals in each of the 100 metres, 200 metres, long jump and 4 × 100 metre relay at the 1936 Berlin Olympics?

8   What type of animal is a Bombay Duck?

9   In which film does the character Travis Bickle appear?

10   What are the four main blood groups? (Positives and negatives not required!)

11   In *Reservoir Dogs*, when Mr Blonde tortures a police officer, which Stealers Wheel song is playing in the background?

12   What is the last day of Christmas called?

13   In business terminology, what does PLC stand for?

14   After a childhood bout of polio, which Mexican artist became known for painting about her experience of chronic pain?

15   In the political acronym NATO, what does the A stand for?

16   Due to how frequently he painted them, which Flemish painter lends his name to an adjective that describes voluptuous, curvy women?

17   The name of which extremely important substance is made from a combination of the Greek words for "acid" and "creation"?

18   "Death spiral" is a term used in which pairs sport?

19   An ECG measures the activity of which organ of the body?

20   Which former member of The Beatles released the 1965 album *Best of The Beatles*?

Easy

Medium

Hard

Answers to QUIZ 55 – Pot Luck

1	52	11	ZZ Top
2	A spring	12	Pearl Harbor
3	Three	13	*Stranger Things*
4	Chess openings	14	Paris
5	Capybara	15	Ramsay Street
6	Hod	16	Andrew Lloyd Webber
7	World Wide Web	17	*Toy Story*
8	Mexico	18	Amsterdam
9	Apple	19	*Lucasfilm*
10	Archduke Franz Ferdinand of Austria	20	*Mousetrap*

1 How many face cards are there in a standard deck?

2 Which now-ubiquitous food item was rumoured to be created when a hungry Earl was too engrossed in his card game to leave and get food?

3 Which traditional British card game includes cards such as Mr Bun the Baker and Mrs Soot the Sweep?

4 Which solitaire game utilising the whole deck and four open "cells" has been included with every release of Microsoft® Windows since 1995?

5 In which card game is "three of a kind" also known as a "prial"?

6 Butler, Elope, Matrix and Panama are all terms used in which card game?

7 Which iconic poker movie sees Matt Damon's Mike McDermott battle heads up with John Malkovich's Teddy KGB?

8 Which American shedding-type card game with a deck featuring "skip" and "reverse" cards shares its name with the Spanish for "one"?

9 In bridge, which is the highest ranking suit?

10 Cards not used in any valid combination in Gin Rummy are known as what?

11 The name of which card game means "basket" in Spanish?

12 Which two jacks look sideways and thus are said to be one-eyed jacks?

13 The "World Series" of which card game has been hosted in Las Vegas annually since 1970?

14 In which card game that uses a pegboard is the winner the first player to score more than 120 points?

15 The King of Hearts is the only king in the deck to lack which feature?

16 How many cards are there in a tarot deck?

17 Which adult party fill-in-the-blank card game originated with a Kickstarter campaign in 2011?

18 In the game of bridge, what is the term for bidding and winning a contract of thirteen tricks?

19 The name of which card game holds the world record for highest-ever starting score in *Scrabble®*?

20 What score is the player trying to achieve in a game of French Baccarat variant *chemin de fer*?

Easy

Medium

Hard

Answers to QUIZ 56 – Brothers

1	Brothers Grimm	11	Zeppo
2	*Band of Brothers*	12	The Doobie Brothers
3	Coen Brothers	13	The Isley Brothers
4	Bee Gees	14	Hemsworth
5	*The Blues Brothers*	15	Emilio Estevez
6	The Allman Brothers Band	16	Chemical Brothers
7	Jonas Brothers	17	Hanson
8	Lehman Brothers	18	The Chuckle Brothers
9	The Everly Brothers	19	The Krays
10	*Super Smash Bros*	20	The Baldwins

58

Easy

Medium

Hard

1   Which James Bond film shares its name with a duck?

2   What is the largest island in the world? (Australia, a continental land mass, does not count!)

3   What word can refer to both a place of education, or a group of fish?

4   Between 1661 and 1715, Louis XIV of France expanded a small château into which royal residence?

5   Which is the lightest type of commercial hardwood?

6   Who was the leader of the Argonauts?

7   If even they existed at all, in what ancient city were the "Hanging Gardens" purportedly located?

8   What was the name of the captain of the Pequod in *Moby Dick*?

9   William Cody was an American soldier and showman who shot to fame under what nickname?

10   Alexander Graham Bell and Sherlock Holmes both had assistants with which name?

11   Who was born on the island of Corsica, exiled to the isle of Elba and died on the island of Saint Helena?

12   Which winter sport uses stones and brooms?

13   Charles Darwin's five-year scientific survey voyage took place on a ship with which animal name?

14   What nickname links Al Capone and Al Pacino?

15   Which unit of measure is equal to six foot, usually with reference to the depth of water?

16   Which Swedish chemist and inventor recorded 355 patents in his lifetime, with his most famous invention being dynamite?

17   Alongside the much smaller Aniene, the city of Rome stands on which major river?

18   Which American actress and pin-up girl said of her own legs, "I became a star for two reasons, and I'm standing on them"?

19   Who was the first person to break the once-thought-impossible four-minute mile barrier?

20   Lady Godiva supposedly rode naked riding through which city?

Answers to QUIZ 57 – Pot Luck

1	John Glenn	11	*Stuck in the Middle With You*
2	Buffalo	12	Epiphany
3	*From Me To You*	13	Public Limited Company
4	William I (aka William the Conqueror)	14	Frida Kahlo
5	*Peter Pan*	15	Atlantic (North Atlantic Treaty Organization)
6	Abraham Lincoln	16	Peter Paul Rubens (such women are "Rubenesque")
7	Jesse Owens	17	Oxygen
8	Fish	18	Figure skating
9	*Taxi Driver*	19	Heart (electrocardiogram)
10	A, B, AB and O	20	Pete Best

ANSWERS ON PAGE 62

Easy

1. What term is used to describe the relative positions of the stars and planets at the time of a person's birth?
2. It is said that which astrological sign can be creative, magnanimous, dramatic, dogmatic and patronising?
3. When a planet moves backwards through the zodiac, what is it said to be in?
4. Which sign of the Zodiac is represented by twins?
5. Arising in the 2nd millennium BC, the earlist recorded system of astrology was by which ancient civilization?
6. Published in 1968, what was the title of Linda Goodman's debut astrology book, the first to make the *New York Times* Best Seller list?
7. In a breakdown of all the US Presidents in history to date, most presidents have been which star sign, thought to be magnetic, receptive and feminine?
8. Which band took its name from the primary elemental and seasonal qualities of the lead singer's star sign, Sagittarius?
9. Having been born on 25th December, Jesus would have been which star sign?
10. Scorpio, Cancer and which other star sign are associated with the element water?
11. Which zodiac sign is represented neither by man nor beast?
12. Described as being witty, intelligent and a great communicator, Gemini is said to be ruled by which planet?

Medium

13. Those born a few days before or after the Sun changes zodiac signs take on the characteristics of both signs and are said to be on what?
14. Which star sign comes after Scorpio but before Capricorn?
15. When the Babylonians defined the zodiac 3,000 years ago, they left out which constellation for symmetry purposes?
16. Which astrologer published *Les Prophéties* in 1555?
17. As the astrological year is different to the calendar year, which is the first sign in the zodiacal year?
18. When a celestial body passes through a sign of a similar nature, it is said to be in what?
19. When a planet is positioned in the zodiac sign opposite the sign it rules (over which it has domicile), it is said to be in what?
20. Optimism is correlated highly with which planet?

Hard

Answers to QUIZ 58 – Card Games

1. 12
2. Sandwich
3. Happy Families
4. Freecell
5. Brag
6. Contract Bridge
7. *Rounders*
8. Uno
9. Spades
10. Unmatched or deadwood
11. Canasta
12. The Jacks of Spades and Hearts
13. Poker
14. Cribbage
15. Moustache
16. 78 (22 in the major arcana, 56 in the minor arcana)
17. *Cards Against Humanity*
18. Grand Slam
19. Bezique
20. Nine

ANSWERS ON PAGE 63

1   Which concentrated fruit soft drink brand takes its name from the Māori for "hello"?

2   Kangaroos, wallabies and indeed all animals with pouches for their young are classified as what order of mammals?

3   In which part of the human body can the labyrinth be found?

4   Which Egyptian-born businessman has owned Harrods department store and Fulham FC?

5   Which Dutch artist's work featured mathematical objects and operations, including impossible objects, reflection and never-ending stairs?

6   What gas is a waste product of photosynthesis?

7   The Rosetta Stone and the Piranesi Vase can both be seen where?

8   Which certified insane English gangster, who spent 42 years in prison for numerous violent offences, later became a television celebrity?

9   Sharing the name with the sitcom about them, what nickname was given to Britain's "Home Guard" during World War II?

10 Which 15th-century Incan citadel on a Peruvian mountainside was made public by Hiram Bingham in 1911?

11 *Around The World In 80 Pints* is the autobiography of which English cricket coach and pundit?

12 Father and son speedsters Malcolm and Donald Campbell both set speed records in cars and boats called what?

13 In which city are the Topkapi Palace and Blue Mosque located?

14 David Beckham and David Mitchell both married women with which first name?

15 A *dacha* is a countryside second home in which country?

16 In the UK, mains electricity is required by law to be delivered at what voltage, within a tolerance of +10% / –6%?

17 Anything described as "aural" is related to which part of the body?

18 What is the pollen-producing part of a flower called?

19 What is the SI unit of conductance, equal to one reciprocal ohm?

20 Between 1963 and 1965, Singapore was a part of which country?

Easy

Medium

Hard

Answers to QUIZ 59 – Pot Luck

1	GoldenEye	11	Napoleon Bonaparte
2	Greenland	12	Curling
3	School	13	HMS Beagle
4	Palace of Versailles	14	Scarface; it was Capone's nickname, and Pacino starred in a film of that name
5	Balsa		
6	Jason	15	Fathom
7	Babylon	16	Alfred Nobel
8	Captain Ahab	17	Tiber
9	Buffalo Bill	18	Betty Grable
10	Watson	19	Roger Bannister
		20	Coventry

Name the villains from the *Doctor Who* TV series. (Not listed in order of scariness.)

Easy

1

2

3

4

Medium

5

6

7

8

Hard

Answers to QUIZ 60 – Astrology

1	Horoscope	11	Libra
2	Leo	12	Mercury
3	Retrograde	13	The cusp
4	Gemini	14	Sagittarius
5	Babylonian	15	Ophiuchus, the serpent bearer
6	*Sun Signs*	16	Nostradamus
7	Scorpio	17	Aries, as the zodiacal year begins on the spring equinox
8	Earth, Wind and Fire	18	Exaltation
9	Capricorn	19	Detriment or exile
10	Pisces	20	Jupiter

1   The idiom "treading the boards" means to do what?
2   Spinach, broccoli, peanuts and liver all contain which acid?
3   What does Rabbi literally mean?
4   Which professional coaching company and authority on etiquette and behaviour was founded in 1769, with the first edition of *The New Peerage*?
5   Media personality and businesswoman Katie Price used to model under what country's name?
6   Robin Williams voiced the Genie in which 1992 animated Disney musical?
7   What is the colour-based term for journalism that contains little or no legitimate news and instead uses eye-catching headlines?
8   Joseph Cyril Bamford founded which British equipment manufacturer in 1945?
9   Convention holds that all areas of which planet are supposed to be named for females?
10 The Bluewater Shopping Centre is in which English county?
11 Giving its name to a pie, Fray Bentos is a port city in which South American country?
12 Which former professional tennis player founded a range of family-oriented health and fitness clubs with an emphasis on tennis?
13 Clive Anderson once described which acerbic art critic as "a man intent on keeping his Christmas card list nice and short"?
14 What does the CB stand for in the name of CB radios?
15 Bombora™, Reyka® and Smirnoff® are brands of which alcoholic drink?
16 Craniate animals all have what?
17 Matelot, tar and hearty are synonyms for people in which profession?
18 Primarily, who played bass guitar in The Beatles?
19 The slang term Smokey, as used for the title of the film *Smokey and the Bandit*, was used by bootleggers to refer to what?
20 After Red Rum four decades previously, which horse became in 2019 only the second to win more than one English Grand National?

Answers to QUIZ 61 – Pot Luck

1	Kia-Ora®	11	David "Bumble" Lloyd
2	Marsupials	12	*Bluebird*
3	Ear	13	Istanbul
4	Mohamed Al-Fayed	14	Victoria
5	M. C. Escher	15	Russia
6	Oxygen	16	230 volts
7	British Museum	17	Ear
8	"Mad" Frankie Fraser	18	Stamen
9	*Dad's Army*	19	Siemens
10	Maccu Pichu	20	Malaysia

Easy

1   Rebuilt and reopened in 2003, what is the name of the large shopping centre in central Birmingham?

2   At which ground do Birmingham City FC play their home games?

3   Which exhibition centre located adjacent to Birmingham International Airport is the UK's largest?

4   Which motorway that runs around the south and east of the city connects Birmingham with Nottingham, Solihull, Tamworth and Redditch?

5   In Birmingham in 1837, Alfred Bird developed the modern egg-free powdered version of what sweet sauce?

6   It is said that which type of curry served in a thin, pressed-steel wok and cooked quickly using vegetable oil was invented in Birmingham?

7   Located in Birmingham, what is the tallest freestanding clock tower in the world?

8   Which reggae and pop band were formed in December 1978 by brothers Ali and Robin Campbell?

9   Cillian Murphy stars as Tommy Shelby in which BBC period crime drama series set in Birmingham?

10 Which Birmingham train station is the UK's busiest interchange station outside London?

11 Which test match cricket venue can be found in a namesake suburb of Birmingham?

12 Which supermarket opened its first British store on 5th April 1990 in Stechford, Birmingham?

13 Often misattributed to Major Walter Wingfield, Spanish-born merchant and Birmingham resident Augurio Perera was the inventor of which sport?

14 Which multinational confectionery firm was founded in Birmingham in 1828?

Medium

15 Between 1906 and 2016, cars from marques including Rover and BMW were assembled at which Birmingham plant?

16 The M6, the A38(M), the A38, the A5127, a railway line, three canals and a river all meet at which interchange?

17 Giving their name to a lunchtime magazine programme, what were the names of the BBC's Birmingham studios?

18 What 2,400-acre National Nature Reserve and large urban park is located 6 miles north of Birmingham city centre?

19 Birmingham is a 92 kilometre-wide impact crater found where?

20 The largest cast iron statue in the world is located in Birmingham, Alabama and is of which Roman god of fire?

Hard

Answers to QUIZ 62 – Doctor Who Villains

1   Daleks
2   The Cybermen
3   The Weeping Angels
4   Ood
5   Sontarans
6   The Master
7   Davros
8   Zygons

1   *The Castle Of Blood, The Monkey King* and *The Saucermen From Mars* were abandoned sequels in which Harrison Ford film series?

2   What colloquial name is given to the American 10 cent coin?

3   The shortest verse in the Bible consists of only which two words?

4   Otalgia affects which part of the body?

5   Rosanna Davidson, daughter of Chris de Burgh, won which title in 2003?

6   Applejack, Rainbow Dash and Fluttershy are all characters from which toy range and media franchise?

7   In which London cemetery are Michael Faraday, Karl Marx, Alfred Lord Tennyson and George Michael all buried?

8   Which other Indonesian island lies to the immediate southeast of Java?

9   Thursday takes its name from that of which Norse god?

10   Because their enamel is hardened with iron, what colour are a beaver's teeth?

11   Eve, The Lemon Pipers and Bob Dylan each had songs with which instrument in the title?

12   The Arctic tern annually migrates from the Arctic to where?

13   *Pipes of Peace* was a single and album for which musician?

14   Robert Plant, Jimmy Page, John Paul Jones and John Bonham formed which band?

15   What type of lightning is cloud-to-ground lightning that exhibits branching of its path?

16   Also known as "hairy cattle", which type of long-haired domesticated cattle can be found throughout the Himalayan region?

17   Ronan Keating and Stephen Gately were the co-lead singers of which Irish boy band?

18   How many bones are there in the adult human body?

19   What was the name of the giraffe used to advertise Toys 'R' Us?

20   *Forbes* magazine named which motor racing driver as the highest-earning sportsman of 2006?

Easy

Medium

Hard

Answers to QUIZ 63 – Pot Luck

1	Act on stage	11	Uruguay
2	Folic acid	12	David Lloyd
3	Teacher	13	Brian Sewell
4	Debrett's	14	Citizens' Band
5	Jordan	15	Vodka
6	*Aladdin*	16	Skulls or braincases
7	Yellow press	17	Sailor
8	JCB	18	Paul McCartney
9	Venus	19	Police officers
10	Kent	20	Tiger Roll

1 Which actor, songwriter, singer and playwright created and starred in the hit Broadway musical *Hamilton*?

2 Which American Vice President shot and killed Alexander Hamilton in a duel on 11th January 1804?

3 Which former Conservative MP was arrested while recording a documentary with Louis Theroux?

4 Deriving from its origins as a school team, what is the unusual name of the professional football team from the town of Hamilton in South Lanarkshire?

5 Margaret Hamilton played the Wicked Witch of the West in which iconic 1939 film?

6 Which Caribbean island nation has Hamilton as its capital city?

7 Linda Hamilton played Sarah Connor in the first two entries of which science fiction action film franchise?

8 Which British comedian and screenwriter of many dozens of shows is also noted for his small 5'2" stature, short neck and missing right thumb?

9 Out of the league with substance abuse problems three years earlier, Josh Hamilton won the 2010 American League MVP award in which sport?

10 Which Colombian striker was Middlesbrough's top scorer in the 1998-99 and 1999-2000 seasons?

11 The largest mass shooting in British history was committed by Thomas Hamilton in 1996 in which Scottish town?

12 On which American bank note does Alexander Hamilton feature?

13 English maid, model, dancer and actress Emma, Lady Hamilton was the mistress of which naval hero?

14 Which artist's intimate relationship with Juan Hamilton, her caretaker 58 years her junior, was an art world scandal?

15 Who pipped Lewis Hamilton on the final lap of the final race to win the 2021 Formula 1 Drivers' Championship?

16 Natasha Hamilton joined which girl group in 1999 to replace Heidi Range?

17 The Canadian city of Hamilton lies on the western edge of which lake that shares its name with the province it sits in?

18 After starring for Scotland in the 1999 World Cup, which Yorkshire cricketer switched allegiance to England for Test cricket, but played only one match?

19 Alexander Hamilton founded which still-extant New York newspaper in 1801?

20 After dropping out, Alexander Hamilton surprisingly endorsed who in the 1800 election, who went on to become the country's third president?

Answers to QUIZ 64 – Birmingham

1	Bullring	11	Edgbaston
2	St Andrew's	12	Aldi
3	NEC	13	Tennis
4	M42	14	Cadbury
5	Custard	15	Longbridge
6	Balti	16	Spaghetti Junction
7	Joseph Chamberlain Memorial Clock Tower	17	Pebble Mill
8	UB40	18	Sutton Park
9	*Peaky Blinders*	19	On the Moon
10	New Street	20	Vulcan

ANSWERS ON PAGE **69**

1   Which cyclist won, but was later stripped of, seven consecutive Tour de France titles?

2   Nava and Savoy are types of which vegetable?

3   Since 2020, the longest commercial flight measured by distance travelled runs between New York and which Asian city-state?

4   Between 1961 and 1963, The Beatles performed 292 times at which music venue in Liverpool?

5   Water is comprised of which two elements?

6   The Whopper is produced by which fast food company?

7   In a 1989 single, Aerosmith find love where?

8   NASA astronauts wear what colour spacesuits during launch and landing of a space shuttle?

9   How many 20-minute periods are there in a professional ice hockey game?

10   What is the name of the bird in the *Peanuts* comic strip?

11   The first officially recognised Test match took place from 15th to 19th March 1877, between which countries?

12   Dippy, the 26-metre long diplodocus skeleton, used to stand in the entrance to which London museum?

13   The world's largest species of frog and spider both take their name from which Biblical character?

14   Margaret Thatcher once described which artist as "that man who paints those dreadful pictures"?

15   "Gooners" are supporters of which London-based football club?

16   In British educational terminology, what does UCAS stand for?

17   Mycroft is the older and smarter brother of which fictional detective?

18   Which Hungarian inventor is best known for mechanical puzzles including the Cube, Magic and Snake?

19   The series *Blackadder Goes Forth* is set during which historical period?

20   According to the proverb, what can you not make without breaking eggs?

Easy

Medium

Hard

Answers to QUIZ 65 – Pot Luck

1	*Indiana Jones*	11	Tambourine
2	Dime	12	The Antarctic
3	"Jesus wept."	13	Paul McCartney
4	The ears	14	Led Zeppelin
5	Miss World	15	Fork Lightning
6	*My Little Pony*	16	Yak
7	Highgate Cemetery	17	Boyzone
8	Bali	18	206
9	Thor	19	Geoffrey
10	Orange	20	Michael Schumacher

ANSWERS ON PAGE 70

Easy

1 What three-word phrase marked the traditional request for the public to leave the House of Commons galleries so that the Chamber could sit in private?

2 Which two-time Best Actress Academy Award winner served as a Labour MP between 1992 and 2015?

3 Which former Labour MP formed the New Party in 1931?

4 As British MPs cannot directly resign their seat, those wishing to quit apply for stewardship of which nominal archaic office?

5 What title is granted to enable people that do not head ministries or have specific responsibilities the right to attend cabinet meetings?

6 Although the role had existed unofficially before, and then notably in the wartime coalition government, who in 1995 became the UK's first *official* Deputy Prime Minister?

7 Which Conservative MP wrote the novel *The Clematis Tree*?

8 Environment Minister Tim Yeo was revealed to have had an affair just after the launch of which Conservative campaign, which advocated traditional values such as decency and courtesy?

9 Which MP for Southend West was murdered in 2021?

10 In office between 1900-22 and 1924-64, which two-time Prime Minister was also the longest serving MP in British history?

Medium

11 Which Labour politician and cabinet minister unsuccessfully attempted to fake his own death in 1974?

12 What is the Irish political equivalent to the British abbreviation, MP?

13 Which MP for North East Somerset holds the record for the longest word said during Parliamentary proceedings?

14 Conservative MP Peter Viggers infamously filed an expense claim for what garden decoration?

15 At the time of his eponymous scandal, John Profumo held what cabinet position?

16 Which trade secretary was forced to resign in 1983 over an illegitimate child, then took out an injunction to prevent her ever being mentioned?

17 Which Irish republican party routinely wins some of Northern Ireland's 18 seats in the UK House of Commons, but refuses to sit or vote in it?

18 Who was the Labour MP for Knowsley North between 1974 and 1986, but latterly became better known for a less-than-stellar broadcasting career?

19 As of 2021, who is the only woman to have served as Speaker of the House of Commons?

20 Which Franco-English writer, historian, orator, poet, sailor, satirist and writer of letters was the MP for Salford South between 1906 and 1910?

Hard

Answers to QUIZ 66 – Hamilton

1	Lin-Manuel Miranda	11	Dunblane
2	Aaron Burr	12	Ten dollar bill
3	Neil Hamilton	13	Lord Horatio Nelson
4	Hamilton Academical	14	Georgia O'Keeffe
5	*The Wizard of Oz*	15	Max Verstappen
6	Bermuda	16	Atomic Kitten
7	*The Terminator*	17	Lake Ontario
8	Andy Hamilton	18	Gavin Hamilton
9	Baseball	19	*New York Post*
10	Hamilton Ricard	20	Thomas Jefferson

1   Which is the world's tallest uninterrupted waterfall?
2   In the American and European markets, the original Nintendo® Game Boy™ came packaged with which puzzle game?
3   Which island group comprises the least populous country in Africa?
4   Which is the most common pub name in Britain?
5   Superstition holds that if which captive birds at the Tower of London are lost or fly away, the Crown will fall and Britain with it?
6   As a household item, what is sodium bicarbonate better known as?
7   What is a baby hedgehog called?
8   Reclassified in 2006, which dwarf planet was previously classed as a planet for less than one of its own years?
9   As of 2021, who is the tallest football player to ever score for England?
10 In the comics, which baby is left on Popeye's doorstep, whom he adopts and raises as his son?
11 According to the Oxford English Dictionary, which is the only English word that ends with "mt"?
12 *Neeps and tatties* is a common dish in which country of the United Kingdom?
13 *Knots Landing* was a spin-off series of which Texas-based soap?
14 The Chinese Gooseberry is also known as which fruit?
15 In the NATO phonetic alphabet, which name is used for the letter C?
16 Usually, rice is grown in fields known as what?
17 What type of animal does Alice follow in *Alice's Adventures in Wonderland*, and Neo follow a woman with a tattoo of in *The Matrix*?
18 Which French cartoon skunk was created by Warner Brothers in 1945?
19 At the 1958 UEFA championships, who became the first England footballer ever sent off during an international match?
20 Since 1945, all new British-built tanks have come with the ability to make what beverage?

Easy

Medium

Hard

Answers to QUIZ 67 – Pot Luck

1	Lance Armstrong	11	England and Australia
2	Cabbage	12	Natural History Museum
3	Singapore	13	Goliath
4	Cavern Club	14	Francis Bacon
5	Hydrogen and oxygen	15	Arsenal
6	Burger King®	16	Universities and Colleges Admissions Service
7	In an elevator	17	Sherlock Holmes
8	Orange	18	Ernő Rubik
9	Three	19	World War I
10	Woodstock	20	An omelette

Easy

1   Stormtroopers are the infantry foot soldiers of the Galactic Empire in which science fiction series?

2   Which TV weather forecaster famously reassured viewers that the Great Storm of 1987 would not hit British shores, hours before it did?

3   What is the name given to tropical storms that form over the Indian Ocean?

4   Named for its founders, what name is given to the rating system that classifies hurricanes based on their sustained wind speed?

5   What term is used for the loosely defined area of Texas, Oklahoma, Kansas and other central US states that are prone to severe storms?

6   Which component of hurricane damage causes the greatest loss of life?

7   On the twelve-level Beaufort scale, which grade of wind force classifies wind speed as a storm?

8   Hurricanes always form above what?

9   Illegal payments to adult actress Stormy Daniels were one of the many scandals plaguing which US President?

10   BBC podcast *The Coming Storm* seeks to explore the origins of which American political conspiracy theory?

Medium

11   What code name was given to the American Air Force's aerial bombing offensive during the first Gulf War?

12   Who starred as Captain Billy Tyne in the 1997 film *The Perfect Storm*?

13   Who wrote the mini-series *Storm of the Century*?

14   The WNBA team nicknamed "The Storm" play in which north-western American city?

15   Which comic book hero rides a horse called Storm?

16   Who starred as Storm in the first four instalments of the *X-Men* film franchise?

17   Which rapper's album *Gang Signs & Prayer* became the first from the grime genre to ever top the UK album chart?

18   Sue Storm, a superhero from the Marvel Comic universe, was initially known by which name?

19   Which Finnish DJ topped the charts with his 2000 instrumental *Sandstorm*, which would later become an internet phenomenon?

20   Lynne Spears's 2008 memoir *Through the Storm* chronicles the ups and downs of parenting who?

Hard

Answers to QUIZ 68 – Members of Parliament

1   "I spy strangers"
2   Glenda Jackson
3   Oswald Mosley
4   Chiltern Hundreds
5   Minister Without Portfolio
6   Michael Heseltine
7   Ann Widdecombe
8   *Back to Basics*
9   Sir David Amess
10   Sir Winston Churchill
11   John Stonehouse
12   TD (*Teachta Dala*)
13   Jacob Rees-Mogg (with floccinaucinihilipilification)
14   Duck house
15   War Secretary
16   Cecil Parkinson
17   Sinn Fein
18   Robert Kilroy-Silk
19   Betty Boothroyd
20   Hilaire Belloc

1   What, simply, is the main ingredient of bread?

2   What word can mean a vein of coal in a mine, a long thin indentation, or a movement of a cricket ball?

3   Flip, flow, bar and pie are types of what?

4   Which borough of Devon, including the resort towns of Torquay, Paignton and Brixham, is nicknamed the English Riviera?

5   Which 2009 Hilary Mantel novel is a sympathetic fictionalised biography on the rapid rise to power of Thomas Cromwell?

6   In 1999, which actor won the Worst Actor of the Century Award at the Razzies?

7   In the event of a tied score at the end of a frame of snooker, how is the victor determined?

8   Roboto, Calibri and Helvetica Bold are all types of what?

9   Which fast food brand is also often known as the Golden Arches?

10 In beer and brewing, what does the abbreviation IPA stand for?

11 Natural gas, coal and oil are all examples of what type of fuel?

12 *Masala*, *paneer* and *chapati* are all from which country's cuisine?

13 Have a break; have which chocolate biscuit?

14 What is the most common road name in the UK?

15 Which archipelagic province of Ecuador is 600 miles off the mainland and is home to species of penguins and tortoises?

16 What is the largest animal in the world today, and, as best as can be attained, the largest animal that has ever existed?

17 Deciduous trees lose their leaves at certain times of the year – which type of tree does not?

18 The lemur is native to which island in the Indian Ocean?

19 Which basketball legend was known as His Airness?

20 Near which pole do Polar Bears live?

Easy

Medium

Hard

Answers to QUIZ 69 – Pot Luck

1	Angel Falls	11	Dreamt (undreamt, daydreamt and redreamt also count as its derivatives)
2	*Tetris*®		
3	Seychelles	12	Scotland
4	The Red Lion	13	*Dallas*
5	Ravens	14	Kiwifruit
6	Baking soda	15	Charlie
7	A hoglet	16	Paddy fields
8	Pluto (a year on Pluto lasts 248 Earth years)	17	White rabbit
9	Peter Crouch	18	Pepé Le Pew
10	Swee'Pea	19	Alan Mullery
		20	Tea

1. In *Blackadder*, what type of plan did Baldrick always seem to have?
2. Which antiques dealer mainstreamed the phrases "Cheap as chips" and "Bobby Dazzler" when he hosted *Bargain Hunt*?
3. In which sitcom did Michelle Dubois regularly say "Listen very carefully, I shall say zis only once"?
4. Which comedian and actor had the catchphrase "Ooh, you are awful ... but I like you!"?
5. "Computer says no" was one of the catchphrases used in which sketch show?
6. Which 21st century sitcom launched the word "bazinga" in the lexicon?
7. "Shut that door!" and "what a gay day" were among the catchphrases of which entertainer and presenter?
8. In which film does Rick Blaine utter the line "Here's looking at you, kid" four times?
9. Paris Hilton trademarked which two-word catchphrase that she had inadvertently become synonymous with?
10. In *Star Trek: The Next Generation*, what was Captain Jean-Luc Picard's customary call to action?
11. Which cartoon character used the catchphrase "By the power of Greyskull"?
12. "Does my bum look big in this?" was the catchphrase of one of the characters of which *Fast Show* actress?

13. Which former judge on *Strictly Come Dancing* made a catchphrase out of how he would say the number seven?
14. Which price comparison website has been advertised by a meerkat saying "simples"?
15. Which catchphrase from Captain Kirk from the original *Star Trek* series passed into popular culture, even though he never actually said it?
16. Which *Doctor Who* actor used the catchphrase "Would you like a jelly baby?" as a greeting?
17. Surly teenager Lauren Cooper and her catchphrase "Am I bovvered?" was a creation of who?
18. In a 2006 poll, Peter Kay's rant about which foodstuff was voted the best one-liner in TV comedy?
19. Complete the introduction by MC Martin Fitzmaurice: "Are you ready? Ladies and Gentlemen! Let's...play..."?
20. Which curly-haired slapstick comedian, popular with children, became known for his catchphrase "Hello, my darlings!"?

Answers to QUIZ 70 – Storms

1	*Star Wars*	11	Desert Storm
2	Michael Fish	12	George Clooney
3	Cyclones	13	Stephen King
4	Saffir-Simpson scale	14	Seattle
5	Tornado Alley	15	Aquaman (Storm is a seahorse)
6	Storm surge	16	Halle Berry
7	Ten	17	Stormzy
8	Oceans	18	Invisible Woman
9	Donald Trump	19	Darude
10	QAnon	20	Britney Spears

ANSWERS ON PAGE 75

1   According to the proverb, a cat has how many lives?
2   A zedonk is the hybrid of which two animals?
3   Francois Mitterand said that which world leader had "the lips of Marilyn Monroe and the eyes of Caligula"?
4   The gander is the male of which animal species?
5   Which city is the world's southernmost national capital?
6   Formerly a slang term for the brain, what political term denotes a body of experts providing advice and ideas on specific political or economic problems?
7   To make a spritzer, wine is mixed with what?
8   Dr Seuss wrote about which feline over the course of five books?
9   *Quidditch Through the Ages* was a 2001 book written by who?
10 The 1994 biography *Obsession* was about which fashion designer?
11 According to the World War II proverb, what did loose lips do?
12 Which is the only body of water with shores on each of Asia, Africa and Europe?
13 Adwaita, the longest-living terrestrial animal in the history of the known world, was what species?
14 Any angle that measures more than 90 degrees and less than 180 degrees is termed as what?
15 Which bird of prey is the national bird of the United States of America?
16 The Rovers Return is the pub found in which soap opera?
17 *H.M.S. Pinafore*, *The Pirates of Penzance* and *The Mikado* were among the 14 comic operas created by which duo?
18 Catherine Earnshaw is the female protagonist in which Emily Brontë novel?
19 Which painter reputedly cut off his left ear after an argument with Paul Gaugain?
20 Which Danish novelist wrote many fairytales, including *The Snow Queen*, *The Emperor's New Clothes* and *The Little Mermaid*?

Easy

Medium

Hard

Answers to QUIZ 71 – Pot Luck

1	Flour	11	Fossil fuels
2	Seam	12	India
3	Chart	13	Kit Kat®
4	Torbay	14	High Street
5	*Wolf Hall*	15	Galapagos Islands
6	Sylvester Stallone	16	Blue Whale
7	The black is put back on the table ("respotted"), and play resumes	17	Evergreen
		18	Madagascar
8	Font	19	Michael Jordan
9	McDonald's®	20	The North Pole
10	Indian Pale Ale		

Easy

1 Which book by the legendary Doyle Brunson has been so influential that it has become regarded as "the Bible of poker"?

2 Which aptly-named accountant won the 2003 World Series of Poker Main Event as an amateur, catalysing the "poker boom" in the following years?

3 Which particular variant of poker is used in the World Series Main Event and is by far the most common televised format?

4 Often nicknamed "the Tiger Woods of poker", which legend of the game has twice been successfully sued by casinos for "edge sorting"?

5 Which 2017 film follows the investigation of an underground poker empire run for celebrities, athletes, business tycoons and the Russian mob?

6 The second series of *Poker Million*, the first televised event to ever have a £1,000,000 prize, was won by which snooker player?

7 Which Channel 4 show beginning in 1999 was the original showcase for the hole-card camera?

8 In 1989, which self-styled "Poker Brat" became the youngest player ever to win the Main Event?

9 What term is given to the fee taken by a poker room for operating a game, scaled to the buy-in and generally equal to 5-10% of the pot in each hand?

10 What term is given to the events of 15th April 2011, when the US government shut down the three largest online poker websites in the country?

11 What name is given to a five-card poker hand with all cards being of the same suit?

12 What catch-all name is given to any poker variant in which each player is dealt a complete hand before the first betting round?

Medium

13 Which form of poker is similar to Seven-card Stud, except the lowest hand wins?

14 Which American gambling icon opened the successful *Horseshoe* casino in downtown Las Vegas?

15 Poker is generally considered to have developed from collaboration between French settlers and Persian sailors in which American city?

16 The starting Hold'em hand of Ace-King is often given the nickname of which former tennis player, on account of it looking good but rarely winning?

17 Which poker legend, who died in 1998, played only 30 major tournaments but won 10 of them, including three Main Events?

18 Which Iranian-American poker player and magician won the then-biggest prize in poker history ($18,346,673) at the 2012 One Drop?

19 Which man, US President between 1969 and 1974, allegedly funded much of his initial Congress run with poker winnings from his time in the Navy?

20 Which Old West law enforcement officer was shot dead at a poker game holding two pair, aces and eights, now known as the Dead Man's Hand?

Hard

Answers to QUIZ 72 – Catchphrases

1	Cunning	11	He-Man
2	David Dickinson	12	Arabella Weir
3	*'Allo 'Allo!*	13	Len Goodman
4	Dick Emery	14	*Compare the Market*
5	*Little Britain*	15	"Beam me up, Scotty" (he did say "Scotty, beam
6	*The Big Bang Theory*		me up" once, but never the exact phrase)
7	Larry Grayson	16	Tom Baker
8	*Casablanca*	17	Catherine Tate
9	"That's hot"	18	Garlic bread
10	"Make it so"	19	"Darts!"
		20	Charlie Drake

1   *The Murder at the Vicarage* marked the first appearance of which fictional detective?
2   Which piece of furniture lends its name to the group of the most senior ministers that meet regularly with the Prime Minister?
3   Charon, Styx, Nix, Kerberos and Hydra are the five known moons of which dwarf planet?
4   What 'F' could be a padded unsprung mattress originating in Japan, or a low wooden sofa bed one could be put on?
5   Save for one letter, what name is shared by a character constantly expected by Vladimir and Estragon, and an Israeli actress?
6   "Reassuringly expensive" was an advertising slogan for which beer?
7   Which talk show host signed off every episode with the catchphrase "take care of yourself, and each other"?
8   Pam Dawber and Robin Williams starred as which hugely popular TV duo?
9   Who joined the cast of *EastEnders* as Alfie Moon in 2002?
10 Most of the vitamin C found in fruits is located in which part?
11 Vodka and coffee liqueur make up which cocktail?
12 Into which sea does the River Nile flow?
13 A nebuchadnezzar holds the equivalent of how many bottles of wine?
14 Under what often-changing name does hip-hop star Calvin Broadus record?
15 In the name of Washington D.C., what does the D.C. stand for?
16 Which Italian car manufacturer uses a trident as its logo?
17 At the height of his political career in the 1990s, who was dubbed "Two Jags" by the tabloid press?
18 Olympic weightlifter Toshiyuki "Harold" Sakata played which henchman in the *James Bond* movie franchise?
19 The story of Noah's Ark appears in which book of the Bible?
20 Where in the human body is the tibia?

Easy

Medium

Hard

Answers to QUIZ 73 – Pot Luck

1	Nine	11	Sink ships
2	Zebra and donkey	12	Mediterranean Sea
3	Margaret Thatcher	13	Aldabra Giant Tortoise
4	Goose	14	Obtuse
5	Wellington, New Zealand	15	Bald Eagle
6	Think tank	16	*Coronation Street*
7	Sparkling water or club soda	17	Gilbert & Sullivan
8	The Cat in the Hat	18	*Wuthering Heights*
9	JK Rowling	19	Vincent van Gogh
10	Calvin Klein	20	Hans Christian Andersen

Identify these winners of TV talent shows, as well as which show they won.

Easy

1

2

3

Medium

4

5

6

7

8

9

Hard

Answers to QUIZ 74 – Poker

1	*Super/System*	11	Flush
2	Chris Moneymaker	12	Draw
3	Texas Hold'em	13	Razz
4	Phil Ivey	14	Benny Binion
5	*Molly's Game*	15	New Orleans
6	Jimmy White (and Steve Davis came third)	16	Anna Kournikova
7	*Late Night Poker*	17	Stu Ungar
8	Phil Hellmuth	18	Antonio Esfandiari
9	Rake	19	Richard Nixon
10	Black Friday	20	Wild Bill Hicock

1 Which new wave band had a 1979 hit with *Video Killed the Radio Star*?

2 What term refers to a man who has lost his wife by death, and who has not subsequently remarried?

3 Mahatma Gandhi, Clive Anderson, Henri Matisse and Andrea Bocelli all trained as what?

4 Which French frozen dessert made from sugar-sweetened water is used between courses to refresh the palate?

5 The alcoholic drink mead is made by fermenting which substance?

6 The Cook Strait separates the North and South islands of which country?

7 Which rapper's real name is Aubrey Graham?

8 Hans Gruber was the antagonist in which movie, which may or may not be considered a Christmas film?

9 Olive Ridley, Hawksbill and Loggerhead are types of which animal?

10 The ancient Greeks had no symbol for which number, which also could not be written in Roman numerals?

11 The Marquess of Queensberry Rules are generally accepted as the rules for which sport?

12 Captain Sensible sang the theme tune to which TV game show?

13 Sierra Leone, Djibouti and Burundi all lie on which continent?

14 Royal College of Art student John Pasche created the anti-establishment tongue and lips logo for which rock band?

15 Two members of the Spice Girls have which first name?

16 In terms of distance from the sun, which planet lies between Jupiter and Uranus?

17 What was the 1990 sequel to the 1987 film *Three Men and a Baby*?

18 Which common English language surname takes its name from a person who makes arrows?

19 In 2008, Google launched which web browser?

20 The Koala's diet consists mostly of the leaves of which tree?

Easy

Medium

Hard

Answers to QUIZ 75 – Pot Luck

1	Miss Marple	11	Black Russian
2	Cabinet	12	The Mediterranean Sea
3	Pluto	13	20
4	Futon	14	Snoop Dogg
5	Godot (*Waiting for Godot* and Gal Gadot)	15	District of Columbia
6	Stella Artois	16	Maserati
7	Jerry Springer	17	John Prescott
8	*Mork & Mindy*	18	Oddjob
9	Shane Richie	19	Genesis
10	The skin	20	Leg – it is the shinbone

Easy

1   Of the Seven Wonders of the Ancient World, how many were located inside the borders of Egypt?

2   Which British archaeologist discovered Tutankhamun's tomb in 1922?

3   Which modern Egyptian city, often called the "world's greatest open-air museum", gives its name to a pyramid-shaped super casino in Las Vegas?

4   Which city, the fifth-largest in the country, is located at the northernmost tip of the Suez Canal?

5   Which city, the third-largest in Egypt after Cairo and Giza, is known as the "Bride of the Mediterranean"?

6   Crucial to the understanding of hieroglyphics, the Rosetta Stone features writing in Egyptian (both glyphic and written) and what other language?

7   Although largely all removed, the pyramids of Giza were all initially covered in what polished sedimentary rock?

8   Which facial fixture is the Sphinx missing?

9   Which Egyptian-American actor played the lead role of Freddie Mercury in the Queen biopic *Bohemian Rhapsody*?

10 Which Egyptian forward won the Premier League Golden Boot award in both the 2017–18 and 2018–19 seasons?

11 Ancient Egyptians believed that the god Anubis weighed which organ of the human body to determine if the person would be allowed into the afterlife?

12 Which Egyptian actor starred in *Doctor Zhivago* and *Lawrence of Arabia*?

13 Lake Nasser was formed by the creation of which dam?

Medium

14 What name is given to the area on the west bank of the Nile that has been found to be home to at least 63 pharaohs' tombs?

15 The popular resort of Sharm El Sheik, on the Red Sea, is particularly noted for what type of holiday activity?

16 In Egyptian mythology, Osiris is married to which goddess, who upon his death was thought to cause the Nile's annual flooding with her tears?

17 Which 27th century BC high priest was regarded as a god of medicine, architecture, fine arts and scribes, and designed the step pyramid?

18 Which three other countries does Egypt border?

19 Deposed in 1953 when he was still only one year old, who was the last King of Egypt?

20 Which pharaoh is credited with joining Upper and Lower Egypt in a single centralised monarchy?

Hard

Answers to QUIZ 76 – Talent Show Winners

1   Candice Brown – *The Great British Bake Off*
2   Lost Voice Guy – *Britain's Got Talent*
3   Bill Bailey – *Strictly Come Dancing*
4   Kevin Simm – *The Voice*
5   Alexandra Burke – *The X Factor*
6   Michelle McManus – *Pop Idol*
7   Lenny Henry – *New Faces*
8   Spike Milligan – *Opportunity Knocks*
9   David Sneddon – *Fame Academy*

1 The sitcom *Frasier* was a character spin-off of which other sitcom?

2 On the pH scale, which number represents maximum acidity?

3 What is the largest land animal on Earth?

4 Douglas Adams and John Lloyd wrote which humorous "dictionary of things that there aren't any words for yet"?

5 What term can be used for an unmarried noblewoman attending a queen or princess, or for a bride's principal bridesmaid?

6 Which word can mean to train someone, as well as being the name of a part of a train?

7 Edina Monsoon and Patsy Stone were the principal characters in which sitcom?

8 The koala is native to which country?

9 In the traditional folk song, what did Yankee Doodle call the feather in his cap?

10 Roy Keane played for which football club between 1993 and 2005?

11 *The Pebbles and Bamm-Bamm Show* was a spin-off from which cartoon series?

12 The International Date Line runs between the South Pole and North Pole through which ocean?

13 Professor Moriarty was the criminal mastermind nemesis of which fictional detective?

14 The E Street Band are the backing group to which singer-songwriter?

15 EA Sports' series of NFL video games take the name of which legendary coach and commentator?

16 Carlos Estevez is better known as which actor?

17 Flopsy, Mopsy and Cotton-tail are the sisters of which anthropomorphic literary character?

18 *Trumpets*, *It Girl* and *In My Head* are among the hits of which R&B singer?

19 Which polymath and Founding Father can count the lightning rod, bifocal glasses and the flexible urinary catheter among his inventions?

20 In which 1997 comedy film do six unemployed men from Sheffield decide to form a male striptease act?

Answers to QUIZ 77 – Pot Luck

1	The Buggles	11	Boxing
2	Widower	12	*Big Break*
3	Lawyers	13	Africa
4	Sorbet	14	The Rolling Stones
5	Honey	15	Melanie
6	New Zealand	16	Saturn
7	Drake	17	*Three Men and a Little Lady*
8	*Die Hard*	18	Fletcher
9	Turtle	19	Chrome
10	Zero	20	Eucalyptus

Easy

1   Currer, Ellis and Acton Bell were the male-passing soubriquets of which venerated Victorian literary novelist sisters?

2   Which two sisters are, as of the end of 2021, the two highest-earning female tennis players of all time?

3   LaVerne, Maxene and Patty formed which singing swing and boogie-woogie group known for their 1941 hit *Boogie Woogie Bugle Boy*?

4   Kourtney, Kim and Khloé make up which reality TV sister trio?

5   The ugly stepsisters are characters in which fairy tale and pantomime?

6   Among other things, what name is shared by a constellation, a London train station and an 1860 play?

7   Singer, songwriter and actress Solange is the lesser-known sister of which global superstar?

8   Jake Shears and Ana Matronic were the vocalists of which pop rock band?

9   Which R&B singing group had hits with *Fairytale*, *He's So Shy*, *Slow Hand* and *I'm So Excited*?

10 Which pop duo and solo artist teamed up to record *Sisters Are Doin' it For Themselves*?

11 Which Anglo-Irish group's biggest hit was 1980's *I'm In the Mood for Dancing*?

12 Which vocal group released the 1979 hit *We Are Family*?

13 Pauline Quirke and Linda Robson starred as sisters Sharon and Tracey in which long-running sitcom?

14 When Mary I died without an heir in 1558, her sister became which Queen of England?

15 Twins Mary-Kate and Ashley, and younger sister Elizabeth, make up which trio of acting siblings?

16 Skipper, Stacie and Chelsea are the three "sisters" of which toy?

17 *Titanic* is still the second largest ocean liner wreck in the world, only beaten by which of her sister ships?

18 Which Russian wrote the play *Three Sisters*?

19 What song's famous melody was written in 1893 by sisters Patty and Mildred Hill?

20 Which venerated actress began performing in vaudeville as a child with her two older sisters, in a group called *The Gumm Sisters*?

Medium

Hard

Answers to QUIZ 78 – Egypt

1	Two (Great Pyramid of Giza, Lighthouse at Alexandria)	11	The heart
2	Howard Carter	12	Omar Sharif
3	Luxor	13	Aswan High Dam
4	Port Said	14	Valley of the Kings
5	Alexandria	15	Diving/snorkelling
6	Ancient Greek	16	Isis
7	Limestone	17	Imhotep
8	Nose	18	Sudan, Libya, Israel
9	Rami Malek	19	Fuad II
10	Mo Salah	20	Menes

QUIZ 81 – Pot Luck

ANSWERS ON PAGE **83**

1   In *Fawlty Towers*, who portrayed John Cleese's wife?
2   Which UK political party came to power for the first time in 1924?
3   The Mekong Delta is in which country?
4   The Medici family are most commonly associated with which Italian city?
5   Cast, pig and wrought are all types of which metal?
6   In the colours of the rainbow, which is next to violet?
7   Something described as "vernal" pertains or occurs in which season?
8   A polygraph machine is also known as what?
9   The Severn Estuary flows into which channel?
10 Which American city is known as Motor City?
11 In a pack of cards, which king is always in profile?
12 On a ship, which side is sheltered from the wind?
13 In 1931, bootlegger and racketeer mob boss Al Capone was sentenced to 11 years in prison for which crime?
14 Which sport is often referred to as "the noble art"?
15 Despite its name, which body of water between Europe and Asia is the world's largest inland lake?
16 *The Rime of the Ancient Mariner* was a major work by which English poet?
17 Epiphany occurs in which month of the year?
18 In England and Australia, the name of which red wine is sometimes used as a synonym for blood?
19 In the *James Bond* stories, by what name is Sir Miles Messervy better known?
20 *Drivers License* was the 2021 debut single for which singer?

Easy

Medium

Hard

Answers to QUIZ 79 – Pot Luck

1	*Cheers*	11	*The Flintstones*
2	Zero	12	Pacific Ocean
3	African elephant	13	Sherlock Holmes
4	*The Meaning of Liff*	14	Bruce Springsteen
5	Maid of honour	15	John Madden
6	Coach	16	Charlie Sheen
7	*Absolutely Fabulous*	17	Peter Rabbit
8	Australia	18	Jason Derulo
9	Macaroni (referring to an 18th century style of continental dress, not the pasta)	19	Benjamin Franklin
10	Manchester United	20	*The Full Monty*

ANSWERS ON PAGE 84

1 Which Category 5 hurricane caused over 1,800 fatalities and $125 billion in damage in the New Orleans area in late August 2005?

2 The eruption of which Indonesian volcano in 1883 was so loud that it deafened sailors 40 miles away?

3 The earthquake that caused the 2004 Indian Ocean tsunami was the world's largest in 40 years – what did it measure on the Richter scale?

4 By estimated death toll, all of the top three famines and four biggest floods in history occurred in which country?

5 Causing an estimated 75-200 million deaths, what term was used for the bubonic plague pandemic occurring worldwide between 1346 and 1353?

6 What name is given to the region of mostly calm weather at the centre of tropical cyclones?

7 What country's name was given to the 1918 influenza pandemic that killed an estimated 17 million to 50 million people?

8 The capital city of which great empire was devastated by a fire that burned for nearly a week in AD 64?

9 In 1923, a massive earthquake killed 99,000 people in Tokyo. The quake, however, was not directly responsible for most of the deaths. What was?

10 The capital city of which island nation was completely destroyed and buried by the eruption of Mont Pelée on 8th May 1902?

11 Which Roman writer witnessed and wrote about the eruption of Vesuvius and the resulting destruction of Pompeii and Herculaneum?

12 While the Richter scale measures the power of the seismic waves, which twelve-point scale measures the intensity of an earthquake by the amount of damage caused?

13 A 518-metre high tsunami, the biggest on record, only claimed five lives, as it struck which sparsely-populated US state?

14 Slab and loose are the two main types of which sudden and potentially disastrous natural process?

15 An estimated 316,000 people were killed when a catastrophic magnitude 7.0 earthquake struck which Caribbean country on 12th January 2010?

16 Following the eruption of the Soufrière Hills volcano, Plymouth, the capital of which British Overseas Territory, was completely buried in ash?

17 Roughly 600 skeletons were found in Roopkund, India, that were eventually determined to have died of skull injuries caused by which weather form?

18 What name is given to the point *within* the earth where an earthquake originates?

19 Tropical storms that form over the Northwest Pacific Ocean have what name?

20 Which African body of water "exploded" in a limnic eruption in 1986, suffocating 1,746 people?

Answers to QUIZ 80 – Sisters

1	Charlotte, Emily and Anne Brontë	11	The Nolan Sisters
2	Venus and Serena Williams	12	Sister Sledge
3	The Andrews Sisters	13	*Birds Of A Feather*
4	Kardashians	14	Elizabeth I
5	*Cinderella*	15	The Olsens
6	Seven Sisters	16	Barbie®
7	Beyoncé Knowles-Carter	17	*Britannic*
8	Scissor Sisters	18	Anton Chekhov
9	The Pointer Sisters	19	*Happy Birthday to You/Good Morning to All*
10	The Eurythmics and Aretha Franklin	20	Judy Garland (whose real name was Frances Ethel Gumm)

1   A lumbar puncture is a procedure carried out on which area of the body?
2   Which ingredient in bread makes it rise?
3   In internet and text parlance, what does the acronym "smh" stand for?
4   Which date is known as Star Wars Day?
5   Which singer experienced a supposed "wardrobe malfunction" during the Super Bowl XXXVIII Halftime Show?
6   On 30th September 1955, which actor was killed in a car accident on the way to a car race?
7   The pop novelty instrumental *Yakety Sax* became widely known through its using as the closing music to which comedy show?
8   As featured in the song, what does the abbreviation YMCA stand for?
9   In the UK, what was imposed in January 1974 to save electricity at the start of the miner's strike?
10 Which position in netball is signified by the letters WD?
11 "Nollywood" is a nickname for which country's film industry?
12 Freeman, Hardy and Willis was a high street retailer of what?
13 Concorde was created as a joint enterprise between Britain and which other country?
14 Which country lies across the Bering Strait from Alaska?
15 Which compound is added to tap water to prevent tooth decay?
16 In addition to the knit, what is the second basic knitting stitch?
17 Which actress is best known for her role of Mercedes McQueen in the Channel 4 soap opera *Hollyoaks*?
18 In the history of the British monarchy, which ruling house followed the Tudors?
19 Purely in terms of average distance from the Sun, which is the closest planet to Earth?
20 Between 2000 and 2011, Jamie Oliver was the public face of which supermarket?

Answers to QUIZ 81 – Pot Luck

1	Prunella Scales	11	King of diamonds
2	Labour	12	Lee side
3	Vietnam	13	Tax evasion
4	Florence	14	Boxing
5	Iron	15	Caspian Sea
6	Indigo	16	Samuel Taylor Coleridge
7	Spring	17	January
8	Lie detector	18	Claret
9	Bristol Channel	19	M
10	Detroit	20	Olivia Rodrigo

1. Rod Serling created which TV franchise, incorporating fantasy, science fiction, suspense, horror and supernatural elements?
2. Lily James and Sebastian Stan starred in which 2022 biographical drama miniseries about a 90's celebrity married couple?
3. Which British TV channel shares its name with the rapper who won Album of the Year at the 2020 Brit Awards?
4. Berk, Boney and Drutt were monsters living in a castle in which 1980s stop-motion children's series?
5. Later a TV medical expert regularly appearing on *This Morning*, which doctor initially rose to fame appearing as Amazon on *Gladiators*?
6. Cage and Fish, a law firm, was the setting for which 1997-2002 comedy-drama series?
7. Far better known for a different soap role, which actress appeared in *Coronation Street* as Mrs Parsons from 1970 to 1971?
8. Which TV producer is credited with creating the "Idol" format of talent shows?
9. Noted for her role on *Modern Family*, which Colombian-American actress was the world's highest paid in 2020?
10. Which adult animated comedy-drama set in Hollywood centres on a depressed anthropomorphic horse?
11. Actor Dermot Morgan died of a heart attack the day after finishing filming the third series of which sitcom?
12. Which near-centenarian actress appeared in *The Mary Tyler Moore Show*, *Hot In Cleveland* and *The Golden Girls*?
13. In which series running between 2016 and 2020 was Kristen Bell welcomed into a highly selective Heaven-like utopia?
14. In the series of the same name, what was Lovejoy's occupation?
15. Siblings Daisy-May and Charlie Cooper star in which mockumentary series set in the Cotswolds?
16. *Woodentop* was a 1983 one-off drama that turned into which long-running soap opera?
17. Claire Foy (series 1 and 2) and Olivia Colman (series 3 and 4) both played who in what?
18. Eugene Levy and Catherine O'Hara star in which show about a bankrupt couple relocating to a town that they initially bought as a joke?
19. In *It's Always Sunny In Philadelphia*, which diminutive actor plays Frank Reynolds, the *de facto* owner of Paddy's Pub?
20. "You are Number 6." "I am not a number; I am a free man!" This exchange was part of the opening narration of which 1960s show?

Answers to QUIZ 82 – Natural Disasters

1	Hurricane Katrina	11	Pliny the Younger
2	Krakatoa	12	Mercalli Scale
3	Nine	13	Alaska
4	China	14	Avalanche
5	Black Death	15	Haiti
6	Eye	16	Montserrat
7	Spain (Spanish Flu)	17	Hail
8	Roman Empire (Rome)	18	Hypocentre
9	Fire	19	Typhoons
10	Martinique	20	Lake Nyos

Easy
Medium
Hard

1 In the Polish version of Scrabble®, how many points is the Z tile worth?

2 Which animal lives in a drey?

3 *What Have You Done for Me Lately*, *Black Cat* and *All For You* were hits for which member of the Jackson family?

4 Faith, Judy and Rinder can all be preceded with which job title to make three television shows?

5 What is the "average" score in an IQ test?

6 Also the name of a TV quiz show, according to the saying, a chain is only as strong as its what?

7 At the very beginning of a chess game, how many different pieces can white move?

8 In snooker, after all reds have left the table, which colour ball is next?

9 Which airline operated flight MH370 that disappeared in March 2014, leading to the biggest search operation in history?

10 Sold for 400 francs, *The Red Vineyard* was the only painting sold in which artist's lifetime?

11 What animal is featured on the main logo of the World Wildlife Foundation?

12 Las Vegas is surrounded on all sides by which desert?

13 In the name of computer games such as *Sim City* or *The Sims*, what does "sim" mean?

14 By what English name is the mountain Yr Wyddfa (pronounced *arr withva*) known?

15 In The Beatles' song *Penny Lane*, what is a nurse selling from a tray?

16 What was the name of the landing module on the Apollo 11 space mission?

17 The FTSE is the stock market index of which country?

18 Under what name was Erich Weiss (1874-1926) better known?

19 On a racing card, what does the abbreviation SP signify?

20 Vilnius is the capital city of which European country?

Answers to QUIZ 83 – Pot Luck

1	Back or spine	11	Nigeria
2	Yeast	12	Footwear
3	Shaking my head	13	France
4	4th May (as in, May the fourth be with you...)	14	Russia
5	Janet Jackson	15	Fluoride
6	James Dean	16	Purl
7	*The Benny Hill Show*	17	Jennifer Metcalfe
8	Young Men's Christian Association	18	The Stuarts
9	Three-Day Week	19	Venus
10	Wing defence	20	Sainsbury's

Easy

1. 17th April 1961 saw the failed invasion of which Cuban coastal area by Cuban exiles, covertly funded by the US Government?
2. Which Marvel comic superhero has a daughter named April Parker?
3. In April 2010, an erupting volcano in which country shut down European air travel for nearly a week?
4. St George's Day is usually celebrated on which date in April?
5. Which Motown legend was shot to death on 1st April 1984 by his father?
6. On which date in April does the Queen's actual (rather than ceremonial) birthday fall?
7. Despite always being ten due to the show's floating timeline, which cartoon character known for his pranks is said to have been born on 1st April 1979?
8. On 18th April 1906, an earthquake and subsequent fire damage destroyed 80% of which west coast American city?
9. On 15th April 1986, the USA began bombing which country in retaliation for Colonel Gaddafi's alleged sponsoring of a terrorist attack ten days earlier?
10. A 1957 April Fool's Day prank by the BBC's *Panorama* jokingly reported that which food grows on trees?

Medium

11. The first Disney theme park in Europe was opened on 12th April 1992 in which city?
12. Referring to the annual deadline for income tax payments, which poet, on whose work the musical *Cats* is based, said "April is the cruellest month"?
13. April Rhodes is a recurring character in which musical comedy-drama television series centred around a school choir?
14. On 26th April 1999, which TV presenter was murdered on Gown Avenue in London for reasons unknown by an unknown assailant?
15. On 19th April 1995, Timothy McVeigh and Terry Murray conspired to blow up a truck bomb on a federal building in which US city?
16. The poem *Home Thoughts From Abroad* that begins with the line "Oh to be in England now that April's there" was written by who?
17. The April 1972 issue of Cosmopolitan sold over 1.5 million copies, thanks to a nude centrefold of whom?
18. First a computer programmer and then later a reporter, April O'Neil was a human ally to which band of fictional anthropomorphic superheroes?
19. Many overseas Vietnamese refer to the week of 30th April as "Black April" in lamentation for the fall of which city in 1975?
20. April Mendez became a three-time WWE Divas Championship winner under which ring name?

Hard

Answers to QUIZ 84 – Television

1	The Twilight Zone	11	Father Ted
2	Pam and Tommy	12	Betty White
3	Dave	13	The Good Place
4	The Trap Door	14	Antiques dealer
5	Zoe Williams	15	This Country
6	Ally McBeal	16	The Bill
7	June Brown (Dot Cotton in *EastEnders*)	17	Queen Elizabeth II in *The Crown*
8	Simon Fuller (not Simon Cowell!)	18	Schitt's Creek
9	Sofia Vergara	19	Danny DeVito
10	BoJack Horseman	20	The Prisoner

1 Which car manufacturer's logo features a green snake and a red cross?

2 Plains, mountain and Grevy's are the three living species of which animal?

3 Tutankhamun and Edward VI shared which nickname, related to their age?

4 In the nursery rhyme, on which day did Solomon Grundy get married?

5 Ipswich is the administrative headquarters of which English county?

6 In cricket, what name is given to the fielder who patrols the boundary behind the slips?

7 As depicted in their logo, how many varieties of Heinz products were there purported to be as of 1896?

8 What are the two forenames of *Narnia* creator C.S. Lewis?

9 Because he considered himself to be the centre of the universe, without equal, King Louis XIV of France was known as what?

10 The Cayman Islands are a self-governing overseas territory of which country?

11 What did a woman named Erika Roe do at Twickenham Stadium during an England vs Australia rugby union match on 2nd January 1982?

12 *Goodbye, Farewell and Amen* was the 1983 final episode of which classic American sitcom, watched by over 105 million people?

13 What fruit flavour does a Bellini cocktail have?

14 Someone who has a lack of red blood cells is suffering from which affliction?

15 Supposedly, the Roman Emperor Caligula made Incitatus a priest; who or what was Incitatus?

16 As heard in the lyrics to *Waltzing Matilda*, what animal is known as a jumbuck in Australian slang?

17 In which Olympic event do competitors use ribbons and hoops?

18 Formerly known as British Honduras, which is the only Central American country where English is an official language?

19 Chairman Mao's "little book", and *This Is Your Life's* big book, were both which colour?

20 Resigning after losing the 2001 General Election, who became only the second-ever leader of the Conversative Party to not become Prime Minister?

Easy

Medium

Hard

Answers to QUIZ 85 – Pot Luck

1	One	11	Giant panda
2	Squirrel	12	Mojave
3	Janet Jackson	13	Simulator or simulation
4	Judge	14	Snowdon
5	100	15	Poppies
6	Weakest link	16	*Eagle*
7	Ten (the eight pawns and two knights; everything else is blocked in)	17	United Kingdom
		18	Harry Houdini
8	Yellow	19	Starting price
9	Malaysia Airlines	20	Lithuania
10	Vincent van Gogh		

Easy

1 The Panama Canal was built to link up which two oceans?

2 With more than 25,000, which ocean contains the most – and indeed the majority – of all the ocean islands in the world?

3 More than 1,000 miles from any continental land mass, Diego Garcia is a British Overseas Territory and important military base in which ocean?

4 What is the name of the strait that separates the Arctic and Pacific Oceans?

5 Into which ocean does the Amazon river flow?

6 Eleven countries border both the Pacific and Atlantic; Mexico, Guatemala, Nicaragua, Costa Rica, Colombia, Russia, Canada, USA, Panama, Honduras and which South American country?

7 The North Sea is the north-eastern edge of which ocean?

8 How many American states border the Pacific Ocean?

9 The name Pacific comes from the Portuguese for "peaceful sea", named by which explorer, whose 1521 voyage was the ocean's first recorded crossing?

10 In 2021, the National Geographic Society finally recognised which ocean as the world's fifth, 64 years after the International Hydrographic Organization had removed its classification as such?

Medium

11 The Pacific and Atlantic oceans meet at which Chilean land mass?

12 Varuna is the god of the ocean in which world religion?

13 Along with plankton (that float) and nekton (that swim), what name is given to organisms that live on, in or near the bottom of the ocean?

14 The Lomonosov Ridge is a major submarine ridge located in which ocean?

15 When it existed hundreds of millions of years ago, the superocean Panthalassa surrounded which supercontinent?

16 The paranormal activities at 112 Ocean Avenue where Ronald DeFeo shot and killed six members of his family formed the story of which novel and film?

17 Which rock band from Birmingham had their chart heyday in the 1990s with hits such as *The Day We Caught The Train*?

18 Named 2012 Album Of The Year by The Guardian, Channel Orange was the debut studio album by which R&B singer-songwriter?

19 Which singer, real name Leslie Charles, had hits in the 1970s and 1980s including *When the Going Gets Tough, the Tough Get Going*?

20 Who played the heist victim Terry Benedict in the 2001 remake of *Ocean's Eleven*?

Hard

Answers to QUIZ 86 – April

1	Bay of Pigs	11	Paris
2	Spider-Man	12	T.S. Eliot
3	Iceland (the volcano was Eyjafjallajökull)	13	*Glee*
4	23rd	14	Jill Dando
5	Marvin Gaye	15	Oklahoma City
6	21st	16	Robert Browning
7	Bart Simpson	17	Burt Reynolds
8	San Francisco	18	Teenage Mutant Ninja (or Hero) Turtles
9	Libya	19	Saigon
10	Spaghetti	20	AJ Lee

QUIZ 89 – Pot Luck

ANSWERS ON PAGE **91**

1   In the *Doctor Who* canon, what does the abbreviation TARDIS stand for?

2   In boxing, what name is given to the left-handed fighting stance, in which the right hand and right foot are set forward?

3   Which jean cut hugs the hips and thighs, then widens from the knee to the hem, flaring out slightly at the ankle?

4   In English, which day of the week is named after the Norse god Tiw or Tyr?

5   *Halal* food is permitted under the dietary rules of which religion?

6   Who appeared at both the London and Philadelphia *Live Aid* gigs?

7   In French, *jeudi*. In German, *Donnerstag*. In Spanish, *jueves*. What is it in English?

8   George IV commissioned which extravagant seaside Royal residence as a discreet location for private liaisons with his long-time companion, Maria Fitzherbert?

9   Burns Night celebrations are usually held on which date in January, the anniversary of the namesake poet's birthday?

10 A tracheotomy is performed on which part of the body?

11 Which animated TV series featured a green dog and a pink cat?

12 Which rectangular type of biscuit shares its name with an Italian general?

13 Which American Olympic swimmer portrayed Tarzan in twelve films, and Jungle Jim in thirteen more?

14 Theodor Geisel wrote many children's books under what pen name?

15 What is the name for the side opposite to the right angle on a right-angled triangle?

16 What breed of dog is the one most often trained as guide dogs?

17 Dresden is the capital city of which state in Germany?

18 The surname of which multiple Wimbledon singles champion is also that of an enemy of the Federation in *Star Trek*?

19 Winning Best Actress for *Howards End* (1992) and Best Adapted Screenplay for *Sense and Sensibility* (1995), who is the only person to win Academy Awards for both acting and writing?

20 The Montgolfier brothers pioneered what form of air travel?

Easy

Medium

Hard

Answers to QUIZ 87 – Pot Luck

1	Alfa Romeo	11	Streak
2	Zebra	12	M*A*S*H
3	The Boy King	13	Peach
4	Wednesday	14	Anaemia
5	Suffolk	15	His favourite horse
6	Third man	16	Sheep
7	57	17	Rhythmic gymnastics
8	Clive Staples	18	Belize
9	The Sun King	19	Red
10	United Kingdom	20	William Hague (the first was Austen Chamberlain)

Who do these icons of lip foliage belong to?

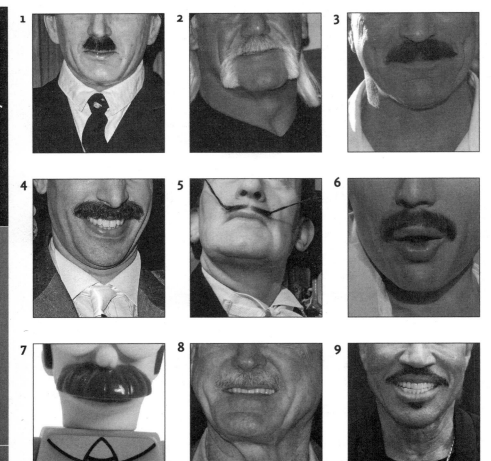

Answers to QUIZ 88 – Oceans

1 Atlantic and Pacific Oceans
2 Pacific Ocean
3 Indian Ocean
4 Bering Strait
5 Atlantic Ocean
6 Chile
7 Atlantic Ocean
8 Five (Hawaii, Alaska, California, Oregon, Washington)
9 Ferdinand Magellan
10 Southern Ocean

11 Cape Horn
12 Hinduism
13 Benthon
14 Arctic Ocean
15 Pangaea
16 *The Amityville Horror*
17 Ocean Colour Scene
18 Frank Ocean
19 Billy Ocean
20 Andy Garcia

1   What term describes the rate at which the speed of an object increases?

2   The Venus de Milo is located in which museum?

3   As of 2021, which is the only song to have sold a million copies in the UK on three separate occasions for three different artists?

4   During which battle did the infamous Charge of the Light Brigade take place?

5   In the English language version of Scrabble®, which is the only letter tile to have a unique points value?

6   As of 2021, what is the world's most populous world city, with over 37 million residents?

7   In the name of the football team, what does QPR stand for?

8   Which defunct furniture retailer, that seemingly always had a sale on, was once so ubiquitous that 60% of British children were said to have been conceived in one of their beds?

9   In betting terminology, what betting style consists of 11 bets of equal value on selections in four separate events: six doubles, four trebles and one four-fold?

10 In the children's stories by Enid Blyton, what was Noddy's job?

11 What is it customary to shout after filling in an entire bingo card?

12 Yarrows, Swan Hunter and Robbs, all now defunct, were British builders of what?

13 Which was the last French city held by England?

14 Zippo Manufacturing Company introduced its first example of what item in 1933?

15 The mouth of the Nile river lies in what country?

16 *Teenage Kicks*, John Peel's all-time favourite song, was the 1978 debut single for which Northern Irish band?

17 Which European capital city lies on the banks of the River Spree, which flows into the Havel, a tributary of the Elbe?

18 Thomas Jackson, a Confederate general during the American Civil War, went by which nickname, now perhaps better known as the name of an LGBTQ+ charity?

19 In investment terminology, what does APR stand for?

20 Which car manufacturer was for a long time advertised by the call and response "Papa!", "Nicole?"

Easy

Medium

Hard

Answers to QUIZ 89 – Pot Luck

1	Time and relative dimensions in space	11	*Roobarb and Custard*
2	Southpaw	12	Garibaldi
3	Bootcut	13	Johnny Weissmuller
4	Tuesday	14	Dr Seuss
5	Islam	15	Hypotenuse
6	Phil Collins	16	Labrador Retriever
7	Thursday	17	Saxony (or *Sachsen*)
8	Brighton Pavilion	18	Borg
9	25th January	19	Emma Thompson
10	Throat	20	Hot air balloons

1. Whose novelty hit *Shaddap You Face* kept Ultravox's *Vienna* off the top spot back in 1981?

2. While they released the strikingly similar *Another Day* and *Think of You*, which pop act never replicated the success of their debut single, *Saturday Night*?

3. Although they released it second to try and avoid being a one-hit wonder, which song by The Vapors was ultimately their only ever top 40 hit?

4. What refrain did the Baha Men yell repeatedly in their 2000 international one-hit wonder?

5. The Knack had an international hit in 1979 with which song, their first and only No.1 in any country?

6. Korean artist Psy created an international phenomenon with which 2012 song, combining a catchy beat and a unique dance?

7. What was the name of the 1995 song in which Chumbawamba ruminated on getting knocked down, but also on getting up again?

8. The Champs achieved a one-hit wonder in 1958 with a song that contained only one word, one sung only three times. Which word?

9. Although often thought to have been recorded by the Beach Boys, the 1963 instrumental *Wipe Out* was performed by which other surf rock band?

10. Norman Greenbaum has not released new material since 1972 as he earns sufficient royalties from which 1969 hit to not need to?

11. Immediately recognisable for its "ooga-chaka" opening refrain, Swedish rock band Blue Swede topped the charts in 1974 with which song?

12. Famous for being the theme tune to *Friends*, *I'll Be There For You* was a one-hit wonder for which group, named after an artist?

13. The hat-wearing Daniel Powter had a much-parodied 2005 hit with which song?

14. Leading to countless prank calls to innocent people with the number, *867-5309 (Jenny)* was a hit for which American power pop band?

15. Despite achieving better success in their native New Zealand, *How Bizarre* was the only international mainstream success for which pop-rap group?

16. Although often mistaken for an individual based on their name, which Danish pop band had an international 2015 hit with *7 Years*?

17. The 2012 multi-platinum-selling single *Let Her Go* was by which English singer-songwriter?

18. The only novel that Margaret Mitchell ever wrote in her life was which celebrated classic?

19. The 1969 Italian film *Medea* was the only non-opera acting role for which legendary soprano, known for her *bel canto* technique?

20. In a 1987 film, Sarah Pickering appeared with Derek Jacobi as which titular Dickens character? She had never acted before, and never acted again.

Answers to QUIZ 90 – Name That Moustache

1. Charlie Chaplin
2. Hulk Hogan
3. Tom Selleck
4. Borat (Sacha Baron Cohen)
5. Salvador Dali
6. Freddie Mercury
7. Ned Flanders
8. John Cleese
9. Lionel Richie

ANSWERS ON PAGE **95**

1   Counting upwards from seven, which is the next prime number?

2   "Rush Hour Crush" is a lonely hearts bulletin section in which free daily newspaper?

3   Which chocolate drink and breakfast cereal has been advertised by a monkey called Quicky?

4   Who was Henry Morten Stanley, Welsh-American explorer and journalist, sent by the *New York Herald* to Africa to find?

5   What are the odds of a coin landing on tails on four consecutive flips?

6   K2, the second-highest mountain on Earth, straddles the border between which two countries?

7   In which London park is the Serpentine recreational lake?

8   In Greek mythology, which King turned everything he touched into gold?

9   Carson City and Las Vegas are found in which US state?

10 Variola is more commonly known as which disease?

11 What is the main ingredient in *borscht* soup?

12 After Barbara Mandell, who became the second female news presenter on British television?

13 What is the only US state to have a one syllable name?

14 Which London landmark was built to commemorate the Great Fire of London?

15 *Pebble in the Sky* and *I, Robot* are the first two books written by which science fiction author?

16 One circuit of a modern outdoor running track is how many metres long?

17 On which street is the Bank of England located?

18 Acetylsalicylic acid is more commonly known as which drug?

19 What kind of creature was the TV character Flipper?

20 Iridology is the study of which part of the body to determine a patient's overall health?

Easy

Medium

Hard

Answers to QUIZ 91 – Pot Luck

1	Acceleration	11	"House!"
2	Louvre	12	Ships
3	*Unchained Melody* (Righteous Brothers, Robson and Jerome, Gareth Gates)	13	Calais
4	Battle of Balaclava	14	Cigarette lighter
5	K (worth five)	15	Egypt
6	Tokyo	16	The Undertones
7	Queens Park Rangers	17	Berlin
8	MFI	18	Stonewall
9	Yankee	19	Annual percentage rate
10	He drove a taxi	20	Renault

Easy

1   Which male former Arsenal and Scotland goalkeeper, later a broadcaster, has the middle name Primrose?

2   Which star of *The Late Late Show*, *Gavin & Stacey* and *The History Boys* has the middle name Kimberley?

3   When Reg Dwight changed his name to Elton John, he also added what middle name, taken from a mythological figure famous for his twelve labours?

4   Which *Pretty Woman* actor's middle name is Tiffany, as it was his mother's maiden name?

5   Which British actor has the middle name Mungo, since it pairs so well with his first name?

6   Famous for the song *Honey to the Bee* and appearing in *Doctor Who*, which British actress and singer was given the middle name Paul?

7   Which British Prime Minister is known by one of his two middle names, the other being 'de Pfeffel'?

8   At various stages in her career, Hillary Clinton has made a point of using her maiden name as a *de facto* middle name. What is it?

9   Which basketball legend had "Bean" as a middle name, derived from his father's nickname in his own playing days, "Jellybean"?

10 Which British-Canadian heavyweight boxing champion and Olympic medallist has the middle name Claudius?

11 Which US president had merely a middle initial rather than a middle name, after his family could not decide on one?

12 Which *Simpsons* character was named after the middle name of former President Richard Nixon?

Medium

13 What does the 'T' stand for in the name of Star Trek character James T. Kirk?

14 *Family Guy* patriarch Peter Griffin's middle name is Löwenbräu, which was a popular 1980s brand of what?

15 Which knighted singer-songwriter goes by his middle name as his first name, James, was the same as his father's?

16 One of Greta Thunberg's middle names is shared with which cartoon character, created by Belgian artist Hergé?

17 Both the second and sixth US presidents were called John Adams, with the latter's middle name invariably included to differentiate them; what is it?

18 A 2017 study by swordandscale.com found that roughly half of the US population to have which middle name have been tried for murder?

19 What name is, by quite some distance, the most popular girl's middle name of all time in the UK?

20 As played by Al Pacino in *The Irishman*, which union leader who disappeared mysteriously had the middle name Riddle?

Hard

Answers to QUIZ 92 – One-Hit Wonders

1	Joe Dolce Music Theatre	11	*Hooked On A Feeling*
2	Whigfield	12	The Rembrandts
3	*Turning Japanese*	13	*Bad Day*
4	*Who Let The Dogs Out?*	14	Tommy Tutone
5	*My Sharona*	15	OMC
6	*Gangnam Style*	16	Lukas Graham
7	*Tubthumping*	17	Passenger
8	*Tequila*	18	*Gone With The Wind*
9	The Surfaris	19	Maria Callas
10	*Spirit In The Sky*	20	*Little Dorrit*

QUIZ 95 – Pot Luck

ANSWERS ON PAGE 97

1   Flautist René Laennec modified one of his own hand-carved flutes to make the first prototype of which diagnostic medical instrument?
2   In *The Dukes of Hazzard*, what was the name of Bo and Luke Duke's car?
3   Which company was formed by the merger of the BOAC and BEA?
4   Which "fossil" composed of a human cranium and an ape jaw was "discovered" by Charles Dawson in 1912, but shown to be a hoax in 1953?
5   The city of Constantinople become known as what, as of March 1930?
6   Trotter's Independent Trading Company was a shady company in which sitcom?
7   Batman lives and operates in which city?
8   What was the name of Michael Jackson's chimpanzee?
9   The Dick King-Smith novel *The Sheep-Pig* was adapted into which 1995 film, named for the lead character?
10 Which fuel company used the slogan "Put a Tiger in Your Tank"?
11 India, Indonesia, the Maldives, Mauritius, Nepal, Pakistan, Seychelles and Sri Lanka all use a currency with which name?
12 Despite also excelling in golf and football, and working as a baseball coach, which cartoon character's best sport was bowling, where he played under the nickname "Twinkletoes"?
13 Savoy, semi-savoy and flat-leaf are the three major types of which leafy vegetable?
14 Which is the yellow Tellytubby?
15 How many wings do all butterflies have?
16 The comedy duo Laurel and Hardy became well known for wearing which style of hat?
17 Scooby Doo's name originates from nonsense scat lyrics in which Frank Sinatra song?
18 Which TV cartoon series features a robot named Bender?
19 Which Netflix show was its most streamed in 2021, with more than 146 million views?
20 Which Grammy-nominated New York rapper, born Earl Simmons, died on 9th April 2021, the same day as Prince Philip?

Answers to QUIZ 93 – Pot Luck

1	11	11	Beetroot
2	*Metro*	12	Angela Rippon
3	Nesquik®	13	Maine
4	Dr David Livingstone	14	The Monument
5	One in sixteen	15	Isaac Asimov
6	Pakistan and China	16	400m
7	Hyde Park	17	Threadneedle Street
8	Midas	18	Aspirin
9	Nevada	19	Dolphin
10	Smallpox	20	Eyes

Easy

1. Typically, what five ingredients go into a Cuban Highball Mojito?
2. Served unmixed in a tall glass, which cocktail is made of tequila, orange juice and grenadine syrup?
3. A mix of ginger ale and a splash of grenadine, garnished with a maraschino cherry, is named for which child actor, who hated it?
4. How do you turn a Black Russian into a White Russian?
5. Which alcoholic drink forms the basis of Batanga, Margarita and Matador cocktails?
6. Which cocktail of absinthe and champagne shares its name with an Ernest Hemingway novel?
7. The name of which cocktail is derived from the Tahitian word for "excellent" or "very good"?
8. What fruit juice is used to make both Cosmopolitans and Sea Breezes?
9. The original version of which cocktail was a mix of American whiskey, vermouth and bitters?
10. Cognac, crème de cacao and cream are combined to create which cocktail?
11. Adding gin to an Americano and removing the soda creates what other cocktail?
12. Popular in French ski resorts, Green Chaud is a mixture of hot chocolate and which liqueur?
13. Often consumed at Christmas time in America, a mix of eggnog with brandy and rum, served hot, is named after which cartoon duo?
14. Made of equal parts vodka, triple sec and lime juice, which cocktail's name translates from Japanese as "Divine Wind"?
15. Vermouth is used in conjunction with which spirit to make a Martini?
16. Adding orange juice to a Perfect Martini creates which other cocktail, named for a borough of New York City?
17. Vodka, peach Schnapps, orange juice and cranberry juice combine to make which cocktail?
18. Pink Lady cocktails get their distinctive colour through the addition of which non-alcoholic ingredient?
19. The Bellini, a combination of peach and prosecco, originated in which Italian city?
20. Because of their similarities, which other cocktail, vibrantly coloured, is sometimes known as Tom Collins's girlfriend?

Answers to QUIZ 94 – Middle Names

1	Bob Wilson	11	Harry S. Truman
2	James Corden	12	Milhouse
3	Hercules	13	Tiberius
4	Richard Gere	14	Beer
5	Hugh Grant	15	Sir Paul McCartney
6	Billie Piper	16	Tintin
7	Boris Johnson	17	Quincy
8	Rodham	18	Wayne
9	Kobe Bryant	19	Louise
10	Lennox Lewis	20	Jimmy Hoffa

QUIZ 97 – Pot Luck

ANSWERS ON PAGE 99

1. "Mother's Ruin" is a nickname for which alcoholic drink?

2. In 1995, which bowler's 7/43 figures were the best ever by an Englishman on Test debut, followed up with a Test cricket hat-trick two tests later?

3. The band Duran Duran took their name from which science fiction film?

4. Garibaldi, Digestive and Ginger Nut are all types of what?

5. Cherilyn Sarkisian LaPierre became internationally successful under what name?

6. Which English city was known by the Romans as Verulamium?

7. "Darby and Joan" is a proverbial phrase used to refer to what kind of relationship?

8. In Roman numerals, what is the total of MD + MD?

9. *Vaquero, gaucho* and *paniolo* are all regional terms from places in the Americas for what profession?

10. Which football league team has the nickname The Blades?

11. Cobs are the male of which creature?

12. What does the American law enforcement acronym CIA stand for?

13. In Venice, what famous structure links the Ducal Palace with the state prison?

14. Bulawayo is the second-largest city in which African country?

15. On a London Underground map, how are interchange stations signified?

16. Vegetation covered in dirt and rock, subjected to pressure and heat over millions of years, creates which mineral fuel?

17. Notorious for a destructive effect on the ozone layer, what does CFC stand for?

18. Guy Gibson was the first Commanding Officer of No. 617 Squadron and thus the leader in which wartime raid?

19. In which South American city were the 2016 Summer Olympics held?

20. A *bathyscaphe* was a manned submersible vessel invented by which Swiss deep-sea explorer?

Easy

Medium

Hard

Answers to QUIZ 95 – Pot Luck

1	The stethoscope	11	Rupee
2	*The General Lee*	12	Fred Flintstone
3	BA – British Airways	13	Spinach
4	Piltdown Man	14	Laa-Laa
5	Istanbul	15	Four
6	*Only Fools and Horses*	16	Bowler hat
7	Gotham City	17	*Strangers in the Night*
8	Bubbles	18	*Futurama*
9	*Babe*	19	*Squid Game*
10	Esso	20	DMX

Easy

1. Which 1972 hit is Alice Cooper's first and only no.1 record in the UK to date?
2. A cooper is a person trained to make what?
3. Alice Beer co-hosted which BBC consumer affairs programme with Anne Robinson in the 1990s?
4. FBI Special Agent Dale Cooper is one of the leading characters in which mystery-horror drama serial created by Mark Frost and David Lynch?
5. Formerly known as Stuart, what is the third-largest town in the Australian Northern Territory?
6. *Blue Weekend* was the first UK no.1 album bestseller for which alternative rock band?
7. Who starred alongside Lady Gaga in *A Star Is Born*?
8. Which English biologist and television presenter has been a professor at the University of Birmingham since 2012?
9. In a still-unsolved mystery, which fugitive famously eluded capture in 1971 by parachuting out of the aeroplane he had hijacked?
10. Which CNN journalist and reporter was the first openly LGBTQ+ person to moderate a presidential debate?
11. Which English actress has credits to her name including *She's Out of My League*, *Men in Black 3* and *Entourage*?
12. Cooper, sportscaster and the older brother of legends Peyton and Eli, is a member of which American NFL family dynasty?

Medium

13. Which 1950 Nevil Shute novel tells the story of a woman who falls for a prisoner and emigrates to Australia with him?
14. A girl called Alice Liddell was the inspiration for the character of Alice in *Alice in Wonderland* and *Through The Looking Glass*, written by who?
15. Which big-haired punk performance poet has performed alongside the Sex Pistols, The Fall, Joy Division, The Buzzcocks and many others?
16. With hits including *No Excuses*, which grunge band formed in Seattle in 1987 had the late Layne Staley on vocals?
17. In 1998, the Dutch Eurodance-pop group Alice Deejay achieved a UK no.2 hit with which song?
18. With 1,296 as of 2020, which actress had the most on-screen kills in cinema history, the majority coming in her role as Alice in the *Resident Evil* series?
19. *Alice* (1990) was the eleventh of thirteen films directed by Woody Allen that also starred who, his wife at the time?
20. Which actor, who won the Best Actor Oscar for *Sergeant York* and *High Noon*, refused the leading male role in *Gone With the Wind*?

Hard

Answers to QUIZ 96 – Cocktails

1	White rum, lime juice, sugar, soda water and mint	11	Negroni
2	Tequila Sunrise	12	Chartreuse
3	Shirley Temple	13	*Tom and Jerry*
4	Add cream	14	Kamikaze
5	Tequila	15	Gin
6	Death in the Afternoon	16	Bronx
7	Mai Tai	17	Sex on the Beach
8	Cranberry juice	18	Grenadine
9	Manhattan (although Canadian whiskey was used during Prohibition)	19	Venice
10	Brandy Alexander	20	Singapore Sling

1 Susie Dent is the resident lexicographer on which daytime game show?

2 Which South American country has Dutch as its official language?

3 Which tech giant launched the Walkman® on 1st July 1979?

4 What word is given to the sound of a bell, especially when rung solemnly for a death or funeral?

5 A 1990 advert for Levi's® jeans helped which Steve Miller Band song to the top of the charts, 17 years after its initial release?

6 Which mode of transport describes a series of camels carrying passengers and goods between points?

7 Centaurs had the head, arms and torso of a man, and the body and legs of which animal?

8 According to the Hebrew Bible, God commanded Abraham to offer which of his sons as a sacrifice?

9 Coney, Flemish Giant and Holland Lop are all which type of animal?

10 On the Celsius temperature scale, at what temperature does water freeze?

11 A 39-mile turf fortification between the Firth of Forth and the Firth of Clyde was built by the Romans and named for which emperor?

12 The world's first public steam railway was built between which two towns in the northeast of England?

13 The Victoria Falls lie on the border between which two African countries, whose names start with the same letter?

14 Betz cells are found in which organ of the body?

15 Due to its proximity to Scone Abbey, which city was considered the capital of Scotland before Edinburgh?

16 Bill Gates and Paul Allen founded which computer technology corporation in 1975?

17 Billy Connolly played banjo and guitar, and Gerry Rafferty sang, in which Scottish folk group?

18 Corkscrew, dappled and weeping are all types of which tree?

19 Flamingos spend about 15 to 30 percent of each day doing what?

20 *Poisson d'Avril* in France is known in Britain as what?

Answers to QUIZ 97 – Pot Luck

1	Gin	11	Swans
2	Dominic Cork	12	Central Intelligence Agency
3	*Barbarella*	13	The Bridge of Sighs (*Ponte dei Sospiri*)
4	Biscuit	14	Zimbabwe
5	Cher	15	White circle with a black border
6	St Albans	16	Coal
7	A devoted elderly married couple	17	Chlorofluorocarbon
8	MMM (1,500 + 1,500 = 3,000)	18	The Dam Busters
9	Cowboy	19	Rio de Janeiro, Brazil
10	Sheffield United	20	Auguste Piccard

Easy

1. Which British fashion designer was instrumental in the 1960s Mod and youth fashion movements, and claims credit for the miniskirt and hotpants?
2. In April 1967, Shirley Preston became London's first what?
3. A mere 22 minutes after the passing of the 1963 Peerage Act, who was the first peer to renounce his title?
4. Named after a suburb of Pardubice in the Czech Republic, which explosive was first manufactured in 1964?
5. In the 1960s, on account of his lifestyle and long hair, which footballer was one of several people to be called "The Fifth Beatle"?
6. Who led his "Family" in the August 1969 murder of Sharon Tate?
7. On 6th March 1964, Cassius Clay changed his name to what?
8. Who was the third member of the 1969 Apollo 11 mission who remained in the command module and never set foot on the Moon?
9. On 9th October 1967, which socialist revolutionary and guerrilla leader was captured and executed by the Bolivian army?
10. Which French philosopher, author, journalist and Nobel Laureate died in a car accident on 4th January 1960?

Medium

11. A key figure of 1960s UK culture, which actress and novelist went on to launch a range of kitchenware?
12. Which monthly music and culture magazine was founded in 1967 by Jann Wenner and Ralph J. Gleason?
13. Published in 1965, eight months after his death, which was Ian Fleming's twelfth and final James Bond novel?
14. Which country's new flag was proclaimed on 28th January 1965 by the country's queen?
15. Nancy Sinatra sang about, and is forever linked to, which item of 60s fashion?
16. On 18th March 1965, who performed the first ever space walk?
17. Who was President of France for all but the last few days of the 1960s?
18. Construction of what began in May 1967 in southwestern Orange County, Florida, and ended four and a half years later?
19. Why was the 1968 Oscars ceremony postponed by 48 hours?
20. Burundi gained independence from which European country on 1st July 1962?

Hard

1   Which traditional Scottish dish consists of meat mixed with suet and oatmeal, boiled in a bag traditionally made of animal stomach?

2   In the story of *Peter Pan*, what was the name of the fairy?

3   Which English city sits on the eastern side of the Mersey Estuary?

4   The Statue of Liberty was a gift to the USA from which country?

5   Stratus, nimbus and cumulus are types of what?

6   The fiddle is an informal name for which instrument?

7   Organic matter used as a fuel for the generation of electricity is known as what?

8   A block of steel, gold or silver, typically oblong in shape, is known as what?

9   What term is given to the scientific study of plants?

10 Isosceles and scalene are types of what?

11 What name is given to a baby hare?

12 Icicle, bowline and barrel hitch are types of what?

13 *Endeavour*, *Adventure* and *Discovery* were the three Royal Navy ships used on the Pacific Ocean voyages of which Captain?

14 Something described as cervine is relating to or resembling which animal?

15 In *The Wizard of Oz*, what was the Scarecrow looking for?

16 How many emirates make up the United Arab Emirates?

17 Laverbread is a traditional delicacy from which country?

18 What name was given by English sailors for the flag flown to identify a pirate ship about to attack?

19 In police terminology, who or what is the CPS?

20 Which English city is known as the City of Dreaming Spires?

Answers to QUIZ 99 – Pot Luck

1	*Countdown*	11	Antonine Wall (not Hadrian; that is a different wall 100 miles further south)
2	Suriname		
3	Sony	12	Stockton and Darlington
4	Knell	13	Zimbabwe and Zambia
5	*The Joker*	14	The brain
6	Caravan or train	15	Perth
7	Horse	16	Microsoft®
8	Isaac	17	The Humblebums
9	Rabbit	18	Willow
10	Zero degrees	19	Preening
		20	April Fool's Day

Can you solve these anagrams for the names of 20 animal species? (In several cases, the answer is more than one word.)

1 ICE OR HORNS
2 LOCO CIDER
3 OWN BARBER
4 ALIEN PHEASANT
5 NO BRAWL
6 LOOPED
7 GENTLE OVERRIDER
8 HALLO TWO MY MOM
9 NIGERIA'S TRIBE
10 MOURNING PEEPER
11 WARLOCK WIPED BIDS

12 HIKING REFS
13 DANG PATINA
14 WAR MOTHER
15 WEAKER RAT THIGHS
16 MELON ACHE
17 A TOWEL, FUNNILY
18 OH, BAD ENERGY
19 NASAL DREAM
20 PRAM WHEELS

Answers to QUIZ 100 – The 1960s

1	Mary Quant	11	Jane Asher
2	Female licensed taxi driver	12	*Rolling Stone*
3	Tony Benn	13	*The Man with the Golden Gun*
4	Semtex	14	Canada
5	George Best	15	Go-go boots
6	Charles Manson	16	Alexei Leonov
7	Muhammad Ali	17	Charles de Gaulle
8	Michael Collins	18	Walt Disney World®
9	Che Guevara	19	The assassination of Martin Luther King
10	Albert Camus	20	Belgium

1. Much used due to the COVID-19 pandemic, The Oxford English Dictionary selected which three-letter truncated word as its 2021 Word of the Year?
2. The Aegean Sea separates which two countries?
3. Which river, the second longest in Europe, flows from the Black Forest to the Black Sea?
4. A Geordie is a native of which English city?
5. The golfer Vijay Singh is from which Oceanic island nation?
6. Which author wrote the *Twilight* series of novels?
7. In the world of investing and commerce, what is an IPO?
8. In the folk tale from the *One Thousand and One Nights* collection, Ali Baba overhears a group of how many thieves?
9. Clint Eastwood appeared as ramrod Rowdy Yates in the first seven series of which Western television series?
10. Despite the name, the Spanish Steps can be found in which city?
11. By quite some way, what is the most common surname in the English speaking world?
12. Scorbutus, a condition caused by deficiency of ascorbic acid (vitamin C), is more commonly known as what?
13. In both Greek and Roman mythology, who was the god of the Sun, music and prophecy?
14. In which year was the United Nations established?
15. Queen guitarist Brian May is also a doctorate holder and lecturer in which scientific field?
16. Blinky, Pinky, Inky and Clyde are a quartet of ghost characters from which video game franchise?
17. Which studio makes both the *Red Dead Redemption* and *Grand Theft Auto* series of video games?
18. What sports car company manufactures the 911 range?
19. Which boy's name is spelled out by the initial letters of five consecutive calendar months?
20. Which Carthaginian general and statesman supposedly crossed the Alps with elephants on the way to war with the Romans?

Easy

Medium

Hard

Answers to QUIZ 101 – Pot Luck

1	Haggis	11	Leveret
2	Tinkerbell	12	Knot
3	Liverpool	13	James Cook
4	France	14	Deer
5	Cloud	15	A brain
6	Violin	16	Seven (Abu Dhabi, Ajman, Dubai, Fujairah, Ras Al Khaimah, Sharjah and Umm Al Quwain)
7	Biofuel or biomass		
8	Ingot	17	Wales
9	Botany	18	Jolly Roger
10	Triangle	19	Crown Prosecution Service
		20	Oxford

What are the common names of these plant species?

Easy

1

2

3

4

Medium

5

6

7

8

Hard

Answers to QUIZ 102 – Animal Anagrams

1	Rhinoceros	11	Black Widow Spider
2	Crocodile	12	Kingfisher
3	Brown Bear	13	Giant Panda
4	Asian Elephant	14	Earthworm
5	Barn Owl	15	Great White Shark
6	Poodle	16	Chameleon
7	Golden Retriever	17	Yellowfin Tuna
8	Woolly Mammoth	18	Honey badger
9	Siberian Tiger	19	Salamander
10	Emperor Penguin	20	Sperm whale

1   *Vache* is the French word for which animal?
2   Snoopy, the cartoon character, is what breed of dog?
3   Diamond and graphite are allotropes of which element?
4   The Colossus – one of the Seven Wonders of the Ancient World – was located on which Greek island?
5   What are the names of all seven of Snow White's dwarves?
6   Ed Koch, Rudy Giuliani and Bill de Blasio have all been mayor of which American city?
7   Dromedary and Bactrian are the two surviving types of which animal?
8   The name of which nationality is used to describe an auction in which the price is reduced until a buyer is found?
9   In 1961, Viv Nicholson became famous when she told the media that she would "spend, spend, spend" after her husband Keith won £152,319 on what?
10   What is the longest river in Australia?
11   OLF units are measurements for which of the senses?
12   Amity Island is the fictional setting of which classic 1975 film?
13   What does WD stand for in the name of the spray WD-40®?
14   Which ex-Royal Navy Town-class light cruiser is now permanently moored as a museum ship on the River Thames in London?
15   Giving its name to a brand of UK food products, which food of the gods supposedly conveyed immortality?
16   The abbreviation of fashion label DKNY stands for what?
17   Who were the only three drivers to win the Formula 1 World Championship in the 2010s?
18   The name of which month of the year is, albeit pronounced slightly differently, also an adjective meaning respected and impressive?
19   If something can be described as noisome, what is it?
20   Which type of animals live in a sett?

Easy

Medium

Hard

Answers to QUIZ 103 – Pot Luck

1	Vax	11	Smith
2	Greece and Turkey	12	Scurvy
3	Danube	13	Apollo
4	Newcastle	14	1945, as a direct response to World War II
5	Fiji	15	Astrophysics
6	Stephenie Meyer	16	*Pac-Man*™
7	Initial public offering	17	Rockstar Games
8	40	18	Porsche
9	*Rawhide*	19	Jason (July, August, September, October, November)
10	Rome	20	Hannibal

1   What term is given to the process of working a dough to produce gluten by repeatedly folding it onto itself?

2   Profiteroles and eclairs are made from which type of pastry?

3   Of what, primarily, is meringue made?

4   Sponge cake with jam and cream in the middle is named for which monarch?

5   What term is used for the outer coloured part of the peel of a citrus fruit when it is used as flavouring?

6   What type of heavy, slightly sweet rye bread has a name which translates as "devil's fart"?

7   The addition of what turns white sugar into brown sugar?

8   Supposedly, which chewable sweet was created by mistake when the baker overstirred an attempt at caramel, and takes its name from her anguished shout after discovering this?

9   Cakes rise in the oven because the baking powder or yeast in the batter produces which gas?

10 17th century folklore holds that which kind of cake will show you who you will marry in your dreams if you place it under your pillow?

11 Pierogi, kreplach, gyoza and jiaozi are all types of what foodstuff?

12 Often associated with Yorkshire and traditionally eaten on Guy Fawkes Night, parkin cake has what flavour?

13 Which fruitcake associated with Easter is distinguished by layers of almond paste or marzipan with eleven balls on the top?

14 In 1921, the Washburn Crosby Company created which female character to promote its flour and baking products?

15 Launched in 1915, what was the first ever brand of consumer cooking products made with temperature-resistant glass?

16 Who was the female judge on the first seven series of *The Great British Bake Off*?

17 Which small rich French sponge cake is baked in a fluted tin or mould and decorated with coconut and jam in a distinctive shell shape?

18 Similar to a brownie but with a caramel and butterscotch taste due to the brown butter used, which baked good shares its name with a new wave band?

19 Which French term describes a water bath placed in the oven to prevent delicate bakes from curdling, cracking or overcooking?

20 Not usually eaten, which dough made from icing sugar and gum tragacanth is used for shaping delicate flowers and other items as decoration?

Answers to QUIZ 104 – Horticulture

1   Sunflower
2   Venus Flytrap
3   Lupin
4   Poppy
5   Gerbera
6   Dahlia
7   Daffodil
8   Allium

ANSWERS ON PAGE 109

1 Fuerteventura is the second-largest of which group of islands?
2 Which is the outermost of human skin's three main layers?
3 By what nickname was criminal Albert DeSalvo better known?
4 In which country is the spa town of Baden-Baden?
5 In 1731, the Scottish mathematician and doctor John Arbuthnot wrote that which vegetable gives urine "a foetid smell"?
6 Oktoberfest begins in which month?
7 In which prehistoric town did the Flintstones live?
8 Arthur Negus was the original presenter of which TV show, which Fiona Bruce became the host of in 2008?
9 If someone suffers from strabismus, what condition do they have?
10 An "astronomical unit" is a unit of measurement equal to the distance between what two objects?
11 What did English technical draughtsman Harry Beck create in 1931 that is still widely used today?
12 Most species of bird have how many toes on each foot?
13 "History will be kind to me, for I intend to write it" was a line spoken by which politician and Nobel Laureate?
14 In old money, how many pence was a groat worth?
15 Which film was derisively called "Walt Disney's Folly", only for it to become the highest-grossing animated film of all time, adjusted for inflation?
16 Football commentator Bjørge Lillelien's famous "your boys took a hell of a beating" diatribe came after which country beat England in a World Cup qualifier?
17 What is the most commonly broken bone in the human body?
18 In aviation, what does VTOL stand for?
19 In the British political system, who receives the largely ceremonial title of Father of the House?
20 In metres, how long is an Olympic-sized swimming pool?

Easy

Medium

Hard

Answers to QUIZ 105 – Pot Luck

1	Cow	11	Smell
2	Beagle	12	*Jaws*
3	Carbon	13	Water displacement
4	Rhodes	14	HMS *Belfast*
5	Grumpy, Sleepy, Happy, Bashful, Sneezy, Dopey and Doc	15	Ambrosia
		16	Donna Karan New York
6	New York City	17	Sebastian Vettel, Lewis Hamilton and Nico Rosberg
7	Camel		
8	Dutch auction	18	August
9	The football pools	19	Smelly and/or unpleasant
10	Murray	20	Badgers

Easy

1. The 1960s Japanese animated series *Kimba the White Lion* is alleged to have been plagiarised by which popular American movie?

2. Ash Ketchum is the protagonist of which popular Japanese franchise?

3. Which was the first Japanese anime to win an Oscar?

4. In 2017, Scarlett Johansson starred in a remake of which Japanese animated movie?

5. Which Oscar-winning actor provided the English language voiceover of the title character in the 2004 Studio Ghibli movie *Howl's Moving Castle*?

6. Fictional anime character Goku from *Dragonball Z* was the ambassador for which sporting event?

7. Which anime series, spanning more than 40 years, inspired a life-size 18-metre, 25-ton, moving "mech" statue in Yokohama, Japan in 2020?

8. Mighty Atom is the Japanese name for which animated character, credited as the first anime to be broadcast in the USA in 1963?

9. Which 2015 anime series is known in Japan as *Wanpanman*?

10. Katsuji Morishita directed an eight-minute animated segment in which 2003 Quentin Tarantino movie?

11. Classic Japanese anime, *The Rose of Versailles*, is based on which major 18th century event in European history?

12. Which Marvel legend co-created and made a cameo in the anime series *Heroman and Reflection*?

13. Which Canadian actor provided the voice of Pikachu in the 2019 movie *Detective Pikachu*?

14. Which Hollywood actor produced and voiced the Japanese anime *Afro Samurai* in 2007?

15. In 1997, *Princess Mononoke* became the highest grossing movie in Japan, beating the record held for 15 years by which Steven Spielberg movie?

16. *Ponyo*, the story of a fish that turns into a girl, is based on which Hans Christian Andersen fairy tale?

17. The 1992 Studio Ghibli movie *Porco Rosso* featured an anthropomorphic version of which animal as the title character?

18. The Wachowskis developed Japanese manga and anime series *Mach GoGoGo* into which 2008 movie?

19. In the 2008 movie *Ponyo*, which food does Ponyo claim to love?

20. Which 1986 song by The Bangles features as the end credits theme for the 2014 anime *Jo Jo's Bizarre Adventure: Stardust Crusaders*?

Medium

Hard

Answers to QUIZ 106 – Baking

1	Kneading	11	Dumplings
2	Choux	12	Ginger
3	Egg whites	13	Simnel
4	Victoria	14	Betty Crocker
5	Zest	15	Pyrex™
6	Pumpernickel	16	Mary Berry
7	Molasses	17	Madeleine
8	Fudge	18	Blondie bars
9	Carbon dioxide	19	Bain-marie
10	Wedding cake	20	Pastillage

ANSWERS ON PAGE 111

1 In the *Star Trek* universe, Vulcans have what colour blood?
2 The drummers of both Duran Duran and Queen had which full name?
3 Daisy Fay Buchanan is a fictional character in which classic 1925 novel?
4 Which French manufacturer makes the Zoe electric car?
5 The art of clipping bushes and hedges into artistic shapes is called what?
6 The seaport town of Cowes is located on which island?
7 Which Australian bird's song is described as laughing?
8 The Boswell family were the focus of which sitcom set in Liverpool?
9 The names of British racehorses are limited to how many characters in length?
10 What name is given to a junction between two nerve cells consisting of a small gap through which impulses are transmitted?
11 If you are in tune with someone, you are said to be on the same what, a distance in physics?
12 How many of the squares on a Rubik's® Cube never move?
13 How did suffragette Emily Davison meet her death in 1913?
14 Referring to the basic skills taught in schools, what are "the three Rs"?
15 Madeira and the Azores are islands belonging to which European country?
16 Which airborne disease causes inflammation in the brain and spinal cord, marked by intense headaches, fever, sensitivity to light and muscular rigidity?
17 The Hatton Garden area of Holborn, London, is famous for the sale of what?
18 Captured and held for ransom by English Colonists in 1613, how was Rebecca Rolfe better known?
19 Highly influential jazz singer Eleanora Fagan was better known by what name?
20 In 1930, which English pilot became the first woman to fly solo from London to Australia?

Easy

Medium

Hard

Answers to QUIZ 107 – Pot Luck

1 Canary Islands
2 Epidermis
3 The Boston Strangler
4 Germany
5 Asparagus
6 September
7 Bedrock
8 *Antiques Roadshow*
9 Their eyes do not point in the same direction (squint)
10 Earth and the Sun; roughly 93,000,000 miles
11 The London Underground map
12 Four (three forward-facing, one backward)
13 Winston Churchill
14 Four
15 *Snow White and the Seven Dwarfs*
16 Norway
17 Clavicle (collar bone)
18 Vertical Take-Off and Landing
19 The longest-serving MP (presumably, a woman would be called Mother of the House, but all holders thus far have been men)
20 50 metres

ANSWERS ON PAGE 112

Easy

1   Which author wrote the *Famous Five* series of novels?

2   What are the five Olympic rings intended to represent?

3   In terms of both depth and surface area, which is the largest of the five American Great Lakes?

4   Prior to the 2015 departure of Zayn Malik, which English-Irish boy band comprised of five members?

5   Complete this list of the *original* 1965 members of the Jackson Five; Michael, Tito, Jermaine, Jackie, _____?

6   Which E4 comedy-drama series focused on a group of five young offenders sentenced to work community service that gain supernatural powers?

7   Clint Eastwood's five *Dirty Harry* films were predominantly set in which American city?

8   Charles Bronson starred as vigilante killer Paul Kersey in the first five releases in which action-crime-drama film series?

9   *Last Blood* (2019) ended this five-part film series; *First Blood* (1982) started it. Which film franchise is this, starring Sylvester Stallone?

10 Jerry Murrell and his four sons founded which fast casual food restaurant chain in 1986?

11 Coined by *Vogue*, the "Big Five" supermodels of the 1990s were Cindy Crawford, Christy Turlington, Linda Evangelista, Naomi Campbell and who?

12 Cui, Borodin, Balakirev, Mussorgsky and Rimsky-Korsakov are considered the "Mighty Five" classical composers from which country?

13 Complete the list of the "Big Five" African animals; lion, leopard, black rhinoceros, African buffalo, _____?

Medium

14 Which American vocal quintet formed via a merger of The Primes and The Distants and are the subject of the Broadway musical *Ain't Too Proud*?

15 Shahada, salat, zakat, sawm and hajj are the five core beliefs or "Pillars" of which major world religion?

16 Which new wave band from Birmingham were dubbed "the Fab Five" by the press in their early days, comparing them to The Beatles?

17 Which German composer wrote five piano concertos, the fifth of which gained the nickname *Emperor*?

18 Which teen drama series gave breakthrough opportunities to Neve Campbell, Lacey Chabert and Jennifer Love Hewitt amongst others?

19 Three films have won the "Big Five" Academy Awards (Best Picture, Director, Actor, Actress and Screenplay); name any one of them.

20 Which opera by Georges Bizet features the *Smugglers Quintet*?

Hard

Answers to QUIZ 108 – Anime

1	*The Lion King*	11	The French Revolution
2	*Pokémon*	12	Stan Lee
3	*Spirited Away* (2001)	13	Ryan Reynolds
4	*Ghost in the Shell*	14	Samuel L. Jackson
5	Christian Bale	15	*E.T. the Extra Terrestrial*
6	Tokyo Olympics 2020	16	*The Little Mermaid*
7	*Gundam/Mobile Suit Gundam*	17	Pig
8	Astro Boy	18	*Speed Racer*
9	*One Punch Man*	19	Ham
10	*Kill Bill: Volume 1*	20	*Walk Like An Egyptian*

QUIZ 111 – Pot Luck

ANSWERS ON PAGE 113

1   How many dots are used in each letter of the Braille system?
2   Who was everyone's first friend on Myspace?
3   Shaggy, Daphne, Velma and Fred are characters in which film and television franchise?
4   Cavity Sam is the featured character in which board game?
5   In computing, what food item describes a data file that relays information about a user's web browsing activities?
6   The Manic Street Preachers' song *Kevin Carter* told the tragic story of a man in what profession?
7   Timothy "Tiny Tim" Cratchit is a character in which Charles Dickens novel?
8   What are the main two political parties in the United States of America?
9   Santorini, Cephalonia and Lesbos are islands of which country?
10 Rapa Nui, also known as Easter Island, is administered by which South American country?
11 Which is the only county in Britain to have two separate coastlines?
12 On what part of your body would *kufis*, *homburgs* and *ayams* be worn?
13 Who managed England to victory in the 1966 FIFA World Cup?
14 So as to avoid accusations of nepotism, actor, producer and director Nicolas Coppola goes by what name?
15 In which country is the Chernobyl nuclear plant?
16 Which famous director was the organiser of the 2012 London Olympic opening ceremony?
17 Minnie Mouse's name is a shortening of what full name, the female version of William?
18 After a takeover in 2014, Beats Electronics – best known for their Beats by Dr. Dre® headphones – has been a subsidiary of which tech giant?
19 The sports of polo, field hockey and jai alai all prohibit what playing style?
20 Which royal house followed the House of Stuarts?

Easy

Medium

Hard

Answers to QUIZ 109 – Pot Luck

1	Green	11	Wavelength
2	Roger Taylor	12	Six (the middle ones on each face)
3	*The Great Gatsby*	13	She was trampled under the King's horse at the Derby
4	Renault	14	Reading, writing and arithmetic
5	Topiary	15	Portugal
6	Isle of Wight	16	Meningitis
7	Kookaburra	17	Jewellery
8	*Bread*	18	Pocahontas
9	18, including spaces	19	Billie Holliday
10	Synapse	20	Amy Johnson

Easy

1 Since 1066, all English – and, since 1707, British – monarchs have been crowned in which London church?

2 How many years after the death of Elizabeth I was Elizabeth II crowned?

3 Who designed Queen Elizabeth II's coronation dress?

4 Which 15th century 12-year-old king ruled for only 86 days before disappearing without a trace, and thus was never crowned?

5 Which ancient symbol of Scottish sovereignty was used for centuries in the coronation ceremonies of Scottish monarchs?

6 Princess Margaret's romance with which RAF officer became news when she was seen plucking fluff from his coat during Queen Elizabeth II's coronation?

7 Which British monarch's coronation ceremony was interrupted when his estranged wife, Catherine of Brunswick, tried to get in?

8 Which English king was crowned twice, in 1216 and 1220, due in part to the regalia allegedly being lost in The Wash by his predecessor, King John?

9 Tasked with catering the coronation banquet of Queen Elizabeth II, Constance Spry and Rosemary Hume created which aptly-named dish?

10 Which large diamond has been set respectively into the crowns of Queens Consorts Alexandra, Mary and Elizabeth?

11 Which English king's coronation was postponed at short notice as he suffered an abdominal abscess?

12 Which Anglo-Irish officer attempted to steal the Crown Jewels from the Tower of London in 1671, and nearly succeeded?

Medium

13 Chosen due to it reportedly being the day most likely to be sunny, what was the date of Queen Elizabeth II's coronation?

14 Since 1386, which Duke also holds the hereditary position of Earl Marshal and thus has the duty of organising coronations?

15 Motifs of which vegetable could be seen on Queen Elizabeth II's coronation dress?

16 The coronation is a hybrid variety of table grape developed in which country?

17 Which man, the fifth US president, attended Napoleon's coronation in 1804, as he was the Ambassador to France at the time?

18 Which city associated with the champagne industry was the site of the coronations of most French kings?

19 The Coronation Stakes horse race takes place on day four of which five-day annual meet?

20 In *Coronation Street*, what is the name of the brewery?

Hard

Answers to QUIZ 110 – Famous Fives

1	Enid Blyton	11	Claudia Schiffer
2	The five continents	12	Russia
3	Lake Superior	13	Elephant
4	One Direction	14	The Temptations
5	Marlon (Randy joined much later, in 1976)	15	Islam
6	*Misfits*	16	Duran Duran
7	San Francisco	17	Ludwig van Beethoven
8	*Death Wish*	18	*Party of Five*
9	*Rambo*	19	*It Happened One Night* (1934); *One Flew Over the Cuckoo's Nest* (1975); *The Silence of the Lambs* (1991)
10	Five Guys (hence the name)	20	*Carmen*

ANSWERS ON PAGE 115

1   In education terminology, what is a BA degree classification?

2   Lufthansa is the flag carrier for and largest airline of which country?

3   The Simpson Desert and Great Victoria Desert can be found in which country?

4   A Sinophile is a lover of which country?

5   In rugby union, which position feeds the ball into the scrum and removes the ball from the back of it?

6   More than 30 threatened or protected species, including the Florida panther and the American crocodile, inhabit which Floridian national park?

7   "My Day at the Zoo" was the first video ever uploaded to which website?

8   *Panthera leo* is the scientific name for which animal?

9   It is the first rule of which film to not talk about the subject in its title?

10   Which unfinished Spanish cathedral finally received its building permit in 2019, 137 years after its construction began?

11   An artist's *magnum opus* is their what?

12   What type of instrument usually has a scratchplate attached?

13   Brontology is the study of which weather phenomenon?

14   Who won the gold medal in the men's 3 metre springboard diving at the 1988 Seoul Olympics, despite having given themselves a concussion hitting the board in the preliminary round?

15   What term is used for the lowest internal portion of the hull of a ship, as well as the water that collects in it?

16   Which classic board game utilises a doubling cube?

17   Prestwick is one of the two international airports in which UK city?

18   How is the letter S represented in Morse code?

19   Starting in the 1980s, Ian Botham advertised which breakfast cereal?

20   Which ingredient in a *soubise* sauce gives it its distinct flavour?

Easy

Medium

Hard

Answers to QUIZ 111 – Pot Luck

1	Six	11	Devon
2	Tom (Anderson)	12	Head
3	*Scooby Doo*	13	Sir Alf Ramsey
4	*Operation*	14	Nicolas Cage
5	Cookie	15	Ukraine
6	Photographer	16	Danny Boyle
7	*A Christmas Carol*	17	Wilhelmina
8	Democrats and Republicans	18	Apple
9	Greece	19	Playing left handed
10	Chile	20	House of Hanover

Easy

1. Which date is considered an unlucky day in Western superstition when it falls on a Friday?
2. How is Friday said in French?
3. The line "Friday night and the lights are low" opens the first verse of which ABBA song?
4. Justin Lee Collins and Alan Carr presented seven series of which Channel 4 comedy variety show?
5. "Black Friday" is the colloquial name for the shopping day immediately after which annual American holiday?
6. *Friday* was the widely-panned 2011 debut self-funded single for which then-13-year-old singer?
7. *Pink Friday* was the 2010 debut studio album by which rapper, real name Onika Maraj?
8. Which agreements signed on 10th April 1998 concerned issues of sovereignty, civil rights, weapons demilitarisation, justice and policing in Northern Ireland, and were a major step in the region's peace process?
9. The *Friday the 13th* slasher film franchise centres on which hockey goalie mask-wearing man as the usual antagonist?
10. The hashtag #ff represents which social media user-driven marketing initiative, used to encourage people to connect with other users?
11. Alan Stillman opened the first of which restaurant chain in New York in 1965 in the express hope that opening a bar would help him meet women?
12. Friday is the name given to an island native by the title character in which Daniel Defoe novel?

Medium

13. Which TV sitcom starring Tamsin Greig, Paul Ritter, Simon Bird and Tom Rosenthal is based around the Goodman family?
14. Which 1980 British gangster film about corruption and IRA fundraising was the breakthrough role for Bob Hoskins?
15. *Friday I'm in Love* was the first ever platinum single for which British rock band?
16. Jamie Lee Curtis and Lindsey Lohan starred as mother and daughter in which 2003 fantasy-comedy film?
17. Which chocolate bar has since 1991 been advertised using the slogan "Get that Friday feeling"?
18. Dedicated Los Angeles police detective Sergeant Joe Friday is the main character in which American radio and TV detective franchise?
19. Shaun Ryder was banned from Channel 4 for nearly 20 years for repeatedly swearing on which early-evening music variety show hosted by Chris Evans?
20. *Carburetion Day* or *Carb Day* is the final practice session held on the Friday before which sporting event?

Hard

Answers to QUIZ 112 – Coronations

1	Westminster Abbey	11	Edward VII
2	350 (1603 to 1953)	12	Thomas Blood
3	Norman Hartnell	13	2nd June 1953 – inevitably, it rained
4	Edward V	14	The Duke of Norfolk
5	Stone of Scone	15	Leeks (to represent Wales)
6	Group Captain Peter Townsend	16	Canada
7	George IV	17	James Monroe
8	Henry III	18	Reims
9	Coronation Chicken	19	Royal Ascot
10	Koh-I-Noor	20	Newton and Ridley

ANSWERS ON PAGE **117**

1   Who rules in a plutocracy?

2   What links Jane Austen's novel *Persuasion*, Tupac Shakur's album *Still I Rise* and Stanley Kubrick's film *Eyes Wide Shut*?

3   When a cricket umpire sticks both hands above his head, what is he signalling?

4   On the flag of Israel, what colour is the star?

5   In an army, which officer, usually commissioned from the ranks, is responsible for administering barracks and looking after supplies?

6   Traditionally, hawthorn blooms in which month?

7   The band Portishead took their name from an area of which English city?

8   In the 1956 FA Cup Final, who broke their neck, but carried on playing?

9   Amritsar is a holy city in which major world religion?

10   Which word can refer to a device used for directions, when used in the singular, or for drawing circles, when used in the plural?

11   Sharing its name with a car rental company, what is the SI unit of frequency?

12   Which planet in our solar system is, by far, the hottest?

13   How many fluid ounces are there in a pint?

14   Famous for mustard, which city is the capital of the Burgundy region of France?

15   Which is the most northern, easterly and westerly state of the United States of America?

16   Mycology is the study of what?

17   Which ancient Greek poet wrote both the *Odyssey* and the *Iliad*?

18   To what period of the day does the adjective crepuscular refer?

19   What is the name for the two lower muscular chambers of the heart that pump out blood?

20   Prior to Elizabeth II, which British monarch had had the longest reign?

Easy

Medium

Hard

Answers to QUIZ 113 – Pot Luck

1	Bachelor of Arts	11	Greatest work
2	Germany	12	Guitar
3	Australia	13	Thunder
4	China	14	Greg Louganis
5	Scrum-half	15	Bilge
6	Everglades National Park	16	Backgammon
7	YouTube	17	Glasgow
8	Lion	18	Dot dot dot
9	*Fight Club*	19	Shredded Wheat®
10	Sagrada Família	20	Onion

Easy

1   According to the proverb, a little of what is a dangerous thing?
2   How do still waters run?
3   One man's meat is another man's what?
4   A proverb states that the hand that rocks the cradle also does what?
5   A change, says the proverb, is as good as what?
6   If speech is silver, what is golden?
7   What do you have to kiss a lot of to find a handsome prince?
8   Complete the proverb; Procrastination is the...?
9   According to the old proverb, who or what is the mother of invention?
10 If he only works and never plays, who becomes a dull boy?
11 According to the proverb, which fruit tastes the sweetest?
12 Which virtue, according to the saying, begins at home?
13 According to the proverb, who or what does the devil make work for?
14 What, according to the proverb, is better than no bread?
15 What is said to be the better part of valour?
16 According to the proverb, who or what should not call the kettle black?
17 What does absence cause to grow fonder?
18 What are birds of a feather said to do?
19 As per the 16th century proverb, there is "many a slip 'twixt" what and what?
20 What two things are said to wait for no man?

Medium

Hard

Answers to QUIZ 114 – Friday

1	13th	11	TGI Fridays
2	*Vendredi*	12	*Robinson Crusoe*
3	*Dancing Queen*	13	*Friday Night Dinner*
4	*The Friday Night Project*	14	*The Long Good Friday*
5	Thanksgiving	15	The Cure
6	Rebecca Black	16	*Freaky Friday*
7	Nicki Minaj	17	Cadbury's Crunchie
8	Good Friday Agreements	18	*Dragnet*
9	Jason Voorhees	19	*TFI Friday*
10	Follow Friday	20	Indianapolis 500

QUIZ 117 – Pot Luck

ANSWERS ON PAGE 119

1 Marrowfat and garden are varieties of which vegetable?
2 Which previously London-based Rugby Union team relocated to Coventry in 2014?
3 *Ashes To Ashes* by David Bowie was a sequel to which previous song of his?
4 In March 2022, which travel company sacked 800 staff to protect the "future viability" of the business, with no forewarning?
5 Which famous upmarket department store opened in 1849 on Brompton Road in Knightsbridge?
6 Which is the only even prime number?
7 How would the year 1988 be written out in Roman numerals?
8 *Future Nostalgia* was the 2020 second studio album for which singer?
9 Which parts of the body are sometimes known as tootsies?
10 In skiing, the braking and turning technique "snowplough turn" is sometimes referred to by which food?
11 Minsk is the capital of which European country?
12 Tom DeLonge, Travis Barker and Mark Hoppus were the original line-up for which pop-punk band?
13 Which American talk show host once gifted a car to every member of her studio audience?
14 Edward Land invented what type of camera, and subsequently co-founded the namesake company?
15 How many Kings of France were named Louis?
16 Which pantomime character is the son of Widow Twankey?
17 Jon Richardson described what as "basically tidying up disguised as sport"?
18 What Greek mythological figure flew too close to the sun and melted his wax wings?
19 Which city lies on the confluence of the rivers Don, Sheaf, Rivelin, Loxley and Porter?
20 The Wailing Wall is located in which city?

Answers to QUIZ 115 – Pot Luck

1	The rich	11	Hertz
2	They were all released posthumously	12	Venus
3	Six runs	13	20
4	Blue	14	Dijon
5	Quartermaster	15	Alaska (a tiny bit of it sticks out across the International Date Line)
6	May	16	Fungi, including mushrooms
7	Bristol	17	Homer
8	Bert Trautmann	18	Evening
9	Sikhism	19	Ventricles
10	Compass/compasses	20	Queen Victoria (1837-1901)

1. From season two of its rebooted format through to series 22, James May was one of the hosts of which BBC motoring show?
2. Prior to becoming UK Prime Minister, Theresa May served in which cabinet post between 2010 and 2016?
3. On 16th and 17th May 1943, RAF 617 Squadron used Barnes Wallis's "bouncing bombs" to attack what type of German infrastructure?
4. On 5th May 1851, Napoleon Bonaparte died in exile on which island?
5. The Acts of Union between England and Scotland took effect on 1st May in which year?
6. Which green gemstone is the birthstone for the month of May?
7. Which Warner Brothers *Looney Tunes* character made his debut in 1954's *Devil May Hare*?
8. David Jason, Pam Ferris and Catherine Zeta-Jones appeared as members of the Larkin family in which 1990s TV series?
9. On 21st May 1881, Clara Barton founded the American branch of which international non-profit humanitarian organisation?
10. Who wrote the coming-of-age novel *Little Women*?

11. Each May, which European country observes National Windmill and Pumping Station Day?
12. An iconic sports photo taken on 25th May 1965 depicts a victorious Muhammed Ali standing over which defeated opponent?
13. Which guitarist and astrophysicist uses a sixpence instead of a pick when playing?
14. Which 1971 Rod Stewart single was ranked no.130 on *Rolling Stones'* list of *The 500 Greatest Songs of All Time*?
15. According to the old idiom, "Marry in the month of May, and you'll surely..." what?
16. Launched on 6th May 1940, what was the first ever public-usage postage stamp?
17. On 25th May 1895, which Irish poet and playwright was convicted of gross indecency and sentenced to two years' hard labour?
18. Henry VIII's second wife was executed at the Tower of London on 19th May 1536 – which one was she?
19. On 3rd May 1494, who "discovered" Jamaica?
20. On 5th May 1961, who became the first American in space?

Answers to QUIZ 116 – Proverbs

1	Knowledge	11	Forbidden fruit
2	Deep	12	Charity
3	Poison	13	Idle hands
4	Rules the world	14	Half a loaf
5	A rest/holiday	15	Discretion
6	Silence	16	The pot
7	Toads/frogs	17	The heart
8	Thief of time	18	Flock together
9	Necessity	19	The cup and the lip (meaning, even when things look certain, they can still go wrong)
10	Jack	20	Time and tide

1 António Guterres, Boutros-Boutros Ghali and Gladwyn Jebb have all served in which international role?

2 Granny Smith apples were originally cultivated on what continent?

3 Comino and Gozo are two of the three inhabited islands that make up which European nation?

4 The artist Banksy is most associated with which city?

5 What title is granted to the wife of an Earl?

6 Hampden Park and Ibrox are football stadiums in which city?

7 Google Translate lists 42 languages in which *ananas* is the name of which fruit?

8 Which TV soap opera is set in the fictional borough of Letherbridge, Birmingham?

9 The name of which international retailer is an acronym that consists of the initials of the founder, the family farm where he was born and a nearby village?

10 What two-word name links TV fitness expert Diana Moran with the British Army's firefighting vehicles?

11 Norman Lawson invented the formula, and Norman Larsen invented the aerosol can, for which lubricant?

12 Which member of The Beatles sang the lead vocals on *With a Little Help From My Friends*?

13 Billie Eilish admitted in an interview that until she was 16, she did not believe which girl band really existed, and were characters invented for a film?

14 "Chirky", "in high snuff" and "gladsome" are antiquated terms for someone feeling what emotion?

15 In darts, what is the lowest score attainable from hitting three different trebles in the same visit?

16 In 2018, Apple acquired which app that can identify music based on only a short sample for a reported $400 million?

17 Which surname, the most common in Ireland, derives from a word meaning sea warrior?

18 To beat George Foreman in their 1974 *Rumble in the Jungle* fight, Muhammed Ali employed what defensive boxing technique?

19 What two items is the Statue of Liberty holding?

20 Norman Bridwell wrote a series of children's books about a big red dog with what name?

Answers to QUIZ 117 – Pot Luck

1	Pea	11	Belarus
2	Wasps	12	blink-182
3	*Space Oddity*	13	Oprah Winfrey
4	P&O Ferries	14	Polaroid
5	Harrods	15	18
6	Two	16	Aladdin
7	MCMLXXXVIII	17	Snooker
8	Dua Lipa	18	Icarus
9	Feet	19	Sheffield
10	Pizza, as the skis point in a pizza slice shape	20	Jerusalem

Drummers are people too. Who are these famous percussionists?

Easy

1

2

3

Medium

4

5

6

7

8
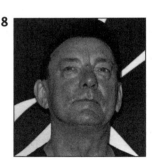

9

Hard

Answers to QUIZ 118 – May

1	*Top Gear*	11	The Netherlands
2	Home Secretary	12	Sonny Liston
3	Dams (they were the *Dam Busters*)	13	Brian May
4	Saint Helena	14	Maggie May
5	1707	15	"Rue the day"
6	Emerald	16	Penny Black
7	Taz/the Tasmanian Devil	17	Oscar Wilde
8	*The Darling Buds of May*	18	Anne Boleyn
9	Red Cross	19	Christopher Columbus
10	Louisa May Alcott	20	Alan Shepherd

1. Panther, Tiger and Panzer were German examples of what in the 20th century?

2. *The Rainbow* (1915) and *Women in Love* (1920), novels about the lives of the Brangwen sisters, were written by who?

3. Which Steven Spielberg comedy film depicts Los Angeles six days after the attack on Pearl Harbour, and is named for the year it is set in?

4. The musical instruction *andante* means to play how?

5. On a box of Kellogg's® Special K® cereal, what colour is the K?

6. What term is given to any obstacle to the spread of flames, especially artificially-created open strips in forests?

7. In the British legal system, what do the initials QC represent?

8. Which of the Spice Girls was known as Baby Spice?

9. From which Fyodor Dostoyevsky novel is the line "you shouldn't have gone murdering people with a hatchet" taken?

10. Which paint brand has since 1961 been advertised by an old English sheepdog?

11. In the nursery rhyme, who or what ran away with the spoon?

12. The roles of which English actress have included Emma Peel in *The Avengers* and Countess Teresa di Vicenzo in *On Her Majesty's Secret Service*?

13. What term is given to a river or stream flowing into a larger river or lake?

14. Julie Christie appeared as Larissa "Lara" Antipova in which 1965 film, based on a Boris Pasternak novel?

15. What term is given to the point against which a lever is placed to get purchase, or on which it turns or is supported?

16. If a triangle has one angle of 32 degrees and another angle of 84 degrees, what is the third angle?

17. In the nursery rhyme, what animal did Tom, Tom the piper's son, steal?

18. Under what stage name was Asa Yoelson better known?

19. Marlon Brando refused to accept his Oscar for *The Godfather* on account of the oppression of which people?

20. By what name is Portuguese West Africa now known?

Answers to QUIZ 119 – Pot Luck

1	Secretary-General of the United Nations	11	WD-40®
2	Australia	12	Ringo Starr
3	Malta – the third island is Malta itself	13	The Spice Girls
4	Bristol	14	Happiness
5	Countess	15	18
6	Glasgow	16	Shazam®
7	Pineapple	17	Murphy
8	*Doctors*	18	The Rope-a-dope
9	IKEA (Ingvar Kamprad, Elmtaryd, Agunnaryd)	19	Torch and book
10	Green Goddess	20	Clifford

1. In 2018, who became the first centibillionaire ever included in *Forbes* magazine's *The World's Billionaires* rich list?
2. Which two founders of Google became billionaires at age 30?
3. Which Russian oligarch owned Chelsea football club between 2003 and 2022?
4. Which British newspaper has curated its own Rich List since 1989?
5. Which man, who amassed his fortune from the Standard Oil company, became the first ever billionaire in 1916?
6. Bill Gates and Warren Buffet founded which campaign to encourage the ultra-wealthy to give their wealth to charity?
7. Which Mexican business magnate was considered the world's richest person between 2010 and 2013?
8. The Walton family is the richest in the USA, with their billions derived from the business of which retailer?
9. Who is the only black female billionaire in the USA?
10. Which entrepreneur claims that he wants to die on Mars; just not on impact?
11. On Thanksgiving 1966, the owner of the Desert Inn in Las Vegas asked which aviation pioneer to leave? Instead of leaving, he bought the hotel.
12. Whitney Wolfe Herd became the world's youngest female self-made billionaire, and also the youngest woman to take a company public, with the IPO of which dating app?
13. Who was the first American to ever take the top spot on the *Forbes World's Billionaires List*?
14. Why did 83 billionaires drop off the 2002 *Forbes World Billionaires List* from the previous year?

15. For a long time, New York City was known as the billionaire capital of the world; in 2017, which other city replaced it?
16. Which Indian steel magnate joined Flavio Briatore and Bernie Ecclestone in buying shares of Queen's Park Rangers in 2007?
17. In 2008, who at 23 become the youngest self-made billionaire?
18. Nearly half of the world's reported 2,095 billionaires as of 2020 were citizens of one of which two countries?
19. Forbes's 2021 rich list names which European country as having by far the highest ratio of billionaires per million people?
20. Bernard Arnault, the richest person in Europe as of 2022, is the chairman and chief executive of which luxury goods company?

Answers to QUIZ 120 – Drummers

1. Keith Moon
2. Ginger Baker
3. Phil Collins
4. Meg White
5. Dave Grohl
6. Buddy Rich
7. John Bonham
8. Neil Peart
9. Travis Barker

1   Mr Rochester, Mrs Fairfax and John Reed are all characters from which classic novel?
2   In broadcasting, what do the initials of the channel CNN stand for?
3   In the nursery rhyme, who killed Cock Robin?
4   Which British royal has the middle names Philip Arthur George?
5   Which children's animated character has the full name of Samuel Peyton-Jones?
6   What name is shared by an Ant and Dec-fronted game show and a Lady Gaga song?
7   How many years are celebrated by a platinum anniversary?
8   In mathematics, a number that is equal to the sum of its positive divisors, excluding the number itself (such as 6 and 28), is called what type of number?
9   Which track and field athletics event features a water obstacle?
10 What are the two official languages of Canada?
11 What is the English term for what are called "thongs" in Australia?
12 Which famed actor's final film role was as Kincade the gamekeeper in the James Bond film, *Skyfall*?
13 In which country does the River Amazon rise?
14 What five-letter word is used for young domestic chicken, turkey, pheasant or other fowl being raised for food?
15 Which is the world's largest species of lizard?
16 Which British Army rank is equivalent to a Flight Lieutenant in the RAF?
17 Which A-list actor retired in March 2022 following a diagnosis of aphasia, affecting his ability to communicate?
18 Opposite sides on standard six-sided die add up to what?
19 Knightsbridge station lies on which London Underground line?
20 Duncan Goodhew was an Olympic gold medallist in which sport?

Easy

Medium

Hard

Answers to QUIZ 121 – Pot Luck

1	Tank	11	The dish
2	DH Lawrence	12	Diana Rigg
3	1941	13	Tributary
4	Fairly slowly	14	*Doctor Zhivago*
5	Red	15	Fulcrum
6	Firebreaks	16	64 degrees
7	Queen's Counsel	17	A pig
8	Emma Bunton	18	Al Jolson
9	*Crime And Punishment*	19	Native Americans
10	Dulux	20	Angola

Easy

1. Which mobile phone manufacturer accounted for 4% of Finland's entire gross domestic product in 2000?
2. On an old-fashioned rotary phone, what number requires the longest turn of the dial?
3. What is the name of Apple's video-calling service?
4. Also the name of a rock supergroup, what is the UK's international dialling code?
5. Which north-eastern English city has its own telephone network, and thus no lines on the BT network?
6. On a telephone handset, which symbol can also be called an octothorpe?
7. Sent in December 1992, the first ever SMS message consisted of which aptly-seasonal two-word phrase?
8. Between 2010 and 2016 and before the advent of the Pixel, which range of phones were considered Google's flagship Android products?
9. Which company made the J-Phone, the first to send picture messages?
10. Which mobile-related technology takes its name from an incorrect translation of the name of the notoriously verbose Nordic King, Harald Blatand?
11. Lollipop, Marshmallow and Oreo are the names of releases of which mobile operating system?
12. The Motorola DynaTAC 8000X, the world's first portable commercial handheld phone, was released in which year?
13. What is the NHS's non-emergency hotline number?
14. On 16th April 1995, which digit was added into almost every single landline number in the UK?

Medium

15. Starting in 1997, which game where players move a growing line that becomes an obstacle to itself appeared on almost every new phone for a decade?
16. Despite the conspiracy theories, which technology standard for broadband networks is predicted to have more than 1.7 billion subscribers by 2025?
17. In the UK, what is the number to dial to get an automated message telling you the last number that called you?
18. Launched in 1936, if you dial 123 on a BT phone and are willing to spend 35p a minute, which service will you get?
19. Alexander Graham Bell suggested people use which phrase to answer the phone (although Mr Burns from *The Simpsons* may be the only one who does it)?
20. Which numerals on the telephone keypad do not have corresponding keypad letters?

Hard

Answers to QUIZ 122 – Rich List

1	Jeff Bezos	11	Howard Hughes
2	Sergiy Brin and Larry Page	12	Bumble
3	Roman Abramovich	13	Bill Gates
4	*Sunday Times*	14	The dot-com bubble burst
5	John Davison Rockefeller	15	Beijing
6	The Giving Pledge	16	Lakshmi Mittal
7	Carlos Slim	17	Mark Zuckerberg
8	Walmart	18	USA and China
9	Oprah Winfrey	19	Monaco (though it does have only three)
10	Elon Musk	20	LVMH (LVMH Moët Hennessy – Louis Vuitton)

1 Over which continent did the hole in the ozone layer form?
2 In the nursery rhyme, who kissed the girls and made them cry?
3 The Jutland peninsula is a part of which country?
4 In Channel 4's *Countdown*, how many letters are selected in each letters game?
5 What is obstetrics the study of?
6 Although they are all unique, snowflakes always have how many sides?
7 In tennis, what is a score of 40 points each called?
8 *L.H.O.O.Q.*, a 1919 artwork by Marcel Duchamp, involved simply drawing a moustache onto what?
9 Microsoft®, although headquartered in Washington, was originally founded in which other state?
10 Libel is a written defamation; what term is used for an oral defamation?
11 Courtney Walsh and Curtley Ambrose played international cricket for which team?
12 Who played the title role in the film *Red Sonja*?
13 The measurement kHz is an abbreviation for what?
14 If a stringed instrument is being played *pizzicato*, how is it being played?
15 LLDs and LLMs are degree classifications in what profession?
16 After which Greek god of sleep was the drug morphine named?
17 What type of device measures radioactivity levels by detecting and counting ionising particles?
18 The volcanic mountain Popocatépetl is located in which country?
19 Zinfandel is a type of which alcoholic drink?
20 The New York Stock Exchange is located on which street?

Easy

Medium

Hard

Answers to QUIZ 123 – Pot Luck

1	*Jane Eyre*	11	Flip flops
2	Cable News Network	12	Albert Finney
3	Sparrow	13	Peru
4	Prince Charles	14	Poult
5	Fireman Sam	15	Komodo dragon
6	*Poker Face*	16	Captain
7	70	17	Bruce Willis
8	Perfect number	18	Seven
9	Steeplechase	19	Piccadilly
10	English and French	20	Swimming

Easy

1   Tungsten has the chemical symbol of W, deriving from what alternative name by which it is more commonly known in Germanic languages?

2   On the periodic table, what is it that tells the reader how many protons are in the nucleus of an atom?

3   Which Russian chemist is widely credited with creating the modern periodic table?

4   What element was named after the Greek word for green?

5   What are the four elements whose names start with I?

6   How many columns are there in the periodic table?

7   Despite its name starting with an A, which element goes by the symbol Sb, deriving from its original Latin name *stibium*?

8   Due to their relatively low levels of radioactivity, helium, neon, argon, krypton, xenon and radon are collectively known as what?

9   If all the elements were written out in alphabetical order, which would come last?

10 Of the 94 elements found in the natural world, which is the rarest, with no more than a few ounces in known existence?

11 The elements in group 17 in modern classification – fluorine, chlorine, bromine, iodine, astatine and tennessine – are collectively known as what?

12 What are the only two letters of the alphabet not to appear in any official element names (i.e. excluding temporary ones)?

13 If the vertical columns of the periodic table are known as groups, what are the horizontal rows called?

Medium

14 Whose theory states that electrons are not located randomly around an atom's nucleus, but reside in specific electron shells?

15 What is the electron capacity of the innermost electron shell?

16 Which are the only two elements that are in liquid state at room temperature?

17 Which is the only element that can have no neutrons?

18 Although it is a silvery-white metal, what element lends its name to a shade of deep blue, and takes its name from the German for goblin?

19 Which was the first element to be produced artificially, as reflected in its name?

20 At approximately 40% of the total mass, what is the most abundant element in the Earth's crust?

Hard

Answers to QUIZ 124 – Phones

1	Nokia	11	Android
2	0	12	1983
3	*Facetime*	13	111
4	+44	14	1 (after the initial 0)
5	Kingston upon Hull	15	*Snake*
6	The hash key	16	5G
7	"Merry Christmas"	17	1471
8	Nexus	18	The speaking clock
9	Sharp	19	"Ahoy hoy?"
10	Bluetooth	20	1 and 0

1   In which English county is the coastal resort of California?

2   Which of Shakespeare's works is often known as "the Scottish play", due to superstitions around its name?

3   What two colours appear on the Ukraine flag?

4   What type of doctor specialises in diagnosing and treating disorders of the colon, rectum and anus?

5   In which city is Sauchiehall Street, a main shopping thoroughfare?

6   What do the initials stand for in the name of the economic body, the IMF?

7   *Ride Wit' Me* was a 2001 hit for which hip-hop star?

8   In the nursery rhyme, what does Thursday's child have?

9   The logo for Hush Puppies® shoes features what breed of dog?

10 Someone described as sinistral is what?

11 What colour is the ribbon on the Victoria Cross?

12 Sting, Stewart Copeland and Henry Padovani formed which rock band in 1977?

13 To what does the Cockney rhyming slang term "dog and bone" refer?

14 In which city was Molly Malone said to sell her cockles and mussels?

15 Early 20th century French sculptor and painter Frédéric Bartholdi is best known for designing what?

16 The skin disease lupus takes its name from the Latin for which animal?

17 Ian Fleming's estate in Jamaica gave its name to which of the James Bond films?

18 The name of the French national anthem is adapted from which port city?

19 In the name of the movie studio, what does MGM stand for?

20 Which environmental campaign group repeatedly blocked the M25 motorway in September 2021?

Easy

Medium

Hard

Answers to QUIZ 125 – Pot Luck

1	Antarctica	11	West Indies
2	Georgie Porgie	12	Brigitte Nielsen
3	Denmark	13	Kilohertz
4	Nine	14	By plucking the strings rather than using a bow
5	Childbirth	15	The legal profession
6	Six	16	Morpheus
7	Deuce	17	Geiger Counter
8	The *Mona Lisa*	18	Mexico
9	New Mexico	19	Red wine
10	Slander	20	Wall Street

1 Which scholarship is an international postgraduate award for students to study at the University of Oxford?

2 The film *The Social Network* tells the story of the founding of Facebook in the dormitories at which prestigious American university?

3 Heads of state of 37 different countries, including British PMs Clement Attlee and Ramsay McDonald, studied at which London-based university?

4 In which US state is Yale University?

5 Yale, Princeton, Harvard, Columbia, Dartmouth, Brown, Cornell and Penn make up which group of esteemed American universities?

6 The prestigious Sorbonne University can be found in which city?

7 Trinity, Corpus Christi and Brasenose are all constituent colleges of which English university?

8 Which Italian city contains the world's oldest university in continuous operation, dating back to 1088?

9 Which university in Edinburgh takes its name from a 16th-century Scottish mathematician?

10 The Open University's administrative headquarters are located in which Buckinghamshire town?

11 Sir John Moores CBE, the founder of the football pools, gives his name to a university in which British city?

12 In American higher education, what name is given to a second-year student?

13 New British universities founded during or since the 1960s and the reclassification of polytechnics in 1992 are colloquially known as what building material?

14 What name is given to the self-selected group of 24 "elite" UK universities that are committed to research and academic standards?

15 Which actor was a college roommate at Harvard with US Presidential candidate Al Gore in 1965?

16 Which knighted comedian, actor, presenter and writer became the Chancellor of Birmingham City University in 2016?

17 Prince William captained which sports team at the University of Saint Andrews?

18 Which female American blues singer was voted "Ugliest Man On Campus" at the University of Texas in 1963?

19 A University of Houston student found a student's union loophole and had which rock group elected "Homecoming Queen" in 1972, the same year as their education-related biggest hit?

20 Previously billed as the New Yardbirds, which band's first gig under their ultimate name was at the University of Surrey on 25th October 1968?

Answers to QUIZ 126 – The Periodic Table

1	*Wolfram*	11	Halogens
2	The atomic number	12	Q and J
3	Dmitri Mendeleev	13	Periods
4	Chlorine	14	Niels Bohr
5	Iodine, iron, indium, iridium	15	Two
6	18	16	Mercury and bromine
7	Antimony	17	Hydrogen
8	Noble or inert gases	18	Cobalt
9	Zirconium	19	Technetium
10	Astatine	20	Oxygen

ANSWERS ON PAGE 131

1. It is said that Napoleon pulling on which part of the body was a coveted gesture of his approval?
2. Which flower is the emblem of the Alzheimer's Society?
3. How many squares are there on a chess board?
4. Named for a folkloric castle, which consortium was the first licensee to run the UK National Lottery?
5. The Sargasso Sea and the Azores island group both lie in which ocean?
6. The Brecon Beacons rise in which Welsh county?
7. Originating from Germany, Trockenbeerenauslese is what type of drink?
8. Having divorced baseball legend Joe DiMaggio, Marilyn Monroe married which playwright?
9. The first line of Jane Austen's *Pride and Prejudice* states that "a single man in possession of a good fortune must be in want of..." what?
10. Also the former name of a delivery company, who was the messenger of the Greek gods?
11. Singer and actor Dino Crocetti achieved fame under what name?
12. When a soldier has gone AWOL, what does AWOL stand for?
13. Usually, Black Forest gateau is made with which fruit as a filling?
14. Room 101 is a location in which dystopian novel?
15. Waterloo, site of the Napoleonic battlefield, is located in which European country?
16. The parietal lobe is in which part of the human body?
17. In animation terminology, what does the abbreviation CGI stand for?
18. In terms of the metaphysical sensor phenomenon, what does ESP stand for?
19. In which novel does the character Major Major Major Major – an army major – appear?
20. In the film classification system, what do the letters PG stand for?

Easy

Medium

Hard

Answers to QUIZ 127 – Pot Luck

1	Norfolk	11	Crimson
2	*Macbeth*	12	The Police
3	Blue and yellow	13	Phone
4	Proctologist	14	Dublin
5	Glasgow	15	The Statue of Liberty
6	International Monetary Fund	16	Wolf
7	Nelly	17	*GoldenEye*
8	Far to go	18	Marseille (*La Marseillaise*)
9	Basset Hound	19	Metro-Goldwyn-Mayer
10	Left-handed	20	Insulate Britain

1   Which LNER A4 Class locomotive broke the world speed record for steam locomotives at 126 mph in 1938?

2   First flying in 2005, what is the world's largest passenger airliner?

3   What call sign is given to any Air Force aircraft on which the President of the United States is flying?

4   More than 3 million models of which car marque were produced in East Germany between 1957 and 1990, with almost no design upgrades in that span?

5   Founded in 1810 as a coffee mill company before going on to sell bicycles and ultimately cars, what is the oldest car company still in business today?

6   What make of car did Doc Brown and Marty McFly use to time travel in *Back To The Future*?

7   At a distance of 1,980 miles, the Orient Express originally ran between which two cities upon its inception in 1887?

8   The O'Jays had a 1972 hit single with a song about which form of romantic transport?

9   Although now just known as Qantas, what does the airline's former acronym QANTAS stand for?

10 Which ultra-low-cost carrier serving flights to Europe and North Africa has its largest bases at Budapest and London Luton airports?

11 In 2001, Liverpool's international airport was renamed in honour of which singer-songwriter?

12 Which former London Underground line closed in 2007 and reopened as part of the Overground network in 2010?

13 Which major international figure travels on an aeroplane with the call sign "*Volo Papale*" and not, as urban legend has it, "*Shepherd One*"?

14 What slightly inaccurate rhyming nickname was given to Howard Hughes's birch-framed H4-Hercules transport plane that flew once for 26 seconds?

15 Nissan offers a 100% electric car with what "green" name?

16 According to the Glenn Miller song of the same name, which train leaves the Pennsylvania station 'bout a quarter to four?

17 Despite the name, Charles Peugeot was named in 2010 as the sales director for which other French motor company?

18 What was unusual about the car entered by Tyrrell in the 1976 Formula 1 Grand Prix season that spawned several imitations?

19 The 1987 film *Planes, Trains & Automobiles* starred Steve Martin alongside which late actor?

20 Which type of British fighter plane shot down a reported 1,294 enemy aircraft in World War I?

Answers to QUIZ 128 – University

1	Rhodes Scholarship	11	Liverpool
2	Harvard	12	Sophomore
3	London School of Economics and Political Science (LSE)	13	Red brick universities
		14	The Russell Group
4	Connecticut	15	Tommy Lee Jones
5	Ivy League	16	Sir Lenny Henry
6	Paris	17	Water polo
7	University of Oxford	18	Janis Joplin
8	Bologna	19	Alice Cooper
9	Edinburgh Napier (John Napier)	20	Led Zeppelin
10	Milton Keynes		

1. In which sport are the playing periods known as chukkas?
2. Ruth Handler, former president of the toy manufacturer Mattel™, is credited with inventing which specific world-famous toy in 1959?
3. Heriot-Watt University is based in which city?
4. Mario and Luigi, sibling stars of the *Super Mario* game franchise, both have what job?
5. Whose execution led to King Philip II of Spain launching the Spanish Armada in 1588?
6. On a clothes label, what is indicated by a square with a circle inside of it?
7. In which river was Jesus baptised?
8. What is the British term for what is known as cotton candy in America?
9. The first line-up of which singing group was comprised of Diana Ross, Florence Ballard, Betty McGlown and Mary Wilson?
10. In Morse Code, what letter is represented by two dashes?
11. Campanology is the art and/or practice of what?
12. Elizabeth Fry and the Howard League are or were both concerned with what?
13. Known as The Big Easy, which golfer's 10 on the first hole of the 2016 US Masters was the worst individual hole score in the tournament's history?
14. What name is given to the larva of a fly?
15. Golda Meir was the fourth prime minister, and the first female one, in which country?
16. *Bouillabaisse* is what type of French fish dish?
17. What do the capitals of Djibouti, Luxembourg and Singapore have in common?
18. In the classic rhyme, when it is raining and pouring, what is the old man doing?
19. In law, what is evidence that does not directly prove something, but allows the fact finder to draw a reasonable inference about it based on the evidence called?
20. What did Judas Iscariot receive in exchange for betraying Christ?

Easy

Medium

Hard

Easy

1. In Disney's *Moana*, who voices Maui, the legendary yet easily annoyed shapeshifting demigod?
2. Who won the Academy Award for Best Supporting Actress for her role as Lisa in 1999's *Girl, Interrupted*?
3. Sancho Panza was the squire to which deluded fictional knight?
4. Who was the member of *Wham!* that wasn't George Michael?
5. Jeremy Piven played Ari Gold, Vincent Chase's abrasive agent, in which HBO comedy-drama series?
6. Who started out as a side character in *The Adventures of Tom Sawyer* before starring in its sequel?
7. Benvolio and Tybalt are cousins to which two title characters?
8. Who is Yogi Bear's blue bow tie-wearing constant companion?
9. D'Arcy Carden starred as Janet, an artificial being who assists the residents, in which fantasy comedy series?
10. The bald and lazy George Costanza was a side character in which American sitcom?
11. Dancer Mark Berry is better known by what mononym?
12. Gadget Hacketwrench, Monty Jack and Zipper were the other three members of which cartoon detective agency?
13. Jean Passepartout is the fictional French valet of which novel's English main character?

Medium

14. Which guitarist has played with both John Mayall's Bluesbreakers and, for two years, The Rolling Stones?
15. From the second release in the franchise onwards, Miles "Tails" Prower was the sidekick fox to which video game character?
16. Faizura Balk became a style icon after her turn as Nancy Downs in which 1996 supernatural film?
17. Who has been in comedy double acts with both Rob Newman and Frank Skinner?
18. Licensed funeral director Bill Moody had a sideline as which aptly-named manager of professional wrestler The Undertaker?
19. Which dinosaur sidekick of Nintendo's® Mario character ultimately landed his own franchise of games?
20. John Goodman played intense Vietnam veteran Walter Sobchak in which 1998 film?

Hard

Answers to QUIZ 130 – Planes, Trains and Automobiles

1	*Mallard*	11	John Lennon
2	Airbus A380	12	East London Line
3	Air Force One	13	The Pope
4	Trabant	14	*Spruce Goose*
5	Peugeot	15	Leaf
6	DeLorean	16	*Chattanooga Choo Choo*
7	Paris and Constantinople (now known as Istanbul)	17	Citroen
8	*Love Train*	18	It had six wheels
9	Queensland and Northern Territory Aerial Services	19	John Candy
10	Wizz Air	20	Sopwith Camel

1 How many holes are there on a standard golf course?
2 How many players are there in a netball team?
3 In snooker, what word is used to describe an unbroken streak of consecutive pots?
4 Which international fugitive was killed in the Pakistani town of Abbottabad in May 2011?
5 Riff Raff is the Transylvanian assistant handyman in which film, later made into a play?
6 Cu is the symbol for which chemical element?
7 In British political parlance, what is an MEP?
8 In weather forecasting, what line joins places of equal pressure?
9 Although the former name is still widely used, the country of Burma officially changed its name in what in 1989?
10 A Portuguese man o' war is what sort of animal?
11 How many days does an Olympic decathlon take place over?
12 Which soft drink was invented by Dr John Pemberton in 1886?
13 St David's Day and St Patrick's Day both fall in which month?
14 The American state of Georgia was named after which George?
15 Marrakesh and Rabat are cities in which country?
16 A cockle is sometimes used as slang for how much money?
17 Which Welsh loanword, which has no vowels in English, can mean a cupboard, cubbyhole, cuddle or hug?
18 In the nursery rhyme about the five little pigs, what did the second little pig do?
19 Which sweets were advertised with the slogan "too good to hurry mints"?
20 In the Bible, who led the children of Israel to the Promised Land?

Answers to QUIZ 131 – Pot Luck

1 Polo
2 Barbie®
3 Edinburgh
4 Plumber
5 Mary, Queen of Scots
6 The item can be tumble dried
7 River Jordan
8 Candy floss
9 The Supremes
10 M

11 Bell-ringing
12 Prison reform
13 Ernie Els
14 Maggot
15 Israel
16 Soup/stew
17 Their name is exactly the same as the country
18 Snoring
19 Circumstantial evidence
20 30 pieces of silver

What are these well-known toys? (Not listed in order of awesomeness.)

Easy

1

2

3

4

Medium

5

6

7

8

Hard

Answers to QUIZ 132 – Side Characters

1 Dwayne "The Rock" Johnson
2 Angelina Jolie
3 Don Quixote
4 Andrew Ridgeley
5 *Entourage*
6 Huckleberry Finn
7 Romeo and Juliet
8 Boo-Boo
9 *The Good Place*
10 *Seinfeld*

11 Bez, from Happy Mondays/Black Grape
12 *Rescue Rangers* (the other two being *Chip 'n' Dale*)
13 *Around the World in Eighty Days's* Phileas Fogg, written by Jules Verne
14 Mick Taylor
15 *Sonic the Hedgehog*
16 *The Craft*
17 David Baddiel
18 Paul Bearer
19 Yoshi
20 *The Big Lebowski*

1   How many hoops are used in a game of garden croquet?

2   Which country's men's field hockey team won six consecutive Olympic gold medals between 1928 and 1956?

3   After Mecca, what city, the final place-of-residence of Muhammad, is the second-holiest city in Islam?

4   Often shortened to DORA, which British law was passed four days after entering World War I to give the government wide-ranging powers such as requisition?

5   What name is given to an ultra wide-angle camera lens that produces strong visual distortion to create a wide panoramic or hemispherical image?

6   David Ben-Gurion was the first Prime Minister of which country?

7   In 1983, which Derby-winning racehorse was stolen from the Aga Khan's stud, never to be seen again?

8   What is the cause of Down's syndrome?

9   On the London Underground map, what colour is the Piccadilly line?

10 To genuflect is to perform what act?

11 If a person is anosmic, which sense do they lack?

12 In the nursery rhyme, which fruit did Little Jack Horner pull out of the pie?

13 The reflexology massage technique sees pressure applied on which area of the body?

14 What word, meaning to make an abrupt movement, was also the name of the butler in *The Addams Family*?

15 Y! is the logo of what internet company?

16 What is the highest number on a standard roulette wheel?

17 Orly airport, the Sacré-Coeur and the Obelisk of Luxor are all to be found in which city?

18 More than 11 miles in length and almost one mile at its widest point, what is the largest natural lake in England?

19 Arthur Scargill is most well known for his time as the President of the National Union of what?

20 The iconic La Scala opera house is located in which Italian city?

Easy

Medium

Hard

Answers to QUIZ 133 – Pot Luck

1	18	11	Two
2	Seven	12	Coca Cola®
3	Break	13	March
4	Osama bin Laden	14	King George II
5	*Rocky Horror Picture Show*	15	Morocco
6	Copper	16	£10
7	Member of the European Parliament	17	Cwtch
8	Isobar	18	Stayed at home
9	Myanmar	19	Murray Mints
10	Jellyfish	20	Moses

1 What are the names of John Lennon's two sons?

2 Which Beatle was the executive producer of the cult 1980s film *Withnail & I*?

3 Which is the final Beatles album when listed alphabetically?

4 What is the name of the 2021 documentary mini-series directed by Peter Jackson which used footage from the *Let It Be* film?

5 Which was the first Beatles album to include instances of backmasking?

6 In which year did The Beatles win an Oscar for their soundtrack on *Let It Be*?

7 The song *Michelle* includes lyrics in which language other than English?

8 Ringo Starr went on to narrate the first two series of which children's TV show?

9 In which park is Strawberry Fields, a large memorial to John Lennon?

10 Paul McCartney wrote and starred in a 1984 film, the title of which was a tribute to which soon-to-be-closed London railway station?

11 Which musician, whose name rhymes with a famous Beatles song, formed the band Wings alongside Paul McCartney?

12 Which was the only double album released by The Beatles?

13 What was the make and model of the white car depicted near the zebra crossing on the famous *Abbey Road* album cover?

14 Which two pop artists designed the album cover for the *Sgt. Pepper's Lonely Hearts Club Band* album?

15 What is the simple name of The Beatles' compilation album which became the best-selling record of the 2000s worldwide?

16 Which no.1 single from 1968 was, at 7 minutes 11 seconds, the longest ever chart-topping song in the UK at time of release?

17 Which 1964 Beatles album consisted solely of Lennon/McCartney compositions?

18 "Sitting on a cornflake" and "Yellow matter custard" are both lyrics from which song?

19 How many Beatles albums appear in *Rolling Stone Magazine*'s 2020 edition of *The 500 Greatest Albums of All Time*?

20 Which Beatles album rated the highest on *Rolling Stone Magazine*'s 2020 edition of *The 500 Greatest Albums of All Time*?

Easy

Medium

Hard

Answers to QUIZ 134 – Toys

1 Yo-yo
2 Duplo®
3 Slinky®
4 Fidget spinner
5 Subbuteo®
6 Tonka Trucks®
7 Sindy®
8 POGs™

ANSWERS ON PAGE **139**

1   What is the name of the official record of daily proceedings in the British Parliament?

2   The New Forest is a local government district in which English county?

3   Which musical term can also, in mathematics, refer to any line that passes through the centre of a circle?

4   Phobos and Deimos are the two known moons of what planet?

5   Pol Pot was a tyrannical leader of which Asian country?

6   In pre-decimal British currency, how many pennies were there in a pound?

7   For her role in 2019's *Judy*, who became only the fourth actress to win a Best Actress Oscar after previously winning Best Supporting Actress?

8   Scottish outlaw and folk hero Rob Roy hailed from which highland clan?

9   In 2022, *We Don't Talk About Bruno* became the first-ever original Disney song to top the UK singles chart; which film's soundtrack is it from?

10 Singaporean-born British violinist Vanessa-Mae took part in the 2014 Winter Olympics in which sport?

11 What colour is the central ring of the Olympic flag?

12 In the acronym LASER, what does the E stand for?

13 Pencil "lead" is actually primarily made of which crystalline form of carbon?

14 The liqueur kirsch is made with which fruit?

15 Which is the only number that is one greater than a square and one less than a cube?

16 Huey Lewis and the News, Jennifer Rush and Frankie Goes To Hollywood all charted high with singles with what name?

17 Which chemical element has the symbol Si?

18 Which American park was the world's first National Park?

19 Which writer, producer and presenter has written two novels about *The Thursday Murder Club*?

20 Which character created by W.E. Johns was a Detective-Inspector of the Special Air Police?

Answers to QUIZ 135 – Pot Luck

1	Six	11	Smell
2	India	12	Plum
3	Medina	13	Feet
4	Defence Of the Realm Act	14	Lurch
5	Fisheye lens	15	Yahoo!
6	Israel	16	36
7	Shergar	17	Paris
8	An extra chromosome	18	Windermere
9	Dark blue	19	Mineworkers
10	Bending the knee	20	Milan

Easy

Medium

Hard

Easy

1. Which station functions as the London terminus for Eurostar services?
2. Finally demolished in 2015, which English town's bus station was once voted the fourth ugliest building in the UK?
3. It is said that which train departs from London's Kings Cross Station on Platform 9 and 3/4?
4. The UK Shipping Forecast is broadcast four times a day on which radio station?
5. Nine Elms and Battersea Power Station were new stations opened on which London Underground line in 2021?
6. Which is the busiest railway station in Bristol?
7. What was the name of the Soviet/Russian space station that operated in low Earth orbit from 1986 to 2001?
8. From which London station would a train travelling to Lancaster leave?
9. The Three Gorges Dam, the largest hydro-electric power station in the world, is located on which river?
10. On a UK General Election day, what time do polling stations close?
11. Michaelwood, Gordano and Bridgewater are all service stations on which motorway?
12. The largest Royal Air Force station in the UK is near to, and named for, which Oxfordshire village?
13. In which US city is Jamaica train station?
14. Pelbury House is the main station for the Central Police in which crime series?
15. Holding up to 1,250 people, which is the largest scientific research station in the Antarctic?
16. Which is the only London Underground station to have London in its name?
17. How much does it cost to buy a train station on a British Monopoly™ board?
18. From 1892 to 1954, nearly 12 million immigrants arrived at which island immigrant inspection station in New York Bay?
19. The New Safe Confinement arch was fixed in place over which nuclear power station in 2016?
20. Which company makes the PlayStation® range of games consoles?

Medium

Hard

Answers to QUIZ 136 – The Beatles

1	Julian & Sean	11	Denny Laine
2	George Harrison	12	*The Beatles (The White Album)*
3	*Yellow Submarine*	13	Volkswagen Beetle
4	*Get Back*	14	Peter Blake and Jann Haworth
5	*Revolver*	15	*One*
6	1971	16	*Hey Jude*
7	French	17	*A Hard Day's Night*
8	*Thomas the Tank Engine*	18	*I Am The Walrus*
9	Central Park, New York City	19	Nine
10	*Give My Regards to Broad Street*	20	*Abbey Road* (no.5)

1   Rodney Marks, an Australian astrophysicist who died from methanol poisoning, is often considered the first person to be murdered where?

2   The prison known until 1990 as Strangeways is in which English city?

3   Before adopting a rota system, David Dickinson and Tim Wonnacott were the two permanent hosts of which BBC antiques show?

4   The government of Slovakia protested which Eli Roth horror film due to the negative portrayal of their country within it?

5   Almost half of the world's golf courses are situated in which country?

6   In 2022, which Deputy Leader of the Labour Party advocated that the police "shoot your terrorists and ask questions second"?

7   How did the reigns of Wilhelmina, Adriana and Beatrix, the three 20th century monarchs of the Netherlands, all end?

8   In Roman mythology, who was the husband of Juno?

9   *Operation Matterhorn* was the 2019 repatriation exercise to bring home 1,400 British tourists stranded after the failure of which travel agent?

10   Chopin Airport is located in which European capital city?

11   In rhyming slang, what is someone described as "mutton"?

12   The 1904 *Entente Cordiale* series of agreements creating a friendly understanding between political powers was signed by which two countries?

13   Fax, the truncated name of the outmoded communications technology, is short for what?

14   *Flying Down to Rio* was a 1933 musical film famous for being the first screen pairing of which dance duo?

15   Upon receiving the Turner Prize in 1995, who said "It's amazing what you can do with an 'E' in A-level art, a twisted imagination, and a chainsaw"?

16   Matt Hancock resigned from which cabinet role in June 2021 after being found to have breached social distancing rules?

17   Gaynor Hopkins, a Welsh singer known for her distinctive husky voice, rose to fame under what stage name?

18   The bassoon is an instrument in which section of the orchestra?

19   A phrase often attributed to Mark Twain states there are three types of lies: lies, damned lies and what?

20   Michaelmas Day falls on the 29th of which month?

Easy

Medium

Hard

Answers to QUIZ 137 – Pot Luck

1   Hansard

2   Hampshire

3   Chord (and if a chord passes through the middle of the circle, it is the diameter)

4   Mars

5   Cambodia

6   240

7   Renee Zellweger (after Meryl Streep, Jessica Lange and Cate Blanchett)

8   MacGregor

9   *Encanto*

10   Skiing

11   Black

12   Emission (light amplification by the stimulated emission of radiation)

13   Graphite

14   Cherry

15   26

16   *The Power of Love*

17   Silicon

18   Yellowstone

19   Richard Osman

20   James "Biggles" Bigglesworth

1. Which fruit is sometimes called the love apple?
2. In 1537, which English King declared via royal charter that 14th February would be the holiday of St Valentine's Day?
3. Who was the Greek equivalent of the Roman god Cupid?
4. Who banned Valentine's Day celebrations in the UK in 1653?
5. In 1929, the Saint Valentine's Day Massacre took place in which American city?
6. Mean-spirited Valentine cards in the Victorian era were often given what alliterative name?
7. The Shrine of the Roman Saint Valentine is found in what European capital city?
8. Which famous building in New York lights up a red heart each St Valentine's Day?
9. Which Scottish Poet Laureate wrote the Valentine's-themed poem *The Bees* for the *Daily Telegraph* in 2010?
10. *Ik hou van jou* is a way to say "I love you" in which language?
11. What social media platform was launched on Valentine's Day 2005 by Steve Chen, Chad Hurley and Jawed Karim?
12. Which British explorer was killed by the natives of Hawaii on 14th February 1779?
13. In the *Simpsons* episode *I Love Lisa*, who does Lisa give a Valentine's Day card to when she sees he has not received any?
14. Johnny Depp and Natalie Portman appeared in the music video for 2012's *My Valentine*, a single by who?
15. Who played Shirley Valentine in the 1989 film of the same name?

16. Because of the national February carnival, in which country is the equivalent of Valentine's Day, "*Dia dos Namorados*", instead celebrated on 12th June?
17. Paris's *Pont des Arts* bridge is regularly covered in what, put on there by couples as a show of love?
18. Other than love and marriage, name one of the many things St Valentine is considered the patron saint of.
19. Master tapes of which band's album *Cigarettes and Valentines* were stolen just before completion, forcing them to start again with a new album, *American Idiot?*
20. After being ejected from a game, which MLB manager disguised himself with sunglasses and a fake moustache and came back in?

Answers to QUIZ 138 – Stations

1	St Pancras International	11	M5
2	Northampton	12	Brize Norton
3	Hogwarts Express, from *Harry Potter*	13	New York City
4	BBC Radio 4	14	*Line of Duty*
5	Northern Line	15	McMurdo
6	Bristol Temple Meads	16	London Bridge (London Fields is overground only)
7	*Mir*	17	£200
8	Euston	18	Ellis Island
9	Yangtze	19	Chernobyl
10	10pm	20	Sony

1   As of 2021, Wolverhampton Wanderers, Burnley, Preston North End and Sheffield United are the only four English football clubs to do what?

2   Albumen is an alternative name for which specific food item?

3   Who sang *It's My Party*, and cried if she wanted to?

4   In 2018, which Australian drag queen won *Celebrity Big Brother*, beating Ann Widdecombe into second place?

5   On 30th March 1981, who did John Hinckley Jr attempt to assassinate?

6   Who was the Roman goddess of love and marriage?

7   A *shinai* is a Japanese sword typically made of bamboo used primarily in which sport?

8   Charlie from *Charlie and the Chocolate Factory* and Hyacinth from *Keeping Up Appearances* share what surname?

9   Which English city was known in Roman times as Duroliponte?

10 LinkedIn™, Twitter™ and Facebook™ all have logos made of which two colours?

11 Which talk show host and politician was born at Highgate tube station?

12 Bloodnok (*The Goon Show*) and Gowen (*Fawlty Towers*) were both fictional characters that held what military rank?

13 In musical notation, what name is given to the five parallel lines around which notes are written?

14 Despite the name, the Spanish Riding School is located in which country?

15 In the Bible, which book follows Matthew?

16 At the time of his death, which daredevil reportedly had 10-12 pounds of metal rods and screws in his body from various bike crashes?

17 *Behind the Candelabra* was a biographical film about which pianist?

18 In 1989, which Japanese electronic giant bought Columbia Pictures?

19 The National Railway Museum is located in which English city?

20 Which giant internet company started life as cadabra.com?

Easy

Medium

Hard

Answers to QUIZ 139 – Pot Luck

1	Antarctica	11	Deaf
2	Manchester	12	Britain and France
3	*Bargain Hunt*	13	Facsimile
4	*Hostel*	14	Fred Astaire and Ginger Rogers
5	The USA	15	Damian Hirst
6	Angela Rayner	16	Health Secretary
7	Abdication	17	Bonnie Tyler
8	Jupiter	18	Woodwind
9	Thomas Cook	19	Statistics
10	Warsaw, Poland	20	September

Easy

1   On the same day Elizabeth II was crowned, 2nd June 1953, word spread that which two men had become the first to summit Mount Everest?

2   On 18th June 1815, Napoleon led a 72,000-strong army into battle with Britain and Prussia near which Belgian village?

3   Which English king signed the Magna Carta on June 15th 1215?

4   Trooping the Colour is held in London annually in June on which London parade ground?

5   The plot of which historical novel, musical and film ends during the 1832 June Rebellion in Paris?

6   Which annual summer music event happens in the last week of June in Somerset?

7   On 12th June 1942, her birthday, which Dutch girl received a diary as a present?

8   *June Is Bustin' Out All Over* is a song from which 1945 Rodgers and Hammerstein stage musical?

9   On 30th June 1859, who became the first person to tight-rope walk across the Niagara Falls?

10 The first public demonstrated flight of which mode of transplant took place on 4th June 1783 in Annonay, France?

11 On June 4th 1989, the Chinese Government sent in troops to clear which public space, which had been occupied by protesters for seven weeks?

12 At 24 hours long, the world's oldest active sports car endurance racing event is held annually in June near which French town?

13 In 2021, Juneteenth (June 19th) became a recognised federal holiday in the USA, commemorating what?

14 What happened to the Cuyahoga River in Ohio, USA, on 22nd June 1969?

Medium

15 June Carter, a famous singer-songwriter in her own right, was also well known for her marriage to who?

16 In the sitcom *Terry and June*, who played title character June Medford?

17 In November 2019, which TV presenter was appointed as the BBC's first Director of Creative Diversity?

18 June Ackland was a character in which TV drama from 1983 until 2007?

19 Who died on 8th June 632 in Medina, Saudi Arabia?

20 On 13th June 1956, which club became the first ever European football champions?

Hard

Answers to QUIZ 140 – Valentine's Day

1	Tomato	11	YouTube
2	Henry VIII	12	Captain James Cook
3	Eros	13	Ralph Wiggum
4	Oliver Cromwell	14	Sir Paul McCartney
5	Chicago	15	Pauline Collins
6	Vinegar Valentines	16	Brazil
7	Dublin	17	Padlocks
8	The Empire State Building	18	The mentally ill, beekeeping, fainting, epilepsy and plague
9	Carol Ann Duffy	19	Green Day
10	Dutch	20	Bobby Valentine (he was rumbled and later suspended for two games)

ANSWERS ON PAGE 145

1   Anhidrosis is a medical condition diagnosed as the inability to do what?

2   The Mendip Hills lie in which English county?

3   Prestidigitator is a synonym for what kind of entertainer?

4   Which of the Teenage Mutant Ninja Turtles wears red?

5   In the Banksy mural *Pulp Fiction*, John Travolta and Samuel L. Jackson are holding which fruit instead of guns?

6   The three biggest cities by population in which US state all begin with the letter C?

7   Chicories are closely related to which other leafy vegetable?

8   The name of which island can also be a sweater, a cow and a potato?

9   The March 1938 *Anschluss* was the annexation of which other European country by Germany?

10 In which month does the Spring Bank Holiday fall?

11 Who was the original keyboardist with the band Squeeze?

12 "Unbelievable Jeff" is the unintentional catchphrase of which television football pundit?

13 The soundtrack to *Guardians of the Galaxy* features which song by 10cc?

14 In the 16th century, which artist spent four years painting the ceiling of the Sistine Chapel in Rome?

15 Saigas, gerenuks and impala are all species of which animal?

16 Sol beer was first brewed in 1899 in which South American country?

17 Sid Vicious was the bass player in which punk band?

18 Which singer, born Noah Kaminsky, controversially appeared in blackface when starring in the remake of *The Jazz Singer*?

19 Gammon, ham and bacon are all meats that come from which animal?

20 Alphabetically, which is the second sign of the zodiac?

Easy

Medium

Hard

Answers to QUIZ 141 – Pot Luck

1	Win all four divisions of the English football league	11	Jerry Springer
2	Egg white	12	Major
3	Leslie Gore	13	Stave or staff
4	Courtney Act	14	Austria
5	Ronald Reagan	15	Mark
6	Juno	16	Evel Knievel
7	Kendo	17	Liberace
8	Bucket (although in Hyacinth's opinion, the pronunciations differed)	18	Sony
		19	York
9	Cambridge	20	Amazon
10	Blue and white		

1   Which British Army officer and writer founded the Scout Movement?

2   Which film star created the annual Sundance Film Festival?

3   Who recorded the 2000 UK Christmas no.1 with *Can We Fix It*?

4   Whose career acting roles have included Boo Radley, Major Frank Burns and Tom Hagen?

5   Which Irish singer-songwriter is the lead singer of the Boomtown Rats, but is perhaps better known for his activism?

6   Which American outlaw was viewed as a "coward" and "traitor" for his 1882 assassination of Jesse James?

7   Nicknamed the "Bard of Ayrshire" and "Ploughman Poet", which Scottish poet's works include *To a Louse* and *To a Mouse*?

8   Which lawyer and member of a reality TV family was on O.J. Simpson's murder trial defence team?

9   Contrary to popular myth, which quiz show presenter did not play the saxophone on Gerry Rafferty's *Baker Street*?

10 Which actress won the Best Actress Oscar for her 2000 role as real-life environmental activist Erin Brockovich?

11 Which big-haired self-proclaimed genius character on *The Simpsons* becomes arch-enemies with Bart?

12 Which actor's credits include *Sling Blade*, *Primary Colors*, *Armageddon*, *A Simple Plan*, *Monster's Ball* and *Bad Santa*?

13 In January 2000, the Zimbabwe Banking Corporation held a promotional lottery with a Z$100,000 first prize jackpot. Who won it?

14 Which American theoretical physicist is often credited with being the "father of the atomic bomb"?

15 In old money, which coin was also known as a bob?

16 Which hip-hop duo had a 2000 hit with *B.O.B. (Bombs Over Baghdad)*?

17 Which filmmaker has directorial credits to his name including *From Dusk Till Dawn* and *Sin City*?

18 Which entertainer was best known for appearing with a canine puppet named Spit the Dog?

19 Until he was surpassed by Ian Botham, who was England's leading all-time Test cricket wicket taker?

20 Which American dancer revolutionised musicals with his distinct style of dance including frequent use of props, signature moves and jazz hands?

Answers to QUIZ 142 – June

1	Edmund Hillary and Sherpa Tenzing Norgay	11	Tiananmen Square
2	Waterloo	12	Le Mans
3	John	13	The ending of slavery
4	Horse Guards Parade	14	It caught fire (that's how much oil and litter was
5	*Les Misérables*		in it)
6	Glastonbury	15	Johnny Cash
7	Anne Frank	16	June Whitfield
8	*Carousel*	17	June Sarpong
9	Jean Francois Gravelot, or "The Great Blondin"	18	*The Bill*
10	Hot air balloon	19	The prophet Muhammad
		20	Real Madrid

Easy

Medium

Hard

ANSWERS ON PAGE 147

1   What is Queen Elizabeth II's surname?
2   Andrew Marr, Emily Maitlis and Jon Sopel all left the BBC to join which radio station?
3   Butterhead, Batavia and Winter Density are all types of which vegetable?
4   The potentially fatal affliction decompression sickness, a risk to SCUBA divers, is more commonly known by what name?
5   Which Japanese car manufacturer makes the Jazz?
6   Whose Twitter™ handle is @Pontifex?
7   In geometry, how many minutes are there in a degree?
8   The national rugby team of which country are known as The Springboks?
9   Davy Jones fronted which pop rock group that was "manufactured" in 1965 by television producers?
10 Which recurring sound heard in the heart through a stethoscope is usually a sign of disease or damage?
11 Bernard Montgomery and Frank Spencer became known for wearing which type of soft, flat-crowned French hat?
12 Focaccia, pita and brioche are all types of what?
13 Errol Brown was the lead singer with which group, named after a drink?
14 *South Park* is set in which American state?
15 "Devil's-bones" is a slang term for what piece of gaming equipment?
16 *Amarillo* is the Spanish word for which colour?
17 The logo of which film studio is a winged horse?
18 In which modern-day country was Marie Curie born?
19 Which London Underground line has the most stations?
20 Snooker players Neil Robertson and Eddie Charlton come from which country?

Easy

Medium

Hard

Answers to QUIZ 143 – Pot Luck

1	Sweat	11	Jools Holland
2	Somerset	12	Chris Kamara
3	Magician	13	*I'm Not in Love*
4	Raphael	14	Michelangelo
5	Bananas	15	Antelope
6	Ohio (Cleveland, Cincinnati, Columbus)	16	Mexico
7	Lettuce	17	The Sex Pistols
8	Jersey	18	Neil Diamond
9	Austria	19	Pig
10	May	20	Aries

1   What forename also describes a spayed female cat?

2   In T.S. Eliot's *Old Possum's Book of Practical Cats*, who was the wise and beloved elderly cat?

3   Which football team from the northeast of England goes by the nickname "The Black Cats"?

4   At 48.5 inches long, Stewie, the world's longest cat, was of which breed, named for an American state?

5   When they are newly born, all kittens have what colour eyes?

6   Panthro, Cheetara and Snarf are characters in which 1980s animated TV series?

7   Mr Bigglesworth was the hairless sphynx pet cat of which movie antagonist?

8   Sean Lock was a team captain on the first eighteen seasons of which comedy panel show?

9   Which Nobel Laureate Austrian-Irish physicist is known partly for his studies of the wave mechanics of orbiting electrons, but also for an imaginary cat?

10 How many kittens were there in what, as of 2021, was the biggest litter of kittens ever recorded?

11 Known as "The Cat in the Hat" for his range of headwear, Jason Cheetham is the lead vocalist of which jazz-funk band?

12 A black cat is an important symbol representing *déjà vu* and impending trouble in which science fiction film series?

13 Félicette was the first and thus far only cat to do what?

14 In Shakespeare's *Romeo and Juliet*, Mercutio repeatedly calls which character the "prince of cats", in reference to his sleek yet violent manner?

15 Which television presenter hosted *SMTV Live* and *Fame Academy* before becoming the last presenter of the original run of *Stars in Their Eyes*?

16 Who plays The Cat in *Red Dwarf*?

17 Which 1997 American romantic comedy-drama film starring Jack Nicholson was known in Hong Kong as *Mr Cat Poop*?

18 Which animal, the largest mammalian carnivore on Madagascar, is often mistaken for a big cat, despite actually being more related to a mongoose?

19 Which cat breed is the only one to be named after a person?

20 Which man – widely recognised as one of the greatest mathematicians and physicists of all time – allegedly also invented the cat flap?

Answers to QUIZ 144 – Bobs and Roberts

1   Robert Baden-Powell

2   Robert Redford, named for his role as the Sundance Kid

3   Bob the Builder

4   Robert Duvall

5   Bob Geldof

6   Robert Ford

7   Robert Burns

8   Robert Kardashian

9   Bob Holness

10 Julia Roberts

11 Sideshow Bob (or, if you'd rather, Dr. Robert Underdunk "Bob" Terwilliger Jr., PhD)

12 Billy Bob Thornton

13 President Robert Mugabe

14 Robert Oppenheimer

15 Shilling

16 Outkast

17 Robert Rodriguez

18 Bob Carolgees

19 Bob Willis

20 Bob Fosse

QUIZ 147 – Pot Luck

ANSWERS ON PAGE **149**

1. With works including *The Thinker*, which French sculptor is generally thought to have brought sculpture into the modern age?
2. *Mad World* and *Everybody Wants to Rule the World* were both UK Top 10 hit singles by which band?
3. Which two Japanese cities were obliterated by atomic bombs in World War II?
4. The name of which martial art means "the way of the sword"?
5. What type of animal is called a *chameau* in French?
6. Whose autobiography *Dear Fatty* is written as a series of letters, mainly to friends and relatives?
7. A rhombus and a trapezium each have how many sides?
8. Which name goes before Rambo, McClane, Spartan, Steed and Wick in the names of action movie characters?
9. Anne Bonny and Mary Read are two of history's few recorded female...what?
10. A castrated horse is known as a what?
11. Belgian-Australian singer-songwriter Gotye and New Zealand singer Kimbra had a worldwide hit in 2011 with which song?
12. In 2017, NASA announced the *Artemis* program, a series of spaceflight missions to where?
13. On a standard dartboard, which number lies directly opposite 5?
14. How did French revolutionary Joan of Arc die?
15. In the *Miss Marple* novels by Agatha Christie, what was Miss Marple's first name?
16. Who was chosen to be Lord Mayor of London on four occasions; 1397, 1398, 1406 and 1419?
17. What is the English equivalent of the Spanish name *Iago*?
18. In the name of the car manufacturer, what do the letters MG stand for?
19. To defenestrate someone or something is to do what?
20. Pascal, C++ and Basic are all types of what?

Easy

Medium

Hard

Answers to QUIZ 145 – Pot Luck

1	Windsor	11	Beret
2	LBC	12	Bread
3	Lettuce	13	Hot Chocolate
4	The bends	14	Colorado
5	Honda	15	Dice
6	The Pope	16	Yellow
7	60	17	TriStar
8	South Africa	18	Poland
9	The Monkees	19	District Line (60)
10	Murmur	20	Australia

Easy

1. Which 2019 musical fantasy film by Tom Hooper lost Universal Pictures between $71 million and $114 million?

2. Despite selling almost half a million units in 13 years, which brand of Hillman car was much derided for its famously poor reliability?

3. Who directed the low-budget films *Bride of the Monster* (1955) and *Plan 9 from Outer Space* (1957)?

4. The final scene of the final episode of which HBO crime drama series controversially faded to black, leaving the fate of the characters ambiguous?

5. Which actor has released 11 albums, ranging from 1967's *The Transformed Man* to 2021's *Bill*?

6. Appearing in his eleventh *Carry On* film, who played the title role in the film *Carry On Columbus*?

7. Which artificial hill in London cost £6 million to build yet was closed after only six months?

8. *Swagger Jagger* was the much-derided 2011 debut single for which singer?

9. Which 2000 John Travolta film won the Worst Picture of the Decade award at the 2010 Razzies?

10. *Bulletproof* was a much-derided video game featuring which rapper as its lead character?

11. Despite having a 95% usage share in 2003, which web browser known for security concerns and spotty performance was finally retired in 2022?

12. Three of the four members of which British girl band made their big screen debut in 2000's *Honest*, regarded as one of the worst films of all time?

13. Geraldo Rivera hosted which 1986 two-hour special hyping up the live discovery of riches, money and bodies, only to find absolutely nothing at all?

Medium

14. Which actor was deemed to have appeared in so many bad films in 2021 that he was awarded his own category at the 2022 Razzies?

15. DJ Mike Read wrote which 2012 biographical musical, which closed after one performance?

16. Which action role-playing video game by CD Projekt was released in December 2020 to much fanfare, yet was notoriously buggy and incomplete?

17. *The Lair of the White Worm* (1911), a candidate for the worst book ever written, was which Irish horror writer's final novel?

18. Which much-hyped Google optical head-mounted display never took off?

19. Denise van Outen starred in which widely-panned 1998 sitcom about three women sharing a flat in London?

20. *Bob Honey Who Just Do Stuff* was a much-derided 2018 political satire book by which actor?

Hard

---

1. In golf, how much under par is a condor?
2. A cat named Church comes back from the dead in which Stephen King novel?
3. Henning Mankell's Swedish detective Wallander has what first name?
4. Prior to a name change in 1990, what were Snickers® bars called?
5. Although they can be almost any colour, sapphires are most often what colour, and give their name to a shade of it?
6. Who recorded the voice of Anna in the Disney film *Frozen*?
7. The asteroid belt is located between which two planets in the solar system?
8. What type of creature is a sculpin?
9. In rhyming slang, what does "rabbit and pork" refer to?
10. The oblique muscles can be found in which part of the human body?
11. Danielle Steel is a prolific author of which literary genre?
12. In 1976, JVC introduced the VHS video format – what did VHS stand for?
13. *The Testaments*, joint winner of the 2019 Booker Prize, was the sequel to which novel?
14. Jean-Jacques Rousseau explored the best way to establish a political community in the face of the problems of commercial society in which 1762 treatise?
15. In the *Harry Potter* universe, what are the Shooting Star, the Nimbus 2000 and the Firebolt?
16. On a calculator, what does the AC button stand for?
17. What service did Jack Dorsey, Noah Glass, Biz Stone and Evan Williams launch in 2006?
18. How many squares are there on a Scrabble® board?
19. The brothers Matt and Luke Goss formed which 80s pop band?
20. Including dewclaws, how many toes in total does the average cat have?

Easy

Medium

Hard

Answers to QUIZ 147 – Pot Luck

1	Auguste Rodin	11	*Somebody That I Used to Know*
2	Tears for Fears	12	The moon
3	Hiroshima and Nagasaki	13	17
4	Kendo	14	She was burned at the stake
5	Camel	15	Jane
6	Dawn French	16	Dick Whittington
7	Four	17	Jacob
8	John	18	Morris Garages
9	Pirates	19	Throw it out of a window
10	Gelding	20	Computer languages

Do you know which fast food chains use these logos?

1

2

3

4

5

6

7

8

Answers to QUIZ 148 – Critically Panned

1	Cats	11	Internet Explorer
2	Imp	12	All Saints
3	Ed Wood	13	*The Mystery of Al Capone's Vaults*
4	*The Sopranos*	14	Bruce Willis
5	William Shatner	15	*Oscar Wilde: The Musical*
6	Jim Dale	16	*Cyberpunk 2077*
7	Marble Arch mound	17	*Bram Stoker*
8	Cher Lloyd (it went to No.1 anyway)	18	Google Glass
9	*Battlefield Earth*	19	*Babes in the Wood*
10	50 Cent	20	Sean Penn

1 E. C. Segar was the creator of which maritime cartoon character?

2 Bettany Hughes and Simon Schama appear on TV in what professional capacity?

3 Sugarloaf Mountain and Christ the Redeemer are both landmarks overlooking which South American city?

4 Euchre, Clab, Clagger and Skat are all games played with what?

5 In Shakespeare's *Macbeth*, who does Macbeth murder through ambition and to appease his wife?

6 In computing, what is a GUI?

7 In internet meme culture, what does the abbreviation "tfw" usually stand for?

8 Keanu Reeves plays a quarterback turned FBI agent turned undercover surfer in which slightly absurd 1991 action film?

9 Which series of religious wars between Christians and Muslims started in 1096, primarily to secure control of holy sites considered sacred by both groups?

10 The American sitcom *Frasier* was set in which city?

11 With hyperinflation raging at more than 2.2 million%, which African country issued $100 billion notes in 2008?

12 For the last years of his life, Galileo was under house arrest for espousing which man's theory of heliocentrism?

13 The flags of Turkey and Tunisia both bear which two celestial symbols of Islam?

14 Which country was formerly known as South West Africa?

15 Which Academy Award-winning actress is also Warren Beatty's sister?

16 An inflatable lifejacket introduced during World War II was named for which shapely actress?

17 A butterfly's chemoreceptors (used to taste in lieu of tastebuds) are located where?

18 Who preceded Ted Hughes as Poet Laureate?

19 Which strict simple-living Mennonite sect was founded by the Swiss preacher, Jakob Amman?

20 In the 1997 film *Bean*, which iconic portrait painting did Mr Bean accidentally ruin?

Answers to QUIZ 149 – Pot Luck

1	Four	11	Romance
2	*Pet Sematary*	12	Video Home System
3	Kurt	13	*The Handmaid's Tale* by Margaret Atwood
4	Marathon	14	*The Social Contract*
5	Blue	15	Broomsticks
6	Kristen Bell	16	"All clear"
7	Mars and Jupiter	17	Twitter™
8	Fish	18	225
9	Talk	19	Bros
10	Abdomen	20	18 (five on each front foot, four on each back foot)

ANSWERS ON PAGE **154**

Easy

1   In *Cats*, the characters move around a set designed to look like what?

2   In which musical does Franklin Delano Roosevelt appear as a character, singing the song *Tomorrow*?

3   Which long-running musical features the song *Food, Glorious Food*?

4   Comedian Stewart Lee co-wrote a musical about which famous talk show host?

5   *I Feel Pretty*, *A Boy Like That* and *Something's Coming* are all songs in which classic musical?

6   The name of a song from *The Sound of Music*, edelweiss is a type of what?

7   The musical *Camelot* features which legendary figure as the lead role?

8   *Spamalot*, the musical comedy adapted from the 1975 film *Monty Python and the Holy Grail*, was written by which of the Pythons?

9   The creators of *South Park* wrote, directed and provided voices for which 2004 puppet musical that satirises big-budget action films and the global implications of US foreign policy?

10   Which musical, based on the play *Pygmalion* by George Bernard Shaw, centres on the character of Eliza Doolittle?

11   Barbra Streisand won the Oscar for Best Actress for playing a girl named Fanny Brice in which hit musical?

12   What is the name of the lead teen character in the musical *Hairspray*?

13   While 1957's *West Side Story* may be his best known, which 1944 work was the first musical written by Leonard Bernstein?

14   The 2018 musical film *A Star is Born* starred Bradley Cooper and Lady Gaga, but which singer was originally set to star?

15   In *Little Shop of Horrors*, what is the name of the carnivorous Venus flytrap plant?

Medium

16   Which 1961 musical tells the story of a real female frontierswoman as its heroine, albeit with a non-historical, somewhat farcical plot?

17   Princeton, Brian and Mrs Thistletwat are characters in which puppet-heavy musical?

18   First staged in 2005, the musical *The Color Purple* is based on a book by which author?

19   *Send in the Clowns* was a song written by Stephen Sondheim for which 1973 musical?

20   What type of vehicle "with a fringe on top" is the subject of a classic show tune in the musical *Oklahoma!*?

Hard

Answers to QUIZ 150 – Fast Food Brand Logos

1   McDonald's®

2   Domino's®

3   Starbucks®

4   Pepsi®

5   Pizza Hut™

6   Taco Bell™

7   Wendy's®

8   Gregg's

1   In darts, what score is known as "Bed and Breakfast"?

2   Bizzy, Wish, Layzie, Krayzie and Flesh make up which hip-hop group?

3   Which berry is regarded as a hybrid of the North American blackberry and the European raspberry?

4   Australian writer and social activist Irina Dunn is credited with the saying "a woman needs a man like a fish needs"…what?

5   Nathuram Vinayak Godse was the assassin of which lawyer and political activist?

6   Which Greek city, the oldest continually inhabited city in Europe, shares its name with a high street retailer?

7   The 100 folds in a *toque* (chef's hat) are supposed to indicate the 100 different ways there are to prepare what?

8   Sciamachy is an alternative name for what warm-up act?

9   Skiing and fencing both take place on surfaces called what?

10 Which sport appears in *Alice in Wonderland*?

11 The Duke of Wellington statue located outside the Gallery of Modern Art, Glasgow, has since 1970 been almost continually adorned with what on its head?

12 Black Périgord, winter and Bianchetto are all types of what edible fungus?

13 Which phenomenon in physics occurs when a fire that has consumed all available oxygen suddenly explodes when more oxygen is made available?

14 The PlayStation® character Crash was which type of marsupial, native to Australia and New Guinea?

15 Now better known as exercise equipment, what machines were used in prisons in early Victorian Britain as a method of exerting hard labour?

16 In the words of Sir John Betjeman, "come, friendly bombs, and fall on"….where?

17 Lena Katina and Julia Volkova formed which Russian music duo, known for the hit *All The Things She Said*?

18 Born Clifford Price, which producer and DJ is known for his pioneering role in the 1990s UK jungle, drum and bass and breakbeat scenes?

19 Beginning in the 1960s, which schoolteacher began an unlikely second career as a self-appointed guardian of British morals, especially on television?

20 Which Scottish boxer became the undisputed light-welterweight champion after defeating José Ramírez in May 2021?

Answers to QUIZ 151 – Pot Luck

1	Popeye	11	Zimbabwe
2	Historians	12	Nicolaus Copernicus
3	Rio de Janeiro	13	Star and crescent
4	A deck of cards	14	Namibia
5	Duncan	15	Shirley MacLaine
6	Graphical User Interface	16	Mae West
7	"That feeling when…"	17	On its feet
8	*Point Break*	18	Sir John Betjeman
9	The Crusades	19	Amish
10	Seattle	20	James McNeill Whistler's *Arrangement in Grey and Black No.1* (more commonly called *Whistler's Mother*)

ANSWERS ON PAGE **156**

Easy

1   In what year did the "canonical five" Jack the Ripper murders take place?

2   In which impoverished area of London did the Ripper murders occur?

3   Of the "canonical five" victims of the Ripper, who was last?

4   Known as the "double event", which two victims of the Ripper were murdered within an hour of each other?

5   Early on in the investigation, the murderer was given what nickname in reference to something that suspect Jon Pizer always wore?

6   A message found written on the wall close to Elizabeth Stride's body blamed which group of people?

7   What body part did Jack the Ripper claim he would cut off and send to police in one of his letters?

8   The "From Hell" letter received by George Lusk came with half of which human organ alongside it?

9   In the film *From Hell* about the Ripper, which actor played the lead role of Chief Inspector Fredrick Abberline?

10   The name Jack the Ripper came from how the first letter sent to the Central News Agency was signed off, but how was it addressed?

11   Which member of the Royal Family was tenuously linked to the Jack the Ripper case?

12   Due to her mood swings, what was Ripper victim Annie Chapman's nickname?

13   Which organisation is it rumoured that Jack the Ripper was associated with?

14   Which artist – who had taken a keen interest in the case – was declared to be Jack the Ripper in a 2002 book by Patricia Cornwell?

15   Bertrand Ashley, Claude Clayton and Ashley Nabokoff were aliases used by which Ripper suspect?

16   What nickname was given to the second postcard received by the Central News Agency, postmarked 1st October 1888?

17   The grave of which Ripper victim no longer exists?

18   Ten years after the last murder, Inspector Frederick Abberline made it known that he believed which man was the Ripper?

19   In his 1996 book *Jack the Ripper, Light-Hearted Friend*, Richard Wallace theorised that which famous author was in fact the Ripper?

20   What was the name of Queen Victoria's Royal Doctor who was once a suspect in the Ripper murders?

Medium

Hard

Answers to QUIZ 152 – Musicals

1	Landfill/junkyard	11	*Funny Girl*
2	*Annie*	12	Tracy Turnblad
3	*Oliver!*	13	*On The Town*
4	Jerry Springer	14	Beyoncé
5	*West Side Story*	15	Audrey II or "Twoey"
6	Flower	16	*Calamity Jane*
7	King Arthur	17	*Avenue Q*
8	Eric Idle	18	Alice Walker
9	*Team America: World Police*	19	*A Little Night Music*
10	*My Fair Lady*	20	Surrey (a type of horse-drawn carriage)

1 Which actress played the lead role in the box-office bomb *Grease 2*?
2 Who was the King of Scotland from 1040 to 1057?
3 1971's *Move on Up* was the biggest UK hit in the career of which soul superstar?
4 The F-117 Nighthawk, the first operational aircraft to be designed around stealth technology, was built by which manufacturer?
5 The Tyrannosaurus rex lived on what would now be classified as which continent?
6 As of 2021, the fastest marathon ever run by someone dressed as a fruit was 2 hours, 58 minutes, and 20 seconds – which fruit?
7 Which British seaside town is the only one to still have three piers?
8 Which headland in southern Wales also gives its name to the district encompassing Oystermouth, Newton, West Cross and Mayals?
9 "NOM" appears on authentic bottles of which spirit?
10 Gumbo is the official cuisine of which American state?
11 In the world of newspapers, what does "op-ed" stand for?
12 What word can mean both the process of a cold weather front overtaking a warm front, or the position of one's teeth when clenched?
13 The Wade-Giles method is a romanisation system for translating which Asian language?
14 On an Ordnance Survey map, what does W stand for?
15 Who was captain of the winning European team at the 2018 Ryder Cup?
16 Yul Brynner was born in which country?
17 The Kaizer Chiefs is a football team in which country?
18 The subscapularis muscle is a part of which joint?
19 Willem De Kooning was a noted artist in which style?
20 Thomas DeCarlo Callaway is better known as which singer and rapper?

Easy

Medium

Hard

Answers to QUIZ 153 – Pot Luck

1	26	11	Traffic cone
2	Bone Thugs-N-Harmony	12	Truffle
3	Loganberry	13	Backdraught
4	A bicycle	14	Bandicoot
5	Mahatma Gandhi	15	Treadmills
6	Argos	16	Slough
7	Eggs	17	Tatu
8	Shadow boxing	18	Goldie
9	Piste	19	Mary Whitehouse
10	Croquet	20	Josh Taylor

1. "Your mind is the scene of the crime" was a tagline to which 2010 Christopher Nolan film?
2. As of 2021, which two films has Steven Spielberg won Best Director Oscars for?
3. After being impressed with his turn in *Return of the Jedi*, George Lucas wrote which fantasy film specifically for Warwick Davis?
4. The Sarah Siddons Award, given for outstanding performances in Chicago theatre productions, was initially a fictional award in which Oscar-winning film?
5. The title of which 1954 film directed by David Lean is an idiom for "no choice at all"?
6. In the 2010 re-make of the classic John Wayne film *True Grit*, who played Rooster Cogburn?
7. Which was the first film in the James Bond franchise to feature an Aston Martin?
8. Which 2016 film tells the story of the title character seeking to return a mystical relic to the goddess Te Fiti?
9. In which Studio Ghibli film do characters catch the Catbus, a large grinning, twelve legged cat with a hollow body that serves as a bus?
10. Frank Sinatra won the Best Supporting Oscar for his role in which film?
11. Al Pacino played Lowell Bergman, producer of CBS's *60 Minutes*, in which 1999 film?
12. Also known as the "King of Venereal Horror" or the "Baron of Blood", which Canadian director's works include *Scanners* and *The Fly*?
13. Who won Best Supporting Actor Oscars for their roles in both *Moonlight* and *Green Book*?
14. Virginia McKenna and Bill Travers starred together in which 1969 film about man's relationship with animal, the animal in question being an otter?
15. The main setting to which 2005 Disney animated film is the town of Oakey Oakes?
16. Mel Gibson starred as the eponymous Mad Max in the first three films of the franchise; who replaced him for the fourth?
17. Legend of film scores John Williams won his first Oscar for which 1971 film?
18. Which two films in the 1990s that had animals in their titles won consecutive Best Picture Oscars?
19. Beatrice Straight won the Best Supporting Actress Oscar for her performance in which film, despite only appearing in it for five minutes?
20. "The Harry Lime Theme" was an instrumental written and performed by Anton Karas for the soundtrack to which 1949 film?

Easy

Medium

Hard

Answers to QUIZ 154 – Jack the Ripper

1	1888	11	Prince Albert Victor, Duke of Clarence and Avondale, oldest son of Edward VII (died before his father)
2	Whitechapel		
3	Mary Jane Kelly	12	Dark Annie
4	Elizabeth Stride and Catherine Eddowes	13	Freemasons
5	"Leather Apron"	14	Walter Sickert
6	Jews (written as "Juwes")	15	Michael Ostrog
7	An ear (he never did it)	16	"Saucy Jacky"
8	Kidney	17	Annie Chapman
9	Johnny Depp	18	Severin Klosowski, also known as George Chapman
10	"Dear Boss"	19	Lewis Carroll
		20	Sir William Gull

QUIZ 157 – Pot Luck

1 Unavailable in other countries, what is the biggest social media platform in China, with over 445 million monthly active users?

2 Between 1513 and 1972, every monarch of which European country was called either Frederick or Christian?

3 The ancient city of Babylon was built along both banks of which river?

4 Cato Fong was the manservant to which fictional film detective?

5 Which two countries found out at the 1936 Olympic Games that they had identical flags?

6 What inscription is engraved on the Victoria Cross?

7 Which Burmese United Nations Secretary-General's name essentially translated to "Mr Clean"?

8 Which boxer was the last to fight Muhammed Ali in 1981, and five years later was beaten by Mike Tyson for his first heavyweight championship belt?

9 The 1915 poem *The Soldier* was written by which English poet?

10 Name any of the three British Prime Ministers who went by their middle name, when their first name was actually James.

11 Which future Best Actress Oscar winner starred as and in *The Next Karate Kid*?

12 "Leatherneck" and "Jarhead" are slang terms for members of which service?

13 The Bay of Campeche is a part of which much larger gulf?

14 The sword-bill is the only bird with a beak longer than its body – what type of bird is it?

15 Which water sport made its Olympic debut at Tokyo 2020?

16 What is the atomic number of calcium?

17 The comedian Gary Delaney married which other comic in 2013?

18 Lawyer and politician Robert Kennedy was assassinated by who?

19 In 1715, Louis XIV of France was succeeded by Louis XV – what relation was he to his predecessor?

20 A 1969 Richard Cawston documentary about whom was watched by approximately 30 million people?

Answers to QUIZ 155 – Pot Luck

1	Michelle Pfeiffer	11	Opposite editorial
2	Macbeth	12	Occlusion
3	Curtis Mayfield	13	Mandarin Chinese
4	Lockheed	14	Well
5	North America	15	Thomas Bjørn
6	Banana	16	Russia
7	Blackpool	17	South Africa
8	Mumbles	18	Shoulder
9	Tequila	19	Abstract Expressionism
10	New Orleans	20	CeeLo Green

ANSWERS ON PAGE **160**

Easy

1   The British Library, Great Ormond Street Hospital, London Zoo, the BT Tower and a pub called "The World's End" are all in which London borough?

2   Which football league team dropped "Borough" from its name in 2010 after 46 years of non-league existence?

3   Which is the only one of London's 33 boroughs to have three professional football clubs?

4   Market Harborough is a market town in which English county?

5   Which actor, filmmaker and entrepreneur became life president of Chelsea FC in 2008 after 28 years as a director?

6   Which 18th century English portrait and landscape artist painted *Mr and Mrs Andrews* and *The Blue Boy*?

7   Which football ground was the scene of a 1989 disaster in which 97 Liverpool fans were crushed to death at an FA Cup semi-final?

8   Which is the only London borough to have a name that begins with M?

9   Gold medallist swimmer Anita Lonsborough was the first female winner of which accolade in 1962?

10   Of the five boroughs that make up New York City, which is the only one that is not on an island?

Medium

11   In bridge, a yarborough is a hand containing no card higher than what value?

12   The Australian soap opera *Neighbours* is set in which fictional suburb of Melbourne, Victoria?

13   As alluded to by its name, which London borough is the only one to be on both sides of the River Thames?

14   Maidstone is the only borough in the UK where what belong to the mayor, rather than the monarch?

15   *Coronation Street* is set in which fictional borough of Greater Manchester?

16   The Holbeck Hall Hotel, which collapsed into the sea live on television on 5th June 1993 after heavy rains caused a landslide, was in which city?

17   Barry Fry has been owner, director, chairman and manager at which Cambridgeshire football club?

18   The former Emperor of France, Napoleon III, is buried in which Hampshire town, famous for its aviation links?

19   The Dukedom of Marlborough is seated at which palace located in the Cotswolds?

20   Which publishing company has a literary fiction imprint called *The Borough Press*?

Hard

Answers to QUIZ 156 – Film

1	*Inception*	11	*The Insider*
2	*Schindler's List* and *Saving Private Ryan*	12	David Cronenberg
3	*Willow*	13	Mahershala Ali
4	*All About Eve*	14	*Ring of Bright Water*
5	*Hobson's Choice*	15	*Chicken Little*
6	Jeff Bridges	16	Tom Hardy
7	*Goldfinger*	17	*Fiddler on the Roof*
8	*Moana*	18	*Silence of the Lambs* and *Dances With Wolves*
9	*My Neighbour Totoro*	19	*Network*
10	*From Here to Eternity*	20	*The Third Man*

1 From its approximate foundation in AD 800, who was the first ruler of the Holy Roman Empire?
2 What was the name of Roy Rogers's horse?
3 Excluding the sun, which is the brightest star in the sky?
4 In Jonathan Swift's 1726 novel *Gulliver's Travels*, which fictional land is occupied by giants?
5 Which actress won three Academy Awards for her performances in *Gaslight*, *Anastasia* and *Murder on the Orient Express*?
6 What is measured by an anemometer?
7 In 1933, which American aviator became the first pilot to fly solo around the world?
8 Originally bred in southwest USA, which breed of horse has a pale golden or tan-coloured hide with a white mane and tail?
9 What five-letter word describes broken rock fragments at the base of a cliff accumulated through periodic rockfall?
10 Scrimshaw is the name given to a type of handcraft created by engraving or carving what?
11 If someone looks at you askance, what are they conveying?
12 Which colour has for centuries been associated with wealth and royalty in Western culture, as well as in Japan?
13 Myology is the study of the structure and actions of what part of the body?
14 Buzkashi, the national sport of Afghanistan, involves horse-mounted players trying to "score" what animal in a goal?
15 Despite being regarded in European culture as the epitome of distance, or sometimes not even real, Timbuktu is a real city in which African country?
16 The diagnostic "stool chart" designed to classify human faeces into seven categories is named for which city?
17 A farmhouse called Stott Hall Farm is situated right in the middle of the Manchester end of which trans-Pennine motorway?
18 Oliver Bierhoff's goal in the Euro 96 final was the first use of which rule in European Championship football?
19 In Spanish, *alcázar* refers to what kind of structure?
20 The Andy Capp cartoon strip has appeared in which newspaper since 1957?

Easy

Medium

Hard

Answers to QUIZ 157 – Pot Luck

1	Weibo	11	Hilary Swank
2	Denmark	12	US Marines
3	Euphrates	13	Gulf of Mexico
4	Jacques Clouseau	14	Hummingbird
5	Liechtenstein and Haiti	15	Surfing
6	"For valour"	16	20
7	U Thant	17	Sarah Millican
8	Trevor Berbick	18	Sirhan Sirhan
9	Rupert Brooke	19	Great grandson – Louis XIV outlived both his son and grandson
10	Harold Wilson, Gordon Brown, Ramsay McDonald	20	The Royal Family

Easy

1 Under EU law, only producers in Spain and Portugal can use which name for a drink of red wine mixed with lemonade, fruit and spices?

2 A wine that has had a quantity of distilled spirit added to it to increase its alcohol content is known as what type of wine?

3 Marlborough and Central Otago are wine-producing regions in which country?

4 Which *vin de primeur*, fermented for just a few weeks and released on the third Thursday of November, is famous for the race to distribute it?

5 A Rehoboam holds the equivalent of how many bottles of wine?

6 Which catch-all term describes the environment in which a wine is produced, including its soil, topography and climate?

7 If a wine has been produced biodynamically, what name does it carry on the bottle as certification, taken from the Greek goddess of grain?

8 A standard case of wine contains how many bottles?

9 While it can be a term used to determine quality, what must simply be the case for a wine to be a "vintage"?

10 The raised dimple on the bottom of a wine bottle, supposedly added to increase surface area, is known as a what?

Medium

11 The wine-producing grape called Syrah in France and much of Europe is instead known in Australia by what other name?

12 Also known as a carboy, what is the name for a narrow-necked bottle holding from 3 to 10 gallons of liquid for fermentation and/or travelling?

13 The act of deliberately leaving botrytis (or grey mould) on grapes to produce sweet honey-flavoured wines is known as what?

14 James May embarked on *Big Wine Adventures* with which wine expert for two BBC television series?

15 Used mostly for wine, what were the tall jugs with two handles and a narrow neck in both ancient Greek or Roman society called?

16 Which word meaning "disaster" is also the name of a straw-covered rounded wine bottle?

17 Winemakers often plant what type of bushes adjacent to their vines as a early warning system for detecting certain types of fungi?

18 Which Greco-Roman god was a nature god of fruitfulness and vegetation, especially of wine?

19 After breaking up with Winona Ryder, which actor had his "Winona Forever" tattoo modified to read "Wino Forever"?

20 Since the late 1990s, which English singer-songwriter has produced Vida Nova wine from his vineyard in the Algarve?

Hard

Answers to QUIZ 158 – Boroughs

1	Camden	11	Nine
2	Stevenage FC	12	Erinsborough
3	Hammersmith & Fulham (Fulham, Chelsea, Queens Park Rangers)	13	Richmond upon Thames
4	Leicestershire	14	Swans
5	Richard Attenborough	15	Weatherfield
6	Thomas Gainsborough	16	Scarborough
7	Hillsborough	17	Peterborough United
8	Merton	18	Farnborough
9	Sports Personality Of The Year	19	Blenheim Palace
10	The Bronx	20	HarperCollins

1   Who was the last amateur men's singles winner at Wimbledon?

2   Winston Churchill stated that which notional barrier stretched from Szczecin (Stettin) in Poland to Trieste in Italy?

3   In the *Winnie the Pooh* poem *The More It Snows (Tiddely-Pom)*, which bit of Pooh keeps growing colder?

4   A toxophilite is a student or lover of which sport?

5   Which American author wrote the commercially and critically successful novel *Slaughterhouse-Five*?

6   Which Italian-born fashion designer introduced her signature colour "Shocking Pink" in 1936?

7   The Japanese chado/sado festival celebrates which beverage?

8   In 2022, who became the first action-sports athlete to win three medals at the same Olympic Games?

9   Penry Pooch was the "real" name of which cartoon detective?

10   In which type of skiing event does the skier make sharp turns around coloured poles?

11   Into which Rome fountain are coins worth approximately €3,000 daily thrown for good luck?

12   Frank Lloyd Wright was a key figure in which industry?

13   Born Ernest Evans, which American rock and roll singer and dancer popularised The Twist dance style?

14   The *Tao Te Ching*, reputedly authored by Lao Tzu, is widely considered the keystone work of which world religion?

15   Which waxy substance, originating as a secretion in the intestines of the sperm whale, is used to make perfume?

16   *Semillon* is a type of which fruit?

17   In maths, how many sides does an icosagon have?

18   Better Boys, Early Girls and Tiny Tims are varieties of which fruit?

19   An agelast is a person who never does what?

20   Roy Harold Scherer was better known as which actor?

Easy

Medium

Hard

Answers to QUIZ 159 – Pot Luck

1	Charlemagne	11	Disapproval or distrust
2	Trigger	12	Purple
3	Sirius or Dog Star	13	Muscles
4	Brobdingnag	14	Goat
5	Ingrid Bergman	15	Mali
6	Wind speed and direction	16	Bristol
7	Wiley Post	17	M62
8	Palomino	18	Golden Goal
9	Scree	19	Fortress/castle
10	Bones	20	*Daily Mirror*

1   In the TV series *The Sopranos*, which late actor played the lead role of Tony Soprano?

2   Who shot and killed Richie Aprile?

3   Which veteran of mafia movies played the role of Phil Leotardo, boss of the Lupertazzi crime family and the chief antagonist in the final season?

4   Which famous actor not only played the part of Tony Blundetto in thirteen episodes, but also directed a further four?

5   Credited as the show's creator and the writer of the most episodes, who nevertheless only directed the first and last episodes?

6   Who declined the role of Carmela Soprano, fearing it would be too similar to her previous role as Karen in *Goodfellas*, instead opting to play Dr Melfi?

7   Which American television network commissioned and produced the show?

8   The term "oogatz" is frequently heard on the show, but what does it mean?

9   What was the name of the prequel film released in 2021 that follows Tony Soprano's teenage years amid civil unrest?

10 Who had to return to Italy after a flirtation with Tony Soprano's wife Carmela?

11 Which country permanently banned Janice from entering after putting her on the Unwanted Persons list?

12 Tony Soprano's uncle Corrado is referred to by what nickname?

13 Michael "Mikey Grab Bag" Palmice shot and killed Brendan Filone when Filone was where?

14 Changing it from "Lollipop", what name did Adriana give the nightclub that she received as a gift from Christopher?

15 On account of his alopecia, what was Tony Soprano's nickname for Artie?

16 In the sixth season, Christopher and Little Carmine pitch Christopher's script, *Cleaver*, to which famous actor?

17 Who sends Tony Soprano an arrangement of flowers at the funeral parlour for his mother's funeral?

18 When he returned to New Jersey, Tony Blundetto was determined to live a legitimate life working as a what?

19 What was the name of Angie and Sal Bompenseiro's dog?

20 To what did a "box of Ziti" refer?

Answers to QUIZ 160 – Wine

1	Sangria	11	Shiraz
2	Fortified	12	Demijohn
3	New Zealand	13	Noble rot
4	Beaujolais Nouveau	14	Oz Clarke
5	Six	15	Amphorae
6	Terroir	16	Fiasco
7	Demeter	17	Rose bushes
8	12	18	Dionysus/Bacchus
9	The grapes are from the same year's harvest	19	Johnny Depp
10	Punt or kick-up	20	Cliff Richard

1 Until it was replaced by the euro, the *litas* was the monetary unit of which country?
2 South American, Mountain, Baird's and Malayan are the four extant types of which mammal?
3 Which Brian scored the first ever goal in the history of the Premier League?
4 *The Fast Show* character Dave Angel was introduced to the music of which Mike Oldfield song?
5 Henry IV deposed and replaced which monarch – his cousin – after they did not allow Henry to inherit the title of John of Gaunt?
6 Which US state is the only one to have a land border with only one other state?
7 In the name of the computer file type, what does RTF stand for?
8 In the *Teenage Mutant Ninja Turtles* franchise, who is the leader of the Foot Clan and the archenemy of the Turtles and Splinter?
9 How was Parisian photographer and visual artist Emmanuel Radnitzky better known?
10 A 1948 Alfred Hitchcock film shares its name with which *Cluedo*® murder weapon?
11 When a solid turns directly to a gas, bypassing the liquid phase, what process has occurred?
12 The Brenner Pass forms the border between which two countries?
13 Which computer game franchise is marketed under the slogan "The Real Driving Simulator"?
14 In the fairytale *Snow White*, what were the seven dwarfs mining for?
15 Tracy Thorn and Ben Watt formed which 1990s music duo?
16 With 22 competitive wins and four honorary wins, who, as of 2021, has won by far the most Academy Awards of any individual?
17 Which Italian-born British architect worked on the Pompidou Centre in Paris, the Lloyd's building and the Millennium Dome?
18 From which flower is the drug *digitalis* obtained?
19 In the world of online video gaming, what is an MMOG?
20 At the world-famous Cooper's Hill Cheese-Rolling and Wake annual event, which cheese is rolled?

Easy

Medium

Hard

Answers to QUIZ 161 – Pot Luck

1	John Newcombe	11	Trevi
2	The Iron Curtain	12	Architecture
3	Toes	13	Chubby Checker
4	Archery	14	Taoism
5	Kurt Vonnegut	15	Ambergris
6	Elsa Schiaparelli	16	Grape
7	Tea	17	20
8	Eileen Gu (gold in Big air and Halfpipe, silver in Slopestyle)	18	Tomatoes
		19	Laugh
9	Hong Kong Phooey	20	Rock Hudson
10	Slalom		

Easy

1. Torvill and Dean won gold at the 1984 Winter Olympics dancing to which one-movement piece by Maurice Ravel?
2. The works of which German composer of the late baroque period include *Air on the G String* and the *Goldberg Variations*?
3. *Clair de Lune* is a piano piece forming the third movement of *Suite bergamasque* by which composer?
4. In classical notation, what does the instruction *da capo* mean?
5. Which Russian composer wrote *Novorossiysk Chimes for Orchestra*, played daily in the namesake city?
6. *Karelia Music* is a work by which composer?
7. Which Puccini opera tells the story of how the Kingdom of Naples's control of Rome was threatened by Napoleon's invasion of Italy?
8. In Camille Saint-Saëns's *The Carnival of the Animals*, which instruments represent the kangaroos?
9. Which Baroque composer died of gangrene after stabbing himself in the foot with a baton?
10. The musical *Rent* is loosely based on which Giacomo Puccini opera?

Medium

11. Which Italian Baroque composer was known as "the red priest" (*il prete rosso*) due to his flaming red hair?
12. Which conductor always appeared on the podium wearing a carnation, earning him the derogatory nickname "Flash Harry"?
13. Ralph Vaughan Williams's *Symphony No 7*, and Peter Maxwell Davies's *Symphony No 8*, were both themed around where?
14. John Belushi, Ed Harris and Gary Oldman have all played which composer in film?
15. Yehudi Menuhin was a virtuoso on which instrument?
16. The eleventh of Edward Elgar's *Enigma Variations* was partially inspired by which animal?
17. Bach, Beethoven and Berlioz were the initial "Three Bs" as anointed by Peter Cornelius; who replaced Berlioz in the later list by conductor Hans von Bülow?
18. Which composer was derisively nicknamed "the little mushroom", as he was less than five feet tall?
19. Which New Zealand singer, who had a 2003 hit with the crossover album *Pure*, has sung in more than a dozen different languages?
20. The words to *Beethoven's Ninth Symphony* were taken from which poem by Friedrich Schiller?

Hard

Answers to QUIZ 162 – The Sopranos

1	James Gandolfini	11	Canada
2	Janice Soprano	12	Junior
3	Frank Vincent	13	In the bath
4	Steve Buscemi	14	*Crazy Horse*
5	David Chase	15	Prince Rogaine
6	Lorraine Bracco	16	Sir Ben Kingsley
7	HBO	17	The FBI
8	Zero	18	Massage therapist
9	*The Many Saints of Newark*	19	Cocoa
10	Furio Giunta	20	$1,000

ANSWERS ON PAGE 167

1   In 1963, less than two years before his death, who became the first ever honorary US citizen?

2   The Admiralty Islands, an archipelago group of 18 islands in the Pacific Ocean, are administered by which country?

3   Created by Steven Galanis, Martin Blencowe and Devon Spinnler Townsend, which website and app allows celebrities to send personalised video messages to fans?

4   "Directing her was like directing Lassie. You need 14 takes to get one of them right." So said Otto Preminger about which actress?

5   Cricket bats are traditionally made from which wood?

6   Although it has subsequently been extended several times, what was the original maximum length of a TikTok video?

7   Which country achieved independence in 1993 after breaking away from Ethiopia?

8   Which UK no.1 single does not mention the song title in its own lyrics, but does mention the title of the record that knocked it off the no.1 spot?

9   Which 16th century French astrologer and supposed oracle also published a recipe for an aphrodisiac called "Love Jam"?

10 LimeWire, Kazaa and Morpheus were all types of what sort of computer program?

11 The names of how many US states contain the letter U?

12 What are the only two extant egg-laying mammals?

13 Be it a fact or a myth, which toy – which dates back to the Ancient Greek civilisation – supposedly originated as a weapon for hunting game?

14 Someone *Sammarinese* comes from which European microstate?

15 Reportedly, music from which children's TV show was used by US officers as a form of torture at Guantanamo Bay?

16 Which keyboardist was a founding member of the Rolling Stones, but was dropped from the line-up for looking "too normal", and instead became a stagehand?

17 By population, what is the third largest democracy in the world, behind India and the USA?

18 In 1924, which French ski resort became the first to host the Winter Olympics?

19 Which of Shakespeare's plays features two sets of identical twins?

20 In *The Magic Roundabout*, what is Dougal's favourite food?

Easy

Medium

Hard

Answers to QUIZ 163 – Pot Luck

1	Lithuania	11	Sublimation
2	Tapir	12	Austria and Italy
3	Brian Deane	13	*Gran Turismo*
4	*Moonlight Shadow*	14	Diamonds
5	Richard II	15	*Everything But the Girl*
6	Maine	16	Walt Disney
7	Rich text format	17	Richard Rogers
8	Shredder	18	Foxglove
9	Man Ray	19	Massively multiplayer online game
10	*Rope*	20	Double Gloucester

Can you name these athletes, who have all won medals for Great Britain at the Olympic Games?

Easy

1

2

3

Medium

4

5

6

7

8

9

Hard

Answers to QUIZ 164 – Classical Music

1	*Bolero*	11	Antonio Vivaldi
2	Johann Sebastian Bach	12	Sir Malcolm Sargent
3	Claude Debussy	13	Antarctica
4	From the beginning	14	Ludwig van Beethoven
5	Dmitri Shostakovich	15	Violin
6	Jean Sibelius	16	A bulldog; he tried to replicate the sound of a dog falling into a river
7	*Tosca*		
8	Pianos	17	Brahms
9	Jean-Baptiste Lully	18	Franz Schubert
10	*La Bohème*	19	Hayley Westenra
		20	*Ode to Joy*

1   In 1557, which Chinese city was leased to the Portuguese, becoming the first European settlement in China?

2   Which chemical element has the symbol Sc?

3   In *The Dukes of Hazzard*, what make of car was the General Lee?

4   In NHL ice hockey, a "Gordie Howe hat trick" is an unofficial accomplishment in which a player records a goal, an assist and what, all in the same game?

5   Hickling, Barton and Martham are all lakes in which English national park?

6   In 2014, the Chinese city of Chongqing opened a lane for people doing what while walking?

7   Dying after only 119 days, which 1827 British Prime Minister had the total shortest period in office?

8   Panama hats originated in which country?

9   Which annual tennis tournament held in early and mid-March in California is often called "the fifth Grand Slam"?

10 On a professional-level squash ball, what colour are the two dots?

11 *Puffinus puffinus* is the scientific name of which bird?

12 Which former Arsenal and Sunderland footballer was nicknamed the Romford Pelé?

13 In law, what type of contract is established from the action and conduct of the parties, rather than stated in oral or written words?

14 What type of RAF aircraft takes its name from a person who engages in persistent attacks on others or incursions into their land?

15 Which actor and comedian made the first-ever withdrawal from a cash machine on 27th June 1967?

16 Often captioned "We can do it!" in a poster campaign, which icon of World War II represented and recruited women working in factories and shipyards?

17 Which Mars chocolate bar was once advertised with the slogan "What's got a Hazelnut in every bite?"

18 Take-Two Interactive develops which series of turn-based strategy games in which players attempt to build an empire to conquer the world?

19 In 1976, which became the only country to not win a single gold medal at a Summer Olympics where they were the host?

20 Actor Omar Sharif represented Egypt internationally at which card game?

Easy

Medium

Hard

Answers to QUIZ 165 – Pot Luck

1	Winston Churchill	11	Eight (Connecticut, Kentucky, Louisiana, Massachusetts, Missouri, South Carolina, South Dakota, Utah)
2	Papua New Guinea		
3	Cameo		
4	Marilyn Monroe	12	Platypus and echidna
5	Willow	13	Yo-yo
6	One minute	14	San Marino
7	Eritrea	15	*Barney & Friends*
8	*Bohemian Rhapsody* (knocked off by *Mamma Mia*)	16	Iain Stewart
9	Nostradamus	17	Indonesia
10	Peer-to-peer file sharing client	18	Chamonix
		19	*A Comedy of Errors*
		20	Sugar

Easy

1 "Reader, I married him" is a famous defiant line from which classic romance novel?

2 George Wickham and Charlotte Lucas are two side characters in which novel?

3 "Look after my heart; I've left it with you" is a quote from which teen fantasy-romance novel?

4 Which 1996 Nicholas Sparks novel tells the story of Allie, a dementia sufferer, who wrote about her love for Noah before she forgets?

5 Often seen in a pink chiffon gown and blonde wig, the books of which contemporary and historical romance author allegedly sold more than two billion copies?

6 Jilly Cooper wrote several romantic novels set in which fictional county?

7 Which Irish writer's works include *The Copper Beech* and *Circle of Friends*?

8 Whose works include *England's Perfect Hero*, *The Black Duke's Prize* and *The Devil Wears Kilts*?

9 Which 2003 Jill Mansell novel is a reworking of Romeo and Juliet?

10 In which novel by Fannie Flagg does Evelyn Couch, a middle-aged housewife, hear the love stories of Ninny Threadgoode, an elderly woman?

11 Who wrote the 1991 novel *Outlander*?

12 Which romance author was recognised by *Guinness World Records* for having a book on the New York Times Bestseller List for 381 consecutive weeks?

Medium

13 Between 1990 and 2019, the RITA Awards were the most prominent award for English-language romance fiction – what replaced them in 2021?

14 *Sweet Ermengarde*, a parody of romantic melodrama, was written by which aptly-named author?

15 The name of which US state derives from a 16th century romance novel about a mythical island populated solely by black women warriors?

16 Roughly 2.5 million old copies of *Mills & Boon* romance novels were pulped and used during the 2003 construction of which British motorway?

17 *The Tale of Two Lovers*, written in 1444, was written by a man called Aeneas Sylvius Piccolomini, who went on to become who/what?

18 In 2000, which man – slightly more famous in other fields – published an allegorical romance novel entitled *Zabiba and the King*?

19 What is different about the 1993 romance novel entitled *Just This Once*?

20 Which fast food chain released a 96-page romantic novella in 2017 entitled *Tender Wings of Desire*?

Hard

Answers to QUIZ 166 – British Olympians

1 Linford Christie
2 Victoria Pendleton
3 Tom Daley
4 Sharron Davies
5 Daley Thompson
6 Alan Wells
7 Alistair Brownlee
8 Justin Rose
9 Christine Ohuruogu

QUIZ 169 – Pot Luck

ANSWERS ON PAGE **171**

1   In 2019, *Forbes* magazine anointed who as the world's youngest self-made billionaire, but one year later released a statement accusing her of forging tax documents to inflate her wealth?

2   Which MP for Stratford-on-Avon replaced Gavin Williamson as Education Secretary in 2021?

3   Insulin, tubulin and myosin are all examples of which large, complex body molecules?

4   The "Galilean" moons of Io, Callisto, Europa and Ganymede orbit which planet?

5   The adjective *pluvial* refers to which sort of weather?

6   The black swan is native to which country?

7   The People's Eyebrow and The People's Elbow were signature moves of which wrestler turned actor?

8   The host country receives an automatic berth to the FIFA World Cup – until 2002, who else did?

9   Which late actor narrated the 1981 series of *Willo the Wisp*?

10 When they first laid eyes on a specimen sent over from Australia, British zoologists thought which unique animal species was a hoax?

11 Playing just his first Test match, which South African batsman faced 376 balls for 110 not out in the fourth innings to deny Australia victory in the 2012 Adelaide Test?

12 In betting parlance, what type of bet is placed at fixed odds before the runners are known on a horse or dog considered likely to be entered?

13 On what date, and in which year, was American Independence Day?

14 "Well, Clive, it's all about the two Ms – movement and positioning." So said which former football manager when working as a commentator for ITV?

15 Which film director, the director of many Laurel and Hardy films, died in 1992 aged 100?

16 Aside from one being ever so slightly longer, which two countries – one a European microstate, one in Asia – have identical flags?

17 A statue of which king riding a horse stands in London's Trafalgar Square?

18 What is the county town of Wiltshire?

19 Mount Ararat – a real-life dormant volcano mentioned in the Bible as being the resting place of Noah's Ark – is located in which country?

20 Magnetite is a common ore of which metallic element?

Easy

Medium

Hard

Answers to QUIZ 167 – Pot Luck

1	Macau	11	Manx Shearwater
2	Scandium	12	Ray Parlour
3	Dodge Charger	13	Implied-in-fact contract
4	A fight	14	*Harrier*
5	Norfolk Broads	15	Reg Varney
6	Using their phone	16	Rosie the Riveter
7	George Canning	17	Topic®
8	Ecuador	18	*Civilization*
9	Indian Wells	19	Canada (Montreal)
10	Yellow	20	Bridge

QUIZ 170 – Ghosts

ANSWERS ON PAGE 172

Easy

1 In Charles Dickens's *A Christmas Carol*, how many ghosts visit Ebenezer Scrooge on Christmas Eve?

2 In 1995, which friendly ghost became the first ever computer-generated character to star in a film?

3 In the 2016 all-female reboot of *Ghostbusters*, who played Dr Jillian "Holtz" Holtzmann?

4 Along with having three whole Shakespeare plays named for him, which English king also appears as a ghost in *Richard III*?

5 In the *Harry Potter* series, which ghost haunted the second-floor girls' bathroom at Hogwarts?

6 Which British children's TV comedy series centred on a company that hired out spirits for various tasks?

7 The ghost of Scratching Fanny was said to haunt which London street?

8 The spirit of Anne Boleyn, beheaded in 1536, is said to haunt which Norfolk residence?

9 Which seventeenth-century merchant ship, often called the world's best-known non-human ghost, is said to haunt the high seas?

10 What links the authorship of Mary Shelley's *Frankenstein*, Lord Byron's *Darkness* and John Polidori's *The Vampyre*?

Medium

11 Which two-tone band released the song *Ghost Town* in June 1981?

12 In which Penelope Lively fantasy novel is a boy plagued by the 17th century ghost of a magical sorcerer who does not want to leave?

13 "Thy bones are marrowless, thy blood is cold". So says which Shakespearean title character to Banquo's ghost?

14 With stairs to nowhere and multiple false toilets, which bizarre house in California was continuously built for 36 years to "confuse spirits"?

15 Which British spiritual medium was best known for his appearances on *Most Haunted* between 2002 and 2010?

16 One of the nicknames of which Welsh boxer was the "Ghost with the Hammer in His Hand"?

17 Called the "best car in the world" by *Autocar* magazine, the Silver Ghost was a 1906 car model made by which manufacturer?

18 Presented as live television, which one-off 1992 BBC paranormal pseudo-documentary attracted an estimated 1,000,000 calls from people who thought it was real?

Hard

19 Poes are ghosts in which video game series that is primarily set in the land of Hyrule?

20 In the vernacular of online dating, what is meant by "ghosting"?

Answers to QUIZ 168 – Romance Novels

1 *Jane Eyre*
2 *Pride and Prejudice*
3 *Twilight*
4 *The Notebook*
5 Barbara Cartland
6 Rutshire
7 Maeve Binchy
8 Suzanne Enoch
9 *Falling For You*
10 *Fried Green Tomatoes at the Whistle Stop Café*
11 Diana Gabaldon
12 Danielle Steel
13 Vivian Awards
14 H.P. Lovecraft
15 California
16 M6 Toll
17 Pope Pius II
18 Saddam Hussein
19 It was written by a computer to imitate the style of Jacqueline Susann
20 KFC

QUIZ 171 – Pot Luck

1 Which Cadbury chocolate bar was advertised on television by comedy duo Reeves and Mortimer with the slogan "it's slightly rippled with a flat under-side"?

2 Which MP for Richmond resigned as Trade and Industry Secretary in January 1986 over the Westland affair?

3 Which Houston-based rapper released her debut studio album *Good News* in 2020?

4 Which Canadian-American invented the game of basketball?

5 In the Netherlands between 1634 and 1637, a bubble saw the individual price of which flower skyrocket to roughly that of a mansion?

6 The historic rock and roll music venues The Filmore and Filmore West were located in which Californian city?

7 What was the name of the author Evelyn Waugh's first wife?

8 The lyrics of REM's *It's The End Of The World As We Know It (And I Feel Fine)* mention four men each with names starting with which two initials?

9 Slayer, Metallica, Megadeth and Anthrax are often considered the "Big Four" of which musical genre, a subgenre of heavy metal?

10 In which American city was Martin Luther King Jr. assassinated?

11 In baseball, what name is given to the feat of one player hitting a single, double, triple and a home run in the same game?

12 In the sphere of blockchain technology and cryptocurrency, what does the abbreviation NFT stand for?

13 Which prolific inventor and less-prolific businessman was nicknamed the Wizard of Menlo Park?

14 Vambrace, sabaton and cuirass are all parts of a what?

15 Julian Lloyd-Webber, Gay-Yee Westerhoff and Jacqueline du Pré all play or played which instrument?

16 Ophiology is the branch of zoology concerning the study of which animals?

17 The Denmark Strait separates which two landmasses, one of which makes up part of the country of Denmark, and the other of which used to?

18 Blunderbuss and arquebus are archaic forms of what?

19 In the English-speaking world, which unofficial unit of measurement is usually considered equal to three miles?

20 What does the Hebrew name prefix "Ben" mean?

Answers to QUIZ 169 – Pot Luck

1 Kylie Jenner
2 Nadhim Zahawi
3 Proteins
4 Jupiter
5 Rain
6 Australia
7 Dwayne "The Rock" Johnson
8 The defending champion
9 Kenneth Williams
10 Duck-billed platypus
11 François "Faf" du Plessis
12 Ante-post
13 4th July 1776
14 Ron Atkinson
15 Hal Roach
16 Monaco and Indonesia
17 George IV
18 Trowbridge
19 Turkey
20 Iron

1 In heraldry, an animal described as "passant" is doing what?

2 Sable is the term used in heraldry to describe which colour?

3 The heraldic term "gules", referring to the colour red, comes from the French *gueules*, meaning what?

4 On a heraldic shield, what is a vertical dividing line called?

5 If things in heraldry are "accosted", what position are they in?

6 A fylfot is a heraldic name for which symbol?

7 Officials who recorded and regulated the use of armorial bearings had what job title?

8 A person's social status can be determined from what part of their coat of arms?

9 A "bar sinister" or "bend sinister" – a broad diagonal stripe from top right to bottom left of a shield in a coat of arms – is said to imply what?

10 Humans, animals or objects placed on either side of a shield and depicted holding it up are known as what?

11 In English heraldry, what is the name given to variations of the original arms of a family, or marks attached to them for the purpose of pointing out branches?

12 In the heraldic symbols of the British royal family, what are the two most common poses for lions?

13 On which European microstate's coat of arms do the keys of Saint Peter appear?

14 A lion is depicted to signify dauntless courage; a bear, strength and cunning. What unlikely animal is intended to signify an invulnerability to attack?

15 There is a unicorn on the arms of Canada. Which other country does it represent?

16 A triangular wedge emerging from the upper edge of a shield and converging to a point near the base is known in heraldry as what?

17 What adjective, which in non-heraldic use means noticeable, is usually applied to a wild beast when borne as if leaping at his prey?

18 Which traditional floral heraldic emblem of England combined the roses of the competing Houses of Lancaster and York?

19 Seen in heraldry, which imaginary creature is represented as a vulture with the head and breast of a woman?

20 What term is used for the abbreviated description of a coat of arms?

Answers to QUIZ 170 – Ghosts

1 Four (Jacob Marley and the spirits of Christmas Past, Present and Future)
2 *Casper*
3 Kate McKinnon
4 Henry VI
5 Moaning Myrtle
6 *Rentaghost*
7 Cock Lane
8 Blickling Hall
9 *The Flying Dutchman*
10 They were all devised as the result of a challenge issued by Byron to see who could write the best ghost story one night when all three were stuck indoors together due to bad weather.

11 The Specials
12 *The Ghost of Thomas Kempe*
13 Macbeth
14 Winchester Mystery House
15 Derek Acorah
16 Jimmy Wilde
17 Rolls-Royce
18 *Ghostwatch*
19 *The Legend of Zelda*
20 Abruptly disappearing without reason or communication

1   In the late 13th century, which Eurasian empire grew to become the then-largest in history, and still ranks second behind only the British Empire?

2   In baseball, which is the only infield position that can be played left-handed?

3   In which Olympic sport do all of the different medal events take place over the same 2,000m course?

4   Which unit of distance is roughly equal to 5,878,625,370,000 miles?

5   Which scientist hosted the television show *Cosmos: A Personal Voyage*?

6   In optics, what is the opposite property of translucency?

7   T.J. Lavin, Dave Mirra and Mat Hoffman were among the most famous competitors in which Olympic sport?

8   Ponyboy and Sodapop are characters in which coming-of-age novel by S. E. Hinton, later made into a film by Francis Ford Coppola?

9   Kate and Helen Richardson-Walsh were an Olympic gold medal-winning married couple that competed in which team sport?

10   Which African lake is the largest in the world to share its name with a national capital city?

11   In 2019, who became the first knighted individual to win the Rear of the Year competition?

12   In Elisabeth Kübler-Ross' five-stage model of grief, what is the second stage, after denial?

13   In 1963, who became the first – and, as of 2021, only – goalkeeper to win the Ballon D'Or?

14   The Iraqi capital Baghdad is split in half by which river?

15   Due to her 1971 decision to withdraw free milk in school for children over eleven, which Education Secretary was derisively nicknamed "Milk Snatcher"?

16   Abel Magwitch is a major fictional character from which Charles Dickens novel?

17   In the British Army ranks, what comes between Colonel and Major General?

18   Thomas, Henry and Albert Pierrepoint all worked what now-obsolete job?

19   Matt Bellamy, Chris Wolstenholme and Dominic Howard founded which rock band in 1994?

20   Adge Cutler was the original frontman of which band?

Easy

Medium

Hard

Answers to QUIZ 171 – Pot Luck

1	Boost	11	Hitting for the cycle
2	Leon Brittan	12	Non-fungible token
3	Megan Thee Stallion	13	Thomas Edison
4	James Naismith	14	Suit of armour
5	Tulip	15	Cello
6	San Francisco	16	Snakes
7	Evelyn – among their friends, they became known as "He-Evelyn" and "She-Evelyn"	17	Greenland and Iceland
		18	Gun
8	LB (Leonard Bernstein, Leonid Brezhnev, Lenny Bruce, Lester Bangs)	19	League
		20	"Son of"
9	Thrash		
10	Memphis		

1. 19th May 1925 saw the births of both civil rights activist Malcolm X and which tyrannical leader of an East Asian country?

2. On 17th March 1975, the same day as will.i.am, which *Desperate Housewives* actress was born?

3. Angelina Jolie and Russell Brand were both born on 4th June of which year?

4. Sylvester Stallone shares 6th July 1946 as a birthday with which man, the 43rd President of the USA?

5. 14th March 1933 saw the births of which actor with the real name Maurice Mickelwhite, and which record producer with the middle name Delight?

6. Actor and director Jason Bateman shares a 14th January 1969 birthday with the drummer of Nirvana and lead singer of the Foo Fighters; name either.

7. Name either the former Israeli Prime Minister or boogie-woogie pianist to be, born on 26th February 1928.

8. 30th November 1955 saw the births of football pundit Andy Gray and which singer, real name William Broad?

9. On 10th April 1992, which Senegalese international striker and *Star Wars* actress were both born?

10. On the same day as football manager Louis Van Gaal, 8th August 1951, which director of *Meet Joe Black* and *Gigli* was born?

11. Electronic musician Moby was born on 11th September 1965, as was Bashar al-Assad, the President of where?

12. Which legend of leg spin was born 13th September 1969, the same day as Tyler Perry?

13. Actress Debra Winger was born on 16th May 1955, as was which woman, one of the most influential gymnasts of all time?

14. Name either of the famous Johns – one a wrestler, one a comedian – born on 23rd April 1977.

15. David Attenborough was born on 8th May 1926, the same day as which insult comic, nicknamed "Mr Warmth" by Johnny Carson?

16. Christmas Day 1957 saw the births of which Irish singer and which football player turned pundit?

17. *Cousin Skeeter* actress Meagan Good was born on 8th August 1981, the same day as which male tennis record-setter?

18. Actor David Threlfall was born on 12th October 1953, the same day as which entertainer, born Leslie Heseltine?

19. Savant Kim Peak was born on 11th November 1951, the same day as which South African golfer, known invariably by a nickname?

20. Teenager Kyle Rittenhouse, who fatally shot two men and became a pariah for US gun rights, was born on 3rd January 2003, as was which activist with the middle name Tintin?

Answers to QUIZ 172 – Heraldry

1	Walking	11	Marks of cadency
2	Black	12	Rampant and passant
3	Gullet or throat	13	Vatican City
4	Pale	14	Tortoise
5	Side by side	15	Scotland (the unicorn is the national animal of Scotland)
6	A cross with perpendicular extensions, i.e. a swastika shape	16	A pile
7	Heralds	17	Salient
8	The helm, atop the shield	18	Tudor Rose
9	Illegitimacy	19	Harpy
10	Supporters or attendants	20	Blazon

Easy

Medium

Hard

1   Pinkie, Dallow and Spicer are all characters in which 1938 Graham Greene novel?

2   *Songs in A Minor* was the debut studio album by which singer-songwriter-pianist?

3   What name is given to any polyhedron with twelve flat faces?

4   In 2020, which comedian briefly changed his name to Hugo Boss?

5   Johnny Cash, Waylon Jennings, Willie Nelson and Kris Kristofferson formed which country supergroup?

6   When a butterfly is in a cocoon and in its pupa stage, what is it called?

7   The name of which prominent Apache leader was used as the name for the US's special operation to seize Osama Bin Laden?

8   In 1990, what became Elton John's first solo UK no.1 single?

9   Who was the first woman to win *TIME Magazine*'s Person of the Year Award (still known as Man of the Year at the time)?

10 Bradley Walsh and Rod Stewart both spent time as youths with which football club?

11 What did Aristotle call "The Master Science"?

12 Who wrote, directed and starred in the 1967 British slapstick comedy film *The Plank*?

13 Which US mail service, using relays of horse-mounted riders with 186 stations, each ten miles apart, operated between Missouri and California in 1860 and 1861?

14 Whose fifth symphony became known as the "*Victory Symphony*", and coincidentally has its first four notes mimicking the Morse code for V?

15 Bunny Ears, Old Lady and Saguaro are all types of what plant?

16 Which German-American pianist, composer, and conductor of jazz and classical music was known to British comedy audiences as "Mr Preview"?

17 Which golfer finished fourth in the 1998 US Open as an amateur, then missed his first 21 cuts as a pro, but later won the 2016 Olympic gold medal?

18 Which animated fish is praised for being one of the few accurate portrayals of neurological anterograde amnesia (inability to form new memories)?

19 Archimedes (after entering a bath and seeing the water rise) and Isaac Newton (after an apple landed on his head) both reportedly shouted which word?

20 Which iconic Alaskan winter event is an annual dogsled race run in March between Anchorage and Nome?

Easy

Medium

Hard

Answers to QUIZ 173 – Pot Luck

1	Mongol Empire	11	Sir Andy Murray
2	First base	12	Anger
3	Rowing	13	Lev Yashin
4	A light year	14	Tigris
5	Carl Sagan	15	Margaret Thatcher
6	Opacity	16	*Great Expectations*
7	BMX racing	17	Brigadier
8	*The Outsiders*	18	Executioner
9	Field hockey	19	Muse
10	Lake Victoria (Victoria is the capital of Seychelles)	20	The Wurzels

Easy

1. In which month of the Islamic calendar do Muslims not eat and drink during daylight hours?
2. Starting daily at 8am, which animals are let loose to run the streets during the Festival of San Fermin in Pamplona, Spain?
3. Which Scottish city has annual festivals for jazz, books, film, art, science and children, as well as a highly successful "fringe"?
4. Nirvana Day, falling annually on 15th February, commemorates the death of which religious leader?
5. Which iconic music festival was billed "an Aquarian exposition" and "three days of peace and music"?
6. Originating in 1968, which annual event was the first music festival in the UK?
7. Ja Rule regrettably endorsed which 2017 fraudulent luxury music festival founded by con artist Billy McFarland on the Bahamian island of Great Exuma?
8. Tons and tons of which fruit are thrown in a big food fight at which annual festival held in the Valencian town of Buñol?
9. The annual Bayreuth Festival celebrates the music of which 19th century composer?
10. Conceived of to promote national recovery, in which year was the Festival of Britain held?

Medium

11. Known also the Festival of Lights, which annual festival is celebrated by Hindus, Jains and Sikhs alike?
12. An American classical music festival based in New York City celebrates the music of "Mostly..." who?
13. What is equal parts a Renaissance fair, a Celtic festival, a musical festival, a literary festival and "the supreme exhibition of the Welsh culture"?
14. Also known as the Festival of Spring, Holi is a festival in which religion?
15. What is the highly unusual "aim" of the Japanese festival of *Naki Zumo*?
16. The Waldo Salt Screenwriting Award is handed out annually at which annual event in Park City, Utah?
17. Attracting approximately 800,000 people annually, which Wisconsin-based festival promotes itself as "The World's Largest Music Festival"?
18. Why was *T in the Park* almost cancelled in 2015?
19. Originally at least, what is *Oktoberfest* a celebration of?
20. During the Esala Perahera festival in Sri Lanka, Buddha's tooth is carried around in a casket on the back of what animal?

Hard

Answers to QUIZ 174 – Born on the Same Day

1. Pol Pot
2. Eva Longoria
3. 1975
4. George W. Bush
5. Michael Caine and Quincy Jones
6. Dave Grohl (same guy)
7. Ariel Sharon or Fats Domino
8. Billy Idol
9. Sadio Mane and Daisy Ridley
10. Martin Brest
11. Syria
12. Shane Warne
13. Olga Korbut
14. John Cena or John Oliver
15. Don Rickles
16. Shane MacGowan and Chris Kamara
17. Roger Federer
18. Les Dennis
19. Fuzzy Zoeller ("Fuzzy" coming from his full name, Frank Urban Zoeller)
20. Greta Thunberg

1. Which actor played Dumbledore in the first two *Harry Potter* movies because his granddaughter vowed never to talk to him again if he declined the role?
2. Shetlands, Chalfonts and Belindas all refer to which affliction in Cockney rhyming slang?
3. In 1991, which actor allegedly stole flowers from train robber Buster Edwards' flower stall for his girlfriend and *Press Gang* co-star Julia Sawalha?
4. Glass Joe, King Hippo and Bald Bull are opponents in which critically acclaimed 1980s video game?
5. With a name meaning "eight standing together", how many islands make up the country of Tuvalu?
6. Juan Catalan's 2003 murder conviction was overturned when it transpired he had an alibi as an accidental background character in which Larry David sitcom?
7. Which singer has had 23 singles chart in the UK as a secondary artist or part of a group, but only 1984's *Somebody Else's Guy* as a solo hit?
8. In 1998, a particularly red cultivar of rhubarb was named after which then-topical politician?
9. Which is the shortest Olympic running race for which a bell is rung to signify the start of the final lap?
10. Nicolas Cage won a Best Actor Oscar for his performance as a suicidal alcoholic in which 1995 film?
11. As of 2021, Len Hutton remains the only person in Test cricket history to be given out in which unusual way?
12. *At Home with the Braithwaites*, *Last Tango in Halifax* and *Happy Valley* were all created by which screenwriter?
13. In 2010, which Finnish legend became the first footballer to have played international football in four different decades?
14. On 1st November 1947, Ossie Schectman scored the first two points in the history of which sports league?
15. *Don't Dream It's Over* and *Weather With You* were hits for which Australian rock band?
16. Which English actress made her film debut in *The Falling* before taking more prominent roles in *Fighting with My Family* and *Little Women*?
17. A character named Nerissa appears in which Shakespeare play?
18. Which comic strip was based on the life of a Melchester Rovers striker?
19. Montezuma I and II were respectively the second and ninth emperors of which ancient empire?
20. A sliotar is the ball used in which sport?

Easy

Medium

Hard

---

1   Jerome K. Jerome wrote an 1889 comic travelogue about how many men in a boat?

2   The *Cutty Sark* was built to carry what sort of cargo?

3   What was the name of Captain Nemo's underwater ship in Jules Verne's *Twenty Thousand Leagues Under the Seas*?

4   Master's mate Fletcher Christian led the famous mutiny on which ship?

5   On a ship, what are the scuppers?

6   Of the three ships (*Santa Maria*, *Niña* and *Pinta*) on Christopher Columbus's first transatlantic expedition, which one did not return, running aground on Christmas Day and broken up for materials?

7   What 'R' is the system of ropes or chains employed to support a ship's masts and to control the yards and sails?

8   What is a "painter" on a boat?

9   On an anchor, what are the triangular flat faces with pointed bills that dig into the ground called?

10   On 13th January 2012, which Italian cruise ship struck an underwater rock, capsized and sank, resulting in 32 deaths?

11   At night, what colour light is shown on the port side of a ship?

12   The Yellow Jack signal flag was historically used to signify a vessel was, or might be, harbouring a dangerous disease. What did it later come to signify?

13   What is the distance between the waterline and the gunwale called?

14   Which former British Royal Navy minesweeper was converted into a research vessel and used by oceanographic researcher Jacques Cousteau?

15   The annual Varsity Boat Race course runs between Putney and which suburban district of Richmond-upon-Thames?

16   In Bram Stoker's *Dracula*, to which North Yorkshire port town does the ship bring Dracula?

17   The clipper ship was replaced by a yacht in the logo of which toiletry brand in February 1992?

18   On 16th March 1978, which oil tanker ran aground off the coast of Brittany?

19   What was the name of the lead boat in a fleet of three robotic lithium battery–powered Autosub Long Range autonomous underwater vehicles commissioned in 2016?

20   The *Queen Mary*, *Queen Elizabeth* and *Queen Elizabeth II* liners were all built in which Scottish shipyards?

Answers to QUIZ 176 – Festivals

1	Ramadan	11	Diwali
2	Bulls	12	"…Mozart"
3	Edinburgh	13	National Eisteddfod of Wales
4	Buddha	14	Hinduism
5	Woodstock	15	To make babies cry
6	Isle of Wight Festival	16	The Sundance Film Festival
7	Fyre	17	Summerfest
8	Tomatoes	18	A pair of ospreys returned to their long-term roost on the site
9	Richard Wagner	19	The royal wedding of King Ludwig I
10	1951	20	Elephant

1   In the 1999-2000 season, who became the only Englishman to ever win the European Golden Boot?

2   Which is the only UK Parliamentary constituency to contain a J in its name?

3   Poppit Sands is at the northern end of which UK National Park?

4   On 30th November 2021, the England women's football team beat Latvia by what score line?

5   What type of meat is used in the Italian dish *osso buco*?

6   Which 1986 film is the only sequel that Martin Scorsese has directed in his career, 25 years after Robert Rossen directed the forerunner *The Hustler*?

7   What does the acronym for the disease AIDS stand for?

8   Who became the first athlete to both light the Olympic cauldron and win a gold medal at the same games?

9   In film, who are the characters Pete Mitchell and Nick Bradshaw better known as?

10 What element was first discovered on the Sun during an eclipse in 1868 and was not found on Earth until 1895?

11 Which is the only London Underground station whose name does not contain any of the letters from the word "underground"?

12 Cinnabar, Bogong and Dingy Footman are species of which animal?

13 Many of which country's postage stamps feature the word *Magyar*?

14 Many of the events in *Treasure Island* take place on which boat, which shares its name with an island divided into two nations?

15 Where on a horse is its poll?

16 Florence Nightingale came to prominence as an army hospital nurse and trainer during which war?

17 Formerly known as On A Friday, which English rock band took their new name from a song by Talking Heads?

18 The United Nations' headquarters are found in which city?

19 In the 2000-01 season, which Portuguese football team broke up the run of 54 consecutive titles won by either Benfica, Sporting Lisbon or Porto?

20 The elderly characters Statler and Waldorf, known for their cantankerous heckling, feature in which sketch comedy ensemble?

Easy

Medium

Hard

Answers to QUIZ 177 – Pot Luck

1	Richard Harris	11	Obstructing the field
2	Haemorrhoids (as in "Piles"; Shetland Isles, Chalfont St Giles, Belinda Carlisles)	12	Sally Wainwright
		13	Jari Litmanen
3	Dexter Fletcher	14	The NBA
4	*Mike Tyson's Punch-Out!!*	15	Crowded House
5	Nine (it was named before the ninth was discovered)	16	Florence Pugh
		17	*The Merchant of Venice*
6	*Curb Your Enthusiasm*	18	*Roy of the Rovers*
7	Jocelyn Brown	19	Aztec
8	Ken Livingstone	20	Hurling
9	800m		
10	*Leaving Las Vegas*		

If you know your knit stitches from your purls, perhaps you can identify these stitching patterns.

1

2

3
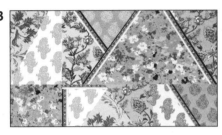

4

5

6

7

8
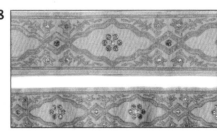

Answers to QUIZ 178 – Boats and Ships

1	Three	11	Red
2	Tea	12	The complete opposite – no disease aboard
3	*Nautilus*	13	Freeboard
4	HMS *Bounty*	14	*Calypso*
5	Holes in the side to allow water to run off the deck	15	Mortlake
6	*Santa Maria*	16	Whitby
7	Rigging	17	*Old Spice*
8	A rope attached to the bow of a boat for tying it to a quay	18	*Amoco Cadiz*
9	Flukes	19	*Boaty McBoatface*
10	*Costa Concordia*	20	John Brown & Company, Clydebank

QUIZ 181 – Pot Luck

ANSWERS ON PAGE 183

1. On the Beaufort scale, what number represents a "fresh breeze"?
2. The films *Blade Runner*, *Total Recall* and *Minority Report* were all based on books by which author?
3. Herbie Hancock, Skinny Hightower and Fats Waller all played which instrument?
4. Which 18th century smuggler and folk hero is often called the "Robin Hood of France"?
5. Jarlsberg cheese originated in which country?
6. Because of its abundant red sandstone, red clay and red chalk buildings, which Moroccan city is nicknamed the Red City?
7. The renminbi is the currency of which country?
8. What hairstyle was Bo Derek credited with making "cross-cultural" when she wore it in the movie *10*?
9. Bruce Willis played a time traveller in which 1995 film?
10. As well as being the fourth-longest river in the continent, which is the longest east-flowing river in Africa?
11. Which Radio 1 DJ was nicknamed the Big Hairy Cornflake?
12. *Cider with Rosie*, *As I Walked Out One Midsummer Morning* and *A Moment of War* are an autobiographical trilogy of novels by which author?
13. Born in Wales, who is the only British Prime Minister whose first language was not English?
14. By starring in *Avatar*, *Avengers: Infinity War* and *Avengers: Endgame*, which actress had appeared in three of the five highest-grossing films of all time as of 2021?
15. ASLEF is a trade union representing workers in which industry?
16. Weddell, ribbon and crabeater are types of which marine mammal?
17. What verb can mean to transport, or the desire to see two specific characters become a couple?
18. Which Burmese Nobel Peace Prize winner spent 15 of the 21 years between 1989 and 2010 under house arrest?
19. On 1st December 1955, which African-American activist refused to give up her seat on the bus to a white passenger in Montgomery, Alabama?
20. Which actress recruited many others to perform an online version of *Imagine* to raise morale during the COVID-19 pandemic, but instead mostly got ridicule?

Easy

Medium

Hard

Answers to QUIZ 179 – Pot Luck

1. Kevin Phillips
2. Jarrow
3. Pembrokeshire Coast
4. England 20 – 0 Latvia
5. Veal
6. *The Color of Money*
7. Acquired Immune Deficiency Syndrome
8. Cathy Freeman, Sydney 2000
9. Maverick and Goose (from *Top Gun*)
10. Helium
11. Balham
12. Moth
13. Hungary
14. Hispaniola
15. Head; it is the bony highest part, behind the ears
16. Crimean War
17. Radiohead
18. New York City
19. Boavista
20. The Muppets

1   The 2,000th star on the Hollywood Walk of Fame was awarded to which Italian actress?

2   Which singing cowboy is the only person to have a star in all five Walk of Fame categories?

3   Which of the Disney Princesses has a star on the Walk of Fame?

4   On Walk of Fame stars, what emblem is used to represent the theatre/live performance category?

5   Listed in the initial group of 500 before being rejected due to character concerns, which actor is the only person to be selected twice for the same star?

6   All living Walk of Fame honourees have since 1968 been required to attend their star's unveiling – which actress-singer-director is the only one that failed to appear?

7   One of only two characters named on their star alongside their actors, Clayton Moore played which fictional western character throughout the 1950s?

8   Which boxer's Walk of Fame star is the only one mounted to a wall rather than the floor, as he did not want his name to be stepped on?

9   Which two US presidents have stars on the Hollywood Walk of Fame?

10 Despite not traditionally meeting the criteria, which NBA legend has a star on the Walk of Fame on account of owning a theatre chain?

11 What links the stars of Julia Louis-Dreyfus, Dick Van Dyke and Mauritz Stiller?

12 In addition to the entire line-up having a star, which two Muppets characters also have individual stars on the Hollywood Walk of Fame?

13 Six members of which family acting dynasty have stars on the Walk of Fame?

14 For which role are the largest group of individuals – an estimated 122 adults and 12 children – represented by a single star?

15 On the walk of fame, a steel art installation entitled *Hollywood and La Brea Gateway* depicts which actress in an iconic pose?

16 Which Spanish singer's Hollywood Walk of Fame star is kept in pristine condition by a devoted band of elderly women?

17 Which man – the director of *The Defiant Ones* and *It's a Mad, Mad, Mad, Mad World* – was the first honouree to have his star laid *permanently*?

18 In 2004, which acting siblings became not only the youngest ever recipients of a star, but also the only twins to share a singular star?

19 Name either of the two novelists to have stars on the Hollywood Walk of Fame.

20 Why was a Southern Californian talk radio host's star covered in flowers and candles in June 2009?

Easy

Medium

Hard

Answers to QUIZ 180 – Needlework

1   Cross stitch
2   Crochet
3   Patchwork
4   Smocking
5   Berlin wool work
6   Cutwork
7   Crewelwork
8   Passementerie

1 What derogatory term was popularised by Mao Zedong to refer to something or someone that appears powerful, but is actually ineffectual?

2 What term is used for a woman employed to provide guidance and support to the mother of a new-born baby, or during the birth?

3 The words *Kaiser* and *Czar* both derive from which name, which became a synonym for Emperor in the Roman Empire?

4 If someone is phlegmatic, how are they acting?

5 Which librarian and educator was so driven by efficiency that he dropped two "redundant" letters from his first name?

6 Which 2019 Taika Waititi comedy-drama film tells the story of a Hitler Youth member who discovers a Jewish girl hiding in their home?

7 Which stock sound effect has been used in more than 400 films and TV shows since 1951, including many blockbusters?

8 Which member of *The Goodies* appeared as a computer operator in *Willy Wonka & the Chocolate Factory*?

9 The Canadian city of London, Ontario, stands on the confluence of which river?

10 Which stuffed toy range emerged as a major collectible during the 1990s not only as toys, but also as a financial investment?

11 Which island's land area is split between Indonesia, Malaysia and Brunei?

12 Joanna Trollope is the fifth-generation niece of which other author?

13 Prior to its dissolution, what was the currency of Yugoslavia?

14 To which category of instruments does the piano belong?

15 Which film and media production company has been advertised since its inception by Leo the lion?

16 In which film does Roger Murtaugh revoke Arjen Rudd's diplomatic immunity?

17 Which South American singer recorded the official 2010 FIFA World Cup Song, *Waka Waka (This Time For Africa)*?

18 Who played Daisy Duke in the original TV series of *The Dukes of Hazzard*?

19 Which alternative Latin name for the Lord's Prayer also gives its name to a type of continuous passenger elevator?

20 The brand "Old Jamaica" is associated with which type of drink?

Easy

Medium

Hard

Answers to QUIZ 181 – Pot Luck

1	Five	11	Dave Lee Travis
2	Philip K. Dick	12	Laurie Lee
3	Piano	13	David Lloyd-George
4	Louis Mandrin	14	Zoe Saldana
5	Norway	15	Train drivers (Associated Society of Locomotive
6	Marrakesh		Engineers and Firemen)
7	China	16	Seal
8	Cornrows	17	Ship
9	*12 Monkeys*	18	Aung San Suu Kyi
10	Zambezi	19	Rosa Parks
		20	Gal Gadot

Easy

1   Which former international cricketing star became Prime Minister of Pakistan in 2018?

2   Which former international footballing star became President of Liberia in 2018?

3   In 2018, Xavier Bettel became the world's first openly gay Prime Minister to win a second term when he was re-elected in which country?

4   Which man proved so popular playing the part of the President of Ukraine in a TV series that he later actually became it?

5   Yoweri Museveni has served as President of which East African country since 1986, removing his constitution's own age and term limits to do so?

6   Which country's President, Gurbanguly Berdimuhamedov, is oddly obsessed with breaking world records?

7   Which President of the Philippines openly campaigned on a pledge to kill millions of drug addicts, and compared himself to Hitler?

8   At aged 34, Sanna Marin became the world's youngest Prime Minister in December 2019 when she was elected as the head of which country?

9   By what nickname was the former President of Haiti, Francois Duvalier, better known?

10 In China, pictures of which children's character are heavily censored, due to their derisory use as a lookalike for President Xi Jinping?

11 Lasting only one month in the job, who in 1841 became the first United States president to die in office?

12 Which country's head of state lives in what is known as the "Blue House"?

13 Sirimavo Bandaranaike became the world's first female Prime Minister in 1960 when she was elected to head which country?

14 Which former German Chancellor's name essentially translates to "healthy cabbage"?

15 Winston Churchill once said that which French President "looks like a female llama who has just been surprised in her bath"?

16 Which former British Prime Minister was a cousin of Rudyard Kipling?

17 "This man has a nice smile, but he has got iron teeth." So said foreign minister Andrei Gromyko about which former USSR President?

18 Which Prime Minister was assassinated on 31st October 1984 by her own bodyguards?

19 On 6th April 1994, the presidents of which two African countries were killed after their aircraft was shot down?

20 Which US President used the campaign slogan "Keep Cool"?

Medium

Hard

Answers to QUIZ 182 – Hollywood Walk of Fame

1   Sophia Loren
2   Gene Autry
3   Snow White
4   Comedy/tragedy masks
5   Charlie Chaplin
6   Barbra Streisand
7   *The Lone Ranger*; the other star is for the Betty Lou character of radio comic, Tommy Riggs
8   Muhammad Ali
9   Ronald Reagan and Donald Trump
10 Magic Johnson

11 They were all initially misspelt; in Stiller's case, the error remained for 28 years
12 Kermit the Frog and Big Bird
13 Barrymore (John, Ethel, John Drew, Drew, and two for Lionel)
14 The Munchkins
15 Marilyn Monroe
16 Julio Iglesias
17 Stanley Kramer
18 Mary-Kate and Ashley Olsen
19 Sidney Sheldon and Ray Bradbury
20 His name was Michael Jackson, and fans were laying their tributes at the wrong star

QUIZ 185 – Pot Luck

ANSWERS ON PAGE **187**

1   What name was given by Allied troops in the South Pacific during World War II to all female English-speaking radio broadcasters of Japanese propaganda?

2   William the Conqueror, Charlemagne and King Edmund were all crowned on which already-significant day?

3   Which Scottish market town is nicknamed "Queen of the South" and plays host to the football team of the same name?

4   With his name also found as the surname of footballer Leon and TV presenter Richard, who was the founder of the Ottoman Empire?

5   In 2018, Arsenal football club entered into a marketing deal with which east African country's government?

6   British forces engaged in the Battle of Tora Bora in December 2001 gave the caves which nickname in honour of a tabloid socialite?

7   Which 400 metre hurdler won 122 consecutive races between 1977 and 1987?

8   Which Indian tea is made by boiling tea leaves with milk, sugar and optional spices, including cinnamon and cardamom?

9   Schubert's eighth, Beethoven's tenth and Borodin's third are all symphonies better known as what?

10 Prague was built on the banks of which river?

11 Which 82-mile linear earthwork roughly follows the border between England and Wales and was originally built to divide Powys and Mercia?

12 The Forbidden City is a palace complex in which modern-day Asian city?

13 Vocalist Ian McCulloch, guitarist Will Sergeant and bassist Les Pattinson were the original members of which band?

14 In Edgar Allen Poe's poem *The Raven*, what is the only word that the titular raven says?

15 Who directed the film *Almost Famous* based on his own experiences as a reporter for *Rolling Stone* magazine in the 1970s?

16 Usually, how many counters does each player have at the start of a game of backgammon?

17 Thomas Chippendale was an 18th century designer and maker of what?

18 Which country uses the international vehicle registration code "E"?

19 Which actor played the 9-year-old Cole Sear in *The Sixth Sense*?

20 In 1982, which company, notable for founding the football pools, was the largest private company in Europe?

Answers to QUIZ 183 – Pot Luck

1	Paper tiger	11	Borneo
2	Doula	12	Anthony Trollope
3	Caesar	13	Dinar
4	Calmly	14	Percussion – although it is full of strings, it is
5	Melville "Melvil" Dewey, the inventor of the		played via a strike
	Dewey Decimal System	15	Metro-Goldwyn-Meyer (MGM)
6	Jojo Rabbit	16	Lethal Weapon 2
7	Wilhelm Scream	17	Shakira
8	Tim Brooke-Taylor	18	Catherine Bach
9	River Thames (fittingly)	19	Paternoster
10	Beanie Babies®	20	Ginger beer

1   Located in the Pacific Ocean, what is the deepest oceanic trench on Earth?

2   It is estimated that which area of Antarctica has not seen rain in two million years?

3   The highest registered air temperature on Earth was 56.7°C, recorded in which American national park?

4   Not including the poles, parts of which desert have not seen rain for 500 years and are the driest places on Earth?

5   What geographical honour is held by the Russian city of Norilsk?

6   Which volcanic island in the South Atlantic Ocean is the most remote point on Earth inhabited by humans?

7   Which is the world's highest free-standing mountain (i.e. not part of a wider range)?

8   The surface of what is 430.5 metres below sea level, thus making it the lowest point on dry land?

9   Which is further away from sea level; the world's highest point, or the world's lowest?

10 What term is given to the region around much of the rim of the Pacific Ocean where many volcanic eruptions and earthquakes occur?

11 Which Eurasian capital city is the lowest-lying national capital in the world?

12 Which country has both the most rainfall of any country, and also the highest degree of biodiversity?

13 Lying on the border of Bolivia and Peru in the Andes, which is the world's highest navigable lake?

14 In July 2007, which TV presenting duo claimed to be the first people in history to reach the 1996 location of the north magnetic pole by car?

15 Which African desert is the world's oldest sand desert and has the highest sand dunes on the planet?

16 Despite lying in the South Atlantic between South Africa and Antarctica, Bouvet Island – the world's most remote – was annexed by which European nation?

17 Which city with a population of more than a million is furthest away from any other city with a population of more than a million?

18 Because the Earth is not a perfect sphere and bulges at the equator, the peak of which Andean stratovolcano is the farthest point on the Earth's surface from the Earth's centre?

19 Which is the only country in the world that is situated on all four main hemispheres?

20 Which is the easternmost town in the United Kingdom?

Answers to QUIZ 184 – International Heads of State

1	Imran Khan	11	William Henry Harrison
2	George Weah	12	South Korea
3	Luxembourg	13	Sri Lanka (then known as Ceylon)
4	Volodymyr Zelensky	14	Helmut Kohl
5	Uganda	15	Charles de Gaulle
6	Turkmenistan	16	Stanley Baldwin
7	Rodrigo Duterte	17	Mikhail Gorbachev
8	Finland	18	Indira Gandhi
9	Papa Doc	19	Rwanda (Juvénal Habyarimana) and Burundi (Cyprien Ntaryamira)
10	Winnie the Pooh	20	Calvin Coolidge

QUIZ 187 – Pot Luck

ANSWERS ON PAGE 189

1. Tom Joad is the protagonist of which John Steinbeck novel?
2. In *Lady and the Tramp*, what breed of dog is Lady?
3. Which Scottish town is the northernmost one on the British mainland?
4. The idiom "bought the farm" means to have done what?
5. Jess Hayes and Max Morley were the winning couple on which 2015 reality dating game show?
6. The phrase "warts and all" – an instruction to his portrait artist to paint him faithfully – is attributed to who?
7. Who is the author of the 2012 book *Gone Girl*?
8. Dulcimers, zithers and psalteries all belong to which family of instruments?
9. Vänern and Vättern are the two largest freshwater lakes in which European country?
10. Blossom, Bubbles and Buttercup are artificially-made superhuman kindergartners better known as who?
11. The first Olympic Games held outside of Europe took place in which American city?
12. How many members sit on a jury in Scotland?
13. In 2016, Hasbro, the makers of *Cluedo*, announced they would be introducing a new character, Dr Orchid, to replace which of the original six?
14. Which musical comedy using puppets (including one of Gary Coleman) has been praised for its approach to themes of racism and homosexuality?
15. An important plot point in which zombie film involves going to *The Winchester*, having a nice cold pint and waiting for it all to blow over?
16. How many musicians perform in a duodecet?
17. Which member of a famous acting dynasty starred in many films including *Jackie Brown* and *Single White Female*, before retiring in 2002 aged 38?
18. *Girl with a Pearl Earring* is one of the 34 surviving paintings attributed to which artist?
19. Condyles are rounded protrusions on the end of what?
20. The scaphoid, lunate, triquetrum, trapezoid, trapezium, capitate, hamate and pisiform are the eight small carpal bones that make up what part of the body?

Answers to QUIZ 185 – Pot Luck

1. Tokyo Rose
2. Christmas Day
3. Dumfries
4. Osman
5. Rwanda
6. Tora Bora Tomkinson (after Tara Palmer-Tomkinson)
7. Ed Moses
8. Chai
9. *Unfinished Symphony*
10. Vltava
11. Offa's Dyke
12. Beijing
13. Echo & the Bunnymen
14. "Nevermore"
15. Cameron Crowe
16. 15
17. Furniture
18. Spain
19. Haley Joel Osment
20. Littlewoods

1   How many dancers take part in a *pas de deux*?
2   Prince Siegfried is the hero in which ballet?
3   The name of which dance derives from the French word for "duck"?
4   With a nickname widely known through a Jerry Jeff Walker song, which tap dancer once held the world speed record for running backwards?
5   Bean Setting, Leap Frog and Laudnum Bunches are types of which dance style?
6   "The dancer's body is simply the luminous manifestation of the soul" is a quote often attributed to which American dancer?
7   Airbaby, jackhammer and 2000 are all moves in which style of dance?
8   Which man, the pre-eminent male classical dancer of the 1970s and 1980s, cameoed in *Sex and the City*?
9   Which Brazilian dance is based on the African Batuque?
10 Which female dancer and star of *Singin' in the Rain* insured her legs for $5 million?
11 Which Gaelic social events are noted for Scottish or Irish folk music and singing, traditional dancing and storytelling?
12 Which actor danced in the music video for Fatboy Slim's single *Weapon of Choice*?
13 The 1237 dancing mania outbreak among German children is said to have been an inspiration for which legendary story?
14 In ballet, what does the term *tombe* mean in English?
15 Burlesque dancer Sally Rand was known for her performances of which dance?
16 Which member of the Rat Pack was noted for his skills as a tap dancer?

17 Jon Heder performed a famous uncut dance finale in which cult comedy movie?
18 "The Carlton", a nerdy arms-heavy dance invariably performed to Tom Jones's *It's Not Unusual*, originated in which TV show?
19 Of the 32 that have them, what dance do 24 US states list as their official "state dance"?
20 In the Bible, Salome demanded what part of John the Baptist's body as a reward for her dancing?

Answers to QUIZ 186 – Extreme Places on Earth

1	Mariana Trench, and in particular, the Challenger Deep	11	Baku
2	McMurdo Dry Valleys	12	Colombia
3	Death Valley	13	Lake Titicaca
4	Atacama Desert	14	Jeremy Clarkson and James May
5	World's northernmost city	15	Namib
6	Tristan de Cunha	16	Norway
7	Mount Kilimanjaro	17	Auckland, New Zealand
8	Dead Sea	18	Chimborazo
9	The lowest – Challenger Deep is 10,929m down, while Mount Everest is 8,848m up	19	Kiribati
10	Ring of Fire	20	Lowestoft

1. Fashion chain H&M originated in which European country?
2. Scotland's first new town in May 1947 was which town, the largest in South Lanarkshire?
3. *Coronation Street*'s iconic *Rovers Return* pub was (fictionally) listed for sale by which online estate agent in 2021, whose signage could be seen outside it?
4. Which heroine of Shakespeare's *Twelfth Night* shares her name with a stringed instrument?
5. Which British comedian recorded a 2001 TV show in which he set out to find and meet 54 people that shared his name?
6. *Mossad* is the secret intelligence service of which country?
7. The important naval passage, the Strait of Magellan, runs through which country?
8. Who directed most of *The Wizard of Oz*, but left towards the end of production to take over the troubled *Gone With The Wind*?
9. The Disney film *Tangled* is a retelling of which classic fairy tale?
10. What colour is pure liquid oxygen?
11. What was E.T.'s favourite candy/chocolate bar?
12. In chess, which is the only piece that can be captured without its square being directly landed on?
13. Belize, Guatemala and Mexico can all be found on which peninsula?
14. As of 2021, which animal gives its name to the first and youngest section of the Scouts?
15. Which unit of mass is abbreviated CT?
16. Not including the end zones, how many yards long is an American Football pitch?
17. Which actor cameos as himself in *Zombieland*, providing refuge to the main characters?
18. The Old Man From Scene 24 and The Black Beast of Aaaaargghh are characters from which 1975 comedy film?
19. What kind of animal are the cartoon characters Pinky and the Brain?
20. Which is the only NBA team that Larry Bird ever played for?

Easy

Medium

Hard

Answers to QUIZ 187 – Pot Luck

1	*The Grapes of Wrath*	11	Saint Louis, 1904
2	Cocker spaniel	12	15
3	Thurso	13	Mrs White
4	Died	14	*Avenue Q*
5	*Love Island*	15	*Shaun of the Dead*
6	Oliver Cromwell	16	12
7	Gillian Flynn	17	Bridget Fonda
8	String	18	Johannes Vermeer
9	Sweden	19	Bones
10	*The Powerpuff Girls*	20	Wrist

Easy

1. *Uncle Tom's Cabin; or, Life Among the Lowly* is a 19th century anti-slavery novel by which American author?
2. Edward Prendick's ship rammed some debris and sank in which H.G. Wells work?
3. Which Irish poet's works include *The Second Coming, Death* and *Leda and The Swan*?
4. The idiom "full of the milk of human kindness" originated in which Shakespeare play?
5. What was the name of Robert Jordan's epic series of 15 books, 704 total chapters and 4.4 million words?
6. Which Charles Dickens novel features the lawyer Mr Jaggers?
7. Which 2005 work by Bill Bryson was widely acclaimed for its accessible communication of science?
8. Who wrote the 2012 dystopian novel *Shades of Grey*, in which social standing is determined by the ability to see colours?
9. Which doctor, author, presenter and advice columnist has written several books on health, including the *Children's Medical Handbook*?
10. Nick Carraway is a fictional character in and the narrator of which 1925 novel?

Medium

11. A satire on the power of the church set in Spain during the Inquisition, which was W. Somerset Maugham's last published novel?
12. Which ancient Greek playwright is often referred to as "the Father of Comedy" and "the Prince of Ancient Comedy"?
13. Sidonie-Gabrielle were the first names of which French novelist, better known by a monomym?
14. The 1881 novel *The Prince and the Pauper* was which author's first attempt at historical fiction?
15. Who wrote the classic 1936 children's novel *Ballet Shoes: A Story of Three Children on the Stage*?
16. *The Cat Who...* is a series of twenty-nine mystery novels featuring a reporter named Jim Qwilleran and his Siamese cats, written by which author?
17. The subtitle of which 1897 H. G. Wells novel reads "A Grotesque Romance"?
18. What novel by Richard Wright tells of Bigger Thomas, a 20-year-old African American living in a Chicago slum who accidentally kills his white employer's daughter?
19. Svengali is a man who seduces, dominates and exploits the title character in which 1895 George du Maurier novel?
20. Prior to his comedy career, which Brighton-based stand-up comedian wrote erotic fiction and performed street juggling?

Hard

Answers to QUIZ 188 – Dance

1	Two	11	Ceilidhs
2	*Swan Lake*	12	Christopher Walken
3	Can-Can	13	*Pied Piper of Hamelin*
4	Bill "Bojangles" Robinson	14	Fall
5	Morris dances	15	Fan dance
6	Isadora Duncan	16	Sammy Davis Jr
7	Breakdancing	17	*Napoleon Dynamite*
8	Mikhail "Misha" Baryshnikov	18	*The Fresh Prince of Bel-Air*
9	Samba	19	Square Dance
10	Cyd Charisse	20	Head

1   What is secreted from sudoriferous glands?

2   *Pac-Man*, *Dirty Harry* and *Clint Eastwood* are all songs by which virtual band?

3   Set on and around the Ponderosa ranch, which TV Western series centres on the wealthy Cartwright family?

4   In 1999, Tony Hawk completed the first ever '900' in which trick-based action sport?

5   Which Disney character first appeared in a Mickey Mouse short in 1932 under the name "Dippy Dawg"?

6   What was the name of the first man in Britain to receive a vaccination for the COVID-19 virus, a name much better known as that of an author and poet?

7   Which US President popularised the expression "the buck stops here", keeping a sign with it written on at his desk?

8   Antarctica is the only continent, and Iceland the only country, to not have any species of which flying insect?

9   Which Australian tennis player gave up tennis for a year in 2015 and played professional cricket, despite her never having played cricket before?

10   The Victoria Falls lie on which African river?

11   Which World War II flying ace claimed at least 23 aerial victories, despite not having any legs?

12   Who wrote the novella *Breakfast at Tiffany's*?

13   In the 2021/22 series, who became the first player to take the most wickets in three consecutive Ashes?

14   The only two square national flags in the world belong to the Vatican City and which other European country?

15   Other than the six main stars of the *Friends* cast, who is the most regular character to appear on the show?

16   Which basketball legend plays co-pilot Roger Murdock in *Airplane!*?

17   Obelisks in Central Park, New York and on the Victoria Embankment in the City of Westminster, London share what name?

18   Who directed *The Dark Knight*?

19   How many loaves of bread is it traditional to have on the table on Shabbat?

20   In *Phone Booth*, which actor plays the caller, whose voice is heard throughout, but who only appears in a brief scene at the end of the film?

Easy

Medium

Hard

Answers to QUIZ 189 – Pot Luck

1	Sweden	11	Reece's Pieces
2	East Kilbride	12	Pawn, via *en passant*
3	Purplebricks	13	Yucatan
4	Viola	14	Squirrel
5	Dave Gorman	15	Carat
6	Israel	16	100
7	Chile	17	Bill Murray
8	Victor Fleming	18	*Monty Python and the Holy Grail*
9	*Rapunzel*	19	Mice
10	Blue	20	Boston Celtics

Easy

1 Whose post-war "New Look" revolutionised women's dress and contributed to the reestablishment of Paris as the centre of the fashion world?

2 Focusing on contemporary trends, Emporio is the second brand created by which Italian fashion family?

3 In 1994, Tom Ford became creative director of which high-end Italian luxury fashion house?

4 The maxim of which French fashion designer was, "luxury must be comfortable, otherwise it is not luxury"?

5 Although best known for his "prairie style" architecture, which designer once quipped that he was almost always black and blue from his own furniture?

6 Which American architectural firm designed the Empire State Building?

7 Coco Chanel and Jean Patou were instrumental in mainstreaming which fashion item, whose advent coincided with that of the Ford Model T car?

8 Francis Ford Coppola made a 1988 film about which car designer, who created the "48", better known as "The Torpedo"?

9 Kenneth Parker's 1939 design of the "Parker 51" became a status symbol – what was a Parker 51?

10 Called the "Queen of Prep", which American designer of brightly coloured dress prints got started when she needed clothes to hide fruit juice stains?

Medium

11 American designer Michael Taylor's extensive use of white walls and natural materials created which look, named for a US state?

12 A 2005 CBS reality show called *The Cut* saw candidates compete *Apprentice*-style for a job with which designer, famous for his red, white and blue sportswear?

13 After production improvements reduced costs by 80%, which light metal, through its ubiquity, became widely associated with the 1930s modernist style?

14 In addition to something much more famous, which Baltic-German jeweller also designed cigarette boxes and carved animals?

15 Dorothy Draper was an anti-minimalist interior decorator whose bright, exuberant colours and large prints on plasterwork saw her credited with the invention of what style?

16 Which Finnish-American designer is best known for his *Womb* and *Tulip* styles of chair, as well as the Gateway Arch in St Louis, Missouri?

17 Which British fashion photographer and interior designer won Oscars for his costume designs for both *Gigi* and *My Fair Lady*?

18 Which fashion designer was alleged to have had an affair with Winston Churchill?

19 What device, with both medical and recreational uses, was first invented in 1833 by Scottish physician Neil Arnott, but not patented until 1971 by Charles Hall?

20 Peter Foy designed the "inter-related pendulum" to create the illusion of stage-flying for which 1954 West End musical?

Hard

Answers to QUIZ 190 – Literature

1	Harriet Beecher Stowe	11	*Catalina*
2	*The Island of Doctor Moreau*	12	Aristophanes
3	W.B. Yeats	13	Colette
4	*Macbeth*	14	Mark Twain
5	*The Wheel of Time*	15	Noel Streatfield
6	*Great Expectations*	16	Lilian Jackson Braun
7	*A Short History of Nearly Everything*	17	*The Invisible Man*
8	Jasper Fforde	18	*Native Son*
9	Miriam Stoppard	19	*Trilby*
10	*The Great Gatsby*	20	Simon Evans

1. Which luxury liner departed on her maiden voyage from Southampton on 27th May 1936?
2. Which American stand-up comedian was arrested seven times for obscenity in the 1960s, one more occasion than he ever appeared on television?
3. Which American author said "Habit is habit, and not to be flung out of the window by any man, but coaxed down-stairs one step at a time"?
4. Juliana became the queen of which European country in 1948, ruling until her abdication in 1980?
5. Although he himself did not think highly of them, which religious movement of Jamaican origin views activist and journalist Marcus Garvey as a prophet?
6. In pre-decimal currency, how many florins were there in a pound?
7. With 14 neighbouring countries, which country has the most borders?
8. Morwongs and lumpsuckers are what type of animal?
9. On an Ordnance Survey map, a red triangle represents what type of establishment?
10. In 1976, the village of Yambuku in the Democratic Republic of Congo was the scene of the first recorded case of which disease, named for a nearby river?
11. Which geothermal spa in south west Iceland has the same name as a 1980 movie starring Brooke Shields and Christopher Atkins?
12. Liberia, the USA and Myanmar are the only three countries in the world not to have officially adopted what?
13. Muruntau, a mine in Uzbekistan's Qizilqum Desert, is the world's largest open-pit mine of which precious metal?
14. What is secreted from lacrimal glands?
15. Which of the apostles asked to be crucified upside-down?
16. In the lyrics of a Johnny Cash song, who, in Gatlinburg in mid-July, stopped for a brew at an old saloon on a street of mud?
17. Of the three Winter Olympic "sliding" sports, which is the slowest?
18. Which man, the 36th President of the USA, was nicknamed "Light Bulb" because of his reported enthusiasm for turning out the White House lights every night?
19. Which NBA legend starred in the 2021 film *Space Jam 2: A New Legacy*?
20. What is the name of the singer and guitarist frontman of the Fun Lovin' Criminals?

Easy

Medium

Hard

Answers to QUIZ 191 – Pot Luck

1	Sweat	11	Douglas Bader
2	Gorillaz	12	Truman Capote
3	*Bonanza*	13	Pat Cummings
4	Vert skateboarding	14	Switzerland
5	Goofy	15	Gunther
6	William Shakespeare	16	Kareem Abdul-Jabbar
7	Harry S. Truman	17	*Cleopatra's Needle*
8	Mosquito	18	Christopher Nolan
9	Ashleigh Barty	19	Two
10	Zambezi	20	Kiefer Sutherland

Can you identify both halves of these famous double acts?

Easy

1

2

3

Medium

4

5

6

7

8

9

Hard

Answers to QUIZ 192 – Designers

1	Christian Dior		11	California Look
2	Armani		12	Tommy Hilfiger
3	Gucci		13	Aluminium
4	Coco Chanel		14	Gustav Fabergé
5	Frank Lloyd Wright		15	Modern Baroque
6	Shreve, Lamb & Harmon		16	Eero Saarinen
7	Little Black Dress		17	Cecil Beaton
8	Preston Tucker		18	Lady Doris Castlerosse
9	A pen		19	Waterbed
10	Lilly Pulitzer		20	*Peter Pan*

1   Who was the mother of King James I of England?

2   The line "Give me your tired, your poor, your huddled masses yearning to breathe free" from a sonnet by Emma Lazarus can be found inscribed on which landmark?

3   Which theoretical physicist was known as the "father of the atomic bomb"?

4   Savile Row in London is a road known for its abundance of what type of business?

5   Who became President of France in May 1995, succeeding François Mitterand?

6   Which planet was visited by the space probe MESSENGER in 2011 after seven years of travel?

7   Dendrophilia refers to having an attraction to what?

8   Libya has borders with Chad, Algeria, Tunisia, Egypt, Sudan and which other country?

9   The first ever Tony award for Best Musical was awarded in 1949 to which Cole Porter production, based on a Shakespeare play?

10   In *Beauty and The Beast*, Lumière is turned into a what?

11   *Atonement*, *Enduring Love* and *Amsterdam* are all novels by which author?

12   French, Butterfly, The Spiderman and Eskimo are all types of what action?

13   A figure of Abe Mitchell, a British golfing legend from the 1920s, can be found on the top of which golfing trophy?

14   Who won the 1976 Eurovision Song Contest for the UK with *Save Your Kisses For Me*?

15   Busbies and Glengarries are both worn on which part of the body?

16   Which British writer coined the phrase "Youth is the most beautiful thing in this world – and what a pity that it has to be wasted on children!"?

17   The Adnams brewery is based in which English county?

18   What type of animal is Jean de Brunhoff's literary character Babar?

19   How many events take place in a tetrathlon?

20   Odontology is the scientific study of the structures and diseases of what?

Easy

Medium

Hard

1   The Isle of Man is famous for its TT motorcycle race. What does TT stand for in this context?
2   Which is the Isle of Man's capital and main seaport?
3   The Great Snaefell Mines primarily produced which metal?
4   What is the name of the northernmost point on the Isle of Man?
5   As the crow flies, what is the nearest country of the United Kingdom to the Isle of Man?
6   Which international online gaming company has headquarters in the town of Onchan on the Isle of Man?
7   "Morrey Mie" is a Manx Gaelic way to say what?
8   Island folklore holds that on 30th April, residents should fix a wooden cross bound with sheep's wool inside their front door. Why?
9   Similar to hurling and shinty, what is the national sport of the Isle of Man?
10 Who won the Isle of Man's only gold medal at the 2006 Commonwealth Games?
11 Which 1275 battle resulted in the Isle of Man falling under Scottish control?
12 Where on the Isle of Man is the so-called Moddey Dhoo or Black Dog ghost the most famous resident?
13 Which comedian lived for 27 years in a house in Andreas, a village on the Isle of Man, and not in Albania?
14 What is the second-largest town on the Isle of Man, behind Douglas?
15 Which BBC radio DJ and presenter was sentenced to three months' imprisonment in 2008 in the Isle of Man for breaching a restraining order?
16 The Great Laxey Water Wheel is also known by which woman's name?
17 Which marsupial species now lives in the wild on the Isle of Man after two of them escaped from a wildlife park in the Curraghs?
18 As of the Isle of Man Food & Drink Festival 2018, what has been crowned the Manx national dish?
19 In June 2021, after a change in the law, the government of the Isle of Man began to offer licenses for production and export of what?
20 Dying in 1265, who was the last Norse King of Mann?

Answers to QUIZ 194 – Double Acts

1   Morecambe and Wise
2   Laurel and Hardy
3   Smith and Jones
4   French and Saunders
5   Little and Large
6   Thelma and Louise
7   Vincent Vega and Jules Winnfield
8   Key and Peele
9   Hale and Pace

ANSWERS ON PAGE **199**

1   Kong Qiu – also anglicised as K'ung Fu-tzu – was the real name of which Chinese philosopher, to whom the quote "only the wisest and stupidest of men never change" is often attributed?

2   Sine, cosine and tangent are terms used in which branch of mathematics that studies angles and distance?

3   A gun can be found on the national flag of which African Commonwealth country, a former Portuguese colony?

4   By surface area, which is the largest Scottish loch?

5   The Pomeranian dog breed takes its name from a region in the northwest of which European country?

6   Which mountain range forms the border between Europe and Asia?

7   Created by L.L. Zamenhof, which is the most widely-spoken "artificial" language?

8   After taking up a career as a novelist after years as a journalist and translator, Mary Ann Evans wrote under male-sounding pen name?

9   Which prolific English romance novelist married two men with the surname McCorquodale?

10   Which six-time world snooker champion became a techno DJ in retirement, performing under the name "DJ Thundermuscle"?

11   What title is used by the wife of a Marquess?

12   Which former First Lady of the United States opened a range of addiction clinics in her name?

13   Which UK river rises near Syresham in Northamptonshire, flows through Buckinghamshire and Bedfordshire, and drains into The Wash?

14   Although becoming a US citizen in 1951, Greta Garbo was born and raised in which European country?

15   Which football team play their home games at the Madejski Stadium?

16   Figaro, Stromboli and Geppetto are all characters in which Disney film?

17   From low to high, which notes are the four strings on a violin normally tuned to?

18   CH is the international vehicle registration code for which country?

19   Galeophobia is a fear of which marine creatures?

20   Denzel Washington's first film as director was which 2002 work, in which he also co-starred?

Easy

Medium

Hard

Answers to QUIZ 195 – Pot Luck

1	Mary, Queen of Scots	11	Ian McEwan
2	The Statue of Liberty	12	Kissing
3	J. Robert Oppenheimer	13	The Ryder Cup
4	Tailors	14	Brotherhood of Man
5	Jacques Chirac	15	The head
6	Mercury	16	George Bernard Shaw
7	Trees	17	Suffolk
8	Niger	18	Elephant
9	*Kiss Me, Kate*	19	Four (shooting, swimming, riding and running)
10	Candelabra	20	Teeth

ANSWERS ON PAGE 200

Easy

1. While their true identity has never been discovered, who – be they an individual or a group of people – is the named founder of bitcoin?

2. Started as a joke, which meme coin features the Shiba Inu dog as a logo and became accepted by Tesla for merchandise sales in 2021?

3. Which electronic information storage technology enables the existence of cryptocurrencies?

4. The name of which animal is used to refer to individuals or entities that hold large amounts of bitcoin, and thus the power to manipulate its value?

5. Which Central American country was the first to grant bitcoin legal tender status?

6. What name is given to any cryptocurrency whose value is tied to an underlying reserve asset, usually a paper currency?

7. What term is used for the process that verifies and adds new transactions to the blockchain for a currency that uses the proof-of-work method?

8. In crypto terminology, an investor who has low risk tolerance and exits a trade at the first sign of risk is said to have what weird type of body part?

9. A group of crypto fans purchased an original work by which artist, only to burn it and sell a digitised version for four times its original value?

10. The smallest denomination of bitcoin is 0.00000001, a unit known as a what?

Medium

11. In January 2021, a man who lost a hard drive with $300 million in Bitcoin on it was refused help in finding it. Where did the hard drive end up?

12. In 2021, which sports league launched the *Top Shot* range of officially licensed collectible NFTs showcasing the best moments from its games?

13. Ross Albricht, known as "Dread Pirate Roberts", was sentenced to life in jail for running which darknet marketplace, where narcotics were bought with cryptocurrency?

14. Instead of proof-of-work, greencoins use what other mechanism to verify transactions on its blockchain?

15. What was the previous name of the famous Los Angeles sporting venue that was renamed the Crypto.com Arena in 2021?

16. In crypto culture, which term that began as a forum typo has become a mantra for a long-term approach to cryptocurrency investing?

17. How many confirmations is considered the safe amount for a bitcoin transaction?

18. What name is given to a wallet that requires two or more keys to send a transaction?

19. Which Japanese coin exchange folded in 2014 after roughly 850,000 bitcoins went missing and were likely stolen, worth approximately $450 million?

20. What is the maximum amount of bitcoins that can ever exist?

Hard

Answers to QUIZ 196 – Isle of Man

1	Tourist Trophy	11	Battle of Ronaldsway
2	Douglas	12	Peel Castle
3	Zinc	13	Norman Wisdom
4	Point of Ayre	14	Ramsey
5	Scotland – its nearest point is only 17 miles away	15	Andy Kershaw
6	PokerStars	16	"Lady Isabella" after the wife of the island's governor at the time it was built
7	"Good morning"	17	Red-necked wallaby
8	To ward off malevolent spirits	18	Queen scallops, or "queenies"
9	Cammag	19	Cannabis
10	Mark Cavendish, cyclist	20	Magnus Olafson

1   Amid protests, Princess Mako left which country's Royal family in 2021 in order to marry a commoner?

2   What everyday (or at least should be everyday) household item did English entrepreneur William Addis invent in 1780?

3   An international summit of which inter-governmental political forum was held at Carbis Bay in Cornwall in June 2021?

4   In which event at the 2020 Olympics did two contestants from two different countries agree to a first-place tie, rather than enter sudden death?

5   Which magic trick was first performed by magician P. T. Selbit on 17th January 1921 at the Finsbury Park Empire theatre in London?

6   "Never a lender nor a borrower be" is a quote from which Shakespeare play?

7   Phrenology, a debunked pseudoscience, involved attempting to identify a person's personality traits by "reading" the contours of which part of their body?

8   The "Glorious Twelfth", marking the first day of the grouse shooting season, falls on the twelfth day of which month?

9   At which English racecourse is the St Leger Stakes run?

10 Although he died from drowning, who was the only member of the Beach Boys that actually surfed?

11 Which 1972 erotic drama film starring Marlon Brando and Maria Schneider was banned in multiple countries?

12 Mario Puzo won the Academy Award for Best Screenplay with the first screenplay he ever wrote, for which film?

13 Which actor, the highest-grossing live-action star of all time, was also an usher at Martin Luther King Jr's funeral?

14 Which Pink Floyd album starts with the words "...we came in?" and ends with the words "Isn't this where...", so as to create an endless loop?

15 What type of bird featured in Guinness® adverts for almost 50 years?

16 Which car marque has used the slogan "The Ultimate Driving Machine" since the 1970s?

17 A periorbital haematoma is more commonly known as what?

18 Blue Mountain coffee comes from which country?

19 In American politics, which animal is used as the symbol for the Democratic party?

20 Which textile is produced from the yarn of the Angora goat?

Easy

Medium

Hard

Answers to QUIZ 197 – Pot Luck

1	Confucius	11	Marchioness
2	Trigonometry	12	Betty Ford
3	Mozambique	13	River Great Ouse
4	Loch Lomond	14	Sweden
5	Poland	15	Reading
6	The Urals	16	*Pinocchio*
7	Esperanto	17	G, D, A, E
8	George Eliot	18	Switzerland
9	Barbara Cartland	19	Sharks
10	Steve Davis	20	*Antwone Fisher*

Easy

1   Which stout was advertised for several years on television using the phrase "Good for you"?

2   Defying its own name, which beer brand reported a 40% increase in UK sales in 2020?

3   What fruit flavouring is used in the Belgian beer, Kriek?

4   The county of Rutland was home to which brewer until 1999?

5   Per the results of a 2019 Kirin Beer University report, which European country drinks, by far, the most beer per annum?

6   What American beer advertises itself as "The King of Beers"?

7   Cobra® beer originated in which country of the Commonwealth?

8   On a German beer bottle, what does *in der Flasche gereift* mean?

9   Which cask size, equivalent to 16-18 gallons, is the unit of choice of CAMRA for calculating beer quantities for festivals in the UK?

10 The 1516 *Reinheitsgebot* regulations governing the ingredients in German beer permitted only which three ingredients to be used?

11 Which beer brand produced Elvis Juice beer until 2020, despite a series of court cases with Elvis Presley's estate?

12 If someone older than 18 but younger than 21 is caught with beer in Arkansas, what, in addition to a fine, is their unusual punishment?

13 Which former world leader once held the world record for downing a yard of ale in the quickest time, a mere 11 seconds?

14 The iconic red triangle of which brewer's logo became the UK's first registered trademark?

15 An annual festival event held since 1974 in which country sees competitors race boats made out of empty beer cans?

Medium

16 Which viscous, beer-like Mexican beverage is made from the fermented sap of the *maguey* plant?

17 Which saint – the "mother saint" of Ireland – is the miracle of turning water into beer attributed to?

18 In ancient Sumerian religious mythology, who was the goddess of beer?

19 Which gas is inside the pressurised widget in a can of beer?

20 In 2021, Alix Blease became head brewer at Gritchie, an independent brewer founded by which film director?

Hard

Answers to QUIZ 198 – Cryptocurrencies

1	Satoshi Nakamoto	11	In a landfill
2	Dogecoin	12	NBA
3	Blockchain	13	The Silk Road
4	Whale	14	Proof-of-stake
5	El Salvador	15	Staples Center
6	Stablecoin	16	Hodl (pronounced to rhyme with "yodel")
7	Mining	17	Six
8	"Paper hands"	18	Multisig
9	Banksy	19	Mt. Gox
10	Satoshi, often shortened to sat	20	21 million

1 The Monmouth Rebellion was a 1685 royal coup attempting to unseat which monarch from the British throne?

2 In which African country is the continent's northernmost point?

3 In 2019, Cressida Cowell, author of the *How to Train Your Dragon* series, was awarded which honorary literary position?

4 What was the full name of the Charles Dickens character, the Artful Dodger?

5 Which Indian state, with the capital Vasco da Gama, was in 1961 the last part of Portuguese India to return to Indian control?

6 Which Thames river crossing lies between Vauxhall Bridge and Westminster Bridge?

7 In which decade was the Irish Potato Famine?

8 Which cult surreal film begins with The Criminologist saying the line "I would like, if I may, to take you on a strange journey"?

9 Tommy Vercetti, Carl Johnson and Niko Bellic are all protagonists in which video game series?

10 Martin Luther King Day is celebrated on the third Monday of which month?

11 An *embouchure* is formed with the mouth to be able to play which family of instruments?

12 Which Austrian composer was known as both "Father of the Symphony" and "Father of the String Quartet"?

13 Which Greek philosopher was sentenced to death by drinking hemlock for corrupting youthful minds and for not believing in the gods of the state?

14 Initially awarded by Columbia University, which award is given across 22 categories in journalism, letters and the arts?

15 Which British polymath co-wrote the *Principia Mathematica* series on the foundation of mathematics, as well as authoring *The Problems of Philosophy*?

16 The Menai Strait divides Anglesey from which mainland Welsh county?

17 What is the national flower of Mexico?

18 Sharing its name with a small animal, what is the SI unit for substance?

19 The Giant's Causeway consists of which type of igneous rock?

20 Situated roughly 30 miles west of the Mendips, which hill range in Somerset was designated the UK's first Area of Outstanding Natural Beauty in 1956?

Easy

Medium

Hard

Answers to QUIZ 199 – Pot Luck

1	Japan	11	*Last Tango in Paris*
2	Toothbrush	12	*The Godfather*
3	The G7	13	Samuel L. Jackson
4	Men's high jump	14	*The Wall*
5	Sawing a woman in half	15	Toucan
6	*Hamlet*	16	BMW
7	The skull	17	Black eye
8	August	18	Jamaica
9	Doncaster	19	Donkey
10	Dennis Wilson	20	Mohair

1 Which Hungarian-born food critic (1915-2010) is said to have raised the standards of British cuisine via his column in *The Daily Telegraph*?

2 During the Great Fire of London, what items did diarist Samuel Pepys bury in his garden to save them from the fire?

3 In 2021, which British television personality launched his own brand of lager named Hawkstone?

4 Which spirit is added to the non-alcoholic Shirley Temple cocktail to make it a "Dirty Shirley"?

5 *Caboc* is a Scottish variant of which food?

6 Pomology is the study of growing what?

7 Which drink's name originated from the Arabic word *qahwa*?

8 In Spanish and Mexican cuisine, what are *albondigas*?

9 Chantenay, Nantes and Danvers are types of which root vegetable?

10 Which fruit is also known as the alligator pear?

11 Bananas grow in bunches that are also known as what?

12 What was Desperate Dan's favourite food?

13 Bok Choy is a Chinese cultivar of which vegetable?

14 Roquefort cheese is made from the milk of which animal?

15 Saffron spice is derived from the flower of which plant?

16 Which chocolate bar has been advertised under the slogan "Why have cotton when you can have silk"?

17 *Adzuki* or *aduki* is a type of what?

18 McVitie's® went to court in 1991 to argue that which of their products was in fact what its name said it was, and not a biscuit?

19 What are onions studded with in a bread sauce?

20 Which Iberian soup made of raw, blended vegetables is served cold?

Easy

Medium

Hard

Answers to QUIZ 200 – Beer

1	Guinness®	11	Brewdog
2	Corona®	12	They might be ordered to write an essay about alcohol
3	Cherry		
4	Ruddles	13	Bob Hawke, former Australian Prime Minister
5	Czech Republic	14	Bass®
6	Budweiser®	15	Australia
7	India	16	*Pulque*
8	Matured in the bottle	17	Saint Brigid of Kildare
9	Kilderkin	18	Ninkasi
10	Water, hops and barley	19	Nitrogen
		20	Guy Ritchie

QUIZ 203 – Pot Luck

ANSWERS ON PAGE **205**

1. What type of light, found in sunlight, has a wavelength shorter than visible light but longer than X-rays?
2. In which fictional village is *Postman Pat* set?
3. Which country is the only one to have a national flag which is neither square nor rectangular?
4. Which country won the first FIFA Women's World Cup in 1991?
5. How many balls are used in a game of Quidditch?
6. When Rudolf Dassler split from his brother Adolf's company, Adidas®, which rival sportswear brand did he go on to found?
7. Which rock family is composed of rocks that have been changed by heat, pressure or chemicals?
8. Consensus holds that the mid-to-late 1990s are the starting birth years and the early 2010s are the ending birth years of which demographic cohort?
9. Which organ filters and stores blood to protect against infection and blood loss?
10. Rugby and Tewkesbury are among the towns standing on which river?
11. Quito is the capital of which South American country?
12. In what decade did Louis Bleriot make the first powered flight across the English Channel?
13. If a bingo caller shouted "Duck and Dive", what number would they be calling?
14. Which two of Henry VIII's wives outlived him?
15. Who did Justin Welby succeed as Archbishop of Canterbury in 2013?
16. Which famous scientist once wrote, "Life is like riding a bicycle. To keep your balance you must keep moving."?
17. What colour is the 'L' in the Google logo?
18. Which full-length 2015 Pixar animated movie is set in the mind of a young girl called Riley Andersen?
19. Tiffi, Mr Toffee, Mr Yeti and Odus the Owl are all characters in which popular mobile game series?
20. What were the two first names of writer P.L. Travers, author of the *Mary Poppins* books?

Answers to QUIZ 201 – Pot Luck

1	James II	11	Brass
2	Tunisia	12	Joseph Haydn
3	Children's Laureate	13	Socrates
4	Jack Dawkins	14	Pulitzer Prize
5	Goa	15	Bertrand Russell
6	Lambeth Bridge	16	Gwynedd
7	1840s	17	Dahlia
8	*The Rocky Horror Picture Show*	18	Mole
9	*Grand Theft Auto*	19	Basalt
10	January	20	Quantocks

1   Previously nomadic, Aztec society finally settled in the early 14th century in which present-day country?

2   Which Spanish conquistador led the 16th century expedition that caused the fall of the Aztec Empire?

3   In 1519, which Aztec emperor was taken prisoner by the Spanish, supposedly without resistance?

4   An important part of Aztec religious worship, human sacrifice, was usually done via the removal of which organ?

5   Aztecs believed dead warriors were reborn as which small species of bird?

6   One side of the *Templo Mayor* was dedicated to Tlaloc, the god of which type of weather?

7   What was the primary language of the Aztec empire?

8   Which dog, also called the *pelon* or "bald dog", was often buried alongside Aztec soldiers?

9   Mictlantecuhtli was the Aztec god of what?

10 Part of the reason for the Aztec empire's collapse was their lack of resistance to which disease, brought by their Spanish conquerors?

11 On the site of modern Mexico City, what was the Aztec capital, the third-biggest city in the world in the early 16th century?

12 Which crop was so important to the Aztecs that there was a god – Centeotl – specifically for it?

13 Xipe Totec, the Aztec god of agriculture and seasons, was depicted wearing what?

14 In Aztec pictograms, what number did a feather represent?

15 Which ancient Aztec temple is the largest pyramid by volume in the world?

16 Due to the belief that it was lord of the animals, Aztec cuāuhocēlōtl warriors dressed as which animal in battle?

17 Which animal was used in Aztec society to describe someone's degree of intoxication?

18 In Aztec society, what type of public service, essentially, were Tēlpochcalli?

19 Which food was used by the Aztecs as a means of trading goods?

20 What was distinct about the Aztec farming technique known as Chinampas?

Answers to QUIZ 202 – Food and Drink

1	Egon Ronay	11	Hands; an individual banana is thus also called a finger
2	Cheese and wine		
3	Jeremy Clarkson	12	Cow pie
4	Vodka	13	Cabbage
5	Cheese	14	Sheep
6	Fruit	15	Crocus
7	Coffee	16	Galaxy®
8	Meatballs	17	Bean
9	Carrot	18	Jaffa Cakes
10	Avocado	19	Cloves
		20	Gazpacho

ANSWERS ON PAGE 207

1   Which 2005 action comedy film was criticised by the Colombian government for erroneously portraying Bogota as a small jungle village with a hot and humid climate?

2   The American Dialect Society anointed which singer's surname as 2015's Most Creative Word, defining it as "a woman who has aged out of being a cougar"?

3   Which Japanese manufacturer's motorbikes were so ubiquitous in Vietnam that the manufacturer's name was often a synonym for one?

4   Who, in 2006, was initially declared the third non-European winner in the history of the Tour de France, but was later disqualified for doping?

5   In the view of most traditional schools, a single honest recitation of which Islamic oath in Arabic is all that is required for a person to become a Muslim?

6   Which comedian appeared in a 1980s new wave group called Seona Dancing?

7   Which American musician popularised an eponymous three-finger banjo picking style, radically different from the traditional way of playing?

8   When he joined Coventry City in 1996, who became the first Brazilian ever to play in the Premier League?

9   Russell Crowe portrayed boxer Jim Braddock in which 2005 film?

10 Mashies, niblicks and brassies are obsolete terms for forms of which pieces of sporting equipment?

11 Which is the only chemical element named for a place in Britain?

12 Which fictional Norfolk-based presenter and DJ has two children called Denise and Fernando?

13 The flowering plant *nepeta cataria* is better known colloquially by what name, due to the stimulating effect it has on certain domestic pets?

14 Coachman, Elddis and Sterckeman are all leading manufacturers of what type of road-going vehicle?

15 Found by Mark King, Mike Lindup and the Gould brothers, which English jazz-funk band had a 1986 no.3 hit with *Lessons in Love*?

16 What name is given to each of the 25 states that make up Switzerland?

17 Which American rock band took their name from the nickname of *The Simpsons* character, Rod Runtledge?

18 Which Briton of Ghanian heritage became the first black head designer of a luxury fashion house when he was appointed creative director of menswear at Givenchy in 2003?

19 On account of its unusual yodel-like sound, which African dog breed is nicknamed the "barkless dog"?

20 "It was a bright cold day in April, and the clocks were striking thirteen." This is the opening line to which novel?

Easy

Medium

Hard

Answers to QUIZ 203 – Pot Luck

1	Ultraviolet	11	Ecuador
2	Greendale	12	The 1900s
3	Nepal	13	25
4	United States of America	14	Anne of Cleves and Catherine Parr
5	Four	15	Rowan Williams
6	Puma®	16	Albert Einstein
7	Metamorphic	17	Green
8	Generation Z or Gen Z	18	*Inside Out*
9	Spleen	19	*Candy Crush Saga*
10	River Avon	20	Pamela Lyndon

Easy

1   Those who doubt the official story of John F. Kennedy's assassination usually believe a second gunman was hidden behind what natural feature?

2   Which conspiracy theory/movement in American far-right politics centres on false claims made by an anonymous individual known as "Q"?

3   During the COVID-19 pandemic, which medicine – used as treatment for river blindness in horses – became the COVID-19 cure of choice in conspiracy circles?

4   From secret bunkers to lizard people, multiple conspiracy theories swirl around which sprawling American international airport?

5   In 2019, NBA star Shaquille O'Neal fuelled rumours that which blind music legend can see?

6   Which of The Beatles was rumoured to have died in 1966 and been replaced by a look-alike?

7   *Behind the Curve* is a 2018 documentary film about believers in which conspiracy, which has been given new life by the internet?

8   What alliterative term describes an act which is orchestrated to appear to be the work of another, often used by conspiracists to accuse governments of staging terrorist attacks?

9   A conspiracy theory states that which Canadian singer died in 2003 and was replaced by a body double named Melissa Vandella?

10   The belief that the world is run by the 18th-century Bavarian secret society known as the Illuminati began as a prank in the letters page of which magazine?

11   Which visible lines in the sky left by aircraft are believed by some to consist of chemical or biological agents released as part of a covert operation?

Medium

12   Conspiracy theorists often claim which Hungarian-born American billionaire investor is a puppet master controlling the global economy?

13   An April 2010 explosion at which oil rig was variously alleged by conspiracists to be sabotage by environmentalists, or a strike by North Korean or Russian submarines?

14   Which former Coventry City goalkeeper learned during his "turquoise period" that he was a "Son of the Godhead"?

15   Periodically, rumours abound that which US political figure, who died in a plane crash in 1999, will return to frontline politics?

16   Part genuine theory, part running joke, there is an online conspiracy that which European country does not really exist?

17   In his lifetime, numerous conspiracy theories surrounded which philosopher and author (1561-1626), claiming he was a member of secret societies?

18   The Skull and Bones Secret Society at Yale University is said to be the controlling force behind which American intelligence service?

19   In his MI5 memoir *Spycatcher*, Peter Wright claimed which British PM was a Soviet agent?

20   Which conspiracy theorist broadcaster lost multiple lawsuits from parents of victims of the Sandy Hook shooting, which he claimed were not real?

Hard

Answers to QUIZ 204 – The Aztecs

1	Mexico	11	Tenochtitlan
2	Hernán Cortés	12	Maize
3	Montezuma II or Moctezuma II	13	Human skin (they really did think about death a lot)
4	Heart; they believed it to be a fragment of the Sun	14	400
5	Hummingbird	15	Great Pyramid of Cholula
6	Rain	16	Jaguars
7	Nahuatl	17	Rabbits – it ranged from very mild intoxication (a few rabbits) to heavy drunkenness (400 rabbits)
8	Mexican Hairless or Xoloitzcuintle		
9	The dead	18	Schools
10	Smallpox	19	Chocolate
		20	It featured "floating islands" of small strips of farmland built in rivers and lake beds

ANSWERS ON PAGE 209

1　*The Black Album*, *The Blueprint* and *Reasonable Doubt* are all albums by which hip-hop star?

2　The second-biggest country by land area in the world, how many time zones does China have?

3　Which Arsenal player only scored seven league goals for the club between 2008 and 2018, but two of them won the Premier League Goal Of The Year award?

4　Buddy Love is the alter ego of the eponymous lead character in which film, played by Jerry Lewis in the 1963 original and by Eddie Murphy in the 1996 remake?

5　Amoretti are representations of which figure in works of art?

6　Famous for a 1970s hostage situation, Entebbe is the main international airport in which African country?

7　Dancer and actress Virginia McMath was better known by what name?

8　Most common among children, the infectious disease varicella is better known as what?

9　Until Russell Westbrook did it four times in five seasons between 2017 and 2021, who had been the only NBA player to average a triple-double back in 1962?

10　The Nile is the longest river in Africa; which is second?

11　*Memories Are Made of This* was the only UK no.1 single for which actor and singer?

12　Who wrote *The Prime Of Miss Jean Brodie*?

13　Carlito Brigante, Frank Serpico and Lefty Ruggiero are all characters played in film by which A-List actor?

14　The pylorus is a valve that joins the lower intestine to which other organ of the body?

15　Due to its use as the name of the title character in Vladimir Nabokov's 1955 novel, what name has come to mean a seductive young girl?

16　James Dean played the emotionally complex loner Cal Trask in which 1955 film?

17　Hot Lips Houlihan, Hawkeye Pierce and Maxwell Klinger were lead characters in which comedy drama series?

18　Dianne Wiest and Shelley Winters are the only two people to have won which Academy Award more than once?

19　Which animal has the largest cranium of any primate in proportion to the mother's pelvis?

20　Which is the only African country to have appeared at the Eurovision Song Contest?

Easy

Medium

Hard

Answers to QUIZ 205 – Pot Luck

1　*Mr and Mrs Smith*
2　Mellencamp (after John Cougar Mellencamp dropped the "Cougar" from his name)
3　Honda
4　Floyd Landis
5　The Shahada
6　Ricky Gervais
7　Earl Scruggs
8　Isaias
9　*Cinderella Man*
10　Golf clubs

11　Strontium (after Strontian in Scotland, where it was first isolated)
12　Alan Partridge
13　Catnip or catmint
14　Caravans
15　Level 42
16　Cantons
17　Fall Out Boy
18　Ozwald Boateng
19　Basenji
20　*1984* by George Orwell

1   AOL bought which social media website for $850 million in 2008, only to sell it back to the original owners for $10 million two years later?

2   Which record label rejected The Beatles in 1962, saying "Guitar groups are on the way out"?

3   Which businessman became notorious for a speech mocking the quality of his jewellery company's products, wiping out £500 million of its value?

4   *Leonard v. Pepsico, Inc* was a case brought to enforce a joke offer to redeem 7,000,000 Pepsi Points for what, valued at $33.8 million at the time?

5   While three investors passed it up, Levi Roots appeared on *Dragons' Den* to secure £50,000 for which product that has grown into a business worth over £30 million?

6   Which now-dissolved company declined the chance to buy Netflix in 2000 for $50 million?

7   Which web services company passed on opportunities to buy each of Google, Facebook™ and YouTube, and instead bought AltaVista and Tumblr?

8   Which company invented digital cameras but did not push them so as to protect their conventional photography sales, and then went bankrupt?

9   After Western Union declined buying the telephone patent for $100,000, which company did Alexander Graham-Bell and partners form?

10 In 1985, Coca Cola® unsuccessfully reformulated their main product under what name?

11 Once the fastest ever company to reach a $1 billion valuation, which marketplace spurned a $6 billion buyout from Google in 2010, and by 2021 lost more than $1.1 million every day?

12 In 1992, which home appliance company promised free airline tickets to anyone who spent at least £100, which cost far them more than it earned?

13 Netflix almost imploded itself back in 2011 when it divided its DVD and streaming subscriptions into different products, with the former trading as what?

14 An oft-cited reason for World Championship Wrestling's downfall was the odd decision to make which actor World Champion for twelve days?

15 Which company licenced the rights to make an *E.T.* video game, but rushed it, suffered huge losses and buried millions of unsold copies in the desert?

16 Which video game company ruined the launch of its Saturn console by oversaturating their market with their Mega CD, 32X and Dreamcast devices?

17 In 2011, News Corp CEO Rupert Murdoch said the $580 million purchase of which social networking site in 2005 was a mistake "in every way possible"?

18 By failing to release a touchscreen device until 18 months after the iPhone was released, which phone manufacturer lost its enormous market share?

19 What name is given to the phenomenon of people cancelling orders for a current product as a result of the company announcing the follow-up product prematurely?

20 A combination of changing the recipe to save money and a strangely violent advertising campaign led to the near demise of which American beer brand?

Answers to QUIZ 206 – Conspiracies

1	Grassy knoll	11	Chemtrails
2	QAnon	12	George Soros
3	Ivermectin	13	*Deepwater Horizon*
4	Denver International	14	David Icke
5	Stevie Wonder	15	John F. Kennedy Jr
6	Sir Paul McCartney	16	Finland
7	Flat Earthers	17	Francis Bacon
8	"False flag"	18	CIA
9	Avril Lavigne	19	Harold Wilson
10	*Playboy*	20	Alex Jones

1 In 2021, who became Scotland's all-time record try scorer in rugby union internationals?

2 Which animal can be found on the flag of Uganda?

3 Which author penned the *Inspector Morse* stories?

4 Steve Harley is the lead singer of which British rock group, whose biggest hit was 1975's *Make Me Smile (Come Up and See Me)*?

5 In February 1935, Wallace H. Carothers first produced which synthetic material?

6 Which former MP wrote the novel *Chasing Men* and the non-fiction work *What Women Want*?

7 Which 1960s beat combo were the first act to reach no.1 in the UK Singles Chart with their first three releases, the third of which was *You'll Never Walk Alone*?

8 In the *Peanuts* comic strip, Belle is the only named sister of which character?

9 Which international rugby union team uses the nickname *Los Pumas*?

10 Which "set piece" is used in rugby union but not in rugby league, where a scrum is used instead?

11 As a part of his starring role in *My Cousin Vinny*, which veteran actor released a rap song called *Wise Guy*?

12 Before embarking on a solo career, who was the lead singer of Kajagoogoo?

13 Twins Melanie and Martina Grant were the supporting hosts on the British version of which children's game show?

14 The Cornish village of Port Isaac becomes the fictional village of Portwenn to serve as backdrop for which regional detective series?

15 Who is the lead singer of British rock band the Stone Roses?

16 Misogamy is the hatred of what?

17 The inclusion of which South African-born player into the English test cricket team's tour of that country caused controversy in 1968?

18 Which English actor/singer was born Michael Dumble-Smith in 1942?

19 Although both starred in *The Godfather Part II*, Al Pacino and Robert de Niro did not appear on screen together until appearing in which 1995 Michael Mann film?

20 Which long-time BBC radio host is credited with introducing the "zoo" format to the UK airwaves?

Answers to QUIZ 207 – Pot Luck

1	Jay-Z	11	Dean Martin
2	One	12	Muriel Spark
3	Jack Wilshere	13	Al Pacino
4	*The Nutty Professor*	14	Stomach
5	Cupid	15	Lolita
6	Uganda	16	*East Of Eden*
7	Ginger Rogers	17	*M.A.S.H.*
8	Chickenpox	18	Best Supporting Actress
9	Oscar Robertson	19	Human
10	Congo River	20	Morocco (1980)

ANSWERS ON PAGE 212

Which of these members of the primate family is which?

Easy

1

2

3

4

Medium

5

6

7

8

Hard

1. Which house in Surrey is the country home of the Earl and Countess of Wessex?
2. The 1893 *New World Symphony* was written by which Czech composer?
3. Which pioneer of the horror film genre and creator of the *Night of the Living Dead* franchise has been called the "Father of the Zombie Film"?
4. How many books are found in the New Testament?
5. If something is described as sagittate, what shape is it?
6. Ludlow, Oswestry and Bridgnorth are all found in which English county?
7. Belfast stands at the mouth of which river?
8. Which professional Dutch football club was founded by the Phillips technology company?
9. Which YouTube personality has embarked on a boxing career that has seen wins over former NBA player Nate Robinson and UFC fighter Tyron Woodley?
10. Which football legend was the manager of Kettering Town FC for 39 days in 2005?
11. The *Dance of the Knights*, a movement in Sergei Prokofiev's ballet, *Romeo and Juliet*, is used as the theme music for which BBC reality talent show?
12. B.B. King's trademark guitar was given which female forename, which it shares with a Kenny Rogers song?
13. What is the most westerly city in the United Kingdom?
14. An inglenook is a recess or partially closed space that adjoins what?
15. Hugo A-Go-Go is the arch enemy of which cartoon superhero?
16. Which childhood acting star latterly formed a comedy hip-hop group named Pizza Underground?
17. Omnium, Madison and Keirin are racing events in which Olympic sport?
18. Amanda Nunes and Ronda Rowsey are among the best all-time fighters in which combat sport?
19. The inspiration for the name Pepsi, the common medical condition dyspepsia is better known as what?
20. Which Irish comedian and actress writes and stars in the sitcom *This Way Up*?

Easy

Medium

Hard

Answers to QUIZ 209 – Pot Luck

1	Stuart Hogg	11	Joe Pesci
2	Crane	12	Limahl
3	Colin Dexter	13	*Fun House*
4	Cockney Rebel	14	*Doc Martin*
5	Nylon	15	Ian Brown
6	Edwina Currie	16	Marriage
7	Gerry and the Pacemakers	17	Basil D'Oliveira
8	Snoopy	18	Michael Crawford
9	Argentina	19	*Heat*
10	The line-out	20	Steve Wright

Easy

1 Hepatocytes are the chief functional cells of which organ of the human body?

2 The primary psychoactive constituent in marijuana is known by which three-letter abbreviation?

3 What term describes the metabolic state that occurs when a body does not have enough carbohydrates or glucose for energy, so it burns fat instead?

4 Used in soaps, drain cleaner and paper, which inorganic compound has NaOH as its chemical formula?

5 Which branch of science concerns the earth's physical structure and substance, history, and the processes that act on it?

6 In *Philosophiæ Naturalis Principia Mathematica*, which English physicist outlined three laws of classical mechanics that describe the relationship between the motion of an object and the forces acting on it?

7 In physics, what word beginning with V is a quantity containing both a magnitude and a direction?

8 With which condition do the sexes of the same species exhibit different characteristics, particularly characteristics not directly involved in reproduction?

9 Metol is an organic compound chemical salt used by hobbyists in which activity?

10 What is a renal calculus better known as?

Medium

11 In 1888, which Austrian chemist discovered an improved method for making pure alumina from low-silica bauxite ores?

12 What does a sphygmomanometer measure?

13 Azidothymidine, Vocabria and Cabenuva are all medicines approved to fight which affliction?

14 When ingested, the amygdalin in which nut breaks down into several chemicals, including cyanide?

15 In 1943, which psychologist created the idea of the "hierarchy of needs", a theory of psychological health predicated on fulfilling innate human needs in priority?

16 Osteoblasts, osteocytes and osteoclasts are three of the four types of cells found in what?

17 A male born with Klinefelter syndrome has an extra what?

18 It is believed that which mineral form of carbon, superheated through entering the Earth's atmosphere, is even stronger than diamond?

19 Sir Christopher Wren was a professor at Oxford University in which scientific field?

20 Which English biochemist separated Vitamin D from cod liver oil and established its potential role in preventing rickets?

Hard

Answers to QUIZ 210 – Primates

1 Chimpanzee
2 Spider Monkey
3 Bushbaby
4 Mandrill
5 Ring-tailed lemur
6 Marmoset
7 Tarsier
8 Emperor Tamarin

1   In which country are the European Courts of Justice based?

2   Which Gilbert & Sullivan comic opera shares its name with a now-obsolete term for the Emperor of Japan?

3   The eponymous mask of the 1994 film *The Mask* is said in the film to be the mask of who, the Norse god of mischief?

4   In the 1970s and 1980s, Feargal Sharkey was the lead singer of which punk band?

5   What was the world's first electronic stock market?

6   In the New Testament of the Bible, which book comes after Apostles?

7   Which is the only medieval English cathedral with three spires?

8   The 2002 Winter Olympics were held in which American state capital city?

9   A man named Alan Mitchell died laughing in 1975 after watching an episode of which comedy show?

10   What term is given to the time period during which legal proceedings may be brought?

11   A statue of Billy Bremner stands outside Elland Road, the ground of which football club?

12   Which George Gershwin opera is set in the fictional South Carolina tenement of Catfish Row?

13   Natural vanilla flavouring comes from which plant family?

14   Across both the Old and New Testaments, how many books are there in total in the Bible?

15   Which Charles Dickens novel is the only one to have more than one narrator and a female narrator?

16   What type of creature is a bummalo?

17   Scaramanga's servant Nick Nack is a character in which James Bond film?

18   The adjective pavonine relates to which animal?

19   Doctor Calico is the villain in which Disney movie?

20   Which is the largest vein in the human body?

Easy

Medium

Hard

Answers to QUIZ 211 – Pot Luck

1	Bagshot Park	11	*The Apprentice*
2	Antonín Dvořák	12	Lucille
3	George Romero	13	Derry
4	27	14	A fireplace
5	Arrowhead-shaped	15	Batfink
6	Shropshire	16	Macaulay Culkin
7	River Lagan	17	Track cycling
8	PSV Eindhoven	18	Mixed martial arts (MMA)
9	Jake Paul	19	Indigestion
10	Paul Gascoigne	20	Aisling Bea

1   Modelled on Swiss physicist Auguste Piccard, what is the name of Tintin's scientist friend?

2   *Hägar the Horrible* and *Hi and Lois* were both written and drawn by who?

3   Which character first appeared in the *King Features* comic strip *Thimble Theatre* on 17th January 1929?

4   In 1996, Marvel and DC Comics combined their universes and characters for a series of adventures, published under what name?

5   Which *Dandy* character was named for how she would spend her time looking into other people's houses?

6   In the namesake comic strip, who was Blondie's husband?

7   Korky the Cat appeared as the front page mascot for which comic for more than 40 years?

8   "It's Clobberin' Time" is the catchphrase of which Marvel Comics character?

9   Who created the *Dilbert* series about an engineer and his office colleagues?

10 Peter O'Donnell created which crime fighter and former crime syndicate leader in 1962?

11 Frank Miller released which controversial graphic novel in 2011 that initially was intended for Batman, but ultimately stood alone?

12 Debuting two years before Superman, which Lee Falk creation was the first costumed superhero?

13 Which comic strip and namesake character made his first appearance in the *Detroit Free Press* on 4th October 1931?

14 At over 8 million copies sold in 1991, what is by far the best-selling comic book of all time?

15 Man-Eating Cow is a character in which comic book parody series?

16 Which star of his own namesake TV show had his own comic strip in the children's magazines *Robin* and *Pippin*?

17 Which comic strip about the Winslow family and their Great Dane was drawn by Brad Anderson from 1954 to 2015?

18 In the *Garfield* stories, what is the name of Jon Arbuckle's farmer brother?

19 Which comic book of 1884 was the first to ever feature a recurring character?

20 *Amazing Cow Heroes* were a series of promotional comics handed out in 2010 by which American restaurant chain?

Answers to QUIZ 212 – Science

1	Liver	11	Karl Joseph Bayer
2	THC (tetrahydrocannabinol)	12	Blood pressure
3	Ketosis	13	AIDS
4	Caustic soda/sodium hydroxide	14	Walnut
5	Geology	15	Abraham Maslow
6	Sir Isaac Newton	16	Bone
7	Vector	17	X chromosome
8	Sexual dimorphism	18	Lonsdaleite
9	Photography	19	Astronomy (he was an architect too, but astronomy came first)
10	Kidney stone	20	Sir Edward Mellanby

1 Which national team made the finals of the Rugby World Cup in 1987, 1999 and 2011, but lost all three?

2 Although now part of Dorset, Bournemouth was in which county until 1974?

3 Which TV wildlife presenter, the subject of a *Scouting For Girls* song, was also the 2002 Ladies World Gurning Champion?

4 Although their last win came back in 1893, which team actually has the third most Scottish FA Cup titles, behind Celtics and Rangers?

5 Most of the moons of Uranus are named after characters in the works of which two English authors?

6 In which Canadian city were the 1988 Winter Olympics held?

7 Which board game takes its name and aim from something its deviser Pat Reid actually did towards the end of World War II?

8 What was the unabbreviated and highly appropriate full name of CC the cat, the first-ever cloned pet?

9 In 2015, Trevor Noah took over from Jon Stewart in hosting which nightly comedy news show on Comedy Central?

10 In darts, to hit a single, double and treble of the same number in the same visit is known by what city name?

11 Which novel by Jane Austen is set in the fictional country village of Highbury?

12 Bajans are people native to or inhabiting which island nation?

13 Francis Shields, runner-up in the 1931 Wimbledon men's singles championship, was the grandfather of which actress and model?

14 The name of which animal translates literally from Mandarin Chinese as "business goose"?

15 In June 2012, after going out for lunch with his family, which British politician left his eight-year-old daughter in the pub?

16 What was the leading cause of death in the US Civil War?

17 What was significant about a man named Laszlo Hanyecz buying two pizzas on 22nd May 2010?

18 In Jewish, Christian and Muslim belief, who led the Hebrew slaves out of Egypt?

19 Who was the original host of *Desert Island Discs*?

20 With the surname at birth of Deeks, which British actress took on her famous stage surname in 1953, inspired by the Queen's coronation?

Easy

Medium

Hard

Answers to QUIZ 213 – Pot Luck

1	Luxembourg	11	Leeds United
2	*The Mikado*	12	*Porgy and Bess*
3	Loki	13	Orchids
4	The Undertones	14	66
5	NASDAQ	15	*Bleak House* (Esther Summerson)
6	Romans	16	Fish
7	Lichfield	17	*The Man with the Golden Gun*
8	Salt Lake City	18	Peacock
9	*The Goodies*	19	*Bolt*
10	Statute of Limitations	20	Vena cava

1   The very first episode of *EastEnders* saw Den Watts, Arthur Fowler and Ali Osman finding the dead body of who?

2   In *Coronation Street*, Deirdre Barlow was sentenced to prison for committing which crime, prompting a national campaign?

3   Which soap became famous for screening the first pre-watershed lesbian kiss on British television?

4   In 2000, three years into its existence, the geographic focus of which soap opera was retconned to Stanley Street, West London?

5   In which village is *Emmerdale* set?

6   Which *Casualty* character has been shot, run down, trapped in a car deliberately driven into the sea, and had three heart attacks?

7   In 2014, which soap became the first other than *EastEnders* or *Coronation Street* to win the Best British Soap award?

8   In April 2006, *Doctors* was the first British TV programme to show what on screen?

9   Which television producer created all three of *Brookside*, *Rownd a Rownd* and *Hollyoaks*?

10 More famous for his appearance in another soap, which actor played Graham Lodsworth for 22 episodes of *Emmerdale Farm* between 1986 and 1987?

11 Which former *Holby City* star won Celebrity Big Brother in 2012?

12 ATV produced which ITV soap opera between 1972 and 1979 that shared a name with – but was otherwise unrelated to – an American counterpart?

13 Which 1980s BBC soap was an attempt to provide a British alternative to glossy American sagas such as *Dallas* and *Dynasty*?

14 Jasper Carrott joked that the cast of which former ITV soap went on strike when they were threatened with rehearsal?

15 Which BBC soap, set amongst the expatriate community in Spain, was beset with problems and cancelled after one year?

16 Which 1980s BBC soap was set aboard a North Sea ferry that sailed from Felixstowe to Gothenburg to Amsterdam, as reflected in the name?

17 1,445 total episodes were written of which soap opera, broadcast on ITV's *ORACLE* Teletext service?

18 Deciding its schedule needed a soap opera set in Scotland, ITV commissioned which 1980 soap opera that ran until 2003?

19 Made and broadcast by the BBC from 1954 to 1957, which family-centric series is often considered to be the first UK soap opera?

20 Launching in 1974, which Welsh-language series is the longest-running television soap opera produced by the BBC?

Easy

Medium

Hard

Answers to QUIZ 214 – Comic Books and Strips

1	Professor Cuthbert Calculus	11	*Holy Terror*
2	Dik Browne	12	The Phantom
3	Popeye	13	*Dick Tracy*
4	Amalgam Comics	14	*X-Men #1*
5	Keyhole Kate	15	*The Tick*
6	Dagwood Bumstead	16	Andy Pandy
7	*The Dandy*	17	*Marmaduke*
8	The Thing	18	Doc Boy Arbuckle
9	Scott Adams	19	*Ally Sloper's Half Holiday*
10	Modesty Blaise	20	Chick-fil-A® – the theory being, if people like cows, they'll eat more chicken

1. What was the soubriquet of Swiss-French architect Charles-Édouard Jeanneret?
2. In 1947, which US President had the first bowling alley installed in the White House?
3. Aidan Turner plays the title character in which 2015 BBC series about a soldier returning from war to his beloved Cornwall to find his world in ruins?
4. Which German player scored the only goal in the 2014 FIFA World Cup Final?
5. Which year is known as the "Year of the three Popes"?
6. Which literary technique involves the repeated use of the same vowel sound?
7. Which significantly eyebrowed man served as Margaret Thatcher's press secretary throughout her eleven years as Prime Minister?
8. Released in 2009, which sandbox video game with deliberately blocky graphics quickly became the highest-selling video game of all time?
9. Which 2020 comedy-drama starring Jason Sudeikis tells the story of an American college football coach who is hired to coach AFC Richmond, a soccer team?
10. In 1979, which MP and former leader of the Liberal Party was the first British MP to stand trial for murder?
11. The perpetually-burning sinkhole named "The Gates of Hell" can be found in which country?
12. To desiccate something is to do what to it?
13. In winning the 2020 Olympic men's breaststroke 100m gold, which British swimmer set a record of having all of the top sixteen fastest times in the event's history?
14. Mikhail Gorbachev and Donald Trump have both starred in adverts for which company, perhaps better associated with Boris Yeltsin?
15. Every year between 2004 and 2018, the winner of the World Touring Car Championship had what first name?
16. Winning the 1964 Formula 1 title and four 500cc motorcycle titles, who is the only person to have won World Championships on both two and four wheels?
17. Ella Marija Lani Yelich-O'Connor is the real name of which singer-songwriter from New Zealand?
18. Now in common usage with a less severe meaning, what word originally meant to kill one in every ten?
19. Who became British Foreign Secretary in May 2010 and held the post for four years?
20. Alison Moyet's first solo album was given what man's forename?

Easy
Medium
Hard

Answers to QUIZ 215 – Pot Luck

1	France	11	*Emma*
2	Hampshire	12	Barbados
3	Michaela Strachan	13	Brooke Shields
4	Queen's Park	14	Penguin
5	William Shakespeare and Alexander Pope	15	David Cameron
6	Calgary	16	Dysentery/diarrhoea
7	*Escape from Colditz*	17	First ever use of Bitcoin
8	Copy Cat	18	Moses
9	*The Daily Show*	19	Roy Plomley
10	Shanghai	20	Barbara Windsor

1   Who hosted *The Generation Game* between 1971 and 1977, and again between 1990 and 1995?

2   Which boxer and rugby union player were the two original team captains on *A Question Of Sport*?

3   Due to writing inconsistencies, which sitcom character's first name was alternately Rachel or Betty, while her cat, Tiddles, kept changing from a he to a she?

4   Which singing superstar wrote, directed and produced the Disney+ TV musical film *Black Is King?*

5   Which American comedy drama/mystery television series was set in Wisteria Lane?

6   Which reality TV series sees business executives taking secret positions within their own company to observe the employees?

7   Under what name did William White find fame as a TV presenter and entertainer?

8   An (unsuccessful) taped audition by Madonna for which 1982 TV series appeared on YouTube in 2012?

9   Debuting in 2019 on Disney+, which Jon Favreau creation was the first live-action series in the *Star Wars* franchise?

10   In the TV series *The Man from U.N.C.L.E.*, which organisation were the primary antagonists?

11   The two stars of which 1970s British sitcom allegedly fell out for 40 years, in part because one of them refused to allow repeats to air on network TV?

12   Which cartoon character has a pet snail called Gary who meows like a cat?

13   Michael J. Fox played the Deputy Mayor of New York in the sitcom *Spin City* for four years; who replaced him for the final two?

14   Which primetime variety show presented by Noel Edmonds was cancelled after the death of a stuntman in a bungee accident?

15   Which tourist village in Gwynedd served as the location for "The Village" in *The Prisoner?*

16   Adding "ver" between the forename and surname of an Icelandic quiz show host gives the name of a four-time winner of which athletic event?

17   Who played fictional detectives Charley Farley and Piggy Malone in the 1972 serial story *Done To Death?*

18   Chingford Steel was a one-time character portrayed by Richard E. Grant in which sitcom?

19   Kathryn Janeway was the ship's captain in which series in the *Star Trek* franchise?

20   Serial killer John Cooper appeared as a contestant on which television game show during his series of murders?

Answers to QUIZ 216 – UK Soap Operas

1	Reg Cox	11	Denise Welch
2	Fraud	12	*General Hospital*
3	*Brookside*	13	*Howard's Way*
4	*Family Affairs*	14	*Crossroads*
5	Beckindale (until 1994), or Emmerdale (from 1994 onwards)	15	*Eldorado*
		16	*Triangle*
6	Charlie Fairhead	17	*Park Avenue*
7	*Hollyoaks*	18	*Take The High Road*
8	A same-sex wedding	19	*The Grove Family*
9	Phil Redmond	20	*Pobol y Cwm*
10	Ross Kemp		

1. Which syndrome, defined by jealousy and fear of infidelity, is named after a Shakespearian character?
2. Who was the first African footballer to win the Ballon D'Or?
3. On which part of the body is a diadem worn?
4. To which country does the island of Komodo, famous for its dragons, belong?
5. Harmattan, simoon and sirocco are types of what weather phenomenon?
6. In 2013, which Pope became the first to resign the papacy in almost six centuries?
7. Australian poet Banjo Paterson wrote the lyrics to which bush ballad, Australia's unofficial national anthem?
8. William Wordsworth, Samuel Taylor Coleridge and Robert Southey were the three main members of which group of poets, named for where they lived?
9. By land area, what is the largest country in Africa?
10. Who did Fabio Capello replace as England football manager in December 2007?
11. Mary Lennox, Mrs Medlock and Dickon are all characters in which Frances Hodgson Burnett novel?
12. Lee Brilleaux was the lead vocalist and harmonica player in which 1970s pub rock band from Canvey Island?
13. Carl Fredricksen is the lead character in which Disney Pixar film?
14. The scene of President Mubarak's 2021 resignation, Tahir Square is in which North African city?
15. Which female vocalist joined Puff Daddy for the 1997 No.1 hit *I'll Be Missing You*, recorded in tribute to her husband, Notorious B.I.G.?
16. Along with the Question Mark Nymphalid of North America, which butterfly's name is also that of a punctuation mark?
17. Along with André Derain, Henri Matisse was a leader in which short-lived artistic school?
18. Which future Prime Minister returned to Parliament after two years away when he was voted MP for Epping in October 1924?
19. In the epilogue of *Harry Potter and the Deathly Hallows*, who becomes Headmaster of Hogwarts?
20. Under English law, what is the minimum number of people required to qualify an unruly disturbance as a riot?

Easy

Medium

Hard

Answers to QUIZ 217 – Pot Luck

1	Le Corbusier	11	Turkmenistan
2	Harry S. Truman	12	Dry it out
3	*Poldark*	13	Adam Peaty
4	Mario Goetz	14	Pizza Hut™
5	1978	15	Sebastien (Loeb 2004-12, Ogier 2013-18)
6	Assonance	16	John Surtees
7	Bernard Ingham	17	Lorde
8	*Minecraft*	18	Decimate
9	*Ted Lasso*	19	William Hague
10	Jeremy Thorpe	20	*Alf*

Easy

1 Published in 1836, which was Charles Dickens's first novel?

2 Which of Dickens's novels was only half-finished at the time of his death?

3 At over 200 million copies sold, it is estimated that which of Dickens's novels is the best-selling novel of all time?

4 Seth Pecksniff, Mrs Gamp and Tom Pinch all appear in which Dickens novel?

5 Which two of Dickens's novels are considered his only two "historical" works?

6 Which Dickens novel begins with the line "Although I am an old man, night is generally my time for walking."?

7 Hablot Knight Browne, an illustrator of many of Dickens's books, worked under what pseudonym?

8 To pay his father's debts, Charles Dickens went to work at the age of 12 in what job, one he later gave to his iconic character Sam Weller?

9 What short nickname given to him by his family did Dickens employ as a pseudonym for some years?

10 The Mantalinis' shop features in which Dickens novel?

Medium

11 The storyline of which Dickens novel centres around the interminable probate case of Jarndyce and Jarndyce?

12 Which Dickens character was based on his father, John Dickens?

13 Which Dickens novel is by far his shortest, and his only novel not to have any scenes in London?

14 In *Our Mutual Friend*, what was the occupation of Mortimer Lightwood?

15 In *Little Dorrit*, what does the etching "D.N.F." on Mrs Clennam's golden watch stand for?

16 In *A Tale of Two Cities*, Charles Dickens coined the first recorded use of the name for what everyday food?

17 Which Dickens novel focused on what happens when a father has a daughter instead of the desired son?

18 In *A Christmas Carol*, what must Jacob Marley carry around forever as a representation of the burdens he forged in his life?

19 What accident caused Charles Dickens to lose his voice for two weeks in 1865?

20 Which word is missing from this quote from *Martin Chuzzlewit*: "There is no such passion in human nature as the passion for _____ among commercial gentlemen"?

Hard

Answers to QUIZ 218 – Television

1	Bruce Forsyth	11	*Whatever Happened To The Likely Lads?* (Rodney Bewes and James Bolam)
2	Henry Cooper and Cliff Morgan		
3	Mrs Slocomb from *Are You Being Served?*	12	SpongeBob SquarePants
4	Beyoncé	13	Charlie Sheen
5	*Desperate Housewives*	14	*The Late, Late Breakfast Show*
6	*Undercover Boss*	15	Portmeirion
7	Larry Grayson	16	*World's Strongest Man* (Magnús Ver Magnússon)
8	*Fame*	17	Ronnie Barker and Ronnie Corbett in *The Two Ronnies*
9	*The Mandalorian*		
10	THRUSH	18	*Rab C. Nesbitt*
		19	*Star Trek: Voyager*
		20	*Bullseye*

1   Which is the only William Shakespeare play to be set in Spain?

2   Edward Woodstock, 14th Century Prince of Wales and eldest son of Edward III, was known by what name?

3   "Fraulein, have my children by any chance been climbing trees today?" is a line from which classic musical film?

4   Although its name was initially an unrelated abbreviation, which Italian car manufacturer's name is also a word for an arbitrary order or decree?

5   Before being renamed after the late President John F. Kennedy, New York International Airport was known as what?

6   Who was the operator of the Magic Roundabout?

7   Which American city is the setting for the 1987 film *Robocop*?

8   In 2000, which London club won the last FA Cup Final held at the old Wembley Stadium?

9   In the 1973 Disney version of *Robin Hood*, which animal represents Robin?

10 What type of insect is a Kentish Glory?

11 In the name of the Russian spacecraft, what does Soyuz mean?

12 In which 1973 James Bond film starring Roger Moore does actress Jane Seymour play Solitaire?

13 Which English author drowned in 1941 by filling her pockets with stones and walking into the River Ouse?

14 How many red stripes are there on the national flag of Thailand?

15 Which poet was buried upright in Westminster Abbey in 1637?

16 The Rum Rebellion of 1808 was the first and only successful military coup in the history of which country?

17 Tobermory is the capital of which Scottish island?

18 A Slippery Dick is what type of creature?

19 *Nighthawks* is the best-known work of which American artist?

20 On a 1982 edition of *Top of the Pops*, Dexy's Midnight Runners performed in front of a picture of which darts player?

Easy

Medium

Hard

Answers to QUIZ 219 – Pot Luck

1	Othello syndrome	11	*The Secret Garden*
2	George Weah	12	Dr Feelgood
3	On the head	13	*Up*
4	Indonesia	14	Cairo
5	Wind	15	Faith Evans
6	Pope Benedict XVI	16	Comma
7	*Waltzing Matilda*	17	Fauvism
8	The Lake Poets	18	Winston Churchill
9	Algeria	19	Minerva McGonagall
10	Steve McClaren	20	12

QUIZ 222 – Hair and Beauty

ANSWERS ON PAGE 224

1 Which animal's name is used to describe a small section of hair that grows at a different angle than the rest of the hair?

2 "Maybe she's born with it; maybe it's…" which beauty brand?

3 What type of piercing has no exit hole?

4 In which ancient culture was it common for high-ranking females to shave their heads bald and wear a wig instead, and sometimes a false beard?

5 As worn by Friar Tuck, what name is given to the part of a monk's or priest's head left bare on top by shaving off the hair?

6 On which part of your body would you wear chatelaine jewellery?

7 In terms of percentage of the population, which country has the most redheads?

8 The rind from the fruit of which tree is extracted to make an essential oil widely used in fragrances?

9 What does having a beard signify in Amish culture?

10 Often used in beauty products, what does a humectant do?

11 Which hairstyle takes its name from a mistress of King Louis XV of France?

12 The name of which hair product comes from the French word for foam?

13 Which make-up brand is advertised as "The make-up of make-up artists"?

14 The feathery layered "wings" hairstyle was popularised in the 1970s by which actress?

15 In Ancient Greece, what powder did wealthy women often sprinkle into their hair?

16 In the world of beauty, Mary Katherine Campbell was the first and only woman to do what?

17 In hairstyling, schizotrichia is better known colloquially as what?

18 In the classic UK version of Monopoly™, how much does a player collect for coming second place in a beauty competition?

19 Eggshells, pumice, ox hooves, charcoal, bark, crushed bones and urine were all used in Ancient Rome as ingredients in what?

20 *Kesh* – meaning uncut hair and beard – is worn as one of the five distinguishing signs of which religion?

Answers to QUIZ 220 – Charles Dickens

1 *The Pickwick Papers*
2 *The Mystery of Edwin Drood*
3 *A Tale of Two Cities*
4 *Martin Chuzzlewit*
5 *Barnaby Rudge* and *A Tale of Two Cities*
6 *The Old Curiosity Shop*
7 Phiz
8 Bootblack
9 Boz
10 *Nicholas Nickleby*
11 *Bleak House*
12 Mr Micawber from *David Copperfield* – he, too, went to debtor's prison
13 *Hard Times*
14 Lawyer
15 "Do not forget"
16 Chips
17 *Dombey and Son*
18 A chain
19 The Staplehurst rail crash
20 Gravy

1   The fat found in new-borns that helps them make heat has what colour for a name?

2   Specifically, a morepork is a species of what?

3   In January 1973, who defeated Joe Frazier to win the Heavyweight World Boxing Championship?

4   The US Declaration of Independence decreed that how many American colonies, which were at war with Britain, were no longer part of the British Empire?

5   Covering the surface of joints, what colour is articular cartilage?

6   Which golf course has both the shortest ("Postage Stamp") and longest ("Turnberry") holes in Open Championship golf?

7   Who played Bill Sykes in the 1968 film *Oliver!*?

8   Which racing driver received the last rites from a priest in 1976, before winning the 1977 Formula 1 World Championship?

9   The title First Lord of the Treasury is inscribed on the letterbox of which address in London?

10 Goalkeeper Peter Bonetti and cricketer Phil Tufnell both had which animal nickname?

11 A *mahout* is a person who works, tends and rides which animal?

12 The French Opera House was opened in 1859 in which American city?

13 Which national team beat Hungary 4-2 to win the 1938 FIFA World Cup?

14 A clarion was the medieval version of which modern day musical instrument?

15 In which country did the De Stijl art movement originate?

16 How many yards are in a modern international mile?

17 Mount Aconcagua, the 189th highest mountain in the world yet the highest outside of Asia, is found in which South American country?

18 What is the name of the headteacher in Roald Dahl's *Matilda*?

19 Which member of the *Monty Python* comedy troupe starred alongside Robbie Coltrane in the 1990 film *Nuns On The Run*?

20 In 1972, who did Bobby Fischer defeat to become the first American World Chess Champion?

Easy

Medium

Hard

Answers to QUIZ 221 – Pot Luck

1	*Love's Labour's Lost*	11	Union
2	The Black Prince	12	*Live and Let Die*
3	*The Sound of Music*	13	Virginia Woolf
4	Fiat	14	Two
5	Idlewild	15	Ben Johnson
6	Mr Rusty	16	Australia
7	Detroit	17	Mull
8	Chelsea	18	Fish
9	Fox	19	Edward Hopper
10	Butterfly	20	Jocky Wilson (they were performing the song *Jackie Wilson Said*)

1. Which canonised peasant girl led the French army during the siege of Orléans in the Hundred Years' War?
2. Saint Patrick is said to have driven which animal from Ireland, chasing them into the sea after they attacked him during a 40-day fast?
3. Saint Stephen's Day is better known as what?
4. Known for its horn riff, American indie pop band Saint Motel had a worldwide hit in 2014 with which song?
5. King James II of Scotland, Edward Jenner, Prince William and Hazel Irvine all attended which prestigious university?
6. Which saint, known as the "Angelic Doctor", has been recognised by the Catholic Church for his theology tome *Summa Theologica*?
7. In art, which saint and gospel writer is often depicted as an eagle, or holding a chalice containing a serpent?
8. With his image commonly worn in pendants and displayed in cars, who is the patron saint of travellers?
9. In addition to being the patron saint of Scotland, Saint Andrew is also the patron saint of which Eurasian county?
10. Named for a city in France, which indie dance band had hits in the 1990s with *You're In A Bad Way* and *He's On The Phone*?
11. Sisters Nicole and Natalie Appleton were two of the four members of which 1990s girl band?

12. Which Scottish former footballer co-presented the topical football show *Saint and Greavsie* between 1985 and 1992?
13. Which former celebrity couple had four children named North, Saint, Chicago and Psalm?
14. Which is the only London Underground station whose name does not contain any letters from the word 'mackerel'?
15. The NFL franchise in which American city uses the nickname "Saints"?
16. Which saint was the first Archbishop of Canterbury and founded the Christian Church in the South of England?
17. Which Catholic friar gave up a life of wealth to live in poverty, and later became associated with patronage of animals and the natural environment?
18. Kingstown is the capital of which Caribbean island nation?
19. Which football team on the south coast of England uses the nickname "The Saints"?
20. The deadliest volcanic event in US history was the eruption of which mountain, in an explosion so powerful that its height was reduced by 1,300 feet?

Answers to QUIZ 222 – Hair and Beauty

1	Cow, as in cowlick	11	Pompadour
2	Maybelline	12	Mousse
3	Microdermal	13	Max Factor
4	Ancient Egypt	14	Farrah Fawcett
5	Tonsure	15	Gold powder
6	The waist	16	Win Miss America twice
7	Scotland (at 13%)	17	Split ends
8	Bergamot	18	£10
9	Marriage and maturity – men start growing beards upon getting married and never shave them thereafter	19	Toothpaste
		20	Sikhism
10	Draws moisture from the air to the skin		

1   The name of which region in India means "Land of Five Rivers"?

2   The *Sipi Tau* ceremonial dance is performed by which nation's rugby union team before each of their international matches?

3   The fictional town of Hawkins is the setting for which Netflix TV drama series?

4   The Battle of Agincourt is central to the plot of which Shakespeare play?

5   How many moons in our solar system are bigger than Earth's Moon?

6   *I Put a Spell on You* was a 1956 hit for which "noisy" singer?

7   Who has appeared on the cover of *Playboy* magazine more times than any other woman?

8   Strangles is a bacterial infection of the respiratory tract in which animals?

9   Which Cornish dish consists of baked pilchards whose heads protrude through the pastry crust?

10 What was the name of the UK's first offshore pirate radio station?

11 "Little Barrel" is the English translation of the nickname given to which artist, on account of him having an overweight older brother?

12 Bolt Head is a headland on the coast of which English county?

13 Which British race track has corners called Brooklands, Maggots and Becketts?

14 In 1956, the first Eurovision Song Contest was held in which country?

15 *Legato* is an instruction to play a piece in what manner?

16 The famous Hollywood sign originally had which four extra letters on the end?

17 *Talipes* is the scientific name for which medical affliction of the foot?

18 What former member of the Spice Girls launched her solo career in 1999 with her debut album *Schizophonic*?

19 What woodwind instrument's name comes from the French term for "high wood"?

20 What element, atomic number 88, was discovered by Marie and Pierre Curie in 1898?

Easy

Medium

Hard

Answers to QUIZ 223 – Pot Luck

1   Brown fat
2   Owl
3   George Foreman
4   13
5   White
6   Royal Troon
7   Oliver Reed
8   Niki Lauda
9   10 Downing Street; it is a title that the Prime Minister also carries
10 The Cat
11 Elephant
12 New Orleans
13 Italy
14 Trumpet
15 The Netherlands
16 1,760 yards
17 Argentina
18 Miss Trunchbull
19 Eric Idle
20 Boris Spassky

Easy

1 Admiral Nelson died upon which ship at the 1805 Battle of Trafalgar?

2 Which conflict saw the only major battle between the main British and German fleets in World War I?

3 Who was the commander of the English forces during the battles against the Spanish Armada?

4 In which battle of the Anglo-Spanish war did Nelson lose his right arm?

5 *Operation Chromite* was the code name for a decisive Korean War battle and land assault at which Korean port city?

6 Occurring during the Russo-Japanese War, which was the first major naval battle of the 20th century, and the first major battle between steel ships?

7 England fought a series of three mostly-naval wars in the seventeenth century against which other European country?

8 Although born in Scotland, who is regarded as the US's first naval hero, largely for his efforts against the British?

9 In World War I, which heavily armed merchant ships with concealed weaponry were designed to lure submarines into making surface attacks?

10 Which battle of 480 BC marked the turning point in the Greco-Persian wars, as Greece destroyed much of the Persian fleet?

11 Who did Octavian defeat at the Battle of Actium to become the undisputed master of the Roman world?

12 On 19th November 1941, which Australian light cruiser was sunk in battle by the German auxiliary cruiser *Kormoran* off the coast of Dirk Hartog Island?

13 Three days before it too was sunk, the German battleship *Bismarck* sank which British battlecruiser during the Battle of Denmark Strait?

14 Who commanded the combined French and Spanish fleet of 33 ships at the Battle of Trafalgar?

15 Used against Carthage during the First Punic War, what name was given to the boarding devices used by ancient Roman warships?

16 At the Battle of Midway, the US lost only one aircraft carrier to Japan's four – what was the name of the sunken US ship?

17 On 17th February 1864, what became the first ever combat submarine to sink an enemy ship?

18 On 22nd June 1807, which US ship was fired upon by HMS *Leopard* for refusing to allow a search for deserters, a key event in the build-up to the war of 1812?

19 In which battle of 1571 in the Gulf of Patras did a coalition of Catholic states arranged by Pope Pius V inflict a major defeat on the Ottoman Empire?

20 Which battle of May 1942 was the first in which aircraft carriers engaged each other, as well as the first in which opposing ships neither sighted nor fired directly at each other?

---

1   Which West African rice dish is typically made in a single pot with long-grain rice, tomatoes, onions, spices, vegetables and meat?

2   Dennis "Thresh" Fong, the world's first professional video gamer, won a Ferrari at the 1997 Red Annihilation tournament playing which game?

3   Robert "Sugar Bear" Jackson is credited with the creation of which dance move, used to signify gang membership?

4   Which singer voiced the part of Gratuity "Tip" Tucci in the 2015 DreamWorks animated film *Home*?

5   A controversial 1971 prison simulation, intended to examine the effects of situational variables on reactions and behaviours, was held at which US university?

6   *Let's Do It, Let's Fall in Love* is a 1928 Cole Porter song written for which musical?

7   In 2022, which goalkeeper was sent off twice in an international match, only for VAR to overturn both of them?

8   Which American president was in office in the year that the *Titanic* sank?

9   Which entertainer of the Regency era struggled with alcoholism and chronic pain, and said of himself, "I am grim all day, but I make you laugh at night"?

10 Which band took their name from a misheard lyric from Prince's 1985 hit single *Raspberry Beret*?

11 What name is shared by a mountainous district in the Peloponnese of southern Greece and, in Greek mythology, the home of Pan?

12 Due to a lack of available land, what entirely normal act is prohibited in the Spanish town of Lanjarón?

13 Coincidentally sharing its name with the sponsor of the event that year, which horse won the 1991 English Grand National?

14 Who, in 2004, became the first DJ to play live at an Olympic Games?

15 Between 1982 and 2021, Boff Whalley was the lead guitarist for which anarcho-punk and folk band?

16 Who played for New Zealand at the 1991 Rugby Union World Cup, then his native Samoa in the 1995 Rugby League and 1999 Union World Cups?

17 In which European city is the Prater public park?

18 Mizaru, Kikazaru and Iwazaru are the names of the trio of characters in which pictorial maxim?

19 Although he lost, which Hungarian-British boxer twice went the distance with Muhammad Ali?

20 The *Avesta* is the main sacred text of which religion?

Easy
Medium
Hard

Answers to QUIZ 225 – Pot Luck

1	Punjab	11	Sandro Botticelli
2	Tonga	12	Devon
3	*Stranger Things*	13	Silverstone
4	*Henry V*	14	Switzerland
5	Four	15	Smoothly
6	Screamin' Jay Hawkins	16	LAND
7	Pamela Anderson	17	Club foot
8	Horses, ponies and donkeys	18	Geri Halliwell
9	Stargazy pie	19	Oboe
10	*Radio Caroline*	20	Radium

1 When drinking fizzy drinks, which constituent compound creates the tingling feeling on the tongue?

2 Which colourless, pungent gas composed of nitrogen and hydrogen is used in fertiliser, fermentation and fridges?

3 Which branch of science is the study of the structure, properties, composition and reactions of carbon-containing compounds?

4 What name is used for a zinc–lead alloy that ages to resemble bronze but is softer, a copper–zinc alloy used for brazing, or for pure zinc?

5 Widely used in the aviation industry, which alloy is formed of aluminium, copper, manganese and magnesium?

6 Which specific now-ubiquitous alloy did Harry Brearly discover by mistake in Sheffield in 1913?

7 Often used as solder, which fusible alloy comprises 50% bismuth, 25–28% lead and 22–25% tin?

8 Any alloy of 92.5% silver and 7.5% other metals (usually copper) added for hardness is known by what name?

9 Bell metal – as the name suggests, commonly used in making bells – is an alloy of which two metals?

10 Alnico is a term for a variety of alloys often used in magnets that contain which three elements as principal ingredients?

11 Which chemical element is always triple-bonded to a carbon atom in cyanide?

12 What is the predominant element in the alloy chromel?

13 18-carat gold consists of what percentage of alloy?

14 With the chemical formula $CaCO_3$, chalk is a naturally occurring form of which compound?

15 Which alloy of mercury is commonly used for dental fillings?

16 Which eutectic alloy composed of gallium, indium and tin melts at -19 °C and thus is liquid at room temperature?

17 To improve thyroid health, compounds of which element are commonly added to table salt?

18 Until the widespread adoption of porcelain, which alloy was the chief material used for producing plates, cups and bowls?

19 In 1929, which man – the "father of molecular biology" – published five rules to predict and explain crystal structures of ionic compounds?

20 Which class of polyphenolic secondary antioxidant metabolites have health benefits for humans and are found in high volume in dark chocolate?

Answers to QUIZ 226 – Naval Battles

1	HMS *Victory*	11	Mark Anthony
2	Battle of Jutland	12	HMAS *Sydney*
3	Lord Howard of Effingham	13	HMS *Hood*
4	Battle of Santa Cruz de Tenerife	14	Admiral Villeneuve
5	Incheon	15	Corvus
6	Battle of Tsushima	16	USS *Yorktown* (CV-5)
7	The Netherlands	17	H.L. *Hunley*
8	John Paul Jones	18	USS *Chesapeake*
9	Q-Ships	19	Battle of Lepanto
10	Battle of Salamis	20	Battle of Coral Sea

1. The picturesque area of Cambridge, England, where the rear grounds of several colleges of the university lie on the River Cam, is known as what?

2. Which socialite sibling and prominent supporter of Nazism, fascism and antisemitism was ironically conceived in a town called Swastika?

3. Which film soundtrack composer won 25 Grammy awards between 1976 and 2020?

4. Taking its name from a horizontal underground plant stem, which philosophical theory is used to describe systems with no clear beginning or end?

5. Between 2002 and 2008, which Scottish football club went from non-league status to the Premiership to liquidation in only six years?

6. As of 2021, who is the only non-UK winner of the World Indoor Men's/Open Singles Bowls Championships?

7. Both Wembley Stadiums were built on the former site of which abandoned folly, inspired by the Eiffel Tower?

8. Who are the only pair of brothers to have won *Match of the Day's* goal of the season award?

9. Which Labour MP became, in 1968, the only woman to have held the cabinet position of First Secretary of State?

10. Which actor has been murdered by the holy trinity of an Alien, a Terminator and a Predator?

11. Ageusia affects which of the senses?

12. Ireland's first ever medal at the Olympic Games came in which artistic field?

13. Which Watford footballer's only England cap came in 2018 and was entirely in stoppage time, meaning he officially played 1 game and 0 minutes?

14. Which team won the 2020 FA Trophy but, as the final had been rescheduled for March 2021 due to the COVID-19 pandemic, held the trophy for only 24 hours?

15. Which American DJ used to throw a cake at an audience member at every show until the lawsuits started coming in?

16. Battledore was the forerunner of which sport?

17. *The Dancing Class* is one of the first of approximately 1,500 lifetime works about dancing by which French realism artist?

18. The band Steely Dan take their name from *Naked Lunch*, a book by which American author?

19. The first capital of Roman Britannia, what is the earliest recorded town in England?

20. According to a French proverb, if you do not want to be deceived, on what date should you get married?

Answers to QUIZ 227 – Pot Luck

1	*Jollof*	11	Arcadia
2	*Quake*	12	Dying
3	Crip walk	13	Seagram
4	Rihanna	14	Tiesto
5	Stanford	15	Chumbawamba
6	*Paris*	16	Va'aiga Tuigamala
7	Allison Becker	17	Vienna
8	William Taft	18	The three wise monkeys who "see no evil, hear no evil, speak no evil"
9	Joseph Grimaldi (see what he did there?)		
10	The Lightning Seeds	19	Joe Bugner
		20	Zoroastrianism

Easy

1   Which explorer was the first European to see, and then name, Victoria Falls?

2   In 1961, who founded the Jewish Historical Documentation Center in Vienna, which concentrated exclusively on the hunting of war criminals?

3   Which Carthaginian military leader lost an eye, kept 37 elephants, threw snakes as weapons and died of a finger infection?

4   Which 14th century ruler of the kingdom of Mali was, in all probability, the richest person who ever lived?

5   On 13th May 1985, Philadelphia police dropped a bomb from a helicopter to destroy a home occupied by which natural law communal organisation?

6   In the Crimean War, which Jamaican housekeeper and nurse opened a convalescent home between Balaclava and Sevastopol?

7   In which year did Aldershot F.C. become the first team to win promotion through the new playoff system, and Rudolf Hess die in Spandau prison?

8   Towards the end of World War I, which Canadian financier was briefly the UK Minister of Information?

9   In 2012, who became the first Hindu to be elected to the US Congress?

10 Which battle of 1265 marked the defeat and death of Simon de Montfort by Prince Edward, later King Edward I?

11 Said to have been the only woman to enlist as a soldier in the British Army during World War I, who enlisted under the alias "Dennis Smith"?

12 Who was the leader of the Visigoths when they sacked Rome in AD 410?

13 King Louis XVI, Marie Antoinette and Maximilien Robespierre were all beheaded in which Parisian public square?

14 Which 1464 battle marked the end of significant Lancastrian resistance in the north of England during the early part of Edward IV's reign?

15 On account of being the first person identified as a carrier, how was Irish cook Mary Mallon known by the media?

16 Which emperor led the Roman Empire during the Marcomannic wars?

17 The United States bought which state for $15,000,000 in 1803?

18 Sefton was a severely injured horse survivor of which 1982 IRA terrorist attack that killed seven other horses and 11 British military personnel?

19 A March 1979 partial meltdown of which power plant was the most significant accident in US commercial nuclear power plant history?

20 Whose April 1775 "midnight ride" to alert the colonial militia of British forces was dramatised in an 1861 Henry Wadsworth Longfellow poem?

Answers to QUIZ 228 – Alloys and Compounds

1	Carbon dioxide	11	Nitrogen
2	Ammonia	12	Nickel
3	Organic chemistry	13	25% (with 75% gold)
4	Spelter	14	Calcium carbonate
5	Duralumin	15	Amalgam
6	Stainless steel	16	Galinstan
7	Rose's metal	17	Iodine
8	Sterling silver	18	Pewter
9	Copper and tin, with more tin than bronze, another copper/tin alloy	19	Linus Pauling
10	Aluminium, nickel and cobalt (hence the name)	20	Flavonoids

QUIZ 231 – Pot Luck

ANSWERS ON PAGE 233

1. Which American jazz poet, known for his work *The Revolution Will Not Be Televised*, also voiced the original "Orange Man" Tango advert?
2. When Jarvis Cocker was questioned by police after invading the stage at the 1996 BRIT awards, which comic served as his solicitor?
3. Which Welsh football legend was nicked "Gigante Buono" during his time in Italy and finished third in the 1959 Ballon D'Or?
4. In 1931, which mathematician published his first incompleteness theorem, showing that arithmetic was not and could never be complete?
5. Fleegle, Bingo, Drooper and Snorky made up which fictional costumed rock band?
6. Forming part of the country's "coffee triangle", which city is the capital of Colombia's *Quindio* department?
7. *Le Bateau*, a paper-cut artwork infamously hung upside-down by the Museum of Modern Art for 47 days in 1961, was by which French artist?
8. When John Glenn returned to space on Space Shuttle mission STS-95 in 1998, how old was he?
9. Which was the first Winter Olympic games to take place in a non-leap year?
10. In a phrase coined by 16th century author John Lyly, what two things begin to smell after three days?
11. Before he was famous, Olly Murs appeared as a contestant on which now-cancelled afternoon game show?
12. Dicky Barrett was the lead vocalist and Ben Carr the specialist dancer in which ska punk band?
13. Which politician – a Junior Health Minister at the time – said in September 1986 that northerners die of "ignorance and chips"?
14. Which town in County Durham is known locally as Bish Vegas?
15. Members of which Christian denomination, which preaches the imminent return of Christ to Earth, tend to live 10 years longer than the average American?
16. Keith Chegwin had a small part as the host of which nudist game show?
17. Which sport is the only one that was designed especially for the Olympic games?
18. Aphagia is the inability or refusal to what?
19. After withdrawing in 1985, which African country is the only one, as of 2021, that is not a member of the African Union?
20. Perhaps better known for its use as a different mode of transport, what name is given to a hot air balloon's basket?

Easy / *Medium* / *Hard*

Answers to QUIZ 229 – Pot Luck

1. The Backs
2. Unity Mitford
3. John Williams
4. Rhizome theory
5. Gretna FC
6. Ian Schuback (Australia, 1992)
7. Watkins' Tower
8. Danny Wallace (1983-84) and Rod Wallace (1993-94)
9. Barbara Castle
10. Bill Paxton
11. Taste
12. Painting (between 1912 and 1948, the Olympic games contained artistic events)
13. Nathaniel Chalobah
14. Salford FC
15. Steve Aoki
16. Badminton
17. Edgar Degas
18. William S. Burroughs
19. Colchester
20. 30th February

231

Easy

1   Which American privately-funded aerospace manufacturer and spaceflight services company was founded in 2000 by Jeff Bezos?

2   Which European Space Agency satellite was, in 2014, the first to make a controlled touchdown on a comet nucleus?

3   What was the first satellite to orbit the earth?

4   The first country to send a person into space was the Soviet Union; the second was the USA. Which was third?

5   The USA refers to space travellers as astronauts, and Russia as cosmonauts. What do China refer to them as?

6   How many NASA space shuttles flew into orbit?

7   Which communication satellite, launched in 1962, successfully relayed through space the first television pictures and telephone calls?

8   Which space exploration "first" took place on 17th July 1975?

9   On 19th April 2021, NASA made the first ever controlled flight of a craft in the atmosphere of another planet when which small helicopter flew on Mars?

10 Although citizens of more than 40 countries have been to space, how many countries, as of 2021, have launched their own crewed spacecraft?

Medium

11 In August 2012, which spacecraft – launched 35 years earlier – became the first spacecraft to cross the heliopause, entering interstellar space?

12 In 2019, who set a new record for the longest continuous time in space by a woman, with 328 days?

13 What was the September 2021 space flight *Inspiration 4* notable for?

14 What was the new record for the highest number of people to be in space at the same time set on 11th December 2021?

15 The first known space burial saw which screenwriter's ashes be the first ever flown into space in 1992?

16 Twelve men have walked on the moon, but none since which year?

17 In 2001, which American engineer paid $20 million to become the first ever space tourist?

18 The *Fédération Aéronautique Internationale* defines the edge of space as being 100 kilometres above mean sea level, a dividing line known as what?

19 Which term is being used to refer to the relative modernity of private spaceflight efforts and the privatisation of spaceflight as a commercial industry?

20 In 2013, cosmonaut Pavel Vinogradov became the first human to do what important, if mundane, act from space?

Hard

Answers to QUIZ 230 – History

1	David Livingstone	11	Dorothy Lawrence
2	Simon Wiesenthal	12	Alaric
3	Hannibal Barca	13	Place de la Concorde
4	Mansa Musa	14	Battle of Hexham
5	MOVE	15	Typhoid Mary
6	Mary Seacole	16	Marcus Aurelius
7	1987	17	Louisiana
8	Lord Beaverbrook	18	Hyde Park and Regent's Park bombings
9	Tulsa Gabbard	19	Three Mile Island
10	Battle of Evesham	20	Paul Revere

1   Berger's disease affects which organ of the body?

2   The first state visit by an Irish president to the United Kingdom was made in April 2014 by who?

3   "Globbits!" was an expression of mild annoyance frequently heard in which 1980s animated children's television series?

4   Which actress appeared as Kate Hedges in *Ali G Indahouse*, as Tara Wilson on *The Practice* and *Boston Legal*, and as Detective Kit McGraw in *Nip/Tuck*?

5   Which celebrated countercultural figure directed the 1978 film *Jubilee*?

6   Named for a year, what is the name of the committee of all backbench Conservative MPs that meets weekly when the Commons is sitting?

7   Which small flightless bird has the largest egg relative to its body size?

8   Which Indonesian low-cost airline is named after an animal?

9   Bailey's Marvel, Van Dyke, Tommy Atkins and Kent are cultivars of which fruit?

10 At age 25, which famous artist volunteered to become pastor to a poor mining village in southwestern Belgium?

11 In 1968, Marcelo Caetano became the Prime Minister of which European country?

12 When given the option of going on a date with any Australian celebrity for the comedy series *It's a Date*, Ross Noble chose who?

13 Queen Mary I of England married the ruling monarch of which other European nation?

14 Which Brazilian striker won the FIFA Women's World Player Of The Year title five years in a row?

15 In 1998, the comedian Richard Herring created a "Saint's day" named for which cartoon villain, intended as "a day for all the lost souls who don't have anyone to love"?

16 John Lithgow and Glenn Close were both nominated for Academy Awards for their roles in which 1982 comedy-drama film starring Robin Williams?

17 Which "new" African capital city grew at the rate of 139% between 2000 and 2010, making it the fastest growing city in the world?

18 Which Japanese style of brazier is charcoal burnt in to provide indoor heating, and is also the name of a grill used for outdoor cooking?

19 Between 1955 and 1958, and again between 1971 and 1984, Dom Mintoff was the Prime Minister of which country?

20 In Ancient Greek legend, which knot was used as a metaphor for an intractable problem, one solved by Alexander the Great?

Easy

Medium

Hard

Answers to QUIZ 231 – Pot Luck

1	Gil Scott-Heron	11	*Wheel of Fortune*
2	Bob Mortimer	12	The Mighty Mighty Bosstones
3	John Charles	13	Edwina Currie
4	Kurt Gödel	14	Bishop Auckland
5	Banana Splits	15	Seventh Day Adventists
6	Armenia	16	*Naked Jungle*
7	Henri Matisse	17	Modern pentathlon
8	77	18	Swallow/eat
9	1994 (Lillehammer)	19	Morocco
10	Fish and visitors	20	Gondola

Easy

1   Ninety Mile Beach, a 55-mile long beach, is in which country?

2   Formerly called the Spice Islands during imperial times, the Molucca or Maluku island archipelago is a part of which country?

3   Taking its name from one of the largest rivers in the nation, the *kwanza* is the currency of which African country?

4   The Comoro Islands (or Comoros) are located in which water channel within the Indian Ocean?

5   What unfortunate thing happened to the New Cholutca River Bridge in Honduras in 1998, just as it was about to open?

6   The Notre-Dame cathedral and Paris's first hospital Hôtel-Dieu sit on which island in the River Seine?

7   Edmund Halley had an observatory on which remote volcanic tropical island, often associated with Napoleon?

8   Which Irish city, the county town of County Louth, sits exactly halfway between Dublin and Belfast?

9   The southernmost point of Iceland, which "new" island formed through a volcanic eruption on 14th November 1963?

10 The Roman city of Lutetia was the predecessor to which modern-day city?

Medium

11 Which subregion of Oceania includes the Arafura Sea, Fiji, Vanuatu, the Solomon Islands, Papua New Guinea, New Caledonia and parts of Indonesia?

12 Which island is scheduled to gain independence from Papua New Guinea by 2027 and become a new state?

13 Which island, the 91st largest in the world, is the last known place where woolly mammoths survived and is a protected nature sanctuary, with zero human population?

14 Considered the world's largest bridge-tunnel complex, a 17.6-mile bridge-tunnel crosses the mouth of which North Atlantic estuary?

15 While he was not the first to posit it, Alfred Wegener's 1912 paper developed the idea that the continents had once formed a single landmass; a theory which he named what?

16 The Swan River runs through which Australian city?

17 The region of Halkidiki is a popular tourist destination located in which country?

18 Which Australian city was almost named "Batmania" after one of its founders, John Batman?

19 When translated, the name of which Asian country means "land of the thunder dragon"?

20 Not to be confused with the Canadian province of a similar name, the Prince Edward Islands belong to which African country?

Hard

Answers to QUIZ 232 – Space Exploration

1	Blue Origin	11	*Voyager I*
2	*Rosetta*	12	Christina Koch
3	*Sputnik I*	13	It was the first spaceflight to orbit Earth with
4	Czechoslovakia		only private citizens on board
5	Taikonauts	14	19
6	Five (*Atlantis, Challenger, Columbia, Discovery,*	15	Gene Roddenberry
	Endeavour; the sixth, *Enterprise*, never went into	16	1972
	orbital flight)	17	Dennis Tito
7	*Telstar I*	18	Kármán line
8	US and Russian astronauts met in space	19	NewSpace
9	*Ingenuity*	20	Pay income taxes
10	Three (USA, Russia, China)		

1 Because of its landscape, certain scenes from *Star Wars, Monty Python's Life of Brian* and *The English Patient* have been filmed in which African country?

2 Which model was the first to appear on three consecutive covers of the Sports Illustrated Swimsuit Issue?

3 Although Judy Garland ultimately landed the role, who was the studio's first choice to play Dorothy in *The Wizard of Oz*?

4 Who wrote the 1981 philosophical treatise *Simulacra and Simulation*?

5 Which actor's six-minute performance in *Network* is the shortest to ever be nominated for Best Supporting Actor?

6 The Jim Carrey film *Yes Man*, in which he vows to "say yes more" for an entire year, is based on a book by which English comedian?

7 The impractical but striking Armadillo boot was a 2010 design by which designer?

8 Famous for its overture, which was Gioachino Rossini's last opera before retiring aged 37?

9 *Maybe Tomorrow* was the theme music to which Canadian TV series about an ownerless dog?

10 Ferroequinology is an obscure term for the (usually recreational) study of what?

11 In horses and dogs, which 'W' is the ridge between the shoulder blades and is the standard place to measure the animal's height?

12 Which American costume designer won a record eight Academy Awards for Best Costume between 1949 and 1973?

13 Megara, Omphale, Deianira and Hebe were the wives of which Greek mythological figure?

14 How many stocks are featured on the Dow Jones Industrial Average market index?

15 Which Egyptian god served as the protector of graves and cemeteries?

16 Fiacres, britzkas and barouches are all what types of transportation?

17 Which is the hottest chilli pepper in the world?

18 On what type of farm did Taylor Swift grow up?

19 The World Stare-Out Championships featured in which 1990s BBC sketch show?

20 Which British comedian and writer had a no.1 hit in Finland in 1958 with a cover of Sheb Wooley's *Purple People Eater*?

Easy

Medium

Hard

Answers to QUIZ 233 – Pot Luck

1	Kidneys	11	Portugal
2	Michael Higgins	12	Ian Smith (Harold Bishop in *Neighbours*)
3	*The Trap Door*	13	Spain (King Philip II)
4	Rhona Mitra	14	Marta
5	Derek Jarman	15	Saint Skeletor's Day
6	1922 Committee	16	*The World According to Garp*
7	Brown kiwi	17	Abuja
8	Lion Air	18	Hibachi
9	Mango	19	Malta
10	Vincent van Gogh	20	The Gordian knot

Can you identify these species of water birds?

Easy

1

2

3

4

Medium

5

6

7

8

Hard

Answers to QUIZ 234 – Geography

1	New Zealand	11	Melanesia
2	Indonesia	12	Bougainville
3	Angola	13	Wrangel Island
4	Mozambique Channel	14	Chesapeake Bay
5	A massive hurricane rerouted the river it was supposed to go over, resulting in a bridge over nothing	15	Continental drift theory
		16	Perth
		17	Greece
6	Île de la Cité	18	Melbourne
7	Saint Helena	19	Bhutan
8	Dundalk	20	South Africa
9	Surtsey Island		
10	Paris		

1 In the 1960s, which Indian yoga guru, the founder of Transcendental Meditation, became Spiritual Advisor to The Beatles?

2 What name is given to the therapy developed by Sigmund Freud that concentrates on early childhood experiences and unconscious problems?

3 The Turkish national drink *Raki* is what flavour?

4 The Iguazu Falls, the world's largest waterfall system, lies on the border between which two South American countries?

5 Of the seven holy cities of Hinduism, which is considered the holiest of them all?

6 The Pyramids of Giza, the *Mona Lisa*, the Parthenon and the Pepsi logo all cohere with which mathematical ratio, approximately equal to 1.618/1?

7 Warfarin prevents blood from clotting by inhibiting the re-uptake of which vitamin?

8 Queen Beatrix airport is located in which Dutch overseas territory in the Caribbean?

9 A body cavity described as "infundibulum" is what shape?

10 In *Peter Pan*, what is Captain Hook's first name?

11 If the adjective "dextral" refers to your right hand, what adjective refers to your left?

12 In 1980, which European country was the first to have a woman democratically elected as Head of State?

13 What is the name of the famous US Military Academy in New York?

14 Which British cartoon strip character created by Reg Smythe is known as *Willi Wacker* in Germany?

15 Who plays Soviet agent Irina Spalko in the 2008 film *Indiana Jones and the Kingdom of the Crystal Skull*?

16 In Jewish culture, what is a *kever*?

17 What type of plant is a *nardoo*?

18 The Koppen System is a classification system for what?

19 The British literary medal that annually recognises "distinguished illustration in a book for children" is named for which 19th century illustrator?

20 Horsetail, punchbowl, cataract and multi-step are all types of which geographical feature?

Answers to QUIZ 235 – Pot Luck

1	Tunisia	11	Withers
2	Christie Brinkley	12	Edith Head
3	Deanna Durbin	13	Heracles
4	Jean Baudrillard	14	30
5	Ned Beatty	15	Anubis
6	Danny Wallace	16	Horse-drawn carriages
7	Alexander McQueen	17	The Carolina Reaper
8	*William Tell*	18	A Christmas tree farm
9	*The Littlest Hobo*	19	*Big Train*
10	Railways	20	Barry Cryer

Easy

Medium

Hard

1   In the story of Lady Godiva, as she rode naked through the streets, which tailor stole a glance and was struck blind?

2   A long-term legend holds that which unexpected animal supposedly lives in the sewers of New York City?

3   The story of the tand-fé (tooth fee), a possible precursor to the tooth fairy, originated in which country in the 13th century?

4   In which Asian country did the legend of the Slit-Mouthed Woman originate?

5   In Middle Ages German legend, it was thought that kissing a donkey would take away which ailment?

6   Which animal is said to lack a tail because it was accidentally shut in the door of Noah's ark?

7   Which earth spirits from Welsh and English lore are said to dress as miners and steal miners' food and tools?

8   Said to be beautiful but shy, which tree-dwelling nymphs are considered friends of the goddess Artemis and punish anyone who damages a tree?

9   In the Alps, the Krampus is a creature that accompanies which famous saint?

10   Similar to werewolves, Cajun legend holds that which creatures prowl the swamps and woodlands around New Orleans?

11   If it rains on St Swithin's Day, how many days is it supposed to rain thereafter?

12   The folklore of several countries holds that handling toads causes which viral skin condition?

13   Which shapeshifting Caribbean folklore character appears as a reclusive old woman by day, and by night is a blood-sucking fireball?

14   In Latin American folklore, which monstrous creature attacks animals and consumes their blood?

15   Hawai'ian folklore describes which procession of gods and ghosts that carry the dead to their new fates on new moon nights?

16   Which creature of Irish folklore appears as a pony, takes riders through marshland and thorns, then throws them into a ditch or pond?

17   Said to lurk in billabongs and creeks, the name of which amphibious monster of Aboriginal folklore is also now used as a general term for an imposter?

18   In folklore, which metal is said to repel ghosts, fairies, witches and other malevolent supernatural creatures?

19   It is said that ants travelling in a straight line means what is about to happen?

20   Bucca, a merman that inhabits mines and coastal communities as a hobgoblin during storms, is a part of the folklore of where?

Answers to QUIZ 236 – Waterfowl

1   Trumpeter swan
2   Mallard
3   Ruddy duck
4   Canada goose
5   Smew
6   Hooded merganser
7   Wood duck
8   King eider

1 In 1901, Guglielmo Marconi received the first transatlantic wireless signal from atop Signal Hill in which Canadian city?

2 In Norse mythology, who or what is Yggdrasil?

3 Colombia is the source of an estimated 85% of the world's total supply of which precious gemstones?

4 Which narrow 580-mile-long stretch of water separates Malaysia from the Indonesian island of Sumatra?

5 Which humanoid alien witch was the principal enemy of the Power Rangers?

6 Which Tuscan city was the birthplace of the composer Giacomo Puccini?

7 Located in the Andes on the border of Chile and Argentina, which stratovolcano is the highest active volcano in the world?

8 Which Pennsylvanian town was abandoned in the 1980s due to the toxic fumes released by a fire in the abandoned coal mines below that continues to this day?

9 Which British TV presenter appeared as Fleance in Roman Polanski's adaptation of *Macbeth*?

10 What is the term for the vertical distance between two matching design elements on a roll of wallpaper?

11 Prior to both of her big breaks, which former actress and famous spouse used to work as a freelance calligrapher?

12 Graphene is an allotrope of carbon consisting of a single layer of atoms arranged in what shape?

13 In 2014, which Pakistani teenager become the youngest-ever Nobel laureate, winning the Peace Prize for her work against the suppression of children?

14 Which 'M' is a term given to a female's first menstrual cycle?

15 In which Asian country's age classification system does everyone get one year older every New Year's Day?

16 A Danish tradition holds that if someone is unmarried on their 25th birthday, they are tied to a lamppost and covered in which spice?

17 Which is the only bird that has nostrils on the end of its beak?

18 Which 1970s fashion designer popularised the wrap dress?

19 Which writer and intellectual called the drug-related death of fellow writer Truman Capote "a wise career move"?

20 The film *Eternal Sunshine of the Spotless Mind* takes its name from a line in *Eloisa to Abelard*, a verse epistle by which 18th century British poet?

Answers to QUIZ 237 – Pot Luck

1	Maharishi Mahesh Yogi	11	Sinistral
2	Psychoanalysis	12	Iceland (Vigdís Finnbogadóttir)
3	Aniseed	13	West Point
4	Argentina and Brazil	14	Andy Capp
5	Varanasi	15	Cate Blanchett
6	The Golden Ratio	16	Tomb or grave
7	K	17	Fern
8	Aruba	18	Climates
9	Funnel-shaped	19	Kate Greenaway
10	James	20	Waterfalls

Easy

1. Which artist created a porcelain sculpture of Michael Jackson and his pet monkey Bubbles?
2. Who painted *Poker Game* in 1894, the origin of the "Dogs Playing Poker" art trend?
3. In accordance with his will, sixty beggars carrying tapers followed around the casket of which Renaissance artist?
4. Painters Raphael and Annibale Carracci, composer Arcangelo Corelli and architect Baldassare Peruzzi are all buried where?
5. In which city is The Whitney art gallery?
6. A 1956 painting by Graham Vivian Sutherland was an official portrait of who, who hated it so much that it was destroyed after his death?
7. Two years after stealing it and keeping it in his apartment, which art thief was caught trying to claim a reward for returning the *Mona Lisa* in 1913?
8. Thomas Cole is generally acknowledged as the founder of which art movement of landscape painters influenced by Romanticism?
9. 1980's *The Times Square Show* was the first major exhibition of which New York City artists' group?
10. In a jealous rage, which famous sculptor attacked his mistress with a knife because she wanted to leave him?

11. Frans Hals's *The Laughing Cavalier* is among the paintings in which museum located in London's Hertford House?
12. Louis Wain was an English artist best known for his drawings of which animals?
13. Who was the artist sister of Virginia Woolf?
14. Which artist famously shared a bed with the poet Max Jacob?
15. In 2014, which American visual artist known for her large-scale multimedia installations was awarded the National Medal of Arts?

Medium

16. Ellen Blakeley is a mosaicist noted for her pioneering use of which material?
17. The world's longest painting is a kilometre-long 2018 painting by Serbian artist Ana Tudor of which river?
18. Antony Gormley, Chien-Ying Chang and Ben Enwonwu are among the notable alumni of which London art school?
19. Painter Gustave Courbet and writer Gustave Flaubert were both key figures in which movement that spanned multiple areas of art?
20. There are only two surviving landscape paintings by El Greco, both of which depict which Spanish city?

Hard

Answers to QUIZ 238 – Folklore

1	Peeping Tom	11	40
2	Alligators (they don't)	12	Warts
3	Iceland	13	Soucouyant
4	Japan (Kuchisake-onna)	14	Chupacabra
5	Toothache	15	Hukai'po or Nightmarchers
6	Manx cat	16	Púca or phooka
7	Knockers	17	Bunyip
8	Dryads	18	Iron
9	Saint Nicholas	19	Rain
10	Rougarou	20	Cornwall

1   The *real*, the basic currency of Brazil, subdivides into 100 what?

2   Which Italian actress was the first person to win an Academy Award for a performance entirely in a language other than English?

3   What does a helixophile collect?

4   Victor Mature and Hedy Lamarr played the title roles in which 1949 Biblical film?

5   The world's largest ice sculpture festival takes place annually in which Chinese city?

6   Which American state is known as the Old Line State or the Free State?

7   The "Night of the Long Knives" in Germany in 1934 is sometimes referred to by which bird's name?

8   In April 1980, the St Paul's Riot broke out in which English city?

9   In 2008, Sarah Stevenson became Britain's first-ever Olympic medallist in which martial art?

10 Sharing his name with Graham Norton's character in *Father Ted*, who was the 1999 World Series of Poker Main Event champion?

11 By what name is the Siamese fighting fish also known?

12 In Greek mythology, who correctly answers the riddle of the Sphynx?

13 In which Eastern European country could you vacation at the resort known as Sunny Beach?

14 The Mamucium Roman Fort Reconstruction is situated in which English city?

15 Bobby Ewing's death was revealed to be a dream sequence in *Dallas*, but not in which spin-off series, which included his death storyline but not the dream explanation?

16 A bridge that opens in the middle, such as Tower Bridge in London, is known as what type of bridge?

17 Which is the only capital city to directly border two other sovereign states?

18 Founded in 1979 and named for its founder, which prize is often referred to as the unofficial Nobel Prize of architecture?

19 Between 1977 and 1991, pop star Lulu was married to which famous hairdresser?

20 Burdened with mental illness throughout his life, King Charles VI of France suffered episodes in which he thought he was made of which substance?

Easy

Medium

Hard

Answers to QUIZ 239 – Pot Luck

1	St John's, Newfoundland	11	Meghan Markle
2	A tree at the centre of the universe	12	Hexagons, or honeycomb-shaped
3	Emeralds	13	Malala Yousafzai
4	Strait of Malacca	14	Menarche
5	Rita Repulsa	15	Korea
6	Lucca	16	Cinnamon
7	Nevado Ojos del Salado	17	Kiwi
8	Centralia	18	Diane von Fürstenberg
9	Keith Chegwin	19	Gore Vidal
10	Repeat	20	Alexander Pope

1   Canberra, the planned capital city of Australia founded in 1913, was designed by which American husband and wife team?

2   Plans are afoot to replace which rapidly-sinking Asian national capital city, which estimates suggest could be one-third submerged by 2050?

3   Bill Gates and local real estate investors have proposed plans for which new "smart city" on the outskirts of Phoenix, Arizona?

4   Due to the extant capital, Malabo, being on an island more than 100 miles from the mainland, which African country commenced building a new capital city in 2017?

5   What name is being used for China's ambitious plan to build road, rail and maritime infrastructure links across Asia and Europe, including several new cities, to boost trade?

6   Naypyidaw, an entirely planned city outside of any state or region, officially replaced which other city as the capital of Myanmar?

7   Which Eurasian country developed a new planned capital city in the 1960s, then renamed it three times between 1991 and 2019?

8   South Korea is building which new city on land reclaimed from the sea?

9   In 2012, what became Scotland's seventh city?

10 In January 1970, which Mexican city consisted of only three people on a coconut plantation?

11 Because of overcrowding and congestion, the seat of government of Malaysia was shifted in 1999 from Kuala Lumpur to which planned city?

12 Although construction began in 2005, the Financial Times in 2018 described which Saudi Arabian new city as "eerily quiet and empty"?

13 Every single building in which Chinese new city is being heavily covered in plants?

14 To ease overcrowding in Lagos, which 100 hectare new city is being created via reclamation of land from the Lagos Lagoon?

15 33 times the size of New York City, which planned Saudi Arabian city is intended to be so large that it will also reach into Egypt and Jordan?

16 If it is completed, which planned city will feature the first 1 km-tall building in human history?

17 Which Chinese new city is being built in a circle around a circular artificial lake?

18 In 2020, a property tycoon approached the government with a proposal to build a city in Ireland called Nextpolis to host 50,000 emigrants from where?

19 Duqm, a small fishing village as recently as 2011, is being heavily urbanised with a view to being the main tourist resort in which country?

20 Pilgrim Street East is a multi-billion reconstruction project in which English city?

Answers to QUIZ 240 – Art

1	Jeff Koons	11	Wallace Collection
2	Cassius Marcellus Coolidge	12	Cats, usually with large eyes
3	Leonardo da Vinci	13	Vanessa Bell
4	Pantheon, Rome	14	Pablo Picasso
5	New York City	15	Ann Hamilton
6	Sir Winston Churchill	16	Tempered glass
7	Vincenzo Peruggia	17	Danube
8	The Hudson River School	18	Slade
9	Colab	19	Realism
10	Gian Lorenzo Bernini	20	Toledo

1   Which Middle Eastern capital city lies at the base of the Alborz mountains?

2   Which English metaphysical poet wrote in his book *Devotions Upon Emergent Occasions* that "no man is an island"?

3   DC Comics character Barbara Gordon has appeared under the names of both Batgirl and which other?

4   In bridge, due to the tradition that the dummy must buy the declarer a drink if they win the last trick with it, which card is known as the Beer Card?

5   Flora Post and Charles Fairford are characters in which 1932 novel by Stella Gibbons?

6   One minute of latitude at the equator is equal to how many nautical miles?

7   Until its closure in 2020, the Museum of Bags and Purses was in which European city?

8   What is the surname of Joe in the children's puppet series *Joe 90*?

9   American photographer Ansel Adams was famous for his black-and-white photographs of what?

10   The travelling funfair known as the "Goose Fair" is held annually in which English city?

11   Which military science fiction computer game series follows Master Chief Sierra-117 "John" through interstellar war?

12   Rivella is a milk whey-based soft drink from which European country?

13   The Nevada portion of which highway is known as the "Loneliest Road in America", on account of how few inhabited places it goes though?

14   In linguistics, what name is given to a situation in which two languages (or two varieties of the same language) are used under different conditions within a community, often by the same speakers?

15   The Heidelberg School was an impressionist art movement of the late 19th century in which country?

16   The medical condition aphakia affects which part of the body?

17   Blue Castello cheese is made in which country?

18   What is the name of the fictional nation in the *Hunger Games* film series?

19   The Great Smoky Mountains are on the border of which two American states?

20   Who was the first ballerina to tour the world?

Easy

Medium

Hard

Easy

1   Oology is the study and/or collection of what?

2   The modern Scottish Parliament Building is situated in which area of Edinburgh?

3   In which hospital was the UK's first operational major trauma centre situated?

4   How is singer Elaine Bookbinder better known?

5   Which large tropical seabird of the gannet family was named for its stupidity in how easily it is caught?

6   John Rzeznik, Robby Takac and George Tutuska were the founders of which American rock band?

7   In the slang of Australia and New Zealand, what term is given to a young man working on a sheep or cattle station to gain experience?

8   Which thick soup is often prepared communally as a social gathering in central and southern USA, including as the basis for civic fund-raisers?

9   Buffalo Bob Smith was the human sidekick to which freckled American marionette, whose namesake programme mixed circus and Western frontier themes?

10 Which professional sports bettor and poker player became owner/chairman of Brighton & Hove Albion FC in 2009?

11 Which MP for Braintree and Minister for Civil Society resigned after multiple sexting allegations?

12 The alamootie, calloo, kjoorlie and doom are all Shetland Island names for what type of animal species?

13 Which quiz game was featured on Channel 4's Teletext service between 1994 and 2009?

14 Grown in the Chinese province of Hupeh, *oopack* or *oopak* is a variety of what?

Medium

15 Although Regina is the capital, which other city is the largest in the Canadian province of Saskatchewan?

16 Keanu Reeves voiced which stuntman character in *Toy Story 4*?

17 On 16th May 1929, Douglas Fairbanks hosted the first Oscar ceremonies at which Hollywood hotel?

18 *Omoo* (1847) was the second travel adventure based on which author's encounters with the peoples of the Marquesa Islands?

19 In the namesake musical, two American tourists stumble upon which mysterious Scottish village that appears for only one day every 100 years?

20 Toucan Sam is the mascot for which Kellogg's® breakfast cereal that was sold in Britain between 2012 and 2015?

Hard

Answers to QUIZ 242 – New Cities

1	Walter Burley Griffin and Marion Mahony Griffin	11	Putrajaya
2	Jakarta	12	King Abdullah Economic City (KAEC)
3	Belmont	13	Liuzhou City
4	Equatorial Guinea	14	Gracefield Island
5	Belt and Road Initiative	15	Neom
6	Yangon	16	Jeddah Economic City (Saudi Arabia)
7	Kazakhstan – Nur-Sultan (2019-present), previously Akmola (1991-1998) then Astana (1998-2019)	17	Nanhui
		18	Hong Kong
8	Songdo	19	Oman
9	Perth	20	Newcastle
10	Cancun		

1 Which fruit is traditionally used to make a Liverpool Tart?

2 The Aqua Tower, the tallest building in the world designed by a woman (Jeanne Gang), is located in which city?

3 If something is said to have been sherardized, which metal has it been coated with?

4 As opposed to an understudy who learns a specific part, what term in theatre is given to a person who, at any given time and at any performance, can appear in whatever role is needed?

5 In Arabian mythology, which species of bird of prey was said to be so large that it could pick up an elephant?

6 The first Victoria and Albert Museum outside London was opened in which city in 2018?

7 What is the name of Acer Inc's range of affordable computers?

8 Which New York socialite, upon receiving an inheritance from her father's death, set about trying to become a soprano singer, despite being notoriously bad at it?

9 The Rock and Roll Hall of Fame is located in which American city?

10 Which 1966 novel by Thomas Pynchon features Oedipa Maas unearthing a conspiracy theory regarding rival mail distribution companies?

11 In Christianity, what name is given to disfigurements on the body that are believed to be in the same place as Jesus's wounds during the Crucifixion?

12 Which 2021 coming-of-age film by Paul Thomas Anderson takes its name from a defunct record store chain in 1970's Southern California ?

13 Which term for the use of emotional tactics to manipulate another individual's reality is derived from the title of a 1938 British stage play?

14 Which Nobel Prize-winning mathematician was in 1965 the first to prove that black holes are a natural consequence of relativity theory and thus truly exist?

15 Giving his name to a musical based around the story, which French minstrel found the imprisoned Richard I by singing a song that only they knew?

16 The phenomenon that poets are more susceptible to mental illness than other creative writers is named for which poet, who committed suicide aged 30 in 1963?

17 Who was the "gentleman thief" character created by E.W. Hornung, brother-in-law of Arthur Conan Doyle?

18 The radical faction of 19th century textile workers which destroyed machinery in protest at forced technological advancement became known as who?

19 Diefenbaker is Fraser's deaf white wolf sidekick in which Canadian comedy drama series of the 1990s?

20 Which Irish rock group were ambushed at a fake checkpoint with three members killed in the town of Bushkill in 1975?

Easy

Medium

Hard

Answers to QUIZ 243 – Pot Luck

1	Tehran	11	*Halo*
2	John Donne	12	Switzerland
3	Oracle	13	US Route 50
4	Seven of diamonds	14	Diglossia
5	*Cold Comfort Farm*	15	Australia
6	60	16	Eyes; it means to be missing a lens
7	Amsterdam	17	Denmark
8	McLaine	18	Panem
9	The American West	19	North Carolina and Tennessee
10	Nottingham	20	Anna Pavlova

1. Which was the first African team to compete in the Cricket World Cup?
2. Which NBA franchise, founded in 1989, has a full name that is an anagram of "interwoven metabolisms"?
3. Which member of boxing's "Fabulous Four" of the 1980s was the only one who defeated each of the other three at least once?
4. The Hopman Cup is a mixed-gender team event in which sport?
5. Which former Watford footballer's name is often used as a pseudonym for artists and activists who wish to remain anonymous?
6. As of the 2018 games in PyeongChang, what is the only Winter Olympic event in which only men compete?
7. Which racehorse, dominant in his short career before prematurely dying in suspicious circumstances, won Australia's Melbourne Cup in 1930?
8. At which Olympic games were women first allowed to compete?
9. In 2010, who became the first club captain of Manchester United from Eastern Europe?
10. In skiing and snowboarding, what does NASTAR stand for?
11. In 2018, which English football team unveiled a household boiler as its new mascot?
12. Which German boxer invented his now world-famous eponymous system of fitness while imprisoned in a British internment camp during World War I?
13. In which winter sport is a tournament called a *bonspiel*?
14. Which tennis player won his only Grand Slam title at the French Open in 1989, beating Ivan Lendl on the way with underhand serves?
15. In dressage terminology, what name is given to a highly collected and cadenced trot done on the spot?
16. Which Chinese athlete won the men's 110m hurdles at the 2004 Olympics, but did not clear a single hurdle across the 2008 and 2012 games combined?
17. A golf course built on sandy soil buffeted by the wind, with few trees and many bunkers, is broadly known as what type of course?
18. Although she never played a game, Lusia Harris was in 1977 the only woman to ever be drafted into which major American sports league?
19. After 25 years as a pro, which English snooker player finally won his first ever ranking tournament at the 2016 Northern Irish Open?
20. Which versatile Sheffield Wednesday player played in the 1993 League Cup Final as a striker, and the 1993 FA Cup Final as a centre back?

Answers to QUIZ 244 – OO

1	Birds' eggs	11	Brooks Newmark
2	Holyrood	12	Duck
3	Addenbrooke's Hospital, Cambridge	13	*Bamboozle!*
4	Elkie Brooks	14	Tea
5	Booby	15	Saskatoon
6	Goo Goo Dolls	16	Duke Caboom
7	Jackaroo	17	Roosevelt Hotel
8	Burgoo	18	Herman Melville
9	Howdy Doody	19	*Brigadoon*
10	Tony Bloom	20	Froot Loops

1 Although they are almost all uninhabited, which European country has the most islands, with more than a quarter of a million?

2 Which Martin Scorsese film features the line "I heard you paint houses", and is based on of a book of the same name?

3 The original motto of which international organisation was "Amidst War, Charity"?

4 On a guitar, which bar provides a modulation effect that rhythmically changes the volume of a signal?

5 Who, in 1997, became the first footballer to ever play a top-division fixture for each of Liverpool, Everton, Manchester City and Manchester United?

6 La Sapienza University is in which European city?

7 Which Greek goddess is the muse of erotic poetry?

8 Which female forename does *Private Eye* magazine use as a nickname for Queen Elizabeth II?

9 Thefts of what protective item are so rife in Beijing that being caught taking one can technically now result in the death penalty?

10 Which 18th century architect laid out the streets of Bath and designed many of its iconic buildings, including St John's Hospital and The Circus?

11 With which instrument would you associate jazz musicians Thelonious Monk and Art Tatum?

12 For the first 132 years of its existence, which yacht club won every edition of the America's Cup?

13 In 1912, King Gustav of Sweden said "Sir, you are the world's greatest athlete" to who, the recipient of the 1912 Olympic Decathlon gold medal?

14 The 1748 signing of the Treaty of Aix-la-Chapelle ended which war?

15 Located on the Zambezi River and sharing its name with the dam that created it, what is the world's largest man-made lake?

16 At the 1968 Mexico Olympics, which American man recorded the first non-wind-assisted electronic sub-10-second performance in the 100 metres?

17 As well as being the name of a cheese, Stinking Bishop is also a type of which fruit?

18 Which royal palace was the birthplace of Queen Victoria?

19 Which American singer was the historical subject of U2's *Angel of Harlem*?

20 In 1896, the shortest-ever war, lasting only 38 minutes, took place between Britain and which sultanate state, now part of Tanzania?

Answers to QUIZ 245 – Pot Luck

1	Lemon	11	Stigmata
2	Chicago	12	*Licorice Pizza*
3	Zinc	13	Gaslighting
4	Swing	14	Sir Roger Penrose
5	Roc	15	Blondel
6	Dundee	16	Sylvia Plath
7	Aspire	17	Arthur J. Raffles
8	Florence Foster Jenkins	18	The Luddites
9	Cleveland, Ohio	19	*Due South*
10	*The Crying of Lot 49*	20	The Miami Showband

1   In the culture of which Balkan country are the head gestures for yes and no reversed?

2   Which Balkan state was the first to achieve complete independence, and also to join the European Union?

3   The name of which left-wing YouTube channel is shared with a 20th century political Ottoman Empire reform movement that sought to replace monarchy with a constitutional government?

4   Which grilled ground beef and pork sausage dish is a national dish of both Bosnia and Herzegovina and Serbia, and is common across the Balkans?

5   In which Balkan country is the Cyrillic alphabet used?

6   The Croatian city of Dubrovnik was the location for scenes set in which *Game of Thrones* city?

7   The presidency in which Balkan country rotates every eight months among three members?

8   Destroyed by shells during the Croat-Bosniak war of 1992-4, which bridge over the Neretva river was rebuilt and reopened in 2004 as a symbol of reconciliation?

9   Which town makes up the entire 12 miles of coastline that Bosnia and Herzegovina has on the Adriatic Sea?

10 What happened to the Pristevka River running through the Kosovan capital of Pristina during the 1950s?

11 Which Greek monarch abdicated his throne twice in 1917 and 1922?

12 Which karst cave system in southwestern Slovenia is the second-longest cave system in the country and one of the top tourism sites?

13 Which city, the first urban settlement in Europe, was erected on the banks of the Danube, near Belgrade?

14 A UNESCO heritage site located in Albania, what is the deepest and oldest lake in Southern Europe?

15 Which international political organisation was founded in Belgrade in 1961 following an agreement at the 1955 Bandung conference?

16 What is the name of the central mountain range of the Balkan Peninsula?

17 What adjective sits in the middle of the name of Avaz Tower in Sarajevo to reflect its style?

18 Founded by Ante Pavelić, what fascist movement nominally ruled Croatia during World War II?

19 Also the First Secretary of the Party of Labour, who was the leader of Albania from 1944 until his death in 1985?

20 Derived from Serbo-Croat for "monument", what term describes multiple "space-age" anti-fascist monuments constructed in Yugoslavia after World War II?

Easy

Medium

Hard

Answers to QUIZ 246 – Sport

1	East Africa, 1975	11	West Bromwich Albion
2	Minnesota Timberwolves	12	Joseph Pilates
3	Sugar Ray Leonard	13	Curling
4	Tennis	14	Michael Chang
5	Luther Blissett	15	Piaffe
6	Nordic combined skiing	16	Liu Xiang
7	Phar Lap	17	Links
8	1900 games, Paris	18	NBA
9	Nemanja Vidić	19	Mark King
10	National Standard Race	20	Paul Warhurst

1   Giving his name to a university there, which American religious leader and politician founded Salt Lake City, Utah?

2   The windsocks on metal plate "hares" frequently seen at greyhound racing tracks in the UK take their name from which Norfolk town?

3   Which is the current geological epoch?

4   Saraya-Jade Bevis is the real name of which former World Wrestling Entertainment superstar?

5   In 2021, which NFL franchise became the first to ever have both a seven-game losing streak and seven-game winning streak in the same season?

6   The equivalent of the French *dauphin*, what was the title given to the heir apparent in the Russian Empire?

7   Glisson's capsule can be found in which organ of the human body?

8   Which quadrennial international multi-sport event is held for competitions or sports not featured in the Olympic Games?

9   The statue of "Grandma" by which famous cartoonist can be seen in Ipswich town centre in England?

10 Rabologists are collectors of what?

11 Which South African won nine golfing major tournaments and became the first non-American to win all four Majors at least once?

12 Made up of five tercets and a quatrain, how many lines are there in a villanelle poem?

13 Which Russian composer's *Symphony No. 7 In C Major* is nicknamed the "Leningrad"?

14 Centred in the middle of the Amazon rainforest, which Brazilian city was the site of the FIFA World Cup's first ever official water break in 2014?

15 The Red Epicure is what type of vegetable?

16 Which Spanish artist, who combined abstract art with Surrealist fantasy, was described by André Breton as 'the most Surrealist of us all'?

17 What is the nickname of Beethoven's *5th Piano Concerto*?

18 Which Russian author wrote the novels *Crime and Punishment* and *The Brothers Karamazov*?

19 Barbra Streisand became the first woman to write, produce, direct, and star in a major studio film with which 1983 romantic musical drama?

20 Discovered in 2005, what is the second-biggest dwarf planet in our solar system, behind Pluto?

Easy

Medium

Hard

Answers to QUIZ 247 – Pot Luck

1	Sweden	11	Piano
2	*The Irishman*	12	New York Yacht Club
3	The Red Cross	13	Jim Thorpe
4	Tremolo	14	War of the Austrian Succession
5	Peter Beardsley	15	Lake Kariba
6	Rome	16	Jim Hines
7	Erato	17	Pear
8	Brenda	18	Kensington Palace
9	Manhole covers	19	Billie Holliday
10	John Wood the Elder	20	Zanzibar

1   Which enigmatic jazz and blues singer-songwriter described his own characteristically gruff voice as "Louis Armstrong and Ethel Merman meeting in Hell"?

2   A 1956 impromptu jam session by Elvis Presley, Jerry Lee Lewis, Carl Perkins and Johnny Cash was released commercially 25 years later under what name?

3   In 2020, which singer became the first man to appear solo on the cover of *Vogue* magazine?

4   Which English singer had been using the name "Napoleon Dynamite" as an alias on some of his albums, decades before the release of the film of the same name?

5   Which South African produced both Shania Twain's *Come On Over* and AC/DC'S *Back In Black*, two of the highest-selling albums of all time?

6   What was the one-word title of the only UK chart single by The Crazy World of Arthur Brown?

7   American-Senegalese singer-songwriter Aliaune Thiam is better known by what mononym?

8   Which song did Bruce Springsteen write, Manfred Mann's Earth Band perform and Mozart feature in the lyrics of?

9   Douglas Robb is the lead singer with which American rock band, known for the single *The Reason*?

10 How was the blues singer born Ella Otha Bates better known?

11 Two members of which group were the only people to perform on both the 1984 and 1989 Band Aid charity singles?

12 Which Igor Stravinsky ballet started an audience near-riot when it premiered in Paris in 1913?

13 Which Belgian electronic music project had a hit in 1989 with *Pump Up The Jam*?

14 With which instrument would you associate Yo-Yo Ma?

15 Which late English singer was born Ronald William Wycherley in April 1940?

16 Which husband and wife recording duo had hits with *Love Will Keep Us Together*, *Do That to Me One More Time* and *Muskrat Love*?

17 In the 1950s and towards the beginning of his career, John Coltrane played with whose jazz quintet?

18 Which English pop singer's 1986 debut hit, *Each Time You Break My Heart*, was also his biggest?

19 Now a theatre, which former Manhattan nightclub was so popular during the disco era that its owner claimed "only the Mafia made more money"?

20 Which moustachioed 1980s singer-songwriter allegedly apprehended the "Rusty Gun Bandit", an Australian stick-up artist?

Answers to QUIZ 248 – The Balkans

1	Bulgaria	11	King Constantine I
2	Greece	12	Postojna
3	Young Turks	13	Vinca
4	Ćevapčići	14	Lake Ohrid
5	Bulgaria	15	Non-Aligned Movement
6	King's Landing	16	Stara Planina
7	Bosnia and Herzegovina	17	Twist
8	Stari Most	18	Ustase
9	Neum	19	Enver Hoxha
10	It was diverted into underground tunnels for hygiene purposes	20	Spomeniks

1. Caviar is made of the pickled roe of which fish?
2. Which country won the men's football 2020 European Championships, yet somehow failed to qualify for both the 2018 and 2022 World Cups?
3. The bean known as the fava bean in America is known by what alliterative name in the UK?
4. In internet parlance, what does the abbreviation tl;dr mean?
5. Nell Gwyn was the long-term mistress of which King of England?
6. The RoSPA is the Royal Society for the Prevention of what?
7. In snooker, which ball is worth five points?
8. The canals of Venice are famous for the prevalence of what type of manually-powered boat?
9. What are the three red properties on a standard UK Monopoly™ board?
10. Founded in 1999 by Aaron Peckham, which website is a crowdsourced repository of definitions for slang words and phrases?
11. What are the four jumping events in field athletics?
12. For 21 years between 1790 and 1811, Dorothea Jordan was a mistress of which future British monarch?
13. Frank Mars, the creator of the eponymous chocolate company, had a horse named what?
14. In June 2018, the monks of Mount Saint Bernard Abbey in Leicestershire became the first in the UK to do what?
15. The world is divided into how many international time zones?
16. What name is shared by a cleaning product, a Greek mythological hero, a programming concept and a Dutch football team?
17. Writer and philosopher François-Marie Arouet, famous for his wit and criticism of Christianity, wrote under what *nom de plume*?
18. By what mononym is entertainer Steven Frayne better known?
19. In *The Simpsons*, Marge is usually wearing what colour dress?
20. Until the Supreme Court was established in 2009, what was the highest court in the British legal system?

Easy

Medium

Hard

1   Often a breakfast food, what is commonly eaten on Shrove Tuesday?

2   Angels on Horseback are an *hors d'œuvre* made of what, wrapped in what?

3   Which brand of Britvic fruit juice has a name that is a pun on the chemical formula for water?

4   Which champagne house produces *Ice Impérial* and *Dom Pérignon* champagnes?

5   What Italian word is used to describe a dish of meat or fish, thinly sliced or pounded thin, and served raw?

6   The name of which Mexican food translates into English as "little donkey"?

7   Named for their respective regions, Cognac and Armagnac are both types of what alcoholic drink?

8   Which traditional British dish is made from cooked potatoes and cabbage, mixed together and fried?

9   An *affineur* is an expert in the production of which food?

10 What Italian name describes both an espresso diluted with hot water, and a cocktail of Campari®, vermouth and a slice of lemon?

11 In polite circles, in which direction should port be passed?

12 Which traditional German Christmas beverage is usually made from red wine, cinnamon sticks, cloves, star aniseed, orange and sugar?

13 What fast food chain has used the slogan "Better ingredients. Better pizza"?

14 Edwina Currie resigned as Junior Health Minister in 1988 after a controversy concerning which food?

15 What 'T' is a type of cylindrical clay oven used originally in northern India and Pakistan?

16 Which Japanese dish consists of fish, shellfish, or vegetables fried in batter?

17 Fuerte, Mexicola and Topa Topa are all varieties of which fruit?

18 In which cooking process is a fruit or vegetable briefly scalded in boiling water, then plunged into cold water?

19 Which dish of meat and smetana takes its name from a wealthy Russian family who financed the annexation of Siberia in the 16th century?

20 Which style of French cuisine takes its name from a ribbon worn by French knights?

Answers to QUIZ 500 – Science

1	Dalton's Law (first observed by John Dalton)	12	Lobotomy
2	P-value	13	He was dead, and Nobels are not supposed to be given posthumously; however, he had died only three days before, and the committee did not know that then
3	The opening of a flower		
4	Mantissa		
5	James Lovelock		
6	Tachyon	14	Alkali metals
7	Dermis	15	Shield volcano
8	Michael Faraday	16	Lambda point
9	Isomers	17	Simon Baron-Cohen
10	Vernix	18	Shoemaker–Levy 9
11	Rubber	19	Teratology
		20	Double chin

1. Athos, Porthos and Aramis formed which literary trio?
2. By what stage name was Margaret Hookham known?
3. What six-letter word names the Mafia's code of silence about criminal activity and a refusal to give evidence to the police?
4. Woofers and tweeters are what type of hardware?
5. What type of sausage, with a name derived from Italian for "pig's brains", is often found in fish and chip shops in the UK?
6. Milla Jovovich appeared as Leeloo in which 1997 science fiction film?
7. Following an amusingly incorrect answer on *Celebrity Mastermind*, what did Greta Thunberg change her Twitter™ name to?
8. How many wings does a mosquito have?
9. At 24 years old, who became the youngest ever UK Prime Minister in 1783?
10. Ski®, Danone and Yeo Valley are all brands of what food?
11. In the song *Two Little Boys*, the boys each had a wooden version of what animal?
12. Which brand of crisps developed by Proctor and Gamble are hyperbolic paraboloid in shape?
13. Arachnophobia is the fear of what?
14. Who was the leader of a fictional gang called "Da West Staines Massiv"?
15. What relationship were Ross and Monica in *Friends*?
16. Chicle, gathered from the sapodilla tree, is used to make what snack?
17. Famously covered by Soft Cell in 1981, *Tainted Love* was originally performed by which female singer in 1964?
18. Which English explorer was executed in 1618, fifteen years after being found guilty of conspiracy against King James I?
19. Which team won their thirteenth rugby league Challenge Cup title in 2021?
20. On which day of the week are British general elections almost always held?

Easy

Medium

Hard

Answers to QUIZ 251 – Pot Luck

1. Sturgeon
2. Italy
3. Broad bean
4. Too long; didn't read
5. King Charles II
6. Accidents
7. Blue
8. Gondola
9. Strand, Trafalgar Square and Fleet Street
10. Urban Dictionary
11. Long jump, high jump, triple jump and pole vault
12. William IV
13. Snickers
14. Brew beer
15. 24
16. Ajax
17. Voltaire
18. Dynamo
19. Green
20. Appellate Committee of the House of Lords

Easy

1. Originally printed in *Harper's New Monthly Magazine*, *Jude the Obscure* was whose final novel?
2. Which Scottish author wrote *The Strange Case of Dr Jekyll and Mr Hyde* and *Treasure Island*?
3. Which Roald Dahl book begins with the line "What a lot of hairy-faced men there are around nowadays"?
4. In which book did John le Carré's intelligence officer character George Smiley make his debut?
5. The inspiration and namesake for which children's book character died in April 1996?
6. Mary O'Hara's 1941 novel *My Friend Flicka* was about a boy's friendship with what type of animal?
7. Beginning with 1979's *A Woman of Substance*, Emma Harte is the protagonist in a series of seven novels by which author?
8. Baroness Orczy wrote about what colour of pimpernel?
9. The Bagnets, Skipoles and Turveydrops are families in which Charles Dickens work?
10. In which novel does Glubbdubdrib, the island of sorcerers, appear?
11. Which titular object in the *Harry Potter* novels was originally found in Vault 713 at Gringott's Bank?
12. In Judith Viorst's 1972 children's book, who has a "Terrible, Horrible, No Good, Very Bad Day"?
13. Which book, with a girl's name for the title, has John Ridd as the male lead and narrator?
14. Which best-selling author also writes adult fiction under the pen name Robert Galbraith?
15. Fodor's is a publisher of English language books about what?
16. Genesis first, Exodus second; what is the third book of the Bible?
17. Which author wrote both *Jurassic Park* and *The Andromeda Strain*?
18. Khaled Hosseini's first novel about class conflict and immigration in Afghanistan had what name?
19. In J.R.R. Tolkien's *The Hobbit*, Smaug is what type of fictional creature?
20. *The Dong With A Luminous Nose* is a love poem by which English poet?

Medium

Hard

Answers to QUIZ 252 – Food & Drink

1	Pancakes	11	To the left
2	Oysters wrapped in bacon	12	Glühwein
3	J2o	13	Papa John's
4	Moët & Chandon	14	Eggs – she claimed British eggs were rife with salmonella
5	Carpaccio		
6	Burrito	15	Tandoor
7	Brandy	16	Tempura
8	Bubble and squeak	17	Avocado
9	Cheese	18	Blanching
10	Americano	19	Stroganoff
		20	*Cordon Bleu*

1 Russian revolutionary Vladimir Ilyich Ulyanov was commonly known as what mononym?

2 Which credit card was advertised under the slogan "your flexible friend"?

3 Frequently mentioned on *I'm Sorry I Haven't A Clue*, which dancer and entertainer was born Henry Ogus?

4 In humans, which is the largest internal organ?

5 Polar explorer Roald Amundsen came from which country?

6 Which multi-armed multimedia corporation was founded in January 1968 by The Beatles?

7 In 1905, who founded the Battle Creek Toasted Cornflake Company?

8 "Put on your red shoes and dance the blues" is a lyric from which David Bowie song?

9 Saracens Mavericks and Loughborough Lightning are teams in which sport?

10 In an advert for *John Smith's* bitter, what "dive" does Peter Kay do in a diving competition?

11 The Rio Grande forms much of the border between which two countries?

12 Snout, hooter and proboscis are all synonyms for what part of the human body?

13 Ajax, PSV Eindhoven and which other football club make up the "big three" in the Dutch Eredivisie?

14 "Snake eyes" is a slang term for what roll of two dice?

15 Which American painter and abstract expressionist is best known for his "drip technique" of pouring or splashing paint from above?

16 In Australia, cars drive on which side of the road?

17 *Pamplemousse* is the French word for which food?

18 Which African country has a one-word name that contains all five vowels?

19 In 2012, which British fighter became the first ever female Olympic boxing gold medal winner?

20 Obviously not including Earth, which planet was first orbited by a man-made object?

Easy

Medium

Hard

Answers to QUIZ 253 – Pot Luck

1	The Three Musketeers	11	Horse
2	Margot Fonteyn	12	Pringles®
3	*Omertà*	13	Spiders
4	Speakers	14	Ali G
5	Saveloy	15	Brother and sister
6	*The Fifth Element*	16	Chewing gum
7	Sharon	17	Gloria Jones
8	Two	18	Sir Walter Raleigh
9	William Pitt the Younger	19	St. Helens
10	Yoghurt	20	Thursday

Easy

1   Which country is surrounded entirely by South Africa?

2   Only two countries in the world are doubly landlocked – Uzbekistan and which small European microstate?

3   Situated on the border between Europe and Asia, which is the world's biggest landlocked country?

4   Which South American country became landlocked in 1904 when Chile annexed its only coastal territory?

5   What is the largest landlocked country in Africa?

6   Which is the largest landlocked county in the United Kingdom?

7   Gaborone is the capital city of which landlocked country in southern Africa?

8   Aside from Bolivia, which is the only other landlocked country in the Americas?

9   Which Asian state is the second-largest landlocked country in the world?

10   Only becoming landlocked in 1993, which African country is the most populated landlocked country in the world?

11   As it touches no ocean, neither do the states it borders, and nor do the states they border, which is America's only triply landlocked state?

12   At a minimum of 1,620 miles from any ocean, which mountainous central Asian country is the most landlocked state in the world?

13   San Marino and the Vatican City, two of the only three countries landlocked by a single country, are completely surrounded by which "host" nation?

14   As of 2022, which is the newest landlocked country, created via a 2011 independence referendum?

Medium

15   Which three continents have no landlocked countries?

16   Which landlocked English county has only two towns; Oakham, the county town, and Uppingham?

17   Which country borders France, Germany, Liechtenstein and Italy, but no sea?

18   As part of a 2005 territorial exchange with Ukraine, which country received a 600-metre long bank of the Danube, which, as an "international waterway", means they are no longer entirely landlocked?

19   The Mekong river is designated an international waterway so that which otherwise-landlocked country – the only one in Southeast Asia – has access to the South China Sea?

20   Which landlocked country sits between South Africa and Mozambique?

Hard

Answers to QUIZ 254 – Literature

1	Thomas Hardy	11	Philosopher's Stone
2	Robert Louis Stevenson	12	Alexander
3	*The Twits*	13	*Lorna Doone*
4	*Call for the Dead* (it was also Le Carré's first novel)	14	J.K. Rowling
5	Christopher Robin (Milne, from *Winnie-the-Pooh*)	15	Travel and tourism
		16	Leviticus
6	Horse	17	Michael Crichton
7	Barbara Taylor Bradford	18	*The Kite Runner*
8	Scarlet	19	Dragon
9	*Bleak House*	20	Edward Lear
10	*Gulliver's Travels*		

ANSWERS ON PAGE **259**

1   Which instrument plays the highest notes in the woodwind family?

2   Which pilot safely landed US Airways 1549 in an emergency landing in the Hudson River on 15th January 2009?

3   One-armed drummer Rick Allen is a member of which rock band?

4   Which of the *Three Tenors* opera singers died on 6th September 2007?

5   Adélie Land is territory claimed by France on which continent?

6   What title is given to the foremost spiritual leader of the Gelug or "Yellow Hat" school of Tibetan Buddhism?

7   Which band released the 1996 hit single *Don't Speak*?

8   What is measured using a Brannock Device?

9   How many fights did Muhammad Ali lose in his professional career?

10 In the namesake song, which city is the *House Of The Rising Sun* located in?

11 Leonard Bernstein's musical *West Side Story* is based on which Shakespeare play?

12 Which revered German toy company, noted for its quality and high price, mostly produces teddy bears today, but initially used to make elephants?

13 What term links the record label named after Duke Reid's sound system, a type of computer malware, and a military "horse"?

14 During the brief period when *Mastermind* appeared on Discovery Channel, who presented it?

15 Ink caps, death caps and agarics are all types of what?

16 The final issue of which lad mag was published on 29th April 2014?

17 Pepsin is produced in which organ of the body?

18 Introduced by Edward Jenner in 1796, the first successful vaccine was for what?

19 What is the basic monetary unit in Bahrain, Iraq, Jordan, Kuwait and Libya?

20 Dr Dre, Ice Cube, Arabian Prince and Eazy-E formed which pioneering 1980s rap group?

Easy

Medium

Hard

Answers to QUIZ 255 – Pot Luck

1	Lenin	11	Mexico and the USA
2	Access	12	Nose
3	Lionel Blair	13	Feyenoord
4	Liver	14	Double one
5	Norway	15	Jackson Pollock
6	Apple Corps	16	Left
7	The Kellogg family	17	Grapefruit
8	*Let's Dance*	18	Mozambique
9	Netball	19	Nicola Adams
10	A running bomb	20	Mars

Easy

1 Appearing on the £20 note issued in July 1970, which playwright was the first historical figure to appear on a British banknote?

2 As of 2022, which monarch's portrait is used on the banknotes of more than 30 countries?

3 Which scientist appeared on the only £1 UK banknote ever issued?

4 Who was the first woman portrayed on the *rear* of a UK banknote (i.e. not the Queen)?

5 Which scientist was included on the £10 note issued in November 2000 in part because his beard made it hard to forge?

6 99% of banknotes in London were revealed in a 1998 study to have traces of what on them?

7 A 50p coin released to commemorate the 2012 Olympics tried to explain what sporting rule?

8 Which advocate for prisoners' rights was the second woman portrayed on the rear of a UK banknote, appearing on the 2002 £5 note?

9 Which composer was featured on the 1999 edition of the £20 banknote, along with Worcester Cathedral, the city he is most associated with?

10 The first polymer version of the £50 note issued in 2021 featured an image of which mathematician?

11 Which way does Queen Elizabeth II face on British coins?

12 Which economist has been on both the £50 note issued by the Clydesdale Bank in Scotland, and the £20 Bank of England note?

13 The Royal Bank of Scotland became in 1727 the first British bank to issue a note featuring a person's face – which monarch was depicted?

14 A set of coins with Harry Potter on them are produced in which British Crown Dependency, but are only legal tender there?

Medium

15 Which US President is depicted on a $1 bank note?

16 Palau issued a silver dollar coin in 2007 with an image of the Virgin Mary; what else was embedded in it?

17 After Joseph Mobutu's tyrannical regime ended in 1997, what was done to the old 20,000-Zaire notes featuring his image?

18 Fiji created a $7 bill featuring images of their gold medal-winning participants in which Olympic sport?

19 Which aptly-named Greek goddess featured on the new five-euro banknote issued in 2013?

20 An example of *Notgeld* (or "emergency money"), a two mark note released in which country in 1921 featured an emblem of a donkey having a poo?

Answers to QUIZ 256 – Landlocked

1	Lesotho	11	Nebraska
2	Liechtenstein	12	Kyrgyzstan
3	Kazakhstan	13	Italy
4	Bolivia	14	South Sudan
5	Chad, which is ever so slightly bigger (486,179 square miles) than Mali (471,044 square miles)	15	North America, Oceania and Antarctica
6	Shropshire	16	Rutland
7	Botswana	17	Switzerland
8	Paraguay	18	Moldova
9	Mongolia	19	Laos
10	Ethiopia (all its coastline was subsumed into the creation of Eritrea)	20	Eswatini (formerly known as Swaziland)

ANSWERS ON PAGE **261**

1 Troops in the ANZAC corps during both World Wars came from which two countries?

2 The temporary hospitals set up across England and Wales amid the COVID-19 pandemic were named after who?

3 What term can refer to either a type of waterfall, or an eye problem?

4 In 1985, which media holding company bought Twentieth Century Fox?

5 Which road sign is the only one in the UK to be octagonal and coloured red?

6 Which French clothing company's logo is a crocodile, after the nickname of its tennis-playing founder?

7 Born James Wight, which veterinary surgeon and author wrote the *All Creatures Great and Small* series, beginning with *If Only They Could Talk*?

8 A 1917 letter from Baron Fisher to Winston Churchill is the first documented use of which now-common abbreviation?

9 Which character was "feared by the bad, loved by the good" in a TV theme song?

10 Which is the busiest train station in Manchester and the UK's third busiest outside of London?

11 Which boxing weight comes between flyweight and featherweight?

12 Raphael Ravenscroft famously played saxophone on which Gerry Rafferty hit?

13 Which former international cricketer won *I'm a Celebrity, Get Me Out Of Here* in 2003?

14 On British stamps, which way does the monarch face?

15 In chess, what is the maximum number of squares that the king can move in at a time?

16 In the world of business, what is the CFO of a business?

17 Dhaka and Dakar are the capital cities of which Asian and African countries respectively?

18 "Slow and steady wins the race" is the moral attributed to which of Aesop's fables?

19 What name is given to the part of a bell tower or steeple in which bells are housed?

20 At an auction, what name is given to the minimum price that a seller is willing to accept?

Answers to QUIZ 257 – Pot Luck

1	Piccolo	11	*Romeo and Juliet*
2	Chesley "Sully" Sullenberger	12	Steiff
3	Def Leppard	13	Trojan
4	Luciano Pavarotti	14	Clive Anderson
5	Antarctica	15	Mushroom
6	Dalai Lama	16	*Nuts*
7	No Doubt	17	Stomach
8	Shoe size	18	Smallpox
9	Five; to Joe Frazier, Ken Norton, Leon Spinks, Larry Holmes and Trevor Berbick	19	Dinar
		20	N.W.A.
10	New Orleans		

1   In January 1964, which band's first UK top ten single, *Glad All Over*, knocked the Beatles' *I Want to Hold Your Hand* off the top spot?

2   Ritchie Neville, Scott Robinson, Sean Conlon, Abz and J were the initial line-up of which boy band?

3   David Howell Evans, better known as the Edge, plays lead guitar in which band?

4   Which pop rock band took their name from "mental" scribblings found on the back page of Jack Kerouac's book *On The Road*?

5   Alongside his acting career, Jared Leto also plays in which rock band?

6   Which band has had hits with *This Love*, *Moves Like Jagger* and, with Cardi B, *Girls Like You*?

7   *What's Up?* – often mistitled *What's Going On?*, the lyrics of its main refrain – was a 1992 international hit for which alternative rock band?

8   Which new wave band was formed by Terry Hall, Neville Staple and Lynval Golding after leaving The Specials?

9   Trent Reznor is the lead singer – and, for the first 28 years of its existence, only member – of which rock band?

10 Niall Horan, Liam Payne, Harry Styles and Louis Tomlinson were four of the founder members of which boy band?

11 Before becoming the presenter of *The Crystal Maze*, Edward Tudor-Pole fronted which punk band?

12 Formed in York in 1990, which alternative rock band had four top 20 hits in 1996, including *Getting Better* and *Going for Gold*?

13 Beginning their career as YouTube stars, which Australian pop rock band rose to international fame by touring with One Direction?

14 Which Belgian/Dutch dance act had 1990s hits including *Get Ready for This*, *Twilight Zone* and *No Limit*?

15 Jimmy Brown and Astro were members of which 1990s band, named after a document?

16 Which rapper's mum, Afeni, was a member of the Black Panther Party?

17 What was the name of Frankie Valli's band?

18 Reportedly, there is no party like one held by which band, who starred in their own BBC television series, *Miami 7*?

19 Jimmy Pursey was the frontman of which punk band, who had a hit with *Hurry Up Harry*?

20 Lol Creme was a founder member of which rock band from Prestwich and wrote their first UK No.1, *Rubber Bullets*?

Easy

Medium

Hard

Answers to QUIZ 258 – On the Money

1	William Shakespeare	11	Right – this is a better question if you don't immediately hunt for a coin when you hear it
2	Queen Elizabeth II		
3	Sir Isaac Newton	12	Adam Smith
4	Florence Nightingale	13	George II
5	Charles Darwin	14	Isle of Man
6	Cocaine	15	George Washington
7	The offside rule in football	16	A tiny vial of holy water
8	Elizabeth Fry	17	To save money on needing to reprint new notes, his face simply got cut out
9	Edward Elgar		
10	Alan Turing	18	Rugby Sevens
		19	Europa
		20	Germany

1   Basildon Bond is a brand of products in which field?

2   What type of animal is a corncrake?

3   Sir Cuthbert Ackroyd bought the first of which government-issued financial instruments on 1st November 1956?

4   Gorgonzola cheese comes from which country?

5   When spoken in British English, which letters of the alphabet have names that do not rhyme with any other? (There are 11 in total.)

6   Topping out at 1,345 metres above sea level, what is the highest mountain in the UK?

7   Robert Menzies was twice the Prime Minister of which country?

8   Between 1961 and 2004, and then from 2011 onwards, Kenneth Sean Carson was the boyfriend of which toy?

9   Which Skye Terrier from 19th-century Edinburgh is legendary for spending 14 years guarding the grave of his owner?

10   In 1967, London Bridge was dismantled and moved to Lake Havasu City in which US state?

11   What was the winged flying horse of Greek mythology called?

12   What colour is the middle vertical band on the Irish flag?

13   Pamela Anderson starred as which title character in a 1994 film that derived its name from a Lucien B. Smith invention of 1867?

14   In geography, what term is given to the joining of two rivers?

15   In educational terminology, what does GCSE stand for?

16   *Mal de mer* is a French loanword to describe what ailment?

17   Michael Henchard was the namesake mayor of which fictional town?

18   Which pigment is responsible for the brown colour of a suntan?

19   In which fairy story does a queen have to guess an imp's name within three days?

20   Who played Lenny Godber, Norman Stanley Fletcher's cell mate in *Porridge*?

Easy

Medium

Hard

Answers to QUIZ 259 – Pot Luck

1	Australia and New Zealand	11	Bantamweight
2	Florence Nightingale	12	*Baker Street*
3	Cataract	13	Phil Tufnell
4	News Corporation, owned by Rupert Murdoch	14	Left – the direction on coins changes with each
5	Stop		monarch
6	Lacoste	15	One
7	James Herriot	16	Chief Financial Officer
8	OMG	17	Bangladesh and Senegal
9	Robin Hood	18	*The Tortoise and the Hare*
10	Manchester Piccadilly	19	Belfry
		20	Reserve

Easy

1 Which French post-Impressionist artist spent ten years in French Polynesia and became best known for his bright landscapes of Tahiti?

2 Which American director has credits to his name including *Boogie Nights*, *Magnolia* and *Punch-Drunk Love*?

3 Which football pioneer became both the first black player to captain the England team and the first black manager of a Premier League club?

4 Which three-time winner of the London Marathon held the Women's World Marathon Record between 2003 and 2019?

5 How was Karol Józef Wojtyla (1920-2005) better known?

6 Who began as an L.A. Lakers cheerleader, became Janet Jackson's choreographer, recorded three albums and then became a talent show judge?

7 Well known as a part of a duet, which singer-songwriter also had a solo hit with *You Can Call Me Al*?

8 Paula Jones, a former Arkansas state employee, sued which US President for sexual harassment?

9 Which record producer and trance DJ produced the theme music used for the first five series of the UK's *Big Brother*?

10 Comedian Paul Martin took which London borough for a surname when joining Equity, as his birthname had already been taken?

11 Which American TV chef came under fire for her "Lady's Brunch Burger," a burger that replaced the bread buns with two doughnuts?

Medium

12 Which Labour Party politician and MP for Brent South between 1987 and 2005 became the UK's first Black Cabinet Minister in May 2002?

13 Which Frenchman became the world's most expensive footballer when he joined Manchester United in 2016 for €105 million?

14 Which late presenter and writer was best known for her "on the bed" interviews on The Big Breakfast?

15 Which theoretical physicist was so taciturn with his words that his surname came to be used as a unit of shyness?

16 Lester William Polsfuss was an American jazz, country and blues guitarist, songwriter, luthier and inventor, better known by what name?

17 *Paul*, a 2011 sci-fi comedy about two geeks who meet a sarcastic alien, was the third big screen collaboration of which two actors?

18 Which dual-code international rugby player represented New Zealand in rugby league and England in rugby union and sevens?

19 Which social media personality rose to fame on Vine before appearing in the Disney Channel series *Bizaardvark*?

20 Paula Fisch was a character, and Paul Whitehouse a creator and lead actor, in which sketch show?

Hard

Answers to QUIZ 260 – Numbered Bands

1	The Dave Clark Five	11	Tenpole Tudor
2	5ive	12	Shed Seven
3	U2	13	5 Seconds Of Summer
4	The 1975	14	2 Unlimited
5	Thirty Seconds To Mars	15	UB40
6	Maroon 5	16	2Pac
7	4 Non Blondes	17	The Four Seasons
8	Fun Boy Three	18	S Club 7
9	Nine Inch Nails	19	Sham 69
10	One Direction	20	10cc

1   Bulldogs, serotines and pipistrelles are types of which animal?
2   Cliff Richard and Marty Robbins had different songs that shared which title?
3   In *Dad's Army*, what was Captain Mainwaring's day job?
4   The abbreviation RSVP stands for what?
5   Which English city is named after the River Lune, which runs through it?
6   BBC Radio 4 replaced which other radio station in 1967?
7   In which musical does the song *Somewhere (There's a Place for Us)* appear?
8   In the British education system, which establishment's name abbreviates to OU?
9   Riyadh is the capital of which Asian country?
10 Since 1980, products by the European car marque Opel have been largely identical to those of which British brand?
11 The Wombles could be found on which London open space?
12 Zimbabwean President Emmerson Mnangagwa has which animal for a nickname?
13 A haberdashery sells items used in what craft?
14 Which letters of the English alphabet depict Roman Numerals?
15 In 1999, which Scottish golfer became the final British winner of the Open in the 20th century?
16 Rudyard Kipling wrote a story about which snake-killing mongoose in 1893?
17 In which stadium did England win the 1966 World Cup Final?
18 Helen Duncan was in 1944 the last woman tried, convicted and imprisoned in the UK for what?
19 From which city did the hamburger originate?
20 In the *Lone Ranger* stories, what was the name of Tonto's horse?

Easy

Medium

Hard

Answers to QUIZ 261 – Pot Luck

1	Stationery	11	Pegasus
2	Bird	12	White
3	Premium bond	13	*Barb Wire*
4	Italy	14	Confluence
5	F, H, L, M, N, O, R, S, X, Y, Z	15	General Certificate of Secondary Education
6	Ben Nevis	16	Seasickness
7	Australia	17	Casterbridge
8	Barbie®	18	Melanin
9	Greyfriars Bobby	19	*Rumpelstiltskin*
10	Arizona	20	Richard Beckinsale

Who are these celebrities, all of whom have admitted to wearing syrups?

1

2

3

4

5

6

7

8

9

Easy

Medium

Hard

ANSWERS ON PAGE **267**

1   The One O'Clock Gun is a time signal fired every day (except Sunday, Good Friday and Christmas Day) at precisely 1pm at which Scottish landmark?

2   In the names of the Met Police and Manchester Met University, "Met" is short for what?

3   Which car manufacturer's name comes from the German for "People's Car"?

4   A half nelson is a move in which sport?

5   What is the main ingredient of guacamole?

6   Of the five hereditary degrees of the British peerage, which is the third highest?

7   Which fictional horse lived in the stables at Birtwick Hall?

8   Which author created the character Sam Spade?

9   "Swinging the lead" is a slang term for what action?

10 In terms of land area, which is the world's largest continent?

11 Post decimalisation, which British coin continued to be legal tender, with a value of 2+1/2 new pence, until 30th June 1980?

12 A man named Michael Maier sent the first known example of what to King James I in 1611?

13 What is the fourth book of the Old Testament?

14 The Gobi Desert is located in which continent?

15 Which Scottish driver finished second in the 2001 Formula 1 Drivers' Championship to Michael Schumacher?

16 Despite the name, Leeds Castle is located in which English county?

17 Anfield stadium was home to which English football club from 1884 to 1891?

18 The animal order *coleoptera*, the largest order of animals on Earth, is solely comprised of what?

19 In the Bible, which king had to decide which of two women was the mother of a child?

20 What is the chemical formula for snow?

Answers to QUIZ 263 – Pot Luck

1	Bat	11	Wimbledon Common
2	*Devil Woman*	12	Crocodile
3	Bank manager	13	Sewing
4	*Répondez s'il vous plaît* – French for "please respond"	14	I, V, X, L, C, D, M (for a mnemonic, "I value xylophones like cows do milk")
5	Lancaster	15	Paul Lawrie
6	Home Service	16	Rikki-Tikki-Tavi
7	*West Side Story*	17	Wembley
8	Open University	18	Witchcraft
9	Saudi Arabia	19	Hamburg (see what they did there?)
10	Vauxhall	20	Scout

QUIZ 266 – 1984

ANSWERS ON PAGE **268**

1. In which European city were the 1984 Winter Olympics held?
2. Which archbishop and theologian won the 1984 Nobel Peace Prize for his work against apartheid?
3. Which important London flood defence was opened on 8th May 1984?
4. Which tiny European country was the last to grant women the right to vote on 1st July 1984?
5. Name any of the three famous English comedic actors who died of heart attacks in 1984 while performing on stage.
6. The music video for which 1984 hit depicted the Cold War as a wrestling match between Soviet leader Konstantin Chernenko and US president Ronald Reagan?
7. Band Aid's *Do They Know It's Christmas?* was written in reaction to the famine in which country?
8. On 13th October 1984, which stony-faced darts player received £102,000 for hitting the first nine-dart finish in televised history?
9. Which Democratic nominee unsuccessfully ran against Ronald Reagan in the 1984 US Presidential election?
10. According to a 1984 Bananarama Song, who was waiting?
11. Kevin Bacon and John Lithgow fight over a ban on dancing and the musical merits of rock and roll in which 1984 film?
12. The retrovirus that caused which disease was finally identified in 1984?
13. Which breakfast cereal did Henry Cooper advertise that he was unable to eat three of in 1984?
14. With which African country did Britain break off diplomatic relations in April 1984 after shootings at their embassy in London?

Medium

15. In what unusual place did a Canadian livestock farmer begin to rent out advertising space in 1984?
16. In which decade was George Orwell's book 1984 written and published?
17. On 22nd June 1984, which transatlantic airline made its maiden flight?
18. On 1st January 1984, which southeast Asian sultanate gained full independence from Britain?
19. Which English athlete won his second consecutive decathlon gold at the 1984 Olympic Games?
20. Autobots and Decepticons were the two rival factions in which range of toys and cartoons first produced by Hasbro in 1984?

Hard

Answers to QUIZ 264 – Name That Toupee

1. William Shatner
2. Al Pacino
3. Elton John
4. Andre Agassi
5. Ted Danson
6. Keira Knightley
7. Sean Connery
8. Katy Perry
9. Lily Savage

ANSWERS ON PAGE **269**

1   An inability to produce a sufficient quantity of insulin is the cause of which medical condition?
2   In which month is the shortest day of the year in the northern hemisphere?
3   Who wrote the 1667 epic poem *Paradise Lost*?
4   As of 2022, which has been the only country to win all three of the Cricket World Cup, Football World Cup and Rugby World Cup?
5   What was notable about soprano Dame Moura Lympany's 1979 appearance – her second – on *Desert Island Discs*?
6   What are the three royal boroughs of London?
7   What word can mean both an area of sandbanks or a group of fish?
8   In which soap opera do the Sugden family appear?
9   Which Shakespeare character enrages and disappoints her father, a Venetian senator, when she elopes with Othello?
10 The first flight of Concorde took place in which year?
11 What was the capital of Yugoslavia?
12 Denis Law played football for which national team?
13 Au is the symbol for which chemical element?
14 In the French monarchy, what title was given to the eldest son of the king?
15 Which adult cartoon series is set in the fictional town of Quahog, Rhode Island?
16 Astrakhan is a fur that comes from which animal?
17 Which is the only insect that produces food eaten by man?
18 The name of which animal is aptly derived from old French for "spine hog" or "thorn pig"?
19 Located on its namesake street, the Monument in London is dedicated to which event?
20 The adjective lupine relates to which animals?

Easy

Medium

Hard

Easy

1 As of 2022, *All About Eve*, *Titanic* and *La La Land* are tied for the most Oscar nominations by a single film with how many?

2 Whose 1971 concept album *What's Going On?* is viewed as a classic of 1970s soul?

3 Despite being their eleventh in four years, which Beach Boys album was so acclaimed that its follow-up, *Smile*, took over 40 years to finish?

4 Sharing his name with an unrelated famous actor, who was the director of *12 Years A Slave*?

5 Hugh Jackman, Jake Gyllenhaal, Viola Davis and Maria Bello starred in which 2013 film about a vengeful father?

6 Antonio Montana was the Cuban immigrant lead character in which 1983 Brian de Palma gangster film?

7 Richard Dreyfuss starred as Roy Neary in which 1977 Steven Spielberg sci-fi film that won an Oscar for Best Cinematography?

8 Which HBO series won 272 different awards during its run, including eight for Maisie Williams alone?

9 Sandra Oh and Jodie Comer portray a cat-and-mouse investigator/assassin relationship in which TV series?

10 As opposed to its 2010 film adaptation that is considered one of the worst ever, which 2005-08 Nickelodeon comedy/fantasy cartoon received critical acclaim for its characters, references, art and mature themes?

11 Benedict Cumberbatch and Martin Freeman star in which modern-day adaptation of a classic Victorian crime drama?

12 Justin Roiland and Dan Harmon created which adult science fiction-themed cartoon sitcom for the Cartoon Network?

13 Which duo won the National Television Award's Most Popular Presenter award every year from 2001 to 2021 inclusive?

14 Which revered work by Leo Tolstoy centres on an affair that causes scandal in the social circles of Saint Petersburg, Russia?

15 Which medical drama, set in the emergency room of the fictional County General Hospital in Chicago, won 116 awards over its 15-year run?

16 *One Hundred Years Of Solitude*, one of the most significant works in the Hispanic literary canon, was written by who?

17 Which 1924 novel by E. M. Forster was selected as one of the 100 great works of 20th century English literature by the Modern Library?

18 Which auteur wrote and directed *A Clockwork Orange*, *Barry Lyndon* and *The Shining*?

19 *Tapestry*, which held the record for most weeks at No.1 by a female artist for more than 20 years, was a 1971 album by which influential singer?

20 Rosanna Arquette and Madonna received praise for which 1985 film about two New York women who meet through the personals section of a newspaper?

Medium

Hard

Answers to QUIZ 266 – 1984

1	Sarajevo	11	*Footloose*
2	Archbishop Desmond Tutu	12	AIDS
3	Thames Barrier	13	Shredded Wheat®
4	Liechtenstein	14	Libya
5	Eric Morecambe, Tommy Cooper or Leonard Rossiter	15	On his cows
6	*Two Tribes* by Frankie Goes to Hollywood	16	The 1940s
7	Ethiopia	17	Virgin Atlantic
8	John Lowe	18	Brunei
9	Walter Mondale	19	Daley Thompson
10	Robert De Niro	20	*Transformers*

QUIZ 269 – Pot Luck

ANSWERS ON PAGE 271

1 In music, how many quavers are there in a minim?
2 A scapegoat describes someone who always takes or gets what?
3 The Vasco da Gama Bridge, Europe's longest bridge, is located in which capital?
4 Honolulu is the capital city of which US state?
5 Leo Baekeland invented the first plastic made from synthetic components in 1909, and patented it under what name?
6 Four different kings called Nebuchadnezzar ruled which ancient empire?
7 Abdicating on 15th March 1917, who was the last Emperor of Russia?
8 In the Bible, who was entrapped by Delilah?
9 It was once etiquette that women were only supposed to shake hands when doing what?
10 Who was the *de facto* host of *The Muppet Show*?
11 Rhinoplasty procedures are performed on which part of the face?
12 What word can refer to a shield or emblem bearing a coat of arms, or the metal plate surrounding a keyhole?
13 Useful in criminology, dactylography is the study of what?
14 Origami is the Japanese art of what?
15 In boxing terminology, what does WBC stand for?
16 Marti Pellow, Graeme Clark, Tom Cunningham and Neil Mitchell formed which soft rock group in 1982?
17 The hybrid language of Pidgin English originally evolved for trade between Britain and which other country?
18 Which football team started life in 1886 as Dial Square?
19 One of the many uses of which word is as the name of a physical junction between two railways lines?
20 In 1982, which snooker player recorded the first televised maximum 147 break?

Easy

Medium

Hard

Answers to QUIZ 267 – Pot Luck

1 Diabetes
2 December
3 John Milton
4 England
5 Every song she picked was her own
6 Kingston upon Thames, Kensington and Chelsea, Greenwich
7 Shoal
8 *Emmerdale*
9 Desdemona
10 1969

11 Belgrade
12 Scotland
13 Gold
14 Dauphin
15 *Family Guy*
16 Sheep
17 Bee
18 Porcupine
19 The Great Fire of London
20 Wolves

Easy

1 Which animal, also known as the earth pig, has a long snout that ends with a pig-like nose, rabbit-like ears and a tail similar to a kangaroo?

2 What name is given to the South African version of an open-fire barbecue that is an important social custom in the country?

3 For the first seven years of its existence, which now-defunct Swedish car manufacturer only painted its cars in green?

4 Which Green Bay Packers legend is, as of 2021, the only quarterback in NFL history with over 400 touchdowns and fewer than 100 interceptions?

5 Which monthly women's fashion magazine is the oldest in US history?

6 Which international fellowship dedicated to helping people achieve sobriety was started in 1935 by Bill Wilson and Bob Smith?

7 Arsenal sealed the permanent signing of which Norwegian international footballer from Real Madrid in August 2021?

8 Which singer, actress, dancer and model married R Kelly at age 15 and died in a plane crash aged only 22?

9 The 1992 foundation treaty of the European Union is often known by what toponym for the Dutch city where it was signed?

10 Which Iraqi-British businessman, advertising mogul and notorious art collector married Nigella Lawson in 2003?

11 Taking its name from the French for "the iguana", what is the alternate name for the Nile monitor, the largest lizard in Africa?

12 Which soul legend voiced the character of Chef in the first few series of *South Park*?

13 What name is shared by the actor who played *Sonny Corleone* in The Godfather and a former *Dragons' Den* entrepreneur?

14 What is the second largest city in Denmark?

15 In the final week of his playing career, which Dutch football legend won a Champions League final and an Eredivisie title playing for Ajax?

16 Which English author was best known for his *Winnie the Pooh* books?

17 Which organisation was initially founded in 1905 to help motorists avoid police speed traps?

18 Which LBC presenter and former political prisoner stood as the Liberal Democrat candidate for the constituency of Hampstead and Kilburn in 2015?

19 After Boris Johnson was admitted to intensive care with COVID-19 in April 2020, who was asked to deputise as Prime Minister?

20 Which German word for a public spa gave its name to an amusement park on the Southend seafront?

Medium

Hard

Answers to QUIZ 268 – Critically Acclaimed

1	14	11	*Sherlock*
2	Marvin Gaye	12	*Rick and Morty*
3	*Pet Sounds*	13	Ant and Dec – the 2000 winner was Michael
4	Steve McQueen		Barrymore
5	*Prisoners*	14	*Anna Karenina*
6	*Scarface*	15	*ER*
7	*Close Encounters of the Third Kind*	16	Gabriel García Márquez
8	*Game of Thrones*	17	*A Passage To India*
9	*Killing Eve*	18	Stanley Kubrick
10	*Avatar: The Last Airbender*	19	Carole King
		20	*Desperately Seeking Susan*

1. What is the largest sand desert in the world?
2. Jane Wyman was the first wife of which American President?
3. Which publishing company has historically colour-coded its books; for example, orange for fiction, blue for biography and green for crime?
4. The Jungfrau is one of the most distinctive sights in which mountain range?
5. During his time alone on *Treasure Island*, which sailor developed an obsessional craving for cheese?
6. By the end of *The Lion King*, who is the king?
7. What colours are the two vertical bands on the Vatican City flag?
8. What forename is shared by former England footballer Bramble, Roman emperor Andronicus and perjurer Oates?
9. The city of Sunderland lies at the mouth of which river?
10. What are the two main flavours in a banoffee pie?
11. In London, where is Poet's Corner located?
12. Who played Luke Skywalker in the *Star Wars* series of films?
13. The Reichstag is a parliament building in which city?
14. Which American sitcom that ran from 2005 to 2009 featured Jason Lee as the title character trying to right wrongs he has made?
15. In the nursery rhyme *Mary Had a Little Lamb*, where did the lamb follow Mary to?
16. Langhorn Creek and the Barossa Valley are wine-producing regions in which country?
17. Ronnie Barker announced his retirement from showbusiness in 1988 in an appearance on which talk show?
18. Which is the only planet in the Solar System that is not named after either a Greek or Roman God?
19. After how many years of marriage is a silver wedding anniversary or jubilee celebrated?
20. What do the letters of the organisation RHS stand for?

Easy

Medium

Hard

Answers to QUIZ 269 – Pot Luck

1	Four	11	Nose
2	The blame	12	Escutcheon
3	Lisbon	13	Fingerprints
4	Hawai'i	14	Paper folding
5	Bakelite	15	World Boxing Council
6	Babylonian	16	Wet Wet Wet
7	Nicholas II	17	China
8	Samson	18	Arsenal
9	Sitting down	19	Points
10	Kermit the Frog	20	Steve Davis

Easy

1   On *The Simpsons*, which actress has voiced Lisa Simpson since the show's inception?

2   Which record producer's works include three Michael Jackson albums, *We Are The World* and the theme tune to *The Fresh Prince Of Bel-Air*?

3   Which television and radio presenter hosted *GMTV* for seventeen years between 1993 and 2010?

4   Tom Jones sang the theme tune to which James Bond film?

5   Which TV chef bought a majority share in Norwich City football club in 1997?

6   A 2016 study by the University of the West of England revealed that Smith is the most common surname in Britain. Jones is second. What is third?

7   Which actor and rapper won the first ever Grammy Award for Best Rap Performance for the song *Parents Just Don't Understand*?

8   After David Prowse's West Country accent was deemed too jovial, who voiced Darth Vader in the original *Star Wars* film trilogy?

9   Which Hollywood power couple met when jointly starring in *Mr and Mrs Smith*?

10   In the first three episodes of *The Matrix* film franchise, which Australian actor played Agent Smith?

11   *White Teeth* was the award-winning 2000 debut novel of which British author?

12   After Duncan Bannatyne left at the end of series 12, who became the sole remaining member of the original *Dragons' Den* investor line-up?

13   James Todd Smith is the real name of which hip-hop and R&B star, whose hits include *Mama Said Knock You Out*?

14   Which Welshman rose to fame as a teenage chorister during the mid-1980s before moving into TV and radio presenting, including ITV's *Daybreak*?

15   Born Vickie Lynn Hogan, which late actress, model and Playboy Playmate appeared in a famous black-and-white advertising campaign for *Guess* jeans?

16   Which Jamaican-American model, singer, songwriter and actress had a hit album and single both called *Slave to the Rhythm*?

17   Which English actress, singer and dancer started out in sitcoms with roles in *The Royle Family*, *Gavin & Stacey* and *Benidorm* amongst others?

18   What is the name of David Bowie's director son, best known for directing *Moon* (2009), *Source Code* (2011), *Warcraft* (2016) and *Mute* (2018)?

19   In 2003, which opening batsman became South Africa's youngest-ever Test cricket captain?

20   Which religious activist and cult leader founded the *People's Temple* in Indiana, before orchestrating a mass suicide pact in a Guyanese commune?

Medium

Hard

Answers to QUIZ 270 – AA

1	Aardvark	11	Leguaan
2	Braai	12	Isaac Hayes
3	Saab – they had bought up the Swedish Air Force's surplus of green paint left over from the war	13	James Caan
		14	Aarhus
4	Aaron Rodgers	15	Frank Rijkaard
5	*Harper's Bazaar*	16	A.A. Milne
6	Alcoholics Anonymous	17	Automobile Association
7	Martin Ødegaard	18	Maajid Nawaz
8	Aaliyah	19	Dominic Raab
9	Maastricht Treaty	20	Kursaal
10	Charles Saatchi		

1 The Decalogue is more colloquially known as what list?

2 Someone utilising scotopic vision can see where?

3 The Royal Military Academy, the British Army's initial officer training centre, is located in which Berkshire town?

4 Which European country were runners-up in both the 1982 and 1986 FIFA World Cups, before winning in 1990?

5 The song thrush bird is also known by which female name?

6 "Fidentia" is the motto of which insurance organisation, which houses the Lutine Bell in its offices?

7 In Scotland, what are Eigg, Muck, Mull, Skye and Rhum?

8 In addition to their other meanings, tulip, coupe and flute are also types of what?

9 As of 2022, what is the only ocean liner still in service in the world?

10 In the pirate song, how many men were on a dead man's chest?

11 Although they are now biennial, how many years after the 1983 debut event were the *second* World Athletics Championships held?

12 "Let your fingers do the walking" was a 1980s advertising slogan for which now-obsolete product?

13 What surname is shared by the first woman to fly across the English Channel, and a 15-year producer of *Tom and Jerry*?

14 Ladbrokes bookmakers has used which two-colour combination throughout its logo history?

15 The Sam Maguire Trophy is the major competition in which sport?

16 After leaving Mudcrutch, whose backing band was the Heartbreakers?

17 What is the fourth letter of the Greek alphabet?

18 A *howdah* is a seat used to ride either a camel or which other animal?

19 *Come Together* and *Here Comes The Sun* are tracks on which 1969 Beatles album?

20 Griffins were said to have the body of a lion and the head of which bird?

Easy

Medium

Hard

Answers to QUIZ 271 – Pot Luck

1	Sahara	11	Westminster Abbey
2	Ronald Reagan	12	Mark Hamill
3	*Penguin Books*	13	Berlin
4	Alps (specifically, the Bernese Alps)	14	*My Name Is Earl*
5	Ben Gunn	15	School
6	Simba	16	Australia
7	White and yellow	17	*Wogan*
8	Titus	18	Earth
9	Wear	19	25
10	Banana and toffee	20	Royal Horticultural Society

1   There are 22 yards in a chain; how many chains are there in a furlong?

2   Prince Charles and Princess Diana officially divorced in 1996 after how many years of marriage?

3   How many US Presidents' images appear on Mount Rushmore?

4   What is the maximum number of greyhounds that can compete in a licensed track race in the UK?

5   In his book *Outliers*, Malcolm Gladwell theorises that anyone can become an expert at anything if they put in how many hours of practice?

6   How many fluid ounces are there in a pint?

7   In tenpin bowling, and under traditional scoring rules, how many consecutive strikes are required to achieve a perfect "300" game?

8   Which Olympic track and field event contains the most events for female competitors?

9   How many holes are there on a traditional artist's palette?

10 A nonagenarian has lived for at least how many years?

11 How many pieces are there in a chess set?

12 How many countries share land borders with Mexico?

13 To the nearest whole number, how many miles are there in a league?

14 In the title of a Gene Pitney song, how many hours is it from Tulsa?

15 How many countries have equal to or less than ten square kilometres of land?

16 According to the Bible, how many years did Methuselah live?

17 How many points are required to win a game of badminton?

18 How many sheets of paper are there in a ream?

19 How many members were there in the 1980s group Thompson Twins between 1982 and 1986?

20 How many days after John F. Kennedy's assassination was his assailant Lee Harvey Oswald also shot?

Easy

Medium

Hard

QUIZ 275 – Pot Luck

ANSWERS ON PAGE 277

1 Which British political consulting firm was found to have acquired the data of some 87 million Facebook™ users in March 2018?

2 Which pair of fictional DC Comic superheroes are often known as the "Dynamic Duo"?

3 The males of which aquatic animal carry the eggs in a pouch and were described in a 2007 study as "promiscuous, flighty, and more than a little bit gay"?

4 In which sport are there playing positions named hooker, flanker and number eight?

5 Which highly potent green anise spirit had by 1915 been made in illegal in the United States, France, the Netherlands, Belgium, Switzerland and Austria-Hungary?

6 "One man's struggle to take it easy" was the tagline to which 1986 teen comedy film?

7 A natural by-product of decay, which colourless gas has a characteristic odour of rotten eggs?

8 Steve Rogers was the alter ego of which Marvel Comics superhero?

9 Which actor won the 2018 Academy Award for Best Actor for his role in *Three Billboards Outside Ebbing, Missouri*?

10 The name of which small breed of Welsh dog is also that of a die-cast model maker?

11 What adjective denotes any land that is capable of growing crops?

12 Which large breed of dog was originally bred by monks to find lost travellers in the Alps?

13 Papal conclaves are convened to elect who?

14 Who played The Wolf in the Quentin Tarantino film *Pulp Fiction*?

15 What is the name of the chef used in adverts for Homepride's flour and cooking sauce range?

16 The okapi is a member of which animal family?

17 Which breakfast cereal was advertised with the slogan "central heating for kids"?

18 Evidence of the production of what drink dates back to roughly 7000 BC, making it the oldest-known alcoholic beverage?

19 19th century medicine frequently used the application of which live animal to the skin in order to initiate blood flow or deplete bad blood?

20 Which fashion designer created the incredibly pointy bustier for Madonna's 1990 *Blond Ambition* tour?

Easy / Medium / Hard

Answers to QUIZ 273 – Pot Luck

1	The Ten Commandments	11	Four
2	In the dark	12	Yellow Pages
3	Sandhurst	13	Quimby (Harriet and Fred)
4	West Germany	14	Red and white
5	Mavis	15	Gaelic football
6	Lloyd's of London	16	Tom Petty
7	Islands	17	Delta
8	Wine glasses	18	Elephant
9	RMS *Queen Mary 2*	19	*Abbey Road*
10	Fifteen	20	Eagle

Easy

1   The crime of betraying one's country, especially by attempting to overthrow the monarchy or government, is known as what?

2   Guy Fawkes, William Penn and Robert Walpole all served prison time in which central London location, which was still in part a jail at the time?

3   The Birmingham Six were convicted of what offence?

4   In 1950, Timothy Evans was convicted and hanged for two murders actually committed by which bespectacled neighbour of his?

5   In Dante's *Inferno*, what crime was committed by those in the eighth circle of Hell?

6   In the criminal murder trial of OJ Simpson, if what item did not fit, Johnny Cochrane said the jury must acquit?

7   During the Napoleonic Wars, a French boat wrecked off the coast of Hartlepool, and locals hanged the only survivor. What was significant about that survivor?

8   In English law, use of the term "larceny" was replaced in 1968 by which new statutory crime?

9   In old English law, no one could be forcibly removed from the sanctuary of a church, not even criminals, unless they committed which crime?

10 In 1953, Derek Bentley was convicted of murder by joint enterprise on account of which four-word phrase, interpreted by the judge as encouragement to shoot, but by his defenders as encouragement to hand over the gun?

11 Victor Lustig, a highly skilled con artist from Austria-Hungary, is best known for "selling" which iconic world landmark, twice?

12 If someone has been convicted of regicide, what crime have they committed?

13 What name was given to the illicit American establishments that sold alcohol during the Prohibition era?

Medium

14 Which former MP lied in court about his involvement with a prostitute to win a 1987 libel case, for which he was convicted of perjury in 2000?

15 In the Victorian era, what did Mary Ann Cotton gain notoriety as?

16 NFL wide receiver Plaxico Burress was in 2008 sentenced to two years in jail for shooting who?

17 For his ability to consistently dodge charges as they would not stick, Mafia capo John Gotti earned what rhyming nickname?

18 On 12th July 2007, who were the unlikely perpetrators in the robbery of the Dar Es Salaam Bank in Baghdad, Iraq, who made out with $282 million?

19 In addition to murder, Surinder Koli, Armin Meiwes and the rapper Big Lurch were all convicted of which strange and thoroughly unpleasant crime?

20 Which high-profile Welsh drug smuggler published an autobiography entitled *Mr Nice*, one of his many aliases?

Hard

Answers to QUIZ 274 – How Many?

1	Ten	11	32
2	15	12	Three (USA, Guatemala, Belize)
3	Four (George Washington, Thomas Jefferson, Theodore Roosevelt and Abraham Lincoln)	13	Three
		14	24
4	Six	15	Four (Vatican City, Monaco, Nauru, Tuvalu)
5	10,000	16	969
6	16	17	15
7	12	18	500
8	The heptathlon (seven)	19	Three; their name came from Tintin
9	One	20	Two
10	90		

1. In which English county is the Jodrell Bank observatory located?
2. Charles Browne Fleet, pharmacist and inventor of the chapstick, also invented what other substance applied to (or rather, in) the body?
3. Shannon Airport serves which European country?
4. Cawl is a Welsh type of – and often, a synonym for – what food?
5. With his 1911 work *Still life with harp and violin*, Georges Braque became the first artist to exhibit works in which art gallery during their lifetime?
6. Bridgeville, California, was in 2003 the first town listed for sale on which online retailer?
7. Roger Moore first played the role of James Bond in which film?
8. Natural hot water from geothermal activity is used to heat roughly 90% of all buildings in which country?
9. Sloops, wherries and dinghies are types of what mode of transport?
10. In London, what are the Tate Modern and White Cube?
11. What style of cloth was illegal in Scotland from 1746 to 1782?
12. Dating back about 7,000 years, which was the first bird to be domesticated by man?
13. Under standard conditions, which metal – with the atomic number three – is the lightest?
14. *Dad's Army* was set during which war?
15. "Iron horse" is an archaic literary term for what mode of transport?
16. Caribou is a type of – and often, a synonym for – what animal?
17. In which country are fireworks said to have originated?
18. The phrase "three strikes and you're out" is derived from which sport?
19. Which Northern Irish TV presenter has credits to her name including *Rip-Off Britain* and *Open House*?
20. As constructed by the Romans and found in abundance underneath Paris in particular, what "C" is a subterranean cemetery of galleries with recesses for tombs?

Easy

Medium

Hard

Answers to QUIZ 275 – Pot Luck

1	Cambridge Analytica	11	Arable
2	Batman and Robin	12	St Bernard
3	Seahorse	13	Popes
4	Rugby union	14	Harvey Keitel
5	Absinthe	15	Fred
6	*Ferris Bueller's Day Off*	16	Giraffe
7	Hydrogen sulphide	17	Ready Brek
8	Captain America	18	Mead
9	Sam Rockwell	19	Leech
10	Corgi	20	Jean-Paul Gaultier

1 From which language do the words aardvark, meerkat and wildebeest come?

2 What word describes a figure of speech in which contradictory terms appear in conjunction, such as "pretty ugly"?

3 The German loanword *verboten* means something is what?

4 The word "quarantine" initially meant an isolation period of how many days?

5 What two-word alliterative phrase of Latin origin means "the other way round"?

6 With more than 430 listed uses, what simple three-letter word has the longest entry in the Oxford English Dictionary?

7 Containing a common forename, what one-word name is given to a criminal who specialises in opening safes?

8 The English name of which country has ten letters, but only one vowel? [Y is hereby not counted as a vowel.]

9 What word is said to be the sincerest form of flattery?

10 What term for a mid-afternoon nap comes from the Spanish word for six?

11 San Francisco humourist Herb Caen invented which word to refer to 1950's and 1960's non-conformists in dress and thought?

12 What two-word name is shared by an 1847 William Makepeace Thackeray novel and a magazine that featured a pregnant Demi Moore on the cover?

13 Traditionally, Alaskan sled drivers shout what word to drive their dogs forwards?

14 What is the defining characteristic of a heterogram or isogram?

15 In rhetoric, what is distinct about the words or lines in an abecedarian work?

16 In what rhetorical device is one part of an object used to represent the whole, such as referring to a car as "wheels"?

17 Which common usage financial word derives from an Italian term for "broken bench"?

18 What term is given to a form of repetition in which a word is repeated immediately for emphasis, such as Tony Blair's "education, education, education"?

19 What term refers to a word that only appears once in a work of or genus of literature, or in a body of work by a particular author?

20 Which Eurasian species of tall annual grass is the only eight-letter word in English to be entirely in alphabetical order?

Answers to QUIZ 276 – Crimes and Criminals

1	Treason	11	The Eiffel Tower
2	Tower of London	12	The murder of a monarch
3	Bombing a pub in 1974; their convictions were overturned in 1991	13	Speakeasys
4	Reginald Christie	14	Jeffrey Archer
5	Fraud	15	A mass murderer
6	Gloves	16	Himself, by mistake; the gun was unregistered
7	It was a monkey	17	The Teflon Don
8	Theft	18	The bank's security guards
9	Sacrilege	19	Cannibalism
10	"Let him have it"	20	Howard Marks

1. By population, what is the largest city in Scotland?
2. "Blood and Fire" is the oddly dark motto of which humanitarian organisation?
3. Bank robber Charles Floyd, killed in a shoot-out in 1934, went by what complimentary nickname?
4. The abbreviation Bt or Bart after a person's name indicate they are a member of which rank of the nobility?
5. Which organs contain fluid known as "vitreous humour"?
6. Although not the official capital city, Colombo is the largest city of which Asian country?
7. Which character in Jules Verne's novel *Twenty Thousand Leagues Under the Sea* takes his name from the Latin for nobody?
8. What name links a cartoon cat, three Popes, one Antipope and a Doctor Who actor?
9. In the name of the UK government scheme for helping 16- to 18-year-olds into employment Introduced in 1978, what did YOP stand for?
10. Steven Bradbury won a gold medal in which Olympic sport by deliberately staying at the back and hoping all the other competitors crashed into each other, which they did?
11. Which annual event held at the Metropolitan Museum of Art in New York is known globally as "Fashion's Biggest Night"?
12. Lawrence Dallaglio spent his entire playing career with which team?
13. The American M4 tank was named after which Civil War General?
14. In 1940, aged 14, which future Cuban leader sent a letter to US President Franklin D. Roosevelt, asking for a ten-dollar bill?
15. In the nursery rhyme *Sing a Song of Sixpence*, what was the queen in the parlour eating?
16. Which English cathedral surpassed the Great Pyramid of Giza for the title of tallest building in the world, and held it for 238 years until its spire collapsed in 1548?
17. Edward the Confessor was king at the start, Harold II was king in the middle, and William the Conqueror was king at the end of which year?
18. Which American city shares its name with the title of a 2002 Oscar-winning musical film?
19. As heard on BBC Radio 4 on the hour, how many pips make up the Greenwich Time Signal?
20. The infectious disease roup affects the respiratory tract of what animals?

Easy

Medium

Hard

Answers to QUIZ 277 – Pot Luck

1	Cheshire	11	Tartan
2	Laxative (now that's a career)	12	Goose
3	Ireland	13	Lithium
4	Soup	14	World War II
5	The Louvre	15	Steam locomotive
6	eBay	16	Reindeer
7	*Live and Let Die*	17	China
8	Iceland	18	Baseball
9	Boats	19	Gloria Hunniford
10	Art galleries	20	Catacomb

Can you identify these musical instruments?

Easy

1

2
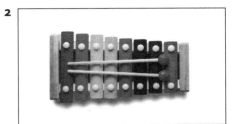

3

4

Medium

5

6
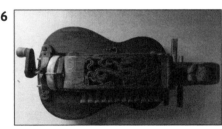

7

8

Hard

Answers to QUIZ 278 – Words

1   Dutch
2   Oxymoron
3   Forbidden
4   40 (from the Italian "quaranta", meaning 40)
5   Vice versa
6   Set
7   Peterman
8   Kyrgyzstan
9   Imitation
10   Siesta
11   Beatnik

12   *Vanity Fair*
13   "Mush" (although "hike" is now increasingly used instead)
14   Every letter in it only appears once (and in a double isogram, every letter appears exactly twice)
15   They are in alphabetical order
16   Synecdoche
17   Bankrupt
18   Epizeuxis
19   Hapax
20   Aegilops

1. Who thus far has been the only man named Oscar to win an Oscar?
2. Ramsay Street is the setting for which soap opera?
3. Ken Aston came up with the idea for which part of a football referee's equipment when stuck in traffic?
4. Which joint connects the foot to the leg?
5. Freestyle and Greco-Roman are the two different Olympic disciplines of which sport?
6. Krishna is a major deity in which religion?
7. "Old Ironsides" was the nickname of which Lord Protector and politician?
8. Pampers®, the nappy brand, is owned and marketed by which multinational consumer goods corporation?
9. What links the playing style of baseball pitcher Pat Venditte, international cricketers Kamindu Mendis and Jemma Barsby, and snooker star Ronnie O'Sullivan?
10. Verona Rupes, a 12-mile high near-vertical drop, is a cliff found on Miranda, a moon of which planet?
11. Coniston Water and Derwent Water are part of which national park?
12. *Sirtaki* or *syrtaki* is a dance originating from what country?
13. Aintree racecourse, the home of the English Grand National, is on the outskirts of which city?
14. Which lyricist collaborated with Andrew Lloyd Webber on notable works including *Jesus Christ Superstar* and *Evita*?
15. Instead of the name most outsiders know them by, members of which organisation refer to it as *La Cosa Nostra*, meaning "this thing of ours"?
16. Which Middle Eastern city gives its name to a type of artichoke?
17. The Babington plot of 1586 was a conspiracy to assassinate which English monarch?
18. The Diet is the legislative body of which country?
19. The River Rhine empties into the North Sea in what European country?
20. What is the highest denomination banknote in circulation in the United Kingdom?

Easy

Medium

Hard

Answers to QUIZ 279 – Pot Luck

1	Glasgow	11	Met Gala
2	Salvation Army (it is meant to refer to the blood of Jesus and the fire of the Holy Spirit)	12	Wasps
3	"Pretty Boy" Floyd	13	(William Tecumseh) Sherman
4	Baronet	14	Fidel Castro
5	Eyes	15	Bread and honey
6	Sri Lanka	16	Lincoln Cathedral
7	Nemo	17	1066
8	Sylvester	18	Chicago
9	Youth Opportunities Programme	19	Six
10	Speed skating	20	Poultry

1   In what is perhaps the ultimate history question, approximately how long ago did the Big Bang take place?

2   Kenneth I is traditionally considered the 9th-century founder of which country, which was then known as Alba?

3   Which US President famously said "I'm not a crook", ten months before resigning due to the Watergate scandal?

4   Indonesia declared independence from which European country at the end of World War II?

5   Which moustachioed peer appeared on a famous World War II recruitment poster, pointing at the viewer?

6   How did the Roman Emperor Claudius die?

7   On 27th May 1977, the worst accident in aviation history took place when two planes collided on the runway on which of the Canary Islands?

8   Which powerful ancient tribe occupied what is now southeast Wales in the first century AD?

9   At the general election of January 1835, which Prime Minister issued the Tamworth Manifesto, the basis for the modern Conservative Party?

10   Erected in 1961, Checkpoint Charlie was a crossing point...where?

11   In the 1820s, which infamous pair of Scottish murderers-for-profit killed their victims to sell their corpses for dissection?

12   Frederick the Great was king of which kingdom, which was dissolved in 1918?

13   Which became the 49th and 50th states of the USA a few months apart in 1959?

14   In 1492, who sighted Cuba, which he thought was China, before landing on Hispaniola, which he thought was Japan?

15   Benazir Bhutto was twice the Prime Minister of which country?

16   No doubt due to the prevalence of them in their local river, which ancient civilisation prayed to Sebek the crocodile god?

17   "Custer's Last Stand" took place at which battle of 25th June 1876?

18   Which ancient religious manuscripts found in 1946 near the Dead Sea are considered one of the most important finds in the history of archaeology?

19   Attempting to celebrate the end of war with Russia in 1807 with a hunt of these animals, Napoleon Bonaparte was instead defeated by a marauding army of what?

20   "The Miracle of 1511" was a protest festival in Brussels in which locals portrayed dozens of pornographic poses using what?

Answers to QUIZ 280 – Instruments

1   Tuba
2   Xylophone
3   Oboe
4   Accordion
5   Gong
6   Hurdy-gurdy
7   Sitar
8   Sackbut

1   Which Scottish city was the venue for the 2014 Commonwealth Games?

2   Maxine Clark founded which retailer that allows customers to customise their own preferred animals, complete with sounds and outfits?

3   Trent Bridge is a cricket ground located on the outskirts of which city?

4   Which brand of injection-moulded plastics is so synonymous with self-assembly model vehicles that products by other manufacturers still tend to be called them?

5   Grandma Moses became famous for taking up what profession at age 78?

6   The Great Barrier Reef lies off the coast of which country?

7   Kalium is an archaic name for which chemical element?

8   Which comedian became the first ever *Celebrity Big Brother* winner in 2001?

9   What do cars use to ignite the fuel with energy from the battery?

10 In 1998, Bill Clinton's Madame Tussauds waxwork had what removed due to persistent vandalism?

11 Which make of Austin car shares its name with a musical term meaning "to go quickly and brightly"?

12 Which Mexican artist produced *Diego and I*, featuring her with her husband's faint image on her forehead?

13 The ureter is a duct that carries urine between which two organs of the human body?

14 In which part of the body are the cruciate ligaments found?

15 What name is shared by singer Richie, dancer and entertainer Blair and footballer Messi?

16 What is the young of a goat called?

17 Foil, épée and sabre are the three types of equipment used in which Olympic sport?

18 Goal shooter, goal attack, centre and wing attack are playing positions in which sport?

19 Speaker's Corner is a feature of which London royal park?

20 What is the primary alkaloid found in the tobacco leaf and the addictive substance in cigarettes?

Easy

Medium

Hard

---

1 In Irish folklore, where are leprechauns said to hide their pots of gold?
2 As of 2022, which Irish singer is the only performer to have won the Eurovision Song Contest twice, in 1980 and 1987?
3 Arthur Griffith was in 1905 the founder of which Irish political party?
4 Which Chilean of Irish descent was the President of Chile from 1817-1823?
5 The most westerly point of mainland Ireland is located in which county?
6 In which Irish county can you kiss the Blarney Stone at Blarney Castle?
7 Located in Dublin, what is the name of Ireland's national theatre?
8 What type of races are run at the Galway Races?
9 Which Irish actor was the fifth man to play James Bond in film?
10 Which Irish boy band's first TV appearance came in 1993 on the *Late Late Show*, where they did some really, really cringey dancing?
11 Irish Bibles of the seventh and eighth centuries pioneered what, a critical factor in the widespread absorption of knowledge?
12 The first film adaptation of which classic Irish novel was banned in Ireland for over three decades for being "subversive to public morality"?
13 Instituted in 1962, the Jacob's Awards were Ireland's first what?
14 A person called Prawo Jazdy was thought to be Ireland's worst motoring offender with hundreds of offences. Why were they never prosecuted?
15 Re-elected in 2004, who was the first president of Ireland to have come from either Northern Ireland or Ulster?

16 Why did the Seán O'Casey pedestrian swing bridge spanning the River Liffey in Dublin not open between 2010 and 2014, as planned?
17 *Light a Penny Candle* was the debut novel of which author, known for her portrayals of small-town Irish life?
18 Which outside centre captained the Irish national rugby team from 2003 to 2012 and is regarded by critics as one of the greatest players of all time?
19 In 1859, at the age of 22, British army officer Lawrence E. Knox founded which newspaper?
20 A Dublin statue representing which character of Irish song is known colloquially as the "Dish with the Fish"?

Answers to QUIZ 282 – History

1	15 billion years ago	11	William Burke and William Hare
2	Scotland	12	Prussia
3	Richard Nixon	13	Alaska and Hawaii
4	Netherlands	14	Christopher Columbus
5	Lord Kitchener	15	Pakistan
6	Poisoning, by Agrippina	16	Ancient Egyptians
7	Tenerife	17	Battle of the Little Bighorn
8	The Silures	18	Dead Sea Scrolls
9	Robert Peel	19	Rabbits
10	In the Berlin wall	20	Snowmen

1 The name of which Japanese car manufacturer literally translates as "three diamonds", as reflected in their logo?

2 "Lung dart" is a pejorative alternative name for what?

3 According to Dutch folklore, where did Hendrik stick his finger?

4 What is the plural of series?

5 Which part of his body did Gene Simmons of KISS insure for $1 million?

6 What is the smallest country in the world?

7 *Foie gras* is made from which part of a duck or goose?

8 In the English version of Scrabble®, assuming no bonuses, how many points would playing the word "CHEESE" score?

9 How many countries have English names that begin with the letter Z?

10 Which giant animal native to Africa can last longer without water than a camel can?

11 What colour is the majority of toilet paper sold in France?

12 What surname is given to the adage "anything that can go wrong will go wrong"?

13 What was the name of the father of footballing siblings Gary and Phil Neville and their netballer sister Tracey?

14 Erythrocyte is a scientific name for what is more commonly known as what?

15 Silent film star Roscoe Arbuckle leant into what potentially unflattering nickname?

16 For obvious reasons, Mars is often known as what colour planet?

17 Prior to their 1998 name change, what were Starburst® sweets – made to make your mouth water – known as?

18 British ska band The Beat had a No.4 hit with which single in 1980?

19 In Scotland, Munros, Corbetts and Grahams are classifications of what?

20 What name is given to the act of stuffing animals for preservation?

Answers to QUIZ 283 – Pot Luck

Easy

Medium

Hard

1   Which reality TV show takes its name from an organisation in George Orwell's 1984?

2   Who rose to TV-presenting fame after finishing in fifth place in the ninth series of *The X Factor*?

3   Who were Alan Sugar's original advisors on the UK version of *The Apprentice*?

4   Multiple suicides, including that of host Caroline Flack, have been committed by stars of which reality show?

5   In 2000, which builder won the first UK series of *Big Brother*, and went on to become a TV presenter?

6   In 2000, which broker was ejected from the first UK series of *Big Brother* for attempted vote manipulation, and went on to become a TV presenter?

7   Jess Wright, Chloe Sims, Lauren Goodger and "Arg" all appear in which reality series?

8   "Sashay away!" is a catchphrase originating on which reality show?

9   Who won both the 2001 series of *Popstars* and the 2008 series of *Dancing on Ice*?

10   In 2014, who refused to parachute into the *I'm A Celebrity...* jungle, and withdrew after only three days?

11   James Tindale, Chloe Ferry, Vicky Pattison and Daniel Thomas-Tuck have all appeared in which reality show?

12   Which chef starred in the reality television series *The Restaurant*, where the prize was, in fact, a restaurant?

13   Who was the first sitting British MP to appear on a reality television show?

14   Arguably Britain's first reality TV star, Maureen Rees was the inadvertent star of which 1997 docuseries?

15   Mike "The Situation" Sorrentino came to prominence as a cast member on which reality TV series?

16   After the departure of Donald Trump, who was the host "entrepreneur" on the final season of the US version of *The Apprentice*?

17   A reality show about which ageing actor trying to revive his career while helping his daughters launch their own careers was cancelled in America after only two episodes?

18   A group of everyday people are left in a remote location and forced to vote each other off to win $1 million on which reality show?

19   *Here Comes Honey Boo Boo* was a spin-off of which other controversial reality show?

20   In what was probably the first-ever reality TV show, which 1970s American series followed the day-to-day life of the Loud family?

---

1   From which country of the United Kingdom did the writer Robert Louis Stevenson hail?

2   How many zeros are in there in ten million?

3   What nationality was the Formula One World Drivers Championship winning father-and-son duo of Graham Hill and Damon Hill?

4   The large amphitheatre known as the Colosseum is located in which European city?

5   Measured by median lethal dose, which snake native to Australia has the most toxic venom in the world?

6   Which facetious engineering unit – one also named for an animal – is defined as a third of one horsepower, or 250 watts?

7   The *haka* dance is associated with which sport?

8   Which Spanish artist had the middle names Diego José Francisco de Paula Juan Nepomuceno María de los Remedios Cipriano de la Santísima Trinidad Ruiz?

9   Which forename is given to baby marsupials, including kangaroos?

10 What suffix do football clubs in West Bromwich, Burton, and Brighton and Hove share?

11 When used as a prefix in Irish surnames, "O'" means what?

12 Which famous highwayman rode a horse called Black Bess?

13 Changi Airport is a major international airport, largely used as an interchange, in which Asian country?

14 Which children's book tells the story of a pig named Wilbur and his friendship with a spider?

15 Sleeping sickness and nagana are transmitted by which African bloodsucking fly?

16 Which American journalist and author of 1967's *Hell's Angels* founded the "gonzo" journalism movement?

17 The "Big Apple" is a nickname for which major world city?

18 Which long grain rice has a name that derives from the Hindi word for "fragrant"?

19 How many months have 31 days?

20 Who wrote *The Canterbury Tales*?

Answers to QUIZ 285 – Pot Luck

1	Mitsubishi	11	Pink
2	Cigarette	12	Murphy's Law
3	In the hole in the dyke	13	Neville Neville
4	Series	14	Red blood cell
5	His famously long tongue	15	"Fatty"
6	Vatican City	16	Red
7	Liver	17	Opal Fruits
8	11 (C=3, H=4, E=1, S=1)	18	*Mirror in the Bathroom*
9	Two (Zambia and Zimbabwe; Zaire was renamed the Democratic Republic of Congo in 1997)	19	Mountains
		20	Taxidermy
10	Giraffe		

Easy

1. With what simple item did Superman disguise himself in order to blend in as an average unassuming newspaper reporter?
2. In 1984, Dick Grayson renounced his role as Robin the Boy Wonder to start out on his own under which superhero moniker?
3. Although initially founded under a different name, in which year was the first Marvel comic released?
4. How did The Joker first meet Harley Quinn?
5. Which singing superstar reportedly wanted to buy Marvel so that he could play the role of Spider-Man himself?
6. Which DC character killed her own father with a kiss?
7. Carter Hall is the secret identity of which DC superhero?
8. Robin developed a romantic relationship with who, his Marvel opponent?
9. Which character in the DC universe was named after a poem?
10. Which former *Doctor Who* companion plays cyborg assassin Nebula?
11. Which former Batman played Spider-Man villain the Vulture?
12. Although he went on to be cast as Loki, which role did Tom Hiddleston initially audition for in *The Avengers*?

Medium

13. Wade Winston Wilson is the full name of which Marvel antihero?
14. While removed from the film series, a plot line in the comics story arc for which Marvel superhero reveals they are actually an alcoholic?
15. As of 2021, which is the only Marvel film not to have a post-credit scene?
16. Which mutant telepath is the self-appointed protector of the Amalgam Universe?
17. Having appeared as both Bane and Venom, which English actor has played antiheros in both the Marvel and DC universes?
18. What was the name of The Justice League's human mascot?
19. One of the languages spoken in Wakanda, Xhosa, is an actual language and one of the official languages of which country?
20. Which Marvel character was originally created by a fan named Randy Schueller in a competition for aspiring writers?

Hard

---

1   Glam rock singer Bernard Jewry enjoyed his best career years under what name, which made him sound like a relative of a David Bowie alter-ego?

2   Which chemical element takes its name from a Greek word for stench?

3   Mayonnaise is thought to take its name after Port Mahón, a town on which Spanish island?

4   What type of weapon was first used in combat on 15th September 1916?

5   Rudolf Hess was the last prisoner remaining in which jail?

6   Rob Lowe starred as Deputy Communications Director Sam Seaborn in which TV series set in the White House?

7   Beriberi is a disease affecting the heart caused by a lack of which vitamin?

8   Nancy Shevell married which English singer/songwriter in October 2011?

9   In musical notation, which sign raises a note above normal pitch?

10 Alan Titchmarsh, Pelé, Ena Sharples and Olivia Newton-John are among the hundreds of cultivars of which plant to be named after people?

11 Which prehistoric period followed the stone age?

12 Which US President compiled a "master list" of political opponents, including a section for "Black Congressmen"?

13 Released in 2011, *Skyrim* was the fifth instalment in which action role-playing video game series?

14 The breakaway British political group "the Gang of Four" founded which political party in 1981?

15 The remains of the ancient city of Troy lie in which modern country?

16 In sleep science, what does REM stand for?

17 In mathematical notation, what is meant by three dots in a triangular formation?

18 Which English band took their name from a 1962 novelty song by Bernard Cribbins?

19 The Treaty of Versailles ended which war?

20 Welsh rarebit is what type of food?

Answers to QUIZ 287 – Pot Luck

1	Scotland	11	Grandson of
2	Seven	12	Dick Turpin
3	British	13	Singapore
4	Rome	14	*Charlotte's Web*
5	Taipan	15	Tsetse
6	Donkeypower	16	Hunter S. Thompson
7	Rugby union – it is performed before matches by the New Zealand national team	17	New York City
		18	Basmati
8	Pablo Picasso	19	Seven (January, March, May, July, August, October, December)
9	Joey		
10	Albion	20	Geoffrey Chaucer

ANSWERS ON PAGE 292

Easy

1. The name of which of Adam and Eve's sons is a homophone for a word meaning having the ability to do something?

2. Which word for bending something over sounds like what a mare has done after she has given birth?

3. Hackman the actor and Harlow the actress have what pair of homophonic forenames?

4. Which Army rank is a homophone of the name of the edible part of a nut?

5. Which homophone could be either an administrative body or given advice, usually professionally?

6. The "Four Candles" sketch based around a series of misunderstandings in a department store was a creation of which double act?

7. Which term for a deceptive or pretend attack sounds like a sudden loss of consciousness?

8. Which stringed instrument's name rhymes with a term for treasure, especially taken from a wartime enemy?

9. "Discreet" means to be subtle, careful and prudent; what does "discrete" mean?

10. What term for an adult male pig also sounds like a dull person to be around?

11. The name of which geometric shape sounds like a story, dialogue, question or statement used in Zen buddhism?

Medium

12. Which is the correct spelling of the three-syllable word that can mean something that is first in order of importance, or the head teacher of a school?

13. Sandra Goodrich used which stage name in her singing career, chosen to sound like a nice holiday destination?

14. What homophone can be either the act of adding extra improvements to something, or a piece of praise?

15. Which heterograph can describe either an object not in motion, or a collection of writing and office materials?

16. What term for a religious teacher sounds just like financial gain?

17. What word for a technique of cooking eggs in water just below boiling point sounds like a word for a young of a certain fish?

18. The name of which animal sounds just like a verb meaning to cater to or indulge someone or something?

19. Abbott and Costello wrote which famous comedy routine about unusually named baseball players and misunderstandings of their fielding positions?

20. Ali G and Benny Hill have both done jokes punning which controversial medical practice with the name of a geographical demograph of young people?

Hard

Answers to QUIZ 288 – Marvel and DC

1	A pair of glasses	11	Michael Keaton
2	Nightwing	12	Thor
3	1939	13	Deadpool
4	She was his therapist	14	Iron Man
5	Michael Jackson	15	*Avengers: Endgame*
6	Poison Ivy	16	Dr Strangefate
7	Hawkman	17	Tom Hardy
8	Jubilee	18	Snapper Carr
9	Solomon Grundy	19	South Africa
10	Karen Gillan	20	Venom

ANSWERS ON PAGE **293**

1. In Alcoholic Anonymous's Twelve Step programme, what is step one?
2. The ambitiously-named theme park Dreamland can be found in which Kentish town?
3. Paul Verhoeven directed which 1997 American military science fiction action film, despite not having read the book it was based on?
4. In *The Hitchhiker's Guide to the Galaxy*, which planet is describe only by two words – "mostly harmless"?
5. The name of which ball game can also refer to someone's senses, especially when they are lost?
6. Which team finished in fourth place in the 1990 World Cup, yet failed to qualify for the 1994 tournament?
7. Which make of SEAT car takes its name from a Balearic island?
8. Which song was The Human League's only ever UK No.1 hit?
9. Married actors Wayne Allwine and Russi Taylor provided the voices to which animated couple for more than thirty years?
10. How many laps are there in a speedway race?
11. *The Lexicon of Love* was the 1982 debut studio album by which English pop band?
12. In the film *Free Willy*, what type of animal was Willy?
13. What is the maximum number of years that can pass between UK General Elections?
14. In Christian tradition, what name is given to the vessel that Jesus used at the Last Supper to serve wine?
15. Which American swimmer won four gold medals and a silver at the 2016 Olympic Games?
16. Which dairy product was the title of a hit single for K-pop band BTS in 2021?
17. The online company Moonpig mainly sells what?
18. Which South African fast food chain uses a red and black rooster as its logo?
19. Aperture, hotshoe and flange are all parts of what?
20. David Nobbs created which fictional salesman played on TV by Leonard Rossiter?

Easy

Medium

Hard

Answers to QUIZ 289 – Pot Luck

1	Alvin Stardust	11	Bronze age
2	Bromine	12	Richard Nixon
3	Menorca	13	*The Elder Scrolls*
4	Tank	14	Social Democratic Party
5	Spandau	15	Turkey
6	*The West Wing*	16	Rapid eye movement
7	B1	17	Therefore
8	Sir Paul McCartney	18	Right Said Fred
9	Sharp	19	World War I
10	Rose	20	Cheese on toast

What do these signs on the United Kingdom road network signify?

Easy

1

2

3

4

Medium

5

6

7

8

Hard

Answers to QUIZ 290 – Homophones

1	Abel	11	Cone/kōan
2	Fold/foaled	12	Principal (not principle)
3	Gene/Jean	13	Sandie Shaw
4	Colonel (kernel)	14	Complement/compliment
5	Council/counsel	15	Stationary/stationery
6	*The Two Ronnies*	16	Prophet/profit
7	Feint/faint	17	Coddling/codling
8	Lute/loot	18	Panda/pander
9	Separate and distinct	19	*Who's on First?*
10	Boar/bore	20	Euthenasia and the "Youth in Asia"

1. Which animal is known in Welsh as *Buwch goch gota*, literally translating to "little red cow"?
2. Brahma, Wyandotte and Plymouth Rock are types of which animal?
3. Starting at the centre and working outwards, what are the five colours of an archery target?
4. From which language did the words bangle, bungalow and thug come?
5. Which Romanian car manufacturer makes the Sandero, Logan, and Duster models?
6. What name is given to an addition or supplement that explains or changes a will?
7. Musicians Hornsby and Springsteen share what first name?
8. One of the most enduring images in cinema, stunt actor Harold Lloyd is seen hanging from what in his 1923 film, *Safety Last!*?
9. Which actor played Del Boy Trotter in *Only Fools And Horses*?
10. Known as a tax haven, which British Overseas Territory island group takes its name from a Carib word for crocodile?
11. What is the antonym of antonym?
12. Which mathematical item is known as *un camembert* in France?
13. In European judo, what is the lowest ranking belt colour?
14. Which long and thin West African country is 295 miles long, only between 15 and 30 miles wide, and entirely surrounded by Senegal?
15. King John set his seal to the Magna Carta on which island?
16. Stewpot was the nickname of which English radio broadcaster and TV presenter?
17. The USSR annexed which three Baltic states in 1940?
18. Which imperial unit of measurement takes its name from the Latin for a thousand?
19. On a standard roulette wheel, which numbers appear in the red segments?
20. What type of subatomic particle is a constituent of the nucleus of every element, except hydrogen?

Easy

Medium

Hard

Answers to QUIZ 291 – Pot Luck

1	Accepting there is a problem	11	ABC
2	Margate	12	A whale (orca, or killer whale)
3	*Starship Troopers*	13	Five
4	Earth	14	The Holy Grail or Holy Chalice
5	Marbles	15	Katie Ledecky
6	England	16	*Butter*
7	Ibiza	17	Cards
8	*Don't You Want Me*	18	Nando's
9	Mickey and Minnie Mouse	19	A camera
10	Four	20	Reginald Perrin

1   In which English county is *Fawlty Towers* set?

2   In which English county was the Wooburn Grange Country Club that was used for the show's exterior shots located?

3   Which *Fawlty Towers* actor was the victim of a prank in 2008 which led to the eventual resignation of the controller of BBC Radio 2?

4   Which character was played by Connie Booth, John Cleese's then real-life wife?

5   Basil's Austin 1100 Countryman car was given a "damn good..." what in the episode *Gourmet Night*?

6   How many episodes of *Fawlty Towers* were broadcast in total?

7   Which show came top of the BBC's 2004 poll series *Britain's Best Sitcom*, where *Fawlty Towers* placed fifth?

8   When Basil purchases a moose's head to hang in the hotel lobby, the Major mistakenly believes it comes from country?

9   Prunella Scales, who played Sybil, is married to which fellow actor?

10   The episode *The Germans* is the only one not to begin with an exterior shot of the hotel. What is visible instead?

11   What type of animal does Manuel wrongly believe his pet rat to be?

12   Who or what does Sybil want to leave in charge of the front desk in *The Builders*?

13   In 2016, John Cleese reprised his role as Basil Fawlty in a series of television adverts for which high street optician?

14   Which actor, also known for his leading role as Lionel in *As Time Goes By*, played Dr Price in series two?

15   What is the occupation of the French guest Mrs Peignoir who flirts with Basil in the episode *The Wedding Party*?

16   In which war did Basil Fawlty supposedly see action?

17   What breed of dog bites Manuel and Polly in the episode *The Kipper and the Corpse*?

18   What phrase does Basil include in his advertisement for the hotel's "Gourmet Night" that leads people to feel insulted and stay away?

19   Which actor, who played Mrs Hudson in the BBC drama series *Sherlock*, featured in the episode *The Anniversary*?

20   In which year was the final episode of *Fawlty Towers* shown?

Answers to QUIZ 292 – Road Signs

1   National speed limit applies

2   Roadworks

3   Slippery road

4   End of goods vehicles restriction

5   No motor vehicles

6   Dual carriageway ends

7   No stopping

8   Give way to oncoming vehicles

1 Which American philosopher, cognitive scientist, critic and a "the father of modern linguistics"?

2 After barely passing a referendum vote, what was legalised fo of Ireland in 1997?

3 In 1960s television adverts, which toothpaste was advertised as confidence"?

4 In the name of the TV production company, what does ITN stan

5 Russian physiologist Ivan Pavlov was known for conditioning exp which animals?

6 In which country are the remains of the ruined city of Carthage?

7 Which toy fad of the late 1990s has a portmanteau name that trans as "egg watch"?

8 In rugby union, what name is given to the forwards on either end o a scrum?

9 What are the two main ingredients of a Bloody Mary?

10 Samantha and Sven are the two non-existent scorers on which Radio 4

11 When purchase tax was abolished in the UK in 1973, what replaced it?

12 When written in English, how many countries have the word Guinea in

13 Basenji, saluki and pinscher are all types of which animal?

14 Airblade™ and Airwrap™ are product lines manufactured by which British te

15 Which strait separates the Isle of Wight and Great Britain?

16 If it was Friday, five o'clock and "Double or Drop" was being played, which show was on?

17 Kryten, Rimmer and Dave Lister are characters in which sci-fi sitcom?

18 Which gold medal-winning gymnast was nicknamed "The Sparrow from Mir

19 Which English football team play at Dean Court?

20 Pasta is made from which crop?

Answers to QUIZ 293 – Pot Luck
1 Ladybird
2 Chick...

QUIZ 285 – Pot Luck

ANSWERS ON PAGE 287

1 The name of which Japanese car manufacturer literally translates as "three diamonds", as reflected in their logo?

2 "Lung dart" is a pejorative alternative name for what?

3 According to Dutch folklore, where did Hendrik stick his finger?

4 What is the plural of series?

5 Which part of his body did Gene Simmons of KISS insure for $1 million?

6 What is the smallest country in the world?

7 *Foie gras* is made from which part of a duck or goose?

8 In the English version of Scrabble®, assuming no bonuses, how many points would playing the word "CHEESE" score?

9 How many countries have English names that begin with the letter Z?

10 Which giant animal native to Africa can last longer without water than a camel can?

11 What colour is the majority of toilet paper sold in France?

12 What surname is given to the adage "anything that can go wrong will go wrong"?

13 What was the name of the father of footballing siblings Gary and Phil Neville and their netballer sister Tracey?

14 Erythrocyte is a scientific name for what is more commonly known as what?

15 Silent film star Roscoe Arbuckle leant into what potentially unflattering nickname?

16 For obvious reasons, Mars is often known as what colour planet?

17 Prior to their 1998 name change, what were Starburst® sweets – made to make your mouth water – known as?

18 British ska band The Beat had a No.4 hit with which single in 1980?

19 In Scotland, Munros, Corbetts and Grahams are classifications of what?

20 What name is given to the act of stuffing animals for preservation?

Answers to QUIZ 283 – Pot Luck

1 Glasgow
2 Build-A-Bear Workshop
3 Nottingham
4 Airfix
5 Art
6 Australia
7 Potassium, hence why its symbol is K
8 Jack Dee
9 Spark plugs
10 The zip on his trousers
11 Allegro (it was perhaps an optimistic name)
12 Frida Kahlo (married to fellow artist Diego Rivera)
13 Kidney and bladder
14 Knee
15 Lionel
16 Kid
17 Fencing
18 Netball
19 Hyde Park
20 Nicotine

Z 296 – July

e did Prince Charles and Lady Diana Spencer get married on 29th July 1981?

da Day, celebrating Canadian independence, is celebrated on which date?

re did people walk for the first time on 20th July 1969?

month of July takes its name from which historical figure?

at organisation did General William Booth found in July 1865 in London?

no became leader of Argentina on 1st July 1974, becoming the first woman in the world

hold the title of President?

ought between 1–3 July 1863, which battle of the American Civil War involved the largest number of casualties and is often described as the war's turning point?

On 2nd July 1937, which female aviator vanished without trace over the Pacific Ocean?

Born in Oldham on 25th July 1978, who was the world's first "test tube baby"?

The July Revolution was an 1830 attempt to overthrow which king of France?

Which Greenpeace vessel was bombed and sunk in Auckland Harbour on 10th July 1985?

12 Published in July 2015, what was the title of Harper Lee's second novel, 55 years after the release of To Kill a Mockingbird?

13 Anders Behring Breivik committed a 22nd July 2011 terrorist attack against the government and population of which country?

14 Which battle of 2nd July 1644 was the largest battle of the English Civil War?

15 How did Claus von Stauffenberg attempt to assassinate Adolf Hitler in the "20th July plot" of 1944?

16 "Knee-high by the fourth of July" is a common saying for farmers in the American Midwest, referring to the desired growth of which crop?

17 What type of weather killed 23 people in Rostov, Ukraine, on 10th July 1923?

18 Who became Governor of The Bank of England in July 2003?

19 Opening on 20th July 1837, what was London's first inter-city railway terminus?

20 In July 2002, who became the first person to fly solo around the world non stop in any type of aircraft?

Answers to QUIZ 294 – Fawlty Towers

1 Devon
2 Buckinghamshire
3 Andrew Sachs
4 Polly Sherman
5 "Thrashing"
6 12
7 Only Fools and Horses
8 Japan
9 Timothy West
10 A hospital

11 Siberian hamster
12 The garden gnome
13 Specsavers
14 Geoffrey Palmer
15 Antiques dealer
16 Korean War
17 Shih-tzu
18 "No riff-raff"
19 Una Stubbs
20 1979

E 288

... Big Brother for attempted vote

...nter?

... Goodger and "Arg" all appear in which reality series?

... a catchphrase originating on which reality show?

who won both the 2001 series of Popstars and the 2008 series of Dancing on Ice?

10 In 2014, who refused to parachute into the I'm A Celebrity... jungle, and withdrew after only three days?

11 James Tindale, Chloe Ferry, Vicky Pattison and Daniel Thomas-Tuck have all appeared in which reality show?

12 Which chef starred in the reality television series The Restaurant, where the prize was, in fact, a restaurant?

13 Who was the first sitting British MP to appear on a reality television show?

14 Arguably Britain's first reality TV star, Maureen Rees was the inadvertent star of which 1997 docuseries?

15 Mike "The Situation" Sorrentino came to prominence as a cast member on which reality TV series?

16 After the departure of Donald Trump, who was the host "entrepreneur" on the final season of the US version of The Apprentice?

17 A reality show about which ageing actor trying to revive his career while helping his daughters launch their own careers was cancelled in America after only two episodes?

18 A group of everyday people are left in a remote location and forced to vote each other off to win $1 million on which reality show?

19 Here Comes Honey Boo Boo was a spin-off of which other controversial reality show?

20 In what was probably the first-ever reality TV show, which 1970s American series followed the day-to-day life of the Loud family?

Answers to QUIZ 284 – Ireland

1 At the end of rainbows
2 Johnny Logan (he also wrote the 1992 winner)
3 Sinn Fein
4 Bernardo O'Higgins
5 Kerry
6 County Cork
7 Abbey Theatre
8 Horse races
9 Pierce Brosnan
10 Boyzone

11 Spaces in between words
12 Ulysses by James Joyce (the ban was lifted in 2000)
13 Television awards
14 They never existed; "Prawo Jazdy" is Polish for "driving license"
15 Mary McAleese
16 Someone lost the remote control
17 Maeve Binchy
18 Brian O'Driscoll
19 The Irish Times
20 Molly Malone

1   With a city for a stage name, which actress's filmography includes 1963's *Tom Jones* and 1969's *They Shoot Horses, Don't They??*

2   Thresher, basking and hammerhead are all types of which animal?

3   What rock are beds of snooker tables traditionally made of?

4   In which sporting event does the winning team move backwards, and the losing team move forwards?

5   What is the smallest planet in the solar system?

6   Starting in 2010, Heston Blumenthal has appeared in adverts for which supermarket?

7   Which oily fish derives its name from an island in the Mediterranean Sea?

8   An ichthyologist is concerned with the study of which animals?

9   Which electronic music duo shares their name with the Russian word for milk?

10 Which comedian has written novels including *Gridlock* and *Blind Faith*?

11 Hamley's toy shop is located on which London street, found on the Monopoly™ board?

12 A spinnaker is used in which activity?

13 In 2010, Zoe Smith became the first Englishwoman to win a Commonwealth Games medal in which sport?

14 Ilex is an alternative name for which family of plants?

15 Which music-themed restaurant chain opened its first venue in Mayfair in 1971?

16 In which part of the body is the sclera located?

17 In Formula 1 racing, what colour flag is waved at a driver being disqualified?

18 The seaside resort of Broadstairs is in which English county?

19 Valerie Adams, Michelle Carter and Gong Lijiao are all Olympic medallists in which throwing event?

20 Which British prime minister was the Public Schools Fencing Champion of 1892?

Easy

Medium

Hard

Answers to QUIZ 295 – Pot Luck

1	Noam Chomsky	11	VAT (value added tax)
2	Divorce	12	Four (Guinea, Guinea-Bissau, Equatorial
3	Colgate®		Guinea, Papua New Guinea)
4	Independent Television News	13	Dog
5	Dogs	14	Dyson
6	Tunisia	15	Solent
7	Tamagotchi™	16	*Crackerjack*
8	Props	17	*Red Dwarf*
9	Vodka and tomato juice	18	Olga Korbut
10	*I'm Sorry I Haven't A Clue*	19	AFC Bournemouth
		20	Durum wheat

Easy

1. Which American comedian, host, actress and writer starred in an eponymous sitcom between 1994 and 1998?

2. Which pinkish Greek and Turkish dip is usually, if not exclusively, made from cod roe and olive oil?

3. A yacht or boat with two equal-sized hulls in a parallel formation is known as a what?

4. The fictional characters Randall Flagg, Gazzo, Predator and Tygra all have what preternatural ability?

5. Which fashion item was initially called the "Atom", with both its former and current name referring to nuclear tests in the 1950s?

6. In *The Adventures of Tom Sawyer*, the title character lives in a small town located near which large river that shares its name with a state?

7. Which Hawaiian dress, a cross between a robe and a shirt, hangs loose from the shoulder and is considered formal dress for weddings?

8. Aristotle, Sherlock Holmes, Scarlett Johansson and Henry Fonda are or were all apiarists, a synonym for what?

9. What term is given to inflammation of the gums?

10. Sara Dallin, Siobhan Fahey and Keren Woodward were the founding members of which pop group?

Medium

11. Which man-made construction links the Atlantic and Pacific Oceans?

12. Although Rabat is the capital, which city is comfortably Morocco's largest by population?

13. What is the indigenous name for Ayers Rock?

14. Charles Manson was said to have been inspired in his crimes by which Beatles song?

15. Which English DJ and presenter of Somali descent was named after the author of *I Know Why The Caged Bird Sings*?

16. What term is given to a one followed by a hundred zeroes?

17. The Labrador Retriever is a dog breed named after a region of what country?

18. Who has hosted the American version of *Wheel of Fortune* for more than four decades?

19. Which vegetable side dish is the national dish of South Korea?

20. Known informally as "The Gong", what is the third-largest city in New South Wales and the tenth-largest in all of Australia?

Answers to QUIZ 296 – July

1	St Paul's Cathedral	11	*Rainbow Warrior*
2	1st July	12	*Go Set a Watchman*
3	The moon	13	Norway
4	Julius Caesar	14	The Battle of Marston Moor
5	The Salvation Army	15	With an exploding briefcase
6	Isabel Perón	16	Corn/maize
7	Battle of Gettysburg	17	Giant hailstones
8	Amelia Earhart	18	Sir Mervyn King
9	Louise Brown	19	Euston
10	Charles X	20	Steve Fossett

Hard

1   Alexey Pajitnov created what very famous video game, which has been released for more different platforms than any other?

2   Zymurgy is a branch of chemistry concerning what process?

3   Movies are "certified fresh" if they achieve above a 75% approval rating on which community film critic website?

4   Gatsometer BV are a Dutch company known for their manufacture of what piece of safety equipment?

5   Who worked as a baker and dishwasher in London hotels before going on to become the first President of Vietnam?

6   Which K-pop band's name would be worth 13 points in snooker?

7   The Dyslexia Research Trust is aptly based in which English city?

8   Which patron saint's day is celebrated annually on 1st March?

9   The London Underground turned how many years old in 2013?

10 The clothing company Blue Ribbon Sports was renamed in 1971 to what?

11 Mel Gibson played a pilot who had been cryogenically frozen for 53 years in which 1992 film?

12 When describing the power of a motor vehicle, what does BHP stand for?

13 Scriptoriums, cloisters and dorters are areas commonly found in what sort of religious complex?

14 What "animal" emblem is on the Welsh flag?

15 Spitalfields, Portobello Road and Camden are all London-based locations of what?

16 Joel David Kaplan, Michel Vaujour, Seamus Twomey and Pascal Payet have all escaped prison by what means?

17 Ahmed Best provided the motion capture and voice of which controversial character in the *Star Wars* franchise?

18 In which American city has the Mardi Gras celebration been held annually since 1827?

19 In the northern hemisphere, all racehorses have the birthdate 1st January; what date do all racehorses have in the southern hemisphere?

20 What was Sarah, Duchess of York's maiden name?

Easy

Medium

Hard

Answers to QUIZ 297 – Pot Luck

1	Susannah York	11	Regent Street
2	Shark	12	Sailing – it is a type of sail
3	Slate	13	Weightlifting
4	Tug of war	14	Holly
5	Mercury	15	*Hard Rock Café*
6	Waitrose	16	The eye
7	Sardine, as in Sardinia	17	Black
8	Fish	18	Kent
9	Moloko	19	Shot put
10	Ben Elton	20	Winston Churchill

Easy

1 The name of all but one episode of *Friends* began with what two words?
2 Which of the six man cast members sat at the kids' table at Monica and Chandler's wedding?
3 To get over her break-up with Richard, what did Monica start making?
4 What is the name of the fellow paleontologist that Ross briefly dates, only to find out she's extremely messy?
5 After Chandler makes out with two of her sisters, too drunk to realise they are different people, which third of Joey's sisters punches him?
6 Joey played the neurosurgeon Dr Drake Ramoray on which daytime television soap?
7 Who stole Ross's monkey Marcel and made him wear a pink tutu?
8 Ross wanted to play which instrument at Chandler and Monica's wedding?
9 When Phoebe married Mike, as her stepfather is unable to get a day release, who walked her down the aisle?
10 Which two actresses have played Rachel's sisters?
11 When Ross made a list comparing Julie and Rachel, he listed only one "con" for Julie. What was it?
12 Much to his embarrassment, what is Chandler's middle name?
13 Which phrase was a new entry in the 2002 edition of the Shorter Oxford English Dictionary due to its popularisation by Joey?
14 What is a "Joey Special"?
15 Which famous and pivotal "mistake" came about only after a genuine mistake by one of the cast during a read-through that the writers decided to keep?

Medium

16 In a desperate attempt to bond when he was trying to get his apartment, what did Ross give to Ugly Naked Guy?
17 What was Rachel's New Year's resolution, which she managed for only two days?
18 After which episode did the producers hire 200 people to take calls from all of the complaints they assumed they would get?
19 In December 1978, Columbus State University hired a man with what name as a professor of paleontology?
20 What was Chandler Bing's job?

Hard

Answers to QUIZ 298 – Only One Vowel

1	Ellen DeGeneres	11	Panama Canal
2	Taramasalata	12	Casablanca
3	Catamaran	13	Uluru
4	Invisibility	14	*Helter Skelter*
5	Bikini	15	Maya Jama
6	Mississippi	16	Googol
7	Muumuu	17	Canada
8	Beekeepers	18	Pat Sajak
9	Gingivitis	19	Kimchi
10	Bananarama	20	Wollongong

1   Who wrote the foundational theoretical text in materialist philosophy, *Das Kapital*?
2   What name is shared by the author who wrote *Cloud Atlas* and one of the stars of *Peep Show*?
3   Gavials or gharials are species of which animal?
4   The tiny "black hole" dungeon in which 123 of 146 British prisoners suffocated on 20th June 1756 was located in which city?
5   Silverstone, Donington and Brands Hatch are venues for what type of sport?
6   Swan Upping is an annual census of the swan population on which river?
7   Paddy Ashdown and Charles Kennedy were both leaders of which political party?
8   *Careless Whisper* was which singer's first solo single?
9   Which American artist produced the *Four Freedoms* series of oil paintings in 1943?
10 From which London railway station do trains to Bristol depart?
11 In mythology, Romulus and Remus were raised by which animals?
12 Hanlon's Razor advises to "never attribute to malice that which is adequately explained by..." what?
13 The Velocipede was an early prototype of what mode of transport?
14 In 1997, Mars admitted that what colour of M&M'S® was included in each packet more than the others?
15 *On Who Wants to Be a Millionaire*, how many questions does a contestant have to answer correctly to win the top prize?
16 *Operation London Bridge* is the codename for the plan of operations in the event of whose death?
17 What is the most common name used in nursery rhymes, including Horner and Sprat?
18 In ice hockey and lacrosse, what term describes a period of the game in which one team has a player temporarily suspended from the game?
19 How many of Henry VIII's wives were called Anne?
20 What four-letter term refers to the part of a knife blade that extends into the handle?

Easy

Medium

Hard

Answers to QUIZ 299 – Pot Luck

1   *Tetris*®
2   Fermentation
3   Rotten Tomatoes
4   Speed cameras
5   Ho Chi Minh
6   Blackpink
7   Reading
8   Saint David
9   150
10 Nike

11 *Forever Young*
12 Brake horse power
13 Monastery
14 A dragon
15 Markets
16 Helicopter – in Payet's case, he has done it three times
17 Jar Jar Binks
18 New Orleans
19 1st August
20 Ferguson

1   The film version of which musical had Catherine Zeta-Jones, Renee Zellweger and Richard Gere in leading roles?

2   The 1953 film adaptation of *Calamity Jane* saw which actress play the title role?

3   Which musical based on a Victor Hugo novel tells the story of Jean Valjean's lifelong struggle to forgo a criminal past?

4   In *The Sound of Music*, Georg and Maria von Trapp have how many children?

5   Benjamin Barker lives above Mrs Lovett's pie shop in which 1973 Stephen Sondheim musical?

6   Zac Efron plays a basketball star and Vanessa Hudgens a shy transfer student in the first entry of which 21st century musical franchise?

7   What are the two opposing gangs called in *West Side Story*?

8   In *Glee*, Sue Sylvester – the antagonist former cheerleading coach and later Vice President of the USA – is portrayed by which actress?

9   Which actor appeared in *Annie Get Your Gun*, *Calamity Jane*, *Kiss Me Kate* and *Seven Brides for Seven Brothers* in a span of only four years?

10 Which trumpeter, vocalist and legend of jazz appeared with his band in the 1956 film *High Society*?

11 Later made into a 2007 film, which 2002 Broadway musical is named after a personal grooming product?

12 The main plot of *Grease* concerns the story of the romance between which two lead characters?

13 In *Willy Wonka and the Chocolate Factory*, as it was the first time they had seen it, the children's reactions to seeing what were genuine?

14 *Rocketman* is a 2019 musical biopic based on the life and music of which superstar?

15 The 2019 backstage musical *Burlesque* starred Christina Aguilera and which veteran pop icon?

16 The most famous scene in 1952's *Singin' in the Rain* saw Gene Kelly dancing around holding what object?

17 Marlon Brando and Frank Sinatra portray gamblers in which 1955 musical film?

18 *Oh, What a Beautiful Mornin'* is the opening song to which musical?

19 While the 1981 musical denied it, the 2006 film *Dreamgirls* more directly acknowledges that its story largely mirrors that of which real-life Motown act?

20 Which 2008 jukebox musical romantic comedy film is based on the songs of pop group ABBA?

Answers to QUIZ 300 – *Friends*

1   "The One" – the only episode that didn't was "The Last One"

2   Ross

3   Jam

4   Cheryl

5   Cookie

6   *Days of Our Lives*

7   Mr Heckles

8   Bagpipes

9   Chandler – she initially asked Joey, but he ends up being the minister instead

10 Reece Witherspoon (Jill) and Christina Applegate (Amy)

11 "She's not Rachel"

12 Muriel

13 "Going commando"

14 Two pizzas eaten one on top of the other

15 Ross calling Emily "Rachel" at the altar

16 Mini muffins

17 To stop gossiping

18 *The One with the Lesbian Wedding* – in total, they only received 11 calls

19 David Schwimmer

20 Unclear, though he works in statistical analysis and data reconfiguration (and not as a transponster, which is not even a word)

1   Closing in 2015, Kellingley was the last operational what in the UK?
2   Which other actor did David Arquette marry in 1999?
3   Ardent, a film production company, was founded in 1993 by who?
4   Ménière's Disease affects which part of the body?
5   Up to two thirds of the total weight of a shark's brain is dedicated to which sense?
6   Which liqueur is added to Drambuie® to make a Rusty Nail cocktail?
7   Which piece of transport infrastructure was first proposed in 1802, but did not open until 1994?
8   What nickname was defender Cesar Azpilicueta given by Chelsea fans, as they found his real name too hard to pronounce?
9   The quokka is indigenous to which country?
10 In 1959, Robert Timm and John Cook set a record for longest continuous plane flight – to the nearest day, how long was it?
11 In what language was the Magna Carta written?
12 In which month did the Russian October Revolution take place?
13 Over how many days is an Olympic decathlon held?
14 On stage in Iowa in 1982, Ozzy Osbourne bit the head off which type of creature?
15 The De Beers group of companies controls more than 80% of the world's supply of what?
16 Which nuts are ground up to make marzipan?
17 Wile E. Coyote would obtain all his traps to try to catch the Road Runner from which company?
18 Charcoal, sulphur and saltpetre are mixed to make which explosive?
19 In what sport was Chris Boardman an Olympic champion?
20 With which hand do British Army soldiers salute? (You can have two guesses.)

Easy

Medium

Hard

Answers to QUIZ 301 – Pot Luck

1	Karl Marx	11	Wolves
2	David Mitchell	12	"…stupidity"
3	Crocodile	13	Bicycle
4	Calcutta/Kolkata	14	Brown
5	Motor sport	15	15 (although, for a brief stretch towards the end of its first UK run, this was reduced to 12)
6	The Thames	16	Queen Elizabeth II
7	Liberal Democrats	17	Jack
8	George Michael	18	Power play
9	Norman Rockwell	19	Two
10	Paddington	20	Tang

Easy

1. What is the surname of Don Vito's crime family in *The Godfather*?
2. In the film *Casino*, which non-Mafia member initially ran the establishment?
3. Near the end of *Scarface*, Tony Montana pulls out an automatic rifle with a grenade launcher and yells what classic line?
4. Joe Pesci refused to come out of retirement a reported fifty times before accepting the role of Russell Bufalino in which Martin Scorsese film?
5. Warren Beatty and Annette Bening starred in which 1991 gangster movie?
6. Viggo Mortensen is an undercover FSB agent working under license from the British government in which 2007 film?
7. Johnny Depp played the role of Joe Pistone, real-life undercover FBI agent who infiltrated the Mafia, in which film?
8. The Notorious B.I.G. used the moniker "Frank White" in many of his songs, one taken from which 1990 gangster film's lead character?
9. Noodles and Max lead a group of Jewish ghetto youths who rise to prominence as Jewish gangsters in which 1984 Sergio Leone film?
10. Martin McDonagh was inspired to write which film about two Irish gangsters hiding in a European city after spending a weekend there?
11. In *The Godfather*, as Rocco gets out of the car after killing Paulie, Clemenza says to leave the gun, but to take what?
12. Memorable for the line "Keep the change, ya filthy animal!", *Angels with Filthy Souls* was a spoof gangster film within which comedy film?

Medium

13. Sylvester Stallone starred in an ill-advised 2000 remake of which classic 1971 Michael Caine crime caper?
14. "If you run, the beast catches you; if you stay, the beast eats you" was the tagline to which 2002 Brazilian gangster film?
15. *The Public Enemy* is a 1931 gangster film featuring a mob boss with what derogatory nickname, based on his appearance?
16. Who played Buddy Russo, "Popeye" Doyle's partner, in *The French Connection*?
17. The Orphans, Baseball Furies, Lizzies and Punks are feuding gangs in which 1971 cult classic?
18. In which film does Marlon Brando regret the fact that he could have been a contender, instead of a bum?
19. Ice Cube, Cuba Gooding Jr., Laurence Fishburne, Nia Long and Angela Bassett were among the cast of which 1991 coming-of-age gangster film?
20. In *Goodfellas*, what is Jimmy Two Times seen getting out of his chair to go and do?

Hard

Answers to QUIZ 302 – Musicals

1	*Chicago*	11	*Hairspray*
2	Doris Day	12	Sandy Olsson and Danny Zuko
3	*Les Misérables*	13	Chocolate room
4	Seven	14	Elton John
5	*Sweeney Todd: The Demon Barber of Fleet Street*	15	Cher
6	*High School Musical*	16	An umbrella
7	Sharks and Jets	17	*Guys and Dolls*
8	Jane Lynch	18	*Oklahoma!*
9	Howard Keel	19	The Supremes
10	Louis Armstrong	20	*Mamma Mia!*

1 Diana Ross duetted with who for the 1981 song *Endless Love*?

2 On letters, what does the abbreviation PS stand for?

3 Which English county used to be divided into sections called ridings?

4 Which pair of bean-shaped organs purify blood in the human body?

5 Which actress played Pussy Galore in *Goldfinger*, Cathy Gale in *The Avengers* and Laura West in *The Upper Hand*?

6 Greens, fairways and bunkers are part of the courses in which sport?

7 Latissimi dorsi muscles are found where on the human body?

8 Which fortnightly satirical magazine was first published in the UK in October 1961?

9 "Bernie Lomax would be the perfect host, except for one small problem: He's dead." This is the tagline to which 1989 film?

10 Which test was invented by and named after the Greek doctor Georgios Papanikolaou?

11 Despite a population of only approximately 17 million people, which European country had almost half a million bikes stolen in 2019?

12 Lockjaw is another name for which disease?

13 AK is the official abbreviation of which American state?

14 What name is shared by a brass instrument and an ice cream cone?

15 In transportation, what does HGV stand for?

16 "What can be asserted without evidence can also be dismissed without evidence" is an epistemological razor accredited to which polemicist?

17 Québec is a province in which country?

18 Nora Batty was Compo's love interest in which long-running TV comedy?

19 Which soft drink has been advertised with the slogan "What's the worst that can happen?"

20 A durian is a famously smelly type of what foodstuff?

Answers to QUIZ 303 – Pot Luck

1	Deep coal mine	11	Latin
2	Courtney Cox	12	November
3	Prince Edward/Earl of Wessex	13	Two
4	Ears	14	Bat
5	Smell	15	Diamonds
6	Whiskey	16	Almonds
7	Channel Tunnel	17	Acme
8	Dave	18	Gunpowder
9	Australia	19	Cycling
10	65 days	20	Right – left is permitted only if the right is incapacitated

Easy

1 Blur, Oasis, Pulp and Suede were considered the "big four" bands of which genre of music?

2 From 1999 to 2011, which "big four" countries were given automatic qualification into the Eurovision Song Contest final?

3 Complete this list of the "big four" Grammy awards: Album of the Year, Record of the Year, Song of the Year and...?

4 *The Little Mermaid, Beauty and The Beast, Aladdin* and *The Lion King* are considered the big four films that led to the resurgence of which company?

5 Which cities play host to what are known as the "big four" fashion weeks?

6 The Hells Angels, Pagans, Outlaws and Bandidos are the "big four" members of what type of club?

7 Sometimes termed the "big four", which four teams dominated Formula 1 racing for three decades, winning every Constructors Championship from 1978 to 2008?

8 In the context of conferences of heads of state after World War I, the term "big four" referred to the UK, the USA, France and Italy; during World War II, which two other countries replaced the latter two?

9 What are considered to be the "big four" international beauty pageants?

10 There are four recognised major governing bodies in boxing; the WBA, the WBC, the WBO and which other?

Medium

11 From approximately 2008 to 2017, who joined the "big three" of men's tennis in many commentators' estimations to make it a big four?

12 A sculpture named the "Big 4" sits outside the London headquarters of which broadcaster?

13 Complete the list of the "big four" annual pay-per-view WWE wrestling events: *Wrestlemania, Summerslam, Survivor Series* and...?

14 In 2007, which "big four" supermarkets had approximately a combined 75% of the market share in the UK?

15 Along with Pearl Jam, Soundgarden and Alice in Chains, which band was considered part of the "big four" bands of grunge music?

16 *Celtic, Cedric, Baltic* and *Adriatic* were the "big four" luxury ocean liners built by which company in the early 20th century, prior to their development of the *Olympic* class?

17 Russell's viper, the krait, the cobra and the saw-scaled viper are the four species responsible for the majority of deaths by snake bite in which country?

18 The Four Companions is a Shia term for the four Sahaba who stayed most loyal to Ali ibn Abi Talib after the death of who?

19 Albert Hawkins, Arthur Neil, Francis Carlin and Frederick Wensley were the "big four" members of which government department after the First World War?

20 Which British motorcycle manufacturer produced the "Big 4" model between 1907 and 1954?

Hard

Answers to QUIZ 304 – Gangster Films

1	Corleone	11	"The cannoli"
2	Sam "Ace" Rothstein, played by Robert De Niro	12	*Home Alone*
3	"SAY HELLO TO MY LITTLE FRIEND!"	13	*Get Carter*
4	*The Irishman*	14	*City of God*
5	*Bugsy*	15	*Putty Nose*
6	*Eastern Promises*	16	Roy Scheider
7	*Donnie Brasco*	17	*The Warriors*
8	*King Of New York*	18	*On The Waterfront*
9	*Once Upon A Time In America*	19	*Boyz n the Hood*
10	*In Bruges*	20	"Get the papers, get the papers."

1 The birth of Moses appears in which book of the Bible?
2 *Haciendas* are South American types of what kind of building?
3 Which of Henry VIII's wives was German?
4 Which former supermodel married Nicolas Sarkozy, at that time the President of France, in 2008?
5 In physics, force times displacement equals what?
6 American physicist Percy Spencer invented which now-ubiquitous kitchen appliance?
7 James W. Marshall's discovery at Sutter's Mill in 1848 started a gold rush in which US state?
8 Helvetica was a former name of which modern-day country?
9 *Manic Monday* was a No.2 in the UK in 1986 for which band?
10 What function does monosodium glutamate have in cooking?
11 To "hit the hay" means to do what?
12 Usually, which is the biggest key on a computer keyboard?
13 What is a female donkey called?
14 Muscovado is an unrefined form of what foodstuff?
15 Who was the lead singer of iconic 1980s pop band Culture Club?
16 Of the 50 French monarchs in history, how many were queens?
17 What colour were Mr Blobby's spots?
18 Of the four tennis Grand Slams, which is the only one to have been played on all three surface types?
19 Doug E. Fresh and Rahzel are both practitioners of which vocal technique?
20 In the musical *Wicked*, what is the first name of the Wicked Witch of the West?

Easy

Medium

Hard

Answers to QUIZ 305 – Pot Luck

Easy

1   Tony Iommi founded the Polka Tulk Blues Band (a name taken either from a brand of talcum powder or a clothing shop) in Birmingham in 1968; what name did they later achieve fame under?

2   Initially called Circus, which Brit pop band then went by Seymour, until the label Food Records made them change it once again?

3   Which surf rock band's first records were done under the name The Pendletones, a pun on Pendleton, a style of woollen shirt popular at the time?

4   Which husband and wife duo of the 1960s and 1970s began their recording careers as Caesar and Cleo before switching to their real names?

5   Which hip hop band, who serve as the house band on *The Tonight Show*, dropped "Square" from their name in 1992?

6   The five members of which manufactured 1990s girl band were originally selected for a band named Touch?

7   Which pop duo were originally known as Tom and Jerry?

8   Prior to 1974, Van Halen went by what other name, unaware that it was already the name of a major British rock band?

9   Kara's Flowers was the name of which band for their first seven years, before changing to their current name to disavow their poppier past?

10 Hardcore punk band the Young Aborigines evolved and renamed to become which hip-hop trio?

Medium

11 The Meggadeaths, the Screaming Abdabs, Leonard's Lodgers, Spectrum Five and Tea Set were all former names of which legendary psychedelic rock band?

12 In between their original name of The Blackjacks, and their penultimate name of The Silver Beatles, what were The Beatles known as?

13 Which trio of singer-songwriting brothers began recording as a skiffle group called The Rattlesnakes?

14 At their first ever gig, Coldplay performed under the name of what pointed marine animal, a name they came up with only an hour beforehand?

15 Which band began as Sweet Children, before changing in 1989 to a new name taken from slang for spending a day doing nothing but smoking?

16 Until forced to change it, Pearl Jam performed under the name of which NBA player?

17 Which band dropped "Transit Authority" from their name in 1969?

18 When Tim Staffel left the band Smile, his replacement, Freddie Bulsara, suggested they rename themselves to what?

19 Which Canadian band were originally called Free Beer, because it helped them draw crowds when playing the bar scene?

20 Polarbear was a former name of which Northern Irish-Scottish rock band, who subsequently changed their name to something polar bears do?

Answers to QUIZ 306 – Big Four

Hard

1	Britpop	11	Andy Murray
2	France, Germany, Spain and the UK; Italy were added in 2011 to make it a Big Five	12	Channel Four
		13	*Royal Rumble*
3	Best New Artist	14	Tesco, Sainsbury's, Morrisons and Asda
4	Disney	15	Nirvana
5	London, Milan, Paris and New York	16	White Star Line (the *Titanic* was one of the *Olympic* class)
6	Outlaw motorcycle clubs		
7	McLaren, Williams, Renault/Benetton and Ferrari	17	India
8	The USSR and China	18	The prophet Muhammad
9	Miss Earth, Miss International, Miss Universe, Miss World	19	Scotland Yard
		20	Norton
10	The IBF		

1   Which politically-minded actress was branded a traitor for her 1972 trip to North Vietnam?
2   Singer-songwriter Abel Makkonen Tesfaye is known professionally as what?
3   Which South American capital city appears in the NATO Phonetic Alphabet?
4   What is the technical name for the gullet, the food pipe that runs between the throat and the stomach?
5   Which other common species of British bird has an intense natural dislike of the owl?
6   The exterior of the Statue of Liberty is made of what metal?
7   Maybach is a luxury car brand that forms part of which German manufacturer's range?
8   Where has a land speed record of 11.2 miles per hour stood since 1972?
9   Which brand of bitters has labels that distinctly do not fit the bottles?
10 What colour was the comic character Korky the Cat?
11 What name is shared by a style of Italian sandwich and a stickers and trading card company?
12 In which 1994 Quentin Tarantino film did John Travolta play Vincent Vega?
13 The largest city in the Indian state of Goa takes its name from which Portuguese explorer?
14 Which musician married his dermatology assistant, Debbie Rowe, in 1996?
15 Who wrote *The Old Man and The Sea*, awarded the 1953 Pulitzer Prize for fiction?
16 Which country has more lakes of at least 25 acres in size than the rest of the world combined?
17 Which car manufacturer owns the Audi, Bentley, Cupra, Ducati, Lamborghini, Porsche, SEAT and Škoda brands?
18 Which colour is found in the names of two London Royal Parks?
19 What is the value of each interior angle in a pentagon?
20 Which coffee made of espresso, chocolate and hot milk shares its name with a city in Yemen?

Answers to QUIZ 307 – Pot Luck

1	Exodus	11	Go to bed
2	Farmhouse	12	Space bar
3	Anne of Cleves	13	Jenny
4	Carla Bruni	14	Sugar
5	Work	15	Boy George
6	Microwave	16	None
7	California	17	Yellow
8	Switzerland	18	US Open
9	The Bangles	19	Beatboxing
10	Flavour enhancer	20	Elphaba

1. In which fictional village is the long-running Radio 4 soap opera *The Archers* set?
2. Which constellation and astrological sign is also known as "The Archer"?
3. A sum of £2,000 is known in UK political circles as an Archer after which man was caught giving a prostitute that amount one morning at Victoria station?
4. Captain Jonathan Archer of Enterprise NX-01 was a major protagonist in which science fiction franchise?
5. In which video game series is Link, an archer, trying to save the eponymous princess title character?
6. Because they could fire further and be reloaded more quickly, which invention was said to have won the Hundred Years War for the English?
7. *The Archer* is the fifth track on the seventh studio album *Lover* for which American singer, whose other hits include *Shake It Off*?
8. FBI agent Sean Archer played by John Travolta seeks vengeance against Nicholas Cage's Castor Troy in which 1997 thriller?
9. In which 1941 American film noir is Sam Spade, played by Humphrey Bogart, investigating the murder of Miles Archer?
10. Worth 1 and 2 points, what colour are the two outer rings on an archery target?
11. Which *Thelma and Louise* actress came 24th in the US national archery qualifiers in 1999, and thus only narrowly missed out on an Olympic berth?
12. In the ancient Olympic games, what tethered animals were used as targets, rather than the boards we would recognise today?
13. Which idiom, meaning being a substitute as distinguished from a regular, originates from the world of archery?
14. Which Swiss folk hero, who was an expert marksman with the crossbow, shot an apple on his son's head?
15. In classical mythology, which Greek god wielded a bow with arrows that caused uncontrollable desire in whomever they hit?
16. Jennifer Lawrence learned archery from scratch to play the role of Katniss Everdeen in which film franchise?
17. There are many different archers in *The Lord of the Rings*, but which elven character, played by Orlando Bloom, was particularly skilled?
18. Which legendary heroic outlaw was a highly skilled archer that stole from the rich to give to the poor?
19. The bow is a feature weapon in which video game, in which Joel Miller is tasked with escorting 14-year-old Ellie across a post-apocalyptic USA?
20. Which notorious British Army officer fought in World War II with a longbow, bagpipes and a Scottish broadsword?

Easy

Medium

Hard

Answers to QUIZ 308 – Bands' Former Names

1	Black Sabbath	11	Pink Floyd
2	Blur	12	The Quarrymen
3	The Beach Boys	13	The Bee Gees
4	Sonny and Cher	14	Starfish (the name lasted only one gig)
5	The Roots	15	Green Day
6	Spice Girls	16	Mookie Blaylock
7	Simon and Garfunkel	17	Chicago
8	Genesis	18	Queen (Freddie Bulsara was Freddie Mercury)
9	Maroon 5	19	Barenaked Ladies
10	Beastie Boys	20	Snow Patrol

ANSWERS ON PAGE 313

1   The White Cliffs of Dover are predominantly made from what?

2   What does Popeye have tattooed on each of his forearms?

3   The film and video game *Happy Feet* feature what animals?

4   Which IRA member was elected the MP for Fermanagh and South Tyrone in April 1981, but died of a hunger strike within four weeks?

5   Situated on the banks of Belfast Lough in Northern Ireland, which still-extant castle was originally built in 1177 by a Norman lord?

6   Who was the mortal enemy of Captain Pugwash?

7   Espadrilles, mules and docksides are all worn on which parts of the body?

8   Which cartoon character's arch enemy was Dr Claw?

9   Brisbane is the capital of which Australian state?

10   16th June is known as "Bloomsday", a day of celebration of the work of which Irish writer?

11   Who recorded tennis's first "Golden Slam" in 1988; the standard Grand Slam, plus an Olympic gold medal?

12   Which 2021 Jane Campion film received 12 Academy Award nominations, but only won one?

13   On a computer keyboard, what is the shortcut for the "paste" function?

14   Who played Doctor Who immediately prior to David Tennant?

15   What makes a disorder congenital?

16   The name of which hobby translates from Japanese as "empty orchestra"?

17   Who came last at the 1988 Australian Open golf championship, but won the 1992 Formula 1 Driver's Championship?

18   In chess, does the white king start on a white or black square?

19   The bonnet ornament on Rolls Royce cars has what name?

20   Stoke-on-Trent and Lichfield are the only two cities located in which English county?

Easy

Medium

Hard

Who are these villains from the world of fiction?

Easy

Medium

Hard

1

2

3

4

5

6

7

8

9

Answers to QUIZ 310 – Archers

1	Ambridge	11	Geena Davis
2	Sagittarius	12	Doves
3	Jeffrey Archer	13	Second string
4	Star Trek	14	William Tell
5	*The Legend of Zelda*™	15	Eros
6	Longbow	16	*The Hunger Games*
7	Taylor Swift	17	Legolas
8	*Face/Off*	18	Robin Hood
9	*The Maltese Falcon*	19	*The Last of Us*™
10	White	20	"Mad" Jack Churchill

1   Geoff Hurst scored three of England's four goals in the 1966 World Cup Final; who scored the other one?

2   Standard & Poor, Moody's and Fitch are considered the Big Three agencies in what area?

3   The break between rounds in professional boxing matches lasts for how long?

4   In which mobile game do players launch different types of birds as projectiles towards green pigs?

5   Which treeless biome – that covers the Arctic regions of Europe, Asia and North America – has subsoil that is permanently frozen?

6   Which high-end watch company has a five-pointed crown as its logo?

7   In the nursery rhyme, what did the Three Little Kittens lose?

8   Which Alpine mountain is the basis of the logo for Toblerone™ chocolate?

9   Pierre Omidyar was the founder of which website, initially called AuctionWeb?

10 Which four southwestern American states meet at the aptly named "Four Corners" region?

11 *Love the Way You Lie*, *Numb* and *The Monster* were all collaborations between which two artists?

12 What colour is the horse on the Porsche logo?

13 Which vegetable is used in the dish Eggs Florentine?

14 Della Street was the secretary to which famous fictional lawyer?

15 Which country, the ninth-largest in the world, has made "Very nice!" its official tourism slogan?

16 Which Australian cricketer caused controversy at a Test match in 1979 by playing with an aluminium bat?

17 For comedic purposes, Jack Benny played which instrument deliberately badly?

18 Sternutation is a scientific name for which body function?

19 What ten-letter word is the longest that can be typed using only the top row of keys on a typewriter?

20 The humerus is a bone in which part of the human body?

Easy

Medium

Hard

Answers to QUIZ 311 – Pot Luck

1   Chalk
2   Anchor
3   Penguins
4   Bobby Sands
5   Carrickfergus
6   Cut-Throat Jake
7   Feet
8   Inspector Gadget
9   Queensland
10 James Joyce (named after the protagonist of his novel *Ulysses*, Leopold Bloom)

11 Steffi Graf
12 *The Power of the Dog*
13 Control + V
14 Christopher Ecclestone
15 If it is present from birth
16 Karaoke
17 Nigel Mansell
18 Black
19 Spirit of Ecstasy
20 Staffordshire

1   In English culinary tradition, which sauce is supposed to be served with roast lamb?

2   Made from fermented soybeans, which Chinese dipping sauce is used for dishes including Peking duck, spring rolls and barbecued pork?

3   In the culinary arts, what is the main ingredient of an *amandine* sauce?

4   Which fish are used in the ingredients of Worcestershire Sauce?

5   What is the cold savoury Cumberland sauce usually served with?

6   What are the three principal ingredients in a Hollandaise Sauce?

7   Which hot pepper sauce takes its name from a state in Mexico?

8   A possibly apocryphal story of the origins of which sauce states that what the two creators initially made was so horrible that they stuck it in their basement, rediscovering it a few years later, and finding they loved it?

9   Which vegetable is the main ingredient used in a *tzatziki* sauce?

10   Which sauce is made with soybeans, roasted grains, water and salt, fermented then brewed?

11   As determined by Escoffier in the late 19th century, what are the five French "mother sauces"?

12   Which "child" of Hollandaise sauce differs in using white wine vinegar instead of lemon juice, and has tarragon and shallots added?

13   Which staple egg-based sauce was invented by the French chef of the Duke de Richelieu in 1756 to celebrate victory in battle?

14   Brown in colour, *bigarade* sauce is traditionally made using which fruit?

15   A *sabayon* is a light sauce traditionally made with egg yolks, sugar and what?

16   Originally, baked beans were served in what sauce?

17   *Sugo di Carciofi*, a sauce often used for gnocchi or pasta, always contains which vegetable?

18   The hangover cure made with raw egg, Worcestershire sauce and seasoning is known as what?

19   Adding grated cheese to a béchamel sauce creates what other sauce?

20   What name is given to a cook who specialises in making sauces?

Answers to QUIZ 312 – Villains

1   Cruella de Vil
2   Jim Moriarty
3   Ming the Merciless
4   Lex Luthor
5   Michael Myers
6   Predator
7   Francisco Scaramanga
8   Skeletor
9   Nurse Ratched

1. Ounce is an alternative name for which animal, the only big cat that cannot roar?
2. In the UK version of the board game *Cluedo®*, what is the name of the victim?
3. The 200th and final episode of which sitcom was set on 31st December 1979?
4. In the Myers-Briggs personality type indicator index, what does I stand for?
5. What was Christophe des Rosiers's contribution to the modern bathroom?
6. What Hebrew word can mean a commandment, or a good deed done for religious duty?
7. Which religious day is known as Ostersonntag in German?
8. Businesswoman and TV presenter Martha Stewart was jailed for what white collar crime in 2001?
9. "Mince pies" is Cockney rhyming slang for which parts of the body?
10. The Mediterranean island of Corsica, near Italy, is governed by which country?
11. In 1998, Guinness World Records recognised the brand "Genius Jeans" as the world's most expensive pair of jeans; which company made them?
12. Which country is 2,670 miles long, but has an average width of only 110 miles?
13. Which are the four Fixed Signs of the Zodiac?
14. Which NASA space shuttle launched the Hubble Space Telescope in 1990?
15. Prince George of Denmark was the husband of which English queen?
16. How many sides are of an equal length in an isosceles triangle?
17. How many children were in Enid Blyton's *Famous Five*?
18. Debuting in 1952, what was the first toy to be advertised on television?
19. Which of London's Royal Parks is almost as large as the other seven put together?
20. Starting in 2007, the Winter Wonderland festival takes place in which London park?

Easy

Medium

Hard

Answers to QUIZ 313 – Pot Luck

1	Martin Peters	11	Eminem and Rihanna
2	Credit rating	12	Black
3	One minute	13	Spinach
4	*Angry Birds*	14	Perry Mason
5	Tundra	15	Kazakhstan, leaning into the Borat thing
6	Rolex	16	Dennis Lillee
7	Their mittens	17	Violin
8	Matterhorn	18	Sneezing
9	eBay	19	Typewriter
10	Arizona, Colorado, New Mexico, Utah	20	Arm

1 In 2014, which boy band became the first to have their first four albums all debut at No.1 in the US album charts?

2 Which boy band topped the UK charts with the incredibly charged *Freak Me* in 1998?

3 Much to brother Mark's chagrin, Donnie Wahlberg was a permanent member of which hugely successful boy band, while Mark left after a few months?

4 Who, in a 1998 hit, were coming with the funk, and repeatedly assured the listener they would make them get down now?

5 *I Can*, the United Kingdom's entry into the 2011 Eurovision Song Contest, was recorded by which boy band?

6 *End of the Road* was a No.1 around the globe for who?

7 JLS, One Direction and Stereokicks all rose to fame via their appearances on which TV show?

8 Westlife had both the 1999 Christmas number one spot and also the last official No.1 single of the 1990s in the UK with which double-A side?

9 *I Swear*, a ballad that had been a hit for country singer John Michael Montgomery in 1993, became an international hit a year later for which boy band?

10 Which boy band were created on the TV series *Popstars: The Rivals*, released the double A-side *Sacred Trust/After You're Gone*, then split without releasing an album?

11 Phone lines were set up by the Samaritans to counsel grieving fans of which boy band when they split up in 1996?

12 Which boy band was named after an area of London?

13 Brothers Nick and Drew Lachey were two of the four members of which multi-platinum-selling boy band?

14 Prior to the teen pop boom of the late 1990s, which Scottish "tartan teen" group of the 1970s were one of the first boy bands?

15 Which fraternal group had acting careers in their own eponymous Disney Channel series, before releasing their first album *It's About Time* in 2006?

16 Which band's 2001 album *No Strings Attached* sold 1.1 million units in its first day and was jokingly called "perhaps the greatest mass spending of allowances in history"?

17 Which R&B-focused boy band had a name deriving from their stated intent to be the 1980s version of the Jackson 5?

18 Jonah Marais, Corbyn Besson, Daniel Seavey, Jack Avery and Zach Herron make up which boy band?

19 Craig Logan was the "third" member of which 1980s boy band?

20 Korean boy band BTS's name stands for Bangtan Sonyeondan – what, literally, does that translate to?

Answers to QUIZ 314 – Sauces

1 Mint sauce
2 Hoisin
3 Almonds
4 Anchovies
5 Cold meats
6 Egg yolk, butter and lemon juice
7 TABASCO®
8 Worcestershire sauce
9 Cucumber
10 Soy sauce
11 Béchamel, velouté, espagnole, hollandaise and tomato
12 Béarnaise sauce
13 Mayonnaise
14 Orange
15 Wine
16 Maple syrup
17 Artichoke
18 Prairie oyster
19 Mornay
20 Saucier

1. Aged only 15, which tennis player rose to prominence with a win over Venus Williams in the opening round at Wimbledon 2019?
2. Which celebrity couple's break-up inspired the hit single *Cry Me a River*?
3. Which palace is the official London residence of the Archbishop of Canterbury?
4. What is the primary ingredient in hummus?
5. What is the fastest *land* animal in the world?
6. Which reptile is known in Central and South America as *pollo de los árboles*, or "chicken of the trees"?
7. What word as an adjective means unstable or unreliable, and as a noun means a rock brought from a distance by a glacier?
8. In humans, the appendix, ear muscles and goose bumps response can be described as vestigial, meaning what?
9. Egypt and Syria united to form which sovereign state in the Middle East from 1958 to 1971?
10. Which multinational company owns the food brands Magnum®, Hellman's and Bovril, among hundreds of others?
11. In Dante's *Divine Comedy*, which ancient Roman poet is the guide through Hell?
12. The Scottish city of Perth lies on which river, the longest in Scotland?
13. Deryck Whibley is the lead singer with which Canadian pop punk band, who had UK hits with *Fat Lip* and *In Too Deep*?
14. Despite the name, the island of Zealand is part of which European country?
15. Where is the Japanese item of clothing known as a *geta* worn?
16. The name of which Japanese sport translate as "gentle way"?
17. At Olympic Games opening ceremonies, which country traditionally enters the stadium first?
18. Hypotension is the medical name for what condition?
19. Mount Logan is the highest mountain in which country?
20. Melanocytes activated by sunlight create which feature of the body?

Easy

Medium

Hard

Answers to QUIZ 315 – Pot Luck

1. Snow leopard
2. Dr Black (known as Mr Boddy in the States)
3. *That 70's Show*
4. Introvert
5. He invented the bidet
6. Mitzvah
7. Easter Sunday
8. Insider trading
9. Eyes
10. France
11. Gucci®
12. Chile
13. Taurus, Leo, Scorpio and Aquarius – they are the four that fall in the middle of seasons
14. *Discovery*
15. Anne
16. Two
17. Four – one of the five was a dog
18. Mr Potato Head
19. Richmond Park (955 hectares versus 980)
20. Hyde Park

Easy

1. Who is the only person to ever score at least 100 points in an NBA game?
2. In 1957, Willie O'Ree became the first and, for 17 years, only black player in the history of which American sports league?
3. Which MLB team was considered blighted by the "Curse of the Bambino", going 86 years between World Series wins before finally winning in 2004?
4. In 2008, which Pittsburgh Penguins center became the youngest captain in NHL history to win the Stanley Cup?
5. Which team lost in four consecutive Super Bowls between 1990 and 1993?
6. Nicknamed "The Dream", which pioneer was the first non-American to be an NBA All-Star, as well as win both the MVP and DPOY awards?
7. Alongside Sandy Koufax, which former Giant is the only man to win multiple World Series, win multiple Cy Young Awards, and throw multiple no-hitters?
8. Which man – the all-time leader in receptions, touchdowns and receiving yards – has scored more points than any other non-kicker in NFL history?
9. Which winger won both the Golden Boot and Golden Ball awards at the 2019 FIFA Women's World Cup?
10. With 46 home runs, 26 steals, and a 3.18 ERA over 23 starts, who in 2021 posted the best two-way season of all time?

Medium

11. Taking inspiration from an assassin in *Kill Bill*, which animalian nickname did Kobe Bryant adopt?
12. Which elite pitching prospect lost his ability to throw strikes during a 2001 NLDS game, but reinvented himself as an outfielder?
13. Which former ice hockey defenceman was the co-founder of an international coffee restaurant chain that takes his name?
14. Recording their 24th championship in 2021, which NHL franchise has, by far, the most Stanley Cup victories?
15. While in college playing basketball for BYU, who also played parts of three baseball seasons with the Toronto Blue Jays before playing in the NBA for 14 seasons?
16. "The Legion of Boom" was the nickname given to the dominant defensive units of which NFL franchise between 2011 and 2018?
17. As of the end of the 2021 season, who is the only player in MLB history to record 100 RBI seasons for five different teams?
18. Which NFL quarterback appeared in a preseason baseball game for the New York Yankees in 2018?
19. Which MLB umpire of 45 years is nicknamed "Cowboy" on account of his country albums and short temper?
20. Which two-time MVP and one-time Super Bowl MVP quarterback is widely hailed as the NFL's greatest ever undrafted player?

Hard

Answers to QUIZ 316 – Boy Bands

1	One Direction	11	Take That
2	Another Level	12	East 17
3	New Kids On The Block	13	98 Degrees
4	5ive	14	Bay City Rollers
5	Blue – it came 11th	15	The Jonas Brothers
6	Boyz II Men	16	NSYNC
7	*The X-Factor*	17	New Edition
8	*I Have A Dream/Seasons in the Sun*	18	Why Don't We
9	All-4-One	19	Bros
10	One True Voice	20	Bulletproof Boy Scouts

ANSWERS ON PAGE 321

1. Paul Coia's voice was the first ever heard on which British TV channel?
2. Ronnie Kray was committed to which high-security psychiatric hospital in Berkshire from 1979 until his death in 1995?
3. Which is the southernmost city in mainland Britain?
4. Fittingly, Hugh Hefner had a species of what animal named after him?
5. Glenn Quagmire is a character in which adult cartoon series?
6. Which of the Mr. Men™ is orange, wears a small blue hat and has incredibly long arms?
7. Hydrocephalus is the build-up of fluid in which organ of the body?
8. Due to its flexibility and fire resistance, which fibrous silicate mineral was widely used as a building material, until it was discovered that it caused cancer?
9. What was the *de facto* middle name of Wolfgang Mozart?
10. 2021's *Don't Shut Me Down* was which band's first UK top 10 single since 1982?
11. Not including its Antarctic territorial claims or any outlying islands, which other country is closest to Australia?
12. To Native Americans, what is a *calumet*?
13. What "G" is a clarified butter made from the milk of a buffalo or cow, used in Indian cuisine?
14. Where on the human body is the vomer bone located?
15. Fighter ace Francesco Baracca, whose plane bore an emblem of a black horse prancing on its two rear hooves, inspired which car manufacturer's logo?
16. Canvey Island and the Isle of Sheppey are islands in which river?
17. The name of which brand of fizzy drink rendered phonetically in Chinese can sound like the words for "bite the wax tadpole"?
18. *Guinness World Records* recognises what as the best-selling copywritten book of all time?
19. Beatrix "The Bride" Kiddo is the lead character in which Quentin Tarantino film?
20. Previously called St Stephen's Tower, what is the name of the London tower in which the bells of Big Ben are housed?

Easy

Medium

Hard

Answers to QUIZ 317 – Pot Luck

1	Coco Gauff	11	Virgil
2	Justin Timberlake and Britney Spears	12	Tay
3	Lambeth Palace	13	Sum 41
4	Chickpeas	14	Denmark
5	Cheetah	15	On the foot
6	Iguana	16	Judo
7	Erratic	17	Greece
8	They have become functionless due to evolution	18	Low blood pressure
9	United Arab Republic	19	Canada
10	Unilever	20	Freckles

1 The teddy bear was invented in honour of, and named after, which US President?
2 Which fictional bear's first outing in literature came in 1924 under the name Edward Bear?
3 The Kodiak bear is native to which American state?
4 What type of coat did Paddington Bear wear?
5 It is said that the polar bear is the only animal to actively hunt what?
6 What colour jumper does Rupert the Bear wear?
7 The brown bear is the official national animal of which European country?
8 In the TV series, who was Yogi Bear's main antagonist, the notably-inconsistently-drawn warden of the park?
9 Which of Shakespeare's plays contains the famous stage direction "Exit, pursued by a bear"?
10 Which is the biggest species of bear in the world?
11 Who plays Huggy Bear in the 2004 film version of *Starsky and Hutch*?
12 Which American golfer used the nickname "the Golden Bear" during his playing career?
13 The bear that inspired the story of Paddington Bear was bought at which famous shop?
14 For years, which fictional bear always had a brown face on the cover illustrations of his books, but a white face inside them?
15 Harry Rossoll created which famous bear character, used in fire awareness campaigns and an advertising icon of the U.S. Forest Service?
16 The NFL team with the nickname the Bears are based in which American city?
17 In which series of books is there a bear character named Iorek Byrnison?
18 Which species of bear has an extended wrist bone that it uses like a thumb to help grip food?
19 Pooky was the name of which cartoon character's teddy bear?
20 In 1995, Magellan T. Bear became the first teddy bear to go where?

Answers to QUIZ 318 – American Sports

1	Wilt Chamberlain	11	Black Mamba
2	The NHL	12	Rick Ankiel
3	Boston Red Sox	13	Tim Horton
4	Sidney Crosby	14	Montreal Canadiens
5	Buffalo Bills	15	Danny Ainge
6	Hakeem Olajuwon	16	Seattle Seahawks
7	Tim Lincecum	17	Gary Sheffield
8	Jerry Rice	18	Russell Wilson
9	Megan Rapinoe	19	Joe West
10	Shohei Ohtani	20	Kurt Warner

1   As of 2021, who is the only male England football player to score in three FIFA World Cups?
2   Name the seven countries whose names in English end in "-stan".
3   Lusophones are speakers of which language?
4   Japan Optical Industries was the original name of which multinational corporation, which specialises in cameras?
5   Often seen in court, what name is given to a person whose job is to transcribe speech in shorthand?
6   Which Italian city did Claude Monet describe in 1908 as "too beautiful to be painted"?
7   Which UK city has metro stations called Byker and St James?
8   The tradition of sending a telegram on someone's 100th birthday began in 1917 with which monarch?
9   What word precedes *Girl* in a 1983 Billy Joel song, and *Funk* in a 2014 Mark Ronson and Bruno Mars tune?
10 What type of energy is harnessed from the sun?
11 Baby whales and baby elephants are both called what?
12 Across all platforms, which messenger program was the most downloaded mobile app in 2019?
13 What year did the UK's Brexit referendum take place?
14 Farrokh Bulsara was the name at birth of which iconic frontman?
15 *thank u, next* was a 2018 break-up song by which singer?
16 In text parlance, what does the acronym TTYL stand for?
17 Who was British Prime Minister from 1997 to 2007?
18 In which country are the remnants of the city of Pompeii located?
19 Whose nicknames included "the father of funk", "the godfather of soul", "Mr Dynamite" and "soul brother number one"?
20 The name of which Pacific Ocean island group literally means "many islands"?

Easy

Medium

Hard

Answers to QUIZ 319 – Pot Luck

1	Channel 4	10	ABBA
2	Broadmoor	11	Papua New Guinea – even at its closest point, New Zealand is more than 1,000 miles away
3	Truro, Cornwall		
4	Rabbit (Hefner had helped fund the research of its discoverer)	12	A peace pipe
		13	Ghee
5	*Family Guy*	14	The face – it is what divides up the two nostrils
6	Mr. Tickle	15	Ferrari
7	Brain	16	River Thames
8	Asbestos	17	Coca-Cola®
9	Amadeus (he was baptised as Joannes Chrysostomus Wolfgangus Theophilus Mozart, but called himself Wolfgang Amadeus Mozart)	18	*Guinness World Records*
		19	*Kill Bill: Volume 1*
		20	Elizabeth Tower

ANSWERS ON PAGE 324

Easy

1   Who served as the creator, writer and executive producer of *Downton Abbey*?

2   In the series, who played Robert Crawley, Earl of Grantham?

3   Which character was originally only meant to be on the show for three episodes, but stuck around due to his "outsider's voice"?

4   The plot of the first series of *Downton Abbey* begins the day after what historical event?

5   Which *Downton Abbey* character died of the Spanish flu?

6   "The business of life is the acquisition of memories. In the end, that's all there is." Which member of the staff said these poignant words?

7   What was the unfortunate name of Robert Crawley's loyal pet Labrador?

8   What are the names of Lord and Lady Grantham's four grandchildren?

9   As seen in the 2012 Christmas episode, to where does the Crawley family travel to visit Lady Rose MacClare in September 1921?

10 After learning Matthew will be able to stand again, who sarcastically said "all this unbridled joy has given me quite an appetite"?

11 Thanks to *Downton Abbey*, demand for what was said to have doubled between 2010 and 2012?

12 To save Downton, which heiress did Lord Grantham marry?

13 Lady Sybil defied societal norms when she married Tom Branson; what role did he work in at the time?

14 Which handsome Turkish diplomat dies of a heart attack in Lady Mary's bed?

15 Later becoming a meme, the sharp retort "sympathy butters no parsnips" was spoken by which character?

Medium

16 What animal nickname does the Marquess of Flintshire, father of Lady Rose MacClare, answer to?

17 Lady Sybil shocked the family when she wore what to the dinner table?

18 In 1867, a document signed in Highclere Castle, the setting for *Downtown Abbey*, led to the foundation of which country?

19 Highclere Castle is owned by the 8th Earl of Carnarvon; his great-grandfather, the 5th Earl and previously the owner, sponsored the 1922 discovery of what?

20 Serving as a plot device when one of them is seemingly stolen, what items does Lord Grantham collect?

Hard

1 The name of which state of matter is used in business parlance for assets which can be immediately turned into cash?

2 Which chocolate bar has been advertised with the slogan, "Get some nuts!"?

3 What do philatelists collect?

4 What is the most commonly diagnosed form of cancer in men?

5 Dugites are a dangerous Australian species of which animal?

6 The Irwell, Irk and Medlock are the three visible rivers in the centre of which English city?

7 The song *Ding-Dong! The Witch Is Dead* comes from which classic film?

8 The name of which US state appears on the label of Jack Daniel's bottles?

9 When HMS Birkenhead wrecked on 26th February 1852 with insufficient serviceable lifeboats for all the passengers, which protocol was spontaneously created?

10 To save changes to a file in Microsoft Word, users can click on an image of which obsolete storage device?

11 After launching on Facebook™ in 2009, which simulation game by Zynga became the most popular game on the site, and held that position for over two years?

12 The unusual method of taking a wicket in cricket generally known as Mankading, after the man who pioneered it, involves what?

13 "It wasn't the airplanes; it was Beauty who killed The Beast" is the last line from which iconic 1933 monster film?

14 In the context of World War II, what were Utah, Omaha, Gold, Juno and Sword?

15 In the nursery rhyme, who could all the king's horses and all the king's men not put back together again?

16 Which clinical psychologist and YouTube personality gave up practising and teaching to write *12 Rules for Life: An Antidote to Chaos*?

17 What is a polygon with eight equal sides known as?

18 Rihanna had a 2007 hit with what piece of weather-proofing equipment?

19 The supercontinent that consisted of all the present continents before they separated is known as what?

20 What two-word term links a Gustav Klimt painting, an Auguste Rodin sculpture, and a moment shared by Britney Spears and Madonna at the 2003 VMA Awards?

Easy

Medium

Hard

Answers to QUIZ 321 – Pot Luck

1	David Beckham	11	Calves
2	Afghanistan, Kazakhstan, Kyrgyzstan, Pakistan, Tajikistan, Turkmenistan and Uzbekistan	12	WhatsApp
		13	2016
3	Portuguese	14	Freddie Mercury
4	Nikon	15	Ariana Grande
5	Stenographer	16	Talk to you later
6	Venice – he did it anyway	17	Tony Blair
7	Newcastle	18	Italy
8	George V	19	James Brown
9	*Uptown*	20	Polynesia
10	Solar		

Easy

1 Jeff Bezos was the founder of which giant internet marketplace?

2 August Horsh named which car company that he founded after a German-to-Latin translation of his surname, which from German to English translates as "hear"?

3 L. Ron Hubbard founded which religion in the early 1950s in which self-awareness is paramount?

4 Founded by and named for the two men who created the American Express® mail business in the 19th century, what bank operates the only two cash machines in Antarctica?

5 Joe C. Thompson founded which chain of American convenience stores, whose name reflects their opening hours?

6 William Wilson founded which pram company in Leeds in 1877, one that later provided the baby carriage to King George VI for Princess Elizabeth?

7 In 1982, Mike Ashley opened his first sport and ski shop in Maidenhead, which later grew into which large retail chain?

8 Which English monarch founded the Order of the Garter in 1348?

9 Fred Phelps founded which controversial "church", known for its homophobic picketing of soldiers' funerals?

10 Berry Gordy was the founder of which record label, the highest-earning African-American business for decades?

11 When Bill Bowerman, an athletics coach who trained 31 Olympic athletes, started making custom shoes for his runners, he founded which sportswear giant?

12 Tim Smit was a co-founder of which brown sign biological destination located in Cornwall?

13 Which brand of chocolate sweet is named for Mars and Murrie, the founders of its parent company?

14 As seen on TV, which naturalist is considered to be the founder of the modern method of freezing food?

15 Which record label was named after its founders, Herb Alpert and Jerry Moss?

16 The Family Federation for World Peace and Unification, often known as the Moonies, was founded by Sun Myung Moon in which Asian country?

17 World War I flying ace Paul McGinness was one of the founders of which southern hemisphere airline?

18 A Canadian educational reformer with the impressive name of Adelaide Hoodless founded which international organisation?

19 In 2004, which English-American musician, DJ, songwriter, producer and record executive was a co-founder of Allido Records?

20 "He who knows others is wise; he who knows himself is enlightened" is a quote attributed to who, often considered the founder of Taoism?

Medium

Hard

Answers to QUIZ 322 – Downton Abbey

1	Julian Fellowes	11	Butlers
2	Hugh Bonneville	12	Cora Levinson
3	Tom Branson	13	The family's chauffeur
4	The sinking of the *Titanic*	14	Kemal Pamuk
5	Lavinia	15	Mrs Patmore
6	Mr Carson	16	"Shrimpie"
7	Isis	17	Big blue billowing harem pants
8	Sybbie, George, Marigold and Caroline	18	Canada
9	Duneagle Castle in The Highlands of Scotland	19	Tomb of Tutankhamun
10	Lady Violet Crawley	20	Snuff boxes

1   A woman named Stella Liebeck sued McDonald's® over the temperature of which item on their menu?

2   The cortex and medulla are parts of which organ of the body?

3   The 7th May 1915 sinking of which liner contributed indirectly to the entry of the United States into World War I?

4   *Brookside* was set in which city?

5   Home to many a conspiracy theory, what is the common name of the highly-classified US Air Force facility in Nevada?

6   On a table football game, what formation do the teams only ever line up in?

7   Which fairy tale character was said to have slept for 100 years?

8   What type of tree produces conkers?

9   In the book and film *Stuart Little*, what kind of animal is Stuart?

10 What magical household item does Aladdin use to fly?

11 Who was the Bengal tiger main antagonist of Rudyard Kipling's *Jungle Book*?

12 At what official residence does the UK's Chancellor of the Exchequer live?

13 According to his business card, which gangster's occupation was actually that of a used furniture salesman?

14 Also called divisionism, which painting technique involves small, distinct dots of colour applied in patterns?

15 The Taj Mahal is located in which country?

16 Which actor starred alongside Kim Basinger in the film *9½ Weeks*?

17 Who was disqualified for biting off part of Evander Holyfield's ear during a WBA Heavyweight Championship boxing match in Las Vegas in 1997?

18 Tawses were banned in schools in Scotland in 1987 – what were they?

19 Bruce Springsteen's *Born to Run* was briefly considered as the official song of which state, before officials realised it was actually about running away from that state?

20 Which actor starred in *The Sixth Sense* as a part of a settlement agreement after an earlier film, *Broadway Brawler*, was cancelled 20 days into shooting due to his behaviour?

Answers to QUIZ 323 – Pot Luck

1	Liquid	11	*Farmville*
2	Snickers®	12	The bowler running out the non-striker
3	Stamps	13	*King Kong*
4	Prostate cancer	14	The five assault beaches that the Allies swarmed on D-Day
5	Snake		
6	Manchester	15	Humpty Dumpty
7	*The Wizard of Oz*	16	Jordan Peterson
8	Tennessee	17	Octagon
9	"Women and children first" – the soldiers stayed on the deck and almost all died	18	*Umbrella*
		19	Pangaea
10	Floppy disk	20	"The Kiss"

What are or were the ring names of these famous grapplers?

1

2

3

4

5

6

7

8

9

Easy

Medium

Hard

Answers to QUIZ 324 – Founders

1	Amazon	11	Nike
2	Audi	12	The Eden Project
3	Scientology	13	M&M's®
4	Wells Fargo	14	Captain (Clarence) Birdseye
5	7-Eleven	15	A&M Records
6	Silver Cross	16	South Korea
7	Sports Direct	17	Qantas
8	Edward III	18	Women's Institute
9	Westboro Baptist Church	19	Mark Ronson
10	Motown Records	20	Laozi/Lao Tzu

ANSWERS ON PAGE 329

1. Caduceus – the traditional symbol of Hermes that features two snakes winding around a staff – is a symbol of what profession?
2. Calderas and fumaroles are features of what natural formation?
3. What colour shirt does Tiger Woods always wear on the last day of golf tournaments?
4. In Einstein's special relativity formula $E = mc^2$, what does the 'm' stand for?
5. Chrissie Hynde is a founder and lead singer of which band?
6. Which *South Park* character has died almost 100 times in the TV series alone?
7. Estimates ranging from 35,000 to 400,000 people are said to make a living from impersonating which singer?
8. Which actress is Tippi Hedren's daughter and Dakota Johnson's mother?
9. In 1981, which non-golfer set the world record for the longest made putt ever televised?
10. Ankara is the capital of which country?
11. As of 2022, what are the only three video games known to have sold over 100 million copies?
12. On a standard British dartboard, what colour is the bullseye, usually?
13. What surname links Rocky Balboa's opponent in Rocky IV, and Malta's only professional snooker player?
14. The tragus is located in which part of the human body?
15. FIDE are the world governing body for what game?
16. What is usually meant by the abbreviation FAQs?
17. The fennec is the smallest breed of which animal?
18. Caries is a disease affecting which part of the body?
19. Who became the first female DJ on BBC Radio 1 in 1970?
20. At the 2010 Wimbledon tennis championships, who won the longest professional match in history, winning the final set 70-68?

Easy

Medium

Hard

Answers to QUIZ 325 – Pot Luck

1	Coffee (as she had suffered serious burns)	11	Shere Khan
2	Brain	12	11 Downing Street
3	*Lusitania*	13	Al Capone
4	Liverpool	14	Pointillism
5	Area 51	15	India
6	1-2-5-3	16	Mickey Rourke
7	Sleeping Beauty (Briar Rose)	17	Mike Tyson
8	Horse chestnut	18	Leather straps used as whips
9	A mouse	19	New Jersey
10	Carpet	20	Bruce Willis

Easy

1 8th August 1963 was the date of which famous heist near Mentmore in Buckinghamshire?

2 When used as an adjective and pronounced slightly differently to the month, what is the meaning of august?

3 Construction of what began on 13th August 1961 in what became commonly referred to in Germany as Barbed Wire Sunday?

4 Who was captured and imprisoned on 5th August 1962 in Howick, KwaZulu-Natal Province?

5 MTV began broadcasting just after midnight on 1st August 1981; what, aptly, was the first music video shown on the channel?

6 In August 1896, what was discovered at Rabbit Creek, a tributary of the Klondike river in Alaska?

7 Which actress and icon of glamour died on 5th August 1962 aged 36 from an overdose of sleeping pills?

8 Prior to being renamed after Augustus Caesar, the month of August was known as Sextilis, meaning what?

9 Which iconic annual Caribbean festival event takes place on the streets of London every August?

10 4th August 2015 saw the announcement on Twitter™ that, after an on-off relationship going back to 1976, which two puppets had broken up for good?

11 Which cartoon aimed at adults but starring children debuted on 13th August 1997?

12 On 31st August 2015, Mount McKinley in Alaska was officially renamed back to what, its native American name?

13 The 19th Amendment to the U.S. Constitution was ratified on 18th August 1920, granting who the right to vote?

Medium

14 Which Caribbean island gained independence from Britain on 6th August 1962, leading to the collapse of the West Indian Federation?

15 Which English Test Cricket captain retired from professional cricket on 29th August 2012?

16 On 2nd August 2018, which tech giant became the first publicly listed American company to reach a value of $1 trillion?

17 Born in 2021, August Brooksbank is a son of which Royal Princess?

18 At Casino de Monte-Carlo on 18th August 1913, the house took millions when the ball in the roulette wheel fell on black how many times in a row?

19 On 13th August 1964, Peter Allen and John Walby became the last two people in Britain to ever be subject to what?

20 Held every August, the 127 Yard Sale (running down Route 127 in America) advertises itself as being the world's longest; how many miles long does it claim to be?

Hard

Answers to QUIZ 326 – Wrestlers

1 Stone Cold Steve Austin
2 The Rock
3 HHH
4 Giant Haystacks
5 Chyna
6 André the Giant
7 Kane
8 Becky Lynch
9 Abraham Lincoln

1 Which are the only two cities in the English county of Somerset?
2 Orange juice, sugar and which spirit make up an Ambassador cocktail?
3 After the death of Henry VIII, who succeeded him as the English monarch?
4 The Uffizi is a museum and art gallery in which Italian city?
5 Why was American president Andrew Jackson's pet African Grey parrot removed from his funeral in 1845?
6 What is the northernmost of the three countries on the Scandinavian peninsula?
7 The multi-sports club Galatasaray is based in which European country?
8 Which is the southernmost country on the Balkan peninsula?
9 The name of which country translates from Spanish as "equator"?
10 Cirrhosis and hepatitis affect which organ of the body?
11 Cynology is the study of which animals?
12 The Clifton Suspension Bridge runs across which river?
13 The city of Geneva is situated in which European country?
14 *The Last of the Mohicans* was written by which author?
15 Caterpillars are the larval stage of which animal?
16 Cape Verde and Guinea-Bissau are former colonies of which European country?
17 Which country has the international car registration code ZA?
18 Which chocolate company produces the Creme Egg?
19 Britt Ekland played Mary Goodnight as the "Bond girl" in which film?
20 The Adi Granth, a collection of nearly 6,000 hymns, is the sacred scripture of which major world religion?

Easy

Medium

Hard

Answers to QUIZ 327 – Pot Luck

1	Medicine	11	*Minecraft, Tetris®, Grand Theft Auto V*
2	Volcanoes	12	Red
3	Red	13	Drago (Ivan and Tony)
4	Mass	14	Ear
5	The Pretenders	15	Chess
6	Kenny	16	Frequently asked questions
7	Elvis Presley	17	Fox
8	Melanie Griffith	18	Teeth; it is tooth decay
9	Sir Terry Wogan	19	Annie Nightingale
10	Turkey	20	John Isner

Easy

1   What term is given to a plant produced by deliberately crossing different parent species?
2   When ripe, what colour is the berry of the coffee plant?
3   16th century German botanist Leonhart Fuchs has which species of plant named after him?
4   What were Dame Edna Everage's favourite flowers?
5   Giving rise to an appropriate adjective, who was the Roman goddess of flowers?
6   What colour flowers does the forsythia plant usually produce?
7   What colour of dye is obtained from the plant woad?
8   In what season should daffodil bulbs be planted?
9   Gregory's Powder is a laxative made from which leafy plant, whose edible stalks are often served in a crumble?
10 *Solanum tuberosum* is the Latin name for which vegetable?
11 From which family of plants do Brussels sprouts come from?
12 Which is the sacred flower of Buddhism?
13 What is the name given to the female reproductive organ of a flower?
14 Oxeye is a type of which flower?
15 Which plant was introduced to the UK in Victorian times as a decoration, but has proved so invasive it is now illegal to allow it to occur in the wild?
16 A pink blend garden rose first introduced in 1998 at the British Embassy in the United States was bred and named in memory of who?
17 If touched, which plant causes a serious chemical reaction that makes skin hypersensitive to ultraviolet light, made doubly dangerous by its likeness to the innocuous cow parsley?
18 What plant-adjacent items were first introduced to Britain from Germany by Sir Charles Isham in 1847?
19 *Papaver Rhoeas* is the scientific name for which common commemorative flower?
20 Beefsteak, plum and cherry are varieties of which common plant?

Medium

Hard

Answers to QUIZ 328 – August

1	Great Train Robbery	11	*South Park*
2	Respected and impressive	12	Denali
3	Berlin Wall	13	Women
4	Nelson Mandela	14	Jamaica
5	*Video Killed the Radio Star*	15	Andrew Strauss
6	Gold	16	Apple
7	Marilyn Monroe	17	Princess Eugenie
8	Sixth	18	26
9	Notting Hill Carnival	19	Capital punishment
10	Kermit the Frog and Miss Piggy	20	690 (it spans six states)

1 Camelopard is an archaic term for which animal species?

2 What is the name of the messaging system involving holding the arms or flags in certain positions according to an alphabetic code?

3 The KGB were the secret police of which former country?

4 Who presents the ITV game show *Tipping Point*?

5 Baby crocodiles and alligators are known as what?

6 Which American state is known as the Golden State, and plays host to the namesake NBA team Golden State Warriors?

7 *Ikebana* is the Japanese art of doing what?

8 Which Savoy opera by Gilbert and Sullivan tells the story of a fairy banished from fairyland for marrying a mortal?

9 In 2014, after performing her first live concerts in 35 years, which recording artist had eight albums in the UK Top 40?

10 "A thing of beauty is a joy forever" is the first line of the poem *Endymion*, written by whom?

11 In the music industry, what does the abbreviation A&R stand for in the role of an A&R man?

12 What term for an embryonic shoot can also refer to a friend?

13 The medical condition glaucoma affects which part of the body?

14 Who played the title character in the 1964 film *Mary Poppins*?

15 At what age does a filly become a mare, and a colt become a horse?

16 Unaware that Robert Thomson had patented a design for one 42 years previously, who in 1888 invented a practical pneumatic tyre from a section of garden hose?

17 Ommetaphobia is the fear of which body part?

18 Selenology is the study of what?

19 What effect does an analgesic drug have?

20 Doctor Who is said to come from which planet?

Answers to QUIZ 329 – Pot Luck

1	Bath and Wells	11	Dogs
2	Tequila	12	Avon
3	Edward VI	13	Switzerland
4	Florence	14	James Fenimore Cooper
5	It kept swearing	15	Butterfly
6	Norway	16	Portugal
7	Turkey	17	South Africa
8	Greece	18	Cadbury
9	Ecuador	19	*The Man with the Golden Gun*
10	Liver	20	Sikhism

Easy

1. The following have all been world champions in which sport? Joe Davis; Ray Reardon; Steve Davis; Ronnie O'Sullivan

2. The following were all boxing champions in which weight class? Jack Dempsey; Ingemar Johansson; Mike Tyson; Tyson Fury

3. The following have all been world champions in which motorsport? Giuseppe Farina; Mike Hawthorn; Alain Prost; Lewis Hamilton

4. The following all won which individual football accolade? Matthias Sammer; Luis Figo; Rivaldo; Lionel Messi

5. The following have all been Olympic medallists in which athletics discipline? Merlene Ottey, Gail Devers, Carmelita Jeter, Shelly-Ann Fraser-Pryce

6. Which of the following have, as of 2022, never won the Premier League? Blackburn Rovers; Leicester City; Chelsea; Tottenham Hotspur

7. As of 2022, which of these countries has never won the Six Nations rugby union tournament? England; Ireland; Scotland; Wales

8. The following teams have all won which American sports championship? Minneapolis Lakers; Boston Celtics; Chicago Bulls; Milwaukee Bucks

9. The following have all been world champions in which athletics discipline? Carl Lewis; Mike Powell; Ivan Pedroso; Greg Rutherford

10. The following have all been world champions in which game? Mikhail Botvinnik; Tigran Petrosian; Anatoly Karpov; Viswanathan Anand; Magnus Carlsen

11. The following have all been world champions in which sport? Gerwyn Price; Rob Cross; Raymond van Barneveld; Phil Taylor

12. As of 2021, which of these people has never won the US Masters golf? Greg Norman; Jack Nicklaus; Phil Mickelson; Tiger Woods

13. The following teams have all won which American sports championship? Buffalo Sabres; Calgary Flames; Toronto Maple Leafs; Montreal Canadiens

14. The following have all been Olympic gold medallists in which athletics event? Marie-José Perec; Shaunae Miller-Uibo; Cathy Freeman; Christine Ohuruogu

15. The following have all been world champions in which sport? Tony Allcock; Alex Marshall; Andy Thomas; Paul Foster

16. The following all won which prestige endurance event? Jacques Anquetil; Bernard Hinault; Marco Pantani; Geraint Thomas

17. The following have all been world champions in which motorsport? Juha Kankkunen; Carlos Sainz; Tommi Mäkinen; Sebastien Ogier

18. The following have all been world champions in which motorsport? Mike Hailwood; Barry Sheen; Valentino Rossi; Marc Marquez

19. The following have all been Olympic gold medallists in which athletics event? Jackie Joyner-Kersee; Denise Lewis; Jessica Ennis; Nafissatou Thiam

20. The following have all been world champions in which nautical sport? Tom Carroll; Andy Irons; John John Florence; Kelly Slater

Medium

Hard

Answers to QUIZ 330 – Plants

1	Hybrid	11	Brassicas
2	Red	12	Lotus
3	Fuchsia	13	Pistil
4	Gladioli	14	Daisy
5	Flora	15	Japanese Knotweed
6	Yellow	16	Diana, Princess of Wales
7	Blue	17	Giant hogweed
8	Autumn	18	Garden gnomes
9	Rhubarb	19	Poppy
10	Potato	20	Tomato

1   Which American city is also known as Beantown?

2   In a chess set, which is the tallest piece?

3   Fenway Park and Wrigley Field are two of the most iconic venues in which sport?

4   In 1932, who became the first non-human to win an Oscar?

5   In the terminology of motor vehicles, what does 4WD stand for?

6   Dry ice is a solid form of which gas?

7   Which measurement is calculated as the distance around the outside of a circle?

8   What colour is the cross on the flag of Greece?

9   Which organisation has the motto "Fidelity, Bravery and Integrity"?

10 Of the eight planets in the solar system, which ones have rings?

11 Which celebrity ran the equivalent of 43 marathons in 52 days in 2009?

12 Porphyrophobia is the irrational fear of which colour?

13 Who was TV's "Crocodile Hunter"?

14 Belfast City Airport was renamed in 2006 after which sportsman?

15 What is a young eel called?

16 What was Mumbai known as before the city's name was changed?

17 Where is the thyroid gland located in the human body?

18 The Great Gazoo was a green floating alien character in which cartoon series?

19 Which English author wrote the *Adrian Mole* series of books?

20 Defeating Kevin Curran in the final, who won the 1985 Wimbledon Men's Singles title, becoming the first unseeded player ever to do so?

Answers to QUIZ 331 – Pot Luck

1	Giraffe	11	Artist and repertoire
2	Semaphore	12	Bud
3	The USSR/Soviet Union	13	Eye
4	Ben Shephard	14	Julie Andrews
5	Hatchlings	15	Four
6	California	16	John Dunlop
7	Flower arranging	17	Eyes
8	*Iolanthe*	18	The moon
9	Kate Bush	19	Pain relief
10	John Keats	20	Gallifrey

Easy

1   Which 1990s SEGA console was known as the Genesis in North America?

2   Which 2017 Nintendo® game console is a hybrid that can be used as both a home console or portable device?

3   Microsoft® launched what brand of motion-sensing input devices for their Xbox range in 2010?

4   To compete with the market dominance of the Game Boy, SEGA added peripheries such as a TV tuner and car charger to which handheld console?

5   A survey conducted in 1990 found that nearly one in three American households owned which games console?

6   Nintendo® began as a company that sold which products?

7   The first "rumble controller" was which 1997 add-on to the standard N64 controller?

8   Which was the first home gaming console that played DVDs, and also the first that used a hard disk for data storage?

9   First released in Japan in 1985, what was SEGA's third generation console?

10 In the world of console gaming, what are or were Game Genie, Action Replay and GameShark?

11 Billed as the "most powerful gaming handheld", which company released the Steam Deck™ gaming device in 2022?

12 Atari® attempted to strike first in the 64-bit market by releasing which console in 1993, which proved a commercial failure?

13 Which indicator of disaster, akin to the Windows "Blue Screen", meant the terminal failure of an Xbox 360?

14 To try and stop kids from eating them, which company adds a layer of the bitter agent denatonium benzoate to its cartridges?

15 Which tech giant's first – and, as of 2022, only – attempted at a video game console came with the 1996 launch of the Pippin?

16 The developers of which console designed its flashing blue light to mimic the call in Morse code of the Japanese Bush Warbler bird?

17 Released in 1998, which was the first console to include a built-in modular modem for internet access and online play?

18 In 1991, arcade company SNK Corporation launched which home console, complete with giant arcade-style controllers, massive cartridges and an even bigger price tag?

19 In 1972, which console was the first commercial home video game console, and the first – and, for many years, only – one to feature removable media?

20 Which new Android-based microconsole raised $8.5 million on Kickstarter in 2012, but was a commercial failure and discontinued by 2015?

Medium

Hard

Answers to QUIZ 332 – Sporting Champions

1	Snooker	11	Darts
2	Heavyweight	12	Greg Norman
3	Formula 1 racing	13	NHL ice hockey
4	Ballon D'Or	14	400m
5	100m	15	Bowls
6	Tottenham Hotspur	16	Tour de France
7	Scotland	17	Rally car racing
8	NBA basketball	18	MotoGP
9	Long jump	19	Heptathlon
10	Chess	20	Surfing

ANSWERS ON PAGE **337**

1 Where does the needle in a compass always point to?

2 David Vine, David Coleman, Sue Barker and Paddy McGuinness have all hosted which BBC television quiz show?

3 Adding one letter to the name of the capital city of Vermont gives the name of which other city, the seventh-largest in France?

4 What liquid is produced by the parotid glands?

5 What clothing item was originally patented under the name C-Curity?

6 British superstition says that to stave off bad luck, you are supposed to do what to a magpie when you see it on its own?

7 In teaching terminology, what does OFSTED stand for?

8 Which colour is used to describe magic used for immoral purposes?

9 Myxomatosis is a viral disease affecting which animals?

10 Michael Hutchence was the lead singer of which Australian band?

11 When Jack and Jill fell down the hill, what did Jack break?

12 In 1796, which US President declined to run for a third term in office, setting a 140-year precedent?

13 Which other country has the USA tried to invade in 1775, 1812 and 1813?

14 Which American city has Major League Baseball teams called the Mets and the Yankees?

15 In addition to the fictional swordsman, Zorro is also the Spanish name for which animal?

16 Oliver Mellors was the title character in which classic novel?

17 Stanley Gibbons is the world's leading merchant and auctioneer of what?

18 In internet parlance, what does a/s/l mean in an introduction?

19 In 1921, who became the first and only unidentified person to be awarded the Victoria Cross?

20 By area, Brazil is by far the largest country in South America; which is second?

Easy

Medium

Hard

Answers to QUIZ 333 – Pot Luck

1	Boston	11	Eddie Izzard
2	King	12	Purple
3	Baseball	13	Steve Irwin
4	Mickey Mouse	14	George Best
5	Four-wheel drive	15	Elver
6	Carbon dioxide	16	Bombay
7	Circumference	17	The neck
8	White	18	*The Flintstones*
9	The FBI (see what they did there?)	19	Sue Townsend
10	Jupiter, Saturn, Uranus and Neptune; the four "gas giants"	20	Boris Becker

Easy

1 Which fruit cake takes its name from a Scottish city situated on the River Tay?
2 Which Scottish fruit cake completely covered with pastry was originally eaten on Twelfth Night, but is also now a regular choice for Hogmanay?
3 Traditional cream teas usually incorporate which slightly sweet plain cake?
4 Which marzipan-covered multi-coloured sponge cake was first baked in 1884 to celebrate a royal wedding?
5 In the UK and Australia, wedding cakes are usually what type of cake?
6 Sponge cake and mascarpone flavoured with coffee and brandy creates which Italian dessert?
7 A pound cake is traditionally made with a pound of each of which four ingredients?
8 Traditionally, the top layer of a wedding cake is saved and eaten on which of two future occasions?
9 In literature, who ate a very small cake with the words "EAT ME" written on it in currants?
10 Sachertorte usually has a layer of which flavour of jam?
11 "Let them eat cake" is a quote often attributed to which wife of King Louis XVI of France?
12 Usually eaten at Christmas, the Madeira-style cake topped with a thick layer of chocolate and decorated with marzipan fruits is named for which African capital city?
13 Which Yorkshire town is famous for its circular liquorice cakes?
14 A sponge cake cube coated in chocolate sauce and rolled in desiccated coconut, Lamington cake comes from which country?
15 Although now eaten on Easter Sunday, simnel cakes were originally eaten on which other occasion?
16 The Dutch mille-feuille cake known as *tompoes/tompouce* cake is traditionally made with which colour icing?
17 Which South Indian steamed rice and lentil cake, usually served with *sambhar*, is often eaten for breakfast in Sri Lanka?
18 "There shall be no more cakes and ale" is a line spoken by Sir Toby Belch in which Shakespeare play?
19 Noel Edmonds and Bruno Brookes disavowed the dangers of the fictional drug Cake in which Channel 4 satire?
20 The chocolate mud cake known as Kladdkaka originated in which country?

Medium

Hard

Answers to QUIZ 334 – Gaming Consoles

1 Mega Drive
2 Nintendo Switch™
3 Kinect
4 Game Gear
5 Nintendo Entertainment System (NES)
6 Playing cards
7 Rumble Pak
8 PlayStation® 2
9 Master System
10 Cheat cartridges
11 Valve
12 Jaguar
13 Red Ring of Death
14 Nintendo®
15 Apple (it lasted two years)
16 Nintendo® Wii
17 SEGA Dreamcast
18 Neo Geo AES (even one of the games, *Steel Battalion*, cost $200, and that was in the 1990s!)
19 Magnavox Odyssey
20 Ouya

ANSWERS ON PAGE 339

1 Due to its proclivity in monarchies across Europe in the 19th and 20th centuries, what is considered the "royal disease"?

2 Cabbage, broccoli, cauliflower, kale, Brussels sprouts and kohlrabi are all types of which plant species?

3 Who was MP for Finchley between 1959 and 1992, then Baroness of Kesteven until her death in 2013?

4 Which political philosophy is founded on public ownership of the basic means of production, distribution and exchange, while allowing for private property ownership?

5 Which film was begun by Stanley Kubrick in the late 1970's yet only finished by Steven Spielberg in 2001?

6 What name is given to a winning tennis serve which is not returned or touched by the opponent?

7 Who was assassinated by Mark David Chapman in 1980?

8 On the date of Queen Elizabeth II's coronation, who was the UK Prime Minister?

9 Until 1980, what were Nobel Prizes made of?

10 In the nursery rhyme named for her, who sat on her tuffet?

11 Which brand of meat pie in a tin takes its name from a Uruguayan port city?

12 Henry II, Henry III and Edward III all had Queen Consorts with what name?

13 A dish described as *à la Clamart* contains which vegetable?

14 In January 2004, which American pop star married her childhood friend Jason Alexander in Las Vegas, a marriage annulled 55 hours later?

15 The racecourses of Lingfield Park and Sandown Park are both located in which county?

16 Reepicheep is a talking mouse in which series of novels?

17 Fanny Crosby was a 19th century household name for writing more than 8,000 what?

18 Which famous London building was largely destroyed by fire on 16th October 1834?

19 Which two football teams compete in the Edinburgh Derby?

20 What is the two-word motto of the Scout movement?

Easy

Medium

Hard

Answers to QUIZ 335 – Pot Luck

1	North	11	His crown
2	*[A] Question of Sport*	12	George Washington
3	Montpelier/Montpellier	13	Canada
4	Saliva	14	New York
5	Zip	15	Fox
6	Salute it	16	*Lady Chatterley's Lover* by D.H. Lawrence
7	Office for Standards in Education	17	Postage stamps
8	Black	18	Age/sex/location
9	Rabbits	19	Whoever is in the Tomb of the Unknown Soldier in Arlington National Cemetery
10	INXS	20	Argentina

1. O'Shea Jackson is the real name of which rapper and actor?
2. Who released the albums *Dreams and Nightmares* and *Dreams Worth More Than Money*, and founded the label imprint Dream Chasers?
3. Which acronym did Drake and Lil Wayne bring into popular vernacular with their song *The Motto* in 2012?
4. After several years out of the spotlight, which "Queen of Rap" returned in 2015 with a cameo at the Super Bowl XLIX halftime show?
5. Upon releasing a reggae album, *Reincarnated,* what did Snoop Dogg change his artist name to, briefly?
6. Which group's album *Once Upon a Time in Shaolin*, the most expensive piece of music ever sold, is almost unique in only ever having one copy made?
7. Which rapper was sued by his own mother in 1999 for $10 million, eventually settling for $1,600?
8. Which rapper is often credited with – and criticised for – pioneering the widespread use of Auto–Tune in 21st century hip hop?
9. Which group won an Academy Award for the song *It's Hard out Here for a Pimp* from the movie *Hustle & Flow*?
10. Who recorded 2019's *Hot Girl Summer*, giving rise to the popular phrase of the same name?
11. When serious world events happen, comedian Dave Chappelle jokingly seeks out the opinions of which 2000s hip hop star?
12. In 1988, who became the first solo female rapper to release a full album?
13. The group The Ferrari Boyz comprises which two rappers?
14. The first ever Grammy award for Best Rap Performance was awarded to which duo in 1989?
15. In addition to their solo careers, Nate Dogg, Snoop Dogg and Warren G formed which hip-hop supergroup?

16. Along with his widow Faith Evans, who recorded *I'll Be Missing You* in memory of The Notorious B.I.G.?
17. Which UK rapper was annoyed by the crease in his *AirForce*?
18. *U.N.I.T.Y.*, a Grammy Award-winning song focused on the disrespect of women, was released by who?
19. Lupe Fiasco, Chance The Rapper and Da Brat all represent which city?
20. Whose hits have included *Donald Trump, Nikes on my Feet, Senior Skip Day* and *Musical Chairs*?

Answers to QUIZ 336 – Cake

1	Dundee cake	11	Marie-Antoinette (although the modern consensus is she never actually said it)
2	Black bun		
3	Scone	12	Tunis
4	Battenberg	13	Pontefract
5	Fruitcake	14	Australia
6	Tiramisu	15	Mothering Sunday/Mother's Day
7	Flour, butter, eggs, sugar	16	Pink
8	The one-year anniversary, or the first child's christening	17	Idli
		18	*Twelfth Night*
9	Alice, from *Alice's Adventures in Wonderland*	19	*Brass Eye*
10	Apricot	20	Sweden

1 Which former topless model inherited $300 million from her late husband J. Howard Marshall II?

2 The 18 species of which animal are the only birds which can swim and dive but cannot fly?

3 Which sportsman was supposed to be the first-ever guest on *This Is Your Life*, but had to be cancelled after newspapers leaked the story?

4 Eccrine and apocrine glands produce what substance?

5 Fatima Whitbread was a world champion and Olympic silver medallist in which sport?

6 If someone is suffering from epistaxis, what is wrong with them?

7 The name of which flightless bird is also that of the mother of Romulus and Remus in Roman mythology?

8 Des Moines is the capital of which American state?

9 Someone described as milquetoast is acting how?

10 The largest city square in the world is located in which country?

11 Mary McAleese, Mary Robinson and Michael D. Higgins have all served as President of which country?

12 Which London Underground station is the only one with a name containing only one vowel?

13 From which country did Suriname gain independence on 25th November 1975?

14 0191 is the telephone dialling code of which region of England?

15 Richard I and John were sons of which other English monarch?

16 "Knock at the door" is a common bingo call for which number?

17 Beth Tweddle represented Britain in which sport?

18 Because of its intense pollution, which Scottish city was nicknamed Auld Reekie?

19 In which Charles Dickens novel is there a case of spontaneous combustion?

20 Escapologist Harry Houdini died a short time after what happened to him?

Easy

Medium

Hard

Answers to QUIZ 337 – Pot Luck

1 Haemophilia
2 Brassica
3 Margaret Thatcher
4 Socialism
5 *A.I. Artificial Intelligence*
6 Ace
7 John Lennon
8 Sir Winston Churchill
9 Solid gold (now they are gold plated)
10 Little Miss Muffet

11 Fray Bentos
12 Eleanor
13 Peas
14 Britney Spears
15 Surrey
16 *The Chronicles of Narnia*
17 Hymns
18 The Palace of Westminster/Houses of Parliament
19 Hearts and Hibernian
20 "Be prepared"

What are the names of these fictional pirates?

Easy

1

2

3

Medium

4

5

6

7

8

9

Hard

Answers to QUIZ 338 – Hip-Hop

1	Ice Cube	11	Ja Rule
2	Meek Mill	12	MC Lyte (with *Lyte as a Rock*)
3	YOLO (you only live once)	13	Gucci Mane and Waka Flocka Flame
4	Missy Elliot	14	DJ Jazzy Jeff & The Fresh Prince
5	Snoop Lion	15	213
6	Wu-Tang Clan	16	Puff Daddy (as he was then)
7	Eminem	17	DigDat
8	T-Pain	18	Queen Latifah
9	Three 6 Mafia	19	Chicago
10	Megan Thee Stallion	20	Mac Miller

1   In which 1985 coming-of-age film do five high school students meet in Saturday detention and discover they have more in common than they assumed?

2   After all species of elephant, what is the next-heaviest land animal in the world?

3   Especially when in its white winter coat, "ermine" is another name for which animal?

4   Following the 2017 general election which resulted in a hung parliament, the Conservative Party signed a confidence-and-supply agreement with which Northern Irish party?

5   Captains Cook, Hook, Kirk and Hewitt all have what first name?

6   What topping must a *pizza funghi* have?

7   In a 1951 post-apocalyptic novel by John Wyndham, which plants try to take over the Earth?

8   Guantanamo Bay is a part of which country?

9   "Connecting People" is a slogan and protected trademark of which telecoms giant?

10 Which is the only continent to have neither snakes nor reptiles?

11 Around one eighth of the motorway network of which country has no mandatory speed limit?

12 Author Gérard de Nerval kept which crustacean as a pet, even going so far as to tie it to string and take it on walks?

13 According to the medieval proverb, where do all roads lead to?

14 Which brand of flavoured rum is named after a 17th-century Welsh pirate?

15 The parents of Azaria Chamberlain claimed in 1980 that what wild animal killed and ate their baby?

16 Which fossil fuel has the least negative effect on the environment?

17 What name was shared by a 20th century Irish artist known for his use of unsettling imagery and an English 16th century philosopher who also served as Lord Chancellor?

18 On 12th March 1951, two otherwise-unrelated cartoon strips both launched, one on each side of the Atlantic, both claiming to be unaware of the other. What name did they both have?

19 Baseball player Randy Johnson, cricketer Jacques Rudolph and tennis player Michael Llodra have all accidentally done what while playing?

20 In law, what Latin term is used to refer to the mental element of a person's intention to commit a crime, or knowledge that their actions/inaction could cause one?

Easy

Medium

Hard

Answers to QUIZ 339 – Pot Luck

1	Anna Nicole-Smith	12	Bank
2	Penguin	13	Netherlands
3	Sir Stanley Matthews (he did appear a few months later)	14	Tyneside
		15	Henry II
4	Sweat	16	Four
5	Javelin	17	Gymnastics
6	They are having a nosebleed	18	Edinburgh
7	Rhea	19	*Bleak House* (the character was Krook Smallweed)
8	Iowa		
9	Timidly	20	A woman, hearing of his reputation for being able to take a blow, repeatedly punched him in his stomach; he then died of appendicitis
10	China (Xinghai Square, covering 270 acres)		
11	Ireland		

Easy

1   The twin towers of which financial centre were struck and felled by hijacked passenger aircraft on 11th September 2001?

2   16th September marks Mexican Independence Day, a day commemorating liberation from which European country?

3   The Great Fire of London started on 2nd September 1666 in which street?

4   Which ship departed Plymouth alone on 16th September 1620, bound for the Americas, with 102 passengers?

5   On what date in 1939 did Britain declare war on Germany?

6   The anniversary of her death, 5th September is the annual feast date of which saint, born Anjezë Gonxhe Bojaxhiu?

7   On 13th September 1902, a burglar named Harry Jackson becomes the first person in Britain to be convicted using what as evidence?

8   Which band released the song *Wake Me Up When September Ends* in 2005?

9   Which actress and monarch died on 14th September 1982 in a car accident?

10   Which American federal holiday is celebrated on the first Monday in September?

11   In September 2003, *Fathers 4 Justice* campaigner Jason Hatch breached Buckingham Palace dressed as who or what?

12   The Treaty of Paris, signed in Paris on 3rd September 1783, officially ended which war?

13   22nd September 1735 saw who, the UK's first Prime Minister, move into 10 Downing Street for the first time?

14   Prime Minister Neville Chamberlain claimed to have achieved what on 30th September 1938 after meeting with Hitler in Munich?

Medium

15   Run at Doncaster each year in September, which is the oldest of England's five "classic" horse races?

16   1st September 1159 saw the death of which man, the only Englishman to become Pope?

17   Which American president was shot and killed on 14th September 1901?

18   Born 5th September 1638 and dying 1st September 1715, which French monarch's reign of 72 years, 110 days is the longest anywhere in history?

19   On account of their name and their lack of championships, which baseball team has long had the nickname "Completely Useless By September"?

20   On 1st September 1969, the Free Unionist Officers Movement gained control of the Libyan government, abolished the monarchy and installed who as head of state?

Hard

Answers to QUIZ 340 – Pirates

1   Captain Jack Sparrow, *Pirates of the Caribbean*

2   Captain Pugwash

3   Captain Hook

4   Long John Silver

5   Dread Pirate Roberts, *The Princess Bride*

6   Captain Flint, *Black Sails*

7   Captain Shakespeare, *Stardust*

8   Morgan Adams, *Cutthroat Island*

9   The Pirate Captain, *The Pirates! In an Adventure with Scientists!*

1 In March 2022, a cargo ship caught fire and sank in the Atlantic Ocean, resulting in a loss of £295 million's worth of what type of cargo?
2 An octogenarian is between how many years old?
3 Aotearoa is the indigenous name for which country?
4 Borlotti and cannellini are types of what?
5 AFIS is a system of identification employed by law enforcement agencies using what?
6 What was the unique ending of the "Battle of Bramall Lane", a football match played between Sheffield United and West Bromwich Albion on 16th March 2002?
7 Something served *parmentier* comes with which vegetable?
8 Which traditional pantomime role is usually played either in an extremely camp way, or by men acting butch in women's clothing?
9 What are the two official languages of Malta?
10 Which bird lays the largest egg, but also the smallest in proportion to its size?
11 Copacabana is both a region and a beach in which South American city?
12 In a 147 maximum snooker break, how many times is the black ball potted?
13 What distinct feature do ungulate animals have?
14 Found in Japan, what are *ryokans*?
15 In 1970, the world's first seat belt law was created in which country?
16 The board game known as checkers in the USA is known as what in Britain?
17 Which metal is the main constituent of the alloy gunmetal?
18 Grenadine, the deep red non-alcoholic bar syrup, is usually made from which fruit?
19 Pruritis is the medical name for which extremely common condition?
20 Which country borders the Dead Sea to the East?

Easy

Medium

Hard

Answers to QUIZ 341 – Pot Luck

1 *The Breakfast Club*
2 Rhinoceros
3 Stoat
4 Democratic Unionist Party
5 James
6 Mushroom
7 Triffids (*The Day of the Triffids*)
8 Cuba
9 Nokia
10 Antarctica
11 Germany (although a limit of 130 km/h is advised, and often required by insurers)
12 Lobster
13 Rome
14 Captain Morgan
15 Dingo (and, despite it being the first-ever known case of death by dingo, they were proved correct)
16 Natural gas
17 Francis Bacon
18 *Dennis the Menace*
19 Killed a pigeon with the ball
20 *Mens rea*

Easy

1   In 2020, which man became the first artist to reach the top 5 of the UK album chart in eight consecutive decades?

2   In 2020, which Welsh singer became the first female artist to chart an album in the top 40 of the UK Albums Chart in seven consecutive decades?

3   The soundtrack to which 1992 film starring Whitney Houston became the first album to sell more than 1 million units in the USA in a single week?

4   Which 1982 Michael Jackson album is, until further notice, the biggest-selling album of all time?

5   In 2005, which former Beatle became the first artist in history to broadcast live music into space?

6   After his death in 2016, which artist had a history-making 19 songs on the American Billboard 200 chart at the same time?

7   In 2014, which Colombian singer became the first person to ever get 100 million likes on Facebook™?

8   As of the 2021 awards, which Irish band has won the most Grammy Awards of any group, with 22?

9   Whose 1997's album *Come On Over* became the biggest-selling studio album of all time by a solo female artist?

10 Who, in 2016, broke Madonna's record for the most No.1 albums in the UK recorded by a solo artist, almost 40 years after his death?

Medium

11 Who is the only artist to have separate top-ten singles as a solo act, as half of a duo, as a third of a trio, as a fourth of a quartet, and as a fifth of a quintet?

12 With 1988's *Where Do Broken Hearts Go*, who became the first artist to have seven consecutive No.1 hits on the US Billboard Hot 100?

13 In 2011, who became the first female to have two top five hits in both the UK single and album charts simultaneously?

14 Who is the only artist to be inducted into the Rock and Roll Hall of Fame three times?

15 *Only Girl (In the World)* was whose fourth number-one song of 2010, making her the first female with four US number-one singles in a calendar year?

16 *Bad Guy* by Billie Eilish ended the record-setting 19-week run at the top of the Billboard 100 singles chart for which Lil Nas X song?

17 In 2019, *Forbes* magazine determined that who had become the first hip-hop billionaire?

18 With her 1978 release *The Kick Inside*, who became the first female artist to write every song on a million-selling album?

19 Supposedly, whose breakthrough album *Calypso* (1956) was the first million-selling record by a single artist?

20 Which Irish vocalist was the first artist to chart at least one new album each year in the UK albums chart for 34 consecutive years?

Hard

Answers to QUIZ 342 – September

1	World Trade Center	11	Batman
2	Spain	12	American Revolutionary War
3	Pudding Lane	13	Robert Walpole
4	The Mayflower	14	"Peace for our time" (He was extremely wrong.)
5	3rd September	15	St Leger
6	Mother Teresa	16	Nicholas Breakspear/Pope Adrian IV
7	Fingerprints	17	William McKinley
8	Green Day	18	Louis XIV
9	Grace Kelly (Princess Grace of Monaco)	19	Chicago Cubs
10	Labor Day	20	Colonel Muammar Gaddafi

1 Which element on the periodic table is represented by the letter H?
2 The holiest day in the Jewish calendar, which holiday celebrates the Jewish Day of Atonement?
3 What colour flag is awarded to a British beach that meets high standards for cleanliness, safety, water quality and amenities?
4 How many points are W tiles worth in the English version of Scrabble®?
5 Rosalind was the first love of which Shakespearean title character?
6 Memorial Stadium and Ashton Gate are football grounds in which British city?
7 The skyscraper at 122 Leadenhall Street in London has what nickname, taken from its likeness to a kitchen utensil?
8 Ablution is another name for which regular act?
9 The remains of which fortification stretch from Bowness-on-Solway to Wallsend, near Newcastle?
10 The underwater city of Bikini Bottom is the setting for which cartoon?
11 Tim Davie, Mark Byford and Greg Dyke have all served as directors-general of which corporation?
12 Which series of fantasy films is based not on a book series, but on a ride at Disneyland®?
13 Which European capital city is known in its native language as *Praha*?
14 How many pairs of chromosomes do humans usually have?
15 If someone self-immolates, what have they done?
16 Which restaurant chain operated an airline between 2003 and 2006, featuring air stewardesses in their branded outfits?
17 John Ronald Reuel were the first names of which English poet and writer?
18 Having appeared in everything from *Footloose* to BT adverts, the game that connect actors via films they have appeared in together is named for who?
19 Carrow Road is the home ground of which English football team?
20 In 2012, which celebrity chef was cautioned by police for repeatedly shoplifting from Tesco?

Easy

Medium

Hard

Answers to QUIZ 343 – Pot Luck

1 Cars (so it was literally cargo)
2 80 and 89 inclusive
3 New Zealand
4 Beans
5 Fingerprints (Automated Fingerprint Identification System)
6 Due to red cards and injuries, Sheffield United had only six players left, forcing the match to be abandoned
7 Potatoes
8 Dame
9 Maltese and English
10 Ostrich
11 Rio de Janeiro
12 16
13 Hooves
14 Inns
15 Australia (initially just in the state of Victoria)
16 Draughts
17 Copper
18 Pomegranate
19 An itch
20 Jordan

Easy

1 How many degrees Fahrenheit is equivalent to 0 degree Celsius?

2 How many teaspoons go into a tablespoon?

3 A lump of platinum in France was between 1889 and 2019 used as the definition for which unit of weight?

4 Depending on what side of the Atlantic you are on, what measurement is equal to either 2,240 lbs or 2,000 lbs?

5 Rod, pole and perch are all names for the same measurement, used in surveying as being equal to a quarter of a what?

6 Cubic decimetres are more commonly known as what measurement of volume, usually for liquids?

7 British scientist Henry Cavendish made the first reliable measurement of what force, late in the 18th century?

8 The prefix "hecto" on compound words means a quantity of how many?

9 What archaic unit of measurement was equal to the distance of the elbow to the tips of the outstretched hand?

10 What was originally defined as being 1/10,000,000th of the distance from the North Pole to the Equator?

11 Henry III lined up three barleycorns in a row to serve as a binding definition for which measurement?

Medium

12 In the term "20/40 vision" to refer to a person's eyesight, what measurement do the numbers refer to?

13 The lux is the SI derived unit of what?

14 In radioactivity, what SI unit is used for the number of decays per second?

15 What travels at 186,282 miles per second?

16 A dioptre is a unit of measurement of the power of what?

17 In millilitres, how much liquid is contained in a standard wine bottle?

18 Primarily used in the precious metals industry, what system of units of mass shares a name with an ancient city?

19 What term for a flat lens made of concentric rings is also used for a unit of frequency equal to 1 trillion Hertz?

20 In some role-playing games, XP – the measure of how much a player or character has endured or learned – stands for what?

Hard

ANSWERS ON PAGE **349**

1   Which Serbian-American engineer and physicist invented the first alternating current motor?

2   Samuel Langhorne Clemens wrote under which pseudonym?

3   In the Tour De France, what colour jersey is worn by the "King of the Mountains"?

4   The Doge's Palace and Bridge of Sighs are landmarks in which city?

5   The New York City neighbourhood of Harlem is named after a city in which European country?

6   Inaccessible Island, a dormant island volcano, is in which ocean?

7   Released in 1937, which was the first full-length traditionally animated feature film, as well as the first Disney animated feature film?

8   The Geologic Time Scale is divided into eons, themselves subdivided into eras, which subdivide into what?

9   Canterbury Cathedral is the oldest in England; which other Kent cathedral is second?

10 In musical notation, what is meant by the instruction *fortissimo*?

11 Which Czech broke his own men's javelin world record with a 98.48 metre throw in May 1996?

12 Rome's International Airport is named after who?

13 Iain Duncan Smith devised which UK social safety net program that merged six different benefits into one?

14 Six of the eight planets in our solar system spin from West to East. Venus rotates East to West. Which planet rotates north to south?

15 What do the flags of Angola, Mozambique, Kenya and Saudi Arabia all feature?

16 The eggs of a robin are which colour?

17 The Comets were the backing group for which early rock and roll star?

18 Italian football club Juventus are based in which city?

19 What name is shared by Norris, a Formula 1 driver, and Calrissian, a *Star Wars* character?

20 The Sandinistas and Contras fought a civil war throughout the 1980s in which central American country?

Easy

Medium

Hard

Answers to QUIZ 345 – Pot Luck

1	Hydrogen	11	The BBC
2	Yom Kippur	12	*Pirates of the Caribbean*
3	Blue	13	Prague
4	Four	14	23
5	Romeo, from *Romeo and Juliet*	15	Set themselves on fire
6	Bristol	16	*Hooter's*
7	Cheese grater	17	J.R.R. Tolkien
8	Washing yourself or bathing	18	Kevin Bacon (Six Degrees of Kevin Bacon)
9	Hadrian's Wall	19	Norwich City
10	*SpongeBob SquarePants*	20	Antony Worrall Thompson

1. Robert Zimmermann is the real name of which singer-songwriter and Nobel Prize winner?
2. Eric Bartholomew used which English seaside town as his stage surname?
3. Singer and presenter Priscilla White subtlety changed her stage name to what?
4. Because it seemed more "saleable", actress Joyce Frankenberg adopted the name of which of Henry VIII's wives?
5. Although still known as Jim to family and friends, comedian James Moir is better known to the public by which name?
6. For her singing career, Marie McDonald McLaughlin Lawrie shortened her name to what four letter word?
7. Regarded as Britain's first teen idol and rock and roll star, how is Thomas Hicks better known?
8. Which actress was born with the surname Zacharenko, had it later changed by her family to Gurdin, and became famous with the surname of a director?
9. Roberta Joan Anderson was the maiden name of which Canadian folk singer?
10. The straight half of a British comedy double act, Thomas Derbyshire performs as who?
11. In the world of pop music, how is Welshman Michael Barratt better known?
12. Convicted murderer and ornithologist Robert Stroud was immortalised by what nickname?
13. Comedian David O'Mahony went by what stage name?
14. Which *Coronation Street* and *Bad Girls* actress was born Shirley Ann Broadbent?
15. The late singer-songwriter John Henry Deutschendorf became famous under which toponym?
16. Terence Wilson, the rapper and "toaster" in reggae band UB40, went by what monoym?
17. Francesco Stephen Castelluccio is the full real name of which falsetto singer?
18. How is Bob van Winkle better known?
19. Melodic rapper Cornell Haynes Jr records his music under what name?
20. Adam Wiles is the real name of the DJ and record producer known professionally as who?

Answers to QUIZ 346 – Weights and Measures

1. 32
2. Three
3. The kilogram
4. A ton – it is 2,240lbs in the UK, 2,000 in North America
5. Chain
6. Litre
7. Gravity
8. 100
9. Cubit
10. A metre
11. Inch – it was previously determined as the width of a man's thumb
12. Feet – it means that person can see things from 20 feet (the first number) what a person with normal vision can read from 40 feet (second number)
13. Illumination
14. Becquerel
15. Light, in a vacuum
16. The optical power of a lens or curved mirror
17. 750ml
18. Troy (though its name derives from Troyes in France)
19. Fresnel
20. Experience points

ANSWERS ON PAGE 351

1 Which drama miniseries depicts the lives of a group of gay men during the HIV/AIDS crisis in London?

2 Which entertainer had a pet named Fanny the Wonderdog?

3 In Spain, who or what are *paradors*?

4 In the NATO phonetic alphabet, Q is represented by which place?

5 Which journalist and broadcaster stepped down as chairman of nascent TV news channel GB News only three months after its launch?

6 In 2004, artist Sam Taylor Wood released a 107-minute video of which famous sportsman sleeping?

7 People diagnosed with coeliac disease have an intestinal hypersensitivity to which protein?

8 The Free Democratic Republic of Formosa was established in 1895 on which island?

9 In tailoring and clothing terminology, an armscye is another word for what?

10 In which board game does a player have 11 chances to guess a sequence of four colours among eight colour choices?

11 Mary of Teck was the spouse of which British monarch?

12 Which major international city was originally founded in 1803 as a penal colony?

13 Bunker Hill was a 1775 battle fought as a part of which war?

14 Willy Lott's Cottage features in several artworks by which English painter?

15 Which common forename also names the weighted mass on the end of a pendulum?

16 By winning the Australian Open in January 2022, which male tennis player set a record for Grand Slam singles victories with 21?

17 Which African country applied to join the European Community in 1987?

18 What are dried plums called?

19 An ortanique is a citrus fruit made as a cross between which two other fruits?

20 When deposed, General Manuel Noriega hid in the Vatican embassy in Panama; how did the US Army drive him out?

Easy

Medium

Hard

Answers to QUIZ 347 – Pot Luck

1	Nikola Tesla	11	Jan Železný
2	Mark Twain	12	Leonardo da Vinci
3	White with red polka dots	13	Universal Credit
4	Venice	14	Uranus
5	Netherlands	15	Weaponry; sword, AK-47, shield and sword respectively
6	Atlantic Ocean		
7	*Pinocchio*	16	Blue
8	Periods	17	Bill Haley
9	Rochester Cathedral	18	Turin
10	Very strongly or loudly	19	Lando
		20	Nicaragua

Easy

1. Between 16th and 28th October 1962, a "missile crisis" concerning the strategic position of nuclear weapons amid the Cold War took place in which country?
2. In the book and film *The Hunt for Red October*, who or what was Red October?
3. On 7th October 1920, who became eligible for admission as full members at Oxford University for the first time?
4. *October* was the name of the 1981 second album of which Irish rock band?
5. On 1st October 1908, which car – the earliest effort to make a car that most people could actually buy – first went on sale?
6. On 21st October 1805, which naval hero was mortally wounded at the Battle of Trafalgar?
7. The United Nations was founded on 24th October 1945; what previous organisation did it replace?
8. The armed conflict fought from 6th to 25th October 1973 between Israel and a coalition of Arab states is commonly named for which religious holiday?
9. Who nailed his "95 Theses" to a church door in Wittenberg, Germany on 31st October 1517, triggering the Protestant Reformation?
10. Who delivered their famous "the lady's not for turning" speech at their party's conference on 10th October 1980?

Medium

11. On 3rd October 1992, which singer ripped up a photo of Pope John Paul II on *Saturday Night Live* as a protest against alleged abuse by the Church?
12. At the height of the global financial crisis in October 2008, against which country did Britain invoke anti-terrorism laws to freeze the UK-based assets of its banks?
13. *The Rumble in the Jungle* legendary boxing match took place on 30th October 1974 between Muhammad Ali and who?
14. Which album topped the UK charts for the second time on 4th October 2019, 49 years and 252 days after the first?
15. Which famous Wild Western shootout took place in Tombstone, Arizona on 26th October 1881?
16. On 9th October 1967, then-Transport Minister Barbara Castle introduced what piece of road safety apparatus?
17. Which government-built airship crashed on 5th October 1930, killing 48 of the 54 people on board?
18. On 17th October 1860, Willie Park Sr. won the first ever professional tournament in which sport?
19. Rower Alex Partridge and hockey player Hannah Macleod had what stolen from them at a nightclub on 25th October 2012?
20. On 31st October 2017, who spoiled the results of *The Great British Bake Off* final on Twitter™, merely hours before it was televised?

Hard

Answers to QUIZ 348 – Real Names

1	Bob Dylan	11	Shakin' Stevens
2	Morecambe (Eric Morecambe)	12	The Birdman of Alcatraz
3	Cilla Black	13	Dave Allen
4	Jane Seymour	14	Amanda Barrie
5	Vic Reeves	15	John Denver
6	Lulu	16	Astro
7	Tommy Steele	17	Frankie Valli
8	Natalie Wood (chosen in tribute to Sam Wood)	18	Vanilla Ice
9	Joni Mitchell	19	Nelly
10	Tommy Cannon	20	Calvin Harris

1 Two straight lines that are always the same distance apart and never touch are said to be in what?

2 Which vowelless word describes the phenomenon of three celestial bodies (such as the sun, moon and Earth during a solar eclipse) forming a straight line?

3 Which part of the brain regulates body temperature, sleep patterns and hunger?

4 Including the goalkeeper, how many players feature in a handball team?

5 Shaun Maloney scored the winning goal for which team in the 2013 FA Cup final?

6 Magellanic, Rockhopper and Humboldt are types of which animal?

7 Which national radio station launched on 30th September 1967?

8 The Khyber Pass sits on the border between which two Asian countries?

9 Death Valley lies in which American state?

10 Madison Avenue and Broadway are found in which borough of New York City?

11 In printing and editing terminology, what is meant by the letters UC?

12 As expressed by Boris Johnson, "wiff waff" was an early form of which modern game?

13 Melanie Sykes appeared as an ice cream seller in a desert in an advert for which beer?

14 On which day of the week does the Queen distribute Maundy Money?

15 The Brink's-Mat heist of November 1983 saw £26 million worth of gold stolen from a warehouse at which airport?

16 What is the highest and most prestigious award of the British honours system?

17 Mina Harker was the main non-title character in which gothic novel?

18 With six weddings to five women and two further engagements, which *EastEnders* character has been married the most times?

19 In which of Shakespeare's plays does Prospero, the rightful Duke of Milan, appear?

20 The tax evasion trial of which Scouse comedian revealed that he kept £336,000 in cash stashed in suitcases in his loft?

Easy

Medium

Hard

Answers to QUIZ 349 – Pot Luck

1	*It's a Sin*	11	George V
2	Julian Clary	12	Sydney, Australia
3	Hotels, owned by the government	13	American Revolutionary War
4	Quebec	14	John Constable
5	Andrew Neil	15	Bob
6	David Beckham	16	Rafael Nadal
7	Gluten	17	Morocco
8	Taiwan	18	Prunes
9	The armhole	19	Orange and tangerine
10	*Mastermind*	20	They blasted heavy metal music at him for ten days straight

1   Which former UK Prime Minister is alleged to have remarked "the best argument against democracy is a five-minute conversation with the average voter"?

2   Upon victory in battle, which Roman general proclaimed "*Veni, vidi, vici*", translating as "I came, I saw, I conquered"?

3   Who promised boxing fans he would "float like a butterfly, sting like a bee"?

4   Which brash football manager once said "I wouldn't say I was the best manager in the business, but I was in the top one"?

5   Who wrote in his memoirs from St Helena, "History is a set of lies that people have agreed upon"?

6   One of the final lines in which film sees Dorothy Gale remark "Oh Auntie Em, there's no place like home"?

7   After an assassination attempt left him badly wounded, who said to his wife, "Honey, I forgot to duck"?

8   In the film *Duck Soup*, who stated "Those are my principles, and if you don't like them...well, I have others."

9   Which British Prime Minister of the 1960s and 1970s observed that "a week is a long time in politics"?

10 The day after the 9/11 attacks, who reportedly said "40 Wall Street actually was the second-tallest building in downtown Manhattan, so now it's the tallest"?

11 "I can resist anything, except temptation" is a quote from *Lady Windermere's Fan*, a play written by who?

12 Which host of *Blankety Blank* once said of his own show, "the prizes are so bad, some people leave them in the foyer"?

13 Amid a 1960s political scandal, who once said "discretion is a polite word for hypocrisy"?

14 "Many young men die at age 25, but are not buried until they're 75." So said which Founding Father?

15 "How lucky I am to have something that makes saying goodbye so hard" was a poignant quote from which children's book character?

16 "I never dreamed about success, I worked for it." So said which fashion designer, the only woman on *Time* magazine's 1998 list of the 20 most influential 20th century "business geniuses"?

17 Which former *Celebrity Big Brother* winner once revealed "I thought the sun and the moon were the same thing; turns out they're not"?

18 "A man who can list on his CV: rapper, comedian, presenter, actor, writer – all after the word 'failed'." Which presenter and comedian said this about Richard Blackwood?

19 In 1973, which Education Secretary said "I don't think there will be a woman Prime Minister in my lifetime"?

20 Which American futurist author wrote, "we have never seen a totally sane human being"?

Answers to QUIZ 350 – October

1	Cuba	11	Sinéad O'Connor
2	A Soviet submarine	12	Iceland
3	Women	13	George Foreman (Ali won)
4	U2	14	*Abbey Road*
5	Ford Model T	15	Gunfight at the O.K. Corral
6	Admiral Lord Nelson	16	Breathalyser
7	The League of Nations	17	R101
8	Yom Kippur War	18	Golf
9	Martin Luther	19	Their Olympic bronze medals; only Macleod ever got hers back
10	Margaret Thatcher	20	Prue Leith (one of the judges)

ANSWERS ON PAGE 355

1   Horses are measured in hands; how many inches are there in a hand?

2   Dale Gribble is a character in which cartoon series?

3   At least seven women were reported to have committed suicide due to the death of which silent movie star in 1926?

4   What is the chemical symbol for the element manganese?

5   The name of the Arctic is derived from the Greek word for which animal?

6   The lateral sulcus or Sylvian Fissure is part of which organ of the body?

7   In the game of Battleship®, five hits are required to destroy which type of craft?

8   In 1968, who became the first English team to win football's European Cup?

9   Winston Churchill described which country as "a riddle, wrapped in a mystery, inside an enigma"?

10   In 2001, Warsaw international airport was named for which composer?

11   Timothy Dalton played the part of James Bond in which two movies?

12   Saltwater, quinkana and Orinoco are all types of what animal?

13   In which iconic London building is the Whispering Gallery located?

14   Before becoming President himself, Joe Biden served twice as Vice President to whom?

15   Dana International, the 1998 Eurovision Song Contest winner, represented which country?

16   Kigali is the capital of which African country?

17   Which 1994 James Cameron film was the first Hollywood film to ever have a $100 million budget?

18   What colour are the "black boxes" on commercial aircraft?

19   Reportedly, which musician once said "I like Beethoven, especially the poems"?

20   O'Hare International Airport is located in which American city?

Easy

Medium

Hard

Answers to QUIZ 351 – Pot Luck

1	Parallel	11	Upper case
2	Syzygy (pronounced si-zi-gee)	12	Table tennis
3	Hypothalamus	13	Boddington's
4	Seven	14	Thursday
5	Wigan Athletic	15	Heathrow
6	Penguin	16	Victoria Cross
7	BBC Radio 1	17	*Dracula*
8	Afghanistan and Pakistan	18	Ian Beale
9	California	19	*The Tempest*
10	Manhattan	20	Ken Dodd

Name these people, whose names all have the initials PP.

1

2

3

4

5

6

7

8

9

Answers to QUIZ 352 – Who Said It?

1	Winston Churchill	11	Oscar Wilde
2	Julius Caesar	12	Les Dawson
3	Muhammad Ali	13	Christine Keeler
4	Brian Clough	14	Benjamin Franklin
5	Napoleon Bonaparte	15	Winnie-the-Pooh
6	*The Wizard of Oz*	16	Estée Lauder
7	Ronald Reagan	17	Chantelle Houghton
8	Groucho Marx	18	Mark Lamarr (who later also called him "Won't Smith")
9	Harold Wilson	19	Margaret Thatcher
10	Donald Trump	20	Robert Anton Wilson

ANSWERS ON PAGE 357

1   Robyn, Roxette and The Cardigans are all musical acts from which country?

2   A dirigible is another name for a what?

3   In the 1930s, the Arlington Experimental hemp farm in Alexandria, Virginia, was cleared in order to build what?

4   Which musician died of a heart attack while playing his signature tune, *Tiptoe Through The Tulips*?

5   In the *Super Mario* video game franchise, what is Mario's surname?

6   Which condition sees facial blood vessels enlarge, giving the cheeks and nose a flushed, red appearance?

7   Which is the only Major League Baseball team in Canada?

8   Crécy was the first major battle in which war?

9   Who was the headline act at the New Year's Eve 1989 concert at Berlin's Brandenburg Gate?

10 What size of paper is twice as big as A5?

11 Which band bought the Clarence Hotel in Dublin in 1992?

12 "Satchmo" was the nickname of which jazz legend?

13 An apterous insect is lacking what?

14 On UK motorways, what background colour do information signs have?

15 Jennifer Aniston's godfather was which other famous actor, who no doubt loved her as a baby?

16 For whatever reason, Australian businessman Clive Palmer is funding the building of an exact copy of what?

17 How old was a man called Hunter Rountree when he robbed a bank in Abilene, Texas on 12th August 2003?

18 Which *Doctor Who* spin-off series had a name that was an anagram of Doctor Who?

19 As mentioned in the war song *Pack Up Your Troubles*, a lucifer is what type of object?

20 On a Monopoly™ board, which colour properties are the cheapest?

Easy

Medium

Hard

Answers to QUIZ 353 – Pot Luck

1	Four	11	*The Living Daylights* and *Licence to Kill*
2	*King of the Hill*	12	Crocodile
3	Rudolph Valentino	13	St Paul's Cathedral
4	Mn (Mg is magnesium; M is unused)	14	Barack Obama
5	Bear	15	Israel
6	Brain	16	Rwanda
7	Aircraft carrier	17	*True Lies*
8	Manchester United	18	Orange (so that they are easier to find)
9	Russia	19	Ringo Starr
10	Frédéric Chopin	20	Chicago

Easy

1 In order to discourage unserious candidates, how much of a deposit is required when submitting nomination papers in a UK general election?

2 Which Labour MP for Sheffield Brightside served as the UK's first blind Cabinet Minister?

3 Albeit only on a temporary basis, who in 1994 became the first woman to lead the Labour Party?

4 In a 2017 interview, what did Theresa May claim was the naughtiest thing she had ever done?

5 Likely due to polio, which US President was paralysed from the waist down, a fact largely covered up during his 12 years in office?

6 In political parlance, what does "NIMBY" stand for?

7 How long does each session of Prime Minister's Questions last?

8 Who was the first British Prime Minister to move into 10 Downing Street without a legal spouse accompanying them?

9 Gordon Brown was forced to apologise to Labour supporter Gillian Duffy after a hot mic caught him referring to her as what?

10 How many readings must a bill have in the House of Commons before being voted on?

11 When Prime Minister Robert Gascoyne-Cecil, Lord Salisbury promoted his nephew A. J. Balfour to Chief Secretary for Ireland, what phrase was spawned?

12 The leadership of which political party was contested in 1995 by two Johns?

13 Other than when being called to speak, when is the only time names are used in the House of Commons?

14 Constituencies in which two rival English cities compete every general election to see which can declare their results the fastest?

Medium

15 Upon becoming the inaugural chancellor of the North German Confederation in 1867, who is said to have stated "Politics is the art of the possible"?

16 In political terminology, "doves" are those who seek to resolve international conflicts without the threat of force; which bird represents the opposite approach?

17 Before entering politics, which Liberal Democrat politician held the British 100 metres record from 1967 to 1974?

18 On a walkabout of Newcastle upon Tyne in 2020, which controversial politician had a milkshake tipped over him?

19 As of 2022, who is the only UKIP candidate to win a seat in a General Election?

20 In 2020, who became the first MP of the Green Party?

Hard

Answers to QUIZ 354 – PP

1 Patsy Palmer
2 Peter Purves
3 Paul Pogba
4 Pete Postlethwaite
5 Pablo Picasso
6 Priscilla Presley
7 Philip Pullman
8 Paul Potts
9 Paula Patton

1   In computing terminology, what does the acronym WYSIWYG stand for?

2   On 17th October 1981 and 25th September 1982, what took place in the car park of the Caesar's Palace hotel in Las Vegas?

3   "Hey, can I try on your yellow dress?" is the final line of which 1982 romantic comedy film?

4   In 2020, who replaced Sandi Toksvig as a presenter of *The Great British Bake Off*?

5   Arthur Jefferson was the real name of which comic actor?

6   Published a few months after his death, 1991's *The Minpins* was the last literary work by which author?

7   A felucca is a type of what mode of transport?

8   In 2016, who stepped down as a *Top Gear* presenter after just one series?

9   Toxaemia is a generic term for what?

10 Which stories of a mischievous schoolboy were written by Richmal Crompton?

11 The English Premier League debuted in which year?

12 Which Scooby-Doo character wears a baggy orange jumper and has a tendency to lose her glasses?

13 Which of Henry VIII's wives had previously been his sister-in-law?

14 Bernard Cribbins and Snoop Dogg have both appeared in TV adverts for which food delivery service?

15 Which Kentish town on the banks of the River Thames lies opposite the Essex town of Tilbury?

16 Vermilion is a shade of what colour?

17 The Sanskrit poem *Bhagavad Gita* is one of the sacred texts of which major world religion?

18 In April 2022, who became the first British No.1 tennis player in either singles or doubles not to have the surname Murray?

19 Which two utilities feature on the standard UK Monopoly™ board?

20 How many rivers are there in Saudi Arabia?

Easy

Medium

Hard

Answers to QUIZ 355 – Pot Luck

1	Sweden	11	U2
2	Airship	12	Louis Armstrong
3	The Pentagon	13	Wings
4	Tiny Tim	14	Blue
5	Mario (and yes, that does mean that Luigi's full name is Luigi Mario)	15	Telly Savalas
		16	The *Titanic*
6	Rosacea	17	91
7	Toronto Blue Jays	18	Torchwood
8	Hundred Years' War	19	Match
9	David Hasselhoff	20	Brown
10	A4		

Easy

1. During *Pokémon Red & Blue*, which Pokémon was nearly hunted into extinction?
2. How can you tell if a Pikachu is female?
3. Which is the only first generation Pokémon that can devolve?
4. When exposed to it, which stone makes Jigglypuff into Wigglytuff?
5. What is the name of the "directory" of Pokémon filled out by players through encountering and capturing them?
6. Which Pokémon wears a skull on its head to conceal its tears?
7. If Charmander's flame on its tail goes out, what happens to it?
8. In the *Pokémon* series, what is the final evolution of Bulbosaur?
9. Which Pokémon evolves into Hitmonchan if Attack is less than Defense, into Hitmonlee if the other way around, and into Hitmontop if they are equal?
10. Which is the first stage evolution of Growlithe?
11. In the *Pokémon* universe, which city has a "Mysterious Blue Aura" surrounding it?
12. Which Pokémon wanders the streets on a nightly basis to look for dropped loose change?
13. Who was the voice of Detective Pikachu in the film of the same name?
14. Which Pokémon's life mainly consists of sleeping and eating, and, when it is awake, eating about 900 pounds of food before going back to sleep?
15. What are the colours of a typical Poké ball?
16. Which 2016 Pokémon mobile game combines the game with the real world and gaming through augmented reality?
17. Which member of Team Rocket once remarked, "we have a proud tradition of failure to uphold"?
18. What was the first Pokémon that Ash caught himself in the wild?
19. In the season two episode *Bulbasaur and the Hidden Village*, which Pokémon did Misty want to catch?
20. To compete with Pokémon, Bandai introduced which range of monsters with their own cards and toys in 1997?

Medium

Hard

ANSWERS ON PAGE **361**

1   In heraldry, "murrey" refers to which colour?

2   At the 1998 *BRIT* Awards, John Prescott was covered in a bucket of water thrown by a member of which band?

3   In cricket, which animal's name is used to reflect when a batsman fails to score any runs?

4   Outside of London, which county has the highest proportion of second homes across England and Wales?

5   The philtrum is a part of what area of the body?

6   Who is the longest-reigning King in English history?

7   Who made his film acting debut in 1981's *Sizzle Beach, U.S.A.* and his directorial debut with 1990's *Dances With Wolves*?

8   It is a running joke in the culture of Aussie Rules Football players to see who can grow the most extravagant example of which hairstyle?

9   Decidophobia is the fear of what?

10 What three-word response did mountaineer George Mallory give to a reporter who asked him why he wanted to climb Mount Everest?

11 Longchamp is a racecourse in which city?

12 How did Jimi Heselden, the owner of the *Segway* robotic transportation company, die?

13 Having been imported by Pablo Escobar, which non-native destructive animal is now wild in the Colombian countryside, leading to a sterilisation programme?

14 In economic terms, what does the acronym GDP stand for?

15 The Koekelberg Basilica, Mannekin Pis and Atomium are all located in which European capital city?

16 In 2000, which model became the face of Yves Saint-Laurent's *Opium* perfume?

17 The board of which game is divided into ranks and files?

18 Pharynx is the scientific name for which part of the body?

19 The tympanic membrane is the scientific name for what part of the body?

20 What type of animal appears in the logo for Bacardi®?

Easy

Medium

Hard

Answers to QUIZ 357 – Pot Luck

1	What you see is what you get	11	1992
2	The Formula 1 American Grand Prix	12	Velma
3	*Tootsie*	13	Catherine of Aragon
4	Matt Lucas	14	Just Eat
5	Stan Laurel	15	Gravesend
6	Roald Dahl	16	Red
7	Boat	17	Hinduism
8	Chris Evans	18	Joe Salisbury
9	Blood poisoning	19	Waterworks and the Electric Company
10	*Just William*	20	Zero

Easy

1. Which Grand Slam tennis tournament was 2021 Sports Personality of the Year winner Emma Raducanu victorious in?

2. What is the relationship between the 1971 and 2006 Sports Personality of the Year winners?

3. As of 2021, who is the only rugby league player to have ever featured in the top three in the Sports Personality of the Year award?

4. 1984 is the only time that more than one individual has won the Sports Personality of the Year award; who won it that year?

5. What was unique about the top three finishers in the 1962 Sports Personality of the Year award?

6. Whose seven winners in seven races at Ascot helped him to a third place finish in the 1996 Sports Personality of the Year award?

7. Which athlete has achieved the most top three finishes without ever winning the Sports Personality of the Year award?

8. Which cricketer's achievement of 19 wickets in an Ashes Test in 1956 helped to earn him that year's Sports Personality of the Year award?

9. As of 2021, how many Formula 1 World Champions have won the Sports Personality of the Year award?

10. As of 2021, who is the only darts player to have ever featured in the top three finishers of the Sports Personality of the Year award?

11. As of 2021, who is the only jockey to have won the Sports Personality of the Year award?

Medium

12. Which broadcaster, best known for his boxing commentaries, presented the Sports Personality of the Year award from 1968 to 1985?

13. Who won the Sports Personality Team of the Year award for 2005?

14. Which golfer only finished second in both the 1969 and 1970 Sports Personality of the Year awards, despite winning Majors in both those years?

15. Greg Rusedski won the Sports Personality of the Year award 1997, with Tim Henman as runner-up; how many career Grand Slam finals did they reach combined?

16. In which country was 2021 Sports Personality of the Year award winner Emma Raducanu born?

17. 2004 Sports Personality of the Year award winner Kelly Holmes won Olympic gold medals in which two Athletics events that year?

18. Barry Briggs finished second in the Sports Personality of the Year award twice in the 1960s for his achievements in which sport?

19. Despite breaking the four minute mile barrier, Roger Bannister only finished second in the inaugural Sports Personality of the Year contest, to who?

20. *The Hydro*, which hosted the 2014 Sports Personality of the Year award ceremony, is an arena in which city?

Hard

1   The north pole of which planet is shaped in an almost-perfect hexagon?

2   Tequila is made from which variety of cactus?

3   Which scoring space is found in the corners of a Scrabble® board?

4   "I've got sunshine on a cloudy day. When it's cold outside, I've got the month of May" are the opening lines to which song?

5   Sam Quek won an Olympic gold medal in which sport?

6   Kelpers are people living in or native to which British Overseas Territory?

7   On account of his poor skills in battle, which English King had the nickname "Lackland"?

8   In computing terminology, what does the acronym LAN stand for?

9   A daffodil appears on the badge of which Welsh county cricket team?

10 Silbury Hill in Wiltshire is the largest what in Europe?

11 Cruciverbalists are lovers of what type of puzzle?

12 In musical terms, what type of note is twice as long as a quaver?

13 Andrea, Sharon, Caroline and Jim formed which Irish sibling band?

14 Which is the largest moon in the solar system?

15 Tofu is made from mashed-up what?

16 Which musical instrument is used in the Guinness® logo?

17 Which actor played Davy Jones in the *Pirates of the Caribbean* film series and Billy Mack in *Love Actually*?

18 Which London borough – also its most populous – has a name which is also a slang term for hair?

19 92220 *Evening Star* was the last example of what built in Britain?

20 Which two London Underground lines run to Heathrow Airport?

Easy

Medium

Hard

Answers to QUIZ 359 – Pot Luck

1	Maroon	11	Paris
2	Chumbawamba	12	He accidentally rode a Segway off a cliff
3	A duck	13	Hippopotamus
4	Norfolk	14	Gross domestic product
5	Lip – it is the ridge in the top lip	15	Brussels
6	George III (1760-1820)	16	Sophie Dahl
7	Kevin Costner	17	Chess
8	Mullet	18	Throat
9	Making decisions	19	Eardrum
10	"Because it's there"	20	Bat

1   Which peacekeeping organisation was in 1917 the recipient of the only Nobel Peace Prize awarded during World War I?

2   Even though he won the 2000 Nobel Prize for Literature, which writer's books are banned in his native China?

3   In which decade was the Nobel Prize for Economics, the most recent addition to the awards, introduced?

4   1922 Physics Laureate Niels Bohr escaped from Denmark to which country by boat during World War II?

5   Which humanitarian organisation won the 2020 Nobel Peace Prize?

6   Which British playwright, whose works included *The Homecoming* and *Victoria Station*, won the 2005 Literature Prize?

7   What was unusual about Jean-Paul Sartre being awarded the 1964 Literature Prize?

8   Which Chilean poet won the 1971 Nobel Prize for Literature, in spite of the judging panel's concerns about his "communist tendencies"?

9   Jonathan Penrose, the brother of 2020 Physics Laureate Roger Penrose, is a ten-time British Champion in what game?

10   V.S. Naipaul, the Literature Laureate in 2001, won the Booker Prize in 1971 for which novel?

11   As of 2022, how many US Presidents have won the Nobel Peace Prize?

12   Who portrayed 1907 Literature winner Rudyard Kipling in the Oscar-nominated 1975 film *The Man Who Would Be King*?

13   The 2004 BBC film *Hawking* contextualised the Nobel Prize-winning achievements of Arno Penzias and Robert Wilson in which decade?

14   Which American singer-songwriter was awarded the 2016 Nobel Prize in Literature?

15   Who won the 1964 Nobel Prize in Chemistry for her work in discovering the structure of Vitamin B12?

16   Which 1934 Nobel Peace Prize Laureate is the only person to have served three different terms in three different decades as leader of the Labour Party?

17   In which country was 2007 Nobel Literature Prize Laureate Doris Lessing born?

18   Yoshinori Ohsumi, a specialist in autophagy, won which Nobel Prize in 2016?

19   Which world leader won the 1990 Nobel Peace Prize?

20   In which year were the first Nobel Prizes awarded?

Easy / **Medium** / **Hard**

1 What name is shared by a former attacking midfielder who played 56 times for England, and the actor who played Sean Wallace in *Gangs of London*?

2 Once a decorative frieze on the Parthenon in Athens, the Elgin Marbles are controversially located in which museum?

3 Jessie the yodelling cowgirl is a recurring character in which animated film series?

4 *Confessions Part II* was a 2004 hit for which R&B singer?

5 Margaret Keenan made the news in January 2021 for what reason?

6 Not counting Greenland, which country has the world's lowest population density, at only five people per square mile?

7 In publishing and word processing, what does kerning refer to in a document?

8 In transportation terms, what links Venice, Melbourne city centre, East Jerusalem Old City and the Channel Island of Sark?

9 A glossectomy is the removal of part or all of which part of the body?

10 In darts, which part of the board is referred to as "The Mad House"?

11 Including the front pincers, how many legs does a lobster have?

12 What did a team led by Robert Ballard find on 1st September 1985?

13 Now usually meant disparagingly, "the old gray lady" is historically a nickname for which major international newspaper?

14 *The Wire* and *Hairspray* are both predominantly set in which US city?

15 Which portmanteau word describes a close but non-sexual relationship between two men?

16 Rapunzel syndrome is an intestinal condition caused by the compulsive eating of what?

17 Which Norwegian explorer and writer led the 1947 Kon-Tiki Expedition across the Pacific Ocean?

18 Constitutionally part of Denmark, which island archipelago lies halfway between Scotland and Iceland?

19 Hartford is the capital of which American state?

20 For the 1986 FIFA World Cup in Mexico, which item of food served as the mascot?

Easy

Medium

Hard

Answers to QUIZ 361 – Pot Luck

1	Saturn	11	Crosswords
2	Agave	12	Crotchet
3	Triple word score	13	The Corrs
4	*My Girl*	14	Ganymede
5	Hockey	15	Soya beans
6	Falkland Islands	16	Harp
7	John	17	Bill Nighy
8	Local Area Network	18	Barnet
9	Glamorgan	19	Steam locomotive
10	Artificial hill	20	Piccadilly and Elizabeth Lines

Easy

1 Which hard rock band had a 1992 hit with *November Rain*?
2 Who was assassinated on 22nd November 1963 in Dallas, Texas?
3 Where did a fire break out on 20th November 1992, causing over £36 million worth of damage?
4 In western Christianity, which feast is celebrated on 1st November?
5 On 10th November 1981, a patent was registered for which board game?
6 On 14th November 1973, who married Captain Mark Phillips at Westminster Abbey?
7 When vandals graffitied the Netflix headquarters in November 2015, what two words did they add to a sign at the entrance?
8 Which particularly bloody and bitter battle of World War I finally ended on 18th November 1916?
9 Which important piece of international infrastructure officially opened for the first time on 17th November 1869?
10 From November 2017, Twitter™ changed its upper limit on characters in a single tweet to how many?
11 In the USA, what holiday is celebrated on the fourth Thursday in November?

Medium

12 The Day of the Dead is an annual holiday celebrated on 2nd November in which country?
13 On the night of 14th November 1940, 449 German Luftwaffe bombers dropped 503 tons of bombs and 881 incendiaries on which city?
14 What burned down on 30th November 1936, 85 years after it was opened for the Great Exhibition?
15 Vladimir Kramnik became the world champion of what in November 2000?
16 Which American-born doctor was hanged at Pentonville Prison on 23rd November 1910 after poisoning his wife and dismembering her body?
17 Which UK government fundraising scheme launched in November 1994?
18 Which fashion designer opened his *Little Black Jacket* photo exhibition in Paris in November 2012?
19 In November 2013, which TV presenter got his first ever tattoo – a scorpion on his shoulder – at the age of 75?
20 Which retailer opened its first new UK store for more than 300 years at St Pancras railway station in November 2013?

Hard

Answers to QUIZ 362 – Nobel Prizes

1	International Red Cross	11	Four (Theodore Roosevelt, Wilson, Carter, Obama)
2	Gao Xingjian		
3	1960s	12	Christopher Plummer
4	Sweden	13	1970s
5	World Food Programme	14	Bob Dylan
6	Harold Pinter	15	Dorothy Hodgkin
7	He declined it	16	Arthur Henderson
8	Pablo Neruda	17	Iran
9	Chess	18	Medicine
10	*In A Free State*	19	Mikhail Gorbachev
		20	1901

1   When it began in July 1995, Amazon only sold what?

2   In 1952, Albert Einstein was offered, but declined, the opportunity to become president of which country?

3   A standard double-six domino set consists of how many tiles?

4   Which video game vendor has a name that is the value of a dime?

5   Actor Thomson, snooker player Virgo and poet Cooper-Clark are all famous Johns from which English city?

6   How many lines are in a sonnet?

7   Makka Pakka, Igglepiggle and the Ninky Nonk are characters in which TV show for toddlers?

8   Which manufacturer produces the Stratocaster® range of guitars?

9   In the name of the optical barcodes technology, what does QR code stand for?

10 What are the three light blue properties on a standard UK Monopoly™ board?

11 What name was given to the 7th December 1972 colour photograph of the entire Earth, the first ever taken by a human?

12 Cuthbert the Caterpillar, a chocolate cake from supermarket chain Aldi, was "sued" by which rival in April 2021?

13 Dai Woodham's scrapyard, once famed for its huge supply of British Rail rolling stock, was located in which town in South Wales?

14 In draughts, how many pieces does each player start with?

15 Derived from their supposed habit of wearing footwear with quiet rubber soles, "gumshoe" is a nickname for someone in what profession?

16 Which Italian green sauce is made of chopped parsley, lemon zest and garlic?

17 As measured in total passenger numbers, what was the world's busiest airport every year between 1998 and 2019?

18 *Guinness World Records* states that whose November 1963 murder was the world's first to ever be televised live?

19 Which one-time WBC heavyweight champion was well known for the phrase "know what I mean, 'Arry"?

20 Which golfer tied for sixth place at the 1998 US Masters at the age of 58?

Easy

Medium

Hard

Answers to QUIZ 363 – Pot Luck

1	Joe Cole	11	10
2	British Museum	12	The wreckage of the *Titanic*
3	*Toy Story*	13	*The New York Times*
4	Usher	14	Baltimore
5	She was the first person in the world to receive a COVID-19 vaccine	15	Bromance
6	Mongolia	16	Hair
7	The spacing between letters	17	Thor Heyerdahl
8	Cars are prohibited	18	The Faroe Islands
9	Tongue	19	Connecticut
10	Double one (because it can drive you mad)	20	A jalapeño pepper called Pique

1 *Toreros* and *matadors* are among the types of participant in which traditionally Spanish entertainment spectacle?

2 In Spanish, which term of address is to be used for a young and/or unmarried lady?

3 In Spanish cuisine, what are *patatas bravas*?

4 Marbella is a resort city on which of the Spanish *costas*?

5 Which novel by Ernest Hemingway was set during the Spanish Civil War?

6 Which Latin dance originated in the folkloric music traditions of the region of Andalusia?

7 In October 2009, who set the all-time appearance record for Spain's most successful football club, Real Madrid?

8 Which city is home to the oldest university in Spain?

9 Between 711 and 1492, which group of North African invaders ruled what is now Spain as a Muslim territory?

10 Which Spanish city features the Bear and the Strawberry Tree Statue, known to locals as *El Oso y El Madrono*?

11 In medieval Spain, which city was noted for its quality steel used in weaponry?

12 In 1099, which Spanish general was reputed to have won his final battle, despite dying before it began?

13 In which Spanish museum can you find over 140 paintings by Francisco Goya?

14 Who was the first – and, as of 2022, only – Spanish actress to have won an Oscar?

15 "The Garlic Wall" is a colloquial nickname for Spain's border with where?

16 Barcelona is the capital of which Spanish province?

17 Which city, the capital of Cantabria, gives its name to one of Europe's biggest banks?

18 Which range of mountains runs along the length of the north coast of Majorca?

19 Often called Spanish opera, what term is given to theatrical plays that contain musical acts, usually with characters representing the working classes?

20 Madrid has been the capital of Spain since 1561, except for a brief period between 1601 and 1606, when which city briefly took over?

Easy | **Medium** | **Hard**

Answers to QUIZ 364 – November

1	Guns N' Roses	11	Thanksgiving
2	John F. Kennedy	12	Mexico
3	Windsor Castle	13	Coventry
4	All Saints' Day	14	Crystal Palace
5	Trivial Pursuit™	15	Chess
6	Princess Anne	16	Dr Crippen
7	"...and chill"	17	The National Lottery
8	Battle of the Somme	18	Karl Lagerfeld
9	Suez Canal	19	David Dimbleby
10	280	20	Fortnum and Mason

1   Where on the body would you wear muffs?

2   James I and Charles I were members of which royal house?

3   Which sci-fi character has been played in film by Leonard Nimoy and Zachary Quinto?

4   Between 2004 and 2017, the Cassini-Huygens space-research mission flew within the orbit of which planet?

5   Chief scout Edward Michael Grylls goes by what animal nickname?

6   What are the first three words of the Bible?

7   Which northern English city was known by the Romans as *Deva Victrix*?

8   According to the proverb, what does a leopard never change?

9   What do Australians call "the dunny"?

10   Breaking a mirror is said to confer how many years of bad luck?

11   The Yukon river runs through which American state?

12   Texel, Dorper and Romney Marsh are types of which farmyard animal?

13   Which Olympic sport takes place in a velodrome?

14   Gemma Collins rose to fame through her appearances on which ITV reality series?

15   On 14th October 1947, Chuck Yeager became the first person in history to break what?

16   Which South American country has *tango* as its national dance and *pato* as its national sport?

17   Who originally presented the UK version of *The Weakest Link* from 2000 to 2012?

18   The adjective Cantonese is often, though not correctly, used as a synonym for which nationality?

19   Since the departure of Jeremy Vine, which BBC current affairs documentary series has been hosted by guest presenters?

20   In English, which country's name comes first alphabetically?

Easy

Medium

Hard

Answers to QUIZ 365 – Pot Luck

1	Books	12	Marks and Spencer's Colin the Caterpillar
2	Israel	13	Barry
3	28	14	12
4	Tencent	15	Private detective
5	Salford	16	Gremolata
6	14	17	Hartsfield–Jackson Atlanta International Airport, USA
7	*In The Night Garden*	18	Lee Harvey Oswald – others, while filmed and televised (including JFK two days before), were not broadcast live
8	Fender®		
9	Quick response		
10	The Angel, Islington; Euston Road; Pentonville Road	19	Frank Bruno
11	The Blue Marble	20	Jack Nicklaus

Easy

1. In the 2009 Disney film *Up*, Carl Fredricksen and Explorer Russell embark on an adventure to which continent?

2. The 1998 release *Up* was the eleventh studio album for which band, whose previous releases included *Automatic For The People*?

3. Which 1968 "kitchen sink" British drama film stars Suzy Kendall as a young woman sacrificing luxuries to "slum it" in a London suburb?

4. Which car manufacturing giant produces the *up!* city car model?

5. "just setting up my twttr" was the first-ever tweet published on Twitter™, written by which co-founder of the site?

6. One of the final lines of which classic film sees Police Captain Louis Renault order his men to "round up the usual suspects"?

7. The song *Pumped Up Kicks* was the breakthrough hit for which American indie pop band in 2011?

8. Leonardo DiCaprio and Jennifer Lawrence star as two astronomers in which 2021 satirical black comedy film?

9. Rick Astley's 1987 hit *Never Gonna Give You Up* became the subject of which internet meme more than two decades later?

10. "What's up, Doc?" was the catchphrase of which Warner Brothers cartoon character?

11. Police officers Adam Hunter, Axel Stone and Blaze Fielding were the playable characters in which 1991 side-scrolling beat 'em up game from SEGA?

12. Developed from the red circle in its logo, the character Cool Spot is an anthropomorphic mascot for which lemon-lime flavoured fizzy soft drink?

Medium

13. "All right, Mr. DeMille, I'm ready for my close-up." is the final line in which Billy Wilder film, as spoken by Norma Desmond?

14. Along with down, charm, strange, top and bottom, up is one of the six "flavours" of what type of sub-atomic elementary particle?

15. "Lock her up" was a much-used slogan in Donald Trump's 2016 US Presidential campaign, referring to who, his Democratic opponent?

16. Every year from 1981 to 2021, which brand of pickup truck was the best selling vehicle in the United States?

17. In bridge, what term is used to refer to playing low to a trick led by the opponents, losing it intentionally, in order to sever their communication?

18. Which British inventor and former stunt man designed and patented the wind-up radio in 1991?

19. In a 2008 survey by Debenhams, which type of push-up bra was almost unanimously voted as the greatest innovation in fashion history?

20. Which African country was formerly known as Upper Volta?

Hard

ANSWERS ON PAGE **371**

1. What colour are the four stars on the flag of New Zealand?
2. Tej Lelvani joined the cast of which BBC business-themed reality TV show in 2017?
3. Who stepped down as the main presenter of *BBC Breakfast* in 2016 after fifteen years?
4. What is the main fruit found in Ribena?
5. Who wrote the 1722 novel *Moll Flanders*?
6. Which English football team plays its home matches at Stamford Bridge?
7. The Newman Society, the Piers Gaveston Society and the Bullingdon Club are all student organisations at which university?
8. Which sport is played at The Oval in London and the Kensington Oval in Barbados?
9. Harley Street in London is regularly associated with which profession?
10. From the group's founding in 1975 until his death in 2015, who was the only continuous member of the band Motörhead?
11. On a standard roulette wheel, what colour is the zero?
12. What forename is also the name of the capital of the Falkland Islands?
13. Part of the Motown sound, which male vocal group had a 1967 hit on both sides of the Atlantic with *Reach Out I'll Be There*?
14. What was Mickey Mouse's original name?
15. What are traditionally made and repaired by a cobbler?
16. The northern hemisphere's summer solstice occurs in which month?
17. Chas Newby, Jimmie Nicol, Neil Aspinall and Brian Epstein were among the people to at various times receive what nickname?
18. Which series of video games first released in 2005 sees players use a guitar-shaped game controller to mimic playing tunes?
19. Which city in Rajasthan, India, has riding breeches named after it?
20. As of 2022, who is the only heavyweight boxing champion to have finished his career undefeated?

Answers to QUIZ 367 – Pot Luck

1	Hands	11	Alaska
2	Stuart	12	Sheep
3	Mr Spock from *Star Trek*	13	Cycling
4	Saturn	14	*The Only Way Is Essex*
5	Bear	15	The sound barrier
6	In the beginning	16	Argentina
7	Chester	17	Anne Robinson
8	Its spots	18	Chinese
9	Toilet	19	*Panorama*
10	Seven	20	Afghanistan

Can you identify these acts, all of whom have won the Eurovision Song Contest?
(No bonus points for songs and countries, but go for it anyway.)

Easy

1

2

3

Medium

4

5

6

7

8

9

Hard

Answers to QUIZ 368 – Up

1	South America	11	*Streets of Rage*
2	R.E.M.	12	7up®
3	*Up The Junction*	13	*Sunset Boulevard*
4	Volkswagen	14	Quark
5	Jack Dorsey	15	Hillary Clinton
6	*Casablanca*	16	Ford F150
7	Foster the People	17	Hold up
8	*Don't Look Up*	18	Trevor Baylis
9	Rickrolling	19	Wonderbra
10	Bugs Bunny	20	Burkina Faso

1   Edvard Eriksen's bronze statue, *The Little Mermaid,* sits in a harbour in which European capital city?

2   In which year did the Battle of Hastings take place?

3   Mount Kilimanjaro is located in which country?

4   What do Americans and Australians call courgettes?

5   Also known as the Pentateuch (from the Greek for "five books"), the Torah is a compilation of what?

6   Which series of children's books featured the Pevensie children, Peter, Edmund, Lucy and Susan?

7   The phrase "crossing the Rubicon" means to pass the point of no return; what is or was the Rubicon?

8   Better known as Canaletto, Giovanni Antonio Canal was an Italian painter from which city?

9   In the *Harry Potter* franchise, who was the half-blood prince?

10 ABBA were formed in which country?

11 The 1818 sonnet *Ozymandias* was written by which English Romantic poet?

12 In the Royal Navy and US Navy, what is the lowest rank of officer?

13 In astronomy, what name is given to planets that do not orbit any star?

14 On a dart board, which number is bottom centre?

15 Which two seas are connected by the Suez Canal?

16 Aniseed comes from which plant?

17 Which actor has been married to both Demi Moore and Mila Kunis?

18 As seen on DVD menus, which country is known as Suomi in its native language?

19 Terry Gilliam directed Johnny Depp and Benicio del Toro in which "stoner" culture film?

20 The exotic dancer and World War I spy better known by the stage name Mata Hari was of what nationality?

Easy

Medium

Hard

Answers to QUIZ 369 – Pot Luck

1	Red (the Australian flag has six white ones)	11	Green
2	*Dragon's Den*	12	Stanley
3	Bill Turnbull	13	Four Tops
4	Blackcurrant	14	Mortimer Mouse
5	Daniel Defoe	15	Shoes
6	Chelsea	16	June
7	University of Oxford	17	"The Fifth Beatle"
8	Cricket	18	*Guitar Hero*
9	The medical profession	19	Jodhpur
10	Ian "Lemmy" Kilmister	20	Rocky Marciano

1   Peter Kay starred as working men's club owner Brian Potter in which sitcom of the 2000s?
2   Which football manager led Nottingham Forest to European Cup victories in both 1978-79 and 1979-80?
3   What name is shared by a football commentator of nine FIFA World Cups, and a former English rugby union hooker?
4   Which actor is the oldest man to have reached the magnetic North Pole on foot, where he says he punched a polar bear on the nose?
5   Alongside roles in *X-Men 2*, *The Long Kiss Goodnight* and *Zodiac*, which Scotsman was the first actor to portray Hannibal Lecter on film in 1986's *Manhunter*?
6   Which broadcaster and professor of particle physics was formerly also the keyboard player for the British bands D:Ream and Dare?
7   Who founded the Rolling Stones in May 1962, was fired by them in June 1969, and died a month later?
8   Which former boy band member once ran over his own head while leaning out of his car to be sick after eating too many baked potatoes?
9   Who managed the Beatles from 1962 until his death in 1967?
10 In film, who was not the Messiah, but a very naughty boy?
11 Prior to going solo, which glam band did Brian Eno play keyboards in?
12 Which guitarist has almost exclusively used a guitar he calls The Red Special since the 1960s?
13 In 2009, who said "Banksy should have been put down at birth. It's no good as art, drawing or painting. His work has no virtue"?

14 Famous for gaffes and giggles, which former Test Match Special commentator broke down in laughter when Ian Botham once failed to get his leg over?
15 Which Scotsman scored 127 goals for Manchester United between 1987 and 1998?
16 Ambroise in the French language version became Brian in the English language version of which TV show?
17 Brian Wilde played Walter Dewhurst (aka Foggy) in which long-running BBC sitcom?
18 Which long-serving BBC foreign correspondent was best known for his coverage of the Falklands war?
19 Glaswegian comedian, author and Twitch streamer Brian Limond performs under what mononym?
20 Brian Belo won the eighth series of which reality TV show?

Answers to QUIZ 370 – Eurovision Winners

1   ABBA
2   Sandie Shaw
3   Buck's Fizz
4   Katrina and the Waves
5   Lordi
6   Dana International
7   Jamala
8   Johnny Logan
9   Gigliola Cinquetti

1   Which comedian's radio and TV series character lived at 23 Railway Cuttings, East Cheam?
2   Brown Willy, on Bodmin Moor, is the highest point in which English county?
3   What colour precedes "Rider" in a work by Wassily Kandinsky and "Boy" in a work by Thomas Gainsborough?
4   Opening in 2017, the Queensferry Bridge crosses which body of water?
5   In the children's book of the same name, what does the Very Hungry Caterpillar eat first on the Monday?
6   Which actor voices the spoken word sequence at the end of Michael Jackson's *Thriller*?
7   An object described as stellate is what shape?
8   In Gioachino Rossini's opera, which character is the titular Barber of Seville?
9   Who was the bass guitarist for the Rolling Stones between 1962 and 1993?
10   Warrigal is an alternative name for which Australian animal?
11   Along with Bob Geldof, who was the co-organiser of the original Live Aid concert?
12   What is the colourful stage name of singer Alecia Beth Moore?
13   How many people sit on the jury in an English courtroom?
14   Wrestler Steve Borden and musician Gordon Sumner share what stage name?
15   What links a 1935 Alfred Hitchcock film and the old Wembley stadium?
16   By what name is the temperature -273.15 degrees Celsius, or 0 degrees Kelvin, better known?
17   *Original Pirate Material* was the breakthrough 2001 album for which act?
18   Stabilo, edding and Sharpie® are all brands of what?
19   With the exception of Liberia, which was the only African country not to be colonised amid the Scramble for Africa?
20   Christopher Cockerell invented which form of transport in the 1950s?

Easy

Medium

Hard

Answers to QUIZ 371 – Pot Luck

1	Copenhagen	11	Percy Bysshe Shelley
2	1066	12	Midshipman
3	Tanzania	13	Rogue planets
4	Zucchini	14	Three
5	The first five books of the Bible	15	Mediterranean Sea and Red Sea
6	*The Chronicles of Narnia*	16	Anise (hence the name)
7	A river in Northern Italy	17	Ashton Kutcher
8	Venice (fittingly)	18	Finland
9	Severus Snape	19	*Fear and Loathing in Las Vegas*
10	Sweden	20	Dutch

Easy

1   During the Crimean War, what did Florence Nightingale help to develop and propagate?
2   In which war was the Gallipoli Campaign fought?
3   During which war did British forces introduce the first concentration camps?
4   The Battle of St Albans started and the Battle of Bosworth ended which war?
5   In World War II, what name was given to the Allies' research and development efforts that produced the first nuclear weapons?
6   At what country estate in Buckinghamshire was the World War II German Enigma code broken?
7   Who were the two competing sides in the English Civil War?
8   Which European country fought a civil war between 1936 and 1939?
9   The Soviet Union's 1979 invasion of which country led to a boycott of the 1980 Moscow Olympic Games?
10 A conflict between Britain and Spain lasting from 1739 to 1748 in the Caribbean Sea had what body part for a name?
11 King Richard III was killed in action at which battle?
12 A British World War II song spoke of "going to hang out the washing" on which German defensive line?
13 The Victoria Cross was introduced in Great Britain on 29th January 1856 to commemorate soldiers in what war?
14 Whose name has became synonymous in America with traitors after he attempted to sell West Point to the British?

Medium

15 Following the sinking of the Battleship Maine in Havana harbour, on which country did the United States declare war in 1898?
16 Why is a man named Stanislav Yevgrafovich Petrov often credited with "saving the world"?
17 During which conflict did the Battle of Goose Green take place?
18 Which Emperor's death in 68 AD led to the first Roman civil war and The Year of the Four Emperors?
19 In which Libyan seaport did Australian forces endure a long siege in World War II?
20 The Peace of Vereeniging ended which war?

Hard

Answers to QUIZ 372 – Brians of Britain

1	*Phoenix Nights*	11	Roxy Music
2	Brian Clough	12	Brian May
3	Brian Moore	13	Brian Sewell
4	Brian Blessed	14	Brian Johnston
5	Brian Cox	15	Brian McClair
6	Brian Cox (the other one)	16	*The Magic Roundabout*
7	Brian Jones	17	*Last of the Summer Wine*
8	Brian Harvey	18	Brian Hanrahan
9	Brian Epstein	19	Limmy
10	Brian Cohen (from *The Life of Brian*)	20	*Big Brother*

ANSWERS ON PAGE 377

1   What designation denotes the "happy medium" between hard and soft on the graphite scale of pencil lead?

2   Fromology is the study of which food?

3   The festival of *Oktoberfest* is held annually in which city?

4   Shiitake is what type of food?

5   Who was the British Prime Minister immediately before David Cameron?

6   Maris Piper, Charlotte and King Edward are varieties of what?

7   Newquay, widely regarded as the surfing capital of the United Kingdom, is located in which county?

8   Which 20th century conflict was described at the time as "The War to End All Wars"?

9   Which 17th century English and Scottish monarch wrote the anti-smoking treatise *A Counterblaste to Tobacco*?

10 In the medical profession, what do the initials GP stand for?

11 How many states make up the United States of America?

12 On 13th March 1991, ten people were killed in a 51-car pile-up on which motorway?

13 Independent local radio station Breezy Radio broadcasts to which country of the United Kingdom?

14 The five-word title of which of William Shakespeare's plays is also a proverb?

15 Which common waste-product gas has the chemical formula CH_4?

16 In music, what term describes the character or quality of an instrument or voice, distinct from its pitch and intensity?

17 Bell's, Jim Beam® and Glenfiddich are all brands of which alcoholic drink?

18 In Arthurian legend, which of King Arthur's knights has an affair with Queen Guinevere?

19 Which pedestrianised shopping street in Soho is noted for its many independent fashion and lifestyle retailers?

20 The extinct bird species dodo was endemic to which island nation?

Easy

Medium

Hard

Answers to QUIZ 373 – Pot Luck

1	Tony Hancock	11	Midge Ure
2	Cornwall	12	Pink
3	Blue	13	12
4	Firth of Forth	14	Sting
5	One apple	15	There were 39 *Steps* from the pitch up to the trophy presentation area
6	Vincent Price		
7	Star	16	Absolute zero – it is as cold as it is physically possible to get
8	Figaro		
9	Bill Wyman	17	The Streets
10	Dingo	18	Pens, specifically marker pens
		19	Ethiopia
		20	Hovercraft

1   In *Star Trek: The Next Generation*, what was the name of Commander Data's cat?

2   Which 1980s rock band were named after a Vulcan Elder?

3   Which cast member of the original series was initially approached to play the role of Spock?

4   The Federation and which other empire were separated by a neutral zone that existed from 2160 until 2387?

5   Which Bajoran is second in command of Deep Space Nine?

6   Despite his English accent, what nationality is Captain Jean-Luc Picard said to be?

7   Which symbiotic humanoid species had a "slug" living inside a pouch?

8   Which Federation Captain forges the first alliance with the Borg, as it was preferable to fighting them?

9   Which quickly-reproducing small round furry creatures do the Klingons consider mortal enemies?

10   At its founding in 2161, the Federation began with which four members?

11   In *Star Trek: Generations*, as he lay dying, what were Captain Kirk's final two words?

12   Who was the first Vulcan science officer aboard the *Enterprise*?

13   Created for the films, which original series actor devised the Klingon language?

14   *Deep Space Nine* was originally a Cardassian mining and refinery station known by what name?

15   Which ancient creature brought the USS Voyager to the Delta Quadrant?

16   21st century human scientist Zefram Cochrane was said to have invented what, integral to the *Star Trek* stories?

17   Which *Star Trek* film featured the first entirely computer generated sequence in cinema history?

18   What recreational facility did the U.S.S. *Enterprise* have on Deck 21?

19   Which event caused almost every warp core in the galaxy to activate and explode at once as most dilithium mysteriously went inert?

20   In *Star Trek: Insurrection*, the region of space in which the Son'a and Ba'ku home planet was located was called what?

Answers to QUIZ 374 – War; What Is It Good For?

1	Modern nursing techniques	12	The Siegfried Line
2	First World War	13	The Crimean War
3	The First Boer War	14	Benedict Arnold
4	War of the Roses	15	Spain
5	The Manhattan Project	16	He was on duty at the Soviet Air Defence Forces when the early–warning system reported that US missiles had been launched – he rightly judged it to be a false alarm and did not fire back
6	Bletchley Park		
7	Roundheads (Parliamentarians) and Cavaliers (Royalists)		
8	Spain	17	Falklands War
9	Afghanistan	18	Nero
10	The War of Jenkins' Ear	19	Tobruk
11	Battle of Bosworth	20	The Second Boer War

ANSWERS ON PAGE **379**

1   What is the more common name for the bird of prey also known as the windhover?

2   Which breed of dog has a name that derives from the French word for earth?

3   When they reach adulthood, Amazon river dolphins are what colour?

4   To which section of the orchestra does the tuba belong?

5   In which English city did the charity Oxfam originate?

6   Which German inventor and publisher introduced printing to Europe in the 15th century with his mechanical movable-type printing press?

7   The mountain known as the Matterhorn straddles the border of which two countries?

8   Which is the largest country situated wholly within Europe?

9   In the *Harry Potter* franchise, what are the names of Harry's parents?

10 For what did Ruth Ellis become nationally famous in Britain in 1955?

11 Which large African mammal gives birth standing up, with the result being that their young enter the world by falling five feet to the ground?

12 Which British politician said in 2016, "I think the people of this country have had enough of experts"?

13 The sting of a stinging nettle comes from the irritant qualities of which acid?

14 Pleurisy affects which organ of the human body?

15 Pinnipeds are mammals with what distinctive type of "foot"?

16 A statue of which actor stands in Leicester Square, London?

17 What forename follows "lazy" in the name of the turntable placed on a table in order to help the distribution of food?

18 Which European country has maintained neutrality in all wars since its independence from the Holy Roman Empire in 1499?

19 In 1942, which writer defined the Three Laws of Robotics, designed to prevent robots harming humans?

20 Often derisively, which sport is sometimes jokingly known as handegg?

Answers to QUIZ 375 – Pot Luck

1	HB (which stands for "hard black")	11	50
2	Cheese	12	M4 – more Brits died in that crash than were killed by enemy fire in the Gulf War
3	Munich		
4	Mushroom	13	Wales
5	Gordon Brown	14	*All's Well That Ends Well*
6	Potato	15	Methane
7	Cornwall	16	Timbre
8	World War I	17	Whisky
9	James I of England/James VI of Scotland (same guy)	18	Lancelot
		19	Carnaby Street
10	General practitioner	20	Mauritius

1. What is the only UNESCO World Heritage site in Northern Ireland?
2. Which two counties does the city of Belfast span?
3. Which ill-fated ship left Belfast's Harland and Wolff shipyards in 1912?
4. The largest freshwater lake in the United Kingdom and Ireland by surface area, which large lake sits in the centre of Northern Ireland?
5. With the top about four feet out of alignment with the bottom, what is Belfast's very own leaning tower?
6. Samson and Goliath are prominent figures on the Belfast skyline; what are they?
7. Which rugby stadium in Belfast is the home of Ulster rugby?
8. Which 19th century manor house plays home to the Northern Ireland Executive?
9. Located in the Ulster Museum, Belfast, who or what is *Takabuti*?
10. If someone from Northern Ireland describes something as "wee buns", what do they think it is?
11. In Northern Irish cuisine, what is yellowman?
12. Northern Irishman Carl Frampton was a former world champion in which sport?
13. Rising in the Mourne Mountains and flowing into Spelga Reservoir, what is the longest river in Northern Ireland?
14. Which poet – who spent 37 years in Northern Ireland and 37 years in the Republic – received the 1995 Nobel Prize in Literature?
15. Which well-preserved Norman castle in County Antrim is the only one on the island of Ireland to have been in continuous use from its first building?
16. The tree-lined Bregagh Road in Ballymoney, also known as the Dark Hedges, featured in which major HBO TV series?
17. Home to the Clinton Centre, which town is the largest in county Fermanagh?
18. In 2002, as part of Queen Elizabeth's Golden Jubilee celebrations, what became Northern Ireland's then-newest two cities?
19. Sixteen bridges, including the iconic Foley's Bridge, cross the Shimna River in which park near Newcastle in County Down?
20. As of 2022, which three Northern Irish sportspeople have won the BBC Sports Personality of the Year Award?

Easy

Medium

Hard

Answers to QUIZ 376 – Star Trek

1	Spot	11	"Oh my."
2	T'Pau	12	T'Pol
3	DeForest Kelley, who instead played Bones	13	James Doohan
4	Romulans	14	Terok Nor
5	Major Keira Neris	15	The Caretaker
6	French	16	Warp drive
7	Trill	17	*Star Trek II: The Wrath of Khan* (it was the Genesis Device demonstration video)
8	Captain Janeway		
9	Tribbles	18	A bowling alley
10	Humans, Vulcans, Andorians and Tellarites	19	The Burn
		20	The Briar Patch

1 "Merchandise 7X" has since 1886 been the "secret ingredient" or "secret formula" of which drink?

2 In old money, how many pence was a tanner?

3 Anthony Robert McMillan OBE is a Scottish actor better known by what name?

4 *Hakuna Matata* is a song from which Disney animated film?

5 The children's character Sir Topham Hatt is better known by what name?

6 In the nursery rhyme, during which season of the year did the Queen of Hearts make the tarts?

7 Which Italian dish consists of rice cooked in stock with ingredients such as vegetables and meat or seafood?

8 Eric Rudolph was a domestic terrorist convicted for the bombing at which 1996 sporting event held in America?

9 Which Greek island is known to its inhabitants as Kerkyra?

10 Pampas grass is native to which continent?

11 Because of their huge thick trunks and (when bare) root-like branches, which tree is also known as the upside-down tree?

12 Lansing is the capital city of which American state?

13 George Bernard Shaw called which man "the only genius to come out of the movie industry"?

14 The umbilicus is the scientific name for which part of the human body?

15 Which Paralympic sport uses a ball fitted with bells?

16 Bluebottle and Eccles appeared as characters in which radio comedy series?

17 Which style of broad-brimmed hat takes its name from the Spanish for shade?

18 In which Oxfordshire royal palace was Winston Churchill born?

19 Who was the first Disney princess not to have been born human, as well as being the first to have her own child?

20 Which American President once said "I've always wondered about the taping equipment. But I'm damn glad we have it."?

Answers to QUIZ 377 – Pot Luck

1	Kestrel	11	Giraffe
2	Terrier	12	Michael Gove
3	Pink	13	Formic acid
4	Brass	14	Lungs
5	Oxford – its original name was the Oxford Committee for Famine Relief	15	Flippers
6	Johannes Gutenberg	16	Charlie Chaplin
7	Switzerland and Italy	17	Susan
8	Ukraine	18	Switzerland
9	James and Lily Potter	19	Isaac Asimov
10	She was the last woman to be hanged	20	American Football

Easy

1   Orange juice is a good source of which vitamin?
2   In chemistry, what is a substance that cannot be split into simpler substances?
3   Emissions from cattle are a major source of which greenhouse gas?
4   In the name of the synthetic polymer, what does the abbreviation PVC stand for?
5   Which is the only chemical element whose English name begins with the letter V?
6   Measured in ohms, what term is used to describe the ability of a component to impede the flow of electrons?
7   Anthropology is the study of what?
8   In the name of various ailments, what does the suffix -itis mean?
9   Which branch of science is concerned with the functioning of living organisms?
10 Which wild plant can cause cirrhosis of the liver when eaten by horses, cows or pigs?
11 What reaction serves as the trigger of an atomic bomb explosion?
12 In computer science, what does USB stand for?
13 Boyle's and Charles' laws are both concerned with the behaviour of what?
14 What is the astronomical term for the Southern Lights?
15 What are the openings in a leaf that allow carbon dioxide into the leaf and oxygen out called?

Medium

16 In 1826, when chemist John Walker picked up a discarded stick in front of his fireplace, what did he inadvertently invent?
17 Produced in 1992, the first genetically modified crop was an antibiotic-resistant type of what plant?
18 Which Cornish chemist invented a miner's lamp, discovered six new elements and discovered the pain-relieving effects of nitrous oxide?
19 Which Swiss physician was the first to isolate nucleic acid, leading to the later identification of DNA?
20 Chemotherapy was inadvertently discovered through the development of what weapon?

Hard

Answers to QUIZ 378 – Northern Ireland

1   Giant's Causeway
2   County Antrim and County Down
3   RMS *Titanic*
4   Lough Neagh (pronounced *nay*)
5   Albert Memorial Clock
6   Giant yellow shipyard gantry cranes
7   Ravenshill
8   Stormont Castle
9   A mummified Egyptian woman who, for whatever reason, is on display unwrapped
10 Easy
11 A bright yellow toffee-like sweet

12 Boxing
13 River Bann/An Bhanna
14 Seamus Heaney
15 Carrickfergus Castle
16 *Game of Thrones* (in which it was known as King's Road)
17 Enniskillen
18 Lisburn and Newry
19 Tollymore Forest Park
20 Mary Peters (1972), Barry McGuigan (1985, who, though born in the Republic, represented Northern Ireland at the Commonwealth Games) and Tony McCoy (2010)

ANSWERS ON PAGE 383

1   Which physicist's "miracle year" of 1905 saw him publish four papers, including his theory of special relativity, that changed understanding of physical concepts forever?

2   A 3.5-mile bus lane existed on which British motorway between 2001 and 2010?

3   Which German football team won the Champions League in 2013 and 2020?

4   Mary Westmacott was a pseudonym used by which famous author?

5   Which American writer wrote both *Stuart Little* and *Charlotte's Web*?

6   What mixed drink cocktail of Scotch whisky and vermouth takes its name from a Scottish folk hero?

7   In which American city is the Golden Gate bridge located?

8   Hell's Belles are a Seattle-based all-female tribute act to which Australian rock band?

9   Jack Ma co-founded which multinational technology conglomerate, named for a character from folk tales?

10 Cadbury's *Heroes* collection of miniature chocolates was introduced in 1999 as a rival to which Mars product?

11 How many athletes are there in an Olympic track relay team?

12 Not counting Russia or Turkey, which country has the biggest population in Europe?

13 The Exxon Valdez oil spill of 1989 occurred off the coast of which American state?

14 Who is the lead singer of Coldplay?

15 Humphrey Bogart won his only Oscar for which 1951 film?

16 Who won the Nobel Peace Prize in 2009, yet even he admitted he did not know why?

17 How many years are there in a semicentennial period?

18 The chemical element hafnium is named after *Hafnia*, the Latin name for which city, where it was discovered?

19 What two toppings typically make up a Hawaiian pizza?

20 Which car manufacturer has sold more than 6 million units of its Prius range of hybrid cars?

Easy

Medium

Hard

Answers to QUIZ 379 – Pot Luck

1   Coca-Cola®
2   Six pence
3   Robbie Coltrane
4   *The Lion King*
5   The Fat Controller from *Thomas the Tank Engine*
6   Summer
7   Risotto
8   The Atlanta Olympics
9   Corfu
10 South America

11 Baobab
12 Michigan
13 Charlie Chaplin
14 Belly button
15 Goalball
16 *The Goon Show*
17 Sombrero
18 Blenheim Palace
19 Ariel, *The Little Mermaid*
20 Richard Nixon – that same taping equipment would later be his downfall

Easy

1. "Duelling Banjos" was a song and a scene from which 1972 film?
2. At one point ranking third all time, which is the highest grossing *Harry Potter* film?
3. Which film was advertised with the slogan "Just when you thought it was safe to go back in the water"?
4. "No dragons were harmed in the making of this movie" is written in the credits of which 2005 film?
5. Alec Guinness played eight different roles in which 1949 comedy film?
6. In the 1991 Disney film *Beauty and the Beast*, what was the Beauty's name?
7. In *The Day of the Jackal*, who played the Jackal?
8. In which film did Renée Zellweger say to Tom Cruise, "you had me at hello"?
9. In standard cinefilm, how many frames are shown per second?
10. Mimi Marquez and Roger Davis are major characters in which musical film, based on a Broadway musical, itself based on an opera?
11. In 1963, who became the first black actor to win the Academy Award for Best Actor for his role in *Lilies of the Field*?
12. What 2012 Ben Affleck film tells a fictionalised account of a real CIA operation to rescue hostages from Iran by making a fake movie?
13. In which film do Abbott and Costello land on Venus?
14. James Bond married Teresa de Vincenzo in which film, which was also George Lazenby's only appearance as him?
15. In which Steven Spielberg film does Tom Cruise investigate "pre-crime" (crime known about before it occurs)?

Medium

16. In which year were the films *Black Panther, Aquaman, London Fields* and *Green Book* all released?
17. David Lean wrote and directed a 1984 historical film about a passage to which country?
18. Which 2019 DreamWorks animated film was banned in the Philippines, Vietnam and Malaysia for depicting the controversial Nine Dash line over the South China Sea?
19. In what kind of environment was the 1958 British war film *Ice Cold In Alex* set?
20. Kirk Douglas appeared as a French World War I officer in which Stanley Kubrick film?

Hard

Answers to QUIZ 380 – Science

1	Vitamin C	12	Universal serial bus
2	Element	13	Gases
3	Methane	14	Aurora Australis
4	Polyvinyl chloride	15	Stomata
5	Vanadium	16	The match – he had been using it to stir a liquid he was trying to make flammable, but the discovery that friction was the key to it working was accidental
6	Resistance		
7	Humans		
8	Infection or inflammation		
9	Physiology	17	Tobacco plant
10	Ragwort	18	Sir Humphrey Davy
11	Nuclear fission	19	Friedrich Miescher
		20	Mustard gas

ANSWERS ON PAGE 385

1. In the names of the furniture items tallboy, highboy and lowboy, the "boy" suffix is derived from the French word *bois*, meaning what?

2. Carmine is a deep shade of which colour?

3. The river Han runs through which Asian capital city?

4. "Louis, I think this is the beginning of a beautiful friendship." is the final line to which classic film?

5. The French loanword *noisette* can refer to chocolate made with which type of nut?

6. The world's longest and busiest subway metro system resides under which city?

7. Which American soul and R&B group had hit singles during the 1970s including *Car Wash* and *I Wanna Get Next to You*?

8. Gary Barlow, Howard Donald, Jason Orange, Robbie Williams and Mark Owen were the founder members of which boy band?

9. Before their international cricket careers, which twins played semi-professional football for Sydney Croatia?

10. At age 40, which goalkeeper captained Italy to the 1982 FIFA World Cup title?

11. Which Italian tenor debuted in a performance of *La Bohème* in April 1961 after giving up his dreams of becoming a goalkeeper?

12. *Laverne & Shirley* and *Mork & Mindy* were both spin-off series from which other TV show?

13. Which 20th-century art movement challenged traditional fine art by including imagery from popular and mass culture, often ironically?

14. In which country of the United Kingdom was Princess Margaret born?

15. Bovine is an adjective relating to which animals?

16. On which river do the towns of Rochester, Chatham and Gillingham stand?

17. In Douglas Adams's *The Hitchhiker's Guide to the Galaxy*, what is the name of the Paranoid Android?

18. When it opened on 14th May 1894, what was the tallest man-made structure in the British Empire?

19. In which county are Woburn Abbey and Woburn Safari Park located?

20. *I Only Want to Be with You* was the first song performed on *Top Of The Pops* in 1964 – who performed it?

Easy

Medium

Hard

Answers to QUIZ 381 – Pot Luck

1	Albert Einstein	11	Four
2	M4	12	Germany
3	Bayern Munich	13	Alaska
4	Agatha Christie	14	Chris Martin
5	E.B. White	15	*The African Queen*
6	Rob Roy	16	Barack Obama
7	San Francisco	17	50
8	AC/DC	18	Copenhagen
9	Alibaba	19	Ham and pineapple
10	*Celebrations*	20	Toyota

These are pictures of what scientists think certain dinosaurs looked like. Can you identify which is which?

1

2

3

4

5

6

7

8

Answers to QUIZ 382 – Film

1	*Deliverance*	11	Sidney Poitier
2	*Harry Potter and the Deathly Hallows – Part 2*	12	*Argo*
3	*Jaws II*	13	*Abbot and Costello Go To Mars*
4	*Harry Potter and the Goblet of Fire*	14	*On Her Majesty's Secret Service*
5	*Kind Hearts and Coronets*	15	*Minority Report*
6	*Belle*	16	2018
7	Edward Fox	17	India
8	*Jerry Maguire*	18	*Abominable*
9	24	19	The North African desert; the title refers to beer that the characters dream of drinking
10	*Rent* (loosely based on Puccini's *La Bohème*)	20	*Paths of Glory*

1   Since 1942, what colour beret is worn by members of the Royal Marines after passing the Commando Course?

2   What three ingredients typically make up a sidecar cocktail?

3   What links the breeding cycles of cowbirds, whydahs, indigobirds and cuckoos?

4   In the names of the government agencies MI5 and MI6, what does the MI stand for?

5   Braintree and Harlow are towns in which English county?

6   Prior to adopting the Euro, the guilder was the former currency of which European country?

7   In the 1990 Tim Burton film, who portrayed Edward Scissorhands?

8   What identifying feature gives catfish their name?

9   Who wrote the 1985 dystopian novel *The Handmaid's Tale*?

10 Nephrology is the study of which organ of the human body?

11 Grandfather, cuckoo and carriage are all types of what household item?

12 Which English international airport was known until 1975 as Ringway?

13 Which motorbike racing legend is nicknamed "The Doctor"?

14 *Tall, Dark and Gruesome* was the autobiography of which horror movie legend?

15 The name of which Italian pasta-like dumpling translates as "knot in wood"?

16 Complete the legal profession saying: "A man who is his own lawyer has…"?

17 The Stanislavski Method is used in what profession?

18 Which Irish-American dancer and choreographer became known for appearing in *Riverdance* before going on to create *Lord of the Dance*?

19 What is examined during an endoscopy?

20 Eton College and Bradfield College are independent private schools in which English county?

Easy

Medium

Hard

Answers to QUIZ 383 – Pot Luck

1	Wood	11	Luciano Pavarotti
2	Red	12	*Happy Days*
3	Seoul, South Korea	13	Pop art
4	*Casablanca*	14	Scotland (specifically at Glamis Castle, Angus)
5	Hazelnut	15	Cattle/oxen
6	Shanghai, China	16	Medway
7	Rose Royce	17	Marvin
8	Take That	18	Blackpool Tower
9	Mark and Steve Waugh	19	Bedfordshire
10	Dino Zoff	20	Dusty Springfield

1   Which important piece of English transport infrastructure opened on 10th January 1863?

2   What did Sir Henry Cole pioneer in 1843 when he was too busy to write Christmas letters to his friends?

3   The Crystal Palace was built in Hyde Park to house which international showpiece event of 1851?

4   The Vaccination Act 1853 made it compulsory for all children born after 1st August 1853 to be vaccinated against which disease?

5   Known as the "Prince Consort", who was Queen Victoria's spouse?

6   In June 1842, Robert Peel's Conservative government introduced which tax?

7   On 9th July 1864, a bank clerk named Thomas Briggs became the first person to ever be murdered where?

8   Which natural product did Victorians use in abundance in skin lotion, wallpaper, dresses, toys, medicines and murder?

9   Which bridge with a red colour scheme did Queen Victoria open on the same day as Holborn Viaduct?

10 Why did the men of Victorian London usually, if not always, wear black clothing?

11 In Victorian times, what was a cracksman?

12 The idea that women fainted from excitement likely originates from the Victorian-era trend for which highly impractical fashion item?

13 In 2004, which Victorian-era nurse was voted the greatest black Briton for her effort to set up the "British Hotel" behind the lines during the Crimean War?

14 In Victorian cuisine, what were "bags of mystery"?

15 What colour clothing was only ever worn by the rich until the 1850s, when teenager William Perkins discovered a cheap synthetic dye?

16 Victorian custom dictated that a lady could only dance a maximum of how many dances with the same man?

17 Which famous Victorian cookery writer published the *Book of Household Management* in 1861?

18 Which disease was the leading cause of death in nineteenth century Victorian England?

19 Those Victorians who could afford it often took *memento mori*, photos of loved ones taken when?

20 In Victorian slang, who or what were "mutton shunters"?

Answers to QUIZ 384 – Dinosaurs

1   Tyrannosaurus Rex
2   Stegosaurus
3   Triceratops
4   Diplodocus
5   Velociraptor
6   Brachiosaurus
7   Archaeopteryx
8   Ankylosaurus

QUIZ 387 – Pot Luck

ANSWERS ON PAGE 389

1. Wyclef Jean, Pras Michel and Lauryn Hill were the members of which 1990s hip hop group?
2. Something described as xanthic resembles which colour?
3. *Yeux* is the French word for which parts of the body?
4. Zara Phillips married which former England rugby union international in 2011?
5. Rihanna, Heidi Klum and Taylor Swift all insured which part or parts of their body?
6. What is the square root of zero?
7. Including all its variant spellings, what is the world's most popular first name?
8. Which animal has a top called a carapace and a bottom called a plastron?
9. Part of the A4, which London road runs from Hyde Park Corner east to its namesake Circus with its famous neon advertising hoardings?
10. The USA's involvement in the Vietnam War spanned five Presidencies; which President finally ended it?
11. Who or what was New York named after in 1665?
12. Despite his tendency to take a deeper look at almost everything, who once said "Sometimes, a cigar is just a cigar"?
13. Which actress's breakthrough role came as Trudy Campbell in the drama series *Mad Men*?
14. The four members of which fictional US Army Special Forces unit were tried by court martial for a crime they had not committed?
15. Which former British Army officer made international headlines in 2020 by raising money for charity by walking the length of his garden 100 times?
16. What term is shared by ceremonial guardians of the Tower of London, and a chain of British pub restaurants?
17. What term refers to both British judokas reaching the rank of 3rd Kyu, and a policy to prevent urban sprawl by keeping land permanently open and not built upon?
18. In which game do players use squidgers to try and squop their opponents?
19. In which game do players have to guess a word from another player's drawing?
20. Candela is the SI unit for what?

Easy / Medium / Hard

Answers to QUIZ 385 – Pot Luck

1. Green
2. Cognac, orange liqueur and lemon juice
3. They are brood parasites, which means they deposit their eggs in the nests of other birds rather than make their own
4. Military Intelligence
5. Essex
6. Netherlands
7. Johnny Depp
8. They have whiskers
9. Margaret Atwood
10. Kidney
11. Clock
12. Manchester International
13. Valentino Rossi
14. Christopher Lee
15. Gnocchi
16. "...a fool for a client"
17. Acting, especially theatre acting
18. Michael Flatley
19. Your insides, usually the digestive tract
20. Berkshire

Easy

1   The month of December contains the summer solstice in which hemisphere?

2   On 2nd December 1804, Pope Pius VII crowned who as Emperor of France?

3   1st December 1990 saw workers from France and Britain meet in the middle of what for the first time?

4   On 29th December 1970, four of Henry II's knights murdered which Archbishop of Canterbury?

5   New Year's Eve is coincident with the Western Christianity feast day for which saint?

6   Who took over from interim Vince Cable as the leader of the Liberal Democrat party in December 2007?

7   The Empire State Building in New York City was illuminated bright yellow on 18th December 2007 to promote which film?

8   Who was assassinated outside the Dakota Building in New York City on 8th December 1980?

9   On 24th December 1814, America and Britain signed which treaty, officially ending the War of 1812?

10 On 21st December 1988, a terrorist bomb exploded on a plane bound for New York, sending it crashing onto which Scottish town?

11 On 9th December 1979, a commission of scientists declared that which disease had been eradicated, the first infectious human disease to be officially so?

12 On Christmas Day 1989, which Romanian dictator and his wife were summarily executed minutes after being found guilty of crimes against humanity?

13 Unruly American colonists emptied the cargo of three ships in Boston harbour in which event of 16th December 1773?

Medium

14 On 15th December 1995, the European Court of Justice issued the "Bosman ruling"; what change did this bring about in football?

15 Which British actor starred in the 2007 Australian family drama film *December Boys*?

16 *December, 1963 (Oh, What a Night)* is a song originally performed by who?

17 NASA's first Mars rover launched on 4th December 1996; what was it called?

18 What was pioneering about the Chelsea team that started against Southampton on Boxing Day 1999?

19 On 20th December 1999, what became the last foreign colony to revert to Chinese rule when Portugal handed over administration?

20 Which Italian fashion house launched the first virtual online museum on 5th December 2011?

Hard

Answers to QUIZ 386 – The Victorians

1	London Underground	11	Burglar
2	Christmas Cards	12	Corsets (which are not good for blood flow)
3	Great Exhibition	13	Mary Seacole
4	Smallpox	14	Sausages
5	Prince Albert of Saxe-Coburg and Gotha	15	Purple
6	Income tax	16	Three
7	On a train	17	Mrs (Isabella) Beeton
8	Arsenic	18	Tuberculosis
9	Blackfriars Bridge	19	After they died
10	The pollution was so bad that anything else would have been pointless	20	The police

1   What name links John Cleese's character in *A Fish called Wanda*, Cary Grant's real name, and, with a slightly different spelling, a designer of more than 20 football league stadiums?

2   Which fictional detective was played on TV for 25 years by David Suchet?

3   In the popular video game series, what colour was Sonic the Hedgehog™?

4   Westeros, Essos and Sothoryos are the fictional continents on which what HBO TV series is set?

5   Who popularised the wearing of t-shirts with his performance and attire in the film *A Streetcar Named Desire*?

6   The death of a woman on 6th May 2019 from which virus was reported to be the first in Norway for almost 200 years?

7   Who wrote the horror novel *It*?

8   The 18th Amendment to the US Constitution banned what from 1920 to 1933?

9   Which fruit is said to keep the doctor away?

10   Which of Queen Elizabeth II's children was the first to get remarried?

11   Sebastian in *The Little Mermaid* and Crazy Joe in *Shark Tale* are both what type of what animal?

12   The name of which English city is often abbreviated to Soton?

13   Blandenburg, Saarland and Lower Saxony are states in which European country?

14   What is the orangey-yellow part of an egg commonly called?

15   Which are the largest muscles in the human body?

16   St Mungo's Cathedral is located in which Scottish city?

17   From which language are the words ketchup, kumquat and tofu derived?

18   Celine Dion won the 1988 Eurovision Song Contest while representing which country?

19   Baja California is a state in which country?

20   *Calcio* is both an old Italian form of, and a current Italian word for, which sport?

Easy

Medium

Hard

Answers to QUIZ 387 – Pot Luck

1	The Fugees	11	The Duke of York, brother of James II, who was King at the time
2	Yellow		
3	Eyes	12	Sigmund Freud
4	Mike Tindall	13	Alison Brie
5	Legs	14	*The A-Team*
6	Zero	15	Captain Sir Tom Moore
7	Mohammad	16	Beefeater
8	Turtle	17	Green belt
9	Piccadilly	18	Tiddlywinks
10	Richard Nixon	19	*Pictionary®*
		20	Luminous intensity

Easy

1   Along with his wife Sylvia, who created the "Supermarionation" puppetry technique in shows such as *Thunderbirds* and *Joe 90*?

2   Ventriloquist Roger De Courcey is best known for his work with which puppet character?

3   When asked who the nicest person he had ever met was, Ronnie Corbett cited which Leicester City-supporting red fox puppet?

4   Which pork pie hat-wearing Muppet character is best known for his poor stand-up comedy skills?

5   Zippy, George and Bungle were the puppet characters alongside Geoffrey Hayes on which children's TV series?

6   Zig and Zag were regular "interviewers" on which Channel 4 morning show, where they taught the Wu-Tang Clan how to fold serviettes?

7   Which puppet is generally regarded as the saviour of morning show *TV-am*, being described as "the only rat to join a sinking ship"?

8   Harry Corbett created which glove puppet character in 1952?

9   Which puppeteer created both *The Muppets* and *Fraggle Rock*, and also directed the film *Labyrinth*?

10 An urban myth says that the nonsense language spoken by which puppet pair was inspired by the noise of a fart in the bath?

11 Originally cancelled in 1996, which British satirical television puppet show was rebooted in 2020?

Medium

12 Gordon Shumway, a puppet character who absolutely loved eating cats, was better known as what?

13 Which marionette lived in a picnic basket and was joined by Teddy, a teddy bear, and Looby Loo, a rag doll?

14 Mossop and Tiddler were the small humanoid creatures living in Marjorie Dawe's garden in which puppet series?

15 Tiger and Kate Kestrel were members of the Earth Defence Squadron in which 1980s series?

16 Who won the 1967 Eurovision Song Contest for Great Britain with the song *Puppet on a String*?

17 First appearing on television in 1946, Annette Mills presented stories with which animal puppet?

18 Dr Mayhem and the Electric Teeth was the house band from which puppet sketch show?

19 Nick Frisbee, a children's in-vision continuity presenter who had a squirrel puppet sidekick he liked to hit, was a creation of which comedian?

20 One of the first British children's shows with characters with regional accents, Hartley Hare, Pig, Topov and the gang were the stars of which series?

Hard

Answers to QUIZ 388 – December

1	Southern	12	Nicolae Ceaușescu
2	Napoleon Bonaparte	13	Boston Tea Party
3	The Channel Tunnel	14	Players could thereafter leave on free transfers once their contracts ran out
4	Thomas Becket		
5	Saint Sylvester	15	Daniel Radcliffe
6	Nick Clegg	16	Frankie Valli and the Four Seasons
7	*The Simpsons Movie*	17	*Pathfinder*
8	John Lennon	18	It was the first time in English football league history that a team had not started a single English player
9	Treaty of Ghent		
10	Lockerbie		
11	Smallpox	19	Macau
		20	Valentino

1 Aged 14, who in 1980 won the *Search for a Star* singing competition, before topping the charts in 1989 with *All Around the World*?

2 In the name of the media company, what does BBC stand for?

3 What colourful nickname did Morgan Freeman's character have in the film adaptation of *The Shawshank Redemption*?

4 In which town is the British version of *The Office* set?

5 Harvey Dent is the alter ego of which DC Comic supervillain?

6 In the physics equation, the mass of an object times its velocity equals what quality?

7 Which is the only igneous rock that can float in water?

8 A frond is a large and divided what?

9 Yogi Bear lives in which fictional park, a pun on the name of a real one?

10 Pantomimes traditionally take place at what time of the year?

11 Which mountain range forms much of the border between France and Spain?

12 A pug is a breed of which domestic pet?

13 Gurdwaras are places of worship in which religion?

14 Which of the British monarch's royal residences is located in Norfolk?

15 TV duo Ant and Dec are originally from which English city?

16 Baker's cysts develop in the back of which joint?

17 What type of animal lives in an apiary?

18 If finders are keepers, what are losers?

19 As of 2022, how many English monarchs have been called Edward?

20 Who presented the first 17 seasons of *Never Mind the Buzzcocks*?

Easy

Medium

Hard

Answers to QUIZ 389 – Pot Luck

1	They are all Archibald Leach (or Leitch)	11	Crab
2	Hercule Poirot	12	Southampton
3	Blue	13	Germany
4	*Game of Thrones*	14	Yolk
5	Marlon Brando	15	Gluteus maximus (the bottom)
6	Rabies	16	Glasgow
7	Stephen King	17	Chinese
8	Alcohol	18	Switzerland
9	Apple	19	Mexico
10	Princess Anne, 1992	20	Football

1   Along with cobras for handles, a representation of which Indian animal appears on the top of rugby's Calcutta Cup?

2   Which tiny cricket trophy is reported to contain (and is named after) the burnt remains of a bail?

3   Traditionally, the winner of the Indianapolis 500 is presented with which non-alcoholic drink?

4   Since 1872, the Claret Jug has been presented to the winner of which annual golfing major?

5   Which fruit appears on the top of the Wimbledon Men's Singles champion trophy?

6   Informally known as the Auld Mug, which sailing trophy is the oldest international competition still active in all of sports?

7   The hefty 89 centimetre-tall Stanley Cup is awarded annually to the winners of which North American sports league?

8   The winner of which "royal" horse race is allowed to actually keep the trophy forever, with the Queen approving a new one each year?

9   A dog called Pickles famously found which stolen trophy under a bush in 1966, just before it was needed?

10   Live lobsters, grandfather clocks and jukeboxes are among the strange prizes given to race winners in which American motor sport series?

11   Which skiing legend won a cow at the Val d'Isere downhill in 2004, which she kept, and a goat at the World Championships five years later, which she didn't?

12   The Green Jacket is awarded to the winner of which prestigious golf tournament?

13   The unique prize of the wife's weight in beer is awarded to the winning pair in which similarly-unique world championship, held annually in Finland?

14   What colour jersey is worn by the leader of the Tour de France?

15   Speedboats, drinks trolleys, carriage clocks and automatic knitting machines were among the prizes on which ITV game show?

16   Dusty Bin was both the mascot and the booby prize on which game show of the 1970s and 1980s?

17   In which comedy series is "the entire Norwich City Council" given away as a prize for choosing the correct hymn?

18   Olympic gold medals are required to actually be made of at least 92.5% of which other metal?

19   Which 16-time World Darts Champion would often sign the board after victories?

20   In Major League Baseball it is considered disrespectful, but what post-home run celebration has become an art form in Korea?

Answers to QUIZ 390 – Puppets and Puppeteers

1	Gerry Anderson	11	*Spitting Image*
2	Nookie Bear	12	ALF (for "Alien Life Form")
3	Basil Brush	13	Andy Pandy
4	Fozzie Bear	14	*The Riddlers*
5	*Rainbow*	15	*The Terrahawks*
6	*The Big Breakfast*	16	Sandie Shaw
7	Roland Rat	17	Muffin the Mule
8	Sooty	18	*The Muppet Show*
9	Jim Henson	19	Brian Conley
10	Bill & Ben, from *Flower Pot Men*	20	*Pipkins*

1. Covered by many artists, the song *Moon River* was originally written by Henry Mancini and Johnny Mercer for which film?
2. Quicksilver is another name for which chemical element?
3. What did the Romans call what is now the modern country of France?
4. The dot above lower case 'i' and 'j' letters is called a what?
5. Epistemology is the study of the theory of what?
6. In the title of the war novel by Stephen Crane, what is a *Red Badge of Courage*?
7. Which country of the UK has more cities; Wales, Scotland or Northern Ireland?
8. How is someone described as "rapacious" acting?
9. Rivalling Google's *Home* and Apple's *Siri*, what is the name of Amazon's virtual assistant?
10. A *croque monsieur* is a hot sandwich of ham and cheese on thick slices of white bread; what is added to make it a *croque madame*?
11. In the law enforcement acronym, what does SWAT stand for?
12. In the name of the medical condition, what does COPD stand for?
13. What name is given to the slight flourishes finishing off a stroke of a letter in certain fonts?
14. Which New Zealand physicist discovered the concept of radioactive half-life, the radioactive element radon and differentiated alpha and beta radiation?
15. Found in some fruits and vegetables, what colour of pigment is lycopene?
16. In some cultures, the foot of which animal is carried as an amulet believed to bring good luck?
17. Who smuggled the Stuart Sapphire out of England as he fled in 1688?
18. Snap, Crackle and Pop have been the mascots of which breakfast cereal since the 1930s?
19. Dustin Hoffman and Meryl Streep fought a custody battle in which five-time Oscar-winning film?
20. Which poet wrote *The Kraken* in 1830?

Easy

Medium

Hard

Answers to QUIZ 391 – Pot Luck

1	Lisa Stansfield	11	Pyrenees
2	British Broadcasting Corporation	12	Dog
3	Red	13	Sikhism
4	Slough	14	Sandringham
5	Two-Face	15	Newcastle
6	Momentum	16	Knee
7	Pumice	17	Bee
8	Leaf	18	Weepers
9	Jellystone Park	19	Eight
10	Christmas	20	Mark Lamarr

1   Mike Myers and Dana Carvey star as a pair of rock music fans who broadcast a public-access television show in which 1992 film?

2   What was the real name of the actor John Wayne?

3   What is the second-most populous city in the state of Indiana, after Indianapolis?

4   Wayne Brady has appeared in almost every episode of the American version of which TV improv comedy show?

5   Which rapper and founder of Young Money Records has released the *Tha Carter* series of albums?

6   Specifically, what does a wainwright make and repair?

7   Fountains of Wayne had a 2003 hit with which coming-of-age pop-punk song, with a video starring model Rachel Hunter?

8   Albert Pennyworth is the butler of which billionaire industrialist and notorious playboy, who serves Gotham City as the vigilante Batman?

9   Which ice hockey legend retired in 1999 as the holder of 61 different NHL records?

10 At 5'2", who is the shortest male dancer ever admitted into the Royal Ballet School?

11 Which man surpassed Bobby Charlton as the leading goal scorer for both Manchester United and the English national team?

12 Born Glyn Geoffrey Ellis, which English rock and pop singer was best known for the 1965 hit *The Game of Love* with the Mindbenders?

13 Which English Romantic landscape artist painted *The Haywain*?

14 Which American serial killer would dress as "Pogo the Clown" at charitable and fundraising events, parades and children's parties?

15 Wayne and Byron Black are Zimbabwean Grand Slam winners in which sport?

16 Behind Alan but ahead of Merrill, Wayne was the second-oldest member of which sibling music group?

17 Which American-Canadian singer and composer has written classical operas, studio albums and set Shakespeare's sonnets to music?

18 Nicknamed "Hawaii 501" during his playing days, Wayne Mardle is now a commentator on which sport?

19 The Saturdays singer Frankie Sandford married which former Chelsea, Southampton, Manchester City and England defender?

20 A highly unusual piece of casting saw John Wayne appear as which Mongol Emperor in the 1956 film *The Conqueror*?

Answers to QUIZ 392 – All About Winning

1	Elephant	11	Lindsey Vonn
2	The Ashes	12	US Masters
3	Milk	13	World Wife-Carrying Championships
4	The British Open/The Open	14	Yellow
5	Pineapple	15	*Bullseye*
6	America's Cup	16	3-2-1
7	NHL ice hockey	17	*Monty Python's Flying Circus*
8	Ascot Gold Cup	18	Silver
9	FIFA World Cup trophy	19	Phil Taylor
10	NASCAR	20	Bat flip

1   Actress Hudgens, singer Carlton and actress/singer Paradis all share what forename?

2   The Los Angeles Times described which man as a "new unknown British Shakespearean actor" shortly after he was cast as Captain Jean-Luc Picard?

3   What are Ġbejna, Gruyère, Gouda and Gorgonzola?

4   Breeding a female horse with a male donkey creates what?

5   The sportswear brand Sondico make clothing and equipment for which sport?

6   In which year did Elizabeth II ascend to the throne?

7   What is the national flower of Wales?

8   The province of Rioja, which gives its name to the namesake wine, is in which European country?

9   Which boxing champion was nicknamed Raging Bull, and was the subject of the namesake film?

10 What are Michaelmas, Trinity and Hilary at the University of Oxford?

11 *Jagged Little Pill* was the platinum-selling debut album for which Canadian singer?

12 TV and radio presenter Dougie Donnelly's career has almost entirely been spent presenting what sort of programming?

13 Which of tennis' four major championships is played on a clay court?

14 What name is shared by the world's first nuclear-powered aircraft carrier, and the main starship in the initial *Star Trek* series?

15 Which English city has football teams called United and Wednesday?

16 Giraffes are only found in the wild on which continent?

17 The Latin phrase "Utrinque Paratus", meaning "Ready for Anything", is the motto of which regiment of the British Army?

18 What sporting event was founded by Baron Pierre de Coubertin?

19 Identity documents which demonstrate a person has permanent residency in the United States are given what colourful name?

20 Whoopi Goldberg lacks what facial feature?

Easy

Medium

Hard

Answers to QUIZ 393 – Pot Luck

1   *Breakfast at Tiffany's*
2   Mercury
3   Gaul
4   Tittle
5   Knowledge
6   A bleeding wound, often interpreted as a sign of bravery
7   Scotland, with eight (Aberdeen, Dundee, Dunfermline, Edinburgh, Glasgow, Inverness, Perth, Stirling). Northern Ireland has six (Armagh, Bangor, Belfast, Derry, Lisburn, Newry) and Wales has seven (Bangor, Cardiff, Newport, St David's, St Asaph, Swansea, Wrexham)
8   Very greedily, especially with regards to money

9   *Alexa*
10 An egg
11 Special Weapons and Tactics
12 Chronic obstructive pulmonary disorder
13 Serifs
14 Ernest Rutherford
15 Red (found in tomatoes, watermelons and others)
16 Rabbit
17 King James II
18 Kellogg's® Rice Krispies
19 *Kramer vs. Kramer*
20 Alfred, Lord Tennyson

Easy

1   Dominic West starred as homicide detective Jimmy McNulty in which highly acclaimed American crime drama series?

2   Set in Dorset, which ITV detective series starred David Tennant and Olivia Colman?

3   Which BBC detective series set in the 1960s stars Martin Shaw and is loosely based on the namesake novels by Alan Hunter?

4   While set on the fictional island of Saint Marie, *Death in Paradise* is in fact filmed on which Caribbean island?

5   Crockett and Tubbs were undercover detectives and the two lead characters in which series?

6   Kenneth Branagh appeared as which compassionate Swedish inspector who suffers from the murders he encounters?

7   Which important ITV detective series of the 1970s took its name from the Cockney rhyming slang for "Flying Squad"?

8   Suranne Jones, Lesley Sharp and Amelia Bullimore take the lead roles in which ITV police procedural, written by Sally Wainwright?

9   Set during and shortly after World War II, Michael Kitchen stars as a reluctant soldier turned detective in which series?

10 Kristen Bell stars as which student who moonlights as a private investigator while progressing through high school and college?

Medium

11 In which 1980s American police procedural did Sharon Gless and Tyne Daley appear in a rare female buddy-cop series?

12 Which Danish/Swedish collaboration begins with the discovery of a mutilated body exactly on the border between the two countries?

13 Helen Mirren portrayed no-nonsense Detective Chief Inspector Jane Tennison in which ITV series between 1991 and 2006?

14 Which two detective series named after David Bowie albums did Philip Glenister star in?

15 Rosemary Boxer and Laura Thyme, the principal characters in the series *Rosemary and Thyme*, ran what sort of business in addition to solving crimes on the side?

16 *Los Angeles*, *New Orleans* and *Hawai'i* are all spin-offs from which US navy-based investigative series?

17 James Garner starred as the taco-binging Pontiac-driving title character in which 1974 detective drama series?

18 In the TV series *Columbo*, what was the name of Columbo's dog?

19 Which five-season series is about a wealthy couple who regularly find themselves as unpaid detectives to solve crimes they become embroiled in?

20 The theme tune to which 1980s American detective series starring Veronica Hamel won a Grammy for Best Instrumental Composition?

Hard

Answers to QUIZ 394 – Waynes

1	*Wayne's World*	11	Wayne Rooney
2	Marion Morrison	12	Wayne Fontana
3	Fort Wayne	13	John Constable
4	*Whose Line Is It Anyway?*	14	John Wayne Gacy
5	L'il Wayne	15	Tennis
6	Carts/wagons	16	*The Osmonds*
7	*Stacy's Mom*	17	Rufus Wainwright
8	Bruce Wayne	18	Darts
9	Wayne Gretzky	19	Wayne Bridge
10	Wayne Sleep	20	Genghis Khan

1   Sea lettuce and dead man's rope are both types of what?

2   Who was the host of the 2021 reboot of the British version of *The Weakest Link*?

3   Which of the Twelve Apostles of Jesus was known as "Didymus", meaning "twin"?

4   A biography of which novelist was titled *Beyond the Thirty-Nine Steps*?

5   What were the Windscale and Calder Works renamed to in 1981?

6   In E.M. Forster's novel *A Room with a View*, in which Italian city is the room?

7   Which short-period comet, the only one visible to the naked eye, was last visible in 1986 and is projected to return in 2061?

8   An egg from a 1980s computer game series, a song by Vic Reeves and a trumpeter with the real name John Gillespie all share what name?

9   In biology, what term describes the process of transformation from an immature form to an adult form in two or more distinct stages?

10   What has an apostate renounced?

11   Philip Glass wrote an opera about which theoretical physicist?

12   In 1999, whose frozen body was found near the summit of Mount Everest, 75 years after he died trying to climb it?

13   In *Coronation Street*, Susan, Jackie, Alma and Linda all married which character?

14   In the world of computing, what is a bug?

15   In weaponry, what is an ICBM?

16   In chess, which piece only moves diagonally?

17   Ophelia and two gravediggers appear in which Shakespeare play?

18   In which slightly macabre game is part of a gallows drawn for every wrong answer?

19   Which English former Formula 1 Driver is now a broadcaster, famous for his pre-race "pit walks"?

20   Who was the first male to feature on a British postage stamp?

Easy

Medium

Hard

Answers to QUIZ 395 – Pot Luck

1	Vanessa	11	Alanis Morrissette
2	Patrick Stewart	12	Sport
3	Cheeses	13	French Open
4	Mule	14	USS *Enterprise*
5	Football	15	Sheffield
6	1952	16	Africa
7	Daffodil	17	Parachute Regiment
8	Spain	18	The (modern) Olympic Games
9	Jake LaMotta	19	Green Cards
10	The names of the teaching terms	20	Eyebrows – she shaves them off as she finds them "itchy"

1   What are considered part of the human skeletal system, but are not bones?
2   What is the only part of the human body with no blood supply?
3   Almost exactly a quarter of the total number of bones in the human body are found where?
4   In humans, which kidney is almost always higher than the other?
5   Which is the largest organ of the human body?
6   Which is the only muscle in the human body to never get conventionally tired?
7   In humans, which is the only bodily organ that can fully regenerate?
8   Someone who could be described as a palmiped has what?
9   Which muscle separates the thorax (chest cavity) and the abdomen (belly cavity)?
10 What colour should healthy human lungs be?
11 Which part of the body is also known as the pollex?
12 Which is the only bone in the human body not directly attached to any other?
13 Borborygmus is the scientific term for what common bodily sound?
14 Which is both the longest and strongest bone in the human body?
15 Although not everyone has it, Darwin's Bump can often be found on which part of the human body?
16 What distinguishes false ribs from fixed ribs?
17 The Circle of Willis is an interconnected series of blood vessels at the bottom of which organ?
18 When someone blushes, which internal organ also turns red?
19 What is the function of the masseter muscle?
20 Which is the only part of the human body that grows faster than hair?

Answers to QUIZ 396 – Television Detectives

1	The Wire	11	Cagney and Lacey
2	Broadchurch	12	The Killing
3	George Gently	13	Prime Suspect
4	Guadeloupe	14	Life on Mars and Ashes to Ashes
5	Miami Vice	15	Gardening
6	Wallander	16	NCIS
7	The Sweeney	17	The Rockford Files
8	Scott & Bailey	18	Dog
9	Foyle's War	19	Hart to Hart
10	Veronica Mars	20	Hill Street Blues

1 Originating from a misconception about how it is transmitted, the name of which disease literally means "bad air"?

2 The Palme d'Or is the highest prize awarded at which international film festival?

3 Saul Hudson is the real name of which metal guitarist?

4 World War II took place between which years?

5 Which food manufacturer makes Nutri-Grain snack bars?

6 Into which estuary do the rivers Trent and Ouse both flow?

7 Although first used in 1874, what did not become mandatory in professional football until 1990?

8 Which Muppet and *Sesame Street* character had a 1970 chart hit with *Rubber Duckie*?

9 In 2020, which fast food company launched a lipstick designed to taste like their product?

10 Which boxing champion was found guilty of draft evasion, stripped of his titles and sentenced to five years in prison, but ultimately never served a day in either the army or jail?

11 On a standard computer keyboard, which letter is located between Z and C?

12 Satirical outlandish factoids about which action movie star have been a meme on the internet since 2005?

13 Which imperial unit of volume is the equivalent of 568ml?

14 Were it hollow, which planet of the solar system could all the other planets theoretically fit inside?

15 By both volume of water and surface area, what is the largest lake in South America?

16 Which continent has the most countries, with 54?

17 What word can refer to the way fabric lies, or a short sleep?

18 Nicolas Jacques Pelletier in 1792 was the first, and Hamida Djandoubi in 1977 was the last person in France to be executed by what method?

19 Which English county is known as "Shakespeare's County"?

20 Gold Hill in Shaftesbury, Dorset was the cobbled street setting for the 1970s "boy on a bike" TV advert for which brand of bread?

Easy

Medium

Hard

Answers to QUIZ 397 – Pot Luck

1	Seaweed	11	Albert Einstein (*Einstein on the Beach*)
2	Romesh Ranganathan	12	George Mallory
3	"Doubting" Thomas	13	Mike Baldwin
4	John Buchan	14	An error in a program
5	Sellafield	15	Inter-continental ballistic missile
6	Florence	16	Bishop
7	Halley's Comet	17	*Hamlet*
8	*Dizzy*	18	Hangman
9	Metamorphosis	19	Martin Brundle
10	Any religious affiliation	20	Edward VII

Identify these famous pugilists.

1

2

3

4

5

6

7

8

9

Answers to QUIZ 398 – Body Parts

1	Teeth	11	Thumb
2	Cornea – it gets its oxygen directly from the air	12	Hyoid, at the root of the tongue
3	In the feet (26 each)	13	Rumbling stomach
4	The left, due to the presence of the liver	14	Femur (thigh bone)
5	The skin	15	Ear
6	The heart	16	They are not directly connected to the sternum
7	Liver	17	Brain
8	Webbed feet	18	Stomach
9	Diaphragm	19	It closes the bottom jaw
10	Pink	20	Bone marrow

1   After controversy in the 2020 Olympics, which sport was removed from the modern pentathlon?

2   At 56 characters in length, what is the longest country name in the world?

3   Where would a Spanish lady wear a mantilla?

4   With the real name Gaius Caesar Augustus Germanicus, which Roman Emperor was instead known by a name that translated as "little boots"?

5   Hermann Maier is a multi-time World and Olympic champion in multiple disciplines of which sport?

6   Completed in 1472, which English cathedral took almost 250 years to build?

7   In weaving, what tool is a spindle-shaped device designed to carry the crosswise threads (weft) through the lengthwise threads (warp)?

8   Malawi and Zambia both use currencies with what name?

9   Limnology is the study of what geographical feature?

10 It is tradition in Italy on Christmas Eve to watch which 1983 Dan Ackroyd/Eddie Murphy film?

11 Which mononymic actress has appeared in a wide range of shows from Disney's *Shake It Up* to HBO's *Euphoria*?

12 Nicknamed "The Scientist", which golfer was the longest average driver on the PGA Tour in both 2020 and 2021?

13 If something is russety, what colour is it?

14 Which TV family lived at 1313 Mockingbird Lane?

15 By what name was the actress Betty Jean Persice better known?

16 Which British singer-songwriter formed the country rock project the Notting Hillbillies in 1988?

17 Longer than shorts but not as long as trousers, which style of pant that ends on the ankle bone takes its name from a Mediterranean island?

18 Now part of HSBC, which defunct high street bank branded itself as "the listening bank"?

19 The short-lived dnL, an attempt to steal consumers from Mountain Dew®, was a caffeinated version of what much longer-lived drink?

20 Which prize has sometimes been described as "The Nobel Prize for Mathematics"?

Easy

Medium

Hard

Answers to QUIZ 399 – Pot Luck

1	Malaria	11	X
2	Cannes Film Festival	12	Chuck Norris
3	Slash	13	Pint
4	1939-45	14	Jupiter
5	Kellogg's®	15	Lake Titicaca
6	Humber	16	Africa
7	Wearing shinpads	17	Nap
8	Ernie	18	Guillotine
9	KFC	19	Warwickshire
10	Muhammad Ali	20	Hovis

1   Who had a 2011 hit with *The Lazy Song*?

2   Lana Del Rey's *Carmen* and ABBA's *Dancing Queen* are both songs about a girl of what age?

3   1990's *A Little Time* was the only UK number one single for which band?

4   A whistled version of which jazz classic is used as the theme tune for the Harlem Globetrotters?

5   *Open Your Heart* was the fourth single released from which Madonna album?

6   *Sour* was the 2021 debut studio album by which singer?

7   Guy Garvey is the lead singer of which Bury-based rock band?

8   *Left of the Middle* was the debut studio album by which Australian singer?

9   Which instrument bears the colloquial nicknames "Hobo Harp", "Reckless Tram" and "Mississippi saxophone"?

10 Psy was the third Korean artist to hold the top two positions in the Billboard 100 simultaneously. Blackpink were third. Which boy band was second?

11 Madonna, Arcade Fire, Little Mix and Leonard Cohen have all recorded songs with the name of which historical figure as the title?

12 Pink Floyd sang about which man, who had the hobby of stealing women's clothes from washing lines?

13 *Where Is the Love* and *The Closer I Get to You* were two of the many duets between Donny Hathaway and which singer?

14 Gary Barlow released which album in 2012 to celebrate the Diamond Jubilee of Queen Elizabeth II?

15 Which electronic musical instrument is played by not quite touching it?

16 *Hybrid Theory* was the 2000 breakthrough album by which nu-metal band?

17 Who were the three musicians to be voted in the top fifty in the BBC's 2002 *Greatest Britons* poll?

18 Welsh rock band The Alarm released the 2004 single *45 RPM* under the guise of which fictitious teenage group?

19 Pat Monahan is the lead singer of which rock band, best known for their 2001 single *Drops of Jupiter (Tell Me)*?

20 *Rock 'n' Roll Gumbo* was the debut album of which New Orleans-based blues musician?

Answers to QUIZ 400 – Boxers

1   Muhammad Ali
2   Frank Bruno
3   Nicola Adams
4   Ricky Hatton
5   Mike Tyson
6   Deontay Wilder
7   Joe Calzaghe
8   Manny Pacquiao
9   Roberto Durán

ANSWERS ON PAGE 405

1   18th century Scottish physician George Cleghorn discovered that quinine could be used to treat which fever?

2   In ancient Greek society, what was a hoplite?

3   Which golfer won his only major at the 1992 US Open?

4   Who in 1964 became the first non-royal to appear on a British postage stamp?

5   Dr Zoidberg and Professor Farnsworth are characters in which animated science fiction television series?

6   On which London Underground line would you find Greenford station?

7   What 'I' is a narrow strip of land with sea on either side, forming a link between two larger areas of land?

8   Which multinational technology company owns the GeForce® brand of computer graphics cards?

9   Ljubljana is the capital city of which European country?

10 Which writer and philosopher wrote the *Father Brown* short stories and the novel *The Man Who Was Thursday*?

11 Which fruit takes its name from a large North African city?

12 Lee Ridley, the winner of *Britain's Got Talent* in 2018, performs under what stage name?

13 Which group reached no.1 in the UK singles chart with *Take On Me*?

14 The Molotov Cocktail was named by the citizens of which country when used on them by invading Soviet forces in World War II?

15 In World War II, to disguise their newly developed radar technology, the Royal Air Force attributed their pilots' success to a heavy diet of which vegetable?

16 The most-aired person on British TV, Carole Hersee, appeared where?

17 Which Middle Eastern appetiser is a thick paste typically consisting of mashed cooked aubergine, olive oil, lemon juice and various seasonings?

18 A "Canadian tuxedo" is a colloquial term for wearing what outfit?

19 Lawyer and human rights activist Peter Benenson founded which advocacy group in 1961?

20 The semispinalis, multifidus and rotatores are muscles in which part of the human body?

Easy

Medium

Hard

Answers to QUIZ 401 – Pot Luck

Easy

1   *Time's* Person of the Year award is a measure of how *influential* one is, rather than necessarily how good; with this in mind, who won it in 1938?

2   Every serving US President since the award's inception has won it, except two; Herbert Hoover, and which man, President between 1974 and 1977?

3   In light of certain financial scandals, Cynthia Cooper, Coleen Rowley and Sherron Watkins won the award in 2002 under which collective name?

4   In 2006, to represent individual internet content creators, which three-letter word was the award's winner?

5   In 2014, the award was given to health care "fighters" who helped stop the spread of which virus epidemic in West Africa?

6   The first non-human choice for the *Time* Man of the Year award was in 1982 for which piece of now-ubiquitous technology?

7   Which US President is to date the only three-time winner of *Time's* Person of the Year?

8   Lawyer Kenneth Starr was a joint winner of the award in 1998, along with which US President, whose impeachment had been triggered by Starr's investigation?

9   In 1949, a one-off Man of the Half Century award was given to which politician and Nobel laureate?

10   Although the attack on Pearl Harbour meant a last-minute change of plan, which Disney character, who had debuted in 1941, very nearly won that year's award?

11   Prior to the award being renamed to the more inclusive Person of the Year in 1999, four women had already won the award. Name any one of them.

12   Who was the first winner of the award in 1927, and essentially who it was invented for, as he had not been on the cover earlier in the year despite his aviation feats?

13   Which entire social class won the award in 1969 reinforcing the implicit American bias?

14   The backlash to the selection of which Asian leader in 1979 has seen all subsequent award winners be less controversial?

15   Since 2019, *Time* has also run a separate Entertainer of the Year award; which singer, rapper and flautist was the inaugural winner?

16   In light of the Arab Spring, Greek austerity protests and other civil unrest around the globe, "The Protester" was the collective award winner in which year?

17   Freedom fighters of which European country were the award's winners in 1956, which was mired in civil war at the time?

18   In 1930, the first non-American chosen for the award was which Asian political and spiritual leader?

19   What was the second non-human choice to win the award in 1988, highlighting an underappreciated issue at the time?

20   A variety of journalists who faced persecution, arrest or murder for their reporting won the award in 2018 under what collective name?

Answers to QUIZ 402 – Music

1	Bruno Mars	11	Joan of Arc
2	17	12	*Arnold Layne*
3	The Beautiful South	13	Roberta Flack
4	*Sweet Georgia Brown*	14	*Sing*
5	*True Blue*	15	Theremin – the note changes based on how
6	Olivia Rodrigo		close you get to it
7	Elbow	16	*Linkin Park*
8	Natalie Imbruglia	17	John Lennon (9th); Paul McCartney (19th); David
9	Harmonica		Bowie (29th)
10	Big Bang	18	The Poppy Fields
		19	Train
		20	Professor Longhair

1 On a horse, what name is given to the sloping part of the foot between the fetlock and the hoof?

2 "Yeezy" is a fashion collaboration between Adidas® and which American rapper and producer?

3 After retiring through back injury in 2015, which former 6'8" England Test cricketer took up weightlifting, and went viral with his body transformation pictures?

4 Which MP for Yorkshire between 1784 and 1812 was a leader of the movement to abolish the slave trade in Britain's overseas territories?

5 In March 2022, which Italian sprinter became the first man to be Olympic 100m champion and World Indoor 60m champion at the same time?

6 Which legendary athlete is best known for his achievement of winning the 5,000m, 10,000m and Marathon at the 1952 Helsinki Olympics?

7 Which is the only member of NATO not to have a standing army?

8 In 2015, which Welshman became the youngest person to receive fifty rugby union international caps, a record broken in 2020 by Vasil Lobzhanidze?

9 Used famously as a lyric in Queen's *Bohemian Rhapsody*, what is the Arabic word that means "in the name of God"?

10 What 'C' is a type of coarse plain-woven cotton cloth, typically plain white or unbleached?

11 Similar to collage, what is described as the craft of decorating objects with paper cut-outs?

12 Which peninsula in Dorset contains Swanage, Corfe Castle, Durdle Door and Studland?

13 Queen Elizabeth II is often credited with the creation of which hybrid dog species, a cross between a Welsh Corgi and a Daschund?

14 Which American sportswear and casual wear company sells product lines including HeatGear® and ColdGear®?

15 What term is given to the code of honour and moral conduct developed by the Japanese samurai?

16 At the 2020 Games, which swimmer became the first British athlete to win four medals at the same Olympic Games?

17 Almost all of California sits on which geological fault line?

18 Which brewer advertised its beers on both TV and radio using the "Real American Heroes/ Real Men of Genius" campaign?

19 Which public sector financial institution was run by the General Post Office before being absorbed into Alliance & Leicester in 2003?

20 The longest species of worm ever found on Earth shares its name with what item of fabric?

Easy

Medium

Hard

Answers to QUIZ 403 – Pot Luck

1	Malaria	11	Tangerine (from Tangiers, Morocco)
2	A soldier	12	Lost Voice Guy
3	Tom Kite	13	A1 (*not* a-ha; their version peaked at no.2)
4	William Shakespeare	14	Finland
5	*Futurama*	15	Carrots
6	Central line	16	On the BBC's test card
7	Isthmus	17	Baba Ghanoush
8	NVIDIA®	18	Double denim (i.e. denim jacket and jeans)
9	Slovenia	19	Amnesty International
10	GK Chesterton	20	Back

1. A young girl named Zoe Roth staring at a burning house and slightly smiling became a meme under what name?
2. Antonio Guillem's photograph representing infidelity "in a playful and fun way" went viral with what name?
3. Restaurateur Nusret Gökçe became a meme in 2017 for the way he prepared and seasoned meat under what name?
4. The Overly Attached Girlfriend character and meme originated in a YouTube video submitted in a contest held by which pop superstar?
5. Which misspelt phrase, mimicking a positive French expression, is often used sarcastically to caption photographs of unappetising food?
6. Prophetically, Cara Cunningham tearfully begged us all to do what in September 2007?
7. On a December 2020 Zoom meeting of the Hanforth Parish Council, who was said to have no authority?
8. In an early 2005 meme, which game character, having been absent during his group's discussion of a meticulous plan, returned and ruined it by charging straight into combat while shouting his own name as a battle cry?
9. Laney Griner uploaded a photograph of her son Sam trying to eat sand in 2007, which became a meme with what title?
10. Which female forename has become a meme as a pejorative associated with uptight, middle-class, do-gooder types who want to speak to the manager?

11. Which anonymous image-based bulletin board has been the genesis of many internet memes since 2003?
12. The woman pictured in the *Woman Yelling at a Cat* meme is Taylor Armstrong, a cast member in which reality show?
13. A group of Ghanaian men dancing became a meme in 2017 because they were carrying what at the time?
14. "Not sure if serious" often captions memes of the squinting eyes of Fry, a character from which cartoon?
15. The reaction meme "aight Imma head out" has which cartoon character getting out of a chair?
16. Memes, songs, a game and a statue were made in honour of which gorilla, shot by zookeepers in 2016 to protect the life of a child?
17. Grogu is the actual name of which fictional character, who went viral under a more descriptive name?
18. Which NBA superstar is the star of a meme in which he walks away, disappointed in a reporter's question?
19. Tardar Sauce, a real cat with a unique facial expression caused by an underbite, was the star of which meme?
20. Which evolutionary biologist invented the term "meme" in his 1976 book, *The Selfish Gene*?

Answers to QUIZ 404 – TIME Persons of the Year

1. Adolf Hitler
2. Gerald Ford
3. The Whistleblowers
4. You
5. Ebola
6. The computer
7. Franklin D. Roosevelt
8. Bill Clinton
9. Winston Churchill
10. Dumbo
11. Wallis Simpson (1936), Queen Elizabeth II (1952), Corazon Aquino (1986), and Soong Mei-ling (1937) as half of a joint award with her husband
12. Charles Lindbergh
13. Middle Americans
14. Ayatollah Khomeini of Iran
15. Lizzo
16. 2011
17. Hungary
18. Mahatma Gandhi
19. The Endangered Earth
20. The Guardians

1　Which chicken dish is named after a battle of the Napoleonic Wars?

2　Which Japanese form of massage therapy is based on the same principles as acupuncture, except with pressure applied using the hands?

3　A *bolo* is a Filipino type of what?

4　Who had a 1956 hit with *Why Do Fools Fall in Love*?

5　*Hashi*, an item used in Japanese cuisine, are better known in English as what?

6　Which 1996 film starring John Travolta takes its name from US military slang for an accident that involves nuclear weapons?

7　Which film director has credits including the action films *Where Eagles Dare* (1968) and *Kelly's Heroes* (1970)?

8　Which Somali model was described by Yves Saint-Laurent as his "dream girl"?

9　Calcium oxide (CaO) is commonly known by what name?

10　What are the three city states (or *Stadtstaaten*) of Germany?

11　What surname is shared by a *Fawlty Towers* resident, Sidney Poitier's character in *In the Heat of the Night* and a cat character in *101 Dalmatians*?

12　Harry Potter is depicted with a scar on his forehead in what shape?

13　Which African country was founded by the American Colonization Society, which believed black people would fare better in Africa than the US?

14　Which short microscopic hair-like vibrating structures move microbes, debris and mucus out of the airways?

15　Which five countries are known as the BRICS countries, considered to be the five economies that will dominate the global economy by 2050?

16　"Crocodile" was only ever a nickname; what was Crocodile Dundee's "real" first name?

17　Coined in 1964, which word describes the pleasant smell of rain on grass after a long period of warm, dry weather?

18　Who was assassinated by John Bellingham?

19　With 114, which English rock band had the highest number of appearances on *Top of the Pops*?

20　Which Mark Twain novel tells the story of Tom Canty, a pauper who lives with his abusive, alcoholic father in Offal Court, off Pudding Lane in London?

Easy

Medium

Hard

Answers to QUIZ 405 – Pot Luck

1	Pastern	11	Découpage
2	Kanye West	12	Isle of Purbeck
3	Chris Tremlett	13	Dorgi
4	William Wilberforce	14	Under Armour®
5	Marcell Jacobs	15	*Bushido*
6	Emil Zatopek	16	Duncan Scott
7	Iceland	17	San Andreas Fault
8	George North	18	Budweiser®
9	Bismillah	19	Girobank
10	Calico	20	Bootlace

1 *Dúirt mé leat go raibh mé breoite* – Irish for "I told you I was ill" – is which comedian's epitaph?

2 Which man, known as "The man with a thousand voices", has the headstone inscription "That's all folks"?

3 Whose epitaph reads "Free at last, Free at last, Thank God Almighty I'm Free at last", citing the lyrics of an African-American spiritual he frequently quoted?

4 Sonny Bono's epitaph features which of his song titles, preceded by the word "And"?

5 Mathematician Ludolph van Ceulen's headstone contains the first 35 digits of which number, which he had dedicated his career to calculating?

6 Which Rat Pack raconteur's epitaph reads "Everybody loves somebody sometime"?

7 "And away we go!" was a catchphrase, album, and ultimately the epitaph of which American comedian and composer, nicknamed "The Great One"?

8 Complete the epitaph found on a headstone in New Mexico; "Here lies John Yeast. Pardon me for…"?

9 Honouring one of his catchphrases, which American comedian's epitaph reads "There goes the neighbourhood"?

10 Which star of *Will Penny* and *Only When I Laugh* has an epitaph that reads "Go away – I'm asleep"?

11 The title of which of Frank Sinatra's songs appears, perhaps ironically, on his epitaph?

12 "O.K…I gotta go now" is on the gravestone of which legendary punk frontman?

13 Which Italian chemist and poet's epitaph simply says "174517", which had been his prisoner number at Auschwitz?

14 Which married vaudeville stars are buried together under a headstone that reads "Together Again"?

15 Which vaudevillian comedian and actor suggested his epitaph read "All things considered, I'd rather be in Philadelphia"?

16 Which member of the 27 Club has "True to your own spirit" written in Greek on his headstone in Paris's Père Lachaise Cemetery?

17 Which novelist, author of *White Fang*, has a non-descript large unshapen rock for a headstone, carrying the epitaph "The Stone the Builders Rejected"?

18 Whose epitaph reads "So we beat on, boats against the current, borne back ceaselessly into the past", the final line of his most famous novel?

19 "A Gentle Man and a Gentleman" is the epitaph of which boxer, who has a fish named after him?

20 After a lifetime of research, renowned Hungarian mathematician Paul Erdős's gravestone reads "I've finally stopped…" what?

Answers to QUIZ 406 – Modern Memes

1	Disaster Girl; Roth later sold the image as an NFT for $500,000	11	4chan
2	Distracted Boyfriend	12	*The Real Housewives of Beverly Hills*
3	Salt Bae	13	A coffin
4	Justin Bieber	14	*Futurama*
5	"Bone apple tea" (as in *bon appétit*)	15	SpongeBob SquarePants
6	"Leave Britney alone!"	16	Harambe
7	Jackie Weaver	17	Baby Yoda
8	LEEROY JENKINS (at least he had chicken)	18	James Harden
9	Success Kid	19	Grumpy Cat
10	Karen	20	Richard Dawkins

1 Which Pacific island nation was originally called the Friendly Islands by Captain James Cook after the congenial reception he received?

2 In Shakespeare's *Hamlet*, the title character gives a speech in a graveyard while holding a skull; whose skull was it?

3 On 9th June 2013, at the age of 15 years and 212 days, who broke a 93-year-old record to become the youngest cricketer to play in a competitive county game?

4 *One-Eyed Jacks* was the only directorial credit for which legendary film actor?

5 Which 1915 epic film by DW Griffith was lauded for its technical virtuosity, but denounced for its content, as it depicts a racially insensitive view of the US Civil War?

6 After tying for first in the team fencing competition at the 1924 Olympics, how did Hungary and Italy settle their differences?

7 Which is the only country in the world with three official, internationally recognised, capital cities?

8 Which former contestant joined *The Chase's* cast of chasers in 2020?

9 Shami Chakrabarti became the director of which advocacy group in 2003?

10 Because it is home to Emirates Airlines and their fleet of Airbus A380 planes, which international airport leads the world in average passengers per flight?

11 Which Welshman won the 1979 World Snooker Championships in what was only his second professional tournament?

12 Which former Formula 1 World Champion has a surname that is also a trick-taking card game?

13 Usually, drag racing strips are how long?

14 The Negev desert covers more than half of the surface area of which Middle East country?

15 In Greek mythology, which fruits were believed to be, and thus known as, "golden apples"?

16 In the name of the website, what does TMZ stand for?

17 After the Sun, which is the next closest star to Earth?

18 Kevin Moran of Manchester United was the first player ever sent off in an FA Cup final; in 2005, which Arsenal player became the second?

19 What was the sequel to the film *Analyze This*?

20 Aureolin, gamboge and jonquil are all shades of which colour?

Easy / **Medium** / **Hard**

Answers to QUIZ 407 – Pot Luck

1	Chicken Marengo	11	Tibbs
2	Shiatsu	12	A lightning bolt
3	Knife	13	Liberia
4	Frankie Lymon & the Teenagers	14	Cilia
5	Chopsticks	15	Brazil, Russia, India, China and South Africa
6	*Broken Arrow*	16	Mick
7	Brian G. Hutton	17	Petrichor
8	Iman	18	Spencer Percival, UK Prime Minister
9	Quicklime	19	Status Quo
10	Berlin, Hamburg and Bremen	20	*The Prince and the Pauper*

Easy

1. Gone are the days when video games came on hardware such as discs; which online storefront operated by Valve is the largest digital distribution platform for PC gaming?

2. In online parlance, which country's name is often used for any attractive, popular men who are successful with women?

3. On Twitch, rather than directly donating money, viewers thank streamers for their work by giving them what virtual currency?

4. Michael C. Hall portrayed a serial killer who would only kill other killers in which *Showtime* TV series?

5. Which video-hosting app did Donald Trump threaten to ban in the USA in July 2020?

6. On 7th September 2016, Apple praised their own "courage" when announcing they were ditching which feature on their next iPhone release?

7. What name links a Danish jewellery retailer and a music streaming service founded in 2000?

8. Reese Witherspoon, Nicole Kidman, Shailene Woodley, Laura Dern and Zoë Kravitz are the "Monterrey Five" that star in which TV series?

9. Credited with pioneering a genre of YouTube videos that focuses on expensive stunts, Jimmy Donaldson is better known as who?

10. The actor Donald Glover is also a recording artist who raps under what name?

11. Heather Feather and GentleWhispering are YouTube channels dedicated to which phenomenon, known by an acronym coined in 2010?

Medium

12. Jack Fincham was half of the winning couple in the fourth series of *Love Island*; who did he couple with?

13. Across all platforms, what was the most streamed single of 2021, with more than 2.17 billion plays?

14. What type of contemporary item made an accidental cameo in episode four of the final season of *Game of Thrones*?

15. Randall Munroe created which webcomic, one the tagline describes as "a webcomic of romance, sarcasm, math, and language"?

16. Latin trap and reggaeton artist Benito Ocasio raps, produces and sings under what name?

17. American actor and filmmaker John Krasinski launched which web news series during the coronavirus pandemic?

18. Snooki, Jwoww and Vinny Guadagnino were cast members on which MTV reality show?

19. Which comedian, actor and star of memes gave up his career as a doctor shortly before rising to fame as Leslie Chow in *The Hangover*?

20. When Jalaiah Harmon was only 14, she became famous after she choreographed which viral dance on TikTok?

Hard

Answers to QUIZ 408 – Epitaphs

1. Spike Milligan
2. Mel Blanc
3. Martin Luther King
4. "[And] The Beat Goes On"
5. π or pi (3.14159265358979323846264338327950288)
6. Dean Martin
7. Jackie Gleason
8. "...not rising"
9. Rodney Dangerfield
10. Joan Hackett
11. "The Best Is Yet to Come"
12. Dee Dee Ramone
13. Primo Levi
14. George Burns and Gracie Allen
15. W.C. Fields (although ultimately it was not used)
16. Jim Morrison
17. Jack London
18. F. Scott Fitzgerald (from *The Great Gatsby*)
19. Jack Dempsey
20. "...getting dumber"

ANSWERS ON PAGE 413

1   In much of European television, the repeated name of which vegetable is used as a sound effect imitating the murmur of a crowd in the background?

2   In internet terminology, what does CSS stand for?

3   The song *Up Where We Belong* won both the Academy and Golden Globe Awards for Best Original Song; which 1982 film was it written for?

4   Which part of the brain does not initiate movement, but contributes to precision and timing, thus controlling balance and coordination?

5   In March 2022, which explorer's ship, *Endurance*, was found on the bed of the Antarctic ocean, 107 years after it sank?

6   The name of which animal is also an initialism used for people regarded as the best ever in their chosen field?

7   *How to Be Champion*, released in 2017, is the first book by which South Shields-born comedian?

8   The numbers *Rich Man's Frug* and *Big Spender* appear in which 1969 Bob Fosse musical film?

9   The Dutch royal family acquired its colourful name from which medieval French town?

10   It is possible to shut Winston the flatulent butler in a walk-in fridge during the introductory level of the second game in which video game series?

11   In the logo for the DreamWorks animation studio, what is the boy holding?

12   Which amorphous clay-like rock is the chief commercial source of aluminium?

13   Before they were famous, Ed Byrne, Amanda Holden, Ortis Deley, Jenni Falconer and Nikki Grahame all appeared as contestants on which game show?

14   Until Boris Johnson became the second, who had been the only UK Prime Minister to have been born outside of the British Isles?

15   The central bank and monetary authority of the United States is known by what two word name?

16   Sir Francis Chichester commissioned which ketch specifically to sail single-handedly around the globe?

17   How many balls are on the table at the start of a game of billiards?

18   After what is London's Fleet Street named?

19   *Suspicion, Notorious, To Catch a Thief* and *North by Northwest* were all directed by Alfred Hitchcock and starred which actor?

20   Josip Broz, communist revolutionary and former president of Yugoslavia, was known by what mononym?

Answers to QUIZ 409 – Pot Luck

1	Tonga	11	Terry Griffiths
2	Yorick's	12	Nelson Piquet Jr
3	Matt Fisher	13	Quarter of a mile
4	Marlon Brando	14	Israel
5	*The Birth of a Nation*	15	Apricots
6	They had an actual duel; Italy won	16	Thirty-Mile Zone
7	South Africa – Pretoria (executive), Cape Town (legislative), Bloemfontein (judicial)	17	Alpha Centauri
		18	José Antonio Reyes
8	Darragh "The Menace" Ennis	19	*Analyze That*
9	*Liberty*	20	Yellow
10	Dubai		

1. The name of which Dutch cheese is also used today as a general term for cheese produced in the traditional Dutch manner?
2. The name of which cheese translated from Italian means "recooked"?
3. King Christian IX, Havarti and Rygeost are cheeses from which country?
4. Just as an oenophile is a connoisseur of wine, what is a connoisseur of cheese called?
5. A 2017 British Nutrition Foundation survey found that 29% of five- to seven-year-olds thought cheese came from where?
6. Generally, mozzarella cheese is what colour?
7. The process of heating milk to kill bacteria prior to its use in cheesemaking is named after which French chemist?
8. Which rolled pancake of Ashkenazi Jewish origin is commonly filled with sweetened cheese, then fried or baked?
9. Manchego cheese is made with the milk of which animal?
10. During an 1851 naval battle between Argentina and Uruguay, when Uruguay ran out of cannonballs, which cheese did they use instead?
11. Legend holds that which French cheese was discovered when a young shepherd left his meal in a nearby cave for several months to chase a beautiful girl?
12. Which broad category of cheese is traditionally used in a Cobb Salad?
13. Which type of strongly-flavoured Italian cheese with bluish-green veins is also the basis of a derogatory nickname for the London Stock Exchange?
14. On account of his body odour, the antagonist in the cartoon *Biker Mice from Mars* is named after which particularly pungent Belgian cheese?
15. With a name meaning "sliced", which Greek cheese is sometimes described as "pickled", as it is cured in brine?
16. Which firm and tangy Swiss cheese is named after a valley in the canton of Fribourg?
17. Which protein is the main one found in milk and, once it coagulates, forms the basis of cheese?
18. Sakura is a Japanese cheese washed in sake, wrapped in bamboo and flavoured with leaves from the sakura tree, a tree which produces which fruit?
19. Which cheese is used in tiramisu?
20. Which strong-smelling soft cheese, usually with an orange rind, takes its name from an Alsace town?

Easy

Medium

Hard

Answers to QUIZ 410 – Modern Culture

1	Steam	11	ASMR (autonomous sensory meridian response)
2	Chad	12	Dani Dyer
3	Bits	13	The Weeknd, *Save Your Tears*
4	*Dexter*	14	A Starbucks cup
5	TikTok	15	xkcd
6	Headphone jack	16	Bad Bunny
7	Pandora	17	*Some Good News*
8	*Big Little Lies*	18	*Jersey Shore*
9	MrBeast	19	Ken Jeong
10	Childish Gambino	20	The Renegade

1   The American superhero thriller and psychological horror film series *Eastrail 177 Trilogy* was written, produced and directed by which auteur?

2   Bugs Bunny and Mickey Mouse have only once officially appeared on screen together; in what film was it?

3   The *krone* is the unit of currency in which two European countries?

4   Before the 2006 death of Proof, how many members were there in the hip-hop group D12?

5   Which English racecourse shares its name with a card game?

6   Scoop, Muck, Dizzy, Roley, Lofty and Wendy formed the "crew" of which building contractor?

7   How many teeth does a fully matured male horse have?

8   The *Guru Granth Sahib* is the central holy scripture of which major world religion?

9   *A Doll's House* and *Peer Gynt* are works by which playwright?

10 How does the official motto of the United States of America, "E Pluribus Unum", translate into English?

11 What is the SI unit of electric charge, equal to the quantity of electricity conveyed in one second by a current of one ampere?

12 In a standard car, only under which circumstance is the driver allowed to go without a seatbelt?

13 John Wayne portrayed Ethan Edwards, a man looking for his abducted niece, in which 1956 western?

14 The 2019 NBA Rookie of the Year and the 2018 winner of the Ballon d'Or both had what forename?

15 Which former NFL star was nearly cast as The Terminator, but was deemed too nice and not plausible enough to be a killer?

16 The musical Miss Saigon was loosely based on which Puccini opera?

17 The inventors of the EchoSonic guitar amplifier and the board game Scrabble® both had what unfortunate surname?

18 Which American fast food chain has an icon modelled after the founder's daughter, Melinda Thomas-Morse?

19 On 11th December 1964, Bertha Franklin shot and killed which soul singer at the hotel she was managing?

20 Which decentralised hacktivist collective is primarily known for "denial of service" cyberattacks against several governments?

Answers to QUIZ 411 – Pot Luck

1   Rhubarb (and yes, it is technically a vegetable, even if it is used like a fruit)
2   Cascading style sheet
3   *An Officer and a Gentleman*
4   Cerebellum
5   Ernest Shackleton
6   Goat (GOAT = greatest of all time)
7   Sarah Millican
8   *Sweet Charity*
9   Orange
10 *Tomb Raider*

11 A fishing rod
12 Bauxite
13 *Blind Date*
14 Andrew Bonar Law
15 Federal Reserve
16 *Gipsy Moth IV*
17 Two; the other cue ball remains off the table until the opponent's first turn
18 The River Fleet (if you've never seen it before, that's because it's underground)
19 Cary Grant
20 Tito

1. The main stadium of the US Open tennis tournament is named after which former winner of the tournament?
2. Which Grenadian sprinter won gold in the men's 400 metres at the 2012 Olympics?
3. "Three in a bed" is a term used in which indoor sport?
4. The National Water Sports Centre is located just outside which city?
5. What is the minimum numbers of players that can be on a football team?
6. While clearly better known as a football show, the first BBC highlights show called *Match of the Day* covered which other sport?
7. How many skittles are used in the game of table skittles?
8. Which northern English football team were originally called Shaddongate United?
9. Which sport has rounds called York, Hereford, American and Portsmouth, amongst others?
10. Which male golfer won his first major at the 2011 US Open?
11. Victor Barna was five times world champion, and Angelica Rozeanu six times, in which sport?
12. "When a man holds you round the throat, I don't think he has come to apologise" is a reported quote from which F1 driver after a 1987 confrontation with Nigel Mansell?
13. In 1924, which country hosted both the Summer and Winter Olympic Games?

14. A *honbasho* is an official professional tournament in which sport?
15. Seating 132,000 people, the largest stadium in the world as of 2022 hosts which sport?
16. Who is the only person in NBA history to have won all of the MVP, NBA Finals MVP, All-Star Game MVP, Rookie of the Year, Coach of the Year and Executive of the Year awards?
17. In which sport is the Thomas Cup an international competition?
18. Which are the only two grounds in England to have hosted an FA Cup Final, an England football international and an England cricket test?
19. Armand "Mondo" Duplantis is a world record holder and gold medal winner in which sport?
20. Doggett's Coat and Badge is both the prize and the name for the world's oldest competition in which sport?

Answers to QUIZ 412 – Cheese

1	Gouda	11	Roquefort
2	Ricotta	12	Blue cheese
3	Denmark	13	Gorgonzola (it is sometimes known as Gorgonzola Hall on account of its colour scheme)
4	Turophile		
5	Plants		
6	White, though it can turn yellow if it has a higher than usual fat content	14	(Lawrence) Limburger
		15	Feta
7	Louis Pasteur (pasteurisation)	16	Gruyère
8	Blintz	17	Casein
9	Sheep	18	Cherry
10	Edam	19	Mascarpone
		20	Munster

ANSWERS ON PAGE **417**

1   In physics, which letter of the alphabet is usually used to represent electric charge?

2   Which chat show host once asked George Best, "Did you ever think, if you hadn't done all that running around playing football, you might not have been so thirsty"?

3   Who was the first actor to be made a life peer?

4   Which Spanish golfer won the US Open in 2021?

5   Popular with prison inmates and celebrities, *The 48 Laws of Power* was the 1998 debut book by which author?

6   A 2021 military coup in which Asian country was inadvertently caught on video by a girl performing a workout routine?

7   Until 1868, which Asian capital city was known as Edo?

8   The Fun Lovin' Criminals' song *Love Unlimited* tells of which R&B singer's exploits as a lifesaver?

9   Grey's Temple, Lincoln's Inn, Inner Temple and Middle Temple are collectively known as what?

10   Which toy, that has become used in a range of namesake sports, takes its name from a pie maker?

11   What name was shared by the author of the Mike Hammer detective novels, and an Irish-American mobster who controlled New York's Hell's Kitchen in the 1960s and 1970s?

12   Which chief minister to Henry VIII was beheaded on orders of the king, who later blamed false charges for the execution?

13   Which type of military aircraft have been derisively nicknamed "Buffs", meaning "Big Ugly Fat Fellows"?

14   Scottish businessman Sir William Alexander Smith founded which international interdenominational Christian youth organisation in 1883?

15   Save for a very slightly different shade of blue, the Romanian flag is nearly identical to the flag of which African country?

16   As of 2021, who is the only man to play in both an NFL Super Bowl and a MLB World Series?

17   The first specimen to be recognised as an early human fossil was discovered in 1856 in which European country?

18   Which gothic fantasy novel series created by Mervyn Peake features the characters Steerpike and Titus Groan?

19   Which rank of the peerage is directly below a duke?

20   Yellowstone National Park is spread across Wyoming, Idaho and which other state?

Easy

Medium

Hard

Answers to QUIZ 413 – Pot Luck

1	M. Night Shyamalan	11	Coulomb
2	*Who Framed Roger Rabbit?*	12	When reversing
3	Denmark and Norway	13	*The Searchers*
4	Six	14	Luka (Doncic and Modric)
5	Newmarket	15	O.J. Simpson
6	Bob the Builder	16	*Madame Butterfly*
7	40	17	Butts
8	Sikhism	18	Wendy's®
9	Henrik Ibsen	19	Sam Cooke
10	"Out of many, one"	20	Anonymous

All of these people go by the first name Charlie – can you name them all?

Easy

1

2

3

Medium

4

5

6

7

8

9

Hard

Answers to QUIZ 414 – Sport

1   Arthur Ashe
2   Kirani James
3   Darts
4   Nottingham
5   Seven – any less than that, and the game is cancelled
6   Tennis
7   Nine, in a pyramid shape
8   Carlisle United
9   Archery
10   Rory McIlroy

11   Table tennis
12   Ayrton Senna
13   France (Paris for the summer, Chamonix for the winter)
14   Sumo wrestling
15   Cricket (Narendra Modi Stadium, India)
16   Larry Bird
17   Badminton
18   The Oval and Bramall Lane
19   Pole vault
20   Rowing

ANSWERS ON PAGE **419**

1   Mikhail Gorbachev instituted which Soviet policy of open discussion of political and social issues in the late 1980s?

2   Which Herman Hesse novel takes the form of a manuscript written by its protagonist, a middle-aged man named Harry Haller?

3   The formula $\pi r^2 h$ calculates the volume of what solid object?

4   Between 1933 and 1947, the Hoover Dam on the Colorado River was instead known as what?

5   In which German city is the European Central Bank located?

6   After losing her singing voice, which legend of stage and screen has moved into voice acting with roles include Queen Lillian, Gru's Mom and Karathen?

7   Which actor, comedian and noted wit once remarked that "military intelligence is a contradiction in terms"?

8   *Passport to Pimlico* was the first in which series of British films, named for a studio and a district of London?

9   In the painting *The Monarch Of The Glen* by Sir Edwin Landseer, what type of animal can be seen?

10 What was the name of Gene Autry's horse?

11 Maria Montessori was best known for her philosophical work in which field?

12 On which day does the Catholic Church celebrate Jesus entering Jerusalem?

13 If a musical note is neither sharp nor flat, what is it?

14 The adjective "buccal" refers to which part of the body?

15 Eau-de-nil (literally, "water of the Nile") is a shade of what colour?

16 After travelling over 5,000 nautical miles, sailors would traditionally get a tattoo of which bird?

17 Who was lost for six days during the 1982 Paris–Dakar rally?

18 Media proprietor and impresario Louis Winogradsky was better known by what name?

19 *I Got Plenty of Nuthin'* is a song from which George Gershwin musical?

20 Brian Connolly, Steve Priest, Andy Scott and Mick Tucker were the best-known line-up of which glam rock band?

Easy

Medium

Hard

---

1 Maurice Micklewhite began his acting career as Michael White before changing it to what?

2 Due to issues with his label, which musician was known alternately as TAFKAP, The Artist, and an unpronounceable squiggle?

3 Rapper and producer Sean Combs changed his performer name to P. Diddy in 2001, and to just Diddy in 2005; what name did he use both before and after these?

4 Which courier service rebranded itself as Consignia in 2001, a move so unpopular that they reverted back to their previous name a year later?

5 Founded as Eboracum in 71 AD, and known as Jórvík in the time of the Vikings, what is this city known as today?

6 Which Scottish highland town has previously been called Maryburgh, Gordonsburgh and Duncansburgh?

7 Which English football team began life as St Mark's (West Gorton), then became Ardwick Association Football Club?

8 Which large south-eastern American city was founded as a railroad terminus called Terminus, then became Marthasville for six years, before adopting its current name in 1843?

9 Home of many NASA launches, the Florida headland known as Cape Canaveral was between 1963 and 1973 known as what?

10 Which publishing imprint was started in 1939 as Timely Comics, had by 1951 generally become known as Atlas, and then evolved into its modern name by 1961?

11 Which actor and singer was born with the surname Crocetti, and boxed under the name Kid Crochet?

12 The capital city of which country was previously known as Hochelaga and Ville-Marie?

13 Which wrestling legend performed as the characters Mankind, Cactus Jack and Dude Love?

14 Formerly known as Petrograd from 1914 to 1924, what was the Russian city of St. Petersburg known as between 1924 and 1991?

15 The dog in which classic cartoon series was known as Spike in 101 episodes, Butch in four, Killer in two and Bulldog in one?

16 Previously RAF Finningley, the airport now known as Doncaster Sheffield was, between 2005 and 2016, named after which folk hero?

17 Which prestigious American university has previously been known as Brown School, Union Institute, Normal College and Trinity College?

18 Between 1760 and 1849, which Japanese artist changed his name at least 30 times?

19 Elston Gunn, Blind Boy Grunt, Bob Landy, Robert Milkwood Thomas, Sergei Petrov and Zimmy are among the many aliases of which Nobel laureate?

20 Born Peter Williams and adopted as James Whitaker, which Lancastrian comedian/presenter's stage surname was a composite of the maiden names of his wife and mother?

Answers to QUIZ 416 – Charlies

1 Charlie Brooks
2 Charlie Sheen
3 Charlie Brooker
4 Charlie Dimmock
5 Charlie Watts
6 Charlie Adam
7 Charlie Parker
8 Charlie Brown
9 Charlie Puth

ANSWERS ON PAGE 421

1 In which fictional county is *The Archers* set?

2 The phenomenon whereby it is more difficult to detect feature changes in an upside-down face than an upright face is named after who?

3 What is measured in becquerel units?

4 In 1982, a Zimbabwean law was passed forbidding citizens from making jokes about which man's name, the first President of the country?

5 Brussels, Calais and Nottingham are or were all renowned for the production of what material?

6 Which mathematician recognised that Charles Babbage's Enigma machine had applications beyond pure calculation and is often regarded as the first computer programmer?

7 Concord is the capital city of which US state?

8 Ruler of Russia, Catherine the Great, was born in which country?

9 The Linke scale is used to measure what?

10 It was said that the mythical Sword of Damocles was suspended by what?

11 The throne of the Emperor of Japan – and, metonymically, the monarchy itself – takes its name from which flower?

12 Not counting the other countries of the United Kingdom, which national capital city is closest as the crow flies to London?

13 By what other name are the Somers Isles better known?

14 Verdaille is a method of painting using shades of which colour?

15 If someone can be described as lachrymose, what do they do often?

16 The surname of which Norwegian military officer, politician and Nazi collaborator has become a synonym for a traitor?

17 Due to the COVID-19 pandemic, 15 of the 19 events on the 2020-21 professional snooker circuit took place in which Buckinghamshire town?

18 Described as a "masterpiece of melodrama", *Drowning Girl* is a 1963 painting in a comic book style by which pop artist?

19 Which is the westernmost province of Canada?

20 Martina Navratilova won 177 women's doubles titles in her career. With which fellow American did she win 79 of them, including 20 Grand Slams?

Easy

Medium

Hard

Answers to QUIZ 417 – Pot Luck

1	*Glasnost*	11	Education
2	*Steppenwolf*	12	Palm Sunday
3	Cylinder	13	Natural
4	Boulder Dam	14	Cheek
5	Frankfurt	15	Light green
6	Julie Andrews	16	Swallow
7	Groucho Marx	17	Mark Thatcher, Margaret's son
8	Ealing Comedies	18	Lew Grade
9	A red deer stag	19	*Porgy and Bess*
10	Champion	20	The Sweet

1. Who won the men's 100 metres at the 1988 Summer Olympics in a world record 9.79 seconds, but later had both achievements stripped for doping violations?

2. In the 1995 World Rally Championship, which manufacturer was caught cheating by giving their Celica model cars an extra 50 brake horsepower?

3. The downfall of which American energy company has seen their name become a byword for willful corporate fraud and corruption?

4. Which former Manchester United footballer was discovered in 2011 to have had an eight-year affair with his brother's wife?

5. Which 2008 heist film starring Jim Sturgess, Laurence Fishburne and Kate Bosworth is based on the true story of the card-counting MIT Blackjack Team?

6. Which country was stripped of the gold at the Sydney 2000 Paralympic Games men's basketball after it emerged several players did not have the learning disabilities they claimed?

7. Six players in the history of Major League Baseball have been caught using what type of modified batting equipment?

8. In 2001, Major Charles Ingram was accused of cheating on which game show?

9. Which cheerful-sounding 1996 pop song is actually about a girl who cheats on her boyfriend, twice, while he joins the military?

10. In *Moonraker*, M charges James Bond with the personal task of determining whether which millionaire villain is cheating at bridge?

11. Which golfer took a four month hiatus from the game starting in 2009 after reports of numerous marital infidelities?

12. On 11th October 2000, which South African test cricket captain was banned for life on match-fixing charges?

13. As he was able to perform integral calculus in his head, which Serbian-American inventor's teachers believed that he was cheating?

14. *How To Cheat at Cooking* was a 2008 cookbook by which television chef?

15. Who did chess world champion Garry Kasparov accuse of cheating after he lost to them in a 1996 match?

16. Up, Up, Down, Down, Left, Right, Left, Right, B, A is a cheat code appearing in dozens of video games produced by which company?

17. Controversy rocked the 2011 world championships of which board game after one player reportedly demanded that Ed Martin be strip-searched in order to locate a missing playing piece?

18. A Yorkshire man named Chris discovered his girlfriend was cheating when Ziggy Stardust told him; who was Ziggy Stardust?

19. What colourful nickname is frequently used to refer to a list of people who are unwelcome in casinos, usually for cheating?

20. Thierry Henry's famous handball sent France to the 2010 FIFA World Cup at the expense of which country?

Answers to QUIZ 418 – Multiple Name Changes

1	Michael Caine	11	Dean Martin
2	Prince	12	Canada (Montreal)
3	Puff Daddy	13	Mick Foley
4	Royal Mail	14	Leningrad
5	York	15	*Tom and Jerry*
6	Fort William	16	Robin Hood
7	Manchester City	17	Duke
8	Atlanta	18	Hokusai
9	Cape Kennedy	19	Bob Dylan
10	Marvel	20	Jim Bowen

Easy

Medium

Hard

1 On what part of the body is a *keffiyeh* worn?

2 Which ABBA song was named after a spotlight used on stage and in stadium concerts?

3 The song *There is Nothing Like A Dame* comes from which musical?

4 Roland Deschain of Gilead is the gunslinger protagonist of which series of Stephen King novels?

5 Which "forbidden art" involves the practice of interpreting the weather or other atmospheric phenomena in order to predict the future?

6 For what was Little Annie Oakley famous?

7 Despite the name, Venetian blinds originated in which country?

8 William Hurt and Marlee Matlin starred in which romantic 1986 film, credited with changing the image of deaf people in popular culture?

9 Which politician provided the spoken-word vocals on Blur's 1997 song *Ernold Same*?

10 Which racecourse located 37 miles southwest of Glasgow hosts the Scottish Grand National?

11 What is the county town of Caithness?

12 Mount Parnassus, in the Pindus mountain range, is located in which country?

13 Complete the Charles Dudley Warner quote, often misattributed to Mark Twain: "Everybody complains about the weather, but nobody..."?

14 By what name was French artist Marie Grosholtz better known?

15 In nautical terminology, what term is used for a thick cable or rope used in mooring or towing a ship?

16 The *Araucaria araucana* tree is more commonly known by which animal name?

17 What is the name of Italy's national airline?

18 Hollie Bradshaw won Team GB's only field athletic medal at the 2020 Olympic Games competing in which event?

19 The varmint Muskie Muskrat was the sidekick of which cartoon lawman?

20 In 1995, who was initially rejected from the role that made him a big star, because of his gingerish hair?

Easy

Medium

Hard

Answers to QUIZ 419 – Pot Luck

1	Borsetshire	11	Chrysanthemum
2	Margaret Thatcher	12	Brussels (197 miles; Paris is 211, Amsterdam is
3	Radioactivity		225, Dublin is 292)
4	Canaan Banana	13	Bermuda
5	Lace	14	Green
6	Ada Lovelace	15	Cry
7	New Hampshire	16	Vidkun Quisling
8	Poland	17	Milton Keynes
9	The blueness of the sky	18	Roy Lichtenstein
10	A single horse hair	19	British Columbia
		20	Pam Shriver

Easy

1   In Leonardo Da Vinci's *The Last Supper*, who is said to be seated immediately to the right of Jesus?

2   The art of making decorative lacework with knotted threads is known as what?

3   Robert Rauschenberg was a painter and graphic artist from which country?

4   Which Flemish artist's home studio in Antwerp opened as a museum to the public in 1946?

5   Which pop artist created his silkscreen Electric Chair series using a press photograph from the Sing Sing Correctional Facility in New York?

6   In which country were the artists Paul Gustav Fischer and Anna Syberg, and the sculptor Bertel Thorvaldsen, all born?

7   Dating from approximately 1504, *Vision of a Knight* was a work by which Florentine painter?

8   The day after agreeing to sell it for $139 million, casino magnate Steve Wynn accidentally shoved his elbow through the canvas of which Picasso painting?

9   *Bowl of Fruit, Violin and Bottle* was a 1914 still life work of which artist?

10 The name of which avant-garde art movement is derived from a French term for "hobby horse"?

11 Hans Van Meegeren forged paintings by many artists, but who in particular was he known for imitating, after selling one of "his" works to Hermann Göring?

12 *Portrait of Dr Gachet* sold at auction for a then-record $82.5 million in May 1990; who painted it?

13 Which famous Baroque artist served as the court painter to King Phillip IV of Spain?

14 *Liberty Leading the People*, a painting commemorating the July Revolution of 1830, was created by which French artist?

Medium

15 The 2011 major solo exhibition at London's Hayward Gallery entitled *Love Is What You Want* consisted of work from which artist?

16 In which English city is the Cartwright Hall civic art gallery located?

17 What is the meaning of the artistic term *impasto*?

18 Henri Matisse described which art movement as "the newspaper of the soul"?

19 Known for her colours and frequent use of polka dots, which Japanese artist has voluntarily lived in a psychiatric hospital since 1975?

20 Which French poet, playwright and art critic is credited with coining the terms "Cubism" in 1911, "Orphism" in 1912 and "Surrealism" in 1917?

Hard

Answers to QUIZ 420 – Cheaters

1	Ben Johnson	12	Hansie Cronje
2	Toyota	13	Nikola Tesla
3	Enron	14	Delia Smith
4	Ryan Giggs	15	*Deep Blue*, the chess-playing computer developed by IBM
5	21		
6	Spain	16	Konami
7	Corked bat	17	Scrabble™; the missing "G" tile later turned up in another player's pocket
8	*Who Wants To Be A Millionaire?*		
9	*Macarena* by Los Del Rios	18	His parrot, who kept saying "I love you, Gary", which he'd clearly learnt somewhere
10	Sir Hugo Drax		
11	Tiger Woods	19	Black Book
		20	Ireland

1 The phrase "Power tends to corrupt, and absolute power corrupts absolutely" is credited to which 19th century historian and writer?

2 Who was the author of *Tarka the Otter*?

3 On which British island group are ceremonies called Up Helly Aa celebrated at the end of the yuletide season?

4 The 1985 documentary film *A.K.* is about which Japanese director?

5 What 'X' describes a garden or landscape created in a style that requires little or no irrigation or other maintenance?

6 What type of jewellery is a torc?

7 Which forensic pathologist is the main protagonist in a series of crime novels by Patricia Cornwell?

8 The majority of longbows throughout European history were made from which wood?

9 Someone described as an Old Wykehamist is an alumnus of which public school?

10 In 1995, which Bath fullback/fly half became the first England player to declare himself a full-time professional rugby union player?

11 Telemark is a turning technique used in which sport?

12 Hamadryas, Guinea, Olive, Yellow, Kinda and Chacma are the six species of which animal?

13 California, Steller, Australian, Galapagos, New Zealand, South American and Japanese are the seven identified species of which animal?

14 Rodney Bewes, Derek Fowlds, Roy North, Howard Williams and Billy Boyle were the straight men to which character?

15 Who won his second golf major with a record eight-shot victory at the 2012 PGA Championships?

16 Alevin, parr and smolt are all stages in the life cycle of which animal?

17 *My Guy* was a 1964 Motown single by which singer?

18 Nicholas Henty Dodd was a famous 1960s British television interviewer and radio DJ working under what pseudonym?

19 Thomas Arnold, developer of the prefect system, was headmaster at which public school?

20 Which Greek mythological heroine would only marry a man who could beat her in a foot race?

Easy

Medium

Hard

Answers to QUIZ 421 – Pot Luck

1	Head; it is an Arab headdress	11	Wick
2	*Super Trooper*	12	Greece
3	*South Pacific*	13	"...does anything about it."
4	*The Dark Tower*	14	Madame Tussaud
5	Aeromancy	15	Hawser
6	Shooting prowess in the Old West	16	Monkey puzzle
7	Japan	17	ITA Airways (Alitalia went out of business in September 2021)
8	*Children of a Lesser God*		
9	Ken Livingstone	18	Pole vault
10	Ayr	19	Deputy Dawg
		20	Colin Firth

Easy

1 In addition to solo work, which guitarist has played in The Yardbirds, John Mayall & the Bluesbreakers, Blind Faith and Derek and the Dominos?

2 Hank Marvin was the lead guitarist in which band from 1958 to 2020?

3 Guitar George, who knows all the chords, is mentioned in the lyrics to which 1970s rock song?

4 The Rock and Roll Hall of Fame described which guitar legend as "arguably the greatest instrumentalist in the history of rock music"?

5 Peter Frampton was so known as the artist who made which guitar effect famous that he now produces a custom line of them?

6 Known as the King of the Surf Guitar, which left-handed guitarist had a backing band known as the Del-Tones?

7 Django Reinhardt, one of the first major jazz talents from Europe, was born in which country?

8 Which guitarist collaborated with Matchbox Twenty vocalist Rob Thomas on the 1999 Grammy-winning song *Smooth*?

9 Eric Bell, Gary Moore and Scott Borham have all played guitar in which band?

10 In 2015, three former members of the Grateful Dead joined with which guitarist to form the band Dead & Company?

Medium

11 Richey Edwards, who went missing on 1st February 1995 and has never been found, was the rhythm guitarist in which band?

12 Which British guitarist played lead guitar on Bob Dylan's 1979 album *Slow Train Coming*, initially unaware of how religious it was?

13 In 1986, who became the first black blues act signed to a major label since Muddy Waters went to Columbia in 1977?

14 Who was the guitarist in the art/glam rock band Be-Bop Deluxe?

15 John Frusciante plays lead guitar, and Flea plays bass, in which Los Angeles-based rock band?

16 Which Canadian folk/rock legend is noted for her use of "weird chords" and has written songs in more than 50 tunings?

17 Whose 1990 album *Passion and Warfare* was described as "the richest and best hard rock guitar-virtuoso album of the '80s" by AllMusic.com?

18 Angus Young of AC/DC almost always performs on stage dressed as what?

19 In which 1961 film did Audrey Hepburn sit on a fire escape and play *Moon River* on acoustic guitar?

20 Which Harvard graduate has played feedback-heavy guitar in each of Rage Against the Machine, Audioslave and Prophets of Rage?

Hard

Answers to QUIZ 422 – Art

1	John the Apostle	11	Johannes Vermeer
2	Macramé	12	Vincent van Gogh
3	The USA	13	Diego Velázquez
4	Peter Paul Rubens ("The Rubenshuis")	14	Eugène Delacroix
5	Andy Warhol	15	Tracey Emin
6	Denmark	16	Bradford
7	Raphael	17	Thickly-applied paint
8	*Le Rêve* or *The Dream*; he later managed to get $155 million for it, so he clearly overcame the struggle	18	Impressionism
		19	Yayoi Kusama
9	Pablo Picasso	20	Guillaume Apollinaire
10	Dadaism		

1 Not including any posthumous anthologies, how many studio albums did The Beatles release in the UK?

2 What term is used to describe areas in the oceans that lack enough dissolved oxygen to support life?

3 What is the county town of the Irish county of Kerry?

4 In addition to being an accomplished jazz pianist, Charles Mingus was a player of what stringed instrument?

5 From 1981 to 1986, which legend of badminton was said to have gone on a 555-game winning streak?

6 In the solar system, which moon is the only one named after a male lover of Jupiter?

7 Coming to power in 2010, who was the first female Prime Minister of Australia?

8 Berry Gordy, Alphonso Mizell, Freddie Perren and Deke Richards were a group assembled to write songs for the Jackson Five under what name?

9 Which Scottish stand-up comedian also does the voiceovers for ITV's *Love Island*?

10 Covering 3.16% of the sky, what is the largest visible constellation?

11 How did Arthur C. Clarke devise the name of HAL, the computer in *2001: A Space Odyssey*?

12 What links a 1955 Dennis Stock photograph of James Dean and a 2004 Green Day single?

13 Named for the legendary Biblical city, Mount Sodom lies alongside which body of water?

14 In 2018, who became both the First Minister of Wales and the Leader of Welsh Labour?

15 In a 2003 Channel 4 poll, which song by the Reynolds Sisters was voted No.91 in a list of the 100 Worst Pop Records of All Time?

16 What is the term for a substance whose structure is built from a large number of similar units bonded together?

17 The first item listed on eBay – or AuctionWeb, as it was at the time – was a broken what?

18 The world's best-selling music notation software uses the surname of which Finnish composer?

19 *Valhalla*, a 2020 action role-playing video game developed by Ubisoft, marks the twelfth instalment in which franchise?

20 The talus bone is located in which area of the human body?

Easy

Medium

Hard

Answers to QUIZ 423 – Pot Luck

1	Lord Acton	11	Skiing
2	Henry Williamson	12	Baboon
3	Shetland Islands	13	Sea lion
4	Akira Kurosawa	14	Basil Brush
5	Xeriscape	15	Rory McIlroy
6	Necklace	16	Salmon
7	Kay Scarpetta	17	Mary Wells
8	Yew	18	Simon Dee
9	Winchester College	19	Rugby
10	Mike Catt	20	Atalanta

1 Which actress's eponymous *Workout* video became the highest-selling VHS tape of the 20th century?

2 Which future monarch was the child of Henry VIII and Jane Seymour?

3 Which actress's career roles have included *Two and a Half Men*, *The L Word*, *Criminal Minds*, *Role Models* and *Paul*?

4 Jane Doe or Jane Roe is used in American law as a placeholder name for an anonymous female party; what name is used as the male equivalent?

5 Known for her hot shooting, whiskey drinking and cross-dressing, American frontierswoman Martha Jane Cannary was better known as who?

6 Which actress starred in *Gentlemen Prefer Blondes* alongside Marilyn Monroe?

7 On 18th April 1963, which 17-year-old actress interviewed the Beatles, and subsequently began a five-year relationship with Paul McCartney?

8 Which singer, songwriter and television presenter from Wakefield rose to fame in 1998 following her appearance on the BBC show *The Cruise*?

9 Using a bizarre accent, which English actress played Daphne Moon on the sitcom *Frasier* from 1993 to 2004?

10 Which two of Jane Austen's novels are set partially in Bath?

11 In the 1847 novel *Jane Eyre* by Charlotte Brontë, what is the home of the male romantic lead, Edward Fairfax Rochester, called?

12 Former fake medium Patrick Jane is the titular main protagonist in which CBS crime drama series?

13 Bette Davis and Joan Crawford starred in which 1962 psychological thriller about an ageing former child star tormenting her paraplegic sister?

14 Which New Zealand director became the second woman to be nominated for (1994), and the third to win (2022), the Academy Award for Best Director?

15 Jane Porter was the love interest of which famous literary character?

16 In the 1997 American war drama film of the same name, who played *G.I. Jane*?

17 Thora Birch plays Jane Burnham, the daughter of Lester, a man struggling wih a mid-life crisis who falls for one of her friends, in which 1999 film?

18 Perry Farrell founded the Lollapalooza festival as a farewell tour for which of his bands?

19 Nancy Kulp played Jane Hathaway, Milburn Drysdale's loyal secretary, in which American TV sitcom of the 1960s?

20 Angie Harmon plays Jane and Sasha Alexander plays Maura as the title characters in which crime drama series?

Answers to QUIZ 424 – Guitarists

1	Eric Clapton	11	Manic Street Preachers
2	The Shadows	12	Mark Knopfler
3	*Sultans of Swing* by Dire Straits	13	Robert Cray
4	Jimi Hendrix	14	Bill Nelson
5	Talkbox	15	Red Hot Chili Peppers
6	Dick Dale	16	Joni Mitchell
7	Belgium	17	Steve Vai
8	(Carlos) Santana	18	A schoolboy
9	Thin Lizzy	19	*Breakfast at Tiffany's*
10	John Mayer	20	Tom Morello

Easy

Medium

Hard

1 Taylor Swift's song *We Are Never Ever Getting Back Together* is rumoured to be about which actor?

2 Which Romanian sculptor created the *Endless Column*, one of three works he produced to commemorate Romanian heroes of World War II?

3 What is the smallest number which, when two is multiplied to the power of it, exceeds a million?

4 Which author died having only gotten as far as the letter Y in her "alphabet" series of mystery novels featuring Kinsey Millhone?

5 TV production company Cosgrove Hall was most associated with which sort of programme?

6 In the 2012 film adaptation of *Les Misérables*, who played Fantine, the mother of Cosette?

7 Which Swedish rock band share their name with a colloquial term for the medical condition urticaria?

8 What name is given to a hymn sung while the clergy and choir are leaving a church at the end of a service of public worship?

9 According to all four canonical gospels, who assumed responsibility for the burial of Jesus after his crucifixion?

10 Before decimalisation, how many old pennies were there in a florin?

11 Which Swedish golfer won the 2016 British Open Championships with a major championship record score of 264?

12 *Ça Plane Pour Moi* is a 1977 three-chord rock song credited to which Belgian performer, even though he did not sing on the record?

13 What four-letter sequence names both a hedge fund that bought Coventry City FC in 2007, and the Finnish national characteristic of stoic determination?

14 Roseate, Sandwich, Common and Arctic are all types of which bird?

15 Grimpeur is a synonym for what type of hobbyist?

16 Damien Chazelle wrote and directed which 2014 film about an aspiring young drummer?

17 Which president of Panama served 17 years in US prison on drug smuggling charges between 1990 and 2007?

18 Foucault's pendulum was the first experiment to give simple, direct evidence of what?

19 Which science fiction TV series featured computers called Zen, Slave, Gambit and Orac?

20 Boll weevils are a major pest of which crop?

Easy

Medium

Hard

Answers to QUIZ 425 – Pot Luck

1	12	11	An abbreviation of Heuristically programmed ALgorithmic computer (the fact that it is a one-letter shift from IBM is a coincidence)
2	Dead zones		
3	Tralee		
4	Double bass	12	Both are called *Boulevard of Broken Dreams*
5	Jahangir Khan	13	Dead Sea
6	Ganymede	14	Mark Drakeford
7	Julia Gillard	15	*I'd Rather Jack*
8	The Corporation	16	Polymer
9	Iain Stirling	17	Laser pointer
10	Hydra	18	(Jean) Sibelius
		19	*Assassin's Creed*
		20	Ankle

1 Who made at least 60 cameos in the Marvel Cinematic Universe before his death in 2018?

2 Which English film director made cameo appearances in 40 of his 54 surviving major films, usually without speaking?

3 Patrick Stewart, Ronnie Corbett, Kate Winslett and Les Dennis all appeared as themselves in which Ricky Gervais sitcom?

4 Which entrepreneur's cameo acting appearances include *Only Fools and Horses*, *Spiceworld*, *Superman Returns*, *Friends* and *Entourage*?

5 Which famous director cameos in *The Blues Brothers* as the county employee who takes Jake and Elwood's money at the end of the film?

6 Which entertainer had an oft-forgotten cameo as villainous bookseller's assistant Swinburne in the 1971 film *Bedknobs & Broomsticks*?

7 John Travolta's mum and sister cameo alongside him in which 1977 film?

8 In which 2000 mock-gangster film starring Sadie Frost, Jude Law and Jonny Lee Miller does former boxer Ricky Grover make a cameo appearance?

9 Which pop superstar guest-starred as bricklayer Leon Kompowsky in a 1991 episode of *The Simpsons*, but went uncredited for contractual reasons?

10 *Rock 'n' Roll*, the eighth album by Motörhead, features a prayer read by which comedian?

11 Who played Jack Sparrow's father in two films of the *Pirates of the Caribbean* series after Johnny Depp openly cited him as an influence for his portrayal?

12 Eminem proudly declares his homosexuality in a cameo in which 2014 film?

13 Actor Stephen Baldwin has a tattoo of the initials of which character, after Miley Cyrus told him he could cameo on the show if he had it done?

14 Which rapper claims his cameo appearance in 1997's *Batman & Robin* was because the studio promised to cast him as the villain in the next movie if he did?

15 Rocker Billy Idol appears in an aeroplane scene and introduces a song over the intercom in which 1998 Adam Sandler comedy?

16 Who received high billing in the advertising for the film *Scream* despite being murdered in the opening scene?

17 While in prison, which world leader was repeatedly forced by US Marines to watch his cameo in *South Park: Bigger, Longer And Uncut*?

18 Which A-List actor agreed to cameo in *Deadpool 2* for just the daily minimum rate of less than $1,000, plus a cup of coffee hand-delivered by Ryan Reynolds?

19 A piece of VT played at the 2012 Olympic Games Opening Ceremony shows who supposedly parachuting out of a helicopter into the Olympic Park?

20 Which 1980s pop star features in an episode of *The A-Team* as himself, erroneously booked to sing at a country and western bar near an oil pipeline?

Easy

Medium

Hard

Answers to QUIZ 426 – Janes

1	Jane Fonda	11	Thornfield Hall
2	Edward VI	12	*The Mentalist*
3	Jane Lynch	13	*What Ever Happened to Baby Jane?*
4	John Doe	14	Jane Campion
5	Calamity Jane	15	Tarzan
6	Jane Russell	16	Demi Moore
7	Jane Asher	17	*American Beauty*
8	Jane McDonald	18	Jane's Addiction
9	Jane Leeves	19	*The Beverly Hillbillies*
10	*Persuasion* and *Northanger Abbey*	20	*Rizzoli & Isles*

QUIZ 429 – Pot Luck

ANSWERS ON PAGE 431

1. In which English city is the cathedral known as "Paddy's Wigwam" located?
2. Which Queen of Spain financed the 1492 voyage of Christopher Columbus?
3. US presidential candidate Pete Buttigieg revealed in 2019 that he had met his husband on which dating app, which markets itself as the only dating app to emphasise long-term connections?
4. Pashto and Dari are the two official languages of which Asian country?
5. In Nelson Algren's novel *A Walk on the Wild Side*, he advises never to play cards with a man called....what?
6. Among the in-joke references in *Private Eye* magazine, who is Beardie?
7. Which European country lost in the final of the 2019 FIFA Women's World Cup?
8. In 1930, and when they were still known as the British Empire Games, the first Commonwealth Games were held in which country?
9. A wimple is a cloth headdress covering the head, neck and the sides of the face still worn by some women of what profession?
10. The twelfth and final labour of Hercules was the capture of which Underworld creature?
11. Tim Campbell was the winner of the first UK series of which reality TV show?
12. *Plastic Hearts* (2020) is the seventh studio album by which American singer?
13. The ozone layer sits in which layer of the atmosphere?
14. *Apicius*, a 5th century AD Roman text, is one of the earliest examples of what type of book?
15. What word can mean a ballet posture with one leg extended backwards at right angles, or an ornamental design of intertwined flowing lines?
16. The book and film *The Wolf of Wall Street* tell the story of which disgraced stockbroker?
17. Lei Wulong and Paul Phoenix are characters from which series of fighting video games?
18. Prior to the Burj Khalifa taking the title in 2009, what had been the world's tallest building since 2004?
19. In dyeing, what name is given to a substance used to bind dyes on fabrics?
20. Whose artworks typically depict a grim, dystopian location in England, usually with *EastEnders* character Phil Mitchell looking on in disgust?

Easy

Medium

Hard

Answers to QUIZ 427 – Pot Luck

1. Jake Gyllenhaal
2. Constantin Brâncusi
3. 20 (2 to the power of 20 is 1,048,576)
4. Sue Grafton
5. Animation
6. Anne Hathaway
7. The Hives
8. Recessional
9. Joseph of Arimathea
10. 24
11. Henrik Stenson
12. Plastic Bertrand
13. SISU/Sisu
14. Tern
15. Rock climber
16. *Whiplash*
17. Manuel Noriega
18. Earth's rotation
19. *Blake's 7*
20. Cotton

We mostly do not use these things any more, but what were they called?

Easy

1
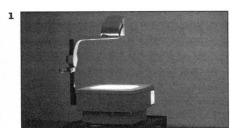

2

3

4

Medium

5

6

7

8

Hard

Answers to QUIZ 428 – Cameos

1	Stan Lee	11	Keith Richards
2	Alfred Hitchcock	12	*The Interview*
3	*Extras*	13	"HM", for Hannah Montana; he never did the cameo and regrets the tattoo
4	Richard Branson		
5	Steven Spielberg	14	Coolio (and if the studio did promise that, they did not follow through)
6	Bruce Forsyth		
7	*Saturday Night Fever*	15	*The Wedding Singer*
8	*Love, Honour and Obey*	16	Drew Barrymore
9	Michael Jackson	17	Saddam Hussein
10	Michael Palin	18	Brad Pitt
		19	Queen Elizabeth II
		20	Boy George

1. Depop and ThredUp are e-commerce platforms for buying and selling what general category of items?
2. In almost all photographs of analogue watches for sale, what "happy" time is the watch set to?
3. In the Bible, Jezebel was married to which king?
4. For the benefit of touch typists, small bumps or ridges called homing bars are often found on which two letters of a computer keyboard?
5. Which London Underground station has the most platforms?
6. Often known as mad cow disease, what do the initials BSE stand for?
7. In the Marvel cinematic universe, Johann Schmidt, the former head of HYDRA, has what codename?
8. Despite being a military march, Julius Fučík's *Entrance of the Gladiators* is nowadays much more commonly heard where?
9. Which portmanteau word describes an individual, group or country using sport to improve their reputation through hosting a sporting event or buying a team?
10. Where in Wales is Britain's Royal Mint situated?
11. Between 1993 and 2011, which country had three consecutive Prime Ministers with the surname Rasmussen, none of who were related?
12. Man Ray, Hugo Ball and Max Ernst were all associated with which deliberately offensive art movement originating from Switzerland?
13. By what name was the singer and actor Terrence Nelhams better known?
14. *Skyward Sword, Ocarina of Time* and *The Minish Cap* are releases in which action-adventure video game series?
15. Which survival game by Hello Games is set in a procedurally generated deterministic open world universe of over 18 quintillion planets?
16. Which Olympic judo medallist, MMA champion and professional wrestler goes by the nickname "Rowdy"?
17. What word means fixed in one place in biology, and attached directly by its base without a stalk in botany?
18. Who played the title character in the 1990s fantasy TV series *Xena: Warrior Princess*?
19. Which French cathedral was designated a World Heritage Site by UNESCO in 1979, which called it "the high point of French Gothic art"?
20. According to Greek myth, Sagittarius is said to be aiming an arrow into the heart of what other constellation?

Easy

Medium

Hard

Answers to QUIZ 429 – Pot Luck

1	Liverpool	11	*The Apprentice*
2	Isabella I	12	Miley Cyrus
3	Hinge	13	Stratosphere
4	Afghanistan	14	Cook book
5	"Doc"	15	Arabesque
6	Richard Branson	16	Jordan Belfort
7	Netherlands	17	*Tekken*
8	Canada	18	Taipei 101
9	Nuns	19	Mordant
10	Cerberus	20	Cold War Steve

1 In the television series *Hi-de-Hi!*, what was the name of the holiday camp?

2 Which religious festival holiday is observed by the kindling of the lights on a nine-branched menorah?

3 In the film *Summer Holiday*, Cliff Richard and the Shadows travelled to Greece via what mode of transport?

4 The holiday resort of Torremolinos is located in what country?

5 Which series of films features the stories of the various holiday adventures of the Griswold family?

6 What do the Pontins holiday company have as their equivalent to Butlin's redcoats?

7 Which Spanish *costa* includes the holiday resort of Benidorm?

8 In 321 AD, which Roman Emperor issued the civil decree that made Sunday a religious holiday?

9 ANZAC Day, Australia's annual holiday to remember fallen soldiers, is held on the 25th of which month?

10 In the United States, which President's birthday is a national holiday, taking place on the third Monday of every February?

11 What are the seven bank holidays common to all countries of the United Kingdom?

12 Japan takes a nationwide public holiday on the third Monday in September in celebration of who?

13 In the Jewish faith, what holiday is also known as the "Head of the World"?

14 Formerly the largest travel agent in tne UK, which company regularly ran TV advertisements of someone being told "Get away!", at which point they would disappear into thin air and end up at a vacation spot?

15 In some Slavic countries, *Pashka* is both a holiday and a food eaten on that holiday. Which?

16 *Día de la Madre* is a Spanish term for which holiday?

17 The Muslim holiday Eid al-Fitr marks the end of what?

18 Many Italians take a week's holiday known as the *Settimana Bianca* (White Week); where do they go?

19 Which South African-born British entrepreneur served as Director General of Hostels to the Ministry of Supply during World War II?

20 *Śmigus-dyngus* is a Roman Catholic holiday in Poland that, on Easter Monday of all days, traditionally involves what unusual courting ritual?

Answers to QUIZ 430 – Obsolete Technology

1 Overhead projector
2 Phonograph
3 Fax machine
4 Traction engine
5 Trebuchet
6 LaserDisc
7 Pager
8 PS/2 port

ANSWERS ON PAGE 435

1   Roger McGough, Mike McGear and John Gorman formed which poetry, music and comedy trio from Liverpool?

2   Lord Birkenhead said, derisively, that Winston Churchill devoted the best years of his life to doing what?

3   "Hacksaw" Jim Duggan was in 1995 the first ever winner of what format of wrestling competition?

4   Which pop star paid £1.67 million for the piano on which John Lennon wrote and composed *Imagine* on, then donated it to The Beatles Story Museum?

5   In which Gloucestershire castle was Edward II murdered?

6   In which needlecraft technique are stitches sewn on the surface of fabric pulled up into tiny tucks?

7   Which letter of the alphabet was essentially invented by Gian Giorgio Trissino in 1524?

8   Lady Day falls on which date in March?

9   Worcester Pearmain is a cultivar of which fruit?

10 What was Dominican friar Tomás de Torquemada's most notable historical contribution?

11 The Kariba Dam is situated on which river?

12 Neither counties nor countries, and neither part of the UK nor overseas territories, Guernsey, Jersey and the Isle of Man are classified as what type of administrative division?

13 *Go the Distance* and *Zero to Hero* are both songs from which 1997 Disney animated musical?

14 In 1885, who became the first actor to receive a knighthood?

15 Before her own solo career, who was the lead singer with The Go-Go's?

16 Although it is broken and has never been used, the Tsarsky Kolokol is the world's biggest example of what?

17 Gudrun Ure starred as the title character in which 1980s children's television show based on books written by Forrest Wilson?

18 Glaskin's Perpetual, Hardy Tarty and Timperley Early are types of which vegetable?

19 The investiture of Charles as Prince of Wales took place at which Welsh castle in 1969?

20 Which Poet Laureate also wrote twenty crime-fiction novels under the pen name Nicholas Blake?

Easy

Medium

Hard

Answers to QUIZ 431 – Pot Luck

1	Clothing	11	Denmark
2	10:10 – the theory being that the hands at that angle look like a smile	12	Dadaism
		13	Adam Faith
3	Ahab	14	*The Legend of Zelda*™
4	F and J	15	*No Man's Sky*
5	Baker Street (10)	16	Ronda Rousey
6	Bovine Spongiform Encephalopathy	17	Sessile
7	Red Skull	18	Lucy Lawless
8	At the circus – it is the "clown" music	19	Chartres
9	Sportswashing	20	Scorpio
10	Llantrisant		

1   More than 500 years after its discovery, the etymology of the name of which continent is still disputed?

2   What plant product is named for the 16th century French ambassador to Portugal, Jean Nicot de Villemain?

3   Which item of clothing is named for the leader of the Charge of the Light Brigade, whose troops wore them?

4   Greek philosopher Epicurus gives his name to epicures, who are lovers of what?

5   Which method of execution was named not for its inventor, but for the man who championed it as a humane alternative?

6   Which hotel is so associated with luxury that its name has become an adjective for something that expensively stylish?

7   President of France from 1969 until his death in 1974, which man gives his name to a structural expressionist modern art museum in Paris?

8   Which German patented a type of rigid airship in 1895?

9   Auguste Escoffier named four different creations (a toast, a peach pudding, a sauce and a chicken dish) after which soprano singer?

10 Which word for an abstention comes from the surname of an English land agent who was ostracised by the Irish after treating them very badly?

11 Which salad is named for a restaurant in Tijuana, Mexico, itself named after its Italian owner?

12 Which German inventor and mechanical engineer has both a combustion engine and the fuel that powers it named after him?

13 Taken from the literary character Don Quixote, how is someone acting if they are being "quixotic"?

14 John T. Thompson invented which submachine weapon in 1918, with the colloquial name for it taken from his nickname?

15 Philidor, Najdorf, Petrov, Evans and Tarrasch are among the hundreds of "opening systems" named after players of what game?

16 Which animal's name is a synonym for repeating things, something the animal is known for?

17 In poetry, which type of four-line biographical verse consists of two rhyming couplets and is invariably designed to make a famous person look absurd?

18 Bowdlerise is a verb that derives from Thomas Bowdler, an English editor; what does it mean?

19 Which unit of length equal to one hundred-millionth of a centimetre, used mainly to express wavelengths and interatomic distances, is named for a Swedish pioneer in that field?

20 What term for a severe law originates from the name of a 7th century BC Athenian legislator who created a written code of law?

Answers to QUIZ 432 – Holidays

1	Maplins	11	New Year's Day, Good Friday, the early May bank holiday, the Spring bank holiday, the Summer bank holiday, Christmas Day and Boxing Day
2	Hanukkah		
3	A red double-decker bus		
4	Spain	12	The elderly
5	*National Lampoon's Vacation*	13	Rosh Hashanah, the Jewish new year
6	Bluecoats	14	Lunn Poly (later Thomson, then TUI)
7	Costa Blanca	15	Easter
8	Constantine I	16	Mother's Day
9	April	17	Ramadan
10	George Washington ("Presidents' Day")	18	The mountains, hence the "white"
		19	Billy Butlin
		20	Boys throw water over girls and spank them with willow branches

ANSWERS ON PAGE 437

1   Which Danish-American comedian and pianist earned the nickname "The Clown Prince of Denmark" for his blend of music and comedy?

2   Which unit of textile measurement is defined as the mass in grams per 9,000 metres of fibre?

3   What was the capital of Portugal between 1808 and 1821?

4   David Balfour was the narrator and main character in two late 19th century novels written by whom?

5   Lasting from 21st February – 18th December 1916, the longest battle of World War I took place in which French city?

6   Bissextile is a word describing what?

7   The Baltimore NFL team takes its nickname from a work by which gothic author?

8   Which national capital city is nearest to the equator?

9   Breaking through as a part of the More Fire Crew, which MC's debut solo single *Pow! (Forward)* reached No.11 in 2004, despite limited airplay?

10 The letters PP appear prominently on the crest of which English football league team?

11 Which jazz vocal group had hits with *Chanson D'Amour*, *Birdland* and *Tuxedo Junction*?

12 In the name of the medical procedure CT scan, what does CT stand for?

13 Which CBS sitcom serves as the prequel to *The Big Bang Theory*?

14 A Dutchman named Anton Geesink was in 1961 the first non-Japanese person to do what?

15 Jello Biafra was the former lead singer and songwriter for which San Francisco punk band?

16 Considered the first widespread internet hoax, a 1994 rumour stated that Microsoft® had purchased which international institution?

17 When used as an adjective, "distaff" refers to what group of people?

18 Egon Madsen was a master of which of the arts?

19 Soleus muscles are located in which part of the human body?

20 Including dormant ones, which country has the most volcanoes?

Easy

Medium

Hard

Answers to QUIZ 433 – Pot Luck

1	The Scaffold	11	Zambezi
2	Preparing impromptu speeches	12	Crown Dependencies
3	Royal Rumble	13	*Hercules*
4	George Michael	14	Sir Henry Irving
5	Berkeley Castle	15	Belinda Carlisle
6	Smocking	16	Bell
7	J	17	*Super Gran*
8	25th	18	Rhubarb
9	Apple	19	Caernarfon
10	He was first Grand Inquisitor of the Spanish Inquisition	20	Cecil Day-Lewis

Easy

1 Which actress, most famous for appearing in the TV series *Charlie's Angels*, died on 25th June 2009, the same day as Michael Jackson?

2 Which aviation pioneer died on 30th January 1948, the same day as Mahatma Gandhi?

3 On the exact same day that saw the passing of second US President John Adams, the *third* President also died – who was he?

4 On the same day Patrick Swayze died, which English celebrity cook and "gastronaut", known for Panama hats and red wine, died of a heart attack?

5 *The Muppets* creator Jim Henson died on 16th May 1990, the same day as which *Rat Pack* member?

6 Name either of the two famous authors that died on the same day as John F. Kennedy.

7 Name either of the two important Russian figures – one a composer, one a political leader – who died on 5th April 1953.

8 Although Orson Welles never directed him, which actor – more famous for *The King and I* – appeared alongside him in the Yugoslav film *Battle of Neretva*?

9 Billy Wilder and Milton Berle both died on the same day as which comic legend, who unsuccessfully auditioned for the role of Tarzan?

10 The 3rd February 1959 aeroplane crash known as "The Day The Music Died" claimed the lives of Buddy Holly, Ritchie Valens, and which other rocker?

11 16th September 1977 saw the deaths of both which frontman of the band T. Rex and which American-born Greek soprano?

12 Learning of her death that morning, which French poet said "Ah, [Edith] Piaf's dead. I can die too", then did exactly that on the evening of 11th October 1963?

13 Which country music legend, known as "The Hag" and for his song *Okie from Muskogee*, died on his 79th birthday?

14 Wrestling legend Chyna died on the same day as which English sitcom star and creator of *Dinnerladies*?

15 Name the two authors to die on 19th February 2016; one a winner of the Strega prize, Italy's most prestigious literary award and the other a 1961 Pulitzer Prize recipient?

16 Actor and comedian Garry Shandling died on the same day as which Dutch football legend, famous for his eponymous "turn"?

17 6th January 1993 saw the dual deaths of which American trumpet virtuoso and which Russian ballet dancer and choreographer?

18 Fred Perry, tennis star and clothing label owner, died on the same day as which actor, who played Blofeld in *You Only Live Twice*?

19 On the same day as the actor Donald Sinden, which loyalist politician and Protestant religious leader finally surrendered?

20 Which Radio 4 comedy musician wrote the song *Try Not To Die, Whatever You Do, The Same Time As Someone More Famous Than You*?

Medium

Hard

Answers to QUIZ 434 – Eponyms

1	America	11	Caesar Salad
2	Nicotine	12	Rudolf Diesel
3	Cardigan (after James Thomas Brudenell, 7th Earl of Cardigan)	13	Unrealistic and impractical
4	Food and drink	14	Tommy Gun
5	Guillotine (not sure I agree)	15	Chess
6	The Ritz (ritzy)	16	Parrot
7	Georges Pompidou (the *Centre Pompidou*)	17	Clerihew (named for Edmund Clerihew Bentley, the pioneer of them)
8	Ferdinand von Zeppelin	18	To censor something
9	Dame Nellie Melba	19	Angstrom (after Anders Jonas Ångström)
10	Boycott (after Charles Boycott)	20	Draconian (Draco)

1   A photo of a Kitti's hog-nosed bat went viral in December 2021 on account of its resemblance to what?

2   Salonga, the largest tropical rainforest reserve in Africa, is located in which country?

3   After beating Italy 1-0 in 1966, which was the first nation from outside Europe or the Americas to progress beyond the first stage of a FIFA World Cup finals?

4   What is the more colloquial name for a graphospasm?

5   At the age of 32, who made his professional football debut in 2018 for Norwegian side Strømsgodset in a friendly match against the Norway national under-19 team?

6   Which actress has portrayed Zainab Masood in *EastEnders* and Mrs Hussein in *Still Open All Hours*?

7   The logo of the Royal Society for the Protection of Birds has an image of which bird?

8   After retiring from cycling, Sir Bradley Wiggins attempted a new career in which other sport?

9   In 2022, which English football league team became the first to ever beat all of the other 91?

10 Which courtship dance of northern Spain features couples clicking castanets and dancing bouncing steps to guitar music in 3/4 or 3/8 time?

11 Track 61 is a private hidden train station underneath which New York City building?

12 In 1906, which Canadian World Heavyweight Boxing champion defended his title twice in one night?

13 Arthur Flegenheimer was the name at birth of which Jewish mobster?

14 Aged only 25, who was appointed as the Creative Director of Paris fashion house Chloe in 1997?

15 In Arthurian legend, what name was given to the vacant seat at the Round Table reserved by Merlin for the knight who would one day be successful in the quest for the Holy Grail?

16 There are four Tate art galleries in the UK. Two are in London; one is in Liverpool. Where is the other?

17 Lord Zedd is a villain in which live-action superhero television series?

18 Ontology is a branch of philosophy concerned with what?

19 What word can refer to a catarrh-causing disease in dogs and other animals, or a type of paint with a glue base?

20 The building housing the London psychiatric hospital derisively nicknamed "Bedlam" was repurposed in 1930 and is now home to what?

Answers to QUIZ 435 – Pot Luck

1   Victor Borge
2   Denier
3   Rio de Janeiro, Brazil
4   Robert Louis Stevenson (*Kidnapped* and *Catriona*)
5   Verdun
6   A leap year
7   Edgar Allen Poe – they are the Baltimore Ravens
8   Quito, Ecuador
9   Lethal Bizzle
10 Preston North End; they stand for *Princeps Pacis* or Prince of Peace

11 The Manhattan Transfer
12 Computerised tomography
13 *Young Sheldon*
14 Win gold at the World Judo Championship
15 Dead Kennedys
16 The Catholic Church
17 Women
18 Ballet
19 Lower leg
20 United States of America (Indonesia has the most active ones)

Easy

Medium

Hard

Easy

1   New Albion was the name of the area of America claimed by Sir Francis Drake for England in 1579; in which state is it now located?

2   Marmolada is the highest peak of which Italian mountain range?

3   Into which bay does the River Ganges flow?

4   Which African country takes its name from its prominent role in the elephant trade?

5   When written in English, which is the only European country to contain one of the four main compass directions in its name?

6   So named for its minimal rainfall, inhospitable conditions and constant heavy surf, in which African country is most of the Skeleton Coast located?

7   Delamere Forest and Harmers Wood are located in which north-western English county?

8   From which country did the USA buy Saint Thomas, Saint John and Saint Croix (now known as the US Virgin Islands) for $25 million in 1927?

9   The Simplon Tunnel runs between which two countries?

10 The Straits of Mackinac connect which two of the Great Lakes of North America?

11 Flemish and Walloon are the two largest ethnic groups of which country?

12 Which historic archaeological city in southern Jordan is noted for how much of its ornate architecture is cut directly into mountain sides?

13 What does the country name Antigua and Barbuda mean in English when translated from Spanish?

14 Which French explorer was the first European to travel inland in North America, and discovered and claimed Prince Edward Island in 1534?

Medium

15 From 1859 to 1975, East Timor was a colony of which European country, before it was invaded by Indonesia?

16 Bahariya, Dakhla, Farafra, Kharga and Siwa are the five largest examples in Egypt of what type of geographical feature?

17 In London, what specific type of geographical features are Tyburn, Effra and Westbourne?

18 The surname of which former President is also the most common county name in the United States?

19 Which country styles itself as "The Land of Fire" due to the large natural gas fires that burn on the shores of the Caspian Sea?

20 Bir Tawil, an area near the unresolved border between Egypt and Sudan, holds what geographical distinction?

Hard

Answers to QUIZ 436 – Died on the Same Day

1	Farrah Fawcett	11	Marc Bolan and Maria Callas
2	Orville Wright	12	Jean Cocteau
3	Thomas Jefferson	13	Merle Haggard
4	Keith Floyd	14	Victoria Wood
5	Sammy Davis Jr	15	Umberto Eco and Harper Lee
6	CS Lewis or Aldous Huxley	16	Johan Cruyff
7	Sergei Prokofiev or Joseph Stalin	17	Dizzy Gillespie and Rudolf Nureyev
8	Yul Brynner	18	Donald Pleasence
9	Dudley Moore	19	Reverend Ian Paisley
10	The Big Bopper	20	Mitch Benn

1   Which property on a UK Monopoly™ board is named for a 21-metre narrow dead-end street with no establishments or shop/house frontages whatsoever?

2   1 million seconds is roughly 11 days. Roughly how long is 1 billion seconds?

3   What was the highly apt name of the Lord Chief Justice of England and Wales between 2013 and 2018?

4   Belém Tower is a coastal 16th-century fortification that serves as a ceremonial gateway to which European city?

5   What was a woman called Lynne Cox's role in the end of the Cold War?

6   Appointed as Leader of the House of Lords in 1981, who was Margaret Thatcher's only female cabinet appointee in her 11 years as Prime Minister?

7   By winning the US Open in 2015 at 33 years and six months, who became the oldest first-time tennis Grand Slam singles winner in the Open Era?

8   Who wrote the iconic work of fiction and socio-political satire *Utopia*, written in Latin and published in 1516?

9   Turbo Island is a "sloap" (a space left over after planning) in which English city?

10 Which legendary actor spent much of the final years of his life getting into arguments on AOL chat rooms?

11 Little Eva (in 1962), Grand Funk Railroad (1974) and Kylie Minogue (1988) all had hits with very different versions of which song?

12 The four stations in the UK version of *Monopoly™* were all served by which of the pre-British Rail "big four" railway companies?

13 Although now used to refer to a non-specific unit of time, what word in medieval times referred to a period of 90 seconds?

14 Mrs Doasyouwouldbedoneby is a fairy character in which partly-satirical 1863 children's novel by Charles Kingsley?

15 Johnny Vaughan presented which Channel 4 2005 hoax show featuring contestants who were told they were being trained as cosmonauts?

16 Up to the inauguration of Joe Biden, who is the only US President not to ever get married?

17 Heather McKay dominated which sport in the 1960s and 1970s, including 16 consecutive British Open titles from 1962 to 1977?

18 The ravens Huginn and Muninn were said to bring news to which Norse god?

19 The Champion Hurdle and Queen Mother Champion Chase are national hunt races held at which racecourse?

20 In *The Simpsons*, Maggie Simpson's first word was voiced by which famous actress?

Easy
Medium
Hard

Answers to QUIZ 437 – Pot Luck

1	A jam doughnut	11	The Waldorf Astoria hotel
2	Democratic Republic of Congo	12	Tommy Burns
3	North Korea	13	Dutch Schultz
4	Writer's cramp	14	Stella McCartney
5	Usain Bolt	15	Siege Perilous
6	Nina Wadia	16	St Ives, Cornwall
7	Avocet	17	*Power Rangers*
8	Rowing	18	The nature of existence
9	Port Vale	19	Distemper
10	*Jota*	20	Imperial War Museum

Easy

1 The 1990s saw the third through eighth releases in which science fantasy game series created by Hironobu Sakaguchi?

2 The best-selling Nintendo 64™ game not developed by Nintendo® themselves was which 1997 adaptation of a film released two years prior?

3 Initially developed for the Amiga, Psygnosis released which puzzle-strategy game in 1991 featuring drone-like animals who would not stop walking?

4 The oddly upbeat "game over, yeeeeaahh!" message from which 1990s racer has become an internet meme?

5 Because of its graphic "fatalities", which 1992 video game was deemed so violent that it prompted a series of US Senate hearings?

6 One of the greatest NBA players of all time appeared in which fighting game, considered one of the worst games of all time?

7 Queen Pulsating, Bloated, Festering, Sweaty, Pus-filled, Malformed, Slug-for-a-Butt was the final boss in which quirky platformer?

8 Two Mega Drive games released in 1991 and 1993 featured which pair of alien rappers from the planet Funkotron?

9 David Hayter voiced the lead character in which 1998 stealth game, and several of its sequels?

10 Named for part of the brain, who was the main villain in the *Crash Bandicoot*® franchise?

11 Chris Redfield and Jill Valentine were the two playable characters in the 1996 first release in which video game series?

12 What kind of animal was Knuckles, who joined the *Sonic the Hedgehog*™ franchise in 1994?

13 In which 1998 game does a firebreathing dragon set out to defeat Gnasty Gnorc?

Medium

14 Which 1998 Nintendo 64™ action-adventure game received perfect scores from the majority of gaming publications that reviewed it?

15 In which 1996 PlayStation® game does an onion in a karate costume teach a dog in a hat how to rap?

16 Which Super Nintendo® game (or perhaps, "game") sold more than 2.3 million copies worldwide and came packaged with a mouse peripheral?

17 What video game franchise began with platform games in 1991 and 1993, before moving to becoming a first-person shooter in 1996?

18 Peter Molyneux and Les Edgar founded which games development company, whose releases included 1994's *Theme Park*?

19 Before making the *Mass Effect* series, Bioware produced which 1998 fantasy role-playing game, inspired by Dungeons and Dragons?

20 Which bandana-wearing "game animal" sulked on an episode of *GamesMaster* in 1996 after losing at *Super Mario*™ 64?

Hard

Answers to QUIZ 438 – Geography

1	California	11	Belgium
2	Dolomites	12	Petra
3	Bay of Bengal	13	Ancient and Bearded
4	Ivory Coast	14	Jacques Cartier
5	North Macedonia	15	Portugal
6	Namibia	16	Oasis
7	Cheshire	17	Underground rivers
8	Denmark	18	Washington
9	Switzerland and Italy	19	Azerbaijan
10	Lake Michigan and Lake Huron	20	It is the only place on Earth that is habitable but not claimed by any government

QUIZ 441 – Pot Luck

ANSWERS ON PAGE **443**

1 Which American sports legend won two gold medals in track and field at the 1932 Summer Olympics, then turned to professional golf and won 10 LPGA major championships?

2 Which frozen food retailer founded by John Apthorp in 1968 was bought out by Iceland in 1989?

3 In linguistics, Toki Pona and Lojban are both types of what?

4 In Roman mythology, who was the goddess of wisdom, war, art, schools, justice and commerce?

5 In November 2012, which Radio 1 DJ mistakenly read out a Top 40 list from four weeks previously?

6 Salop is a former name of which English country?

7 The 15.5 mile-long King Fahd Causeway series of bridges and causeways provides a road link between which two countries?

8 "Probably the worst scholar Eton ever sent us – a buffoon and idler." So said ancient historian Oswyn Murray about who?

9 Leslie Grantham played Danny Kane, the co-owner of a nightclub, in which series?

10 In 2018, which African country changed its capital city from Bujumbura to Gitega?

11 A *mezuzah* – a parchment inscribed with religious texts – should be affixed to which part of a Jewish house?

12 Which natural pigment containing iron oxide and manganese oxide and used in painting is yellowish-brown in colour?

13 In 1992, American financier John Bryan was controversially photographed kissing whose toes?

14 Which Iraqi architect was known as the "Queen of the Curve"?

15 In 1906, which daily newspaper coined the term "suffragette"?

16 "The object of nature is man. The object of man is style." This was the unofficial mantra of which 20th century art movement?

17 Built by Charles Morton in Lambeth in 1852, where is often considered the first true music hall?

18 Euclid is associated with which branch of mathematics?

19 What was the main cause of the two-week Music Hall Strikes of 1907?

20 What was the name of the artist brother of the Brontë sisters?

Answers to QUIZ 439 – Pot Luck

1	Vine Street	11	*The Loco-Motion*
2	31.1 years	12	London and North Eastern Railway (LNER)
3	Lord Judge (his name was Igor Judge)	13	Moment
4	Lisbon	14	*The Water-Babies, A Fairy Tale for a Land Baby*
5	She swam across the Bering Strait between Alaska and Russia, drawing praise from both sides	15	*Space Cadets*
		16	James Buchanan
		17	Squash
6	Baroness Young	18	Odin
7	Flavia Pennetta	19	Cheltenham
8	Sir Thomas More	20	Elizabeth Taylor
9	Bristol		
10	Marlon Brando		

1   Which 1986 contamination incident caused an estimated $700 billion of damage, making it the most expensive single incident in human history?

2   Which extreme weather event of 2005 was estimated to have cost more than $125 billion in damages across the Americas?

3   While moving it out of a studio, movers dropped and broke Angela Hewitt's one-of-a-kind $194,000 Fazioli F278; what type of instrument was it?

4   What fell off a derailed train into Clark Fork River near Alberton, Montana on 6th July 2014?

5   On 4th August 2020, a large amount of ammonium nitrate stored in port in which Asian capital city exploded, causing at least $15 billion in property damage?

6   Including compensation, refloating, towing and scrapping costs, the total cost of the 2012 sinking of which cruise liner was estimated at $2 billion, more than three times the $612 million construction cost of the ship?

7   Which company had to pay $20.8 billion in fines alone for their negligence in causing the *Deepwater Horizon* environmental disaster of 2010?

8   How did a 15-centimetre tear appear in the $130 million Pablo Picasso painting *The Actor (L'acteur)* in 2010?

9   French state-owned railway company SNCF found that 2,000 new trains they had ordered at a cost of €15 billion in 2014 were unusable. Why?

10   The July 1988 sinking of which North Sea oil rig caused more than £1.7 billion in damage?

11   In 1999, NASA's $125 million interplanetary weather satellite, the *Mars Orbiter*, was destroyed through what simple human error?

12   Which £18.2 million London structure was £2 million over budget, opened two months late, was closed after two days and did not reopen for two years?

13   How did IT engineer James Howells lose £300 million in 2013?

14   Aggrieved repair shop owner Marvin Heemeyer caused $7 million of damage in a 2004 rampage when he demolished numerous buildings with a modified what?

15   Which motoring journalist's career has seen him write off both a record-setting Vampire dragster and a £1.2 million Rimac Concept One car?

16   A 2008 earthquake in which country killed around 68,000 people, left at least 4.8 million homeless, and resulted in around $86 billlion of damage?

17   In 2011, after aquaplaning and crashing his ultra-rare McLaren F1 supercar, which actor received a record-breaking £910,000 insurance payout?

18   In 2012, what fresco character was said to resemble "a crayon sketch of a very hairy monkey in an ill-fitting tunic", following a botched restoration by a Spanish amateur?

19   The most expensive aviation accident in history, what type of US Air Force aircraft crashed in Guam in 2008 at a cost of $1.4 billion?

20   To settle lawsuits brought by 46 US states, the "big four" manufacturers of what product agreed to pay a minimum of $206 billion over 25 years?

Answers to QUIZ 440 – 1990s Computer Games

1	*Final Fantasy®*	11	*Resident Evil* (or, in Japan, *Biohazard*)
2	*Goldeneye*	12	Echidna
3	*Lemmings*	13	*Spyro™ the Dragon*
4	*Sega Rally*	14	*The Legend of Zelda™: Ocarina of Time*
5	*Mortal Kombat*	15	*PaRappa the Rapper™*
6	*Shaq-Fu*	16	*Mario Paint*
7	*Earthworm Jim*	17	*Duke Nukem*
8	Toejam and Earl	18	Bullfrog Productions
9	*Metal Gear Solid* (he played Solid Snake)	19	*Baldur's Gate*
10	Dr Neo Cortex	20	Dave Perry

1 Which MLB player retired in 2016 having hit a record 25 Grand Slams?

2 In April 2021, which former NFL tight end set a world record by catching a football dropped from a helicopter hovering at 600 feet?

3 Liechtenstein is too small to have an airport; the airport of which city (in a different country) is the nearest?

4 Gordon Pirie was an Olympic silver medallist in which track event?

5 A cricket stadium named after Libyan leader Colonel Gadaffi is located in which country?

6 Green Room, Sushi Roll and Superman are all terms from which sport?

7 Capable of holding up to 10,000 people, which Ibizan nightclub is the world's largest?

8 What musical key is a piece written in if it has five flats?

9 The Riftwar Cycle is a series of fantasy novels by which American writer?

10 Known for the gap in her teeth, who in 1973 signed a then-record $250,000 annual modelling contract with Revlon?

11 The Glands of Zeis are found in which part of the human body?

12 Which country has the country code top-level domain extension of .kh, despite having neither letter in its name?

13 Which entertainer got his big break in 1905 when he roped a wild bull that had broken out of the Madison Square Garden arena and began climbing into the stands?

14 The entirety of which world capital city was chosen as a UNESCO World Heritage Site in 1964 due to its modernist architecture?

15 Of which Canadian province is St John's the capital?

16 Who did Private Eye magazine refer to as the Bouncing Czech?

17 Of all the fences in the Aintree Grand National, which two are only jumped once?

18 "Parrotheads" are fans of which country-rock singer?

19 Which 26-time winner of the Champion Jockey title is the only flat jockey to have been knighted?

20 Reflecting its country of origin, what do the initials in the name of the global financial institution ING stand for?

Answers to QUIZ 441 – Pot Luck

1	"Babe" Didrikson Zaharias	11	The front door
2	Bejam	12	Sienna
3	Artificial languages	13	Sarah Ferguson, then the Duchess of York
4	Minerva	14	Zaha Hadid
5	Greg James	15	Daily Mail
6	Shropshire	16	De Stijl
7	Saudi Arabia and Bahrain	17	Canterbury music hall
8	Boris Johnson	18	Geometry
9	The Paradise Club	19	Working conditions, including less pay for more work
10	Burundi	20	Branwell

What name do these DJs broadcast and/or perform under?

Easy

1

2

3

Medium

4

5

6

7

8

9

Hard

Answers to QUIZ 442 – That Looked Expensive

1   Chernobyl disaster
2   Hurricane Katrina
3   Piano
4   Three Boeing 737s
5   Beirut, Lebanon
6   *Costa Concordia*
7   BP
8   A woman taking an art class fell on it
9   They were too wide for the majority of the rail network's platforms
10   *Piper Alpha*

11   NASA used metric units of measurement, while a contractor used imperial
12   Millennium Bridge
13   He inadvertently threw away a hard drive containing the encrypted key to the 7,500 Bitcoins he owned
14   Bulldozer; he called it the *Killdozer*
15   Richard Hammond
16   China
17   Rowan Atkinson
18   Jesus Christ
19   B2 Stealth Bomber; the pilot survived
20   Cigarettes

1   Tritium is an isotope of which element?

2   *Hadith* is a collection of the words and actions of which religious figure?

3   Which London Underground station closed in 1994 when the cost of replacing the lifts was considered too expensive?

4   Which Greek astronomer wrote the *Almagest*, a foundational astronomy manual used for hundreds of years?

5   Which actor was the second person to report the death of Osama Bin Laden, and was only 47 seconds shy of the scoop?

6   Which age of Earth's history included the Triassic, Jurassic and Cretaceous Periods?

7   Azote is an archaic name for which chemical element?

8   Calico cloth was invented in and named for the town of Calicut in which country?

9   Winning in 1939 for *Boy's Town*, who was the first actor to win two consecutive Best Actor Oscars?

10   Which Portuguese woman introduced the fork to Britain, popularised tea, married Charles II, and banned flowers from Royal parks after learning he was picking them for his mistresses?

11   At one point home to almost every manufacturer in existence, which American city is regarded as the pinball machine capital of the world?

12   What year is found on the labels on bottles of Smirnoff® vodka?

13   Between 264 and 146 BC, the Punic Wars were fought between who?

14   Originating in ancient India, what sort of pastime is *pachisi*?

15   In the *Harry Potter* universe, F.A.R.T. – the fringe movement for wizards who prefer to wear robes at all times in public – is an abbreviation for what?

16   The statue of Eros in Piccadilly Circus commemorates which Victorian reformer?

17   The Anti-Homosexuality Act 2014 introduced a punishment of life in prison for "aggravated homosexuality" in which African country?

18   In horticulture, which technique involves interlacing branches to form a hedge or provide cover for an outdoor walkway?

19   A man named Johannes Ostermeier patented which piece of equipment used in the photographic process in 1930?

20   Ahead even of Paris, which is the largest French-speaking city in the world?

Easy

Medium

Hard

Answers to QUIZ 443 – Pot Luck

1	Alex Rodriguez	11	Eyelid
2	Rob Gronkowski	12	Cambodia – the Kh comes from Khmer, the national language
3	Zurich, Switzerland		
4	5,000m	13	Will Rogers
5	Pakistan	14	Brasilia, Brazil
6	Surfing	15	Newfoundland
7	*Privilege*	16	Robert Maxwell
8	D flat	17	The Chair and the Water Jump
9	Raymond E. Feist	18	Jimmy Buffett
10	Lauren Hutton	19	Sir Gordon Richards
		20	International Netherlands Group

1. Known for his work on *Mock the Week*, which comedian also released a couple of videos of cricketer impressions entitled *Creased Up*?

2. When working as a morning radio DJ in 1998, Jon Culshaw was able to blag his way into talking to Tony Blair on the phone by pretending to be who?

3. In BBC One's 2003 Christmas special *Posh and Becks' Big Impression*, who played Posh?

4. The first run of which puppet-based impressions show won ten BAFTA Television Awards, and two Emmy Awards in 1985 and 1986 in the Popular Arts category?

5. Rob Brydon and Steve Coogan traded impromptu impressions in which 2010 sitcom featuring slightly fictionalised versions of themselves as restaurant reviewers?

6. Which Scouse comedian got his big break through doing an impression of Mick Jagger at the 1970 Royal Variety Performance?

7. Usually seen in dramatic roles, which actor had a career redux when he became the go-to guy for impressions of Donald Trump on *Saturday Night Live*?

8. Jan Ravens and Debra Stephenson were among the talent on which comedy impressions show, broadcast first on BBC Radio 4 and later BBC Two?

9. Which impressionist featured in the BBC's *The Big Impression* for four seasons, and had his name in the title for the first three?

10. Known for his impression of Bill Clinton, which mimic and *Simpsons* voice actor was shot and killed by his wife in May 1998?

11. Which A-List actor started out performing impressions on the Toronto comedy club circuit, earning the nickname Rubberface?

12. Kevin Pollak, Bradley Cooper and Jim Caviezel are among the many, many people to have their own impressions of which actor, known for his fragmented way of speaking?

13. Which French Impressionist painter, famed for *A Bar at the Folies-Bergère*, died of a gangrenous leg in 1883?

14. Which mimic's once-substantial TV career began to struggle when the people he impersonated (such as Eddie Waring and Harold Wilson) faded from public view?

15. Which Canadian singer had an international hit with *That Don't Impress Me Much* in 1998?

16. *First Impressions* was the original title of which Jane Austen novel?

17. Invariably, every British television impressionist of the 1970s did a version of which sitcom character, usually including the phrase "oooh Betty"?

18. Matt Damon regularly does impressions of which actor on his talk show appearances, which always involve plans to take his shirt off?

19. *The Imitation Game* – a 2018 ITV game show in which impressionists went head-to-head – was hosted by which prolific presenter?

20. Which ground-dwelling Australian bird has a spectacular talent for mimicking sounds it hears, including tractors, chainsaws and camera flashes?

Answers to QUIZ 444 – DJs

1. Tony Blackburn
2. Carl Cox
3. Zane Lowe
4. Pete Tong
5. Avicii
6. deadmau5
7. Annie Mac
8. David Guetta
9. Frankie Knuckles

ANSWERS ON PAGE 449

1. Hit by a bus in 1949 and told he may never walk again, which golfer won three of the four majors in 1953?
2. One of the Wonders of the Ancient World, the Colossus of Rhodes was a statue of which Greek god?
3. Construction of which castle on the island of Anglesey began in 1294, but halted in 1330, and survives to this day unfinished?
4. Mr and Mrs Spoon were characters in which UK children's television series?
5. Gainsboro is a pale tone of which colour?
6. In Irish culture, what is a gombeen man?
7. Car manufacturer Honda developed which variable valve timing system, known by a four-letter acronym?
8. What natural landmark did businessman Peter De Savray narrowly outbid the National Trust for in 1987, buying it for £7 million?
9. The philosopher Francis Bacon called what "the purest of human pleasures"?
10. To absterse something or someone is to do what to it?
11. Yvon Petra, the 1946 Wimbledon men's singles champion, was the last person to win wearing what?
12. Calvados and Dubonnet combine to make which cocktail, named for a luxury car?
13. A five-mile extension of which UK motorway costing £457 million opened in June 2011?
14. Which American pop rock band featured on the 2007 Timbaland hit *Apologize*?
15. Strangers Gate, Pioneers Gate and Engineers Gate are among the twenty entrances to which famous park?
16. Mount Toubkal is the highest peak of which African mountain range?
17. In Australian slang, what are budgie smugglers?
18. Mintonette was the original name of what sport upon its invention in 1895?
19. Found commonly in leafy vegetables, pyridoxine is the scientific name for which vitamin?
20. The Kenbak-1, released in early 1971, is considered to be the world's first what?

Easy

Medium

Hard

Answers to QUIZ 445 – Pot Luck

1	Hydrogen	11	Chicago
2	The prophet Muhammad	12	1864
3	Aldwych	13	The Roman Republic and Ancient Carthage
4	Ptolemy	14	Board game
5	Dwayne "The Rock" Johnson	15	Fresh Air Refreshes Totally
6	Mesozoic era	16	Lord Shaftesbury
7	Nitrogen	17	Uganda
8	India	18	Pleaching
9	Spencer Tracy	19	The flash
10	Catherine of Braganza	20	Kinshasa, Democratic Republic of Congo

Easy

1. In the parlance of the circus, which type of performer can be referred to as a funambulist?
2. What name is given to the large tents in which traveling circuses traditionally take place?
3. On 12th November 1859 at the Cirque Napoleon in Paris, Jules Leotard became the first to perform what circus trick?
4. Founded in Canada, which circus has performed all over the world with tours such as *Quidam*, *Alegria* and *Saltimbanco*?
5. Auguste, Whiteface, Tramp and Character are the four recognised types of which circus performer?
6. In 2009, Bolivia was the first country in the world to ban what in circuses?
7. Which literary character's name was the stage name of Charles Sherwood Stratton, a circus performer noted for his small size?
8. Who opened the circus *The Greatest Show on Earth* in Brooklyn in 1871?
9. Before becoming an actor, which star of *Super Mario Bros* worked in the circus for a year as a clown, ringmaster and fire-eater?
10. Performing as Madame Pauline de Vere, Ellen Chapman was in 1848 said to be the first female circus performer to ever do what?

Medium

11. Which ancient society is said to have created the first circuses?
12. Which family of seven siblings founded and gave their name to a famous travelling circus that ran for 146 years?
13. Early circuses of modern times were almost exclusively made up of what type of act?
14. Merrylegs the performing dog appears at Mr. Sleary's circus in which Charles Dickens novel?
15. In circus industry terminology, what is a "mechanic"?
16. The Hartford circus fire on 6th July 1944 was the worst fire in the history of circus to date; what about the tent it was held in made it so bad?
17. *Circus* was a 2008 single and album by which pop superstar?
18. Opening in Philadelphia on 3rd April 1793, which was the first circus in America?
19. Why did P.T. Barnum call the exits on signage at his exhibitions the "egress"?
20. What is unique about the Flying Fruit Fly Circus located in Albury, New South Wales, Australia?

Hard

Answers to QUIZ 446 – Impressions

1	Rory Bremner	11	Jim Carrey
2	William Hague	12	Christopher Walken
3	Ronni Ancona	13	Édouard Manet
4	*Spitting Image*	14	Mike Yarwood
5	*The Trip*	15	Shania Twain
6	Freddie Starr	16	*Pride and Prejudice*
7	Alec Baldwin	17	Frank Spencer
8	*Dead Ringers*	18	Matthew McConaughey
9	Alistair McGowan	19	Alexander Armstrong
10	Phil Hartman	20	Lyrebird

1. Which Poet Laureate wrote the 1833 lyrical ballad *The Lady of Shalott*?
2. Which US state capital contains a full-scale replica of the ancient Parthenon of Athens?
3. To prove that time of descent was independent of mass, Galileo Galilei dropped heavy lead spheres from what landmark?
4. What do Fred Flintstone and Betty Rubble have on their face that Wilma Flintstone and Barney Rubble lack?
5. In which UK seaside town did ABBA win the 1974 Eurovision Song Contest with *Waterloo*?
6. At around 4,600 square miles as of 2022, which country has reclaimed the most land from the ocean?
7. To raise funds to convert an unused primary school into a community centre, what did the Scottish village of Embo do on 16th July 1988?
8. In February 2022, which Russian tennis player became the first man outside of the "Big Four" (Federer, Nadal, Djokovic, Murray) to hold the men's world No.1 ranking since Andy Roddick in February 2004?
9. In 2022, which became the first team to have played in the English Premier League to subsequently get relegated from the Football League?
10. On being ordered to surrender the town of Bastogne by the Germans, which US general famously replied "nuts"?
11. Kratos is the main protagonist in which video game series?
12. In August 2021, which English football club launched *Tangerine TV*, a reference to their distinctive kit colour?
13. Which tennis player died of AIDS in 1993, contracted from a contaminated blood transfusion after a heart bypass operation?
14. Which late former lead singer of Queens of the Stone Age had a voice described as being "as scratchy as a three-day beard"?
15. Which *Empire* actor was sentenced in March 2022 to 150 days in jail for staging a fake hate crime against himself?
16. Having invested his playing wages into pharmaceuticals, which former Arsenal midfielder was said to be worth $14 billion in 2020?
17. In English footballing terms, what are the "Cockney Firestarters", "Bushwhackers" and "Her Majesty's Service"?
18. 19-year old Canadian musician Taylor Mitchell became in 2009 the only adult known to have ever been killed in an attack by what animals?
19. Aprosexia is an inability to do what?
20. In 1733, John Kay invented what machine, an important step toward automatic weaving?

Easy

Medium

Hard

Answers to QUIZ 447 – Pot Luck

1	Ben Hogan	11	Trousers
2	Helios, god of the sun	12	Bentley
3	Beaumaris	13	M74
4	*Button Moon*	14	OneRepublic
5	Grey	15	Central Park, New York City
6	A wheeler-dealer/grifter	16	Atlas Mountains
7	VTEC (which somehow stands for Variable Valve Timing & Lift Electronic Control)	17	Swimming trunks
8	The Cornish headland of Land's End	18	Volleyball
9	Gardening	19	B6
10	Cleanse/purge	20	Personal computer

Easy

1   Which part of the human anatomy shares its name with a punctuation mark?

2   What is the proper name for the & symbol?

3   In mathematics, the factorial arithmetic operation is denoted by which punctuation symbol after a whole number?

4   Which four letter word beginning with D can mean to move rapidly, and is also the name of a punctuation mark?

5   In HTML mark-up language, which symbol is used to begin a "tag"?

6   What term refers to a set of dots (…) in speech that replace words that are superfluous or able to be understood from context?

7   In most English speaking countries, commas are used to break numbers into thousands (i.e. 10,000). In most non-English speaking countries, a full stop is used (10.000). What does the International Bureau of Weights and Measures recommend?

8   Which world leader's surname is also the name for a diacritical mark of a long horizontal bar placed above a letter for a long vowel sound?

9   Looking like a filled-in, backwards letter P, which punctuation mark is used as a non-printing character to denote the start of a new paragraph?

10 Bang, ecphoneme, shriek, pling and gasper are all alternative names for which punctuation mark?

11 ¿What is the only language that uses an inverted question mark at the beginning of a question and the normal question mark at the end?

Medium

12 Founded with the specific aim of "preserving its correct use", the "protection" society for which punctuation mark was shuttered by its 96-year-old founder in December 2019?

13 In chess notation, what two punctuation marks denote a move that is dubious but potentially interesting?

14 Which punctuation mark is represented by a comma under a dot?

15 Which is longer; an em dash, or an en dash?

16 The optional comma that follows the penultimate item in a list of three or more items and precedes the word "and" is named for which city?

17 A missing hyphen in a line of code caused which NASA spacecraft to fail and crash, five minutes into its July 1962 launch?

18 Often seen in comic strips, what name is given to any string of typographical symbols (such as @&*&!) used in place of any obscenities?

19 Lynne Truss had a 2003 Christmas hit with which book about punctuation, whose title was based on a joke about pandas?

20 Martin Speckter introduced a new symbol of a ! and a ? merged as a way of ending rhetorical questions with a single character – what did he call it?

Hard

Answers to QUIZ 448 – The Circus

1	Tightrope walker	12	The Ringling brothers
2	Big Top	13	Horsemanship
3	Flying trapeze	14	*Hard Times*
4	*Cirque du Soleil*	15	A safety harness
5	Clown	16	It had been waterproofed with a paraffin and gasoline mix
6	The use of any animals		
7	Tom Thumb	17	Britney Spears
8	P.T. Barnum	18	Ricketts' Circus
9	Bob Hoskins	19	So that patrons would follow thinking it was an exhibit, accidentally leave the arena, and have to pay again to get back in
10	Put her head in a lion's mouth		
11	The Romans		
		20	All the performers are children

ANSWERS ON PAGE 453

1 In which play do Jack Worthing and Miss Prism appear?

2 Who designed the R-4, which became the world's first mass-produced helicopter in 1942?

3 The Robert Burns Centre is located in which southern Scottish town?

4 *Country of the Blind* and *Quite Ugly One Morning* are novels by which Scottish writer?

5 What shingle ride links the Isle of Portland to the mainland coast of Dorset?

6 "By Strength and Guile" is the motto of which special forces unit?

7 What geographic honour is held by the Peruvian town of La Rinconada?

8 Built for the Festival of Britain, which Grade I listed concert hall near Hungerford Bridge was the first post-war building to be listed?

9 Voiceover artist Marcus Bentley is most famous for his work on which TV show from 2001-18?

10 What is the longest river found entirely in Wales?

11 Margarita Carmen Cansino was the real name of which actress, known as "The Love Goddess"?

12 Held in 1844, the first ever international cricket match was contested between which two unlikely countries?

13 During the 1980s, which manufacturer of household electrical goods began using the slogan "The appliance of science"?

14 Opened in 1827, which was the first suspension bridge to span the River Thames?

15 Venetian painter Jacopo Robusti was better known by what nickname, meaning "little dyer"?

16 *Coco de mer*, the largest seed of any plant measuring up to 12 inches long, is a seed of what type of tree?

17 Where would you find aglets?

18 Who won the 1906 Nobel Peace Prize for his arbitration in resolving the Russo-Japanese War?

19 What distinguishing feature identifies *millerighe* pasta?

20 Chitterlings are a foodstuff made from what part of an animal, usually a pig?

Easy

Medium

Hard

Answers to QUIZ 449 – Pot Luck

1 Alfred, Lord Tennyson
2 Nashville, Tennessee
3 The Leaning Tower of Pisa
4 Whites to their eyes
5 Brighton
6 China
7 Declared independence from the UK (it lasted one day)
8 Daniil Medvedev
9 Oldham Athletic (who were in the Premier League for its first two seasons, 1992-94)
10 General McAuliffe

11 *God of War*
12 Blackpool
13 Arthur Ashe
14 Mark Lanegan
15 Jussie Smollet
16 Mathieu Flamini
17 Hooligan "firms" (for Charlton Athletic, Millwall and Rangers respectively)
18 Coyotes
19 Concentrate
20 Flying Shuttle

1 In the context of someone's habits of working, what does M.O. stand for?

2 Through discovering the use of carbolic acid to improve the hygiene of surgical operations, which surgeon is considered the father of antiseptic surgery?

3 *Operation Desert Shield* was the first phase of which war of the early 1990s?

4 In the board game *Operation*, which part of the patient's body lights up if a player touches the metal edge with the tweezers while removing a body part?

5 On which English motorway can lorries be parked as a part of *Operation Stack* to prevent disruption?

6 Which Burmese city was returned to Allied control during World War II through the airborne and amphibious attack known as *Operation Dracula*?

7 What is removed in a hysterectomy?

8 *Operation Meetinghouse*, the single most destructive bombing raid in human history, commenced on 8th March 1945 on which city?

9 ROBODOC was the first surgical robot to have widespread use in what type of joint replacement operation?

10 Which scissors-like surgical tool is used in many surgical procedures to control bleeding?

11 Lingual frenectomies are performed to correct ankyloglossia, a bodily anomaly better known as what?

12 The product of an integer and all the integers below it is determined by which mathematical operation?

13 After her 1982 emergency operation to remove a fish bone from her throat, who joked "the salmon have got their own back"?

14 Although ultimately not used, *Operation Olympic* was an Allied World War II planned invasion of where?

15 In the *Fawlty Towers* episode *The Germans*, Sybil was in hospital for an operation on an ingrowing toenail; what does Basil wish it was for instead?

16 After becoming seriously ill during an Antarctic expedition in 1961, a Soviet surgeon had to operate on himself, blindly feeling around, to remove what?

17 Derived from the Ancient Greek for "cut", what word describes the fear of surgical operations?

18 *Operation Moolah* was a Korean War effort by the USA that offered $100,000 and political asylum for anyone who could steal what?

19 Mastoidectomy, myringotomy and the Mustardé technique are all operations performed on what part of the human body?

20 Behind breast augmentation and reduction, the third-most common cosmetic surgery in the UK in 2019 was blepharoplasty, a procedure on what?

Easy / Medium / Hard

Answers to QUIZ 450 – Symbols and Punctuation

1 Colon
2 Ampersand
3 An exclamation mark
4 Dash
5 <
6 Ellipses
7 Neither – instead, leave a space
8 Emmanuel Macron
9 Pilcrow
10 Exclamation mark
11 Spanish
12 Apostrophe
13 ?! (in that order)
14 Semi-colon
15 Em dash (used to separate extra information or mark a break in a sentence)
16 The Oxford comma
17 Mariner I
18 Grawlix
19 *Eats, Shoots & Leaves*
20 An interrobang

ANSWERS ON PAGE 455

1 According to the Talmud, who was the first wife of Adam, before Eve?

2 If immersed in water and properly heated gradually to just below boiling point, which other soft mineral closely resembles marble and is often used as a substitute?

3 Which comedian created the interview podcast series *Under the Skin*?

4 Cubby Broccoli and Harry Saltzman set up which production company in 1961 for the purposes of financing and producing the James Bond films?

5 In his play *Cymbeline*, William Shakespeare remarked that which Welsh natural harbour was a "haven"?

6 In gangster culture, what is being referred to when talking about vigorish or vig?

7 In a Japanese restaurant, what would you get if you ordered *unagi*?

8 Tasseography or tasseology is a fortune-telling method done using what?

9 Which battle was fought two days before Waterloo?

10 The garganey is a rare British species of what type of bird?

11 What word is given to the astronomic time span that runs from new moon to new moon?

12 For an April Fool's prank, in 1998, Burger King marketed a burger specifically for what type of people?

13 Which now-defunct manufacturer produced the Amiga range of personal computers?

14 Godfrey Hounsfield shared the 1979 Nobel Prize for Physiology for his development of which computerised diagnostic technique?

15 In 1975, which comedian had a No.1 hit with *D.I.V.O.R.C.E.*?

16 Which public-private partnership – created to reduce the British national debt through slave trading – had its bubble burst in 1720, causing economic meltdown?

17 Back, slip, zigzag and buttonhole are all types of what?

18 In September 2021, which Spanish fashion brand released *Trompe-L'Oeil* sweatpants with the illusion of plaid boxers sticking out the top for a price of $1,190?

19 *Operation Market Garden* was an unsuccessful Allied military operation during the Second World War fought in which country?

20 Paul Morel is the central character of which D.H. Lawrence novel?

Easy
Medium
Hard

Answers to QUIZ 451 – Pot Luck

1	*The Importance of Being Earnest*	11	Rita Hayworth
2	Igor Sikorsky	12	USA and Canada
3	Dumfries	13	Zanussi
4	Christopher Brookmyre	14	Hammersmith Bridge
5	Chesil Beach	15	Tintoretto
6	Special Boat Service	16	Palm
7	Highest permanent town in the world, 5,100 metres above sea level	17	On the ends of shoelaces
		18	Theodore Roosevelt
8	Royal Festival Hall	19	Grooves down the sides – *millerighe* means "a thousand lines"
9	*Big Brother*		
10	Tywi or Towy	20	Intestines

Easy

1. Which country is often described colloquially and in media as "down under"?
2. If the weather is said to be "chucking it down", what is it doing?
3. The Oxford Down is a domesticated breed of which animal?
4. Fittingly, *Countdown* presenter Colin Murray was born and raised in which Northern Irish county?
5. Hazel, Fiver, Bigwig and Blackberry are among the anthropomorphic main characters in which 1972 Richard Adams book?
6. Which rock band achieved a no.8 hit in both the UK and the US with the 2005 hit *Sugar, We're Goin' Down*?
7. The phrase "27 up, 27 down" describes how to achieve a "perfect game" in which sport?
8. *Down Down*, released in 1974, was the only UK no. 1 hit single for which prolific rock band?
9. What name links an HBO sports comedy starring Danny McBride as Kenny Powers, and a Jerry Reed song from the *Smokey & the Bandit* soundtrack?
10. Which 1999 book and 2001 film tell the story of the US military's controversial 1993 raid on the Somalian capital, Mogadishu?
11. *The Devil Went Down to Georgia*, a song about winning a golden fiddle from Satan, is a song first written and performed by which country group?
12. Which star of the 1986 film *Down and Out in Beverly Hills* was in 1992 voted *People* magazine's Sexiest Man Alive?
13. *SmackDown* is a flagship weekly television show for which global entertainment company?
14. Which range of chalk hills extends for about 260 square miles across Hampshire and Sussex?
15. Due to its apt chorus refrain, which 2013 EDM/trap song by DJ Snake and L'il Jon featured in a series of 2021 adverts for British Gas?
16. According to the song from *Mary Poppins*, a spoonful of what is said to make the medicine go down?
17. In which sport do teams of 11 players get four "downs", or attempts, to move a ball forward ten yards?
18. Serj Tankian, Daron Malakian, Shavo Odadjian and John Dolmayan are members of which Armenian-American metal band?
19. Which actress's career roles include *Upstairs, Downstairs*, *The Pink Panther Strikes Again*, *Rough Cut* and *North and South*?
20. *DownBeat* magazine administers a Hall of Fame for which genre of music?

Medium

Hard

Answers to QUIZ 452 – Operations

1. *Modus operandi* (loosely translated as manner of operation)
2. Joseph Lister
3. Gulf War
4. Nose
5. M20
6. Rangoon
7. Uterus
8. Tokyo
9. Hip; its job was to precision-carve the new socket joint
10. Haemostat
11. Tongue tie
12. Factorial
13. Queen Elizabeth, the Queen Mother
14. Japan, who surrendered before it began
15. An ingrowing tongue
16. His own appendix
17. Tomophobia (hence the suffix -tomy)
18. A Soviet MiG-15 fighter plane
19. Ear (the Mustardé technique involves pinning them back)
20. Eyelids

ANSWERS ON PAGE **457**

1   The scientific name for which snake is exactly the same as its name in common usage?

2   *Young Hearts Run Free* was a 1976 disco hit for which American soul singer?

3   In the legal profession, what is the act of calumny?

4   Which building at the centre of Islam's most important mosque, the Masjid al-Haram in Mecca, is the most sacred site in Islam?

5   Which movement of people believe (or want to believe) they are not under the jurisdiction of any government, and thus are immune to taxes, fines, etc?

6   Who first converted magnetism into electricity in 1831?

7   The actor and playwright Jean-Baptiste Poquelin became famous under which one-word stage name?

8   The story of the lost island of Atlantis comes from two dialogues written in approximately 360 BCE by which Greek philosopher?

9   The Davis Strait separates Canada from where?

10 The New Caledonia island group located roughly 750 miles east of Australia is a territory of which European country?

11 Which *The Man from U.N.C.L.E.* actor also wrote the intro and riff to Dr. Dre's hit *The Next Episode*?

12 The 1973 Chevrolet Impala was the first car to ever come with what feature?

13 Which Asian capital city was granted the royal title of "Distinguished and Ever Loyal City" by King Philip II of Spain?

14 The solo piano piece *Bagatelle No. 25 in A minor* by Ludwig van Beethoven is more commonly known as what?

15 In 1668, who created the earliest known functional reflecting telescope?

16 Which former *X Factor* finalist won the tenth series of *I'm a Celebrity... Get Me Out of Here!* in 2010?

17 What was the cause of the June 1966 crash of the $1 billion prototype XB-70 *Valkyrie* aircraft?

18 What was unusual about the exhibited works of artist Pierre Brassau at the Gallerie Christinae in Göteborg, Sweden?

19 Identifying the presence or absence of which inherited protein on the surface of red blood cells determines the compatibility of blood types?

20 In Yiddish slang, what is a *meshuggener*?

Easy

Medium

Hard

Answers to QUIZ 453 – Pot Luck

1	Lilith	11	Lunation
2	Alabaster	12	The left-handed
3	Russell Brand	13	Commodore
4	Eon Productions	14	CT Scan
5	Milford (hence the name of the subsequently-established town at the site, Milford Haven)	15	Billy Connolly
		16	South Sea Company
6	The interest on a loan	17	Stitch
7	Eel	18	Balenciaga
8	Tea leaves	19	The Netherlands
9	Battle of Quatre Bras	20	*Sons and Lovers*
10	Duck		

1. Which Old West lawman, bartender and customs agent was best known for killing the fugitive Billy the Kid in 1881?
2. On 8th November 1974, which peer disappeared after being suspected of murder, never to be seen again?
3. Robert Leroy Parker and Harry Alonzo Longabaugh were better known as who?
4. Which former teacher and prison officer turned up alive in December 2007, five years after he was believed to have died in a canoeing accident?
5. In the film *The Fugitive*, who was the namesake fugitive?
6. The only fugitive on the FBI's Most Wanted list to be captured in Britain, who was apprehended trying to fly to Africa two months after assassinating Martin Luther King?
7. Who was found in a hole in the ground on 13th December 2003 in the town of ad-Dawr?
8. What extreme body modification tactic did John Dillinger employ to try and evade capture?
9. After killing nine people in his Chicago "murder hotel", which serial killer fled to Canada with three of someone else's children?
10. Which political process means to hand over a fugitive or accused to the jurisdiction of the foreign state in which the crime was committed?
11. Which famous pair of fugitives had the surnames Parker and Barrow?
12. Which British robbery fugitive sang backing vocals on *Carnival in Rio* by German punk band Die Toten Hosen?
13. Which outlaw and stagecoach robber of the 1870s and 1880s was known for leaving behind poetic messages after his robberies?
14. The FBI's Ten Most Wanted Fugitives list was the creation of which director of the bureau?
15. In 1806 and while still a teenager, which Baron of Rochdale published *Fugitive Pieces*, his first volume of poetry?
16. On 18th September 1975, the FBI captured which fugitive heiress in a San Francisco apartment?
17. Which Harvard professor and 1960s psychedelics guru was on the run and living as a fugitive in Algeria in 1970?
18. A fugitive Cary Grant blends in with the crowd at Grand Central Station in which Alfred Hitchcock film?
19. Experiment 626, a fugitive alien, is a title character under a different name in which animated film series?
20. Who, in Genesis 4:14, said "I will be a restless wanderer on the earth, and whoever finds me will kill me", thus becoming the original fugitive?

Answers to QUIZ 454 – Down

1	Australia	11	The Charlie Daniels Band
2	Raining	12	Nick Nolte
3	Sheep	13	WWE wrestling
4	County Down	14	The South Downs
5	*Watership Down*	15	*Turn Down for What*
6	Fall Out Boy	16	Sugar
7	Baseball	17	American football
8	Status Quo	18	System of a Down
9	*East Bound/Eastbound & Down*	19	Lesley-Anne Down
10	*Black Hawk Down*	20	Jazz

1   Which course at the ski resort of St Moritz is often considered to be the birthplace of modern-day skeleton bobsleigh?

2   As of 2022, which Australian tennis star is the only player, male or female, to win a Grand Slam of all four major singles titles in the same calendar year, twice?

3   Real estate developer Mary Anderson invented what part of a car in 1903, but never profited from it, as her patent had expired before they became standard?

4   Which British artist is famous for "spin paintings", created on a spinning circular surface, and "spot paintings", rows of randomly coloured circles?

5   Who was the first Disney princess to have a tattoo?

6   In 2005, London's Strand Theatre was renamed after which Welsh actor and composer, who had lived above it for 38 years?

7   When someone's pulse is taken at the wrist, which artery is being felt?

8   Which literary title character owns a mandolin called Antonia?

9   A boom in the farming and eating of which animal is helping many Peruvian peasant farmers living below the minimum wage get out of poverty?

10   If you hit every segment on a dart board once, what does it add up to?

11   After Henry Ford left to start his new company, Ford, which other car maker was formed from the remnants of his previous business, the Henry Ford Company?

12   Which then-extant country banned hand gliding in 1980 for fear its citizens might use them to escape?

13   Which is the only animal to have four kneecaps?

14   Who won an Oscar for their role in an English language film in which they only spoke eight words in English?

15   The Bedchamber Crisis, concerning selection of the next Prime Minister, occurred very early in the reign of which monarch?

16   The largest football stadium in the world, the Rungrado 1st of May Stadium, is located in which country?

17   The name of which US state scores the hypothetical highest Scrabble® score, at 25?

18   Supposedly, because of its beauty and variety of wildlife, Winston Churchill called which country "the Pearl of Africa"?

19   Named for a Greek statesman, what term describes a victory that takes so much out of the victor that it is tantamount to defeat?

20   By what single word name is the Boeing 787 aircraft known?

Answers to QUIZ 455 – Pot Luck

1	Boa constrictor	13	Manila, Philippines (named after him)
2	Candi Staton	14	*Für Elise*
3	Slander	15	Sir Isaac Newton
4	The Kaaba or Ka'bah	16	Stacey Solomon
5	The sovereign citizen movement	17	The manufacturer of its engines wanted it in a
6	Michael Faraday		mid-air photo with four other planes they had
7	Molière		built engines for, and two of them collided
8	Plato	18	Pierre Brassau was a chimpanzee; it was done
9	Greenland		as a hoax to see if any critics would (or would
10	France		care to) notice
11	David McCallum	19	Rhesus factor
12	Airbags	20	A person acting crazy

1   *Dreams from My Father* is a 1995 memoir by which US President that explores his childhood in Honolulu?

2   Referencing his biggest solo single, which boy band member released the autobiography *Life Is A Rollercoaster*?

3   Harold Pinter married which biographer, whose career included works on Marie Antoinette, Charles II and Mary, Queen of Scots?

4   Better known as a novelist and critic, which American "New Journalist" also produced biographies on Marilyn Monroe and Lee Harvey Oswald?

5   *Pulling No Punches* was the subtitle of which politician's 2008 autobiography, seven years after he famously punched a man who threw an egg at him?

6   Marshall Terrill wrote a 1993 biography called *Portrait of an American Rebel* about which Hollywood star?

7   Donald Spoto's book *The Dark Side Of Genius* was a biography of which legendary film director?

8   *Neither Shaken Nor Stirred* by Andrew Yule was a biography of which James Bond actor?

9   The book *Of Molecules and Men* profiled which molecular biologist, whose work proved pivotal to our modern understanding of DNA?

10 *My Wicked, Wicked Ways* was the ghost-written autobiography of which notoriously hard-living actor, who died in 1959?

11 Which actor wrote the autobiography *A Funny Thing Happened on the Way to the Future*, referencing his most famous role?

12 *Nottingham Evening Post* writer Duncan Hamilton's 2007 biography *Provided You Don't Kiss Me* profiled which football manager?

13 Geoffrey Ward's 2004 book *Unforgivable Blackness* details the life of which early 20th century boxing trailblazer and the racist society he fought in?

14 Which surrealist Spanish artist, with his typical humility, entitled his autobiography *Diary Of A Genius*?

15 The biographical film and book *Lady Sings the Blues* tell the story of which blues legend?

16 Taking its name from a song she covered in 1965, which singer's autobiography was entitled *I Put A Spell On You*?

17 Which former Conservative party leader has written biographies on William Pitt the Younger and William Wilberforce?

18 Which folk singer was the subject of Marc Eliot's 1979 biography *Death of a Rebel*?

19 What classic novel is mentioned in a 2002 biography of Shania Twain even though she and the novel's author are unrelated?

20 Which African-American writer collaborated with Malcolm X himself on *The Autobiography of Malcolm X*?

Answers to QUIZ 456 – Fugitives

1	Pat Garrett	11	Bonnie and Clyde
2	Lord Lucan	12	Ronnie Biggs
3	Butch Cassidy and the Sundance Kid	13	Black Bart
4	John Darwin	14	J. Edgar Hoover
5	Dr Richard Kimble	15	Lord Byron
6	James Earl Ray	16	Patty Hearst
7	Saddam Hussein	17	Timothy Leary
8	Deliberately burned his fingers in acid to try and remove his fingerprints. (It did not work – they grew back.)	18	*North by Northwest*
		19	*Lilo & Stitch* [626 is Stitch]
		20	Cain
9	HH Holmes		
10	Extradition		

1. Advertising agency Goodby, Silverstein & Partners created which slogan for the California Milk Processor Board in 1993?
2. Exemplifying his stance as an existentialist philosopher, what did Jean-Paul Sartre define as hell?
3. Which Italian cathedral was built between 1386 and 1965, and contains more than 3,000 statues?
4. In April 2022, which TV presenter announced he had installed a urinal in his flat?
5. Specifically, what do nidologists study?
6. Which class of racing yacht has the same name as a Shakespeare play?
7. The Twitter™ feed of which columnist and author was added to the list of English A-Level set texts in 2013?
8. Which Nintendo® open-world video game series sees players living in a village inhabited by various anthropomorphic animals doing things such as fishing and fossil hunting?
9. Since 1973, Wilberforce, Humphrey, Sybil, Freya and Larry have held which official position in the UK Government?
10. First published on 11th March 1702, what was the first British daily newspaper?
11. When it was under German occupation, what was the Polish city of Wroclaw called?
12. From a transportation point of view, what do Downing Street, Disneyworld, the city of Mecca and Maccu Picchu have in common?
13. Cultivation of which crop was banned in France in 1748 because it was thought to spread disease, especially leprosy?
14. Woodford Aerodrome is a former airport near which English city?
15. In 1987, who become the first man to break the one-minute barrier for the 100m breaststroke in a 25m pool?
16. Which actress received the Golden Globe Award for New Star of the Year for her role in 1959's *Rio Bravo*?
17. Which boy band had a number two hit in the UK charts with *Crazy for You* in 1994?
18. Guipure is a type of what material?
19. Cachalot, deriving from the French for "big teeth", is an alternative name for which marine animal?
20. Who wrote the novel *The Phantom of the Opera*, on which the stage musical is based?

Easy / Medium / Hard

Even in monochrome, can you identify these species of moths and butterflies?

Easy

1

2

3

4

Medium

5

6

7

8
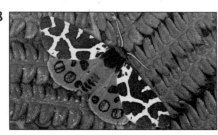

Hard

Answers to QUIZ 458 – Biographies

1	Barack Obama	11	Michael J. Fox
2	Ronan Keating	12	Brian Clough
3	Lady Antonia Fraser	13	Jack Johnson
4	Norman Mailer	14	Salvador Dali
5	John Prescott	15	Billie Holliday
6	Steve McQueen	16	Nina Simone
7	Alfred Hitchcock	17	William Hague
8	Sean Connery	18	Phil Ochs
9	Francis Crick	19	*The Adventures of Tom Sawyer*
10	Errol Flynn	20	Alex Haley

1 The former principality of Wallachia is now a part of which Eastern European country?

2 In *The Birth of Venus* by Sandro Botticelli, what is Venus standing on?

3 *Fireflies* was the 2009 debut single for which American electronica project?

4 Which Shakespeare play – admittedly with disputed authorship – is based on *The Knight's Tale*, one of the *Canterbury Tales*?

5 Derived from Eve, what does the name Zoe mean?

6 Secchi discs – black and white circular discs used to measure water transparency – are also used as markers on what type of safety test devices?

7 Campbell-Stokes recorders measure what meteorological phenomena?

8 Heptadecagons have how many sides?

9 The constitution of which South American country lists 37 official languages, six of which are extinct?

10 A British building is automatically "listed", and thus protected from development, if it was built before which year?

11 Serigraphy is a fancy term for what type of printing?

12 What name is given to those responsible for hand-walking racehorses to cool them down after races and workouts?

13 *Rigadoon, branle* and *gavotte* are French types of what?

14 What name is given to the bonds that join amino acid molecules together to form proteins?

15 In addition to being one of the Seven Wonders of the Ancient World, the Pharos of Alexandria was also the first known example of what?

16 Which French recipe consists of a finely chopped mixture of mushrooms, onions, herbs and black pepper?

17 In 301 AD, after the baptism of King Trdat III, which Eurasian country became the first in the world to formally adopt Christianity?

18 What rhyming name was given to the widespread fear and moral outrage in 1980s America resulting in many abuse allegations made against day care centres?

19 "Glamorous Glennis" was the nickname given to the X-1 supersonic aircraft flown by whom?

20 Which Scottish-sounding surname is used in cinematic terminology for an object or character in a film or story that serves as a plot trigger, if not much else?

Answers to QUIZ 459 – Pot Luck

1	"Got milk?"	11	Breslau
2	"Other people"	12	It is illegal to fly over them
3	Milan Cathedral/Duomo of Milan	13	Potatoes
4	Adrian Chiles	14	Manchester
5	Birds' nests	15	Adrian Moorhouse
6	[The] Tempest	16	Angie Dickinson
7	Caitlin Moran	17	Let Loose
8	*Animal Crossing*	18	Lace
9	Chief Mouser to the Cabinet Office – they are the cats that have lived at 10 Downing Street	19	Sperm whale
10	*Daily Courant*	20	Gaston Leroux

1   Which TV series follows the Halliwell sisters who, after the tragic death of their mother, discover they are powerful witches?

2   In *The Lion, The Witch, and The Wardrobe*, what was the White Witch's name?

3   The best-known book on witches, which treatise of 1486 detailed how to spot, investigate and punish witches?

4   In Homer's *The Odyssey*, the witch Circe drugs a band of Odysseus's men and turns them into what?

5   When Reverend Samuel Parris's daughter got sick and a doctor declared she had been struck by witchcraft, a mass hysteria broke out, resulting in which 1692 event?

6   *The Witch's Curse* is the subtitle to which Gilbert and Sullivan comic operetta?

7   Which witch-hunter claimed the office of Witchfinder General, having been responsible for the executions of over 100 alleged witches between 1644 and 1646?

8   Which Catholic Pope first acknowledged the existence of witches in 1484 and gave permission to do whatever it took to move against them?

9   Ozzy Osborne recorded a 1980 song about which English occultist, who founded the Thelemite religion in the early 20th century?

10   In her research into witch-cult theory, historian Margaret Murray described witchcraft as being divided into covens of how many members?

11   George Burroughs, a minister executed for witchcraft at the Salem witch trials, recited what during his execution, something it was believed a witch could never do?

12   Jill Murphy wrote and illustrated which series of children's books about a girl who attends a witch school?

13   A traditional Wiccan besom (witch's broom) has bristles made from twigs of which wood?

14   In a 1951 Gregory Peck film, who captained the sloop *The Witch of Endor*?

15   Nicole Kidman and Sandra Bullock play witch sisters in which 1998 film?

16   What did the Cajuns of New Orleans believe would happen to an evil witch when she died?

17   In 1990's *The Witches*, who played the part of Miss Eva Ernst, the Grand High Witch?

18   Whose series of fantasy books features a witch called Rhea of the Coos?

19   72-year-old Scottish woman Jane Yorke was, in 1944, the last person convicted under the 1735 Witchcraft Act. What was her punishment?

20   Helen Nicoll wrote, and Jan Pieńkowski illustrated, which children's books about a witch whose spells always seem to go wrong, and her striped cat?

Answers to QUIZ 460 – Moths and Butterflies

1   White Admiral Butterfly
2   Comet Moth
3   Small Tortoiseshell Butterfly
4   Io Moth
5   Eighty-eight Butterfly
6   Giant Leopard Moth
7   Zebra Longwing Butterfly
8   Garden Tiger Moth

1 The slang term "Shanks's pony" refers to what type of transportation?

2 Imre Nagy was a communist politician who served as *de facto* Prime Minister of which country?

3 In *Cheers*, what was Ernie Pantouso's nickname?

4 In 1978, who became the first female artist in UK history to go to number one on the Official Singles Chart with a song she had written herself?

5 Williamine is a brandy distilled from which fruit?

6 What is the SI unit for "dose equivalent", i.e. radiation exposure?

7 David Davis, Dominic Raab and Steve Barclay were the three holders of which now-non-existent Cabinet role?

8 In which 1991 Terry Gilliam film did Robin Williams play a "shock jock" who tries to find redemption by helping a man whose life he inadvertently shattered?

9 In the names of places such as Chipping Norton, what does the prefix "Chipping" mean or represent?

10 Which man, the winner of the 2005 World Snooker Championship, claims to be the only person to ever achieve a 147 snooker break, a nine-dart finish and a golf hole in one?

11 Before expanding into novels, Zoe Sugg became a YouTube celebrity under what name?

12 In October 1977, when baseball player Dusty Baker hit a home run, he and his team mate Glenn Burke spontaneously invented which celebratory gesture?

13 Which Asian country depends almost entirely upon wood for fuel?

14 *Karoshi* is a Japanese word for the country's problem of death through what?

15 The world's smallest painting measures merely 2.3mm by 2.3mm; what does it use as a canvas?

16 In 2019, a man with which "Interesting" name became President of Elon Musk's Boring Company?

17 As distinct from a diuretic, a herb or drug described as "diaphoretic" elicits what bodily reaction?

18 On 1st May 1950, Gwendolyn Brooks became the first African American to ever win what prize?

19 Literally meaning "circumciser", what name is given to a person who performs the Jewish rite of circumcision?

20 Which series of beat-'em-up computer games features characters such as Dhalsim, Ryu and Zangief?

Easy / Medium / Hard

Answers to QUIZ 461 – Pot Luck

1 Romania
2 A giant scallop shell
3 Owl City
4 *The Two Noble Kinsmen*
5 Life
6 Crash test dummies
7 The hours of sunshine bright enough to burn a hole through a card
8 17
9 Bolivia
10 1700
11 Screen-printing
12 Hot walkers
13 Dance
14 Peptides
15 Lighthouse
16 *Duxelles*
17 Armenia
18 Satanic Panic
19 Chuck Yeager
20 MacGuffin

ANSWERS ON PAGE 466

Easy

1   Which economist's work *The General Theory of Employment, Interest and Money* fundamentally changed economic policies of governments?

2   Known as the "father of economics", which Scotsman wrote *An Inquiry into the Nature and Causes of the Wealth of Nations* in 1776?

3   Which term, derived from casino gaming, refers to the stocks of a large, well-established company with a dependable reputation?

4   In the venture capital industry, the name of which fictional animal is used to describe a privately held start-up company with a value of over $1 billion?

5   Which economic theory states that tax breaks and benefits for corporations and the wealthy will filter through to all?

6   Scottish historian Thomas Carlyle coined which derogatory slang term for economics?

7   Which international financial institution was created at the 1944 Bretton Woods Conference?

8   Who was the first woman to serve as both the US Treasury Secretary and the 15th chair of the Federal Reserve?

9   Which South American country spiralled into hyperinflation, starting in 2016?

10   Which economic indexing concept was introduced by the King of Bhutan in 1972 as an alternative to GDP?

Medium

11   Which economic philosophy entails total reliance on the markets with no government intervention?

12   Which animal's name can refer to both a business unit that has a small market share in a mature industry, or a chronically underperforming stock?

13   Two consecutive quarters of negative economic growth results in what?

14   In January 2021, a short squeeze resulted in a 1,500% increase in the share price of which electronics retailer?

15   The monetary principle that "bad money drives out good" is known as whose law?

16   Iain Macleod coined which term for the distressing combination of a stagnant economy and rising prices?

17   What name is shared by an unexpected and extremely negative event in the stock market, and a 2010 Natalie Portman film?

18   Which intergovernmental organisation of 13 oil-producing countries was formed to coordinate policy and stabilise oil markets?

19   Named for a Scottish statistician, what term is used for goods whose demand rises with increases in its price, and vice versa?

20   Who won the Nobel Economics Prize in 1976 for his research on income and consumption and his developments in monetary theory?

Hard

Answers to QUIZ 462 – Witches

1	*Charmed*	11	The Salem Witch Trials
2	Jadis	12	*The Worst Witch*
3	*The Malleus Maleficarum*	13	Birch
4	Pigs	14	Captain Horatio Hornblower.
5	The Lord's Prayer	15	*Practical Magic*
6	*Ruddigore*	16	She would return as a *cauchemar*, or "nightmare witch", and attack the sleeping
7	Matthew Hopkins		
8	Innocent VIII	17	Anjelica Huston
9	Aleister Crowley	18	Stephen King, *The Dark Tower* series
10	13	19	A £5 fine
		20	*Meg and Mog*

1   In 2010, Achieng Ajulu-Bushell became the first black woman to represent Great Britain internationally in which sport?

2   Nick Denton founded which blog and media company that closed in 2016, bankrupted by a libel action taken by Hulk Hogan?

3   *SOS* by Rihanna, *Zoosk Girl* by Flo Rida feat. T-Pain and *Centerfold* by Pink all sample which 1980s hit?

4   Which 177-mile walking trail runs from Sedbury in Gloucestershire to Prestatyn in Derbyshire?

5   The membrane that lines the outside of human bones is called what?

6   Which roadside restaurant chain was founded in 1973 to compete with Little Chef, but had all its outlets converted into *Little Chefs* or closed by 1997?

7   The Rock of Gibraltar is made primarily of which sedimentary rock?

8   What is the largest natural lake in Wales?

9   Which trainspotter became famous for his videos in 2020 due to his enthusiasm for the subject and extensive use of fish-eye lenses?

10   In needlework, which stitch is also sometimes called *petit point*?

11   Still in existence today, what was England's first purpose-built football stadium, opened in 1892?

12   The Cliffs of Moher and Burren National Park are situated in which Irish county?

13   Sir Francis Drake "singed the King of Spain's beard" with raids on which Spanish port city?

14   In the 2015/16 season, which Thai snooker player missed the final black of a 147 break in professional competition twice in four months?

15   In the name of the video format, what does SECAM stand for?

16   *Operation Jubilee* was the codename for the 1942 Allied amphibious attack on which German-occupied port in northern France?

17   Barbara Hepworth was best known for which type of art?

18   In 1885, which chemist and microbiologist administered the first successful anti-rabies inoculation?

19   Which Gloucestershire town, that stands at the confluence of the rivers Severn and Avon, was the site of one of the decisive battles of the Wars of the Roses on 4th May 1471?

20   In Greek legend, which prophetess was the foreteller of doom?

Easy

Medium

Hard

Answers to QUIZ 463 – Pot Luck

1	Your own feet/legs	11	Zoella
2	Hungary	12	The high five – both said they did not know they were going to do it
3	The Coach	13	Nepal
4	Kate Bush, *Wuthering Heights*	14	Overwork
5	Pear	15	A matchstick end (and for what it's worth, it's a picture of Dame Edna Everage)
6	Sievert	16	Steve Davis
7	Secretary of State for Exiting the EU	17	Sweating
8	*The Fisher King*	18	A Pulitzer Prize, for *Annie Allen*, a book of poetry
9	Market	19	Mohel
10	Shaun Murphy	20	*Street Fighter*

Easy

1. After a revolution, who overthrew Cuban military dictator Fulgencio Batista and seized power on 1st January 1959?

2. Argentinian writer Jorge Luis Borges described which war of the 1980s as "a fight between two bald men over a comb"?

3. Despite him serving as Prime Minister four times during her reign, Queen Victoria did not like which man, once saying "he speaks to me as if I was a public meeting"?

4. The future King Charles II went into exile following his defeat in which battle, the final one of the English Civil War?

5. Tommie Smith and John Carlos caused controversy by doing what at the 1968 Summer Olympic Games during the medal ceremony for the 200m?

6. Henri Paul died in which tragic 20th century event?

7. Edward V and the 9-year-old Duke of York – the Princes in the Tower – were captured, detained and supposedly murdered in the Tower of London by who?

8. With an estimated 28,000 slain, which battle of 29th March 1461 is considered the bloodiest ever on English soil?

9. During the American Civil War, General Sherman embarked on a campaign of continuous destruction intended to cripple the South's war-making capacity; what fiery name did it become known by?

10. The Third Defenestration of Prague on 23rd May 1618 symbolically marked the start of which war?

11. Scandal emerged in the 1960s about the safety of thalidomide, a drug that had been prescribed to alleviate what symptom in pregnant women?

Medium

12. Who was the leader of the Visigoths when they sacked Rome in 410 AD?

13. After pilot Commander Jeremiah Denton was shot down over Vietnam and captured in 1965, what famous feat did he perform as a POW?

14. Which 1912 "discovery" of human remains in a gravel pit in Sussex, that supposedly provided the missing link between apes and humans, proved to be fraudulent?

15. Still in existence today, which city was the capital of the Incan Empire from the 13th century until the 16th-century Spanish conquest?

16. Who did Charles Guiteau assassinate in July 1881?

17. Which leader and enemy of the Romans was nicknamed "The Scourge of God"?

18. In which 1954 battle did the Vietminh defeat the French and end their influence in Indochina?

19. In 1902, which German became the first historian to win the Nobel Prize in Literature largely due to his work *A History of Rome*?

20. What was the codename of the last-minute US operation to evacuate American civilians and at-risk Vietnamese citizens from Saigon in 1975?

Hard

Answers to QUIZ 464 – Economics

1	John Maynard Keynes	11	*Laissez-faire*
2	Adam Smith	12	Dog
3	Blue chip	13	A recession
4	Unicorn	14	GameStop
5	Trickle-down economics	15	Gresham's Law
6	"The Dismal Science"	16	Stagflation
7	International Monetary Fund (IMF)	17	Black Swan
8	Janet Yellen	18	Organization of the Petroleum Exporting Countries (OPEC)
9	Venezuela	19	Giffen goods
10	Gross National Happiness	20	Milton Friedman

1 Sir Ronald Ross became the first British Nobel Laureate when he won the prize for Physiology or Medicine in 1902 for his work on the transmission of which disease?

2 To try and get away from their poor reputation, delivery company Hermes announced in 2022 they would rename themselves to what?

3 Which three African countries have shields on their flags?

4 Which phrase for a strong-willed or domineering woman originates from the lead character in Henry Rider Haggard's 1886 novel *She: A History of Adventure*?

5 Which formula is used by the UK Treasury to calculate the annual block grants for the Scottish, Welsh and Northern Irish governments/executives, relative to that of England?

6 What ñame is giveñ to the grapheme that goes over the letter N in Spañish and õver some võwels in Põrtuguese?

7 "When Matisse dies, [he] will be the only painter left who understands what colour is." So said Pablo Picasso about which Belarusian-French artist?

8 Whose 1974 album *Ma! (He's Making Eyes at Me)* made her the youngest person in history (10 years old) to have an album in the top ten of the UK Albums Chart?

9 Which 19th-century British polymath wrote the poem *The Tyger* and painted the artwork *The Ghost of a Flea*?

10 Lady Gaga, Jennifer Lopez, Garth Brooks and Amanda Gorman all sang at which US President's inauguration?

11 Which Asian capital city is known as the "rickshaw capital of the world"?

12 On account of his enormous size, which 1980s and 1990s American footballer player was nicknamed "The Refrigerator"?

13 Which barbecue-flavoured pork sandwich has been on and off McDonald's® menu since 1985, except in Germany, where it is permanent?

14 As of 2022, who has been the only African driver to win the Formula One World Championship?

15 In the building and aerospace trades, what does FRP stand for?

16 The largest percentage of the Earth's non-glacial fresh water supply in any single country can be found where?

17 Who wrote in his 1951 novel *Foundation*, "Violence is the last refuge of the incompetent"?

18 Popular in the 1990s, American taekwondo practitioner Billy Blanks developed which fitness system incorporating martial arts techniques?

19 Which branch of mathematics deals with complex systems whose sensitive behaviours lead to strikingly great consequences, such as the Butterfly effect?

20 In addition to describing any bygone period when everything was happy and peaceful, "halcyon" is also a poetic name for which bird?

Easy

Medium

Hard

Answers to QUIZ 465 – Pot Luck

1	Swimming	11	Goodison Park
2	*Gawker*	12	County Clare
3	*Tainted Love* by Soft Cell	13	Cadiz
4	Offa's Dyke Path	14	Thepchaiya Un-Nooh
5	Periosteum	15	Sequential Colour and Memory
6	*Happy Eater*	16	Dieppe
7	Limestone	17	Sculpture
8	Llyn Tegid	18	Louis Pasteur
9	Francis Bourgeois	19	Tewkesbury
10	Tent stitch	20	Cassandra

1   Which author of *The History Boys* declined both a CBE and a knighthood, saying it would be like wearing a suit every day for the rest of his life?

2   Which eccentric theoretical physicist declined a knighthood as he did not want to be regularly addressed by his first name?

3   Which author of *Howard's End* and *A Passage to India* declined a knighthood in 1949?

4   "It's not a club you want to join when you look at the villains who've got it." So said which man, director of *Kes*, declining an OBE in 1977?

5   Which 1960s radical artist declined a knighthood in 1990, but accepted the freedom of the city of Bradford and, later, an Order of Merit?

6   Which army officer and writer declined both a CBE and a knighthood in protest at Britain's double-crossing of the Arabs he was so associated with?

7   Which Yorkshire novelist and playwright refused both a knighthood and a peerage before accepting an Order of Merit in 1977?

8   "There is nothing more agreeable in life than to make peace with the Establishment – and nothing so corrupting", said which historian when declining his knighthood?

9   Declining an Order of Merit in 1946, who said "Merit in authorship could only be determined by the posthumous verdict of history", 21 years after accepting the Nobel Prize for Literature?

10 Which politician was the last non-royal to be offered a dukedom, and even selected the title of Duke of London, before his son Randolph dissuaded him?

11 Who declined a knighthood in 1887 as well as three offers to join the Privy Council, one each before, during and after his three terms as the second PM of Australia?

12 "I don't take honours", wrote which author in her diary after declining a Companion of Honour award in 1933, 33 years before her widower Leonard did the same?

13 23 years after first declining one due to her disapproval of Tony Blair, which socialist *Isadora* actress accepted a damehood in 2022?

14 Which man, the author of *Crash*, forcefully declined his CBE, calling the honours system a "charade that helps to prop up the top-heavy monarchy"?

15 Which *Guardian* and *Radio Times* columnist declined a CBE for services to journalism in 2000?

16 Which Lancastrian matchstick man artist holds the record for the most declined honours, with five?

17 Which sitcom writer returned her OBE in 2002 in protest after a CBE was awarded to the managing director of CRO Huntingdon Life Sciences, who conduct testing on animals?

18 In declining his honour, which typically self-effacing director stated, "An OBE is what you get if you clean the toilets well at King's Cross station"?

19 Which comedian declined an OBE saying "Why would I want that?", but does have a chlamydia ward for koalas at the Australia Zoo named for him?

20 Which author of both children's and adult literature declined an OBE in hopes of a knighthood, so that he could go by the title "Lady"?

Answers to QUIZ 466 – History

1	Fidel Castro	11	Morning sickness
2	Falklands War	12	Alaric
3	William Gladstone	13	While being interviewed on television for political
4	Battle of Worcester (he was said to have hidden		purposes to say how well he was being treated,
	in an oak tree, hence the pub name The Royal		he blinked the word "torture" in Morse code
	Oak)	14	The Piltdown Man
5	The Black Power salute	15	Cusco, Peru
6	The death of Princess Diana; he was the driver	16	James Garfield, US President
7	The Duke of Gloucester, who became Richard III	17	Attila the Hun
8	Battle of Towton	18	Dien Bien Phu
9	The "Scorched Earth" policy	19	Theodor Mommsen
10	Thirty Years War	20	*Frequent Wind*

ANSWERS ON PAGE 471

1   In mythology, who was banished by his son, Jupiter?

2   Until 1996, the Indian city of Chennai was known as what?

3   Dylan Kwabena Mills is the real name of which rapper?

4   Which MP for Redcar served as Northern Ireland Secretary at the time of the Good Friday Agreement?

5   Before reinventing himself as a country singer, Darius Rucker was the frontman for which multi-platinum rock band?

6   The Storting is the supreme legislature of which country?

7   In which French city are the headquarters of INTERPOL located?

8   Nigel Blackwell and Neil Crossley formed which folk-punk band in Birkenhead in 1984?

9   Dave Brock founded which English rock band, whose albums include *All Aboard the Skylark* and *Space Ritual*?

10 *Hérisson* is a French and heraldic term for which animal?

11 Which French ski resort includes the Vallorcine and Grands Montets ski areas?

12 Which philosopher wrote the treatise on structures of society and government *Leviathan* in 1651?

13 In which Wilkie Collins novel does the villain Count Fosco appear?

14 The legislative body known as the Welsh Parliament in English is known as what in Welsh?

15 In Britain, which public service ceased on 12th June 1921?

16 Moksha Patam, an ancient Indian game, formed the basis for which Western board game?

17 *Never Have Your Dog Stuffed: And Other Things I've Learned* is a 2005 autobiography by which actor?

18 On which river is the rocky cliff of the Lorelei located?

19 In roofing, what is the name for the horizontal boards that cover the underneath of the overhanging roofline?

20 The label Reprise Records was founded in 1960 by which singer and actor?

Easy

Medium

Hard

ANSWERS ON PAGE 472

1. In Mozart's *The Marriage of Figaro*, who does Figaro marry?
2. Which was Beethoven's only opera?
3. The Bugs Bunny cartoon *Rabbit of Seville* features music from a famous opera by which composer?
4. In George Bizet's *Carmen*, the title character works in what type of establishment?
5. What is the English translation of the name of *La Scala*, the famous opera house?
6. In *The Shawshank Redemption*, Andy Dufresne is punished by Warden Norton for playing a duettino from which opera through the prison yard?
7. First performed in 1893, what was Giuseppe Verdi's final opera?
8. Verdi's *Aida* was commissioned in 1869 by the Khedive of Egypt to mark the opening of what?
9. In which opera does US Navy Lieutenant Benjamin Pinkerton arrange to marry a fifteen-year-old Japanese bride, Cio-Cio-San?
10. Johann Sebastian Bach's *Schweigt stille, plaudert nicht* ("Be still, stop chattering") is a miniature comic opera describing an addiction to what?
11. Aged only nine, which composer – who later composed *The Fiery Angel* and *Igrok* – produced his first opera, *The Giant*?
12. In which opera is Prince Tamino persuaded by the Queen of the Night to rescue her daughter Pamina from Sarastro?
13. Which Danish architect designed the Sydney Opera House?
14. Based on John Bunyan's 1678 allegorical work of the same name, *The Pilgrim's Progress* was which composer's last opera?
15. *The Flight of the Bumblebee* is an orchestral interlude in the opera *The Tale of Tsar Sultan*, composed by who?
16. In *The Phantom of the Opera*, how does the Phantom sign his name at the end of messages?
17. Which opera ends with the line "Mimi, Mimi!"?
18. Which London theatre was built expressly to house Gilbert & Sullivan operas?
19. Which notorious British murderer appears in Alban Berg's *Lulu*?
20. *The Anvil Chorus* is a chorus from which 1853 Verdi work?

Easy

Medium

Hard

Answers to QUIZ 468 – Declined Honours

1	Alan Bennett	11	Alfred Deakin
2	Paul Dirac	12	Virginia Woolf
3	E.M. Forster	13	Vanessa Redgrave
4	Ken Loach	14	J.G. Ballard
5	David Hockney	15	Polly Toynbee
6	T.E. Lawrence	16	L.S. Lowry
7	J.B. Priestley	17	Carla Lane
8	A.J.P. Taylor	18	Michael Winner
9	George Bernard Shaw	19	John Oliver
10	Winston Churchill	20	Roald Dahl

1 The carnation is the national flower of which country?

2 Which city's name is used to described mystery illnesses experienced abroad by US government officials and military personnel?

3 Which BBC newsreader successfully sued the BBC in 2019, alleging she had been paid less than male peers?

4 Which publishing magnate was nominated for a 2010 Razzie for Worst Supporting Actor while playing the role of himself?

5 The Battle of Shiloh was a part of which war?

6 In 2020, which pair of equivalent names remained the most popular names for boys and girls born in England and Wales for the fifth consecutive year?

7 As of the inauguration of Joe Biden, who is the only US president to have a PhD degree?

8 Behind only the ostrich and the emu, what is the third-tallest extant bird species?

9 The opposite of hibernation, what word describes the long dormant periods for some animals during hot and dry seasons?

10 What is the surname of professional ring announcer brothers Michael (known for boxing and wrestling) and Bruce (UFC)?

11 Signs above or below letters indicating a difference in pronunciation, such as accents and cedillas, are classified as what?

12 England rugby international players Billy Vunipola and Maro Itoje both attended which public school?

13 Appropriately, considering it was run five days before a general election, which horse won the English Grand National in 1992?

14 In folk medicine, which plant – also called knitbone – is used in wound healing, particularly broken bones, torn muscles, sprains and aches?

15 Which 2022 film starring Jessica Chastain has a title which refers to the codename of an 18th century female spy?

16 Which two stars of *Multi-Coloured Swap Shop* got married after meeting on the programme?

17 Marble is formed by the metamorphosis of which sedimentary rock?

18 Prior to Cardiff, what was the capital of Wales?

19 A library in Magdalene College, Cambridge is named for which diarist, who bequeathed his collection of 3,000 books and manuscripts there?

20 Which car manufacturer's logo is based on the Pleaides star cluster?

Easy
Medium
Hard

Answers to QUIZ 469 – Pot Luck

1	Saturn	11	Argentière
2	Madras	12	Thomas Hobbes
3	Dizzie Rascal	13	*The Woman in White*
4	Mo Mowlam	14	Senedd
5	Hootie & the Blowfish	15	Sunday post
6	Norway	16	Snakes and Ladders
7	Lyon	17	Alan Alda
8	Half Man Half Biscuit	18	The River Rhine
9	Hawkwind	19	Soffit boards
10	Hedgehog	20	Frank Sinatra

Easy

1   Which former *Victoria's Secret* model is credited with pioneering and popularising the "horse walk"?

2   Which tennis player won the French Open in 1997, 2000 and 2001, but never advanced beyond the quarters in any other Grand Slam?

3   Nicknamed "The Brazilian Bombshell", which samba singer, dancer, Broadway actress and film star was known for her signature fruit hat outfit?

4   Which defensive midfielder captained Brazil to the 1994 FIFA World Cup title?

5   Which lyricist wrote the 1988 novel *The Alchemist*, the all-time best-selling book by a Brazilian writer?

6   Which racing driver won the Formula One World Drivers' Championship in 1988, 1990, and 1991?

7   Which former UFC Middleweight Champion set the record for the longest title reign in UFC history at 2,457 days?

8   Which man, the 38th president of Brazil, called the COVID-19 pandemic a "fantasy" and a "measly cold", even after he himself contracted it?

9   Along with Diego Maradona, which football legend was one of the two joint winners of the FIFA Player of the (20th) Century award?

10 Which *Victoria's Secret* model became in 2012 the only celebrity to ever star in two Super Bowl commercials in one game?

Medium

11 Which racing driver won the Formula One World Drivers' Championship in 1972 and 1974?

12 Which economist and politician served as the president of Brazil from 2011 to 2016, becoming the first Brazilian woman president?

13 Which American singer and actress known for hits such as *Walk On By* and *Don't Make Me Over* emigrated to Brazil in 1994?

14 Which Brazilian sailor has won two gold medals, two silver medals and a bronze from five Olympic Games?

15 The leading scorer in Olympic and World Cup history, with the longest ever professional career at 29 years, who is arguably the best basketball player to never play in the NBA?

16 Which architect was a key figure in the development of modern architecture and designed much of Brasilia, the nation's planned capital city?

17 Which Brazilian director's works include *City of God*, *The Constant Gardener* and *The Two Popes*?

18 Six men are instructed by a white-suited, evil kingpin to kill 94 men across the world in which 1976 Ira Levin novel, later made into a 1978 film?

19 Which composer combined indigenous melodic and rhythmic elements with Western classical music in works such as *Bachianas Brasileiras*?

20 Which actress's work includes appearing as Inara Serra in *Firefly*, Vanessa in *Deadpool*, and Jessica Brody in *Homeland*?

Hard

Answers to QUIZ 470 – Opera

1	Susannah	11	Sergei Prokofiev
2	*Fidelio*	12	*The Magic Flute*
3	Gioachino Rossini	13	Jørn Utzon
4	Cigarette factory	14	Ralph Vaughn Williams
5	The staircase	15	Nikolai Rimsky-Korsakov
6	*The Marriage of Figaro*	16	O.G. (Opera Ghost)
7	*Falstaff*	17	*La Bohème*
8	The Suez Canal	18	The Savoy
9	*Madame Butterfly*	19	Jack the Ripper
10	Coffee	20	*Il Trovatore*

ANSWERS ON PAGE **475**

1   Which Australian-British gay rights campaigner twice tried to perform citizen's arrests on Zimbabwean President, Robert Mugabe?

2   The Sussex country house of Glyndebourne is associated with which of the arts?

3   Sabian, Zildjian, Meinl and Paiste are the "big four" manufacturers of what instruments?

4   In which sport is the Bledisloe Cup contested annually by Australia and New Zealand?

5   In 2006, what unwanted item did William Shatner sell to an online casino for $25,000, donating the money to a housing charity?

6   In a namesake series, which TV doctor is so overtly based on Sherlock Holmes that he too lives at 221B Baker Street?

7   *Glad to Be Gay* was a 1978 song by which British punk rock/new wave group?

8   Who wrote the 1856 novel *Madame Bovary*?

9   How many members of Team GB won gold on the day known as "Super Saturday" at the 2012 London Olympics?

10 In chess, what word of German origin describes any situation in which the obligation to make a move is a serious disadvantage?

11 Mirabel International Airport serves which North American city?

12 The *Mr Bean* TV series was produced between 1990 and 1995; how many episodes were made?

13 The term "Cyborg" originated as a portmanteau of which two other words?

14 Julian Huxley, brother of the novelist Aldous, was the first director of which United Nations specialised agency?

15 Dee Snider was the lead singer and songwriter of which heavy metal band?

16 In which 1988 film were one-line actors listed in the credits by the line they spoke, including one credited as "It's Enrico Pallazzo!"?

17 Margaret Walker, Katherine Johnston and Tony Cornforth developed which sign and symbol language programme, and named it after themselves?

18 Which animation studio is known for stop-motion clay animation productions such as *Wallace and Gromit*, *Shaun the Sheep* and *Morph*?

19 Which World War II American assault was unique among Pacific War Marine battles in that American total casualties exceeded those of Japan?

20 Which internet service provider was until 2010 an arm of the Carphone Warehouse?

Easy

Medium

Hard

Answers to QUIZ 471 – Pot Luck

1	Spain	11	Diacritics
2	Havana Syndrome	12	Harrow
3	Samira Ahmed	13	Party Politics
4	Hugh Hefner, for the film *Miss March* – he later claimed "maybe I didn't understand the character"	14	Comfrey
		15	*The 355*
		16	John Craven and Maggie Philbin
5	American Civil War	17	Limestone
6	Oliver and Olivia	18	Machynlleth
7	Woodrow Wilson (in history)	19	Samuel Pepys
8	Cassowary	20	Subaru
9	Aestivation		
10	Buffer		

1. On 13th April 1668, who became the first ever Poet Laureate, and the only one to have the title taken away?
2. The first Poet Laureate to also work as a DJ, who founded the band The Scaremongers?
3. Who was Poet Laureate between 1843 and 1850, during which time he wrote no poetry at all?
4. Laureate from 1968 to 1972, which English poet was the father of a multi-Oscar-winning actor?
5. Upon his appointment in 1999, who vowed to only hold the post for ten years, breaking the 300-year tradition of Poet Laureates holding the title for life?
6. St Pancras railway station features a bronze statue of which poet by the sculptor Martin Jennings?
7. Which of the "Lake poets" was appointed to the position of Poet Laureate by George III in 1813?
8. Poet Laureate between 1930 and 1967, which poet also wrote children's books, including *The Midnight Folk* and *The Box of Delights*?
9. In the role from 1913 to 1930, which Poet Laureate was a doctor by training, achieving literary fame only late in life, largely in the form of adding words to hymns?
10. Appointed in 2009, who is the first known LGBTQ+ Poet Laureate?

11. Appointed in 1718 at the age of 30, who was – and still is – the youngest appointed Poet Laureate?
12. The only two appointed Poet Laureates between 1850 and 1913 shared what first name?
13. Laureate from 1790 to 1793, whose appointment was considered a reward for political favours rather than artistic merit, and was derided as a poetaster?
14. Which Poet Laureate's last published work before his death in 1998 was *Birthday Letters*, which detailed his relationship with his wife?
15. Which Poet Laureate, not much respected by his peers, wrote an "Apology" for his life in 1740?
16. In his time in the role, which Poet Laureate defended other Laureates in a comic poem *A Pathetic Apology for All Laureates, Past, Present, And To Come*?
17. In 1681, which future Poet Laureate heavily rewrote Shakespeare's *King Lear* to give it a happier ending?
18. Who turned down the position of Poet Laureate in 1984 on grounds of ill health, dying the following year?
19. The second official Poet Laureate, which man introduced the custom of producing poems for the new year and the monarch's birthday?
20. Which man, appointed Poet Laureate in 1715, was considered the first editor of the works of William Shakespeare?

Answers to QUIZ 472 – Famous Brazilians

1	Gisele Bündchen	11	Emerson Fittipaldi
2	Gustavo Kuerten	12	Dilma Rousseff
3	Carmen Miranda	13	Dionne Warwick
4	Dunga (Carlos Caetano Bledorn Verri)	14	Robert Scheidt
5	Paulo Coelho	15	Oscar Schmidt
6	Ayrton Senna	16	Oscar Niemeyer
7	Anderson Silva	17	Fernando Meirelles
8	Jair Bolsonaro	18	*The Boys From Brazil*
9	Pele	19	Heitor Villa-Lobos
10	Adriana Lima	20	Morena Baccarin

1   Which former England international striker has invented a percussion instrument called "The Dube"?

2   Marsh gas is an alternative name for which natural gas?

3   The first ever appearance of *The Simpsons*, 1st April 1987, was also the birth date of which women's tennis Grand Slam winner?

4   Named after its inventor, Arpad Elo, the Elo ranking system is a series of mathematical calculations designed to determine rankings in which board game?

5   *The Penguin News* is the weekly newspaper of which British overseas territory archipelago?

6   At which Summer Olympic games did the heptathlon replace the pentathlon?

7   On a 1999 episode of *Have I Got News For You*, Paul Merton once joked that which bathroom personal hygiene item was two days before D-Day?

8   What is, by far, the most abundant element in the universe?

9   In 1991, who became the first woman ever to join The Magic Circle?

10   Which Austrian driver won the 1970 Formula 1 Drivers' Championship in 1970, despite being killed in an accident in the tenth of thirteen races?

11   Epaulets or epaulettes are ornamental tassels worn on which part of the body?

12   In both German and Dutch, the suffix '-berg' in a place name refers to what type of geographical feature?

13   Devizes is a historic market town in which English county?

14   In November 2014, which music megastar pulled her entire catalogue from Spotify as an act of protest against the service's ad-funded "free" tier?

15   The gothic horror novel *The Pit and the Pendulum* was written by which author?

16   At the 2001 British Open, which golfer – tied for the lead at the time – was deducted two shots when his caddy placed an extra club in the bag?

17   "Passions" for all four New Testament gospels were written by which composer?

18   Varig was the first – and for 53 years, only – international airline from which country?

19   The Dally M Awards, Harry Sunderland Trophy and Albert Goldthorpe Medal are all awarded in which sport?

20   Actress Mary Miller, muse of Rodgers and Hammerstein, was the mother of which similarly-famous actor?

Answers to QUIZ 473 – Pot Luck

1	Peter Tatchell	11	Montréal
2	Opera; it is the venue for the annual Glyndebourne Festival Opera	12	Only 15, surprisingly
3	Cymbals	13	Cybernetic and organism
4	Rugby union	14	UNESCO
5	Kidney stone	15	Twisted Sister
6	House	16	*Naked Gun*
7	Tom Robinson Band	17	Makaton
8	Gustave Flaubert	18	Aardman Animations
9	12	19	Battle of Iwo Jima
10	Zugzwang	20	TalkTalk

QUIZ 476 – Television

ANSWERS ON PAGE 478

1. Which artist designed the logo for the children's show *Blue Peter*?
2. Which film star broke his four top front teeth when he fell on his gun filming an episode of the TV series *Gunsmoke*?
3. Which major news story of 1986 was broken by the BBC on *John Craven's Newsround* by stand-in presenter Roger Finn?
4. Jack Warner played the title character in all 432 episodes of which police procedural?
5. KITT was the sleek black crime fighting Pontiac Trans-Am featured in *Knight Rider*; what did KITT stand for?
6. Harold Gould played two of Rose Nylund's boyfriends in which American sitcom?
7. Victoria Justice, Daniella Monet and Ariana Grande starred in which 2009 Nickelodeon sitcom about an aspiring singer?
8. Which Sky panel show won the 2019 BAFTA for Best Comedy?
9. Saoirse-Monica Jackson portrayed Erin Quinn on which black comedy Channel 4 sitcom?
10. Which actress played the title role in the Netflix comedy *Unbreakable Kimmy Schmidt* from 2015 to 2019?
11. Which game show is hosted by Danny Dyer in the UK and Chris Hardwick in the USA?
12. Zach Galifianakis plays himself in the 2019 Netflix Original spin-off of what antagonistic talk show?

Medium

13. Bill and Ben were the forenames of the husband and wife lead characters in which 1990s BBC sitcom?
14. Characters from which sitcom appeared in a sequel called *It Sticks Out Half a Mile*?
15. Which children's magazine show that ran from 1972 to 1982 informed viewers about the latest cinema releases?
16. Who hosted the Sky One version of *Jeopardy* from 1995 to 1996?
17. Which comedian and TV presenter wrote and starred in the short-lived ITV sitcom *Shane*?
18. Which ITV police drama of the 1980s starred Jill Gascoine as Detective Inspector Maggie Forbes?
19. Averaging 13 million viewers per episode, which show had the highest British television viewings ratings in 2016?
20. Which American accordionist and bandleader hosted a namesake TV programme with a style that came to be known as "champagne music"?

Hard

Answers to QUIZ 474 – Poet Laureates

1. John Dryden
2. Simon Armitage
3. William Wordsworth
4. Cecil Day-Lewis
5. Andrew Motion (and he stuck to his word)
6. John Betjeman
7. Robert Southey
8. John Masefield
9. Robert Bridges
10. Carol Ann Duffy
11. Laurence Eusden
12. Alfred (Lord Tennyson 1850-1892 and Austin 1896-1913)
13. Henry James Pye
14. Ted Hughes
15. Colley Cibber
16. William Whitehead
17. Nahum Tate
18. Philip Larkin
19. Thomas Shadwell
20. Nicholas Rowe

QUIZ 477 – Pot Luck

ANSWERS ON PAGE 479

1. Which Welsh cyclist won gold medals at both the European Championships 2020 and the Track Cycling World 2020?

2. The Lost River Range, a child of the larger Rocky Mountains range, spans which American state?

3. FL Studio, Reason and Pro Tools are all software programs classified as DAW; what does DAW stand for?

4. As a reward for being the best selling singer-songwriter of all time, Guinness World Records awarded Sir Paul McCartney a disc made from which unusual element in 1979?

5. Czechia, Hungary, Poland and Slovakia have formed which cultural and political alliance to advance co-operation in military, cultural, economic and energy matters?

6. In 1977, who became the first player from the Republic of Ireland to win the UK Snooker championship?

7. Which singer, actor, presenter and West End star is the son of a member of vocal harmony group, The Southlanders?

8. What type of creatures are Geri and Freki, Odin's companions, in Norse mythology?

9. Which future European monarch won a gold medal in the 6 metre sailing event at the 1928 Olympic Games?

10. Located 5,000 light-years away, which region of space has been measured at -272.15 °C, making it the coolest natural place in the known universe?

11. In 1919, which pianist was elected Prime Minister of Poland?

12. Which programming language is named after an island in the Baltic Sea?

13. In which battle of the American Revolutionary War were the British commander, Wolfe, and the French commander, de Montcalm, both killed?

14. In 480 BC, which king led an army of 6,000 to 7,000 Greeks from many city-states, including 300 Spartans, that thwarted the Persians in the Thermopylæ pass?

15. As of 2021, which shot-putter had achieved more than a third of all the 22 metre throws in history, and later set both the indoor and outdoor world records?

16. *Umarell* is a term used for the bizarre Italian phenomenon of retired men spending their time standing around, hands behind their back, doing what?

17. For two years between 1928 and 1930, after an acquisition, the Bank of America instead went by which country's name?

18. Northwich, Nantwich, Middlewich, Winsford and Sandbach are all towns in Cheshire known for the mining of what?

19. Fleuve, Monchino and Warlander are breeds of which animal?

20. Spanakopita is a filo pastry traditionally stuffed with feta cheese and which vegetable?

Answers to QUIZ 475 – Pot Luck

1	Dion Dublin	11	Shoulder
2	Methane	12	Hill or mountain
3	Maria Sharapova	13	Wiltshire
4	Chess	14	Taylor Swift
5	Falkland Islands	15	Edgar Allen Poe
6	1984	16	Ian Woosnam
7	Bidet	17	Johann Sebastian Bach
8	Hydrogen	18	Brazil
9	Debbie McGee	19	Rugby league
10	Jochen Rindt	20	Larry Hagman

1. Army psychiatrist Doc Daneeka denies Captain John Yossarian's request to leave the army in which satirical 1961 novel?

2. *Call Me Anna* is the autobiography of which 1963 Academy Award-winning actress?

3. James Boswell is best known for writing the 1791 biography of which other writer?

4. Betty Blueskin, Count Kidney Face, Jeremiah Dry-Boots and Penelope Firebrand were among the 198 known pen names of which English writer?

5. Which fictional newspaper in Evelyn Waugh's *Scoop* is also the name of a news website that focuses on politics and pop culture?

6. Robert Lewis May wrote which Christmas story while working as a copywriter in a department store?

7. What unusually-named fictionalised autobiography by Robert M. Pirsig tells the story of a cross-country trip with his son?

8. Capitalising on the fascination with African exploration at the time, *Five Weeks in a Balloon* was an 1863 adventure novel by which French science fiction writer?

9. Which famous semi-autobiographical novel was published under the pseudonym Victoria Lucas?

10. Which American writer won the 2011 Pulitzer Prize for Fiction for her novel *A Visit from the Goon Squad*?

11. Known for *And Suddenly It's Evening* and *Day After Day*, which Italian poet won the Nobel Prize for Literature in 1959?

12. Which 1977 Toni Morrison novel follows the life of Macon "Milkman" Dead III, an African-American man living in Michigan?

13. *The Man of Property* is the first book in *The Forsyte Saga*, a series about an upper-middle-class family, written by who?

14. Which 2005 Charles C. Mann work looks at the Americas before the arrival of Columbus and concludes that pre-Columbian peoples were more numerous and prosperous than previously thought?

15. Ruth Patchett is the infamous anti-heroine of which Fay Weldon novel?

16. "He was soon borne away by the waves, and lost in darkness and distance." This is the last line of which classic novel?

17. Taken from an architectural term for the principal face of a building, what name is given to an illustration facing the title page of a book?

18. What two words append the name of all entries in the series of introductory technology reference books noted for their distinctive yellow and black covers?

19. Salman Rushdie's first full-length non-fiction book, *Jaguar Smile*, tells of his travels to which country?

20. *Death of a Poet* was an 1837 poem by Mikhail Lermontov written as a reaction to the death of which of his peers, the great-grandson of an Ethiopian prince?

Answers to QUIZ 476 – Television

1	Tony Hart	11	*The Wall*
2	Harrison Ford	12	*Between Two Ferns*
3	The Space Shuttle *Challenger* disaster	13	*2point4 Children*
4	*Dixon of Dock Green*	14	*Dad's Army*
5	Knight Industries Two Thousand	15	*Clapperboard*
6	*The Golden Girls*	16	Paul Ross
7	*VICTORiOUS*	17	Frank Skinner
8	*A League of Their Own*	18	*The Gentle Touch*
9	*Derry Girls*	19	*The Great British Bake-Off*
10	Ellie Kemper	20	Lawrence Welk

Easy

Medium

Hard

ANSWERS ON PAGE 281

1   Born Alexander Minto Hughes, who was the first white recording artist to have a reggae hit in Jamaica?

2   Which security guard helped evacuate the area of the bombing at the 1996 Summer Olympics, was hailed as a hero, became considered a suspect by the FBI, yet was ultimately exonerated?

3   Which American President was so good at (American) football that he was offered a professional contract with the Green Bay Packers NFL team?

4   In marine biology, what is milt?

5   Kibo, Mawenzi and Shira are the three volcanic cones on which mountain?

6   In an analysis of the Oxford English Corpus, of the 60 most commonly used words in English, which is the only one to have more than one syllable?

7   Christina Ciminella was the name at birth of which country singer?

8   Sir Martin Frobisher, seaman and privateer, made three voyages to the New World looking for what?

9   Because it counts the year of Jesus's birth differently, which African country is currently eight years behind the rest of the Gregorian calendar?

10 What derogatory internet slang term for a rude alpha male is also the name of an ancient inland African sea?

11 In pottery, what food item is used to describe any pottery that has been fired in a kiln without a ceramic glaze?

12 If wearing kimono to a wedding, convention states that what form of thonged Japanese traditional footwear should be worn?

13 The name of what mode of transport is given to a small irregular white cloud that passes around Neptune approximately every 16 hours?

14 Which *Saturday Night Live* performer has dated Ariana Grande, Phoebe Dynevor, Margaret Qualley, Kim Kardashian, Kaia Gerber and Kate Beckinsale?

15 *The birdcatcher am I* and *Hell's vengeance boils in my heart* are songs from which Mozart opera?

16 In finance, what three-letter term is given to an option that gives the holder the right to sell an asset, at a specified price, by a specified date to the other party?

17 Boards for which solved two-player strategy board game dating back to the Roman Empire are sometimes printed on the back of checkerboards?

18 To commemorate the University of Breslau giving him an honorary PhD, Johannes Brahms composed which overture?

19 What name is shared by the patron saint of medical social workers and a British Olympic relay silver medallist?

20 Timothy Matlack, an assistant to the Secretary of the Congress, was most likely the author of what document?

Answers to QUIZ 477 – Pot Luck

1	Elinor Barker	11	Ignace Jan Paderewski
2	Idaho	12	Kotlin
3	Digital audio workstations	13	Battle of Quebec
4	Rhodium	14	King Leonidas I
5	Visegrád Group	15	Ryan Crouser
6	Patsy Fagan	16	Offering unwanted advice to builders
7	Gary Wilmot	17	Bank of Italy
8	Wolves	18	Salt
9	King Olav V of Norway (6 metres was the length of the boat, not the race)	19	Horse
10	Boomerang Nebula or Bow Tie Nebula	20	Spinach

1   Freetown, the capital of Sierra Leone, is twinned with which northeast English city, winner of the 2017 UK City of Culture title?

2   The tiny village of Whitwell in Rutland is (unilaterally) twinned with which major European capital city, on account of them both having a river?

3   In 2012, the Scottish village of Dull twinned with which synonymous town in Oregon, USA?

4   With 64, which Russian city is said to have the most sister cities in the world, including with its namesake in Florida?

5   England's second-biggest city and Alabama's second-biggest city share what name?

6   St. Paul is the capital city, Minneapolis is the biggest city, and the Minneapolis-St. Paul region is known as the "Twin Cities" region in which US state?

7   As it straddles the border of two states, there are two Kansas Cities. One is in Kansas; the other is the largest city in which neighbouring state?

8   Containing Eccles, Worsley, Swinton, Walkden and Pendlebury, which metropolitan borough of Manchester gained the status of a city in 1926?

9   What was the name of the first capital of united ancient Egypt, now lying in ruins, which the second-biggest city in Tennessee is also named after?

10   The oldest university in the USA and the second-oldest university in Britain both reside in cities with which name?

11   The capital city of Oregon should not be confused with which identically-named town in Massachusetts, where the famous witch trials took place?

12   Which Wiltshire town, not exactly noted for its opulence, was officially twinned with Walt Disney World for one year on account of having a magic roundabout?

13   The small Somerset town of Wincanton is twinned with Ankh-Morpork, a fictional city state in the *Discworld* series of novels written by whom?

14   United by how devastated both were by wartime bombing raids, Coventry is twinned with which German city?

15   Lalibela, the twelfth century capital of Ethiopia known for its churches, is twinned with which "spiritual" Somerset town?

16   The largest cities in the American states of both Maine and Oregon have what shared name?

17   The capital city of Libya and the second-largest city in Lebanon share which name, which translates as "three cities"?

18   Which West Yorkshire town was half of the world's first ever official town twinning arrangement in 1920?

19   In 1873, a new capital was formed in which European country by the amalgamation of three cities?

20   The Murray River separates which interstate twin cities, one north of the river in New South Wales, one on the south bank in Victoria?

Answers to QUIZ 478 – Literature

1   *Catch-22* by Joseph Heller
2   Patty Duke (whose legal first name was Anna)
3   Dr Samuel Johnson
4   Daniel Defoe
5   *The Daily Beast*
6   *Rudolph the Red-Nosed Reindeer*
7   *Zen and the Art of Motorcycle Maintenance: An Inquiry into Values*
8   Jules Verne
9   *The Bell Jar* by Sylvia Plath
10   Jennifer Egan
11   Salvatore Quasimodo
12   *Son of Solomon*
13   John Galsworthy
14   *1491: New Revelations of the Americas Before Columbus*
15   *The Life And Loves Of A She Devil*
16   *Frankenstein; or, The Modern Prometheus* by Mary Shelley
17   Frontispiece
18   "...For Dummies"
19   Nicaragua
20   Alexander Pushkin

1 In the name of the picture file format, what does JPEG stand for?

2 Who replaced Judas Iscariot as an apostle after Judas's suicide?

3 In which river did the Pied Piper of Hamelin drown the rats?

4 Which pop punk band's 2004 album *Chuck* is named after the volunteer UN peacekeeper who helped them evacuate their hotel during heavy fighting in the Democratic Republic of Congo?

5 Also the name of a Ponzi scheme cryptocurrency exchange, a quadriga was an early form of what?

6 On steam locomotives, wootten and belpaire are types of what?

7 Sharing its name with a French port city, which fungicide consists of equal parts of copper sulphate and lime?

8 Which European country has not lost any casualties in war on its own turf since the Turkish Abductions of 1627?

9 The white Hungarian grape *furmint* is the principal grape in which dessert wine?

10 Lemniscate is an alternative name for what mathematical symbol?

11 Shatranj is an old Persian predecessor of which game?

12 Which music hall entertainer was nicknamed "The Prime Minister of Mirth"?

13 "Bottomry" is an old legal term used to refer to borrowing money in which industry?

14 Name any three of the four British horse racecourses whose names do not contain any letter of the word "race".

15 Which A-List Hollywood actor purchased an oil/water separation machine from the United States government in 1995, the same year he starred in a relevant film?

16 Immediately prior to being shot, whose last words were "they couldn't hit an elephant at this distance"?

17 Which doctor was struck off the medical register for his 1998 study that falsely claimed a link between the MMR vaccine and autism?

18 After winning the public vote on *Opportunity Knocks* a record seven times, which singing duo topped the bill at the 1973 Royal Variety Performance?

19 Which English physicist was awarded the 1935 Nobel Prize in Physics for his discovery of the neutron?

20 Which Welsh referee retired in December 2020 as the world record holder for the most rugby union test matches refereed?

Easy

Medium

Hard

Answers to QUIZ 479 – Pot Luck

1	Judge Dread	11	Biscuit
2	Richard Jewell	12	Zori
3	Gerald Ford	13	The Scooter
4	Fish semen	14	Pete Davidson
5	Mount Kilimanjaro	15	*The Magic Flute*
6	About	16	Put
7	Wynonna Judd	17	Nine men's Morris
8	The North-west Passage	18	*Akademische Festouvertüre* (Academic Festival Overture)
9	Ethiopia	19	John Regis
10	Mega Chad	20	The American Declaration of Independence

Easy

1   After appearing as Felicity "Flick" Scully on *Neighbours*, who entered the music industry with her debut single *Kiss Kiss*?

2   Which *Neighbours* character developed a singing career to mimic/help launch that of the actress that played her, Delta Goodrem?

3   Which *EastEnders* actor, born David Sutton, tried his hand at music with a cover version of Michael Jackson's 1972 song *Good Thing Going*?

4   Which *EastEnders* actor and TV presenter has released three albums – two before joining the soap, and one during his 2017 hiatus?

5   A couple on screen, and then in real life, which *Neighbours* stars recorded *Especially for You*?

6   Who bookended three years on *EastEnders* with time with the pop group Milan, and a solo career that included the no.1 hit *Perfect Moment*?

7   Who had a one-album solo career between stints as Nick Tilsley in *Coronation Street* and Kyle Kelly on *Hollyoaks*?

8   Which man had a no.1 single with *Every Loser Wins* in 1986, concurrent with his career playing Simon Wicks on *EastEnders*?

9   Anita Dobson had a 1985 hit with which song that took its main riff from the *EastEnders* theme tune?

10   Which actress, who played Hayley Smith Lawson on *Home and Away*, released an eponymous pop music album in 2002?

Medium

11   Kevin Kennedy was in an 80s band named Paris Valentinos, and released a 2000 single, *Bulldog Nation*. Which character did he play for 20 years in Coronation Street?

12   Who had early 1990s hits with songs such as *Mona* and *Amanda* alongside appearing in both *Neighbours* and *Home and Away*?

13   After three years as Hattie Tavernier in *EastEnders*, which actress had a UK no.4 hit with *Sweetness*?

14   Gayle and Gillian Blakeney had a no.74 hit in Australia in 1991 with *All Mixed Up*, released concurrently with their time playing which *Neighbours* twins?

15   Almost immediately after leaving her role as Emily Shadwick in *Brookside* in 2003, who had a no.6 UK chart hit with *Baby I Don't Care*?

16   Who played Emma Jackson on *Home and Away* between 1989 and 1990 before beginning a music career with her debut studio album, *Love and Kisses*?

17   Between stints as Jambo Bolton in *Hollyoaks* and Harvey Gaskell in *Coronation Street*, who had a 1998 no.5 hit with a cover of *When I Need You*?

18   Bill Tarmey had four albums make the charts between 1993 and 2001, but who did he more famously play on *Coronation Street* for 31 years?

19   Who had a stage and solo career around a four-year stint as Izzy on *Neighbours*?

Hard

20   Which rapper appeared as a wheelchair-bound basketball star in 100 episodes of Canadian teen soap *Degrassi: The Next Generation*?

Answers to QUIZ 480 – Twin Towns and Cities

1	Kingston upon Hull	11	Salem
2	Paris	12	Swindon
3	Boring	13	Terry Pratchett
4	St Petersburg	14	Dresden
5	Birmingham	15	Glastonbury
6	Minnesota	16	Portland
7	Missouri	17	Tripoli
8	Salford	18	Keighley
9	Memphis	19	Hungary (Budapest formed by the merger of Buda, Pest and Obuda)
10	Cambridge	20	Albury-Wodonga

1. Used in drafting for copying a drawing on a different scale, as well as adjustable bathroom mirrors, what name is given to a mechanical linkage that can compress or extend like an accordion, forming a characteristic rhomboidal pattern?
2. Vaticide is the act of killing who?
3. In 1981, who became the first Cuban, Latin American, person of African descent and person from a Western country other than the USA to go into space?
4. In the name of the instrument of litigation, what does SLAPP stand for?
5. Tahliah Debrett Barnett is the real name of which "genre-bending" rapper?
6. The Dunmow Flitch award is given each year to who?
7. Which teenage girl's magazine was first published in January 1964 and ran until July 1993?
8. From 1927 until her retirement in 1943, who was the only female director working in Hollywood?
9. What is – or at least, used to be – the purpose of the black stripe on a "lollipop" road crossing safety sign?
10. Anne Frances Robbins was the name at birth of which First Lady of the United States?
11. In Greek mythology, who was the mother of Castor and Pollux?
12. The National Audubon Society is concerned with the protection of what?
13. Symbolics, a defunct computer manufacturer headquartered in Cambridge, Massachusetts, owned the world's first what?
14. Among many others, what do footballers Alan Smith, Paolo Rossi, Thomas Muller and Gheorghe Popescu have in common?
15. What was the highly unlikely name of baseball star Madison Bumgarner's high school girlfriend?
16. Called the Super Bowl of winter sports, which male-only variant of ski jumping takes place on bigger, steeper hills, on which competitors are not allowed to practice?
17. Dubai-based Alex Hirschi is an Australian social media celebrity, presenter and vlogger of motoring content under what name?
18. *I Giorni* (2001), *Nightbook* (2009) and *In a Time Lapse* (2013) are all solo albums by which Italian pianist and composer?
19. The British Government entered into a contract in 1993 with which security firm to provide security for prisons, only to be embarrassed after a series of security blunders, including escapes?
20. *Adventure Galley* was the ship of which pirate/privateer?

Easy

Medium

Hard

Answers to QUIZ 481 – Pot Luck

1. Joint Photographic Experts Group, the name of the organisation that developed it
2. Matthias
3. Weser
4. Sum 41
5. Chariot
6. Fireboxes
7. Bordeaux mixture
8. Iceland
9. Tokaji
10. The infinity symbol
11. Chess
12. George Robey
13. Shipping – the bottom of the ship was used as collateral, thus forfeiting the boat if the loan was not repaid
14. Goodwood, Huntingdon, Ludlow, Plumpton
15. Kevin Costner
16. General John Sedgwick, Union Army general during the American Civil War
17. Andrew Wakefield
18. [Lennie] Peters & [Dianne] Lee
19. Sir James Chadwick
20. Nigel Owens

Easy

1. Which primatologist and leading chimpanzee expert disproved the idea that only humans could construct tools?

2. The European Space Agency's Mars rover is named for which British chemist, who was instrumental in discovering the structure of DNA?

3. Elizabeth Garrett Anderson (Britain) and Elizabeth Blackwell (America) were the first women in their respective countries to receive what?

4. Which 1968 Nobel Laureate developed new drugs to fight AIDS (AZT), organ rejection (azathioprine), herpes (acyclovir) and leukemia (Purinethol)?

5. Who became the only woman to win an unshared Nobel Prize for Medicine in 1983 for her discovery that some genes could be mobile?

6. Austrian-Swedish physicist Lise Meitner was a part of the team that discovered which reaction?

7. Grace Hopper was a pioneer in which scientific field?

8. Who was the first woman in England to have an official government position, and the first woman to be paid for her work in astronomy, but *not* the first to discover a comet?

9. For developing the STP protocol that joins networks together, which network engineer was known as "the mother of the internet"?

10. For her research into chirped-pulse amplification – ultrashort yet extremely high-energy laser pulses – who in 2018 became the third woman to win the Nobel Prize in Physics?

11. Which Hollywood actress patented and pioneered the signal-hopping technology that formed the basis for Wi-Fi, GPS and Bluetooth?

Medium

12. In the 1950s and 1960s, which African-American mathematician calculated flight trajectories, by hand, for NASA missions?

13. For her work proposing the nuclear shell model of the atomic nucleus, who became the second female Nobel laureate in physics in 1963?

14. A 2021 study found that which European country is home to the largest number of women scientists and engineers?

15. Whose book *Silent Spring* went a long way to raising public awareness of environmental concerns, and led to a ban on DDT?

16. In the mid-19th century, Martha Coston developed what safety device, one that is still used by armed forces today?

17. Dr Virginia Apgar invented the eponymous Apgar Score; what is it used for?

18. Which prolific novelist was part of a three-person team that designed the first aircraft-towed airmail delivery glider?

19. Françoise Barré-Sinoussi received the 2008 Nobel Prize in Physiology or Medicine for her discovery of what, 25 years previously?

20. Which politician worked as a research chemist for J. Lyons and Co. in Hammersmith and was part of a team developing emulsifiers for ice cream?

Hard

---

1. On a typical table tennis paddle, what is the name of the layer between the blade and the rubber?

2. Mother and daughter Finty Williams and Judi Dench voice characters in which children's cartoon about young mouse who loves ballet?

3. In 2007, which South American tennis player became the first – and, as of 2021, only – player to beat Rafael Nadal, Novak Djokovic and Roger Federer in the same tournament?

4. Distinct from the British Poet Laureate, what title is given to the national poet of Scotland?

5. Bruce Oldfield, Willi Smith and Rahul Mishra all work in what artistic field?

6. First held in 1963, the Royal Horticultural Society runs which annual campaign, which aims at creating a more beautiful Britain?

7. Hector Hugh Munro satirised Edwardian society under what mononymic pen name, shared with a species of monkey?

8. Sharing its name with a sportswear brand, what belt can British boxers earn if they win four championship contests in the same weight division?

9. Which engineer's career included designing the Crystal Palace exhibition hall, and cultivating the now-ubiquitous Cavendish banana?

10. Which rapper achieved viral success as an internet meme with her satirical 2018 single *Mooo!*, in which she claims to be a cow?

11. In Greek Mythology, Zeus transformed into which bird in order to seduce Leda?

12. On a tandem bicycle, what military term describes the rider in front?

13. Which "third" denomination of Islam is the largest in Oman and Zanzibar, and is also practised in Algeria, Tunisia and Libya?

14. In *Gulliver's Travels*, Gulliver's first ship had which animal for a name?

15. Bryology is the study of what?

16. *L'esprit de l'escalier* is a French term used in English for the predicament of thinking of what?

17. Which football "player" manipulated his way into a 13-year professional career in his native Brazil, but never played a single match, always somehow finding an excuse?

18. Which abbey on the Wye River in Wales was immortalised in a poem by William Wordsworth?

19. Which 19th-century French writer and Pat Gibson lookalike is best known for the novels *Le Rouge et le Noir* and *La Chartreuse de Parme*?

20. Clotho, Lachesis and Atropos formed which trio of Greek weaving goddesses, who assigned individual destinies to mortals at birth?

Easy

Medium

Hard

Answers to QUIZ 483 – Pot Luck

1	Pantograph	12	Birds
2	A prophet	13	.com domain name
3	Arnaldo Tamayo Méndez	14	All played for their country, while having the most common surname in their respective countries (England, Italy, Germany, Romania)
4	Strategic lawsuit against public participation		
5	FKA Twigs		
6	The year's happiest newlywed couple	15	She was also called Madison Bumgarner, and the two are not related
7	*Jackie*		
8	Dorothy Arzner	16	Ski flying
9	To write on the number plates of anyone who refuses to stop	17	Supercar Blondie
		18	Ludovico Einaudi
10	Nancy Reagan	19	Group 4
11	Leda	20	William Kidd

Identify these national dress costumes and items, and their countries of origin.

1

2

3

4

5

6

7

8

Answers to QUIZ 484 – Women in Science

1	Jane Goodall	11	Hedy Lamarr
2	Rosalind Franklin	12	Katherine Johnson
3	Medical degrees	13	Maria Goeppert-Mayer
4	Gertrude Elion	14	Norway
5	Barbara McClintock	15	Rachel Carson
6	Nuclear fission	16	Signal flares
7	Computer science	17	It is an evaluation for the welfare of newborn babies
8	Caroline Herschel (although she is often credited with the comet thing, it is inaccurate)	18	Dame Barbara Cartland (she was also the first to fly it)
9	Radia Perlman	19	Human immunodeficiency virus (HIV)
10	Donna Strickland	20	Margaret Thatcher

Easy

Medium

Hard

1   Which Ancient Macedonian general became pharaoh of Egypt and founded a namesake dynasty in approximately 305BC?

2   Which award-winning podcast, that blends investigative journalism with non-fiction storytelling, is the most downloaded podcast of all time, as of 2021?

3   Which French fashion designer created the Angel and Alien brands of fragrances?

4   For which Sunday newspaper was Clement Freud briefly a football correspondent?

5   What unit of risk is defined as a one-in-a-million chance of death?

6   Which inner city area of Manchester is known for its "Curry Mile"?

7   The Guatemalan quetzal, the Honduran lempira and the Nicaraguan córdoba are currencies that all have fractional units with what name?

8   In 1984, who won the Nobel Prize for Chemistry for his development of methodology for chemical synthesis on a solid matrix?

9   Something described as quisquilian is considered what?

10 In Greek Mythology, which daughter of Demeter was abducted by Hades, causing Demeter to create the seasons?

11 Who won the 1946 Australian Junior Boys 110 Yards Backstroke Championship?

12 Behind Spanish and Portuguese, and ahead of English, what is the third most widely-spoken language in South America?

13 Norman Rockwell created over 300 covers for which American weekly magazine?

14 Brewshed, Iceni and Roughacre are all breweries in which county?

15 Which horse won the 2014 English Grand National?

16 Towards the end of her life, which American actor worked as a cocktail waitress in a women-only hotel, saying "I like people. I like to talk to them"?

17 Also known as cattle plague, which infectious disease of cows and buffalo was declared eradicated in 2011?

18 Lodged, courant, trippant and springing are adjectives used to describe depictions of animals in various positions in what historical art?

19 Which of Christopher Marlowe's plays was his only one set in England?

20 In the film *The 40 Year Old Virgin*, while having his chest waxed, Steve Carell shouts which singer's name in pain?

Easy

Medium

Hard

Answers to QUIZ 485 – Pot Luck

1	Sponge	11	Swan
2	*Angelina Ballerina*	12	Captain
3	David Nalbandian	13	*Ibadi*
4	Makar	14	Antelope
5	Fashion design	15	Mosses and liverworts
6	Britain in Bloom	16	The perfect reply, slightly too late
7	Saki	17	Carlos Kaiser
8	Lonsdale	18	Tintern Abbey
9	Sir Joseph Paxton	19	Stendhal
10	Doja Cat	20	The Fates

ANSWERS ON PAGE 490

Easy

1   What type of traditional Italian and French folk song is famously sung by Venetian gondoliers?

2   Albeit probably not true, which famous folk song was said to have been written by Henry VIII?

3   Which Irish folk group took their name from a co-founder of the United Irishmen, who led a rebellion against British rule in 1798?

4   In folk music, Dave Guard, Bob Shane and Nick Reynolds performed under what name?

5   Which Canadian singer-songwriter wrote the anti-war folk song *Universal Soldier* in 1964?

6   Yarrow, Stookey and Travers were the surnames of which folk trio?

7   Which folk dance originating in Bohemia, in double time with a hop on the fourth beat, became a popular ballroom dance in the mid-nineteenth century?

8   Known by her first name only, Martin Luther King Jr. called which singer the queen of American folk music?

9   A style of folk music played on concertina, hand saw and goatskin drum called "rake-n-scape" originates from which island nation?

10 On account of its appearance, which instrument often used in folk music is sometimes affectionately known as the "hubcap guitar"?

11 What controversial moment in folk music history happened at the 1965 Newport Folk Festival?

12 What duo's album *At the Gate of Horn* is considered one of the most influential folk albums of the early 1960s?

13 Which ballad was written by English songwriter Frederic Weatherly in 1913 and set to the traditional Irish melody of *Londonderry Air*?

Medium

14 In 2006, BBC Radio 2 listeners voted which album by Fairport Convention as the most influential folk album of all time?

15 Which long-running folk group released an album in 2013 entitled *Wintersmith*, inspired by a Terry Pratchett book?

16 Named onomatopoeically for the sound of the gendang drum, which style of Indonesian dance and folk music originated on the island of Java?

17 Which man, known as the "Rochdale Cowboy" after his 1975 hit single, went on to present Radio 2's folk show for 15 years?

18 What is the most suitable time signature for a jig?

19 The folk instrument known as *cláirseach* in Irish and *clàrsach* in Scottish Gaelic is what type of instrument?

20 Which folk musician contracted toxoplasmosis after trying to give a sheep the kiss of life on his Hereford farm?

Hard

Answers to QUIZ 486 – National Dress

1   Tracht, Austria and Germany
2   Kilt, Scotland
3   Hanbok, Korea
4   Huipil, Mexico
5   Djellaba, Morocco
6   Kimono, Japan
7   Cheongsam, China
8   Gho, Bhutan

ANSWERS ON PAGE **491**

1   Combining a culture and an animal, which term refers to the Irish economy from the mid-1990s to the late 2000s and its rapid economic growth fuelled by foreign investment?

2   Becky Bloomwood is the main protagonist in which series of novels by Sophie Kinsella?

3   Which player scored for both sides in the 1981 FA Cup Final between Tottenham Hotspur and Manchester City?

4   In which 1990s children's television show did Auntie Mabel (played by Lynda Baron) travel the world in a small polka dot aeroplane?

5   In optics, what name is given to the effect whereby the position or direction of an object differs when viewed from different positions?

6   For a couple of years at the start of the millennium, which alcoholic drink was advertised by Tom, a dancing cat?

7   Leigh Francis wrote and performed which Channel 4 television sketch show that lampooned popular culture with often surreal, abstract toilet humour?

8   What was the only completed opera by Hungarian composer Béla Bartók?

9   In internet parlance, what is QQ often used to imitate?

10 Played by Selena Gomez, Alex Russo is the main protagonist of which 2007 Disney fantasy sitcom?

11 On a ship, what name is given to a crane used to raise and lower lifeboats?

12 The Bonifay brothers, Shane and Parks, are two of the most famous competitors in which water sport?

13 Which Austrian ski resort celebrates Christmas by throwing a tree into the lake, then sending a team of divers to rescue it?

14 Peaking in the late 19th century, which Italian literary and operatic movement strove to bring realism to the opera house and written word?

15 Of the twelve prophets of the Jewish Hebrew Bible, which was known as the "Prophet of Doom"?

16 Which man was a pretender to the throne of Henry VII of England in 1487, claiming to be the 17th Earl of Warwick?

17 Which daughter of Marie and Pierre Curie was half of the second married couple to win a Nobel Prize, her parents being the first?

18 Name either of the two countries, both in Africa, whose circulating currency's division units are not based on a power of ten.

19 A silhouette of what appears in the centre of the flag of Lesotho?

20 Especially popular in Italian ski resorts, which drink is made with brandy, advocaat and whipped cream?

Answers to QUIZ 487 – Pot Luck

1	Ptolemy (Ptolemy I Soter)	11	Rolf Harris
2	Serial	12	Quechua
3	Thierry Mugler	13	The Saturday Evening Post
4	The Observer	14	Suffolk
5	Micromort	15	Pineau de Re
6	Rusholme	16	Veronica Lake
7	Centavo	17	Rinderpest
8	Robert Bruce Merrifield	18	Heraldry
9	Worthless	19	Edward II
10	Persephone	20	Kelly Clarkson

1 Who wrote the 1980s films *The Breakfast Club*, *Weird Science* and *Ferris Bueller's Day Off*?

2 David Spade, Dennis Miller and Christopher Walken starred in which 2001 American adventure comedy film about a janitor?

3 2020's *Be Water* is a documentary about the life of which film star?

4 In which film did Elvis Presley play his only double role?

5 Which composer wrote the musical scores for the films *Braveheart*, *Casper*, *Apollo 13*, *Jumanji*, *Jade* and *Balto*, all in 1995?

6 Which actress and singer is best remembered for starring in the *Road to* films alongside Bing Crosby and Bob Hope?

7 Which film directed by Terry Gilliam was inspired by Chris Marker's 1962 short film *La Jetée*?

8 *Run to You* and *Queen of the Night* were the fourth and fifth singles released from the soundtrack to which film of the 1990s?

9 *The Bear and the Bow* was the name in development of which Pixar animated film?

10 Don Bluth was working on a fully computer animated film about which band, that, had it been completed, would have predated *Toy Story* by about eight years?

11 Which English actress overcame a childhood stutter to become a successful actress, with her first credited role being Isolda in 2003's *Boudica*?

12 Princess Atta is the primary female character in which animated film?

13 Which 1944 film had the tagline "From the moment they met it was murder"?

14 In the American Film Institute's 2006 list of the Greatest Movie Musicals, which came first?

15 *Somewhere My Love (Lara's Theme)* is the name given to a leitmotif written for which 1965 film?

16 In *Goldfinger*, what name did Auric Goldfinger give to his team of all-female pilots?

17 Complete the tagline featured on Swedish posters for *Life of Brian*; "So funny it was…"?

18 In the film of the same name, who was Dumbo's diminutive best friend?

19 Tom Holland plays Nathan Drake in the 2022 Hollywood adaptation of which video game franchise?

20 Tom Hanks wrote, directed and starred in which 1996 film about a one-hit wonder band?

Answers to QUIZ 488 – Folk Music

1	Barcarolle	11	Bob Dylan played electric guitar for the first time
2	*Greensleeves*		
3	The Wolfe Tones	12	Bob Gibson and Harrison Camp
4	The Kingston Trio	13	*Danny Boy*
5	Buffy Sainte-Marie	14	*Liege and Lief*
6	Peter, Paul and Mary	15	Steeleye Span
7	Polka	16	Dangdut
8	Odetta (Holmes)	17	Mike Harding
9	The Bahamas	18	6/8
10	Dobro	19	Harp
		20	Roy Harper

1   Who released the album *Old Ideas* in 2012?

2   Particularly associated with jewellers and watchmakers, what name is given to a small magnifying glass which is worn or held close to the eye?.

3   What do footballer Masal Bugduv, basketball player Ivan Renko and ice hockey player Taro Tsujimoto have in common?

4   Scotland's national motorsport centre is located at which racing circuit in Fife?

5   In Arthurian legend, who is the father of Sir Kay that takes in an infant Arthur?

6   Which British sculptor designed the Angel of the North?

7   Whose theorem states that every symmetry of a physical system has a conserved quantity associated with it?

8   Between 10-12 February 1746, which British peer was asked to form a government, but was unable to find more than one person who would agree to serve in his cabinet?

9   Robert Lindsay played a South London young Marxist "urban guerrilla" in which John Sullivan sitcom?

10 If someone has been manumitted, what happened to them?

11 Which Neolithic farmstead in the Orkney islands is, at roughly 6,200 years old, probably the oldest preserved stone house in northern Europe?

12 In addition to being a type of shrub, "Wilson's Wonder" is also the name of a kind of which nut tree?

13 John Lennon and Yoko Ono founded which conceptual "country" to circumvent Lennon's deportation order from the USA?

14 Although its origins are unclear, The Curse of Scotland is a nickname for which playing card?

15 Which six-time world amateur boxing champion became a sitting MP in the Indian Parliament in 2016?

16 When a mugger threatened him with "Look, bud! I said your money or your life!", how did the comedian Jack Benny respond?

17 In 2002, the shipping forecast area of Finisterre was renamed to what, a name taken from the captain of *HMS Beagle*?

18 Which singer eventually admitted to surreptitiously running an Instagram™ account dedicated solely to the review of onion rings?

19 Travelling at speeds up to 268 miles per hour, what is the world's fastest public train?

20 Which small French wine region in east Burgundy shares its name with a single malt Scotch whisky?

Easy

Medium

Hard

---

1   What type of farm animal is a German Landrace?

2   Cattle, sheep and goats are ruminants, which means they all have four distinct chambers in which internal organ?

3   What name is given to the process of pulling a deep tine through the ground to remove compaction?

4   A *kibbutz* is a communal farm or settlement in what country?

5   On a fertiliser label, what does NPK stand for?

6   Farms which specialise in rearing livestock rather than growing crops are known as what?

7   The eggs laid during a single nesting period and fertilised at the same time are known as what?

8   His name perhaps better known as that of a band, which 18th century horticulturalist published the book *Horse Hoeing Husbandry*?

9   The six farmhands arrested in Dorset in 1834 for creating a *de facto* trade union became known as what?

10 The West Yorkshire towns of Wakefield, Morley and Rothwell form the boundary of which farming area?

11 Equal to one chain by one furlong, which unit of land area was originally thought of as being the area of land one man and a team of oxen could plough in one day?

12 Kindred, Steptoe and Windich are all cultivars of which major cereal grain?

13 Harvesting a crop in such a way that the roots and the lower parts of the plant are left uncut to allow regrowth is called what?

14 In lambing, what is the abbreviation ADG used to refer to?

15 Which breed of cow is the biggest producer of milk in the United Kingdom?

16 What name is given to the curved blades on a plough that serve to turn over the furrow?

17 What term is given to a cockerel deliberately neutered to improve the quality of its meat?

18 Banner Lane in Coventry was for over 50 years Britain's biggest producer of what piece of farming equipment?

19 If a heavily pregnant, broad backed ewe is "rigwelted", what has happened to her?

20 Which 18th century Acts of Parliament saw farmland hedged and fenced off into smaller fields, creating property rights on once-common grounds?

Easy

Medium

Hard

1 Toprock, downrock, power moves and freezes are the four main elements of which type of dancing?

2 *Guerrillero Heroico*, an iconic photograph of Che Guevara, was taken by which Cuban photographer?

3 Star NHL players Evander and Patrick, despite being unrelated, share what surname?

4 Which Irish swimmer won all four of her country's medals at the 1996 Olympics amid doping allegations?

5 *Rushen Coatie* is, essentially, the Scottish version of which fairy-tale?

6 *Tiffany's*, *Versace* and *Chanel* are among the names of stores on which famous Beverly Hills street?

7 Natalie Portman's film debut came when she was 11 years old in which film, in which she learns the hitman trade?

8 Which portmanteau word describes a lack of motivation, feelings of guilt and a sense of isolation affecting wealthy young people?

9 Which American sportsman is the only commoner (i.e. non-monarch) to appear on a Scottish banknote while still alive?

10 Which American poet and fascist collaborator played a significant role in developing imagism?

11 Which American author wrote the novel *Jaws*, on which the film was based?

12 Which 1949 film reunited Fred Astaire and Ginger Rogers after ten years, but only after Judy Garland was fired at the last minute?

13 In the terminology of Oxbridge universities, what does it mean to rusticate a student?

14 Which two contestants from the second series of UK *Big Brother* got married after leaving the house?

15 Wily Kit and Wily Kat were twin characters on which children's cartoon show?

16 The Australian city of Darwin lies on the Beagle Gulf, which opens out into which sea?

17 Gabriel Janka created an eponymous "hardness" test for what type of material?

18 In African-American culture, which weeklong celebration held in the USA over the Christmas period honours cultural heritage and traditional values?

19 Which 2008 deck-building card game is themed around monarchs racing to claim, develop and defend land?

20 Feijoada, a stew of black beans with pork or other meat and vegetables served with rice, is the national dish of which country?

Easy

Medium

Hard

Answers to QUIZ 491 – Pot Luck

1	Leonard Cohen	11	Knap of Howar
2	Loupe	12	Walnut
3	They don't actually exist, and were all hoaxes	13	Nutopia
4	Knockhill	14	Nine of diamonds
5	Sir Ector	15	Mary Kom
6	Antony Gormley	16	"I'm thinking it over."
7	Emmy Noether	17	FitzRoy
8	Lord Bath	18	Lorde
9	*Citizen Smith*	19	The Shanghai Maglev
10	They were freed from slavery	20	Jura

Easy

1   What type of crystals are used for timing in watches and electronics?

2   What type of crystal is the hardest substance found on Earth?

3   Orbuculum is an alternative name for what?

4   Crystals found in Australia of which mineral date back 4.4 billion years and thus hold vital information about Earth's earliest days?

5   A crystal anniversary celebrates how many years of marriage?

6   Which port city in Ireland is most famous today for its crystal factory?

7   The Cave of the Crystals, a treasure trove containing some of the largest natural crystals ever found, is located in which country?

8   In crystal systems, how many basic crystal shapes or lattices can all crystals be categorised within?

9   What name is given to the tendency of crystalline materials to split along definite crystallographic structural planes?

10 What was the surname of the father and son team who won the 1915 Nobel Prize in Physics for their services in the analysis of crystal structure by means of X-rays?

11 In crystal healing, how many basic chakras are there said to be?

12 What name is given to the process of cutting a gemstone to give it a flat face, thereby refracting light and maximising its beauty?

13 *Don't It Make My Brown Eyes Blue* was a 1977 US no.2 and UK no.5 hit for which singer?

14 What is rose quartz said to symbolise in crystal healing?

15 In folklore, which gemstone was said to protect sailors and guarantee a safe voyage, as well as being the treasure of mermaids?

Medium

16 Which horror franchise originates with a series of murders at Camp Crystal Lake?

17 Which Premier League footballer was suspended for eight months after jumping into the crowd to kick a Crystal Palace fan in 1995?

18 Which actor and nine-time host of the Oscars ceremony played one game for the New York Yankees in March 2008 at the age of 59?

19 When Richard O'Brien left his hosting duties on *The Crystal Maze* in 1993, which singer replaced him until the show's 1995 cancellation?

20 With supposedly less than 50 known samples in the entire world, what is the rarest crystal?

Hard

Answers to QUIZ 492 – Farming

1	Pig	11	Acre
2	Stomach	12	Barley
3	Subsoiling	13	Ratooning
4	Israel	14	Average daily gain
5	Nitrogen, phosphorous, potassium/potash	15	Holstein
6	Pastoral farms or ranches	16	Mould boards
7	A clutch	17	Capon
8	Jethro Tull	18	Massey Ferguson tractors
9	The Tolpuddle Martyrs	19	She is stuck on her back
10	The Rhubarb Triangle	20	The Inclosure/Enclosure Acts

1 In Greek mythology, which hero was called "Tamer of Horses"?

2 What was the Roman epithet for Hecate, the Greek goddess of magic, crossroads, necromancy, the night and the moon?

3 Which straight-billed small wading bird is unusual in that the female is more brightly coloured than the male?

4 The Russian city of Nizhny Novgorod was formerly known as what?

5 American physician Tom Waddell, a decathlete who competed at the 1968 Summer Olympics, later founded which competition?

6 In his autobiography, which British comedian claimed to have been given the responsibility of guarding Nazi war criminals at Spandau prison?

7 Tim Cahill did not make his debut for Australia until 2004, deemed ineligible having played for which island nation's under-20 team ten years previously?

8 Which Richard Strauss one-act opera was banned in Britain until 1907?

9 In surfing terminology, if someone is "hanging eleven", in what way are they surfing?

10 The Devil's Punch Bowl is in which English county?

11 Luke Pritchard is the lead singer of which British indie band?

12 Which Swiss novelist, notably of children's stories, is best known for her book *Heidi*?

13 The speed of a computer mouse is measured in which apt unit?

14 The exception to the league's maximum of 32 owners per team rule, which community-owned NFL franchise has over 360,000 stockholders?

15 The aitchbone of cattle is which part?

16 Named after a slang term for attacks between gangs, which style of rap music is defined by its dark, violent and nihilistic lyrical content?

17 Who painted 1992's *The Singing Butler*, which became Britain's best-selling art print?

18 Francis Hodgson Burnett wrote which novel about an American boy who turns out to be the long-lost heir of a British fortune?

19 Clarence E. Mulford wrote a series of short stories and novels based on which fictional cowboy character?

20 The inaugural video game in which series sees Commander Shepard, an elite human soldier, try to stop a rogue agent from galactic invasion?

Easy

Medium

Hard

Answers to QUIZ 493 – Pot Luck

1	Breakdancing	11	Peter Benchley
2	Alberto Korda	12	*The Barkleys of Broadway*
3	Kane	13	Suspend them
4	Michelle Smith	14	Helen Adams and Paul Clarke
5	*Cinderella*	15	*ThunderCats*
6	Rodeo Drive	16	Coral Sea
7	*Léon: The Professional*	17	Wood
8	Affluenza	18	Kwanzaa
9	Jack Nicklaus	19	*Dominion*
10	Ezra Pound	20	Brazil

1   Which term for an appetiser translates from French into English as "sofa"?

2   In the Middle Eastern grain salad *tabbouleh*, which herb is traditionally the main ingredient?

3   Which dish of lobster in Cognac is either named after the eleventh month in the French Republican calendar, or a play that was named after that first?

4   Popular from the 16th to 19th centuries, which whipped cream and lemon dessert of Cornish origin is typically flavoured with white wine or sherry?

5   Which three vegetables make up a standard *mirepoix*?

6   It is said that leaving two chopsticks standing out of a bowl of rice signifies what?

7   The grilled pork shoulder sandwich bondipan originated in which country?

8   In the Basque country, what type of snack (or *pintxo*) is a *Gilda*?

9   In a Moscow Mule, after the vodka and lime juice, which other ingredient is said to add the "kick" associated with a mule?

10 Which cooking technique involves covering meat with cornflour, egg white, sesame oil and salt before cooking it?

11 In 1915, who said "We are fighting Germans, Austrians and drink, and as far as I can see, the greatest of these deadly foes is drink"?

12 *Horiatiki* salad is generally made with pieces of tomatoes, cucumbers, onion, feta cheese and olives, dressed with salt, olive oil and which herb?

13 Although often associated with the city of Reims, which adjacent French town is best known as the principal *entrepôt* (or port) for Champagne wines?

14 The "vinegar" available in many fish and chip shops in Britain is not in fact vinegar, and is not allowed to be sold as such – what three-word name should it instead go by, as seen on the packaging?

15 With a name meaning "on the ground" in Spanish, what liquid-ageing process utilises fractional blending in such a way that the final product is a mixture of ages?

16 What do the bilberry, blaeberry, wimberry, whortleberry, urts, hurtleberry, huckleberry, myrtleberry, whinberry and fraughan have in common?

17 *Balut*, a street food widely consumed in Vietnam and the Philippines, contains what animal product?

18 Which popular flavoured rice dish served across Indonesia, with meat and vegetables added, has a name literally meaning "fried rice"?

19 During World War II, to keep up public morale, which quintessentially English dinner was one of the few foods that were never rationed?

20 In 2000, which man took over as CEO for the Christian non-profit organisation *Food For The Poor*, despite his extremely unfortunate name for the job?

Answers to QUIZ 494 – Crystals

1	Quartz	11	Seven (root, sacral, solar plexus, third eye, heart, throat, crown)
2	Diamond		
3	Crystal ball	12	Faceting
4	Zircon	13	Crystal Gayle
5	15	14	Love and harmony
6	Waterford	15	Aquamarine
7	Mexico	16	*Friday the 13th*
8	Seven	17	Eric Cantona
9	Cleavage	18	Billy Crystal
10	Bragg	19	Edward Tudor-Pole
		20	Taaffeite

Easy *Medium* *Hard*

1   Which mixture of nitric and hydrochloric acids earned its name from medieval alchemists for its ability to dissolve gold?

2   Also called "shape poetry", which building material's name is used to describe poetry whose visual appearance matches the poem's topic?

3   Sitting Members of Parliament Pete Wishart, Ian Cawsey and Sir Greg Knight formed a rock band in 2003 with which apt music-related name?

4   Overshadowed by man's first steps on the Moon the day after he arrived, who became the first person to row solo across any ocean when he crossed the Atlantic in 180 days in 1969?

5   As opposed to 13, as it is in England, which number is considered unlucky in Italian culture?

6   Emmanuel Frémiet's equestrian statue of Joan of Arc is located in which Parisian public square?

7   Which team turned up for a 1997 Premier League game at Highfield Road without their kit and had to borrow Coventry City's away strip?

8   Which Russian footballer scored all six goals of his international career in the 1994 World Cup, enough to win a share of the Golden Boot award?

9   Which grey corrosion-resistant form of bronze containing zinc gives its name to a dull bluish-grey colour?

10   In particle physics, fundamental fermions are classified as either quarks or which other subatomic particle?

11   Which ship did Japan surrender on to end World War II, as well as Steven Seagal save from a group of mercenaries in the 1992 film *Under Siege*?

12   Known for his blue eyes and smooth baritone voice, which singer founded and fronted The Dubliners?

13   The first two series of the American version of *The Cube* were hosted by which retired NBA legend?

14   Mount Rushmore National Memorial was designed and worked on for 14 years by which American sculptor?

15   Which 1980's English electronic band formed in Wirral, Merseyside, was founded by Paul Humphreys and Andy McCluskey?

16   A highly toxic protein, ricin is obtained from the pressed seeds of which plant?

17   Oxidoreductases, transferases, hydrolases, lyases, ligases and isomerases are the six categories of what?

18   With only six ships in it, which European country's navy is known as the Merevägi?

19   Which French daily afternoon newspaper's title translates into English as 'the world'?

20   Ingrid Bergman was the mother of which Golden Globe-winning Italian-American actress?

Easy

Medium

Hard

Answers to QUIZ 495 – Pot Luck

1	Hector	11	The Kooks
2	Trivia	12	Johanna Spyri
3	Phalarope	13	Mickeys
4	Gorky	14	Green Bay Packers
5	Gay Games	15	Buttocks
6	Bernard Manning	16	Drill
7	Samoa (Western Samoa at the time)	17	Jack Vettriano
8	*Salome*	18	*Little Lord Fauntleroy*
9	Nude	19	Hopalong Cassidy
10	Surrey	20	*Mass Effect*

Easy

1. Also known as the first chair, which member of the orchestra comes on stage first, before the conductor, and serves as the "concertmaster"?
2. Who wrote the 1945 composition *The Young Person's Guide to the Orchestra*?
3. Originating from Saharan Africa, which instrument features in a modern orchestra as, essentially, a bass xylophone?
4. What instrument is sometimes called the clown of the orchestra because of its jovial timbre?
5. Despite being profoundly deaf, Evelyn Glennie is the world's first full-time classical soloist in which part of the orchestra?
6. Which UK city is the home of the Britten Sinfonia chamber orchestra?
7. Historically, orchestras tended to be almost exclusively male, with the exception of the player of which instrument?
8. The Hallé Orchestra has since 1996 been based at which concert venue?
9. Without using harmonics, which orchestral instrument can play the highest note?
10. In the normal layout of a modern symphony orchestra, the players of which instrument sit directly in front of the conductor?
11. Developed in the mid-19th century, which brass instrument features in some late Romantic and 20th century orchestra ensembles, sometimes playing parts marked for "tenor tuba"?
12. Which conductor and cellist, conductor of both the New York Philharmonic Orchestra and from 1943 until his death the Hallé Orchestra, died in 1970?
13. The principal player of which instrument is generally considered the leader of an orchestra's brass section?
14. Founded in 1448, which orchestra claims to be the world's oldest?

Medium

15. *Gamelan* refers to a traditional percussion orchestra and musical instruments used within one in which country?
16. As opposed to philharmonics, smaller-sized orchestra ensembles of between 25 to 50 musicians are generally referred to as what?
17. A 1983 report by Philip Mason found that which country's orchestra (with 85 members) was bigger than its army (80)?
18. Which musical note do orchestras always tune to?
19. In the Boosey & Hawks system of orchestral instrumentation shorthand, what instruments would be called for in the note "3.2.2.3"?
20. What was notable about the Portsmouth Sinfonia orchestra of the 1970s?

Hard

Answers to QUIZ 496 – Food & Drink

1	Canapé	11	David Lloyd George
2	Parsley	12	Oregano
3	Lobster Thermidor	13	Epernay
4	Syllabub	14	"Non-brewed condiment" (not that you would ever ask for that)
5	Onions, celery and carrots		
6	Death	15	Solera
7	Argentina	16	They are all the same berry, just with different regional names
8	Salty peppers and anchovies, usually on a skewer		
		17	Duck embryo
9	Ginger beer	18	*Nasi Goreng*
10	Velveting	19	Fish and chips
		20	Robin Mahfood

QUIZ 499 – Pot Luck

ANSWERS ON PAGE 251

1 In *Aesop's Fables*, who removed the thorn from the lion's paw?

2 John Kenneth Galbraith was a noted writer in which sphere of social science?

3 The song *Baubles, Bangles and Beads* comes from which 1953 Charles Lederer and Luther Davis musical?

4 In 1943, the whole population of about 150 of which Wiltshire village was evicted to provide an exercise area for American troops preparing for invasion?

5 *Barlinnie Nine*, a single-movement orchestral composition by the Finnish composer Osmo Tapio Räihälä, is dedicated to which controversial Scottish footballer?

6 Which world-famous ballerina was arrested in Panama in 1959, accused of trying to orchestrate a coup against the government?

7 Since 1939, which football league team has played home games at Highbury Stadium? [The answer is *not* Arsenal.]

8 After being turned down for a part in *Dances with Wolves*, Michael Van Wijk appeared on British TV in the 1990s as which character?

9 Antiziganism is the fear or hatred of which group of people?

10 Peaking at roughly 340lbs, who was the heaviest US President?

11 After leaving Apple, Steve Jobs founded which American technology company that specialised in higher-education workstations?

12 How many letters are there in the Hawaiian alphabet?

13 Which provisional capital is known as "Canada's English city", "Little England" and "The Garden City"?

14 The Rainhill Trials of October 1829 were designed to find the best version of which new form of power?

15 Which bishop is considered third in seniority in Britain?

16 With a name referring to a specific place, what was the name for the musicians that dominated US music in the late 19th and early 20th centuries?

17 Which 16-year-old Lemhi Shoshone woman helped the Lewis and Clark Expedition explore the Louisiana Territory?

18 Which US navy ship exploded in Havana Harbor in 1898, an attack initially blamed on the Spanish but now viewed by conspiracists as a "false flag operation"?

19 Taylor Swift's debut single had the name of which other country and music singer?

20 What homemade headwear has become a byword for paranoia, belief in pseudoscience and conspiracy theories?

Easy

Medium

Hard

Answers to QUIZ 497 – Pot Luck

1	Aqua regia	11	USS *Missouri* (BB-63)
2	Concrete poetry	12	Ronnie Drew
3	MP3	13	Dwyane Wade
4	John Fairfax	14	Gutzon Borglum
5	17	15	Orchestral Manoeuvres in the Dark
6	Place des Pyramides	16	The castor oil plant
7	Chelsea	17	Enzymes
8	Oleg Salenko	18	Estonia
9	Gunmetal	19	*Le Monde*
10	Leptons	20	Isabella Rossellini

Easy

1. Whose law states that the total pressure of a mixture of gases is equal to the sum of the partial pressures of the individual component gases?

2. In hypothesis testing, what letter is used to represent the chance that, assuming the null hypothesis is true, results can be observed and validated?

3. In relation to plants, anthesis describes what process?

4. What "M" describes the decimal part of a logarithm?

5. The Gaia hypothesis that all living things have a regulatory effect on the Earth's environment that promotes life overall was postulated by which chemist?

6. What term for a hypothetical particle that moves faster than light has become more broadly used in fiction as a "sciency" word of no particular meaning?

7. Forming the interior part of the cutis, what layer of body tissue consists of papillary and reticular layers?

8. Who first proposed and developed the laws of electrolysis?

9. In organic chemistry, what name is given to chemical compounds which always have the same molecular formulae but different structural formulae?

10. What name is given to the waxy covering of an embryo that protects it from amniotic fluid?

11. Isoprene, nitrile and butyl are all types of what substance?

12. Portuguese neurologist Antonio Egas Moniz won the 1949 Nobel Prize for Medicine for what now-discredited surgical procedure?

13. Despite a 1974 rule that was supposed to prohibit it, what was notable about Ralph Steinman's winning of the 2011 Nobel Prize in Medicine?

Medium

14. What name is sometimes given to the elements in Group 1 of the Periodic Table, due to the pH levels when they are added to water?

15. Which of the three major volcano types produces low-viscosity lava that spreads far from the source, forming a gently-sloping large volcanic structure?

16. The temperature at which normal fluid helium I makes the transition to superfluid helium II is named for which Greek letter?

17. In 1985, which Cambridge professor formulated the mind-blindness theory of autism?

18. Which comet collided with Jupiter in July 1994, the first direct observation of a Solar System collision?

19. Which branch of science is concerned with the development of malformations or serious deviations from normal organisms?

20. Buccula is the scientific term for what usually undesirable feature of the human body?

Hard

Answers to QUIZ 498 – Orchestra

1. The leader of the first violin section (i.e. the best violin player)
2. Benjamin Britten
3. Marimba
4. Bassoon
5. Percussion
6. Cambridge
7. The harp
8. The Bridgewater Hall
9. Piccolo
10. Violas
11. Euphonium
12. Sir John Barbirolli
13. Trumpet
14. The Royal Danish Orchestra
15. Indonesia
16. Chamber orchestras
17. Monaco
18. A – this is also enshrined into international law in the Treaty of Versailles
19. 3 flutes, 2 oboes, 2 clarinets, 3 bassoons
20. It was the "worst orchestra in the world," an experiment consisting of players without musical training and/or first time instrument players